Windows 98:
The Complete Reference

John Levine
Margaret Levine Young
Doug Muder
Alison Barrows

Osborne **McGraw-Hill**

Berkeley   New York   St. Louis   San Francisco
Auckland   Bogotá   Hamburg   London   Madrid
Mexico City   Milan   Montreal   New Delhi   Panama City
Paris   São Paulo   Singapore   Sydney
Tokyo   Toronto

Osborne **McGraw-Hill**
2600 Tenth Street
Berkeley, California 94710
U.S.A.

For information on translations or book distributors outside the U.S.A., or to arrange
bulk purchase discounts for sales promotions, premiums, or fundraisers, please contact
Osborne McGraw-Hill at the above address.

Windows 98: The Complete Reference

1234567890 AGM AGM 901987654321098

ISBN 0-07-882343-9

Publisher
  Brandon A. Nordin

Editor-in-Chief
  Scott Rogers

Acquisitions Editor
  Megg Bonar

Project Editor
  Janet Walden

Editorial Assistant
  Stephane Thomas

Technical Editor
  Stuart McClure
  Joel Scambray

Copy Editor
  William McManus

Proofreader
  Emily Wolman

Indexer
  Valerie Robbins

Computer Designer
  Jani Beckwith
  Roberta Steele
  Michelle Galicia

Illustrator
  Brian Wells

We dedicate this book to our children,
Sarah Willow Levine Saxon, Margaret Virginia Young, and
Christopher Isaac Young—a new generation of cousins.

About the Authors

John Levine is the author of many worldwide best-selling titles including the multimillion seller, *The Internet For Dummies*. He also lectures and consults on the Internet and is a frequent speaker at computer conferences and training events. John previously hosted a call-in radio show about the Internet and now serves as sewer commissioner in his village in upstate New York. He holds a Ph.D. in computer science from Yale University.

Margaret Levine Young is the best-selling author of over two dozen books with various coauthors, including John Levine on *The Internet For Dummies*. In addition to teaching and giving lectures on the Internet, Margaret writes a regular column called "Webwise" for *Seven Days* in Burlington, VT. She holds a B.A. in computer science from Yale University.

Acknowledgments

John and Margy would like to thank Megg Bonar, Scott Rogers, Stephane Thomas, Janet Walden, and many others at Osborne/McGraw-Hill for making this book happen. We also thank our hard-working coauthors: Doug Muder for writing Chapters 5, 8-10, 13, and 23-25; Alison Barrows for writing Chapters 4, 7, 12, 19-20, and 29-32; and Kathy Warfel for writing Chapters 26 and 38. We also got helpful information from Matt Ronn about LAN topics and Allen Smith about NetMeeting. Thanks are also due to Spider Graphics of Trumansburg, New York for the design of the CD-ROM.

Contents

Part I

Working in Windows 98

Part II

Managing Your Disk

Part III

Configuring Windows for Your Computer

Part IV

Windows 98 on the Internet

■■|| 22   Connecting to PPP and SLIP Accounts   473

Part V

Networking with Windows 98

Part VI

Windows Housekeeping

Introduction

Windows 98 is the latest and probably the last of Microsoft's desktop Windows systems. Its heritage includes Windows 95, Windows 3.1, Windows 3.0, 2.1, 2.0, all the way back to Windows 1.0 in the mid-1980s. As you might expect of a system with such a long and distinguished lineage, Windows 98 has an enormous variety of functions and features, including graphics, networks, disk management, e-mail, word processing, DOS compatibility, sound and video, the Internet and World Wide Web, and a fairly credible multiuser Hearts game. This book helps you to make sense of the world of Windows 98, finding your way through all the new and sometimes confusing options, and to make the best use of the facilities that Windows 98 offers.

(If you're wondering why we say Windows 98 is the last version of desktop Windows, we say that because Microsoft claims that all its future systems will be built around versions of Windows NT.)

Who Is This Book for?

This book is for everyone who uses Windows 98, and especially for people who use it to do their day-to-day computing. You may already have Windows 98 installed on your computer, or you may be considering upgrading a Windows 95 or Windows 3.1 system to Windows 98. You may have a lot of experience with other computer systems, or Windows 98 may be your first exposure to computing.

Your computer may be the only one in your home or office, or it may be one of many on a local area network. You probably have a modem or network card, although Windows 98 works perfectly well without either.

If your computer is attached to a large network, we don't expect you to be the network manager, but if you're in a small office with two or three computers, we tell you how to set up a small but usable Windows 98 network. If you have a modem, we discuss in considerable detail what's involved in getting connected to the Internet, because Windows 98 (unlike previous versions of Windows) includes all the software you need to use the Internet.

What's in This Book?

Near the end of this Introduction, you'll find a section titled "New Features in Windows 98," which provides an overview of Windows 98's features, highlighting changes and additions made since Windows 95.

Part I: Working in Windows 98

Part I covers the basics of using Windows 98. We recommend that everyone at least skim this section, because even users familiar with Windows 95 will benefit from knowing about the new features offered by Windows 98.

Chapter 1 starts with the basics of working in Windows 98: using the mouse and managing your windows. Chapters 2 and 3 explain how to run programs and how to install programs, beyond those included with Windows 98. Chapter 4 discusses Windows 98's simple but useful text and word processing programs, and Chapter 5 describes the other accessory programs, such as the address book and calculator. Chapter 6 covers the extensive Help system, both for Windows 98 and application programs. Chapter 7 looks at the many ways to move and share information between and among programs.

Part II: Managing Your Disks

All the information in your computer is stored in disk files and folders. Part II helps you get your files, folders, and disks under control.

Chapters 8 and 9 cover day-to-day file and folder operations, including how to use Windows Explorer and Folder windows to manage your files. Chapter 10 discusses the all-important topic of *backups*, making copies of your files in case hardware or software failure wipes them out. Chapter 11 discusses disk setup, both removable disks and new hard disks that you may add to your computer.

Part III: Configuring Windows for Your Computer

Windows 98 is extremely (some would say excessively) configurable. Part III tells you what items you can configure and makes suggestions for the most effective way to set up your computer.

Chapter 12 covers the *Start menu*, the gateway to the features of Windows 98. Chapter 13 details the *desktop*, the icons and other items that reside on your screen. Chapter 14 explains your keyboard and mouse (yes, lots of options exist just for the mouse), and Chapter 15 tells you how to add and set up additional hardware on your computer. Chapter 16 covers printing, including setting up printers and installing fonts. Chapters 17 and 18 examine Windows 98's extensive sound and video multimedia facilities. Chapter 19 highlights the special features that are useful to laptop computer users. Chapter 20 covers the accessibility features that make Windows 98 more usable for people who may have difficulty using conventional keyboards and mice, seeing the screen, or hearing sounds.

Part IV: Windows 98 on the Internet

Windows 98 offers a complete set of Internet access features, from making telephone or network connections to e-mail and the World Wide Web.

Chapter 21 explains the intricacies of setting up a modem to work with Windows 98, and Chapter 22 tells you how to use that modem to create and set up an account with an Internet service provider or online service. Chapter 23 describes Outlook Express, the program that handles your e-mail. Chapters 24 and 25 cover Internet Explorer, Microsoft's web browser, as well as Netscape Navigator, the world's most popular web browser. Chapter 26 describes FrontPage Express, a program that enables you to create simple web pages of your own. Chapter 27 examines online chatting and conferencing with Microsoft Chat and NetMeeting, and Chapter 28 discusses the other Internet applications that come with Windows 98.

Part V: Networking with Windows 98

Windows 98 has extensive built-in networking features. You can set up your Windows 98 machine as a client in a large network, as a server in a small network, or as both.

Chapter 29 introduces local area networks, including key concepts such as client-server and peer-to-peer networking. Chapter 30 walks you through the process of creating a small network of Windows 98 systems, while Chapter 31 discusses Windows 98 as a client on a larger NetWare or Windows NT network. Chapter 32 tells you how to share printers and disk drives among your networked computers. Chapter 33 covers the limited security features that Windows 98 provides.

Part VI: Windows Housekeeping

Windows 98 is sufficiently complex that it needs some regular maintenance and adjustment, which is covered in Part VI.

Chapter 34 tells you how to keep your disk working well, and how to use the facilities that Windows 98 provides to check and repair disk problems. Chapter 35 covers *disk compression*, schemes to store more data on your disk at the cost of slower access. Chapter 36 explains how to use tuning features to adjust your computer for maximum performance, and Chapter 37 reviews the process of troubleshooting hardware and software problems. Chapter 38 describes the other Windows 98 resources available on the Internet and elsewhere, including Windows Update, which can automatically identify and install updated or corrected Windows components.

Part VII: Behind the Scenes: Windows 98 Internals

Part VII covers a variety of the more advanced Windows 98 topics.

Chapter 39 describes the configuration and control files that Windows 98 uses, and Chapter 40 describes the *Registry*, the central database of program information that is central to Windows 98's operation. Chapter 41 covers DOS compatibility and the facilities that Windows 98 provides to run even the oldest DOS programs. Chapter 42, the final chapter, concludes with the *Windows Scripting Host*, a sophisticated system to automate frequently performed tasks.

Appendix, Glossary, and Instructions for Installing the Book's CD-ROM

Appendix A describes how to install Windows 98 as an upgrade to a Windows 95 or 3.1 system. The Glossary describes all the terminology you need to know to understand Windows 98 completely. And, at the very back of this book, you'll find a page of instructions for how to install the accompanying CD-ROM. (For more information on this book's CD-ROM, see "About This Book's CD-ROM" later in this Introduction.)

Conventions Used in This Book

This book uses several icons to highlight special advice:

A handy way to make Windows 98 work better for you.

An observation that gives insight into the way that Windows 98 and other programs work.

Something to watch out for, so you don't have to learn the hard way.

When we refer you to related material, we tell you the name of the section that contains the information we think you'll want to read. If the section is in the same chapter you are reading, we don't mention a chapter number. If you find yourself skipping around the book, consider reading the text on-screen using the CD-ROM (see the next section).

When you see instructions to choose commands from a menu, we separate the part of the command by vertical bars (|). For example, "choose File | Open" means to choose File from the Menu bar, then choose Open from the File menu that appears. If the command begins with "Start |", then click the Start button on the Taskbar as the first step. See "Giving Commands" in Chapter 2 for the details of how to give commands.

About This Book's CD-ROM

The CD-ROM in the back of this book contains the entire text of the book as a set of several hundred interlinked web pages that you can display with Internet Explorer or Netscape Navigator. Our goal is for the web pages on the CD-ROM to be your reference and tutorial companion as you use your Windows 98 system.

For instance, as you read in Chapter 24 about web pages and you want to know more about how to write them, you can click a link on the CD's Chapter 24 coverage to jump to Chapter 26's coverage of FrontPage Express, Windows 98's web editor. The CD makes it easy to follow links from topic to topic until you get the information you need—without flipping to the back of the book to consult the index!

Wherever the book says "See Chapter so-and-so," the CD-ROM has a link that you can follow with a single click. In the printed book, we refer you to related information by saying "see Chapter 18" or referring to other sections in the current chapter. The CD-ROM version of the book has been coded—using Web-style hyperlinks—to provide references to related topics. When you read the book on CD, you can click links to jump directly to the section of the book that contains the related information.

We've also added other useful links both within the book and to external resources on the World Wide Web. For example, if Microsoft's web site has more information about a topic, we provide you with a clickable link to the page you want. We also provide Internet addresses for companies that provide Windows-compatible products and information. The book also has its own web site (at **http://net.gurus.com/win98tcr**) where you'll find the latest Windows 98 information we think you'll find useful.

The key to the CD-ROM version of the book is the electronic Glossary page that you'll find one click away from the CD's opening screen. This Glossary provides an alphabetical list of Windows-related and Internet-related terms, each linking to the section of the book that introduces that concept. To learn about a topic, find the term in the glossary and follow the link into the text.

A page of instructions at the very back of this book describes how to install and use the CD-ROM.

Talk to Us

We love to hear from our readers. Drop us an e-mail note at **win98tcr@gurus.com** to tell us how you liked the book, or just to test your e-mail skills. Our mail robot will answer right away, and the authors will read your message when time permits (usually within a week or two).

Also visit our web site at **http://net.gurus.com/win98tcr** for updates and corrections to this book.

New Features in Windows 98

Windows 98 looks a lot like Windows 95, but it includes many small yet significant improvements. Microsoft makes the Internet much easier to use from Windows 98 by adding a suite of new Internet programs. Microsoft also responded to feedback from customers by making Windows easier to use, and by providing support for lots of new hardware.

The following is a run-down of some of the most important new features in Windows 98.

New Internet Support in Windows 98

Getting connected to the Internet—through an Internet service provider (ISP), online service, or your organization's private network—is much easier in Windows 98. You can sign up for an online service, open an account with one of a few national U.S. Internet providers, or configure Windows for an Internet account you already have. Once you are connected, Windows 98 also comes with many Internet applications, such as an e-mail program, web browser, chat program, and video conferencing program.

Internet Connection Wizard

Microsoft added the Internet Connection Wizard to later versions of Windows 95 (part of the OSR 2 version of Windows 95). This Wizard, shown in Figure 1, comes standard with Windows 98 and displays a list of national Internet service providers (ISPs) that have phone numbers in your area code.

Improved Dial-Up Networking

Dial-Up Networking, which connects your computer to an Internet account, now supports *multilink channels*—combining two connections into one fast connection. The new scripting feature lets you connect automatically to accounts that have nonstandard login sequences. You can also tell Dial-Up Networking to connect without waiting for you to click the Connect button, a feature many Internauts have been waiting for.

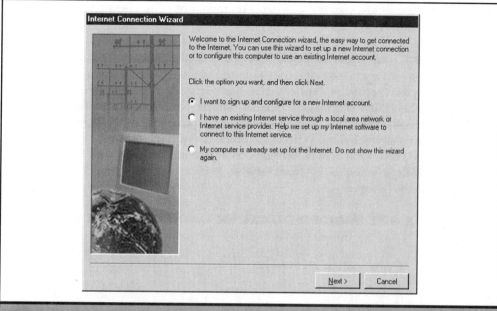

Figure 1.   *The Internet Connection Wizard helps you connect to an existing account or open a new one*

Built-In Sign-Up Programs for Online Services and ISPs

U.S. versions of Windows 98 come with sign-up programs for five of the most popular types of accounts: America Online, CompuServe, Microsoft Network (MSN), Prodigy Internet, and AT&T WorldNet. International versions may come with sign-up programs for providers in your country. Look in the Online Services folder on the Windows 98 desktop.

Built-In World Wide Web Browser

When we wrote this book, Microsoft was planning to ship Internet Explorer 4, Microsoft's free web browser, with Windows 98, but legal action by the U.S. Department of Justice threw those plans into doubt. Regardless of how the legal wrangling turns out, if you don't get Internet Explorer or Netscape Navigator, the world's most popular browser, with your copy of Windows 98, downloading either or both of these browsers is easy (if you don't have them already).

Microsoft Outlook Express for Internet E-Mail

Outlook Express, which comes with Windows 98, replaces Microsoft Internet Mail as Microsoft's basic Internet e-mail program. Windows 98 no longer comes with Microsoft

Exchange or Microsoft Fax, so fax support is no longer built in. Third-party fax programs for Windows 95 still work.

Microsoft FrontPage Express for Creating Web Pages

FrontPage Express is a stripped-down version of Microsoft's FrontPage web page editor. You can use FrontPage Express (shown in Figure 2) in a what-you-see-is-what-you-get (WYSIWYG) manner to create simple web pages; its Personal Home Page Wizard steps you through creating a personal home page. When you are done, you can use the Web Publishing Wizard to copy your web pages to a web server. If your computer is on a local area network, you can use the Personal Web Server to publish your web pages on the LAN; otherwise, you can use it to test a web site before uploading it to the Internet.

NetMeeting and Microsoft Chat for Internet Chatting

Microsoft Chat is an IRC (Internet Relay Chat) client that lets you participate in IRC conversations on public and private IRC servers. For more serious conferencing, NetMeeting lets you meet with other Internet users by text chat, voice chat, video

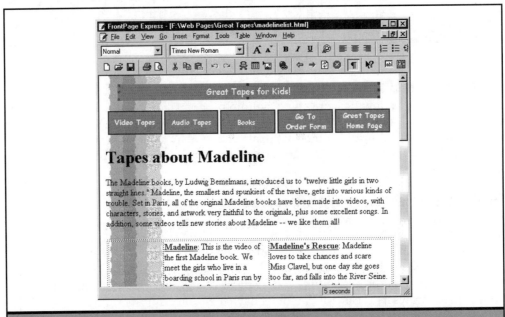

Figure 2.   *FrontPage Express is a what-you-see-is-what-you-get web page editor*

conferences, and scheduled meetings. NetMeeting also includes a whiteboard feature, as well as the ability to collaboratively run almost any application, allowing all the members of the meeting to see and share the application's window.

Channels for Updating Information Automatically from the Internet

You can now subscribe to a web site, and your web browser will automatically visit the site on a scheduled basis and check for new or updated content. Your browser can download the new pages or notify you that they are available. You can also subscribe to *channels*, web sites that provide not only web pages, but also screen savers, information tickers, animated advertisements, and other applets, by using the Channel bar on your desktop.

Virtual Private Networking for Connecting to Private Networks from ISP Accounts

Windows 98's Dial-Up Networking now includes Virtual Private Networking— support for Point-to-Point Tunneling Protocol (PPTP), which allows Internet users to connect through the Internet to private networks such as internal corporate networks.

More User Interface Options

Windows 98 looks and feels almost exactly like Windows 95—as long as you stay with the default Classic style desktop. If you want the desktop to act more like a web page, you can switch to Web style. Windows 98 also contains many usability enhancements, such as a configurable Taskbar and a wizard to configure your Start menu.

Web Style Desktop

If you are used to browsing the Web, you might like the Windows desktop, Folder windows, and Windows Explorer to work like a web page—no double-clicking required. In Web style, shown in Figure 3, single-clicking an icon opens a folder or runs a program. To select an icon, just hover the mouse pointer over the icon.

Active Desktop for Displaying Web Pages on the Desktop

Along with selecting a pattern or graphic file to display on your desktop, Active Desktop allows you to display one or more web pages. The web pages are *live*—meaning their links work. For example, an organization can create a "daily news" web page that all employees display on their Windows 98 desktops; links from that web page could be designed to take employees to forms, memos, announcements, and other information. You can use web pages for the background of windows, too; Figure 3 shows the new look of the Windows 98 Control Panel.

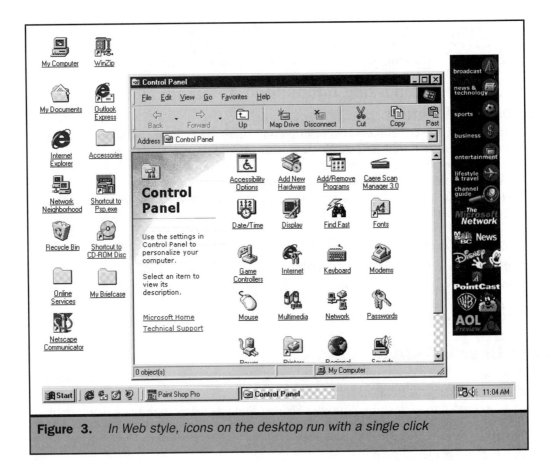

Figure 3. *In Web style, icons on the desktop run with a single click*

Configurable Taskbar

Like Windows 95, the Windows 98 Taskbar contains the Start button, task buttons (for each program that is running), and the system tray, which contains tiny icons at the right end of the Taskbar. Windows 98 lets you add other configurable toolbars to the Taskbar, too. The new Quick Launch toolbar appears at the left end of the Taskbar.

Better Housekeeping Tools

Housekeeping—keeping your hard disk cleaned up, and solving hardware and software problems—is never pleasant, but Windows 98 comes with some new programs that make these tasks easier. For example, Disk Cleanup deletes unnecessary temporary files to keep your hard disk from filling up.

Maintenance Wizard for Scheduling Routine Disk Tune-Ups

The Maintenance Wizard asks a series of questions, and then schedules Windows' housekeeping programs—ScanDisk, Disk Cleanup, and Disk Defragmenter—on a regular basis.

Built-In Backup Program

Microsoft Backup enables you to back up all files, selected files, or newly modified files to backup tape, network drives, floppy disks, or other backup media.

Windows Update over the Internet

As Microsoft updates Windows 98, some updates may be available for downloading on Microsoft's web site on the Internet. The Windows Update program helps you find and download updates to Windows and its driver files.

Other Improvements

Microsoft included several other useful programs and features in Windows 98, too.

FAT32 for Storing Data More Efficiently on Large Disks

The format of Windows disks was inherited from MS-DOS and is not designed for very large disks. Windows 95 can't handle a logical disk greater than 2GB, and the larger the disk, the more space that is wasted when you store small files. FAT32 is a new format that is designed for large hard disks of 500MB and up. Windows 98 can convert existing hard disks to FAT32, moving your files to the new format.

More Built-In Multimedia Support

Windows 98 comes with numerous programs—such as ActiveMovie and Media Player—that let you record and play audio and video files, including audio files in MIDI format. You can also use the DVD Player to play digital video disks, and NetShow with your web browser to play streaming audio and video files from the Internet.

Built-In TV Viewer

If your PC has a TV tuner card and a connection to a television antenna, cable, or satellite dish, you can watch television on your computer screen, either on the whole screen or in a window. The confusingly named WebTV for Windows program has a program guide, too, to make finding your programs easy. You can customize the program to list only your favorite channels.

Support for Multiple Monitors

Mac users have long been able to spread their desktop across two or more displays. Now Windows users can, too—you can configure up to eight monitors to give yourself more screen real estate.

Public and Private Address Directories (LDAP)

Public and private address directories allow organizations to create directories that Windows can use to find e-mail addresses and addresses for NetMeeting connections. You use the Find | People command to look up people in public and private address directories. Windows 98 supports LDAP (Lightweight Directory Access Protocol) for searching address directories, including "white pages" web sites on the Internet.

Windows Scripting Host for Automating Windows Tasks

If you need to repeat a series of commands or a program regularly, you can use the new Windows Scripting Host to run scripts written in JavaScript or VBScript.

Part I

Working in Windows 98

The Complete Reference

Chapter 1

The Basics of Windows 98

W indows is the most widely used computer program in the world. And Windows 98 is the latest version of Windows. Most of the software written for personal computers—indeed, most of the software written for any computer—is written for computers running Windows.

This chapter explains what Windows 98 is, and explains the objects you see on the Windows 98 screen—including the desktop, icons, the Taskbar, the Start menu, and windows. It also explains the Windows 98 Control Panel, a collection of programs that let you control how Windows 98 and your computer work. Many Control Panel programs run *Wizards*, special programs that step you through the process of creating or configuring an object on your computer. Properties are another way of choosing settings for the objects in your computer. This chapter also describes how to start Windows 98, shut it down, and suspend Windows' operation when you're not using your computer.

What Is Windows 98?

Windows 98 is the latest desktop version of Microsoft's Windows series of programs. Together with DOS, which comes with Windows 98, it is an *operating system*, a program that manages your entire computer system, including its screen, keyboard, disk drives, memory, and central processor. Windows also provides a *graphical user interface*, or *GUI*, which allows you to control your computer by using a mouse, windows, and icons. You can also use the keyboard to give commands; this book describes both methods.

You can upgrade to Windows 98 from Windows 95, which Windows 98 closely resembles, from Windows 3.1, or from any version of DOS. You can also buy a computer with Windows 98 pre-installed. Once Windows 98 is installed, you can run Windows 98-compatible *application programs* (programs for getting real-world work done).

Windows 98 comes with a lot of other programs, including utilities that help with hard-disk housekeeping, Internet connection software (Dial-Up Networking), software for connecting to several online services, an e-mail program, a web browser, a simple word processing program (WordPad), several games, and dozens of other programs.

What Appears on the Screen?

Like previous versions of Windows, Windows 98 uses windows to display information on your screen, and icons to provide pictorial buttons for you to click. Windows 98 has a *Taskbar*, a "mission control" for your computer, which is an enhanced version of the Taskbar in Windows 95. All of these objects appear on the Windows 98 desktop—your screen.

What Is the Desktop?

Windows 98 uses your screen as a *desktop*, a work area on which you see your programs. The desktop can contain windows, icons, and the Taskbar. You can think of the icons and windows that appear on your screen as "sitting" on your metaphorical

What Hardware Do You Need?

Windows 98 requires the following computer hardware:

- A 386, 486, Pentium, Pentium Pro, Pentium II, or compatible CPU.

- At least 16MB of RAM memory (although your system will run very slowly with less than 32MB).

- A hard disk with at least 200MB free, depending on which options you choose to install (you may need more for temporary files).

- A CD-ROM drive or diskette drive, from which to install Windows 98 and other software (these drives are not required if your computer is connected to a local area network or the Internet).

- A screen, keyboard, and mouse or other pointing device.

- If you plan to listen to sounds played by Windows 98 and other programs, you need a sound board and speakers attached to your computer (see "Configuring Windows to Work with Sound" in Chapter 17).

- If you plan to use your computer to connect to the Internet, you need a modem and a phone line, a cable modem and cable connection, or a local area network (LAN) connection.

Welcome to Windows 98!

Open the Welcome to Windows icon on the Windows 98 desktop (that is, either click or double-click the icon, depending on how Windows 98 is configured) for an introduction to Windows. If the icon doesn't appear, choose Start | Programs | Accessories | Tips and Tour (that is, click the Start button, choose Programs, then choose Accessories from the drop-down menu that appears, then choose Tips and Tour). You see a menu with the following options:

- Register your copy of Windows 98 via the Internet, using the Registration Wizard. (This option disappears once you register.)

- Discover Windows 98 by taking a tour.

- Tune up your system, using the Tune-Up Wizard (see "Scheduling Your Disk Housekeeping Programs" in Chapter 34).

- Read notes about this release of Windows 98.

For other information about Windows, use its online help system.

desktop. You may also see the Channel bar, a special kind of window (see "What Are Subscriptions and Channels?" in Chapter 25).

See Chapter 2 for an explanation of what windows are and how to use them.

What Style Is Your Desktop?

Your desktop can be configured in one of two *styles*, or in a custom-designed combination of the two:

■ **Web style**   Your desktop looks and acts much like a web page, as shown in Figure 1-1. Icon labels are underlined, like web page links. Filenames in Folder

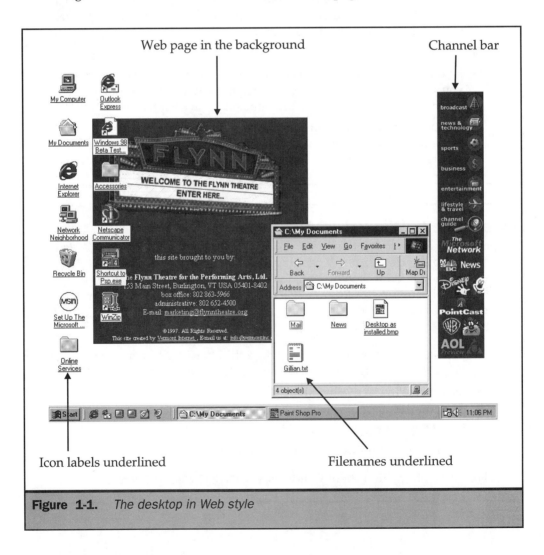

Figure 1-1.   *The desktop in Web style*

and Windows Explorer windows are underlined, too. To run a program or open a file, click the icon or filename once. To select an icon or file, just let the mouse pointer rest on the object.

■ **Classic style**   Your desktop looks and acts just like the Windows 95 desktop, as shown in Figure 1-2. Icon labels are not underlined, nor are the filenames in Folder or Windows Explorer windows. To run a program or open a file, double-click the icon or filename. To select an icon or file, click the object once.

■ **Custom style**   Your desktop looks and acts as you want it to look and act. For example, you can create your own combination of Web and Classic styles (see "Choosing Web Style, Classic Style, or Something in Between" in Chapter 8).

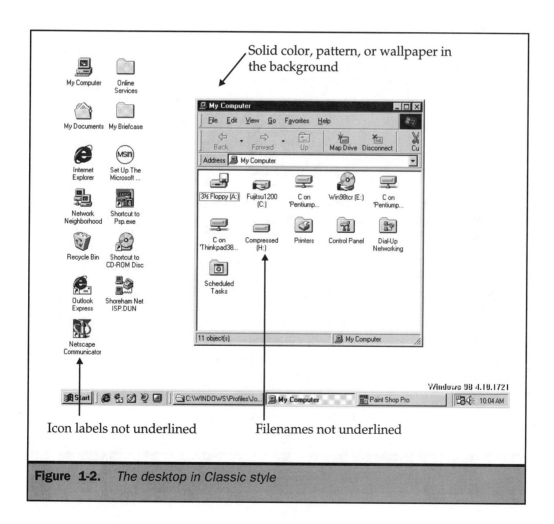

Figure 1-2.   *The desktop in Classic style*

Table 1-1 shows how to run a program, open a file, or select an object in Web style and Classic style.

In this book, when the instructions say to run a program, open a file, or select an object on the screen, follow the instructions in Table 1-1.

To choose the style for your desktop, you choose View | Options from a Folder window, as described in the section "Choosing the Style of Your Desktop" later in this chapter.

 In this book, we indicate command choices from the menu bar like this: "Choose View | Options," rather than saying "Choose View from the menu bar, and then choose Options from the View drop-down menu that appears."

What Is an Icon?

An *icon* is a little picture on your screen. When you click the icon, or select the icon with the keyboard and then press ENTER, something happens. Windows 98 uses icons, such as the example shown here, to represent programs, files, and commands.

Throughout this book, the instructions tell you what icons you can expect to see, what happens when you click them, and when to use them.

Task	Web Style	Classic Style
Run a program using an icon	Click the icon for the program	Double-click the icon for the program
Open a file using an icon or filename	Click the icon for the file or the filename	Double-click the icon for the file
Select an object	Move the mouse pointer to the object for a moment, but do not click	Click the object

Table 1-1. *How to Run Programs, Open Files, and Select Objects on the Desktop*

Tip   *Many programs provide labels for their icons. Icon labels may appear just below the icon, or may appear in a little box when you rest the mouse pointer on the icon for a moment.*

Icons on your desktop that include a little back arrow in a little white box in the lower-left corner of the icon are *shortcuts,* and represent files or programs on your computer (see "What Is a Shortcut?" in Chapter 9).

What Is the Taskbar?

The *Taskbar* is a row of buttons and icons that usually appears along the bottom of the screen (see Figure 1-3). You can configure Windows 98 to display the Taskbar along the top or side of your screen. You can also tell Windows to hide the Taskbar when you aren't using it.

The Taskbar has several parts:

- The Start button, which is usually at the left end of the Taskbar.
- The Task Manager, which contains buttons for each window that is open on the desktop.
- The toolbar area, which can contain one or more toolbars (sets of buttons). Figure 1-3 shows the Quick Launch toolbar.
- The system tray, which contains icons for some Windows 98 programs and folders, including the system clock.

Chapter 12 describes how to use and configure the Taskbar and its toolbars.

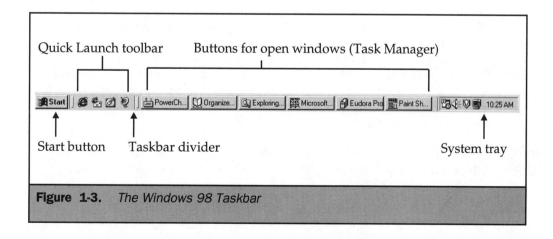

Figure 1-3.   *The Windows 98 Taskbar*

What Is the Start Menu?

When you click the Start button on the Taskbar, the Start menu, shown here, appears.

The Start menu lists commands and additional menus that list most or all the programs that you can run on your computer. You can use the Start menu to run almost any program installed on your computer.

   The Start menu usually includes the Windows Update, Programs, Favorites, Documents, Settings, Find, Help, Run, and Shut Down commands. Other commands may also appear on the menu. For example, if you install Microsoft Office 97, its installation program adds two commands to the Start menu: New Office Document and Open Office Document. You can customize which programs appear on the Start menu and how they are arranged. See "What Is the Start Menu?" in Chapter 12 for how to use and configure the Start menu.

   In this book, we indicate Start menu commands like this: "Choose Start | Help" to tell you to click the Start button and choose the Help command from the Start menu.

What Is the Task Manager?

The *Task Manager*, shown here, is the part of the Taskbar that shows a button for each program that is running.

If a program displays more than one window, more than one button may appear. On each Task Manager button, Windows 98 displays the icon for the program and as much of the program name as can fit. Some programs display other information on the Task Manager button; for example, Notepad displays the name of the text file open in the Notepad window.

Click a window's button to *select* that window, that is, make that window active (see "What Is Multitasking?" in Chapter 2). You can also right-click a button to see the *system menu*, a menu of commands you can give regarding that window, including opening and closing the window (see "What Is the System Menu?" in Chapter 2).

What Are the Icons in the System Tray?

The *system tray* (or *systray*), shown here, appears at the right end of the Taskbar, and contains a group of tiny icons along with the system clock.

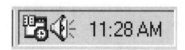

Some programs add icons to the system tray. Windows 98 usually displays these icons:

- **Task Scheduler** Double-click this icon to tell Windows to run programs on specified days at specified times (see "Running Programs on a Schedule Using Task Scheduler" in Chapter 2).

- **Volume** Click this icon to control the volume of your computer's speakers, if any (see "Controlling the Volume, Balance, and Tone" in Chapter 17). Click the desktop to close the little window that appears. Double-click the icon to set the volume and balance of the speakers when they are used to play sounds from various sources.

- **System Clock** The system clock shows the current time according to your computer's internal clock (see "Setting the Date and Time" in Chapter 14). When you move the mouse pointer to the clock, after a moment, the current date appears, too.

To find out the name of an icon, move the mouse pointer to the icon, without clicking. In a moment, the icon's label appears. To change the settings for the program that displays the icon, or to exit the program, double-click the icon or right-click the icon and choose a command from the menu that appears.

What Is the Mouse Pointer?

The *mouse pointer* indicates what object on the screen will be affected when you click a mouse button. As you move the mouse, trackball, or other pointing device, the mouse pointer moves, too. A separate indicator, the *cursor*, which usually appears as a blinking vertical line, shows where text you type will appear (see "Configuring Your Mouse" in Chapter 14).

How Do You Configure Windows and Other Programs?

To use Windows 98 effectively, you'll need to configure Windows and the other programs that you run to work with your computer's hardware and with each other. You'll encounter these concepts:

- Properties, which are settings for many different objects in your computer's hardware and software.
- The Control Panel, which lets you see and change many properties and other settings.
- Wizards, which are programs that help automate the processes of installing hardware, installing software, and configuring software.

What Are Properties?

Every object in Windows 98—the hardware components of your computer, software programs, files, and icons—has *properties*, the settings that affect how that object works. For example, a file might have properties such as a filename, size, and the date the file was last modified.

You can see the properties of most objects by right-clicking the object. Windows 98 displays a Properties dialog box, and may let you change some of the settings, depending on the type of object. Figure 1-4 shows the properties of an icon on the desktop.

What Is the Control Panel?

The *Control Panel*, shown in Figure 1-5, is a window that displays icons for a number of programs that let you control your computer, Windows 98, and the software you have

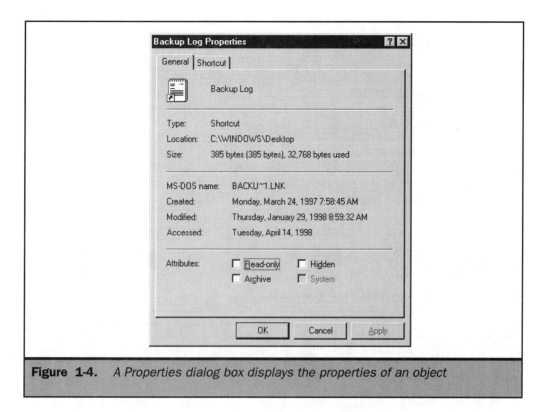

Figure 1-4.   *A Properties dialog box displays the properties of an object*

installed. These programs help you see and change the properties of many parts of Windows 98.

To see the Control Panel, choose Start | Settings | Control Panel. The icons in the Control Panel window may include these programs, depending on what Windows 98 components and other software you have installed:

- **Accessibility Options**   The Accessibility Properties dialog box lets you configure Windows 98's keyboard, sound, display, mouse, and other options, for people with disabilities. This icon appears only if you installed Accessibility options when you installed Windows 98 (see Chapter 20).

- **Add New Hardware**   The Add New Hardware Wizard configures Windows 98 when you add new hardware to your computer system (see Chapter 15).

- **Add/Remove Programs**   The Add/Remove Programs Properties dialog box helps you install new programs or uninstall programs you no longer use (see Chapter 3).

- **Date/Time**   The Date/Time Properties dialog box lets you set the date, time, and time zone where you are located (see Chapter 14).

- **Display**   The Display Properties dialog box controls the appearance, resolution, screen saver, and other settings for your display (see Chapter 13).

Figure 1-5.   *The Control Panel window*

- **Fonts**   The Fonts window lets you install new screen and printer fonts (see Chapter 13).

- **Game Controllers**   The Game Controllers dialog box lets you install games (see Chapter 14).

- **Internet**   The Internet Properties dialog box contains settings for your web browser and Internet connection (see Chapter 24).

- **Keyboard**   The Keyboard Properties dialog box contains settings that control your keyboard and the cursor (see Chapter 14).

- **Modems**   The Modems Properties dialog box contains settings for how your modem works, and helps you diagnose problems (see Chapter 21).

- **Mouse**   The Mouse Properties dialog box lets you define the buttons on your mouse, and lets you choose how fast you need to double-click, what your mouse pointer looks like on-screen, and whether moving the mouse leaves a trail (see Chapter 14).

- **Multimedia**   The Multimedia Properties dialog box contains settings for the audio, video, MIDI, and audio CD settings of your computer (see Chapter 17).

- **Network**   The Network dialog box contains settings you use when configuring a local area network. It also contains settings for connecting to the Internet (see Chapter 29).

- **Passwords**   The Passwords Properties dialog box lets you set a password for using Windows on your computer, user profiles if more than one person will use the computer, and other security settings (see Chapter 33).

- **Power Management**   The Power Management Properties dialog box contains controls to set when Windows 98 automatically turns off your monitor, hard disks, and other computer components to save electricity. Laptops have additional power usage options that Window 98 can handle (see Chapter 19).

- **Printers**   The Printers dialog box includes icons for each printer to which you have access, as well as an icon for adding a new printer (see Chapter 16).

- **Regional Settings**   The Regional Setting Properties dialog box lets you tell Windows 98 the time zone, currency, number format, and date format you prefer to use. Not all programs follow the settings you choose, but many do (see Chapter 14).

- **Sounds**   The Sounds dialog box lets you assign a sound to each Windows event, or events in other programs. For example, you can set your computer to play a fanfare when your e-mail program receives new messages (see Chapter 17).

- **System**   The System Properties dialog box lets you use the Device Manager to change advanced settings for each hardware component of your computer. You can also optimize the performance of your computer (see Chapter 15).

- **Telephony**   The Dialing Properties dialog box contains settings that control how Windows 98 dials the phone using your modem (see Chapter 21).

- **Users**   The Enable Multi-user Settings Wizard helps you set up user names and passwords so your computer can be used by more than one person. Each person's user name can store that person's desktop settings (see Chapter 33).

You may see additional icons if you have installed additional hardware or software on your computer.

What Is a Wizard?

Windows 98, like many other Microsoft programs, includes many *Wizards*, programs that step you through the process of creating or configuring something. For example, the Internet Connection Wizard leads you through the many steps required to set up a Dial-Up Networking connection to an Internet service provider (ISP).

Wizards include instructions for each step, telling you what information you must provide, and making suggestions regarding what choices to make. Most Wizards display window after window of information and questions, with Back, Next, and Cancel buttons at the bottom of each window. Figure 1-6 shows a window displayed by the Microsoft Windows 98 Registration Wizard. Fill out the information requested by the Wizard, and then click the Next button to continue. If you need to return to a previous Wizard window, click the Back button. To exit the Wizard, click the Cancel button. The Wizard's last screen usually displays a Finish button, since there's no "next" screen to see.

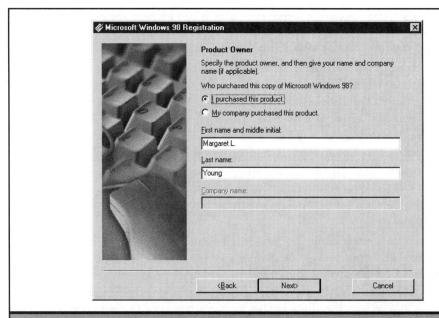

Figure 1-6. *Wizards step you through configuring parts of Windows or other programs*

Starting Up Windows 98

On most systems, Windows 98 starts automatically when you turn on the computer. You see whatever messages your computer displays on startup, followed by the Windows 98 "splash screen" (clouds and a logo). If your computer is on a local area network or is set up for multiple users, you also see a logon screen; type your user name, press TAB to move the cursor to the password box, type your password, and press ENTER.

If your computer system has been suspended, Windows hasn't been shut down; instead, it is "sleeping." To start up where you left off, just resume operation of your computer, which usually is accomplished by moving the mouse, pressing a key (such as the SHIFT key), or opening the cover of a laptop.

Shutting Down Windows 98

When you need to turn off the computer, you must shut down Windows first. Shutting down Windows allows Windows to close all its files and do other housekeeping tasks before terminating.

To shut down Windows, choose Start | Shut Down (or click the desktop and press ALT-F4, or press CTRL-ESC and choose Shut Down). You see the Shut Down Windows dialog box, shown in Figure 1-7. Your Shut Down Windows dialog box may contain different options if your computer is connected to a local area network or has a suspend mode.

Choose Shut Down and click OK. Windows displays a message when you can safely turn off the computer. Don't turn off the computer until you see this message.

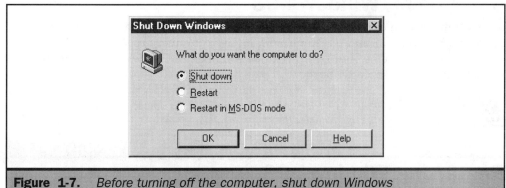

Figure 1-7.   *Before turning off the computer, shut down Windows*

When Can You Turn Off the Computer?

We recommend that you *not* turn off the computer when you are done using it. Windows 98 likes to perform housekeeping tasks when you aren't using the computer, so it's a good idea to leave it on even when you're not working. You can schedule programs to run at specified times—for example, you can schedule Windows 98 to collect your e-mail at 7:00 a.m. every morning (see "Running Programs on a Schedule Using Task Scheduler" in Chapter 2).

Many computers power down the screen, hard disk, and fan after a set time of inactivity. The computer itself, however, is still running. If your screen doesn't power off automatically, you should turn off your screen when you aren't using the computer. Computer screens use the lion's share of the electricity consumed by the computer, and it's bad for the screen to display the same image for hours at a time.

Setting Windows to Shut Down by Itself

Windows includes *OnNow*, technology that allows Windows to power down the computer when nothing is happening and to power back up when the computer is needed again, if the computer's hardware permits. To use OnNow, choose Start | Settings | Control Panel. In the Control Panel window, open the Power Management icon (see "Managing Your Computer Power" in Chapter 19).

Suspending Windows 98

Some computers have a *suspend* or *stand by* mode in which the computer remains on, but the disk drives, fan, and screen turn off. If your computer has such a mode, a Stand By option appears on the Shut Down Windows dialog box. To switch your computer to suspend mode, choose Start | Suspend.

To wake up a computer that has partially powered itself down, move the mouse around without clicking, or press the SHIFT key a few times.

Restarting Windows 98

Many programs require that you restart Windows after installing the program to ensure that the program's components are correctly loaded. To restart Windows, save all the files you are editing (if any), exit your programs, and choose Start | Shut Down. Choose Restart on the Shut Down Windows dialog box, and then click OK. Windows exits and reloads.

It's not a bad idea to restart Windows every day or so. Windows' housekeeping isn't perfect, and it may lose track of some system resources over time (see "What Are System Resources?" in Chapter 36). Restarting Windows ensures that the maximum system resources are available for your use.

Choosing the Style of Your Desktop

You can choose whether to use Web style, Classic style, or your own Custom style for your desktop. Follow these steps:

1. Choose Start | Settings | Folder Options. You see the Folder Options dialog box.

2. If the General tab isn't selected, click it.

3. In the Windows Desktop Update box, click Web style, Classic style, or Custom. If you click Custom, click the Settings button to create your own custom style.

You can define additional settings to control the style of your desktop and the Folder windows on the desktop (see "Choosing Web Style, Classic Style, or Something in Between" in Chapter 8).

Displaying Properties

To display the properties of almost anything you see on the screen in Windows 98, right-click the item and choose Properties from the menu that appears. You see a dialog box, with a title that usually includes the word "Properties." If the object has too many properties to fit in a dialog box, tabs may run along the top of the dialog box; click a tab to see the settings on that tab.

For example, to see the properties of the Windows 98 desktop, right-click the desktop in a place where it is not covered by icons or windows. You see the Display Properties dialog box (see "What Are Display Properties?" in Chapter 13). When you are done looking at the properties shown, and possibly changing some of the properties that can be changed, click OK to save your changes or Cancel to cancel them and exit from the dialog box.

Chapter 2

Running Programs

Running Windows 98 itself doesn't get you very far. The point of Windows is to let you run programs that help you get work done. To take advantage of Windows' ability to *multitask* (do several things at the same time), this chapter explains how to run several programs at the same time and how to switch among them. Because programs display information in windows, you also learn how the windows work that you see on your screen.

You can tell Windows 98 to start programs for you, and you can control the size and location of the windows in which programs run. Once a program is running, you can give commands using the mouse and keyboard. This chapter also explains how to configure Windows 98 to automatically launch the programs you always use, so you're ready to work as soon as you start Windows, how to schedule programs to run at pre-set times, and how to define shortcut keys for quick-starting programs you use frequently.

What Are Windows and Programs?

Windows 98 manages the keyboard, screen, disks, and programs that make up your computer. As you learn about Windows 98, you need to understand what windows and programs are, and you may run across the terms *processes* and *tasks*, which are related.

What Are Programs, Applications, Processes, and Tasks?

A *program* is a sequence of computer instructions that perform a task. Programs are stored in *program files*, which have the filename extension .exe or .com (see "What Are Extensions and File Types?" in Chapter 8). When you run a program, your computer executes the instructions in the program file. Under Windows 98, several programs can run at the same time.

Programs can do several things at once; for example, a word processing program may be able to print one document while you edit another. One program can run several *tasks* or *processes* at the same time. Running several tasks is called *multitasking*. Windows 98 itself uses multitasking, running tasks that monitor the hard disk, screen, and keyboard, update the onscreen clock, and run programs on a schedule, for example.

An *applications program*, or *application*, is a program that does real-world–oriented work. Word processors, spreadsheets, and databases are widely used types of applications. A *systems program* does computer-oriented work. Printer drivers (that control the actions of a printer) or disk scanners (that check disks for errors) are examples of system programs.

This chapter describes how to run programs (see "Starting Programs"). There's also a section on how to control the size and shape of the windows that programs display (see "Controlling the Size and Shape of Your Windows").

What Are Windows and Dialog Boxes?

A *window* is a rectangular area on the screen that displays information from a running program. Under Windows 98, each program displays information in one or more windows (see "What Do the Parts of Windows Do?"). Some windows are divided into sections called *panes*.

A *dialog box* is a special kind of window that allows you to change settings or give commands in a program. For example, in most programs, when you give a command to open a file, you see an Open File dialog box that lets you specify which file you want to open.

While a program displays a dialog box, you must exit the dialog box before continuing to use the program. Most dialog boxes include buttons to exit, including buttons with names like OK, Close, and Cancel (see "Choosing Settings on Dialog Boxes").

16-Bit vs. 32-Bit Applications

Older personal computers process data 16 bits at a time. These 16-bit computers are based on older *CPUs* (central processing units), like the Intel 8088 and 80286.

Newer personal computers process data 32 bits at a time. These 32-bit computers are based on newer CPU chips, like the Intel 80386, 80486, Pentium, and Pentium Pro.

DOS and Windows 3.1 (and earlier versions of Windows) run on both 16-bit and 32-bit computers. Windows 95, Windows 98, Windows NT, and OS/2 all require 32-bit computers.

Some programs are designed to run with DOS and Windows 3.1; these programs are called *16-bit applications*. Other programs are designed to work with Windows 95, Windows 98, Windows NT, and OS/2, and are called *32-bit applications*.

As a Windows 98 user, you can run both 16-bit and 32-bit applications. When you have a choice, run the 32-bit version of a program, though; it takes better advantage of your 32-bit computer, and usually runs faster and has more capabilities than the 16-bit version.

What Do the Parts of Windows Do?

Figure 2-1 shows a program (this example shows WordPad, a simple word processor that comes with Windows 98) running in a window. Although what's inside the

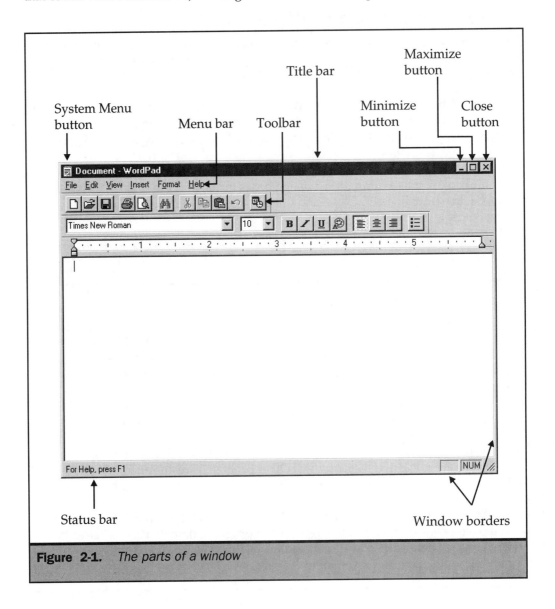

Figure 2-1.   *The parts of a window*

window frame changes from program to program, most windows you see in Windows 98 include the following components:

- **System Menu button**   Displays a menu of commands you can use to move and resize your window (see "Controlling the Size and Shape of Your Windows").
- **Title bar**   Displays the title of the window and provides a way to move the window around within the screen (see "Moving a Window").
- **Minimize button**   Shrinks the window to an icon on the Taskbar (see "Minimizing a Window").
- **Maximize or Restore button**   When you click the Maximize button, the window expands to cover the whole screen (see "Maximizing a Window"). Once a window has been maximized, the Maximize button disappears and is replaced by the Restore button. When you click the Restore button (with two overlapping rectangles), the window shrinks to its previous size and the Maximize button reappears.
- **Close button**   Closes the window and exits the program (see "Closing Windows").
- **Menu bar**   Provides a row of menus you can use to choose commands (see "Giving Commands").
- **Toolbar**   Provides a row of buttons you can click to give commands (see "Giving Commands").
- **Status bar**   Displays information about the program. Some programs let you give commands by clicking parts of the status bar.
- **Scroll bar**   Provides a way to "pan" your window up and down or left and right to show information that doesn't fit in the window (see "What Is a Scroll Bar?").
- **Window borders**   Provide a way to drag around the edges of the window to change the size and shape of the window (see "Changing the Size and Shape of a Window").

What Sizes Can Windows Be?

A window can be in one of three states:

- *Maximized*, taking up the entire screen, with no window borders (see "Maximizing a Window").
- *Minimized*, so that all that appears is the window's button on the Taskbar (see "Minimizing a Window").

■ *Restored*, that is, displayed with window borders, as shown in Figure 2-1 (see "Restoring the Window to Its Previous Size"). You can change the height and width of restored windows. Most windows on your screen are restored windows.

You can switch between these three windows sizes without stopping the program that displays the window. For example, you can minimize the WordPad window shown in Figure 2-1 without interrupting the WordPad program; when you restore or maximize the WordPad window, the WordPad program picks up where you left off.

Minimize windows when you want to unclutter your desktop without exiting programs. The choice between maximizing programs and running them in windows is a matter of taste. If your screen is small or low-resolution, maximize your windows so that you can see their contents as clearly as possible. If you have a large, high-resolution screen, you can run your programs in windows so that you can see several programs at the same time. Another advantage to running programs in windows is that you can copy information from one window to another by using the mouse.

What Is the System Menu?

The *System Menu button* is a tiny icon in the upper-left corner of each window. The icon shows which program you are running (if you happen to recognize the icon). When you click the box, you see the *System menu*, as shown here:

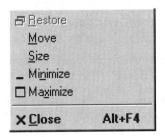

You can also display the System menu by pressing ALT-SPACEBAR or by right-clicking the title bar of the window.

The commands on the System menu do the following:

■ **Restore** Resizes the window to its previous size; this command is available only when the window is maximized. This command does the same thing as the Restore button (see "Restoring the Window to Its Previous Size").

■ **Move** Lets you move the window around on your screen by using the cursor keys. This command does the same thing as dragging the window's title bar with the mouse (see "Moving a Window"). Press ENTER to finish moving the window.

- **Size**   Lets you change the size of the window by using the cursor keys. This command does the same thing as dragging the window borders with the mouse (see "Changing the Size and Shape of a Window").

- **Minimize**   Minimizes the window, shrinking it to a small icon. This command does the same thing as the Minimize button (see "Minimizing a Window").

- **Maximize**   Maximizes the window to cover the whole screen. This command does the same thing as the Maximize button (see "Maximizing a Window").

- **Close**   Closes the window. This command does the same thing as the Close button (see "Closing Windows").

What Is the Menu Bar?

The *menu bar* is a row of one-word commands that appears along the top of a window, just below the title bar. When you choose a command on the menu bar, another menu, called a *drop-down menu*, usually appears (see "Choosing Commands from the Menu Bar").

Each drop-down menu is named after the command that displays it. For example, most programs include a File command as the first command on the toolbar. Choosing the File command displays the File menu, a list of commands that have something to do with files, such as opening, closing, or saving files (see Figure 2-2).

If your screen doesn't have room for the entire drop-down menu to appear, you see a downward-pointing triangle at the bottom of the submenu; click the arrow to see the rest of the menu.

Other information may appear next to commands on menus:

- Commands that have a rightward-pointing triangle to their right display another menu.

- Commands that have an ellipsis (three dots) after them display a dialog box.

- Some commands represent an option that can be turned on or off. A command of this type has a check mark to its left when the option is on (selected) and no check mark when the option is off (not selected). For example, a View menu might have a Status Bar command that is checked or unchecked, controlling whether the status bar is displayed. To turn an option on or off, choose the command; the check mark appears or disappears.

- Some menus contain several options, only one of which may be selected. A large dot appears to the left of the selected option. To select an option, choose the command; the dot appears to its left.

- For some commands there is a button on the toolbar that performs the command. On the drop-down menu that contains the command, the toolbar button appears to its left, just as a reminder.

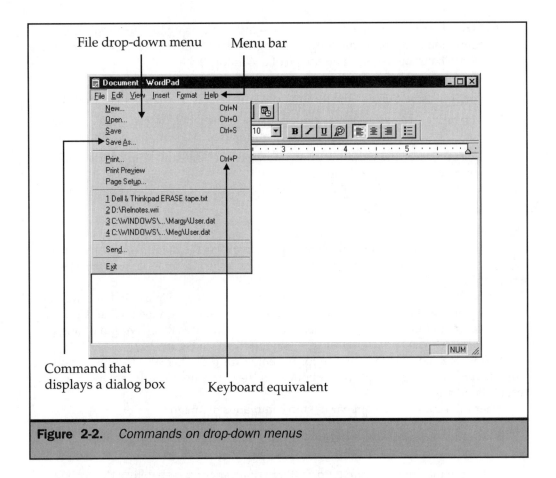

File drop-down menu   Menu bar

Command that
displays a dialog box   Keyboard equivalent

Figure 2-2. *Commands on drop-down menus*

■ Some commands have a keyboard shortcut. For example, many programs
provide the key combination CTRL-S as a shortcut for choosing the File menu
and then the Save command. Keyboard shortcuts appear to the right of
commands on drop-down menus.

*In this book, instructions for choosing commands from the menu bar appear as
follows: Choose File | Open.*

What Is a Scroll Bar?

Many programs display objects that are too large to fit in the program's window.
For example, the WordPad program that comes with Windows 98 can edit documents

that are much larger than can fit on the screen. Most programs provide *scroll bars*, as shown here, to let you choose which part of the document you want to see in the program's window.

Scroll bar ———————

For Help, press F1

Scroll bars may be horizontal (running along the bottom edge of a window) or vertical (running down the right edge of a window). All scroll bars have arrow buttons at each end and a sliding gray box somewhere in the scroll bar; some programs display scroll bars with additional buttons. The length of a vertical scroll bar represents the entire length of the document you are viewing, and the sliding box represents the part of the document that you can currently see. For horizontal scroll bars, the width of the scroll bar represents the entire width of the document.

To change which part of the document you can see, click the arrow button at one end of the scroll bar, or click and drag the sliding gray box along the scroll bar.

What Is Multitasking?

The heart of Windows 98 is its ability to *multitask*, that is, to run several programs at the same time. Some programs run several tasks simultaneously; for example, many word processors can format one document for printing while letting you edit another document.

To run more than one program at the same time, just go ahead and run one program, then another, then another. The first program you run continues to run when the second program starts. Each program runs in its own window; some programs create more than one window. Each window can be minimized, maximized, or restored (see "Controlling the Size and Shape of Your Windows"). A button appears on the Taskbar for each program.

One window is always *on top*, which means it is the *active window*. The title bar of active window is a different color than the title bars of all the other windows on your screen; in the default Windows 98 color scheme, the title bar of the active window is blue while the other title bars are gray (see "What Is a Desktop Scheme?" in Chapter 13). Where the active window overlaps with another window, the active window obscures the other window. Figure 2-3 shows several programs running at the same time; the active window is Calculator, a program that comes with Windows 98 (see "Using Calculator" in Chapter 5).

Whatever you type on the keyboard is directed to the program in the active window. The programs in the other windows continue to run, but they don't receive input from your keyboard until you make them the active window.

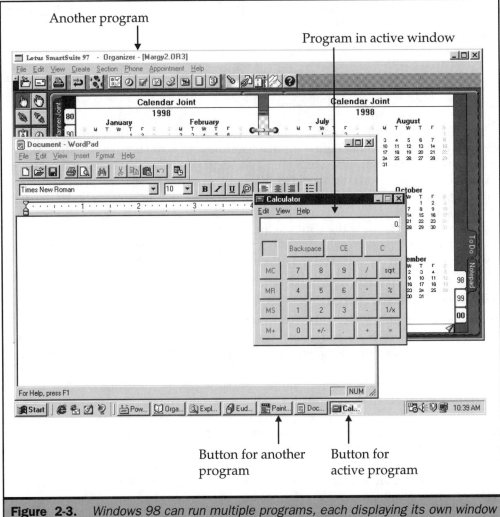

Figure 2-3.   *Windows 98 can run multiple programs, each displaying its own window*

Starting Programs

Windows gives you many ways to start a program, including: clicking its icon on your Windows desktop, choosing it from a menu, clicking a document you want to edit or view by using the program, clicking the name of the file that contains the program, and typing the program name into a Run or DOS window. Each method is described in one of the following sections.

Starting Programs from the Desktop

If an icon for the program appears on your Windows 98 desktop, click the icon either once or twice to run the program. If the labels under the icons on your desktop are underlined, your desktop is configured in Web style, so just click once. If the labels are not underlined, your desktop is configured in Classic style, so double-click. You can control whether you need to single- or double-click icons to run programs by setting your view options (see "Choosing the Style of Your Desktop" in Chapter 1.)

Another way to start a program from the desktop is to select the icon (in Classic style, click the icon once; in Web style, rest the mouse pointer on the icon without clicking). Then press ENTER.

You can change the name, graphic, and action of a desktop icon (see Chapter 13).

Starting Programs from the Start Menu

Chapter 1 describes the Start menu, including the all-important Start button. To launch a program from the Start menu, click the Start button. You see the Start menu, as shown here:

Your Start menu may have additional options, depending on which programs you have installed.

When your mouse pointer is on a menu name, the menu appears to its right. Point to menus until you see the name of the program that you want to run; then click the program name. Most programs appear on the Programs menu, while many Windows utility programs appear on the Settings menu. Other programs appear on submenus of the Programs menu. You may need to try several menus to find the one that contains the program you want. You can always press ESC to cancel the menu you are looking at (moving your mouse pointer off the menu usually cancels the menu, too).

For example, WordPad appears on the Accessories submenu of the Programs menu. To run WordPad, choose Start | Programs | Accessories | WordPad.

You can rearrange the programs on your Start and Programs menus so that the programs you most frequently run appear on the Programs menu rather than on a submenu (see "What Is the Start Menu?" in Chapter 12). You can also create desktop icons for any programs on these menus (see "Designing and Decorating Your Desktop" in Chapter 13).

 You can change the order of the items on the Start and Programs menus by dragging them up and down on the menus. If you don't intend to reorganize your menus, don't click and drag the commands on them! See "Editing the Start Menu" in Chapter 12 for how to configure your menus.

Starting Programs by Opening Files

Windows 98 knows which programs you use to open which types of files. For example, it knows that files with the .doc extension are opened using Microsoft Word. Windows 98 displays the names of files in a Windows Explorer or Folder window. If the filenames are underlined, your desktop is configured in Web style, so you single-click the filename to open it. If the filenames are not underlined, your desktop is configured in Classic style, so you double-click the filename. You can control whether you need to single- or double-click filenames to run programs by setting your view options (see "Choosing the Style of Your Desktop" in Chapter 1).

When you click or double-click a filename, you are telling Windows 98 to run the appropriate program to handle that file (if the program isn't already running), and then to open the file in that program. If an icon for a file appears on your desktop, clicking or double-clicking the icon tells Windows 98 to do the same thing.

For example, if your desktop is configured in Classic style and you double-click a file with the extension .mdb (a Microsoft Access database file), Windows runs Microsoft Access and opens the database file.

If you try to open a file for which Windows doesn't know which program to run, you see the Open With dialog box, shown in Figure 2-4. Choose the program that can open the type of file you clicked; if the program doesn't appear on the list, click the Other button to find the filename of the program. If you always want to run this program when you click this type of file, leave the check mark in the Always Use This Program To Open This File check box. Optionally, you can type a description of the

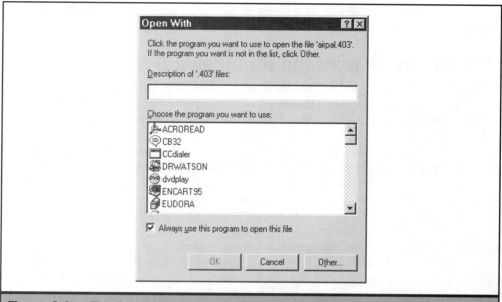

Figure 2-4.   *The Open With dialog box lets you tell Windows which program can open the file you clicked*

type of file in the Description box: this description appears when you choose View | Details in a Folder window (see "What Are Folder Windows and Windows Explorer?" in Chapter 8). Then click OK.

You can control which program runs for each type of file (see "Associating a Program with a File Extension" in Chapter 3).

If you want to open a file using a different program from the one that Windows automatically runs, hold down the SHIFT key while you right-click the filename, then choose Open With from the menu that appears. Windows displays the Open With dialog box shown in Figure 2-4, and you can choose the program you want to run.

Starting Programs by Clicking Program Filenames

Programs are stored in files, usually with the filename extension .exe. Windows 98 displays the names of program files in Windows Explorer or Folder windows.

As mentioned earlier, if the filenames are underlined, your desktop is configured in Web style, so single-click the filename of the program you want to run. If the filenames are not underlined, your desktop is configured in Classic style, so double-click to run the program. (You can control whether you need to single- or double-click filenames to run programs by setting your view options (see "Choosing the Style of Your Desktop" in Chapter 1).

For example, if your desktop is configured in Classic style and you double-click the filename Mspaint.exe, Windows runs the Microsoft Paint program.

Starting Programs from the Run Dialog Box

Before Windows, there was DOS, which required that you type the filename of a program and press ENTER to run the program. If you prefer this method, it still works in Windows 98. Choose Start | Run, and you see the Run dialog box, shown in Figure 2-5.

To run a program, type its filename into the Open box. Alternatively, click Browse to locate the filename. Then press ENTER or click OK. Windows runs the program.

Depending on the program, you may need to type additional information after the filename. For example, to run the FTP program (an Internet file transfer program that comes with Windows 98), type **ftp**, followed by a space and the name of a computer on the Internet (like ftp.microsoft.com). When you press ENTER, Windows runs the FTP program by using the additional information you typed.

If you've typed the filename in the Open box recently, click the downward-pointing button at the right end of the Open box and choose the filename from the list that appears.

Starting Programs from DOS

Serious DOS enthusiasts may want to see the old-fashioned DOS prompt (usually C:\>) before typing the filename of the program they want to run. To run programs from the DOS prompt, choose Start | Programs | MS-DOS Prompt. (Alternatively, you can choose Start | Run, then type **command** and press ENTER.) You see an MS-DOS Prompt window, a window that looks like the screen of a computer running DOS. Type the filename of the program you want to run and press ENTER.

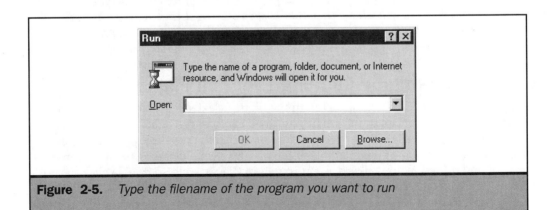

Figure 2-5.   *Type the filename of the program you want to run*

When you are done using the MS-DOS window, close the window by clicking the Close button (the X button in the upper right corner of the window). You can run DOS commands at the DOS prompt, too (see "Starting DOS Programs" in Chapter 41).

Controlling the Size and Shape of Your Windows

Your programs display their information in windows, and if you run several programs at the same time, you can end up with many windows displayed at the same time. Windows 98 lets you control the size and position of most windows, so that you can arrange your open windows to see the information you want to view (see "What Sizes Can Windows Be?").

Moving a Window

The *title bar* is the colored bar that runs along the top of the window. To move a window, click anywhere in the title bar of the window, except for the System Menu button or the buttons at the right end of the title bar. Next, drag the window to the place where you want it to appear. Release the mouse button when the window is located where you want it.

You can use the keyboard to move a window, too: press ALT-SPACEBAR to display the System menu, press M to choose the Move command, press the cursor keys to move the window, and then press ENTER when the window is located where you want it.

Minimizing a Window

A button appears on the Task Manager section of the Taskbar for each program that is running (see "What Is the Task Manager?" in Chapter 1). To minimize a window— make a window disappear, leaving nothing but its Taskbar button—click the window's Minimize button, the leftmost of the three buttons on the right end of the title bar. Alternatively, click the window's System Menu button and choose Minimize from the menu that appears.

You can minimize a window by using the keyboard, too: press ALT-SPACEBAR to display the System menu and press N to choose the Minimize command. You can also minimize a window by right-clicking the window's button on the Taskbar and choosing Minimize from the menu that appears.

Minimizing All Windows

You can minimize all the open windows on your screen by right-clicking a blank area on the Taskbar, and then choosing Minimize All Windows from the shortcut menu that appears. Using only the keyboard, you can press CTRL-ESC then ESC to select the

Taskbar; then press ALT-M to minimize all windows. If the Show Desktop icon appears on your Taskbar, you can click this icon to minimize all your windows, too. (See "What Is the Taskbar?" in Chapter 12 for a description of the Quick Launcher toolbar).

To reverse this command, right-click a blank area on the Taskbar and choose Undo Minimize All.

Maximizing a Window

To maximize a window—expand it to cover the whole screen—click the window's Maximize button, the middle button on the right end of the title bar. Alternatively, click the window's System Menu button and choose Maximize from the menu that appears. When a window is maximized, its Maximize button is replaced by the Restore button, which returns the window to the size it was before you maximized it.

If the window is currently minimized and you want to maximize it, right-click the button on the Taskbar for the window and choose Maximize from the menu that appears.

You can maximize a window by using the keyboard, too; press ALT-SPACEBAR to display the System menu and press X to choose the Maximize command. You can also maximize a window by right-clicking the window's button on the Taskbar and choosing Maximize from the menu that appears.

Restoring the Window to Its Previous Size

After you've maximized a window, you can restore it—return it to its previous size. Click the window's Restore button to restore the window. Alternatively, click the window's System Menu button and choose Restore from the menu that appears. The Restore button appears (as the middle button on the right end of the title bar) only when the window is maximized.

If the window is currently minimized and you want to restore it, click the button on the Taskbar for the window.

You can restore a window by using the keyboard, too; press ALT-SPACEBAR to display the System menu and press R to choose the Restore command. You can also restore a window by right-clicking the window's button on the Taskbar and choosing Restore from the menu that appears.

Arranging All Windows

If you'd like to see all the windows on your desktop at the same time, you can ask Windows 98 to arrange them tastefully for you. Right-click a blank area of the Taskbar and choose one of the following commands from the menu that appears:

- **Cascade Windows**   Opens all the windows such that they are overlapping, with their upper-left corners cascading from the upper-left corner of the screen, down and to the right.

- **Tile Windows Horizontally**   Opens all the windows with no overlapping, with each window extending the full width of the screen and one window below another.

- **Tile Windows Vertically**   Opens all the windows with no overlapping, with each window extending the full height of the screen and one window next to another.

If you choose one of these commands by mistake, you can undo the command by right-clicking a blank area of the Taskbar and choosing Undo Tile or Undo Cascade from the menu that appears.

 If four or more windows are open, Tile Windows Horizontally and Tile Windows Vertically arrange the windows the same way—in a grid.

Changing the Size and Shape of a Window

If a window is minimized or maximized, you can't change its size or shape: Maximized windows always take up the entire screen, and minimized windows always appear only on the Taskbar. When a program is restored (running in a window), you can change both the size and the shape (height and width) of the window by using the *window borders*.

To change a window's height or width, click the border around the window and drag it to the place where you want it. If you click along a top, side, or bottom border, you move one window border. If you click the corner of the window border, you move the borders that intersect at that corner (see Figure 2-6). When your mouse pointer is over a border, it changes to a double-pointed arrow, making it easy to tell when you can start dragging.

You can resize windows by using only the keyboard, if that's your preference. To resize a window, press ALT-SPACEBAR to display the System menu, and press S to choose the Size command. Next, press cursor keys to adjust the window size, and then press ENTER to select that size.

Closing Windows

In the upper-right corner of almost every Windows 98 window, you see a button with an X—the Close button. Clicking the Close button performs the same action as choosing File | Close from the window's menu. If the program appears in only one window (the usual situation), closing the window exits from the program, the equivalent of choosing the File | Exit command.

If you'd rather use the keyboard, you can close many windows by pressing CTRL-F4. To close a window and exit the program, press ALT-F4.

If the window is minimized, you can close the window without restoring it first. Right-click the button on the Taskbar for the window and choose Close from the menu that appears.

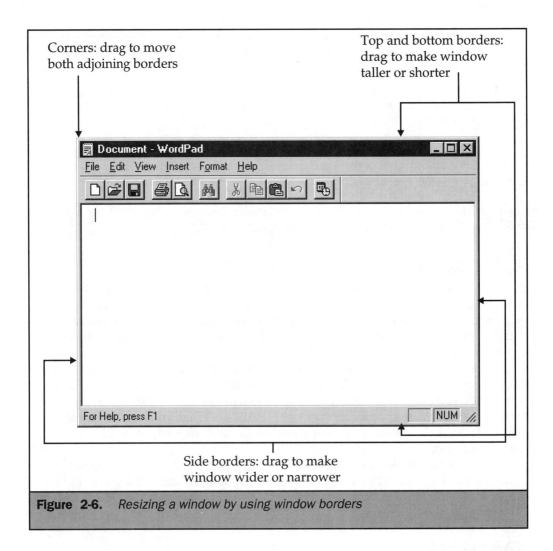

Corners: drag to move
both adjoining borders

Top and bottom borders:
drag to make window
taller or shorter

Side borders: drag to make
window wider or narrower

Figure 2-6.   *Resizing a window by using window borders*

Giving Commands

Almost every Windows program lets you issue commands to control what the
program does. For example, the WordPad program includes commands to create a
new document, save the document you are working on, print the document, and exit
the program (among its many other commands). Most programs provide several ways
to issue commands, including choosing commands from menus and clicking icons on
the toolbar.

If the program you are running lets you view a document, spreadsheet, web page, database, or other material, the entire item you are viewing may not fit in the program's window. Many programs also include scroll bars, which provide a way to move the material you are viewing within the program's window (see "What Is a Scroll Bar?").

Choosing Commands from the Menu Bar

You can choose commands from the menu bar by using your mouse or the keyboard (see "What Is the Menu Bar?").

Using the Mouse to Choose Commands

To choose a command from the menu bar, or to choose a command from any drop-down menu, click it. For example, to choose the File | Open command, click the word "File" on the menu bar, and then click the word "Open" on the File drop-down menu.

When a drop-down menu is being displayed, you can see a different drop-down menu by clicking a different command on the menu bar. To cancel a drop-down menu (that is, remove it from the screen), click somewhere outside the menu.

Tip *If you are used to using a Macintosh, you can choose commands from menus the same way as you do on a Mac: Click and hold down the mouse button on the menu bar command, move the mouse down the drop-down menu to the command you want, and then release the mouse button.*

Using the Keyboard to Choose Commands

In most programs, one letter of each command in each menu is underlined. For example, most programs underline the F in File on the menu bar. To choose a command from the menu bar by using the keyboard, follow either of these steps:

- Hold down the ALT key while you type the underlined letter of the command you want. To choose a command from a drop-down menu, press the underlined letter for that command. For example, to choose the File | Open command, press ALT-F, and then O.

- Press and release the ALT key. The first command on the menu bar is selected and appears enclosed in a box. Press the underlined letter of the command you want. For example, to choose the File | Open command, press ALT, and then press F, and then O.

Tip *You can mix using the mouse and keyboard to choose commands. For example, you can use the mouse to click a command on the menu bar, and then press a letter to choose a command from the drop-down menu that appears.*

To cancel all the drop-down menus that appear on the screen, press the ALT key again. To back up one step, press the ESC key.

 Pressing F10, in most programs, selects the first command on the menu bar (usually the File command); press ENTER to select the command and see its drop-down menu.

Finding Out More About Commands

When displaying a submenu, many programs display more information about each command as you point to the commands with your mouse. The additional information usually appears in the status bar, the gray bar along the bottom edge of the window.

Clicking Buttons on the Toolbar

Most (but not all) Windows programs display a *toolbar*, a row of small buttons with icons on them, just below the menu bar; for example:

Clicking a toolbar button issues a command, usually a command that you also could have issued from the menu bar.

To find out what a toolbar button does, rest the mouse pointer on the button but don't click. After a second, a small label, sometimes called a *tool tip*, appears near the button, naming or explaining the button. Some programs display text along with icons on their toolbar buttons, for people who like words with their pictures.

 Some programs let you move the toolbar to other locations, including into a separate floating window. Try clicking in a blank part of the toolbar and dragging it to another location in the program window.

Choosing Commands from Shortcut Menus

Windows 98 and most Windows 98-compatible programs display special menus, called *shortcut menus*, when you click with the right mouse button. The shortcut menu displays commands appropriate to the object that you clicked. For example, if you right-click a file in Windows Explorer, the shortcut menu that appears contains commands you can perform on a file, such as Open, Delete, Copy, and Rename:

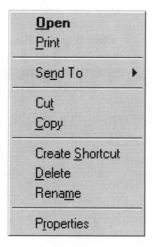

Commands on shortcut menus contain the same symbols (ellipses, triangles, and toolbar buttons) that appear on drop-down menus (see "What Is the Menu Bar?").

After you have displayed a shortcut menu, you can choose a command from the menu by clicking the command (with the left mouse button) or pressing the underlined letter in the command. To cancel a shortcut menu, click outside the menu or press the ESC key.

 You can't tell where shortcut menus will appear, or what will be on them. To use shortcut menus, just right-click the item that you want to work with, and see what appears!

You can display a shortcut menu by using only the keyboard; select the item that you want to right-click; then press SHIFT-F10 to display the shortcut menu. Use the UP-ARROW and DOWN-ARROW keys to select the command you want, and then press ENTER to select it, or choose ESC to dismiss the menu.

Choosing Settings on Dialog Boxes

Many commands display *dialog boxes*, windows that contain settings from which you can choose (see "What Are Windows and Dialog Boxes?"). Dialog boxes (like the ones shown in Figures 2-7 and 2-8) may also include a menu bar, a toolbar, and buttons that display other dialog boxes.

When a dialog box is displayed, choose the settings you want. When you are done, click the OK or Close button to dismiss the dialog box. You can also click the Close

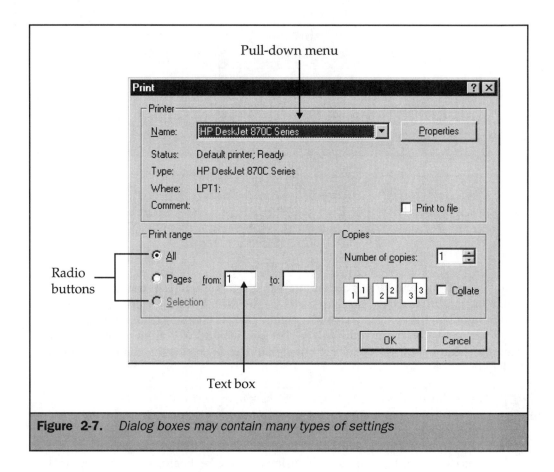

Figure 2-7.   *Dialog boxes may contain many types of settings*

button in the upper-right corner of the window. If you don't want to keep the changes you have made, click the Cancel button or press the ESC key.

> **Tip**   *You can get help about the settings in some dialog boxes by clicking the question-mark button in the upper-right corner of the dialog box, and then clicking the setting about which you want help. If the window doesn't have a question-mark button, click the Help button, if there is one, or press F1. Another method for obtaining help is to right-click the setting you need information about, and then choose the What's This? command from the shortcut menu that appears.*

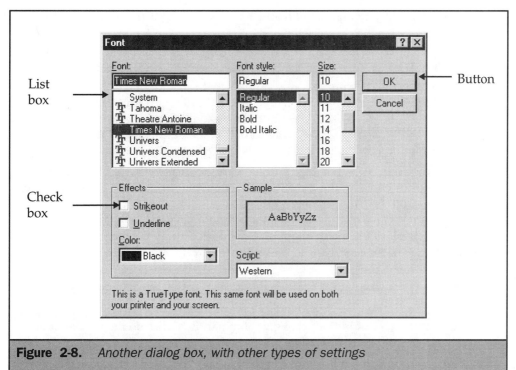

Figure 2-8.   *Another dialog box, with other types of settings*

Settings on Dialog Boxes

Dialog boxes contain various types of settings, and different software companies use different types of settings. The following are the most common types of settings in dialog boxes:

■ **Text box**   A box you can type in. To change the text in a text box, click in the box and edit the text. To replace the text with new text, select the entire contents of the box and type the new text. Some text boxes accept only numbers, and have tiny up- and down-arrow buttons that you can click to increase or decrease the number in the box.

■ **List box**   A box that contains a list of options, one of which is selected. If the list is too long to fit in the box, a scroll bar appears along the right side of the box. To select an option from the list, click it. When a list box is selected, you can use the UP-ARROW or DOWN-ARROW keys to select an option. Some list boxes include a text box just above them, so that you can type an entry in the text box or click an entry from the list box—your choice.

■ **Check box**   A box that can either be blank or contain a check mark (or X). If the check box is blank, the setting is not selected. To select or deselect a check box, click it. When a check box is selected, you can press SPACEBAR to select or deselect it.

■ **Radio button**   A group of round buttons that can either be blank or contain a dot. If the button contains a dot, it is selected. Only one of the buttons can be selected at a time. To select one button in a group of radio buttons, click it. When a button in a group of radio buttons is selected, you can press cursor-motion keys on the keyboard to select the button you want.

■ **Pull-down menu**   A box with a downward-pointing triangle button at its right end. The box displays the currently selected setting. To choose a setting, click in the box or on the triangle button to display a menu; then click an option from the menu. When a pull-down menu is selected, pressing the DOWN-ARROW key usually displays the menu of options; if it does display the menu, press DOWN-ARROW repeatedly until the option you want is highlighted, and then press ENTER.

■ **Menu bar**   A row of commands, such as the menu bar at the top of a program window.

■ **Toolbar**   A row of buttons that give commands, similar to the toolbar at the top of a program window.

■ **Command button**   A box you can click to perform a command. Most dialog boxes include an OK or Close button, and a Cancel button. If the label on the command button ends with an ellipsis (three dots), the button displays another dialog box. One command button on each dialog box is the default command button, and has a darker border. Pressing ENTER has the same effect as clicking this button. When a command button is selected, you can press SPACEBAR to perform its command.

Except for command buttons, most settings have labels (explanatory text) to the left or right (or occasionally above) the setting.

Some dialog boxes have too many settings to fit in the window, so they contain several pages, or *tabs*, of settings. Figure 2-9 shows a dialog box with tabs running along the top of the dialog box. When you click a tab, the rest of the dialog box changes to show the settings that are associated with that tab.

Moving Around a Dialog Box

One setting in the dialog box is selected, which means that it is currently active. The selected setting is affected if you press a key on the keyboard. The selected setting is highlighted or outlined, depending on the type of setting.

Here are ways to select a setting in a dialog box:

■ Click the setting which you want to select.

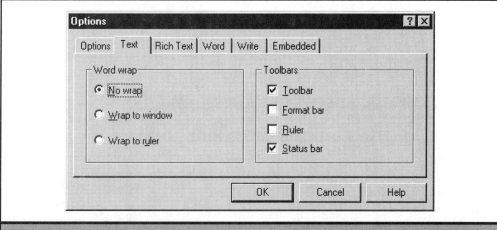

Figure 2-9.   *Each tab along the top of a dialog box displays a different group of settings*

- Press the TAB key to select another setting, usually below or to the right of the current setting. Press SHIFT-TAB to select the previous setting.

- If the setting which you want to select has an underlined letter in its label, hold down the ALT key while you type that letter. For example, to select a setting labeled Save In, press ALT-I.

- If the dialog box has tabs along the top, you can see the settings associated with another tab by clicking that tab or by pressing CTRL-TAB or CTRL-SHIFT-TAB. To select a tab along the top of the dialog box, click the tab, or press the ALT key and type the underlined letter in the label on the tab. Once you select a tab, you can use the LEFT-ARROW and RIGHT-ARROW keys to display the settings for each tab.

Open, Save As, and Browse Dialog Boxes

The Open, Save As, and Browse dialog boxes in most programs have some special settings. All three dialog boxes provide you with a way of choosing a disk drive, a folder, and a file to open, save, or run. The standard versions of these dialog boxes have a special toolbar, as shown in Figure 2-10.

Most Open, Save As, and Browse dialog boxes have the following settings:

- **Look In or Save In pull-down menu**   The Open and Browse dialog boxes contain a Look In pull-down menu that lets you specify the folder that contains the file you want to open. The Save As dialog box contains a similar Save In pull-down menu that lets you specify the folder into which you want to save a file. Pressing F4 usually moves to this menu.

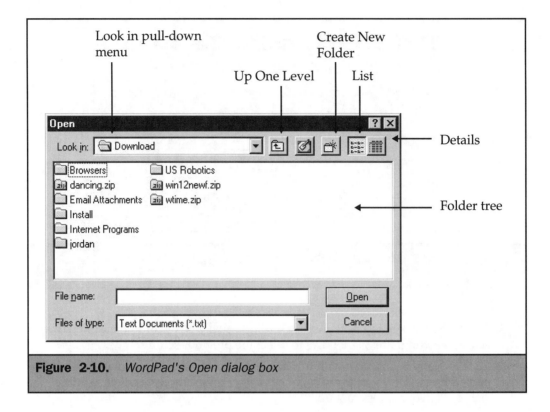

Figure 2-10. *WordPad's Open dialog box*

- **Folder tree** This large list box displays the current contents of the folder you selected in the Look In or Save In pull-down menu. Press F5 to update the contents of the folder tree if you think it has changed (see "What Is the Folder Tree?" in Chapter 8).

- **Up One Level button** Clicking this button changes which folder is named in the Look In or Save In box by moving up one level in the folder tree (to the folder's parent folder). The folder tree listing is updated, too. You can also press BACKSPACE to move up the folder tree one level.

- **Create New Folder button** Clicking this button creates a new folder within the current folder (see "Creating Files and Folders" in Chapter 8).

- **List button** Clicking this button displays in multiple columns the names of the files and folders in the folder tree, with no other information.

- **Details button** Clicking this button displays in a single column the names of files and folders in the folder tree, along with file sizes, file types, and the date the file or folder was last modified.

Switching, Exiting, and Canceling Programs

Windows 98 lets you run many programs at the same time, each in its own window. You can exit from one program while leaving other programs running, and you can choose which program's window is the active window—the window you are currently using.

Switching Programs

To *switch programs*—choose another window as the active window—you can:

- Click in the window for the program.
- Click the button for the window on the Taskbar. If the window was minimized, clicking its button returns the window to its size before it was minimized.
- Press ALT-TAB until the window you want is active. (Or press ALT-SHIFT-TAB to cycle through the open windows in the reverse order.)
- Press ALT-TAB and don't release the ALT key. A window appears with an icon for each program that is running, with the program in the active windows highlighted, as shown here:

Great Tapes for Kids: A Catalog of the Best Child

The name of the highlighted window appears at the bottom of the window. To switch to a different program, keep holding down the ALT key, press TAB to move the highlight to the icon for the window you want, and then release the ALT key.

Exiting Programs

Most programs provide several ways to exit, including some or all of these:

- Choose the File | Exit command from the menu bar.
- Click the Close button in the upper-right corner of the program's window. If a program displays multiple windows, close them all.
- Press ALT-F4.
- Click the System Menu button in the upper-left corner of the program's window and choose Close from the menu that appears.
- Right-click the program's button on the Taskbar and choose Close from the menu that appears.

If you have trouble exiting from a program, you can use the Close Program dialog box, described in the next section.

Canceling Programs

When you are running several programs at the same time, you can exit a program in the usual ways (see "Exiting Programs"). For example, click the Close button for all the windows that the program displays, or choose File | Exit.

Another way to exit a program when multiple programs are running is to press CTRL-ALT-DEL to display the Close Program dialog box (shown in Figure 2-11). This dialog box lists all the tasks that are currently running (see "What Are Programs, Applications, Processes, and Tasks?"), including a number that you probably have never heard of. Windows 98 itself runs a number of tasks with names like Sage and Systray.

To cancel a program, click the program name on the Close Program dialog box; then click the End Task button. If you were using the program to edit a file, you may lose some work.

Note   *The Close Program dialog box is designed for canceling programs that have "hung"—stopped responding to the keyboard or mouse. If no program is hung, Windows may not display the dialog box when you press CTRL-ALT-DEL. To avoid losing unsaved work, always try exiting a program by clicking its Close button, pressing ALT-F4, or choosing File | Exit before resorting to the Close Program dialog box.*

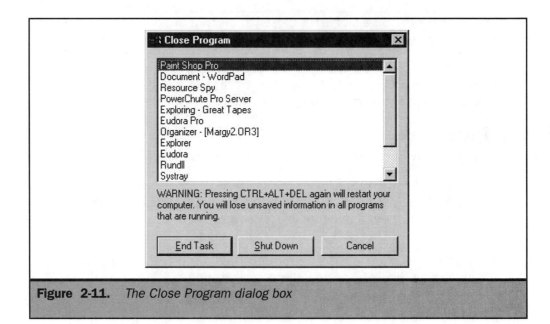

Figure 2-11.   *The Close Program dialog box*

Running Programs When Windows 98 Starts

When Windows 98 starts up, it looks in the C:\Windows\Start Menu\Programs\ Startup folder for shortcuts to programs (see "What Is a Shortcut?" in Chapter 9). If any programs or shortcuts to programs are stored in this folder, Windows 98 runs them automatically when it is done starting up.

For example, you can use this Startup folder to run your word processor and e-mail programs automatically each time you start Windows 98. Just create a shortcut in your Startup folder (see "Making Shortcuts" in Chapter 9).

Running Programs on a Schedule Using Task Scheduler

Task Scheduler is the program that Windows 98 uses to check the files and folders on your hard disk automatically. You can also use the Task Scheduler program to run almost any program at a specified time on a regular basis. When you schedule a task, you must specify the following information:

- What program you want to run.

- How often you want to run it (daily, weekly, monthly, when your computer starts, or when you log on).

- What time you want the program to start running. For weekly and monthly schedules, you also specify what day to run the program to start.

When Task Scheduler is running, its icon appears in the system tray at the right end of the Taskbar.

Scheduling a Program

To tell Task Scheduler to run a program on a regular schedule, follow these steps:

1. Look at the Scheduled Tasks window by choosing Start | Programs | Accessories | System Tools | Scheduled Tasks. Or double-click the Task Scheduler icon in the system tray on the Taskbar. You see the Scheduled Tasks window, shown in Figure 2-12.

2. Open the Add Scheduled Task item that appears in the Name column of the Scheduled Tasks window. (If it's underlined, click it once. Otherwise, double-click it.)

3. Windows 98 runs the Add Scheduled Task Wizard, which takes you through the steps required to schedule tasks to run automatically. Follow the prompts on the screen, clicking Next to move to the next step.

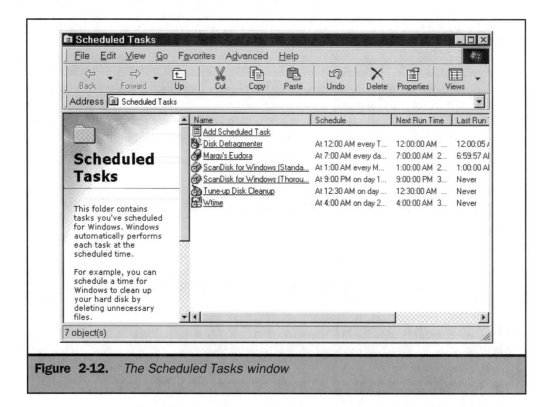

Figure 2-12. *The Scheduled Tasks window*

4. When the Add Scheduled Task Wizard displays all the information that you have specified about the program's schedule, including the name of the program and when you want it to run, click the Finish button. The program appears on a new line in the Scheduled Tasks window.

Be sure to leave your computer turned on all the time, so that when the scheduled time arrives, Windows 98 runs your program. If your computer is off (or Task Scheduler isn't running) when the time comes, the program doesn't run.

 When you schedule a task, Windows 98 creates a file with the extension .job in the C:\Windows\Tasks folder.

Canceling a Scheduled Program

If you decide that you no longer want Windows 98 to run the program automatically, open the Scheduled Tasks window, select the line for the program, and then click the Delete button on the toolbar (the big X). When Windows 98 asks you to confirm that you want to delete the file for this job, click Yes.

To cancel running all scheduled programs, choose Advanced | Stop Using Task Scheduler. No scheduled programs will be run until you choose the command Advanced | Start Using Task Scheduler. Alternatively, you can pause the scheduler program by choosing Advanced | Pause Task Scheduler to temporarily skip running scheduled programs, then choose Advanced | Continue Task Scheduler to resume. It's a good idea to pause Task Scheduler while you are installing new software, for example, so that installation isn't interrupted.

Configuring a Scheduled Program

You can configure other settings for a scheduled task. Click or double-click the line for the task in the Scheduled Tasks window (or select the line, then click the Properties button on the toolbar; or right-click the program name and choose Properties from the menu that appears). You see a dialog box with all the settings for the scheduled program (see Figure 2-13).

Click the Settings tab to tell Windows 98 to delete the job after running it, run the program only if the computer has been idle for a specified number of minutes, stop the program if the computer is in use, or skip running the program if the computer is

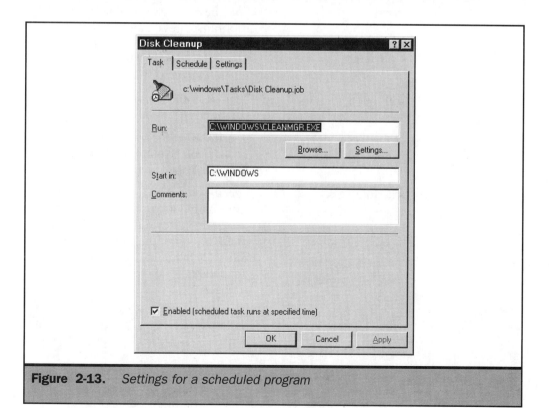

Figure 2-13. *Settings for a scheduled program*

running on batteries. Table 2-1 lists all the settings you can specify when you schedule a program to run.

Tab on Dialog Box	Setting	Description
Task	Run	Specifies the path name (and optional parameters) to run the program. If the path name includes spaces, enclose the entire path name in double quotes.
Task	Browse	Displays a Browse dialog box to allow you to choose the filename of the program you want to run.
Task	Settings	Displays the settings dialog box for the program specified in the Run box.
Task	Start In	Specifies the default folder for the program's files (some programs require files other than the program file, and this setting tells the program where to look for them).
Task	Comments	Provides space for you to type comments (ignored by Windows).
Task	Enabled	Specifies that the task is scheduled. To suspend scheduling the task, clear this check box.
Schedule	Schedule Task	Specifies the frequency that the task runs: daily, weekly, monthly, once, at system startup, at login, or when idle. The rest of the settings on the Schedule tab of the dialog box depend on which frequency you choose.
Schedule	Start time	For daily, weekly, monthly, or one-time tasks, specifies the time that Windows starts the program.

Table 2-1. *Settings for a Scheduled Task*

Tab on Dialog Box	Setting	Description
Schedule	Advanced	Displays the Advanced Schedule Options dialog box, shown in Figure 2-14, in which you can specify an end date or number of repetitions.
Schedule	Show multiple schedules	When this check box is selected, a box appears at the top of the Schedule tab from which you can pick from a list of the schedules you have defined.
Settings	Delete the scheduled task when finished	Specifies that Windows deletes the program after running it (useful only for programs you have scheduled to run only once).
Settings	Stop the scheduled task after *xx* hours *xx* minutes	Specifies the maximum number of hours and minutes that the scheduled program can run. If the program is still running after the specified amount of time, Windows stops the program.
Settings	Only start the scheduled task if computer is idle for *xx* minutes	Specifies that Windows should start the task only after the specified amount of time with no keyboard or mouse usage.
Settings	If the computer is not idle at scheduled start time, retry for *xx* minutes	Specifies that if the computer was not idle when Windows tried to start the program, the number of minutes during which Windows should try to run the program if the computer becomes idle.
Settings	Stop the scheduled task if computer is in use	Specifies that Windows stop the program if you begin to use the computer.

Table 2-1. *Settings for a Scheduled Task* (continued)

Tab on Dialog Box	Setting	Description
Settings	Don't start scheduled task if computer is running on batteries	Specifies that Windows not start the task if the computer is running off of batteries. Some programs, especially disk housekeeping programs like ScanDisk, perform lots of disk access, which can run down your computer's batteries.
Settings	Stop the scheduled task if battery mode begins	Specifies that Windows stop the program if your computer switches from external power to batteries.

Table 2-1.   *Settings for a Scheduled Task* (continued)

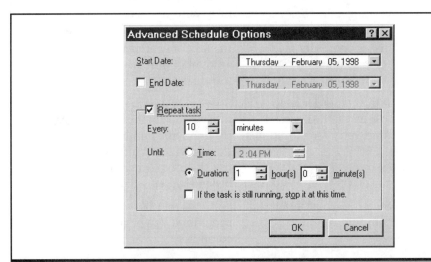

Figure 2-14.   *Advanced settings for daily, weekly, monthly, or one-time tasks*

Other Scheduling Options

You can ask Task Scheduler to let you know how its scheduled programs are doing. If you want to be notified when Task Scheduler is unable to run a scheduled program, choose Advanced from the Scheduled Tasks window's menu bar and make sure that a check mark appears to the left of the Notify Me Of Missed Tasks option (if no check mark appears, choose the option from the menu).

You can look at a log file of the results of scheduled programs by choosing Advanced | View Log from the Scheduled Tasks menu bar. Windows displays the log file, which is stored in text format in C:\Windows\Schedlog.txt, using Notepad. Log entries look consist of several lines of text, as shown here:

```
"ScanDisk for Windows (Standard test).job" (SCANDSKW.EXE)
    Started 8/16/98 5:00:19 PM
    Finished 8/16/98 6:39:58 PM
```

The first line describes the program and the subsequent lines report on the outcome of running the program.

Running Programs Using Shortcut Keys

If there is a shortcut for a program, you can define *shortcut keys* to run the program (see "What Is a Shorcut?" in Chapter 9). Windows shortcut keys for programs are always a combination of the CTRL key, the ALT key, and one other key, which must be a letter, number, or symbol key.

To define shortcut keys for a program:

1. Right-click the program's shortcut and choose Properties from the menu that appears.
2. Click the Shortcut tab on the properties dialog box for the shortcut.
3. In the Shortcut Key box, press the key you want use in combination with the CTRL and ALT keys. For example, press M to specify CTRL-ALT-M as the shortcut keys. To specify no shortcut keys, press SPACEBAR.
4. Click OK.

Once you define shortcut keys for a program, you can press the keys to run the program.

If another program uses the same combination of keys, that combination of keys no longer performs its function in the program; instead the key combination runs the program to which you assigned the shortcut keys. Luckily, few programs use CTRL-ALT key combinations.

Chapter 3

Installing Programs

W indows 98 comes with a number of useful programs, and many new computers come with lots more software pre-installed. But you'll want to install some programs yourself, sooner or later. For example, you might want to install some of the programs included on the Windows 98 CD-ROM that may not have been installed on your system.

Or you may want to do just the reverse—uninstall programs that you no longer use, or that have gone out of date. Windows 98 comes with a built-in system for installing and uninstalling programs.

What Happens During Installation and Uninstallation?

Before you can install a program, you have to get it—you have to buy or download the program. You may receive a program on a CD-ROM, as a stack of floppy disks, or as a file downloaded from the Internet. Once you have a program, you install it, usually by running an installation program to copy the program to your hard disk and configure it to run on your system.

Many programs arrive in the form of an *installation file*, or *distribution file*, which is a file that contains all the files required for a program to run, along with an installation program. You can download (copy) installation files from the Internet or other sources. If your computer is connected to a local area network, the installation file may be stored on a network hard disk (see Chapter 32). The files that make up the program are usually compressed to take up less space (see Chapter 35).

What Happens During Program Installation?

Most programs come with an installation program named Setup.exe or Install.exe. When you install a program, the installation program usually does the following:

- Looks for a previous version of the program on your hard disk. If it finds a previous version, the program may ask whether you want to replace the previous version.

- Creates a folder in which to store the program files. Most installation programs ask where you'd like this folder. Some installation programs also create additional folders within this folder. Windows 98 creates a folder named Program Files, usually in C:\. We recommend that you install all of your programs in folders within the Program Files folder.

Microsoft and some other software vendors have the bad habit of creating programs that are installed in locations other than your Program Files folder. You can't do much about this; the additional folders clutter up your root folder, but they don't do any harm.

■ Copies the files onto your hard disk. If the program files are compressed, the installation program uncompresses them. Usually, the installation program copies most of the files into the program's folder, but it may also put some files into your C:\Windows, C:\Windows\System, or other folders.

■ Checks your system for the files and hardware it needs to run. For example, an Internet connection program might check for a modem.

■ Adds entries to the Windows 98 Registry, to tell Windows with which types of files the program works, in which files the program is stored, and other information about the program (see Chapter 40).

■ Adds a command for the program to your Start menu. It may also add an icon to your Windows 98 desktop, to make running the program easy for you. You can change the position on the Start menu of the command for the program, get rid of the command, or create a command if the installation program doesn't make one (see "Reorganizing the Start Menu" in Chapter 12). You can also create a shortcut icon on the desktop if the installation program hasn't done so, or move or delete the program's shortcut (see "Making Shortcuts" in Chapter 9).

■ Asks you a series of questions to configure the program for your system. The program may ask you to type additional information, like Internet addresses, passwords, or software license numbers.

Every installation program is different, because it comes with the application program, not with Windows 98. If your computer is connected to a local area network or the Internet, the installation program may configure your program to connect to other computers on the network.

What Happens During Program Uninstallation?

The perfect uninstallation program exactly undoes all the actions of the program's installation program, removing all the files and folders the installation program created, and putting back everything else to where it was originally. Unfortunately, we've never seen a perfect uninstallation program. But most uninstallation programs do an acceptable job of removing traces of a program from your system.

Which Windows 98 Programs Might Not Be Installed?

Windows 98 comes with a lot of programs and options, all of which aren't necessarily installed on your system. The following is a list of some of the optionally installed programs that come with Windows 98:

■ Accessibility programs that make Windows 98 and your computer more usable for people with physical disabilities (see Chapter 20).

- Accessories that include games as well as useful items such as Quick View, System Monitor, System Resource Meter, and Windows Scripting Host.

- Communications programs that include Direct Cable Communication, HyperTerminal, Microsoft Chat, and Virtual Private Networking.

- Disk tools that include Backup and FAT32 Converter.

- Multilanguage support for many languages, including Baltic, Central European, and Cyrillic languages, and Greek and Turkish.

- Multimedia programs that include DVD Player, NetShow Player, and other sound- and video-related programs, as well as Web TV for Windows (see Chapters 17 and 18).

- Decorative programs you can use to jazz up the desktop, windows, icons, and even the mouse pointer, such as Desktop Themes and Animated Cursors (see Chapter 13).

You can install these programs by using the Add/Remove Programs icon in the Control Panel (see "Installing and Uninstalling Programs That Come with Windows 98").

Installing Programs

Windows 98 has a program called Add/Remove Programs that helps you find and start the installation program for a new program. However, you can skip this step and run the installation program yourself, if you know how. Some older DOS and Windows 3.1 programs don't come with installation programs, and you have to perform the actions of an installation program yourself.

Installing Programs Using the Add/Remove Programs Program

Using Add/Remove Programs to install a program is a good idea, because Windows 98 adds the program to the list of programs you've installed, making it easier to uninstall the program later. Follow these steps to use the Add/Remove Programs command to help you install a program:

1. Choose Start | Settings | Control Panel. You see the Control Panel window.

2. Run the Add/Remove Programs program. If the icons are underlined, your desktop is configured in Web style, so click the icon once. If the icons are not underlined, your desktop is configured in Classic style, so double-click the icon. You can control whether you need to single- or double-click icons to run programs (see "Choosing the Style of Your Desktop" in Chapter 1).

3. You see the Add/Remove Programs Properties dialog box, shown in Figure 3-1. If the Install/Uninstall tab isn't selected, click it. The box in the lower half of the

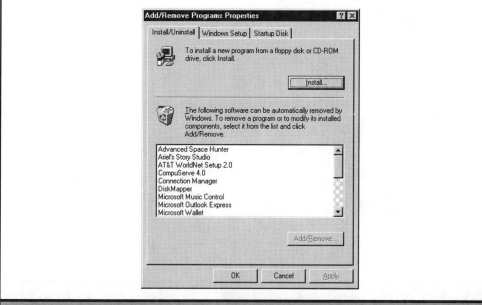

Figure 3-1. *The Install/Uninstall tab of the Add/Remove Programs Properties dialog box*

window lists the programs you have already installed on your system, including Windows 98 itself.

4. Click the Install button.

5. If you are installing a program from a floppy disk or CD-ROM, insert the disk or CD-ROM into its respective drive and click Next. If you are installing a program from a file on your hard disk or on a network drive, just click Next. Windows 98 looks on any floppy disk or CD-ROM in your drives for an installation program (that is, a program named Setup.exe or Install.exe). If Windows 98 finds an installation program, you can skip to step 8.

6. If Windows 98 doesn't find an installation program, you see the Run Installation Program dialog box, shown in Figure 3-2.

7. Click the Browse button and specify the installation file you want to run in the Browse window (see "Open, Save As, and Browse Dialog Boxes" in Chapter 2).

8. When the path name of the installation program appears in the Command Line For Installation Program box, click the Finish button. The installation program runs. Follow the instructions on the screen to install the program.

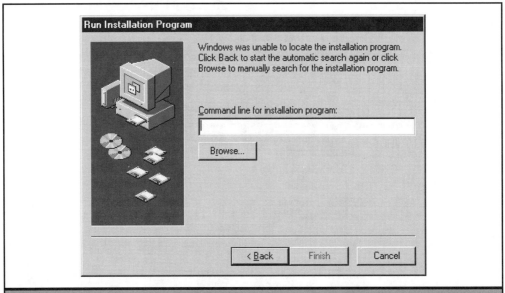

Figure 3-2. *If Add/Remove Programs can't find your installation program, you can specify where it is located*

Once you've installed a program, the program name usually (but not always) appears on the Add/Remove Programs Properties dialog box's list of programs that you can uninstall.

Running an Install or Setup Program

If you know the path name of the installation file for the program you want to install, you can run the installation program directly (see "Starting Programs" in Chapter 2). Follow the instructions on the screen to install the program.

Installing Programs Without Installation Programs

Some older programs, such as those designed to run with Windows 3.1 or DOS, do not have installation programs. Instead, the programs are delivered as a set of files. Some older programs arrive as a *ZIP file*, a file that contains compressed versions of one or more files.

To install a program from a ZIP file, you need an unzipping program; our favorite is WinZip. You can download the latest version of WinZip from the Internet at **http://www.winzip.com**. WinZip comes with its own commands for unzipping (uncompressing) and installing the files in the ZIP file.

To install a program that you receive as a set of files or as a ZIP file, follow these steps:

1. Create a folder in which to store the program files (see "Creating Files and Folders" in Chapter 8). We recommend that you create the folder in the C:\Program Files folder, or in whichever folder you use to store program files. Each program usually should be stored in a separate folder.

2. Copy the files into the folder you just created. If you are installing from a ZIP file, unzip the file by using WinZip or another uncompressing program and put the files into the new folder.

3. Take a look at the list of files to find files with the .exe or .com extension; these are executable programs. If one file is named Setup.exe or Install.exe, run it. Then follow the instructions on the screen. The installation program may ask you a series of questions to configure the program for your system. If one file is named Readme.txt (or some other name that suggestions that it contains instructions), read the contents of the file; if its extension is .txt, click or double-click the filename to see the file in WordPad.

4. Otherwise, look for an executable file with a name like the name of the program; this may be the program itself. For example, if you are installing a program called Spam Hater, you might find a filename such as Spamhate.exe. To run the program, click or double-click the program name. The first time you run the program, it may ask you for information with which to configure the program for your system.

Finishing Installing a Program

After you install a program, you may still need to configure it to work with your system. Many programs come with configuration programs that run automatically, either when you install the program or when you run the program for the first time.

To make the program easier to run, you can add it to your Start menu (see "Reorganizing the Start Menu" in Chapter 12). If the program has an installation program, the installation program may do this for you.

You can also add a shortcut for the program to your Windows 98 desktop (see "Making Shortcuts" in Chapter 9). The program's installation program may have created a shortcut already. You can create shortcuts right on the desktop or in a folder.

Installing and Uninstalling Programs That Come with Windows 98

If you want to install some of the programs that come on the Windows 98 CD-ROM, follow these steps:

1. Choose Start | Settings | Control Panel. You see the Control Panel window.

2. Run Add/Remove Programs.

3. Click the Windows Setup tab. You see a list of the types of programs that come with Windows 98, as shown in Figure 3-3. The check box to the left of each type of program is either blank (meaning that none of the programs of that type are selected), gray with a check mark (meaning that some but not all of the programs of that type are selected), or white with a check mark (meaning that all the programs of that type are selected). The selections show which Windows 98 programs have already been installed.

4. To select additional programs, click the type of program to install (scroll down the components list to see the rest of the program types). A description of the programs appears in the Description box. A few items on the Windows Setup tab of the Add/Remove Programs Properties dialog box have only one program of that type, such as Web TV for Windows. Most of the items on the list include a number of programs, and the Description box tells you the total number of programs of that type and how many are selected.

5. To select all the programs of that type, click the check box to the left of the item. To select some of the programs, click the Details button to see the list of programs of that type. Click each of the programs you want to select, and then

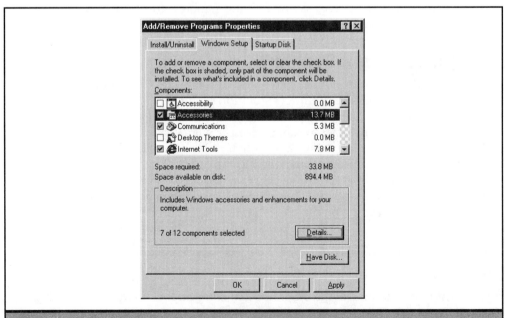

Figure 3-3. *You can install additional programs from the Windows 98 CD-ROM*

click the OK button to return to the Windows Setup tab of the Add/Remove Programs Properties dialog box.

6. You can uninstall previously installed programs at the same time that you install new programs. To uninstall a program, deselect it; that is, clear the check in its check box by clicking the box.

7. After you have selected all the programs you want installed and have deselected all the programs you don't want installed, click the OK button. Windows 98 determines which programs you are installing, which you are uninstalling, and copies or deletes program files appropriately.

8. Depending on which programs you install, you may need to restart Windows when the installation is complete, and you may be directed to run Wizards or other configuration programs to set up the new programs.

Associating a Program with a File Extension

Many programs create, edit, or display files of a specific type. The file type is denoted by the *extension*, the part of the filename that follows the last dot in the filename. For example, the Notepad program (a text editor that comes with Windows 98) works with text files that usually have the extension .txt (see "What Are Extensions and File Types" in Chapter 8). When you open a file with the extension .txt, Windows 98 knows to run Notepad.

The Windows 98 Registry stores *file associations*, information about which program you use to edit each type of file. Installation programs usually store this information in the Registry, but you can, too. Chapter 40 describes how to view and edit the Registry.

Creating or Editing an Association

To associate a file type with a program (or change the program associated with a file type), you use the File Types tab on the Folder Options dialog box. Follow these steps:

1. Choose Start | Settings | Folder Options. You see the Folder Options dialog box.

2. Click the File Types tab, shown in Figure 3-4.

3. In the Registered File Types list, click the type of file you want to associate with a program. When you select a file type, more information about that file type appears in the File Type Details box, including the extension.

4. Click Edit. You see the Edit File Type dialog box, shown in Figure 3-5. This dialog box displays the information that the Registry knows about this file type, including the icon to use for files of this type, a description of the file type, its MIME type (used for attaching files to e-mail messages), and the default extension for files of this type. The Actions box lists the tasks that Windows 98 knows how to perform for files of this type: open, print, edit, and other actions. For each action, you can tell Windows which program to use.

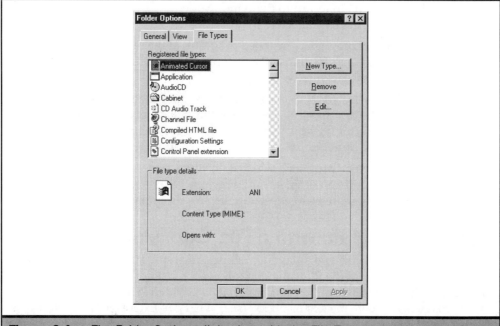

Figure 3-4.   *The Folder Options dialog box with the File Types tab selected*

5. Click the Open entry in the Actions list, and then click the Edit button. (If no Open entry appears, click the New button and type **open** in the Action box of the New Action dialog box.) You see a dialog box entitled Editing Action For Type, followed by the name of the file type (see Figure 3-6). The Application Used To Perform Action box contains the command line that Windows 98 executes when you open files of this type. The command line usually consists of the full path name of a program, possibly followed by a space and %1. The %1 represents the name of the file you want to open; that is, this command runs the program and tells the program to open the file you double-clicked. See the next section for more information about actions.

6. To change the program used to open files of this type, you can edit the command line in the Application Used To Perform Action box. Alternatively, you can click the Browse button to select the file that contains the program. Don't worry if you eliminate the %1 from the command line; Windows 98 adds it for you (although it may not appear in the dialog box).

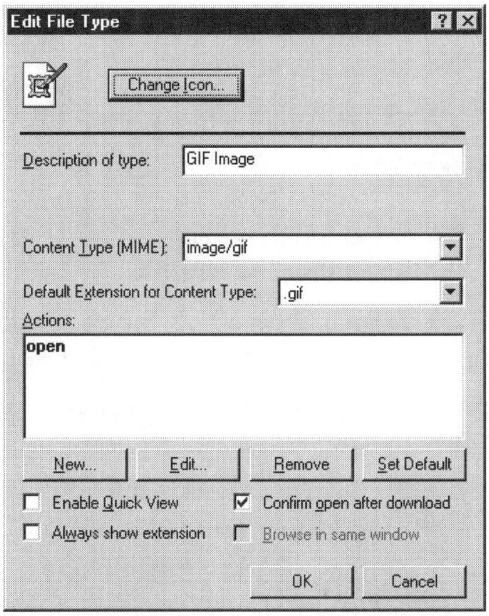

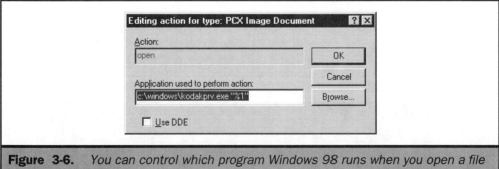

Figure 3-5. *The Edit File Type dialog box*

7. Click OK to return to the Edit File Type dialog box.

8. Choose the other settings for this file type (see Table 1-1).

9. Close the Edit File Type dialog box, then the Folder Options dialog box.

Figure 3-6. *You can control which program Windows 98 runs when you open a file of a specified type*

Setting	Description
Icon	Specifies the icon that appears in Windows Explorer and Folder windows for files of this type. Click Change Icon to choose a different icon.
Description of type	Specifies the description that appears in Windows Explorer and Folder windows when you display details about the file.
Content Type (MIME)	Specifies the MIME type for this type of file, used for attaching files to e-mail messages (see Chapter 23).
Default Extension for Content Type	Specifies the usual filename extension for files of this type.
Actions	Lists the actions that Windows 98 knows how to perform for files of this type. Click New to add an action, Edit to change the selected action, or Remove to delete an action.
Set Default	Returns the settings for this file type to the settings that Windows 98 suggests.
Enable Quick View	Specifies whether the Windows 98 Quick View program can display files of this type (see "Looking at Files Using Quick View" in Chapter 4).
Always show extension	Specifies that the extension always appears after filenames of this type when listed in Windows Explorer or Folder windows.
Confirm open after download	Specifies to open files of this type after downloading.
Browse in same window	Specifies that if the program that opens this program is already running, you want to open the file in the existing program window rather than opening another window.

Table 3-1.   *Settings on the Files Types Tab of the Folder Options Dialog Box*

Once you have created or corrected the Open action for a file type, when you open a file of that type Windows 98 runs the program that you specified.

Actions Associated with File Types

For each file type, you can define as many *actions* as you want. For example, you can define one action that opens files of that type and another action that prints files. There are two types of actions:

- **Regular actions** These actions are listed on the shortcut menu that appears when you right-click filenames in Windows Explorer or Folder windows. For example, when you right-click a filename with extension .txt, the Open command appears on the shortcut menu; the Open action associated with the .txt file type determines what this Open command does.

- **DDE actions** DDE stands for *dynamic data exchange*, which is a method for programs to exchange information. These actions define how data can be moved from one program to another using DDE (see "What Is DDE?" in Chapter 7). DDE actions do not appear on the shortcut menu when you right-click filenames.

When you create or edit an action for a file type as described in the preceding section, you see the New Action or Editing Action For Type dialog box. If the Use DDE check box is not selected, it is a regular action and the dialog box (shown in Figure 3-6) has two settings:

- **Action** Specifies the name of the action, which appears in the Edit File Type dialog box and on the shortcut menu you see when you right-click filenames of this type. You don't have to capitalize the first letter of the action: Windows 98 capitalizes the first letter of the action name when it appears on the shortcut menu. You can choose a letter to be underlined on the shortcut menu: precede the letter with an ampersand (&). You can choose a command from the shortcut menu by typing the underlined letter.

- **Application Used To Perform Action** Specifies the program to run to perform this action on this type of file.

When the Use DDE check box is selected, the action is a DDE action, and the New Action or Editing Action For Type dialog box looks as shown in Figure 3-7. You see four additional settings:

- **DDE Message** Specifies the DDE command for this action.

- **Application** Specifies the DDE application string to start a DDE link with the program. If this box is blank, Windows runs the program specified in the Application Used To Perform Action box.

- **DDE Application Not Running** Specifies the DDE command to use if the program (specified in the Application box) is not already running. If this box is blank, Windows sends the same command specified in the DDE Message box.

- **Topic** Specifies the DDE topic string to start a conversation with the program. The default DDE topic string (used if this box is blank) is "System".

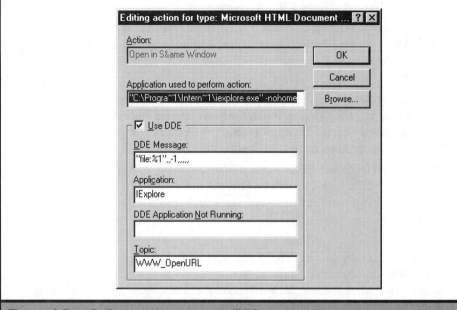

Figure 3-7. *Defining actions that use DDE commands*

Uninstalling Programs

If you don't use a program, you may want to uninstall it to free up space on your hard disk. You may also want to uninstall older versions of programs before installing new versions. You can use the Add/Remove Programs program to remove some programs; some programs come with uninstall programs; and some programs require you to delete files manually.

Uninstalling Programs Using the Add/Remove Programs Program

When you want to uninstall a program, first check whether it appears on the Add/Remove Program Properties dialog box. If the program does appear in this dialog box, use Add/Remove Programs to uninstall the program, following these steps:

1. Choose Start | Settings | Control Panel. You see the Control Panel window.

2. Run Add/Remove Programs. You see the Add/Remove Programs Properties dialog box, shown in Figure 3-1. If the Install/Uninstall tab isn't selected, click

it. The box in the lower half of the window lists many of the programs you have already installed on your system.

3. In the list of installed programs, click the program you want to uninstall, and then click the Add/Remove button. Windows 98 uninstalls the program, while messages appear to let you know what's happening.

If the program doesn't appear on the Add/Remove Programs Properties dialog box, you have to uninstall the program by using another way, as described in the following section.

 Sometimes Windows can't uninstall a program, usually because it can't find all the files it needs to perform the uninstall.

Running an Uninstall Program

Many programs come with uninstall programs, usually named Uninstall.exe. Look for an uninstall program in the same folder where the program is stored. Run the program, and then follow the directions on the screen.

Uninstalling Programs Without Installation Programs

What if a program doesn't appear on the Add/Remove Programs Properties dialog box, and doesn't come with an uninstall program? You can delete by hand the program files and the shortcuts to the program. You may not delete every last file connected with the program, but the remaining files usually won't do any harm. Before deleting anything, check the program's documentation for instructions. Be sure to back up your hard disk (see Chapter 10) before uninstalling a program by hand, in case you delete a file that your system needs.

To delete the program files, determine which folder contains them. The easiest way to find out where the program is stored is to look at the properties of a shortcut to the program (see "What Is a Shortcut?" in Chapter 9). Right-click a shortcut to the program on your desktop, in a folder, or in the C:\Windows\Start Menu\Programs folder. Choose Properties from the menu that appears; then click the Shortcut tab on the Properties dialog box for the program. The Target box contains the full path name of the executable file for the program.

To delete the program, delete the folder that contains the program files and all the files in it (see "Deleting Files and Folders" in Chapter 8). Then delete the shortcuts to the program, so that the program doesn't appear on your desktop, in any folders, or on your Start menu, as described in the following section.

If at all possible, use a program's uninstaller instead of just deleting all the files, since the uninstaller is safer and more comprehensive.

Finishing an Uninstallation

After uninstalling a program, you may see shortcuts to the program lying around on your desktop, in folders, or in your Start menu. Delete these shortcuts by right-clicking the shortcut and choosing Delete from the menu that appears, or by dragging the shortcut into the Recycle Bin on the desktop.

The
Complete
Reference

Chapter 4

Working with Documents in Windows 98

Although word processing isn't glamorous, it is, and probably forever will be, one of the most popular uses for a computer. Windows 98 comes with two tools for working with text documents—the first is the unsophisticated Notepad, and the second is the semi-full-featured WordPad. Quick View, another accessory that comes with Windows 98, can display files in a variety of formats. A fourth tool that you may find useful is the free Microsoft Word Viewer, which lets you see and print documents created and formatted with Microsoft's full-featured word processor, Word. The Word Viewer is useful if you don't own Microsoft Word, or if you receive a document saved with a version of Word that is newer than the one you own. Word Viewer may not come with Windows 98—you may have to download it from Microsoft's web site, or you may find it hidden on your Windows 98 CD-ROM.

Reading Text Files with Notepad

Notepad is a holdover from Windows 3.0. Back in the Windows 3.0 era, configuration information was stored in text files that regularly needed to be edited, and Notepad could edit these files. In the intervening releases of Windows, editing configuration files has become a task more often done automatically by installation programs or manually by system administrators and hackers than by people simply trying to make their computers work the way they want.

Notepad, however, remains available in Windows 98. Using Notepad is the simplest way to edit a text file—sure, you can use a full-fledged word processor, but doing so often is more trouble than it's worth. So use Notepad to edit any *text file* (also called an *ASCII file*)—that is, files that contain only letters, numbers, and special characters that appear on the keyboard. A text file can't store formatting such as bold and italics, for instance.

Running Notepad

To run Notepad, choose Start | Programs | Accessories | Notepad. (Or you can choose Start | Run to display the Run dialog box, then type **notepad** and press ENTER.) Notepad looks like Figure 4-1: just a window with a menu.

The following sections offer some information about and tips on using Notepad.

COPYING, MOVING, AND PASTING TEXT   You can copy or move text to or from the Windows Clipboard using the Edit | Copy, Edit | Cut, and Edit | Paste commands (see "What Is Cut-and-Paste?" in Chapter 7).

DOCUMENT SETTINGS   To change the setup of the document when you print it, choose File | Page Setup (this command isn't available if you haven't installed a printer in Windows 98). Use the Page Setup dialog box (shown in Figure 4-2) to change margins, page orientation, and paper size. (In the Orientation box, Portrait prints on

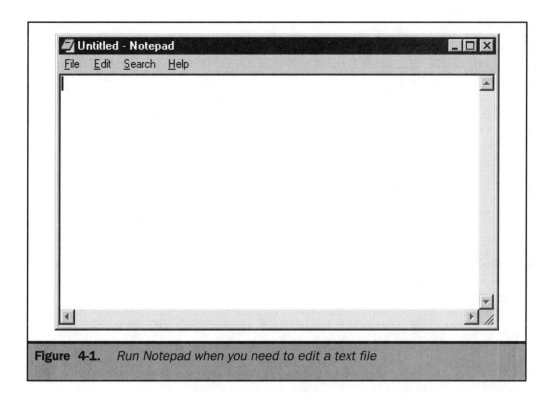

Figure 4-1. *Run Notepad when you need to edit a text file*

paper in the usual way; Landscape prints sideways on the page, with the lines of text parallel to the long edge of the paper.) If you have more than one printer, you can select the one to use. Use the Header and Footer text boxes to add headers and footers to your documents. You can type plain text, or you can use these codes:

&f   Displays the name of the file

&p   Displays the page number

&d   Displays the current date

&t   Displays the current time

&&   Displays an ampersand

&l   Left-justifies the text after this code

&c   Centers the text after this code

&r   Right-justifies the text after this code

FILE TYPES   Choose File | Open to see the Open dialog box. Change the Files Of Type option to All Files if the file you want to open does not have the .txt extension.

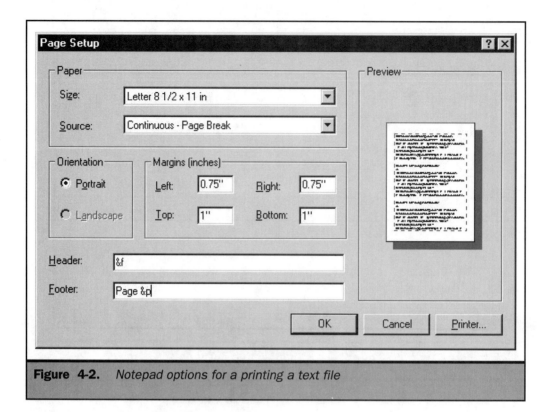

Figure 4-2.   *Notepad options for a printing a text file*

FONTS   Notepad normally uses the FixedSys font, a fixed-pitch font, to display text files. You can change the font by choosing Edit | Set Font to display the Font dialog box, then setting the font, style, and size. The font you choose doesn't affect the font Notepad uses, typically Courier, when you print the file.

LOG FILES   Create a log file by typing **.LOG** in the top-left corner (the very beginning) of your Notepad file (be sure to use capital letters). Each time you run Notepad and open the file, Notepad enters the current time and date at the end of the file. You can then type an entry for that time and date.

PRINTING   Print the text file by choosing File | Print. Notepad prints the file with the filename at the top of each page and a page number at the bottom.

SAVING FILES   Save the text file you are editing by choosing File | Save. To save it with a name you specify, choose File | Save As to display the Save As dialog box (see "Open, Save As, and Browse Dialog Boxes" in Chapter 2).

SEARCHING FOR TEXT   You can search for a string of text by choosing Search │ Find to display the Find dialog box, then typing the string you're looking for into the Find What text box. Click the Match Case check box if you want Notepad to find only text that matches the capitalization of the text you typed. You can also specify whether to search forward or backward in the file by clicking the Up or Down radio button. Start the search by clicking the Find Next button. To search for the same string again, press F3 or choose Search │ Find Next.

TIME AND DATE   You can insert the current time and date (according to your computer's clock) at the cursor by choosing Edit │ Time/Date, or by pressing F5.

UNDO   If you make a mistake, you can reverse your last edit choosing Edit │ Undo.

WORD WRAP   As you work with a document, you may want to turn on the *word wrap*, so that Notepad breaks long lines of text up onto multiple lines on the screen. When word wrap is off, each paragraph appears as a single long line (unless it contains carriage returns). Turn on word wrap by choosing Edit │ Word Wrap. Notepad then wraps lines like a word processor wraps lines, so that no line is wider than the Notepad window. Notepad's word wrap feature doesn't add carriage return characters to the text file when you save it, nor does it affect the way the file appears when printed.

Files You Can Edit with Notepad

The standard file extension for text files is .txt, and when you click or double-click a .txt file in Windows Explorer or a Folder window, Windows runs Notepad to view the files. Notepad works fine for text files up to a maximum size of about 40K. If you try to open a larger file with Notepad, it suggests using WordPad instead.

Windows associates a number of other types of files with Notepad, too, because these files contain only text and are usually small enough for Notepad to handle. These files types include

- Configuration files, such as files with the extension .ini (see "Windows Initialization Files" in Chapter 39)
- Dial-Up Networking scripts
- Log files, with the extension .log, which many housekeeping programs create (see "Creating and Using Logon Scripts" in Chapter 22)
- Setup information files, which come with many installation programs and have the extension .inf

Taking Advantage of Free Word Processing with WordPad

WordPad is a great little word processor if your needs are modest—and the price can't be beat! Open WordPad by choosing Start | Programs | Accessories | WordPad. (Or you can choose Start | Run to display the Run dialog box, then type **wordpad** and press ENTER.)

> **Note**   *WordPad is usually installed along with Windows 98. If not, insert your Windows 98 CD-ROM or floppy disk, open Control Panel, run Add/Remove Programs, click the Windows Setup tab, choose Accessories from the list of types of components, click Details, and choose WordPad from the list of Accessories (see "Installing and Uninstalling Programs That Come with Windows 98" in Chapter 3).*

WordPad does not offer many of the advanced features that you get in Microsoft Word or Corel's WordPerfect—notably missing is a spell checker. But WordPad does offer many of the formatting tools that you need to create a spiffy letter, memo, or essay. Many of the commands and keyboard shortcuts are the same as those in Microsoft Word, which makes them easy for many people to remember. The version of WordPad that comes with Windows 98 can open documents created by versions of Word up through Word 97 (Word 8). And since WordPad is a small program, it loads quickly. You can see WordPad in Figure 4-3.

Opening and Saving Files with WordPad

With WordPad, you can open and edit a document that is saved in any one of a variety of formats, including documents saved with Word 97 (WordPad cannot preserve all of Word 97's formatting, however). To open a document, choose File | Open, and use the Files Of Type option on the Open dialog box to choose the type of document you want to open.

When you're saving a document to pass on to a friend or coworker, choose File | Save to use the existing filename or File | Save As to specify the filename. Be sure to save the document in a format that your friend's or coworker's software can open. Here's a rundown of the file formats WordPad can use to save a document:

- **Word 6.0 for Windows**   Anyone who has Microsoft Word 6.0 or later (version 6.0 was the last version for Windows 3.x) can read a file in this format. In addition, anyone with WordPad can read this file, even if they only use Windows 95. Word 6.0 came out quite a while ago, so any major word processing package can convert a Word 6.0 document and keep its formatting intact. Word 6.0 format is the default WordPad format. This format preserves all the formatting WordPad can create.

Ruler bar

Toolbar

Format bar

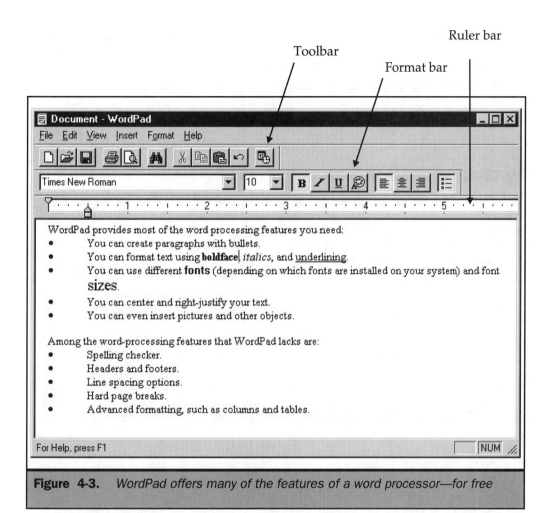

Figure 4-3. *WordPad offers many of the features of a word processor—for free*

■ **Rich Text Format**   If Word 6.0 is not a compatible file format, chances are good that Rich Text Format (.rtf) is compatible. Formatting is preserved in a rich text document, but the files tend to be much larger than .doc files.

■ **Text Document**   When you save a file in plain text format (with the extension .txt), you lose all formatting, but you preserve all text in the ANSI character set (a standard set of codes used for storing text).

■ **Text Document—MS-DOS Format**   When you save a file in MS-DOS text format (also with the extension .txt), you lose all formatting, but you preserve all text in Microsoft's extended ASCII character set, which includes various accented characters and smiley faces. Use this format only if you want to use the text in a Windows or DOS application, but not if you plan to send the file to a Mac, UNIX, or other non-Microsoft system.

■ **Unicode Text Document**   Unicode allows you to use characters from practically every language on Earth, from Latvian to Japanese. But make sure that your recipient has a Unicode-compatible program before you save Unicode documents.

Formatting with WordPad

Use the options on the format bar (the row of buttons below the toolbar) to format a document in WordPad. If you don't see the format bar (or WordPad's other bars—the toolbar, ruler bar, or status bar), use the View menu to display them.

Formatting in WordPad works like this:

■ Select the text you want to format, using your mouse. Or choose Edit | Select All (or press CTRL-A) to select the entire document.

■ Click the button or give the command for the type of formatting you want to apply.

The following sections describe some of the formatting options in WordPad.

BULLETS   To format a paragraph with a bullet, click anywhere in the paragraph and click the Bullets button at the very end of the format bar, or choose Format | Bullet Style. To format more than one paragraph, select the paragraphs before clicking the Bullets button.

INDENTS   To indent a paragraph, click in the paragraph (or select several paragraphs) and choose Format | Paragraph to display the Paragraph dialog box. You can type a measurement from the left or right margin, or for the first line only. You can also specify that the paragraph is left-aligned, right-aligned, or centered. When you click OK, the margin indicators on the ruler bar move to show the current margins for the paragraph your cursor is in.

TABS   To set tab stops, choose Format | Tabs. You see the Tabs dialog box. Set a tab stop by typing a measurement from the left margin and clicking the Set button. The tab stop appears on the list of tab stops that are set for the current position in the document. To delete a tab stop, select it from the list and click the Clear button. When you click OK, little L-shaped tab indicators appear on the ruler bar to show the location of tab stops.

TEXT: FONTS, SIZE, AND COLOR   To change the font, font size, or color of the selected text, click the Font or Font Size box on the format bar and choose the font or font size from the list that appears. Or choose Format | Font to display the Font dialog box, shown in Figure 4-4. Choose the font, font size, color, and whether you'd like the text to be bold, italic, underlined, or struck out. If you have installed multilanguage support, you can also choose the script (alphabet). Then click OK. You can also choose settings from the Font dialog box without selecting text, before you type the text you want to format; use the Font dialog box again to turn the formatting off.

You can also format text by using keystroke combinations: CTRL-B to bold, CTRL-I to italicize, and CTRL-U to underline. You can use these keystrokes after you've selected text, or before you type the text you want to format (press the key combination again to turn the formatting off).

Printing Your WordPad Document

To print your document, click the Print button, the fourth button on the toolbar, or choose File | Print, or press CTRL-P. You see the Print dialog box, in which you can select the printer, which pages to print, and the number of copies.

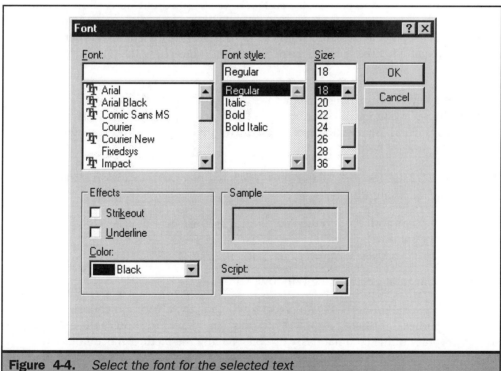

Figure 4-4. *Select the font for the selected text*

You may want to preview the document before you print it (see exactly what it will look like on paper). To preview your document, click the Print Preview button, the fifth button on the toolbar, or choose File | Print Preview. The WordPad window shows approximately how the printed page will look. You can click the Zoom In button to get a closer look, click Print to begin printing, or click Close to return to the regular view of your document.

You can also format the page by choosing File | Page Setup to display the Page Setup dialog box. Use the Page Setup dialog box to change margins, paper orientation, and paper size.

WordPad Extras

WordPad has a couple of additional features you may find useful:

COPYING, MOVING, AND PASTING TEXT   Use the Windows Clipboard to copy and move text within WordPad, and between WordPad and other applications (see Chapter 7). Choose Edit | Copy, click the Copy button on the toolbar, or press CTRL-C to copy selected text to the Clipboard. Choose Edit | Cut, click the Cut button on the toolbar, or press CTRL-X to move selected text to the Clipboard. Choose Edit | Paste, click the Paste button on the toolbar, or press CTRL-V to copy information from the Clipboard to the current cursor location. If you are pasting information other than text into your document, choose Edit | Paste Special to choose how the information should appear.

DATE AND TIME   Insert the current date and time into your document by clicking the Date/Time button, the last button on the toolbar, or by choosing Insert | Date and Time. The Date and Time dialog box appears, from which you can choose the format for the date, time, or both.

INSERTING OBJECTS   Insert an object (such as a picture) into a WordPad document in one of the following ways:

- Dragging the object into the WordPad window from Windows Explorer or any Folder window
- Using Insert | Object and choosing the type of object you want to insert
- Pasting an object from the Windows Clipboard

You can see the properties of an object by clicking the object and choosing Edit | Object Properties or pressing ALT-ENTER. If you insert a picture, you can use WordPad's simple graphic editing commands by double-clicking the picture; the annotation toolbar appears at the bottom of the WordPad window. You can also move an object in your document by clicking and dragging it to a new location.

REPLACING TEXT   You can replace specific text with other text throughout your document by choosing Edit | Replace or pressing CTRL-H. You see the Replace dialog box. In the Find What box, type the text to be replaced. In the Replace With box, type the text to be inserted. You can click the Match Whole Word Only and Match Case check boxes to tell WordPad which instances of the text to match. Click Find Next to find the next instance of the text in the Find What box, then Replace to replace this instance with the Replace With text. To replace all the rest of the instances in your document, click Replace All.

SEARCHING FOR TEXT   You can search for text by using the Find button on the toolbar, which has a picture of binoculars on it, or by choosing Edit | Find or pressing CTRL-F. Use the options on the Find dialog box to find only the whole word, or to match the case of the contents of the Find What text box. To search for the same information again, press F3 or choose Edit | Find Next.

UNDO   Undo your last action by clicking the Undo button, the second-to-last button on the toolbar, by choosing Edit | Undo, or by pressing CTRL-Z.

Setting WordPad's Options

You can configure WordPad by choosing View | Options to display the Options dialog box, shown in Figure 4-5. Table 4-1 shows the settings for the tabs in this dialog box.

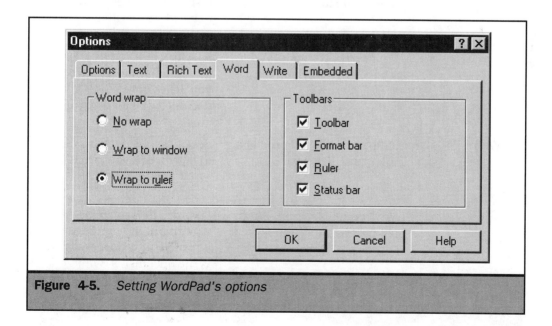

Figure 4-5.   *Setting WordPad's options*

Tab	Setting	Description
Options	Measurement units: Inches, Points, Centimeters, and Picas	Specifies how you'd like to see and set measurements.
Options	Automatic word selection	Specifies that when you select part of a word, you want to select the whole word.
Text	Word wrap: No wrap, Wrap to window, and Wrap to ruler	Specifies how to break long paragraphs into lines when you are editing normal text files.
Text	Toolbars: Toolbar, Format bar, Ruler, and Status bar	Specifies which toolbars to display when you are editing normal text files.
Rich Text	Word wrap: No wrap, Wrap to window, and Wrap to ruler	Specifies how to break long paragraphs into lines when you are editing rich text files (with extension .rtf).
Rich Text	Toolbars: Toolbar, Format bar, Ruler, and Status bar	Specifies which toolbars to display when you are editing rich text files (with extension .rtf).
Word	Word wrap: No wrap, Wrap to window, and Wrap to ruler	Specifies how to break long paragraphs into lines when you are editing Word documents (with extension .doc)
Word	Toolbars: Toolbar, Format bar, Ruler, and Status bar	Specifies which toolbars to display when you are editing Word documents (with extension .doc).
Write	Word wrap: No wrap, Wrap to window, and Wrap to ruler	Specifies how to break long paragraphs into lines when you are editing Windows Write documents (with extension .wri).

Table 4-1. *Settings in WordPad's Options Dialog Box*

Tab	Setting	Description
Write	Toolbars: Toolbar, Format bar, Ruler, and Status bar	Specifies which toolbars to display when you are editing Windows Write documents (with extension .wri).
Embedded	Word wrap: No wrap, Wrap to window, and Wrap to ruler	Specifies how to break long paragraphs into lines when you are editing embedded documents.
Embedded	Toolbars: Toolbar, Format bar, Ruler, and Status bar	Specifies which toolbars to display when you are editing embedded documents.

Table 4-1. *Settings in WordPad's Options Dialog Box (continued)*

Looking at Files Using Quick View

Quick View lets you take a look at files in a variety of formats, including text files and some graphics files. To use Quick View, run Windows Explorer or open a Folder window. (For example, choose Start I Programs I Windows Explorer.) Select a file you want to take a look at. Choose File I Quick View from the Windows Explorer or Folder window menu bar. Alternatively, you can right-click a filename and choose Quick View from the shortcut menu that appears. Quick View displays the file you selected in the Quick View window, shown in Figure 4-6.

If the Quick View command doesn't appear, either Quick View isn't installed or you've selected a file of a type that Quick View can't display. Quick View is not automatically installed as part of the standard Windows 98 installation. To install it, insert your Windows 98 CD-ROM or the first Windows 98 floppy disk, open Control Panel, run Add/Remove Programs, click the Windows Setup tab, choose Accessories from the list of types of components, click Details, and choose Quick View from the list of Accessories (see "Installing and Uninstalling Programs That Come with Windows 98" in Chapter 3).

Quick View can't edit files, only display them. If you have installed a program that can edit the type of file you are looking at using Quick View, you can choose File I Open File for Editing or click the leftmost icon on the toolbar. Windows runs the program that can edit the file you are looking at. For example, if you are looking at a text file using Quick View, the leftmost toolbar button runs Notepad.

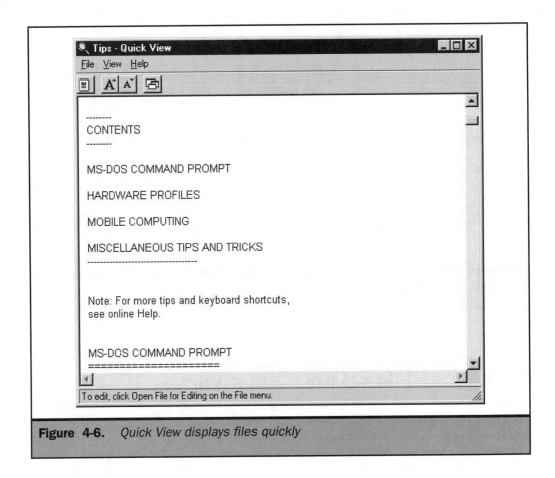

Figure 4-6. *Quick View displays files quickly*

Here are a few other things that Quick View can do:

■ When you are looking at a text file, choose View | Font to display the Font dialog box and change the font Quick View uses to display the file. Or click the Increase Font Size or Decrease Font Size buttons on the toolbar (the second and third buttons) to make the font larger or smaller.

■ Display an entire page of information by choosing View | Page View.

■ If you are looking at a series of files using Quick View, you can tell Quick View to use the same window, replacing the previous file with the new file. Choose View | Replace Window.

You can control which types of files can be displayed by Quick View. Choose Start | Settings | Folder Options, then click the File Types tab to see a list of the types of files that Windows 98 knows about (see "Associating a Program with a File Extension" in Chapter 3). Choose a file type, click Edit, and click the Enable Quick View check box; when this box is selected, the Quick View command appears on the File menu in Windows Explorer and Folder windows.

Reading with Word Viewer What You Could Not Otherwise Read

Microsoft Word Viewer enables you to read and print Word 97 documents with all of their formatting. It is not part of Windows 98, but you can get it in at least two ways:

- Download it for free from Microsoft's web site at **http://www.microsoft.com/word/internet/viewer/viewer97/**. Look in the section on Filters and Viewers for the latest version of the Word Viewer. Be warned that the installation file is large—over 4MB—so it may take a while to download.

- Install it from a Windows 98 CD-ROM. In the \Tools\Viewers folder, run the Wd97vw32.exe program to install Word Viewer.

Word Viewer provides all of Microsoft Word's sophisticated features for viewing and printing a document—you can see the document in Outline view, use the Master Document view feature to jump around a long document, and see headers, footers, columns, and tables as they look in Microsoft Word, for example. Word Viewer does not, however, allow you to edit the document, although you can cut-and-paste text from the Word Viewer window to WordPad or another word processor by using the cut-and-paste techniques described in Chapter 7.

Be aware, though, that you won't be able to copy all the formatting. If you're doing extensive work with the document, print it first so that you can see the document formatting. (Print the document by choosing File | Print. Change any options, as needed, on the Print dialog box and click OK.)

The installation program for Word Viewer may not create a shortcut on your desktop to run Word Viewer, and it may not add Word Viewer to your Start or Programs menus, either. If you don't see a Word Viewer icon on your desktop or command on your Start | Programs menu, run Word Viewer using one of the following methods:

■ Choose Start | Run, then click the Browse button to find the Wordview.exe file in the C:\Program Files\WordView folder.

■ In Windows Explorer or a Folder window, click or double-click the WordView.exe filename (see "Starting Programs by Clicking Program Filenames" in Chapter 2). Click if you use Web style for your desktop, or double-click if you use Classic style (see "Choosing the Style of Your Desktop" in Chapter 1).

If you plan to use Word Viewer often, consider creating a desktop shortcut for the program or adding the program to your Start or Programs menu (see "Making Shortcuts" in Chapter 9).

Figure 4-7 shows the Word Viewer 97 window. Notice the lack of a toolbar. All commands in Word Viewer are given by using the menu bar or keyboard shortcuts.

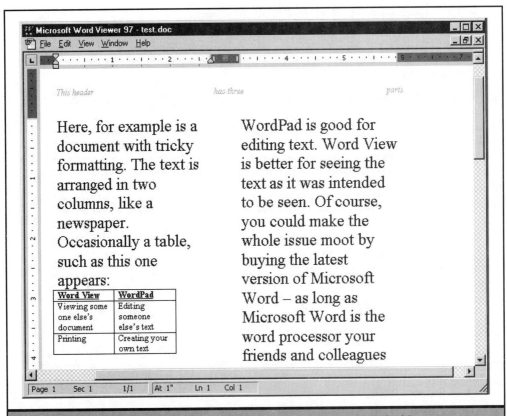

Figure 4-7. Word Viewer allows you to view a document created with Microsoft Word

The Windows 98 CD-ROM has two other viewers, too, stored in the \Tools\Viewers folder. The Viewer.exe program displays Microsoft Excel spreadsheet files, and the Ppview97.exe program displays Microsoft PowerPoint presentations.

Choosing Your View

Word Viewer offers you the choice of five views. If you're familiar with Microsoft Word, you're probably familiar with these views (but if you're familiar with Microsoft Word, you probably don't need the Word Viewer). These are your different options, and what each is good for:

- **Normal**   Shows the document without headers, footers, or margins.

- **Online Layout**   Shows the document with the background colors or textures that are visible when the document is saved as a web page.

- **Page Layout**   Shows the document as it will appear on paper—headers, footers, and margins are visible. This view shows you almost what the document will look like when it is printed—some non-printing marks may be visible in Page Layout view, and headers and footers appear in gray, not black as they will on paper.

- **Outline**   Displays an outline of the document using headings. You can choose to see all text in the document, or only headings to a given level.

- **Master Document**   Displays the document in two panes: One pane is a listing of headings in the document in outline format, the second pane is the document itself. You can navigate the document by clicking a heading in the left pane to see that part of the document in the right pane.

Choose the view you want to use by using the View menu.

You may also want to change the zoom in Word Viewer. A larger zoom factor makes the document larger on the screen; a smaller zoom factor makes the document smaller. The zoom does not affect the way the document looks on paper. To change the zoom, choose View | Zoom to display the Zoom dialog box. Use the radio buttons in the Zoom To portion of the Zoom dialog box, or choose your own zoom by using the Percent option.

Finding the Text You Want To Read

The Microsoft Word format provides a number of ways to navigate within a document, as well as between documents. Here's how the choices work:

- Use Master Document view—you see a clickable outline of the document in the left pane. Click a heading in the outline to see the complete text in the right pane (this feature works only when the document is formatted with the built-in heading styles).

■ Find the table of contents in the document, if one exists. Click a page number in the table of contents to go to that page.

■ Documents may contain links to web pages or other documents. Click hyperlinked text, which usually appears blue and underlined, to follow the link.

■ Choose Edit | Find (or press CTRL-F) to find specific text in the document.

Getting Word Viewer Help

Word Viewer does not have a traditional help system. Instead, it has a document file named Readme.doc in Word format, stored in the WordView program folder (which is C:\Program Files\Wordview, if you installed the application in the suggested location). Help may also be available online—use the web address that was given earlier in the chapter to find the Word Viewer.

Chapter 5

Using Accessories

Windows 98 comes with a number of useful accessories, in addition to the word processing accessories discussed in the previous chapter. Microsoft Paint and Kodak Imaging work with images. You can keep yourself amused with games such as Free Cell, Hearts, Minesweeper, and Solitaire. The Phone Dialer and Calculator do exactly what their names suggest. The Character Map helps you find obscure characters to jazz up your text files and documents. And Address Book can store the e-mail addresses, mailing addresses, phone numbers, and other information about your coworkers and friends.

Working with Images

Not so many years ago, putting a picture into a text document was pretty exotic. Text was text, and pictures were pictures—newspapers and magazines might mix them together, but that was for the professionals. But now, a web page without images is considered boring, and it's no big deal to attach photos to e-mail, or to use your computer to send an image file as a fax. Ordinary people need to have some tools for creating and working with images.

Windows 98 provides two such tools: Microsoft Paint and Kodak Imaging. Paint is relatively unchanged since Windows 95, but Imaging is new with Windows 98. In general, Paint is a better drawing and drafting tool, while Imaging is designed for cropping and annotating photos.

Drawing Pictures Using Microsoft Paint

Microsoft Paint is to images what WordPad is to text documents—a simple but versatile tool for creating and editing. You can use it to make diagrams for presentations or to crop your online vacation photos; your five-year-old can use it as a coloring book, or your ten-year-old can use it to draw moustaches on the Mona Lisa.

To run Paint, choose Start | Programs | Accessories | Paint. Figure 5-1 shows the parts of a Paint window.

Opening and Saving Files

Paint opens files in the following image formats: bitmap (.bmp), tagged image file (.tif), JPEG (.jpg), and GIF (.gif). Files created or edited by Paint can be saved as bitmap files in a variety of color schemes (monochrome, 16 color, 256 color, 24-bit color), as well as JPEG and GIF.

Selecting Objects

With the Select tool chosen (by clicking the dotted rectangle button in the Tool box), you can select objects inside the drawing area just as you select objects inside a Folder window: by enclosing them in a rectangle. Move the pointer to one corner of the

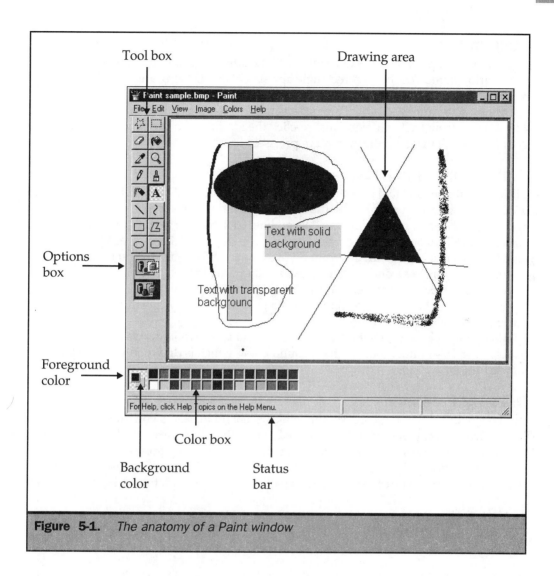

Tool box

Drawing area

Options box

Foreground color

Color box

Background color

Status bar

Text with solid background

Text with transparent background

Figure 5-1.   *The anatomy of a Paint window*

rectangular area that includes the objects you want to select, hold the mouse button down, move to the opposite corner of the area, and release the mouse button.

The Free-Form Select tool (the dotted star button in the Tool box) allows you to select objects and parts of objects inside a region of any shape. Drag the cursor to trace out any curve. Either close up the curve, or Paint closes it up automatically with a straight line. The enclosed region is now selected, and can be moved by dragging or by cutting-and-pasting.

Zooming

To zoom in on a portion of the drawing area, click the Magnifier tool (the magnifying glass button in the Tool box). A rectangle appears in the drawing area. Position the rectangle to enclose the area you want to zoom in on, and then click.

Annoyingly, after zooming, Paint selects the tool you were using before you zoomed. To zoom back out, you must re-click the Magnifier tool, or choose View | Zoom to control the magnification more precisely.

Drawing Lines and Curves

Clicking with the Line tool (the straight line button in the Tool box) nails down one end of a line; the other end moves with the cursor. When the line is where you want it, click again to fix the other end. To make a curved line, click the Curve tool (the wiggly line button in the Tool box), and begin by drawing a straight line, as you would with the Line tool. Then, click-and-drag a point on that line to make a curve. You have the option of dragging a second point to make another kink in the curve.

When the Line or Curve tools are selected, different line thicknesses appear in the Options box, just below the Tool box. Select a new thickness by clicking the line thickness you want.

Using the right mouse button with the Line and Curve tools draws in the background color rather than the foreground color, which is drawn in with the left mouse button.

Drawing Freehand

Paint has four tools in the Tool box that make freehand marks as you drag them: Pencil, Brush, Spray Can, and Eraser. Pencil makes thin lines, Brush makes thick lines, and Spray Can sprays a pattern of dots. You can choose among three densities of Spray Can dot patterns by clicking the pattern you want in the Options box. Just as its name suggests, the Eraser erases anything in its path, replacing it with the background color.

Making Shapes

These four tools in the Tool box make shapes: Ellipse, Rectangle, Rounded Rectangle, and Polygon. The simplest shape to make is a rectangle:

1. Click the Rectangle tool (the solid, not dotted, rectangle button).

2. Click in the drawing area where you want one corner of the rectangle located.

3. Drag to where you want the opposite corner of the rectangle located. When you release the mouse button, Paint creates the rectangle.

You use the Ellipse and Rounded Rectangle tools in a manner similar to the Rectangle tool.

The Polygon tool makes figures with any number of sides:

1. Click the Polygon tool (the L-shaped polygon button).

2. Click inside the drawing area where you want one corner of the polygon located.

3. Each click defines the next corner of the polygon. For the first side, you must click and drag; for subsequent sides, just click.

4. Double-click the last corner. Paint closes up the polygon automatically.

Coloring Objects

Control the colors of objects by using the Color box at the bottom of the Paint window. The two colored squares at the far left of the Color box show the current foreground and background colors, with the foreground square on top of the background square. Any object that you construct using the left mouse button has the foreground color, while objects made using the right mouse button have the background color.

To choose a new foreground color, left-click the square of the new color in the Color box. To choose a new background color, right-click the square of the new color. You can match the color of any object in the drawing area by using the Pick Color tool (the eyedropper button in the Tool box). Select the tool, and then click the object whose color you want to match. Left-clicking changes the foreground color to match the object, right-clicking changes the background color to match the object.

To color within an outlined area, such as a rectangle or an ellipse, select the Fill With Color tool (the tipped paint can button), and click within the area. Right-click to fill with the background color. Using the Fill With Color tool on an area that is not outlined colors the whole "sheet of paper"—the area outside of any enclosed region.

Adding Text

Click the Text tool (the button with the *A*), and drag across the part of your picture where you want the type to appear. Paint displays a rectangular text box for you to type in. A font selection box appears above the text box so that you can select the font, size, and style of the text. Click inside the text box and type. Click outside the text box when you are done typing.

The Options box below the Tool box gives two choices for using the Text tool. The top choice makes a solid background for the text box, using the background color. The bottom choice makes a transparent background.

Flipping, Rotating, and Stretching

Commands on the Image menu flip, rotate, or stretch the entire image or the selected part of the image. Choosing Image | Flip/Rotate opens a dialog box from which you can choose to flip the image horizontally or vertically, or rotate it by any number of degrees. Choosing Image | Stretch/Skew opens another dialog box from which you can stretch the image horizontally or vertically by any percentage, or slant it by any number of degrees.

Cropping Images

You can crop an image—remove unwanted material around the edges of a picture. To crop an image, use the Select tool to enclose the area of the image that you want to keep. Choose Edit | Copy To to save the selected area as a new file. Type the filename and click Save. The original image is unaffected.

Annotating Images with Kodak Imaging

Scanners, digital cameras, clip art CDs, and the Internet give computer users access to countless images, which you can print out, insert into your documents, or display on your web pages. But even though a picture is worth a thousand words, the impact of a picture can sometimes be improved by the addition of a few words, some highlighting, and maybe a few lines drawn on top, either straight or freehand. Kodak's Imaging for Windows is a tool for this job. You can run Imaging by choosing Start | Programs | Accessories | Imaging.

If you click or double-click a graphics file to run Kodak Imaging, you may run its display-only cousin instead, Kodak Preview (see "Viewing Images").

Imaging has four toolbars, which are shown in Figure 5-2. Any or all of these toolbars can be made to disappear by selecting View | Toolbars, and checking the appropriate boxes in the Toolbars dialog box. You can choose the standard Windows file commands (New, Open, Save, Save As, and Print) from the File menu, or by clicking the appropriate buttons on the Standard toolbar.

Acquiring Images

Kodak Imaging can open files in a large number of formats: bitmap (.bmp), tagged image file (.tif), JPEG (.jpg), GIF (.gif), Fax (.awd), PCX (.pcx), DCX (.dcx), XIF (.xif), and WIFF (.wif). If your system has a TWAIN-compliant scanner (*TWAIN* is a standard for communications between scanners and computer software), Imaging can take an image directly from the scanner. You must first select your scanner by choosing File | Select Scanner and picking the scanner from the list that appears. To scan an image, choose File | Scan New. Your scanner's driver displays its dialog box; click the Preview, Scan, or other button to scan the image, which appears in the Kodak Imaging window.

Rotating Images

At the center of the Imaging toolbar are the Rotate Left and Rotate Right buttons. Each button rotates the image 90 degrees. One button undoes the action of the other, and four clicks of either button restores the image to its original orientation.

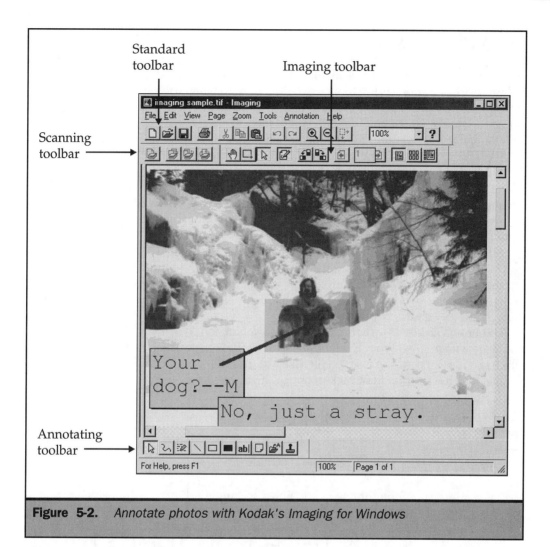

Standard
toolbar

Imaging toolbar

Scanning
toolbar

Annotating
toolbar

Figure 5-2.   *Annotate photos with Kodak's Imaging for Windows*

Zooming

The Standard toolbar contains three Zoom buttons (Zoom In, Zoom Out, and Zoom To Selection) and a Zoom display window, with a drop-down list of standard zoom percentages. Zoom In (the magnifying glass and plus sign button) doubles the size of the image in all dimensions; Zoom Out (the magnifying glass and minus sign button) halves the image. When a portion of the image has been selected (with the Select Image tool), Zoom to Selection expands the selected portion to fill the entire window.

The Zoom display window shows the current zoom percentage, with 100% corresponding to actual size. Change the zoom by typing any number into the display, or by choosing a preset percentage from the drop-down list.

Annotating Images

Imaging has an Annotating toolbar (shown in Figure 5-3) for annotating images. Most of the basic tools resemble those available in Paint, and they work the same way: Click the appropriate button on the toolbar, and the cursor changes to represent the corresponding tool. Use the tool to annotate the image by clicking-and-dragging to define the area in which you want the annotation. Once they have been created, annotations can be selected, moved, or stretched, just like elements in a Paint image.

The Select, Freehand Line, Straight Line, and Text tools are almost identical to the corresponding Paint tools. Imaging has two rectangle tools (Hollow and Filled), whereas Paint has only one. (In Paint, Transparent and Filled are options for a single Rectangle tool.) Highlighter is a third kind of rectangle tool, one whose filling is translucent, resembling what a highlighter pen does to an image on paper. The dog in Figure 5-2 is highlighted.

Attach Note is a tool similar to Text. You use it by dragging a rectangle across the part of the image where you want the note to be located, and then clicking inside the rectangle and typing the note. Unlike Text, however, the attached note has a background color that obscures the original image, as if a stick-on note has been posted there. Figure 5-2 shows two attached notes.

Text From File inserts an entire text file as an annotation. When you click a location in the image with the Text From File tool, an Open window appears, allowing you to choose which text file to insert. The inserted file, like text that you type into a window created by the Text tool, has a transparent background, as if you are typing over the image.

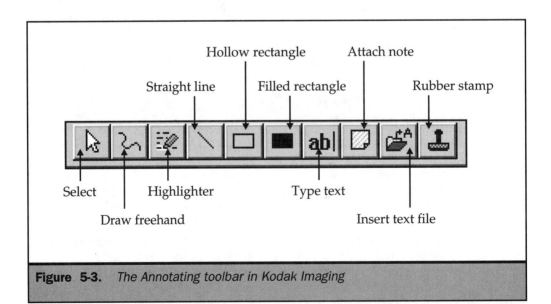

Figure 5-3. *The Annotating toolbar in Kodak Imaging*

Rubber stamp has four options: Approved, Draft, Received, and Rejected. Select one when you click the tool. Clicking the tool on the image "stamps" the corresponding message onto the image in that location. All the options but Draft include the date automatically, as in "Received 10/17/98."

When you are satisfied with your annotations, you can incorporate them into the image by selecting Annotations | Make Annotations Permanent.

Changing Tool Properties

Each of the annotation tools has properties that you can change. Open a tool's Properties box by right-clicking the tool button and selecting Properties. The Properties box of any drawing tool lets you adjust the color and/or line width of the drawing, and the Properties box of any text tool controls the font and size of the text, as well as the color of the background.

Viewing Images

You can open images for viewing alone by using the Kodak Preview program. Windows uses this program for displaying many types of graphics files. The Kodak Preview program doesn't appear on the Start or Programs menus; to run it, open the filename Kodakprv.exe in the C:\Windows folder. You see the Imaging Preview window, which looks just like the regular Imaging window but with fewer commands and toolbars. If you decide that you want to edit the image after all, choose File | Open Image For Editing from the menu bar, or press CTRL-E.

Playing Games

Games have been an important part of the personal computer experience from the very beginning. Even people who are intimidated by serious tools, such as word processors and spreadsheets, can be enticed into learning games—and the basic computer skills that the games require.

Windows 98 provides four free games: Free Cell, Hearts, Minesweeper, and Solitaire. These games aren't state-of-the-art, animated, 3-D multimedia games, but nonetheless, they are surprisingly effective at making time pass quickly, and they can be useful tools for acclimating new computer users to the mouse, keyboard, and Windows. You can play these games by choosing Start | Programs | Accessories | Games.

Note   *Games may not be not installed. If they don't appear on the Start | Programs | Accessories menu, you can install them from the Windows 98 CD-ROM or floppy disks. Choose Start | Settings | Control Panel, run Add/Remove Programs, click the Windows Setup tab, and choose Accessories from the list of Windows 98 components, click Details, and choose Games (see "Installing and Uninstalling Programs That Come with Windows 98" in Chapter 3).*

Playing Free Cell

Free Cell is one of the many variants on 52-card solitaire. The program begins with an empty board. To deal a hand, choose Game | New Game. The rules are described in Help | Help Topics.

Help declares: "It is believed (although not proven) that every game is winnable." If you want to keep trying a game of Free Cell until you win, keep track of its game number on the title bar. Whenever you want to try again, choose Game | Select Game and enter that game number.

Playing Hearts

This is the popular four-person card game. You can play this game as solitaire (with the computer playing the other three hands), but Microsoft wrote this game to show off some networking capabilities in an earlier version of Windows, so the first questions you are asked when you start the game make sense only if you are on a local area network (see Chapter 29).

Your first choice is whether to join a game someone else is dealing on your network, or to deal a new game. If you choose to join a game, you are asked the name of the dealer's computer. If you choose to deal, you can wait for three other players to join your game via the network, or you can press F2 at any time and have the computer play all the hands that haven't been claimed yet.

If you aren't on a network, there are no other games to join, and other players are not going to show up to join your game. Choose to deal your own game, and then press F2 right away to have the computer play the other three hands.

The Help menu contains a good description of the rules of Hearts.

Playing Minesweeper

Minesweeper is a one-person logic-puzzle game whose beginner level is shown in Figure 5-4. Begin play by clicking one of the squares in the grid. If it is a mine, you lose. If not, you get some information about where the mines are—the square you clicked (and possibly some others) is uncovered, revealing a number. The number tells you the number of mines in adjacent squares. The more squares you uncover without hitting a mine, the more information you acquire to help you not click a mine next time.

When you have deduced that a certain square is a mine, leave a marker there by right-clicking. You win when you have uncovered all the squares except the ones with mines.

Two numbers appear above the playing field, on either side of the smiley face. The left number is the number of markers you have left. (If you've placed all your markers accurately, it is also the number of mines left to find.) The right number is the number of seconds since you clicked your first square.

The game has three levels: Beginner, Intermediate, and Expert. The more difficult levels have more squares and a higher percentage of mines.

Figure 5-4.   *Minesweeper: don't get blown up!*

Playing Solitaire

Solitaire is a 52-card solitaire game. Rules are described rather tersely in the Help Topics—we suggest finding a good book of Hoyle. Scoring, in particular, is not described at all, though choosing Game | Options allows you to choose between standard scoring and Vegas scoring.

The score and time of your game is displayed on the status bar.

Using Phone Dialer

If your computer is connected to a phone line, Phone Dialer can dial calls for you. If, in addition, you have a microphone and speakers, your computer may be able to replace your phone entirely. To access Phone Dialer (shown in Figure 5-5), choose Start | Programs | Accessories | Communications | Phone Dialer.

Dialing the Phone

Phone Dialer works like a telephone with speed-dial buttons. Enter a phone number into the display either by typing, clicking the numbered buttons, or cutting-and-pasting from a document. Dial the displayed number by clicking the Dial button.

A list of recently dialed numbers drops down when you click in the display window—redial a number by selecting it and clicking Dial. Dial any number assigned to your speed-dial buttons by clicking the button.

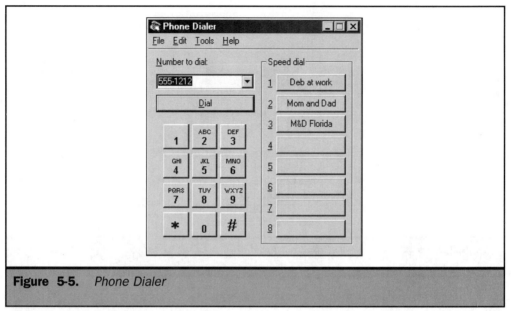

Figure 5-5. *Phone Dialer*

Storing Phone Numbers

Assign a number to one of the eight speed-dial buttons by clicking an unassigned button. Enter the number and a recognizable nickname into the appropriate windows of the Program Speed Dial dialog box, and then click either Save or Save and Dial. Reassign a speed-dial button by selecting Edit | Speed Dial. When the Edit Speed Dial dialog box appears, click the button you want to reassign, and type the new nickname and number in the fields at the bottom of the box. Then click Save.

Logging Your Phone Calls

Phone Dialer can keep a log of your phone calls. Choose Tools | Show Log to display the Call Log window, shown here:

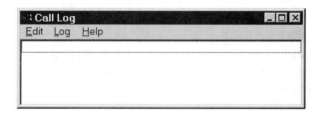

To tell Phone Dialer to keep a log of your calls, choose Log | Options from the Call Log window's menu bar. The Call Log Options dialog box has two check boxes: Incoming Calls and Outgoing Calls. Select the options you want, then click OK. You can close the Call Log window by using its Close button. Reopen the window any time you want to look at the call log.

 Most modems can't inform Phone Dialer about incoming calls, so the Incoming Calls option may not work. If you choose to log outgoing calls, Phone Dialer can track only those calls you dial using the program.

Configuring the Phone Dialer

If you use dialing properties to store your area code, calling cards, and other dialing information, you can use these features from Phone Dialer (see "What Is a Dialing Location?" in Chapter 21). Choose Tools | Dialing Properties to see or change these properties.

If your computer has more than one modem, choose Tools | Connect Using to choose which modem to dial. Choose the modem from the Line box, then click OK.

Using Calculator

Windows 98's Calculator is really two calculators: The unintimidating Standard Calculator that does simple arithmetic, and a more complicated Scientific Calculator. To use either of them, choose Start | Programs | Accessories | Calculator. The Calculator program opens in Standard View. To use the Scientific Calculator, choose View | Scientific.

You can use the Calculator in conjunction with other programs, such as word processors, by cutting and pasting numbers from a document into the Calculator, doing a calculation, and then cutting and pasting the result back into a document (see "What Is Cut-and-Paste?" in Chapter 7). You can also enter numbers into the calculator by clicking its buttons, or by typing the numbers into the display window by using the keyboard. If you mis-enter a digit, click the Calculator's Back button. The CE and C buttons stand for Clear Entry and Clear, respectively.

Using the Standard Calculator

The Standard Calculator (shown in Figure 5-6) adds, subtracts, multiplies, divides, takes square roots, calculates percentages, and finds multiplicative inverses. It has a one-number memory.

Performing Arithmetic

To perform an arithmetic calculation, enter the calculation as you would type it, left to right, as in

3+5=

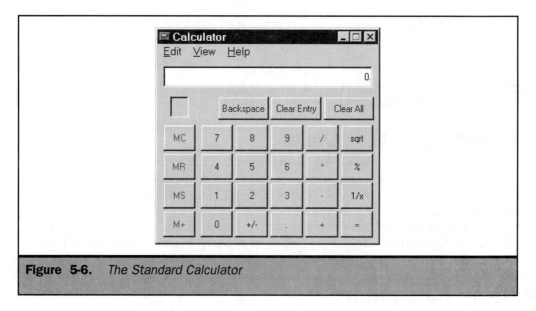

Figure 5-6.   *The Standard Calculator*

To compute a percentage, make the percentage the second number in a multiplication. For example, to figure 15 percent of 7.4, enter

7.4×15%

The 1/x button computes the multiplicative inverse of the displayed number.

Storing Numbers in Memory

The four buttons on the left side of the Standard Calculator control its memory. To store the currently displayed number in the memory, click the MS (memory store) button. An M appears in the box above the MC button to show that the memory is in use. The memory holds only one number, so storing another number causes the calculator to forget the previously stored number. Clicking MC (memory clear) clears the memory. To recall the number stored in memory, click MR (memory recall). Clicking the M+ button adds the displayed number to the number in memory, and stores the result in the memory.

Using the Scientific Calculator

The Scientific Calculator (shown in Figure 5-7) is considerably larger, more powerful, and more complex than the Standard Calculator. Anything you can do on the Standard Calculator works exactly the same way on the Scientific Calculator, except that the Scientific Calculator has no % or sqrt key. (Compute square roots by clicking x^2 when the Inv box is checked.) In addition, you can perform calculations in a variety of number systems, do logical operations, use trigonometric functions, and do statistical analyses.

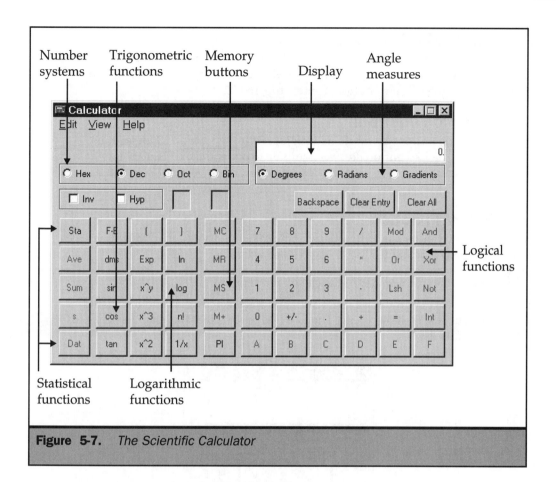

Figure 5-7. *The Scientific Calculator*

Number Systems and Angle Measures

The Scientific Calculator can work in Dec (decimal, the default), Bin (binary), Oct (octal), or Hex (hexadecimal) number systems. Its A-F buttons are actually number buttons, used to enter hexadecimal (base-16) numbers. Choose among number systems by using the radio buttons on the left side of the top row.

You can use the radio buttons just to the right of the number-system buttons to choose among the different ways of measuring angles: degrees (the default), radians, and gradients. When using degrees, the DMS button converts a decimal number of degrees into degrees-minute-seconds form. To convert back, check the Inv box and click DMS again.

The F-E (fixed-exponential) button toggles between fixed-point notation and scientific notation. When entering a number in scientific notation, click the Exp button before entering the exponential part.

Trigonometric Functions

Trigonometric functions are computed with the Sin, Cos, and Tan buttons. Use the Inv and Hyp check boxes to compute inverse or hyperbolic trigonometric functions. The PI button (below the memory buttons) enters the first 32 digits of π.

Logarithmic Functions

The Ln and Log buttons compute natural logarithms and base-10 logarithms, respectively. The Exp button *does not* compute exponentials. (It is used for entering numbers in scientific notation.) Compute exponentials by using Ln with the Inv box checked.

Statistical Functions

In order to use the statistical functions of the calculator, you must first enter a list of numbers, which constitutes the data. To enter a data list:

1. Enter the first number in the calculator display.

2. Click the Sta button. The statistics buttons are activated and a statistics box opens, as shown here. The n=6 line reports that there are 6 entries in the data list.

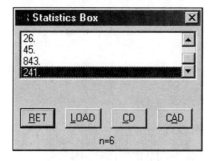

3. Click the Dat button. The number in the calculator display appears in the statistics box.

4. Enter the rest of the data, clicking Dat after each entry.

Once you have entered a data list, Ave computes the average of the entries, Sum computes their sum, and S computes their standard deviation.

You can see the statistics box at any time by clicking Sta. To edit the data list, use the buttons at the bottom of the statistics box: LOAD copies the highlighted number back to the calculator display; CD deletes the highlighted number from the data list; and CAD clears the data list.

Logical Functions

When the Bin radio button is chosen, the calculator works in the binary (base-2) number system, and the buttons And, Or, and Not perform the bitwise logical operations that their names suggest. The Xor button does exclusive or, and Lsh does a left shift. Perform a right shift by clicking Lsh with the Inv box checked.

Other Functions

The Int button finds the integer part of a number. When Inv is checked, the Int button finds the fractional part of a number.

Compute squares and cubes with the X^2 and X^3 buttons. Compute other powers with the X^y button.

The N! button computes factorials of integers. If the displayed number has a fractional part, N! computes a gamma function.

The Mod button does modular reductions, for example:

12 Mod 5 = 2

Getting Help

In addition to the Help Topics on the Help menu, you can find out what any button on the calculator does by right-clicking it and selecting "What's This?".

Using Special Characters with Character Map

Do you need to use unusual characters, like Æ, Ö, or ®? The Character Map accessory can help you find them.

Character Map may not be installed as part of the standard Windows 98 installation. If it doesn't appear on the Start | Programs | Accessories | System Tools menu, you can install Character Map from the Windows 98 CD-ROM or floppy disks. Choose Start | Settings | Control Panel, run Add/Remove Programs, click the Windows Setup tab, and choose the System Tools entry in the list of Windows 98 components, click Details and choose Character Map (see "Installing and Uninstalling Programs That Come with Windows 98" in Chapter 3).

1. Open Character Map by choosing Start | Programs | Accessories | System Tools | Character Map. You see the Character Map window shown in Figure 5-8.

2. Select a font from the Font list. The characters available in this font appear in the Character Map window, arranged in a 7x32 grid.

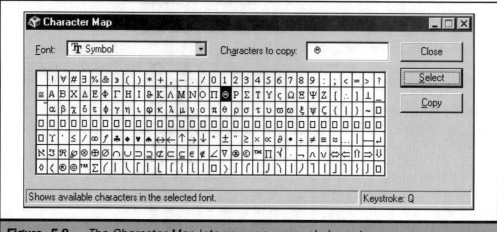

Figure 5-8. *The Character Map lets you use unusual characters*

3. Double-click the character you want to use, or single-click it and then click Select. The character appears in the Characters To Copy box.

4. When you have displayed all the characters that you want from this font in the Characters To Copy box, click Copy. Character Map copies the characters to the Windows Clipboard (see Chapter 7).

5. Paste the characters into a document using a command in the program you use to edit that document. (Most programs use Edit | Paste or CTRL-V to paste from the Clipboard.)

You can remove characters from the Characters To Copy box by clicking in the box and either backspacing over the characters or deleting them.

If you just want to know what keystroke corresponds to a given character in a font, single-click the character in step 3, and look at the bottom-right corner of the Character Map window. In Figure 5-8, for example, you discover that the keystroke Q in Symbol font corresponds to the Greek letter theta, ⊖.

Storing Addresses in the Address Book

One of the first things people did when personal computers were invented was to store lists of addresses on them. It makes sense—the old-fashioned little black book quickly gets filled with scratch-outs as people move or change phone numbers or get a new e-mail address, and you always end up wishing you had left a little more space between Sloane and Smith.

The next good idea in address management was to make the address book into a system utility so that any program could access it. You shouldn't have to keep one list of addresses for your word processor, another for your e-mail program, and a third for your personal information manager. And you shouldn't have to wonder which list has the most recent phone numbers.

The Windows Address Book is still not the perfect realization of this idea, but it is a definite step in the right direction. It keeps track of just about anything you would want to keep track of, provides a space for notes, and is accessible from Internet Explorer, Outlook Express, and NetMeeting. As software is updated for Windows 98, other programs will probably take advantage of its capabilities.

Unfortunately, Microsoft Exchange, the e-mail client that Microsoft introduced with Windows 95, has its own address book. Current versions of Word and Outlook are set up to work with Exchange instead of with Windows 98's Address Book. Outlook Express uses Address Book.

Running Address Book

You can access Address Book either from another program—like Internet Explorer, Outlook Express, or NetMeeting—or by choosing Start | Programs | Internet Explorer | Address Book. You see the Address Book window shown in Figure 5-9. The window lists the people you have entered into the address book with the name, e-mail address, and phone numbers for each person.

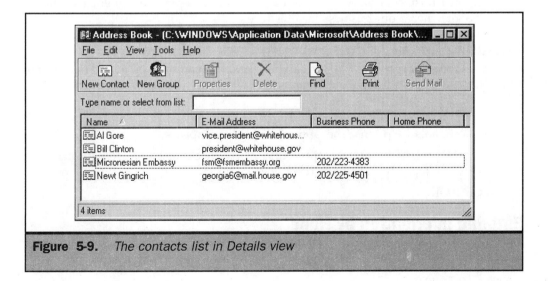

Figure 5-9.   *The contacts list in Details view*

Entering Information into Address Book

You can get information into Address Book in three ways: importing information from your current address book program, capturing it automatically from Outlook Express, or entering it by hand. Once you have a list of contacts in your Address Book, you can organize them into groups.

Importing Addresses and Business Cards from Other Programs

You may already have an address book defined in another program. Address Book can import addresses from the following programs:

- Eudora Pro or Light (through version 3.0)
- LDIF-LDAP Data Interchange Format
- Microsoft Exchange
- Microsoft Internet Mail for Windows 3.1
- Netscape Address Book (versions 2 or 3)
- Netscape Communicator (version 4)
- a text file

Selecting File | Import | Address Book starts an Import Wizard to guide you through the process. In many cases, the Wizard can find the other address book on its own.

Virtual business cards (.vcf files) can also be imported into Address Book. Select File | Import | Business Card (vCard). A Browse window opens so that you can tell Address Book where your business card files are.

Capturing E-mail Addresses from Outlook Express

If you use Outlook Express as your e-mail program, you can set it up to add names and e-mail addresses to Address Book automatically whenever you reply to a message.

1. Open Outlook Express (see Chapter 23).
2. Select Tools | Options. The Options dialog box appears.
3. On the General tab of the Options dialog box, check the box Automatically Put People I Reply To In My Address Book.
4. Click OK.

Entering Information by Hand

To enter a new contact into Address Book, click the New Contact button on the toolbar. A blank Properties dialog box appears. Type in any information you want recorded,

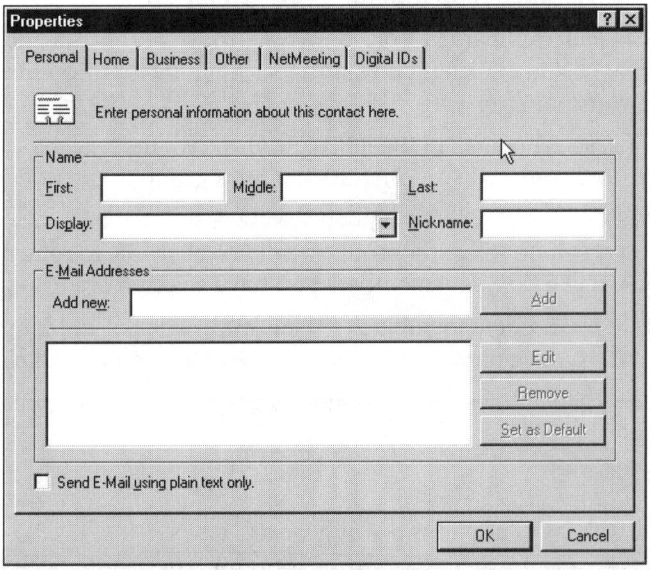

Figure 5-10. *Detailed information about a contact*

and leave blank any line you want. To add or change information about an existing contact, select the contact on the address list and click the Properties button. The Properties dialog box appears, as shown in Figure 5-10 (above). Enter or edit information on any of its six tabs.

Address Book lets you keep track of several e-mail addresses for a single person, with one of them specified as the default. To add a new e-mail address, type it into the Add New line of the E-Mail Addresses box on the Personal tab. Then click the Add button. The new e-mail address appears in the list just below the Add New line.

To set one of a person's e-mail addresses as the default, select it from the list of e-mail addresses on the Personal tab of the Properties dialog box associated with that person's name. The click the Set As Default button.

Defining Groups

It can be confusing to have your customers, your coworkers, and your child's piano teacher all on one big alphabetical list. Address Book allows you to give your contact list some structure by defining groups of contacts that have something in common. To define a group:

1. Click the New Group button on the Address Book toolbar. A Group Properties dialog box opens.

2. Type a name for the group into the Group Name line.

3. Click the Select Members button. A Select Group Members window appears. Your contact list is in its left pane, and its right pane will contain the members of the new group.

4. One by one, select names in the left pane and click the Select button to add this name to the group. You can add an entire group to the new group in the same way.

5. When you are done selecting group members, click OK to return to the Group Properties dialog box. The members you have selected are listed.

6. If you want to add new members to the group, click Select Members again. If you want to remove names from the list, select the names and click Remove.

7. Jot a note into the Notes box to remind yourself what these contacts have in common.

8. Click OK.

A contact can appear in any number of groups.

Looking Up Information in Address Book

When you open Address Book, the first thing you see is the contact list, as shown in Figure 5-9.

Viewing the Contact List

Address Book offers you the same choice of views that Windows Explorer or a Folder window does: Large Icon, Small Icon, List, and Details. Choose among them on the View menu. The differences between Large Icon, Small Icon, and List are fairly trivial: Large Icon uses a large index card icon, and lists contacts in rows; Small Icon uses a small index icon and lists contacts in rows; List uses a small index card icon and lists contacts in columns. Details view uses small icons and presents the name, e-mail address, home phone number, and business phone number of each contact in four columns.

Sorting the Contact List

In any of the views, you can sort contacts according to any of the information displayed. In Small Icons, Large Icons, and List views, only the name is shown, so contacts can be listed according to first or last name, in ascending or descending order. Make these choices by choosing View | Sort By.

In Details view, you can list contacts according to name, e-mail address, home phone number, or business phone number. As in the Details view in Windows Explorer, click the head of any column to list contacts according to that column in ascending order. To list in descending order, click the column head a second time. To tell Address Book whether the Name column should be ordered according to first name or last name, choose View | Sort By.

Looking Up Detailed Information

Each contact has an associated Properties dialog box (see Figure 5-10). To view the Properties dialog box for a contact, double-click the person's entry in the contact list. Table 5-1 lists the properties you can store for each person in your Address Book, along with the name of the tab on the Properties dialog box on which the setting appears.

Tab	Setting	Description
Personal	Name (First, Middle, Last, Nickname, and Display)	Specifies the person's name. The Display box shows how the person's name appears in the address list.
Personal	E-Mail Addresses	Specifies one or more e-mail addresses for this person. To add a new address, type it in the Add New box and click the Add button. One address is the default (the address to use when sending e-mail to this person).
Personal	Send E-Mail Using Plain Text Only	Specifies that messages to this person contain plain text only, not HTML-formatted messages.
Home	Street Address, City, State/Province, Zip Code, and Country	Specifies the person's home mailing address.
Home	Phone, Fax, and Cellular	Specifies the person's home phone numbers.
Home	Gender	Specifies the person's gender (the default setting is "Unspecified").
Home	Personal Web Page	Specifies the URL of the person's home page.
Business	Company, Job Title, Department, and Office	Specifies where this person works.
Business	Street Address, City, State/Province, Zip Code, and Country	Specifies the person's business address.

Table 5-1. *Properties of Address Book Entries*

Tab	Setting	Description
Business	Phone, Fax, and Pager	Specifies this person's business phone numbers.
Business	Business Web Page	Specifies the URL of this person's business home page.
Other	Notes	Specifies other information about the person.
Other	Group Membership	If you have added this person to one or more groups, lists the group names.
NetMeeting	Conferencing E-Mail	Specifies the address to use when contacting this person via Net Meeting. This is frequently the same as the person's e-mail address.
NetMeeting	Conferencing Directory Servers	Specifies the NetMeeting directory servers the person uses (see "Connecting to a Directory Server" in Chapter 27). One of the directory servers is the default, to be used when contacting this person via NetMeeting.
Digital IDs	Select An E-Mail Address	Specifies the e-mail address to which the person's digital ID (certificates) is associated. When you import a digital ID into Address Book, you specify the e-mail address to associate it with.
Digital IDs	Digital IDs associated with the selected e-mail address	Specifies one or more digital IDs (certificates) for that e-mail address. Click Import to import a digital ID from a file (which usually has the extension .pub). Click Export to export the selected digital ID to a .pub file.

Table 5-1.   *Properties of Address Book Entries* (continued)

Viewing Groups

A long contact list is easier to grasp when it is divided into groups (see "Defining Groups"). To view your contact list by group, check the Groups List item on the View menu. The contact list window divides, with a groups list (similar to the folder tree in the left pane of Windows Explorer) in the left pane.

In the left pane, select the group you want to examine, and the right pane shows the list of contacts in that group. To see the entire contact list again, click Address Book at the top of the groups list.

Looking Up People from the Start Menu

Another way to use the Address Book window is to choose Start | Find | People. You see the Find People window, shown in Figure 5-11. Make sure that the Look In box is set to Address Book, then type in what you know about the person and click Find Now. See section "Setting Up Additional Directory Services" for how to use the Find People window to search other address directories.

Contacting People

Select a person from the address list and click the Send Mail button on the toolbar or choose Tools | Send Mail. Your default e-mail program ought to start to compose a message to the person you selected. Unfortunately, Address Book doesn't correctly read the default e-mail program that you can set in the Internet Properties dialog box (see "Setting Your Mail and News Programs" in Chapter 23). Instead, Address Book

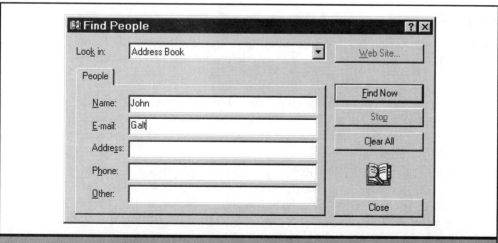

Figure 5-11.   *Finding people in your Address Book or in other directory services*

may try to run Microsoft Outlook or Microsoft Exchange to send e-mail. This limitation may be fixed in future versions of Address Book.

If you use NetMeeting to call people over the Internet, you can select a person from the address list and choose Tools | Internet Call to contact the person using NetMeeting (see "Conferencing Using Microsoft NetMeeting" in Chapter 27).

Printing Information from Address Book

You can print information from the Address Book in three formats:

- Memo, which prints all the information Address Book has about the selected contact(s).

- Business Card, which prints only the information from the Business tab of the contact(s) Properties box.

- Phone List, which prints a list of phone numbers of the selected contact(s).

To print:

1. Select contacts from the contact list. Select blocks of names by holding down the SHIFT key while you click the names. Select individuals scattered throughout the list by holding down the CTRL key. Select a group by clicking its name in the contact list (not the group list). Select all contacts by choosing Edit | Select All.

2. Click the Print button on the toolbar. A Print dialog box appears.

3. Select the Memo, Business Card, or Phone List from the Print dialog box.

4. Click OK.

Exporting Names and Addresses from Address Book

You can also export names and addresses from Address Book in Microsoft Exchange Personal Address Book format, in a comma-delimited text file, or as Business Cards (vCards):

- **Microsoft Exchange Personal Address Book Format**   Choose File | Export | Address Book, choose Microsoft Exchange Personal Address Book from the list that appears, and click the Export button. Choose the Microsoft Exchange profile to use, then click OK.

- **Text File**   Choose File | Export | Address Book, choose Text File (Comma Separated Values) from the list that appears, and click Export. The CSV Export Wizard runs. Specify the name of the file in which you want to store the exported addresses, then click Next. Select the information you want to include for each person, then click Finish.

■ **Business Card or vCard**   Select the person whose information you want to export, then choose File | Export | Business Card (vCard). Specify the name and folder where you want to store the business card and click Save.

Setting Up Additional Directory Services

When you choose Start | Find | People, you see the Find People window shown in Figure 5-11. In addition to searching Address Book entries, you can search other *directory services*—listings of names, e-mail addresses, and other information. These directory services may be public, such as the web-based service Four11 (at **http://www.four11.com**). Or they may be private, such as the employee directory for a large organization.

Window 98 comes with a number of public directory services already set up—click the Look In box in the Find People window to see a list. When you choose a directory service, the boxes in the Find People window adjust to match the types of entries that the directory service can accept.

You can tell Windows 98 about other directory services, for example, for your organization. Windows 98 can work with any LDAP-compatible directory service. (*LDAP* stands for Lightweight Directory Access Protocol.) To configure Windows to work with an additional directory service, run Address Book or Outlook Express, then choose Tools | Accounts. (In Outlook Express, described in Chapter 23, click the Directory Service tab.) You see the Internet Accounts window, shown in Figure 5-12, listing the directory services that Windows 98 knows about.

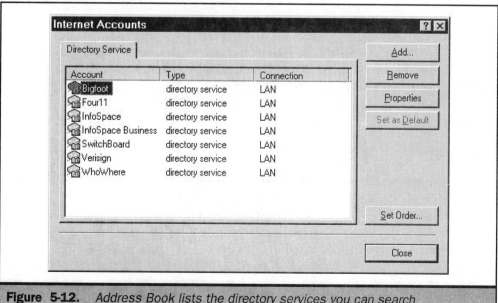

Figure 5-12.   *Address Book lists the directory services you can search*

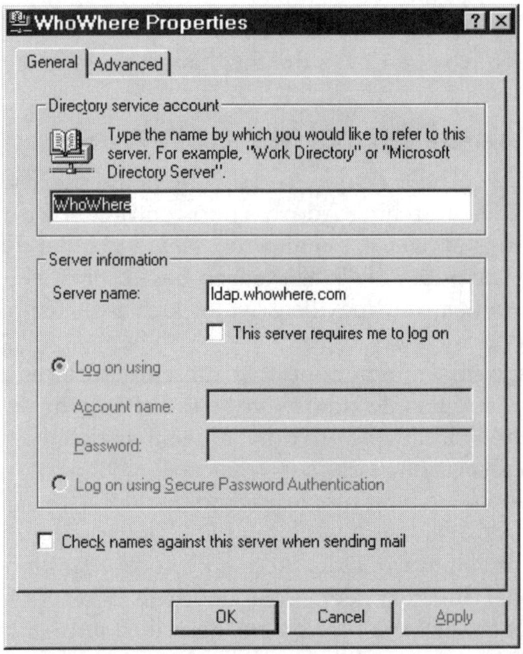

Figure 5-13. *The properties of a directory service*

To change the properties of an existing directory service, click the Properties button. You see the Properties dialog box for the service, as shown in Figure 5-13 (above). Table 5-2 lists the properties you can set for a directory service.

Setting	Description
Directory service account	Specifies the name to appear in the Find People window and other lists of directory services.
Server name	Specifies the Internet host name or IP address (numerical address) of the computer on which the LDAP server runs.

Table 5-2. *Properties of a Directory Service*

Setting	Description
This server requires me to log on	Specifies whether the directory service requires an account name and password or other authentication.
Log on using, Account name, and Password	When selected, specifies the account name and password to use when connecting to this directory service.
Log on using Secure Password Authentication	When selected, specifies that the directory service might prompt you for an account name and password when you connect.
Check names against this server when sending e-mail	When checked, specifies that all addresses in all outgoing mail from Outlook Express or other LDAP-aware mail programs be checked against the entries in this directory service for accuracy. If you check this setting for more than one directory service, you can control the order in which directory services are checked by clicking the Set Order button in the Internet Accounts window.
Server port number, Directory service (LDAP)	Specifies the port on the directory service's Internet host computer to which you connect for directory service information. The default LDAP port number is 389.
This server requires a secure connection (SSL)	When checked, specifies that you must connect to this directory service using SSL (Secure Sockets Layer).
Search timeout	Specifies how long for Windows to wait for a response from the directory service (up to one minute).
Maximum number of matches to return	Specifies the maximum number of responses to accept from the directory service.
Search base	Specifies the base (root) of the directory service to search (required by some directory services). The base specifies a subset of the entire directory.
Use simple search filter	When checked, specifies that the directory service using a simpler searching method that the method that is usually used.

Table 5-2. *Properties of a Directory Service (continued)*

To add a new directory service, click the Add button in the Internet Accounts window. The Internet Connection Wizard runs, and asks for some of the information listed in Table 5-2.

To remove a directory service you no longer use, select the service in the Internet Accounts window and click the Remove button.

Chapter 6

Getting Help

Windows has always come with *online help*—helpful information stored on your computer that you can look at using the Windows Help system. Windows 98 comes with online help, too, but this help is "online" in two senses: The help system includes help files that are stored on your computer's hard disk, as well as a connection to online help information via the Internet. You look at the online help stored on your own computer by using Windows Help, as described in this chapter.

To see the additional information about Windows 98 offered via the Internet, you use your web browser and your Internet connection. Chapter 22 describes how to get connected to the Internet, Chapter 24 explains how to use the Web, and Chapter 38 describes sources of information about Windows 98, including Microsoft's Windows Update and Support Online web sites.

What Is Windows Help?

Windows 98 online help is a set of screens of information about Windows 98 itself and the accessories that come with it. Other programs you install may come with their own online help, too.

Displaying Help Screens

To look at Windows 98 online help, click Start | Help. You see the Windows Help window, shown in Figure 6-1. The left half of the window shows the Contents, Index, or Search tab to help you find the information you need, and the right half displays the help information you find.

Reading Help Topics

When you click the Contents tab, a list of topics appears in the left pane, and the text about that topic appears in the right pane. If a topic has a little closed-book icon to its left, clicking the topic displays a list of subtopics, and the book icon changes to an open book. You can hide the list of subtopics by clicking the open-book icon or by clicking the minus sign to its left. Scroll the listing up and down, using the scroll bar, to find the topic you want.

If a topic has a question mark to its left, click the topic to display information about that topic in the right pane of the Windows Help window. At the bottom of the help text, you may see a Related Topics link; click this link to go to a topic on a related subject. If there is just one related topic, Windows Help displays it. If more than one appear, you see a little menu of topics from which you can choose. Help text may also include links that run the program that the text is talking about.

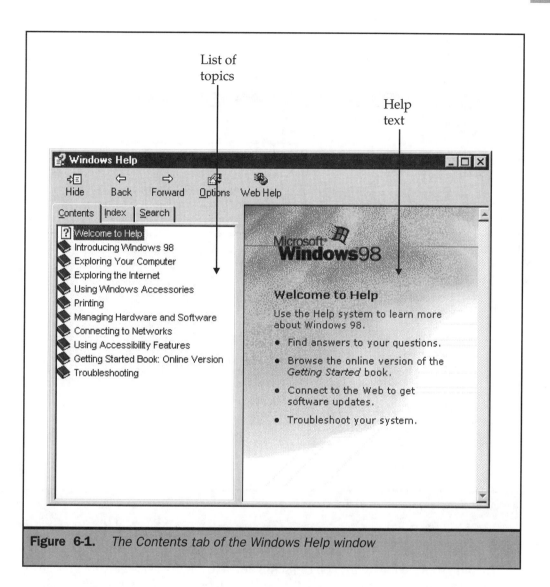

Figure 6-1.   *The Contents tab of the Windows Help window*

Looking Up Topics in the Help Index

When you click the Index tab in the Windows Help window, the left pane displays an alphabetical index of help topics, shown in Figure 6-2. The first time you click the Index tab, you see the "Preparing index for first use" window, which can take several minutes to disappear.

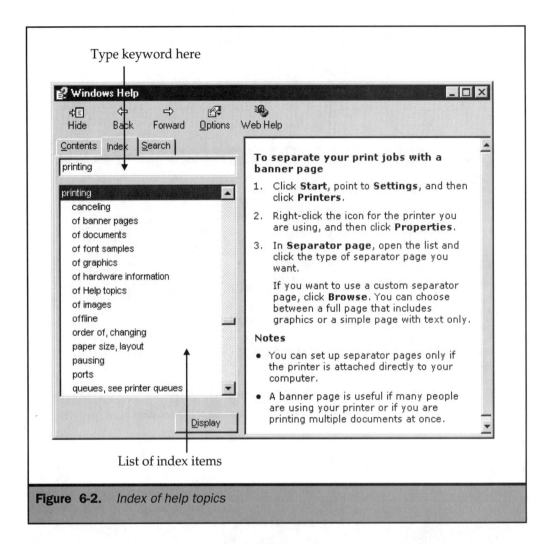

Figure 6-2. *Index of help topics*

To find a topic in the index, you can scroll down it, but the list is very long. Instead, you can type a word in the box above the list. As you type the word, Windows Help finds the first entry in the index that begins with the letters you typed. Then, scroll down the list to see all the entries that start with that word.

When you find a topic of interest, double-click the index entry. If there is only one help topic about that index entry, Windows Help displays it in the right pane. If there is more than one help topic, you see a Topics Found window, as shown next, with a menu of topics to choose from; double-click a topic, or single-click a topic and click Display.

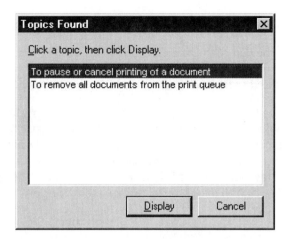

Searching for Topics

Not every term appears in the Windows Help index. You can search for words or phrases wherever they appear in the text of Windows Help, whether or not an index entry exists for that word or phrase. Click the Search tab in the Windows Help window, type a word or phrase in the box, and click the List Topics button. A list of topics appears in the Select Topic To Display box. Double click a topic to display it.

Copying Help Information to Other Programs

You can use the cut-and-paste techniques to copy information from the Windows Help window to other programs (see "What Is Cut-and-Paste?"in Chapter 7). Select the part of the text in the right pane of the Windows Help window that you want to copy. If you want to copy the entire help topic, right-click in the right pane and choose Select All from the menu that appears. Then right-click in the page and choose Copy from the menu that appears. Windows copies the text to the Windows Clipboard. Now you can paste the text into a document by using the Edit | Paste command in the program you use to edit the document.

Other Help Options

Here are other things you can do in Windows Help:

- You can click the Back button on the Windows Help toolbar to move to the previous topic you displayed, or click the Forward button to return to the next topic you displayed before clicking Back.

- If you don't want to see the left pane of the Windows Help window, click the Hide button on the toolbar; click the Show button to display the left pane again.

- To print a help topic, choose Options | Print from the menu bar.

- You can read the text of the brief Windows 98 *Getting Started* manual online using Windows Help. In the index, search for **help**, then choose the Microsoft Windows 98 Getting Started Book from the menu that appears.

- You can change the colors and background used in the right pane of the Windows Help window. Because Windows Help is a special version of Internet Explorer, you customize Windows Help by running Internet Explorer, choosing View | Internet Options, clicking the General tab, and clicking the Color button (see "What is Internet Explorer?" in Chapter 24). Choose the options you want to appear in the right pane of the Windows Help window, then click OK.

- If you want to see extra help information about using the keyboard, open the Accessibility Properties dialog box, click the Keyboard tab, and select the Show Extra Keyboard Help In Programs check box (see "Setting Keyboard Accessibility Options" in Chapter 20). Then click OK.

Looking at Online Help About Other Programs

Most Windows-compatible programs have two ways of displaying Help screens:

- Choose Help, or Help | Contents, or Help | Topics from the menu bar

- Press the F1 key

In Windows 95, both methods run a program called Winhelp to display help screens. Windows 98 replaces Winhelp with the browser-like Windows Help program, although Winhelp is still included (in the C:\Windows folder) for older programs that still use it.

 The Windows 98 Help program displays compiled help modules with the extension .chm. The Windows 95 Winhelp program displays help files with the extension .hlp.

Finding Out What an Onscreen Object Is

Many dialog boxes in both Windows 98 and application programs have a small button with a question mark in the upper-right corner, next to the Close button. This Help button lets you find out what an object is. Click the question mark Help button, then click an item in the dialog box—an icon, button, label, or box. A small window appears with a description of the object you clicked. To dismiss the window, click anywhere in the dialog box.

Another way to display information about an item on the screen is to right-click it. If a menu appears including the What's This command, choose it. Alternatively, select the item that you want information about and press the F1 key.

Chapter 7

Copying, Moving, and Sharing Information Between Programs

W indows 98 provides two methods of sharing data between different Windows application programs (although each method has variations): You can cut or copy, and then paste, using the Windows Clipboard, or you can use OLE, Object Linking and Embedding. In general, cutting and pasting (or its variant, drag-and-drop) works well for the simpler tasks—moving text from one application to another, for instance. OLE is useful when you want all the features of one type of program to take care of an object in another program. For example, if you want to display an Excel spreadsheet in a Word document, and you want to be able to update a complicated formula and display the correct answer in the Word document, then you need to use OLE.

Which Windows 98 Features Enable You to Share Data Among Programs?

Copying or moving information from one location to another within a program is easy, using the cut-and-paste commands that almost all Windows programs support. Cutting-and-pasting uses the Windows 98 Clipboard to store information temporarily. Moving or copying information between programs is easy, too, using the Clipboard. You can use the Clipboard Viewer to look at what's on the Clipboard (described in the next section). Some programs let you drag information from one location to another, too, using your mouse.

What Is Cut-and-Paste?

Cut-and-paste is a feature of Windows that lets you select information from one file and move or copy it to another file (or another location in the same file). Cut-and-paste works by storing information temporarily on the Clipboard (described in the next section). The following cut-and-paste techniques enable you to copy or move information within or between almost any Windows application:

- **Cut** Removes selected information from its current location and stores it (temporarily) on the Clipboard.
- **Copy** Copies selected information and makes a (temporary) copy of it on the Clipboard.
- **Paste** Copies all the information on the Clipboard to the location of the cursor in the active application.

To move information, you select it, cut it to the Clipboard, and then paste it in the new location. To copy information, you select it, copy it to the Clipboard, and then paste it in the new location (see "Cutting, Copying, and Pasting").

What Is the Clipboard?

The easiest way to move information within an application, or from one application to another, is to use the Windows *Clipboard*, a handy little tool that works in the background, saving text, numbers, pictures, or whatever you cut or copy, and allowing you to paste that material somewhere else.

You can use the Clipboard to move or copy text, a range of spreadsheet cells, a picture, a sound, or almost any other piece of information that you can create with a Windows application. The Clipboard can hold only one chunk of information at a time, so you have to either paste it somewhere else right away, or not cut or copy anything else until you've pasted the information where you want it. If you cut or copy another chunk of information, it replaces the information already on the Clipboard.

What Is the Clipboard Viewer?

The Clipboard Viewer is a program that displays the current contents of the Clipboard (see "Using the Clipboard Viewer to Look at What's on the Clipboard"). The Clipboard can contain one item at a time, and the Viewer displays it. You can't edit what's on the Clipboard, but you can save it as a *clipboard file*, with extension .clp, or open a clipboard file, putting the contents of that file on the Clipboard.

What Is Drag-and-Drop?

Drag-and-drop is another method of moving or copying information from one file to another, or to another location in the same file. To move information from one location to another, select it with your mouse and drag it to its new location.

Not all programs support drag-and-drop. Some programs copy the information you drag rather than move it. Some programs let you choose whether to move or copy the information (for example, a program may let you copy the information by holding down the CTRL key while dragging).

What Is OLE?

OLE (Object Linking and Embedding) is far more flexible and can be far more complicated than cut-and-paste or drag-and-drop. OLE allows you to use all of your software applications to create an integrated document. For instance, you may want to create an annual report that includes these components:

- Text that you create and format by using a word processor, such as Microsoft Word or Corel's WordPerfect.

- A company logo that is stored in a graphics file created by Adobe Photoshop, Paint, or some other graphics application.

- Data and calculations on operating costs that are stored in a Microsoft Excel or Lotus 1-2-3 spreadsheet.

- Graphs and charts, which may come from your spreadsheet package or another graphics package.

These components may not reflect exactly what *you* want to do, but the point is the same—if you want to combine the output of different applications, OLE offers many advantages over the Clipboard. Why? Because, when you use OLE, the original program retains ownership of the object, and you can use the program to edit the object. For instance, if you use OLE to embed a portion of a spreadsheet in a word processing document, you can always use the spreadsheet application to edit the object. If, instead, you use the Clipboard to copy the numbers from the spreadsheet, and then you paste the numbers to the word processor, they would just sit in the word processor, oblivious to their origins—you could use only the tools available in the word processor to edit the numbers. If you changed the original spreadsheet, the numbers in the word processing document wouldn't change.

In OLE, an *object* refers to a piece of information from one application that is placed in a *container file* created by another application. For example, a spreadsheet or graphic is an object when it is included in a word processing document. OLE actually is two similar methods of sharing information between applications—embedding and linking. Sticking with the previous example, *embedding* means putting the spreadsheet object in the word processing document (container file) and asking the word processor to take care of storing the object. So, although the word processor allows you to edit the spreadsheet object by using the spreadsheet application, the spreadsheet object is stored with the word processing document. *Linking*, on the other hand, allows the object to retain a very close relationship with its origins—so close, in fact, that if the numbers in the original spreadsheet file change, the linked spreadsheet object in the word processing document changes to match. This occurs because the word processing document doesn't really contain the object it displays—it just contains a reference to the file where the information is stored.

Whether you choose to embed or link objects, the process is similar: You create an object in one application, and then link or embed the object into another application (see "Sharing Information Using OLE").

Although using OLE to link files can be wonderfully convenient and can save you hours of revisions, it should be used judiciously. If you will ever move the file containing linked objects, or send it to someone, you must make sure that one of the following occurs:

- The linked files get moved or sent, too.

- The linked objects will not get updated. This means that the host application won't go looking for the information in the linked file.

■ You edit the links so that the host file knows where to find the source files for the linked objects.

Otherwise, your beautifully organized and time-saving document will become a complete mess. If you are going to move a document with linked objects in it, you need to know how to maintain links, a topic covered later in this chapter.

If you don't need the automatic updating you get with linked objects (for instance, if the source file is not going to change, or if you don't want the object to reflect changes), or if you know you are going to move or send files, then stick with embedded objects—they're easier to maintain.

Some applications allow you to link one file to another in a different way—by using a hyperlink (see "What Is the World Wide Web?" in Chapter 24). A hyperlink actually takes you from one file to another, opening the application for the second file, if necessary.

What Are Scraps?

Not everyone finds scraps useful, but if you need them, they may be a life-saver. *Scraps* are OLE objects that have been left on the desktop or in a folder. You can keep a scrap on the desktop or in the folder or, at some later point, drag it to another application. A scrap has an icon that looks like this:

Scrap icons all look the same, but their names give you a clue as to which application created them. For instance, a scrap from Word or another word processor is called a *Document scrap*, a scrap from Excel is a *Worksheet scrap*, and a scrap from Quattro Pro is a *Notebook scrap* (using the Quattro Pro terminology).

To create a scrap, drag some information to the desktop, or copy it to the Clipboard, and then paste it to the desktop (by right-clicking the desktop and choosing Paste). When you open a scrap on the desktop, the application that created the information opens to display it: single-click the scrap if your desktop is in Web style, and double-click if it is in Classic style (see "Choosing the Style of Your Desktop" in Chapter 1). You can drag a scrap into a different application to create an OLE object out of it.

What Is DDE?

As mentioned in "Actions Associated with File Types" in Chapter 3, DDE stands for *dynamic data exchange*, and it's another way for programs to exchange information. With DDE, the programs send messages among themselves. For example, when you open a .doc filename in Windows Explorer, the program uses DDE to send a message to an already running copy of Microsoft Word, so that the file opens in the current Word window rather than starting up a second copy of Word. You can control what DDE messages your programs send, but programming is required.

Sharing Data Through the Windows Clipboard

To use the Clipboard to move or copy information within or between files, or to share information between programs, you cut or copy the information from one window and paste it in another. You can also use the Clipboard Viewer to see what's on the Clipboard.

Cutting, Copying, and Pasting

You can cut, copy, and paste information by using the following methods (some methods may not work in some applications):

- **Menu**   Choose the Edit menu's Cut, Copy, and Paste commands.
- **Keystrokes**   Press CTRL-X to cut, CTRL-C to copy, and CTRL-V to paste.
- **Buttons**   Many applications have toolbars with Cut, Copy, and Paste buttons, as shown here:

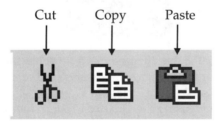

Cut   Copy   Paste

(The Cut and Copy buttons may be disabled if you haven't selected information in the window, and the Paste button may be disabled if no information is on the Clipboard.)

- **Mousing**   Many applications provide shortcut menus that include the Cut, Copy, and Paste commands. Right-click an object to see a shortcut menu.

The following steps explain how to copy or move text from one location to another:

1. Select the information you want to copy or move.

   You can select information by highlighting it with the mouse or by holding down the SHIFT key as you use the arrow buttons. The help system of the application that you're using will contain more information regarding how to select in that application.

   Be careful when you have information selected. Depending on the application, you can inadvertently replace the whole selection by typing a character or space, or by pressing the DEL or BACKSPACE keys. Usually, a simple click deselects the information, ending the danger.

   Tip   *If you are afraid you deleted something by mistake, press CTRL-Z to undo the change in most programs.*

2. If you want to copy the information, press CTRL-C, click the Copy button, or choose Edit | Copy. If you want to move the information, press CTRL-X, click the Cut button, or choose Edit | Cut.

   If you are copying, you don't see any change on the screen when you give the Copy command. If you are cutting, however (which is useful if you want to move information), the selected information will disappear from the screen—it is now stored on the Clipboard.

3. Move the cursor to the place you want the information to appear. This may mean changing applications by clicking a button on the Taskbar, or even opening a new application. As long as you don't cut or copy anything else, or turn off the computer, the information will be available to be pasted to a new location.

4. Paste the text by pressing CTRL-V, by clicking the Paste button, or by choosing Edit | Paste. The information you cut or copy appears at the location of the cursor.

Once you have cut or copied information onto the Clipboard, you can make multiple copies of it by pasting it as many times as you want.

Tip   *Information on the Clipboard does take up RAM, limiting the resources that your computer has available to do other things. Therefore, if you cut or copy a lot of information to the Clipboard, paste it quickly, and then cut or copy something small, one letter or word, for instance, which will replace the large chunk of information on the Clipboard with the letter or word, thus making most of the RAM available again. You can also use the Clipboard Viewer to delete the information on the Clipboard.*

Using the Clipboard Viewer to Look at What's on the Clipboard

You don't have to take for granted that the information you want is on the Clipboard—you can actually look at it by opening the Clipboard Viewer. You may want to use the Clipboard Viewer to do the following:

- See the information on the Clipboard.
- Save the information.
- Delete the information.

To open the Clipboard Viewer, choose Start | Programs | Accessories | System Tools | Clipboard Viewer. Alternatively, you can open a clipboard file (with extension .clp) from Windows Explorer or a Folder window. The Clipboard Viewer looks like Figure 7-1, and shows the current contents of the Clipboard, which you can paste into almost any application.

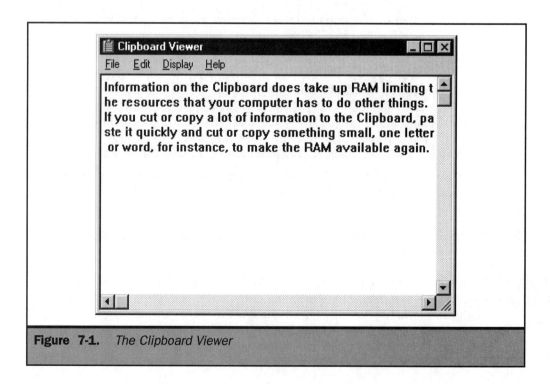

Figure 7-1. *The Clipboard Viewer*

You may have to install the Clipboard Viewer—it isn't always automatically installed (see "Installing and Uninstalling Programs That Come with Windows 98" in Chapter 3). Open the Control Panel, open Add/Remove Programs, click the Windows Setup tab, click System Tools from the list of components, click Details, and choose Clipboard Viewer.

If the contents of the Clipboard Viewer look strange, they may be displayed in the wrong format. Use the Display menu to choose an appropriate display format. The display format does not affect the way the information on the Clipboard is saved or pasted into another application—the display format affects only the display in the Clipboard Viewer.

You can save the contents of the Clipboard by using File | Save As on the Clipboard Viewer menu. Clipboard Viewer saves the information in a clipboard file with extension .clp in the Clipboard's own format. Open a saved clipboard file by choosing File | Open. The Clipboard Viewer can open files saved in the Clipboard format only —you can give them a different extension, but the file is still in .clp format. When you open a clipboard file and the Clipboard already contains information, Clipboard Viewer asks you to confirm that you want to delete the current contents of the Clipboard.

To delete the contents of the Clipboard, choose Edit | Delete or press the DEL key. Deleting the contents of the Clipboard releases RAM for other uses.

 You can't cut-and-paste information from the Clipboard Viewer window—the information is already on the Clipboard!

Capturing Screens Using the Clipboard

Many products can take a *screen shot*, a picture of whatever is on the screen. This book is filled with screen shots that are used as figures. If you need to create a screen shot, you can use the Clipboard to create one. Use the PRINT SCREEN key that appears on your keyboard—it often is above the cursor control keys with the SCROLL LOCK and PAUSE keys. You can take two different kinds of screen shots:

- A picture of the whole screen by pressing PRINT SCREEN
- A picture of the active window by pressing ALT-PRINT SCREEN

Figure 7-2 shows a picture of a window in the Clipboard. Once the picture is on the Clipboard, you can paste it somewhere else. You may want to paste the picture into a graphics program, such as Paint (which comes with Windows 98), so that you can save it in a graphics file format, and use it later (see "Drawing Pictures Using Microsoft

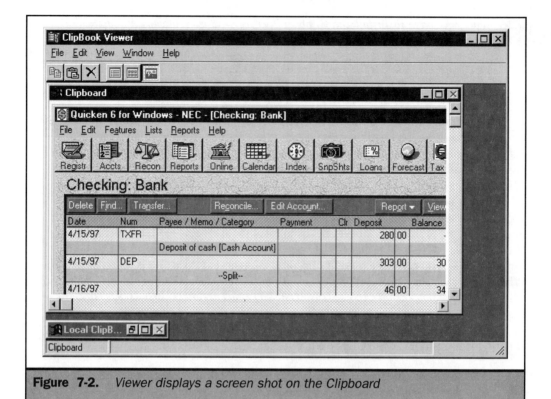

Figure 7-2. *Viewer displays a screen shot on the Clipboard*

Paint" in Chapter 5). Or you may want to paste it into a file, such as a word-processing document containing an explanation of that screen or window.

Sharing Information Using OLE

To use OLE to share information, you create OLE objects and then embed or link these objects in files (see "What Is OLE?").

Creating Linked or Embedded Objects

The way you link or embed an object depends on the application programs you are using—the program into which you want to embed or link the object. Most programs have a menu command to create an object by using OLE, but you may have to use the online help system to find the command. In Microsoft Word, for instance, you can use Insert | Object to create an object by using OLE. The following two techniques may also work: dragging-and-dropping and using Edit | Paste Special—neither technique is supported by all applications.

Embedding an Object by Dragging and Dropping

The easiest way to embed an object is to drag the information from one program and drop it in the other program. For this method to work, both applications must support drag-and-drop embedding. Check the documentation for the program that contains the information you want to embed. When dragging the information you want to embed, use the same technique you use to copy selected information *within* the application: Some applications require that you hold down the CTRL key while dragging the information. For instance, in Excel, you have to click and drag the border of the selected area to move or copy it.

Follow these steps to use drag-and-drop embedding:

1. Select the information you want to embed.

2. Use drag-and-drop to drag the selected information to the other application; use the same drag-and-drop technique that you use to copy information within an application. If the second application is not visible on the screen, you can drag the information to the application's Taskbar button—hold the mouse pointer there for a second, and the application window opens.

3. Drop the information where you want it—if the application supports OLE, you automatically create an embedded object.

You may be able to specify that the information be linked rather than embedded (the usual default when OLE drag-and-drop is supported) by holding down the SHIFT key. Try it to see whether the application you are using supports this feature.

Linking or Embedding an Object Using Paste Special

You may want a little more control over the object than you have when you drag and drop it—to achieve more control over the object, use the Edit | Paste Special command found in many applications. The procedure is much like using the Clipboard to cut and paste, except that you paste by using OLE instead, as follows:

1. Select the information you want to link or embed.

2. Press CTRL-C or CTRL-X to copy or cut the information (or use another method to copy or cut).

3. Move the cursor where you want the object to appear.

4. Choose Edit | Paste Special. You see a dialog box similar to the one shown in Figure 7-3.

Choose the correct application from the choices displayed. Make sure to chose the application that you want to use to edit the object—in the figure, that is Microsoft Word. If you choose another option, you will not be using OLE—instead, you will be using the Clipboard to do a simple paste of information from one application to another.

5. Choose the correct setting to either embed the object in the new file or link the two files together.

To embed the object, choose the Paste option; to link the object, choose the Paste Link option. Figure 7-4 shows the settings to embed a Microsoft Word object into a Corel Quattro Pro spreadsheet. Figure 7-4 shows the settings to link a Corel Quattro Pro spreadsheet into a Microsoft Word document. Other applications may have Paste Special dialog boxes that look different from these.

6. Change the Display As Icon setting, if necessary. If you choose to display the object as an icon, you don't see the information itself—instead, you create a

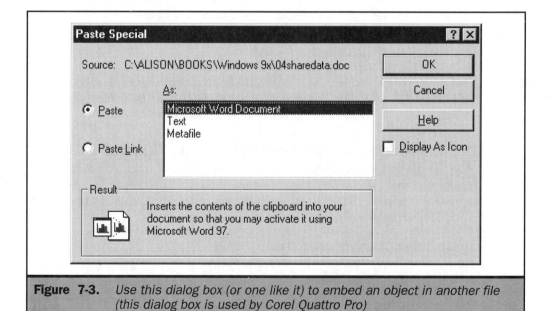

Figure 7-3.   *Use this dialog box (or one like it) to embed an object in another file (this dialog box is used by Corel Quattro Pro)*

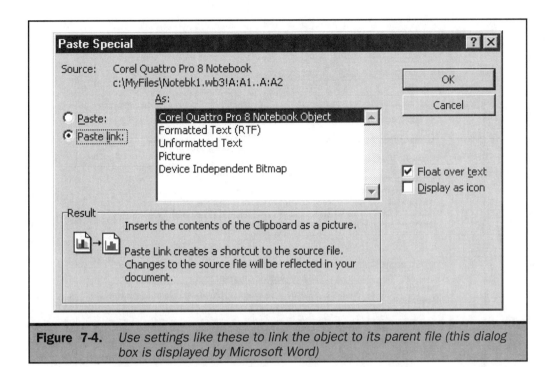

Figure 7-4. *Use settings like these to link the object to its parent file (this dialog box is displayed by Microsoft Word)*

packaged object that will show the information it contains only when you open its icon (see "What Is OLE?").

7. Click OK to link or embed the object. You see the object in the container file, as in Figure 7-5.

Editing a Linked or Embedded Object

Editing a linked or embedded object is simple—in most applications, you just double-click the object. For other applications, you may need to right-click the object to display a menu with an edit option, or change modes so that you are in edit mode (check the help system of the application containing the object, if you're having trouble). Once you've figured out how to edit the object, the object's application opens, and the menu and toolbars of the window in which the object appears are replaced by the menu and toolbars of the application assigned by the registry to that file type (usually the application used to create the object). In other words, if you are editing an Excel object in a Word document, double-click the object to display Excel's

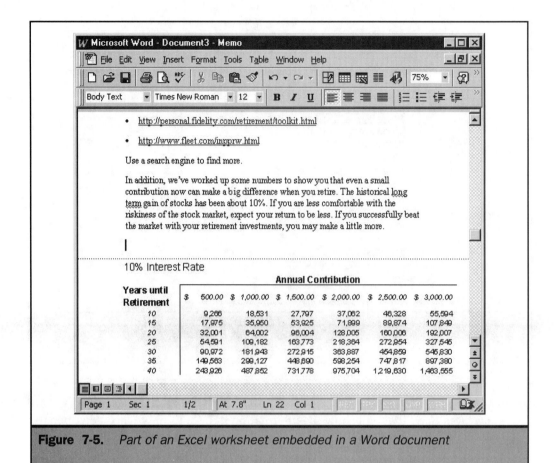

Figure 7-5.   *Part of an Excel worksheet embedded in a Word document*

menu and toolbars in Word's window, as in Figure 7-6. You can edit the object by using that application's tools. When you're done, click outside the object to reinstate the regular menu and toolbars, or choose File | Update or Exit. If you are asked whether you want to update the object, answer Yes.

If the object is linked, rather than embedded, you can also edit the object by editing the source file itself. If the file containing the object is also open, you may have to update it manually to see the new information in the object. Closing and opening the file containing the object may be the easiest way to update the object.

Delete an object by single-clicking it to select it—you will probably see a box around it—then press the DELETE or BACKSPACE key.

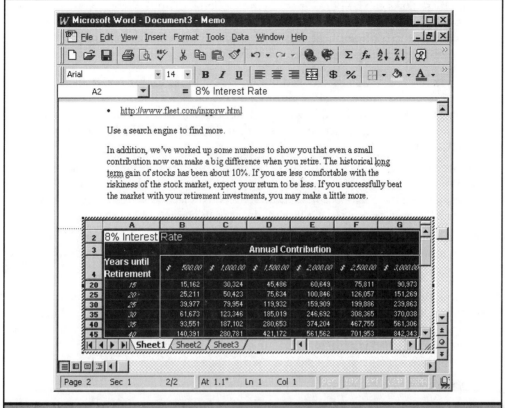

Figure 7-6.   *Edit the Excel object in a Word document by using the Excel menu and toolbars that appear when you double-click the object*

Maintaining OLE Links

If you decide to use a link to put an object in a file, rather than embedding the object, you may have to do some maintenance if the linked file or the file containing the link moves to a new location. A link is usually updated each time the file containing the object is opened or printed. *Updating* means that the current information from the linked file is brought into the object.

If the location of a file changes, you may need to "lock" the link so that the last available information is retained, break the link so that the object becomes an embedded object rather than a linked object, or edit the link so that the correct path and filename are referenced. The exact commands may differ by application (check the online help), but usually there's one dialog box like the one displayed in Figure 7-7, where all these tasks can be performed. In most Microsoft applications, you can display the dialog box by choosing Edit | Links. The following list explains how to do these three tasks in a Microsoft application. Other applications work in a similar way, but may have different names for the dialog box buttons and options.

- **Lock the link** Use the Locked option on the Links dialog box to lock the selected link. You can select multiple links to lock by CTRL-clicking or SHIFT-clicking additional links. A locked link will not be updated. To check whether a link is locked, select the link and see whether the Locked option is checked.

- **Break the link** Use the Break Link (or Cancel Link) button to break a link. When you break a link, the link disappears from the Links list, and you can no longer use the original application to edit the object. A better choice, often, is to lock the link, or replace the linked object with an embedded object.

- **Edit the link** Use the Change Source button to edit the link. This allows you to redirect the link to a different file, or to the same file stored in a different location.

Another option is to set up the file to update the links only when you tell it to do so by specifying manual updating. The Links dialog box has an Update option that allows you to specify automatic or manual updating. If you set this option to manual, the links are updated only when you display the Links dialog box and click the Update Now button.

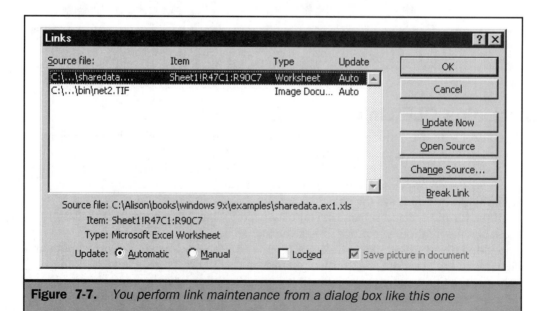

Figure 7-7. *You perform link maintenance from a dialog box like this one*

Part II

Managing Your Disk

Chapter 8

Using Files and Folders

Computers are tools for working with information—creating it, accessing it, and rearranging it. Windows 98 stores information in files, and organizes those files into folders. Everything you do with your computer involves files and folders.

This chapter describes the basic file-and-folder skills that you need in order to operate your computer day-to-day. The next chapter discusses the longer-term issues involved in managing your files efficiently. The present chapter explains the anatomy of the windows in which you manipulate files and folders, and their common toolbars. It tells how to use Windows Explorer and Folder windows to create, select, name, open, move, copy, and delete files and folders. You will also learn the easiest ways to undo or recover from common mistakes.

What Are Files and Folders?

Files and folders are two of the most fundamental concepts of the Windows operating system. No matter what you use your computer for, you create and organize files and folders as soon as you decide to save your work. If you have worked with any other operating system, you undoubtedly are already acquainted with the concept of a file. You probably are familiar with folders as well, though you may know them as *directories*. If you are not already familiar with files and folders, spending a small amount of time learning their properties will serve you well.

What Is a File?

A *file* is any collection of related information that is given a name and stored on a disk so that it can be retrieved when needed. A file may contain any kind of information: a program or application (WordPad, for example, is in a file called Wordpad.exe.); a document; a part of a document, such as a table or an illustration; a sound or piece of music; a segment of video; or any number of other things.

Many files are part of the Windows system itself. Windows 98 uses files to store the information that it needs to function, such as information regarding the appearance of your desktop, the kind of monitor or printer you use, the various dialog boxes and error messages, or how to display different fonts. Similarly, the applications on your computer typically have a number of auxiliary files in addition to the file containing the main program. Some of these files, for example, contain the choices you make about the program's optional settings. When you change these settings, you are not altering the program itself; you are editing some of its auxiliary files.

What Is a Folder?

Because of all the files associated with Windows and the various applications on your computer, your hard drive contains hundreds, or even thousands, of files before you begin creating files of your own. (If your computer is part of a network, you may have access to millions of files.) You would have no hope of keeping track of all those files if they were not organized in some efficient way. In Windows 98 (as in most other major operating systems), the fundamental device for organizing files is the folder.

Technically, a *folder* is just a special kind of file—one that contains a list of other files. The files on the list are said to be *in* the folder, and each file is allowed to be in only one folder. A folder can be either open or closed. When it is closed, all you see is its name and the folder icon, as shown here:

When a folder is open, it has its own window, and the files contained in the folder are displayed in the window (see "What Is a Folder Window?").

The terms "file" and "folder" were chosen to remind you of a more familiar information retrieval system—the filing cabinet. Like the folders in a filing cabinet, the folders in Windows 98 are named objects that contain other objects. For example, a Windows folder named Budget might contain four spreadsheet files for First quarter, Second quarter, Third quarter, and Fourth quarter.

What Is the Folder Tree?

The organizational power of the folder system comes from the fact that it is *hierarchical*, which means that folders can contain other folders. This feature allows you to organize and keep track of a great many folders, without overstraining your memory or attention.

If Folder A is inside Folder B, Folder A is a *subfolder* of B. Any folder can contain as many subfolders as you want to put there, but each folder (like each file) is contained in only one folder. And so, a diagram showing which folders are contained in which other folders looks something like a family tree. This diagram is called the *folder tree*, or sometimes the *folder hierarchy*. Windows Help calls it the *folder list*.

Figure 8-1 shows the top levels of the folder tree as they appear in the left pane of a Windows Explorer window. At the top of the folder tree (the founder of the Folder family, so to speak) is the desktop. Immediately under the desktop are My Computer, the Internet, Network Neighborhood, Recycle Bin, and My Briefcase, plus whatever files and folders you might have copied to the desktop. The manufacturer of your computer may also have put some files or folders on your desktop.

Underneath My Computer are icons representing all of your system's storage media: hard drives, floppy drives, CD-ROMs, and so on. (Your system configuration may differ somewhat from that pictured in Figure 8-1.) Also under My Computer are a number of special folders: Printers, Control Panel, Dial-Up Networking, and Scheduled Tasks. These special folders behave a little differently from other folders, and are covered in other chapters.

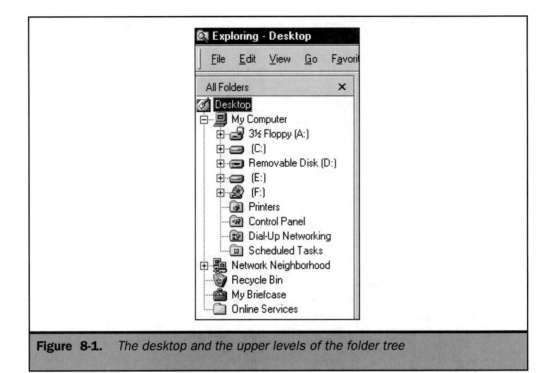

Figure 8-1. *The desktop and the upper levels of the folder tree*

What Are Folder Windows and Windows Explorer Windows?

Windows 98 provides two ways to view and manipulate files and folders: Folder windows and Windows Explorer windows. They share a common set of toolbars, and allow you to do the same things. In general, you will find that simple operations are easier in a Folder window, while more complicated operations are easier in a Windows Explorer window. Which type of window you prefer for any particular operation is a matter of personal taste. (The two types of windows are described further in the next two sections.)

These two tools replace the File Manager and Program Manager applications that are used in Windows versions 3.1 and earlier. File Manager and Program Manager are still part of Windows 98, if you want to use them, but they are no longer necessary. Most people who take time to learn the Windows 98 interface prefer it to the Windows 3.1 tools. If you have never used File Manager or Program Manager, we recommend that you ignore them. If you are used to File Manager, you can access it by opening the file C:\Windows\Winfile.exe, and if you like Program Manager, you can open C:\Windows\Progman.exe.

What Is a Folder Window?

Opening My Computer, or any of the folders that you move to the desktop, produces a *Folder window,* as shown in Figure 8-2. (*My Computer* is a folder that contains items for each disk drive on your computer, along with a few other special subfolders.) The window's title bar displays the name of the open folder. Immediately beneath the title bar are the menu bar and the toolbars. The main window displays icons corresponding to all the files and folders contained in the open folder. The contents of subfolders do not appear in the window. At the bottom of the Folder window lies the status bar, which shows the number of objects in the folder, how many objects are hidden, and the amount of space that the folder takes up on its disk. You can make the toolbars or status bar appear or disappear by toggling the Toolbar or Status Bar commands on the View menu.

The folder in Figure 8-2 is shown with the Web view option off (see "What Is the Web View of a Folder?"). (The same folder with Web view on is displayed later in the chapter in Figure 8-5.) See "Working with Folder Windows and Windows Explorer Windows" later in this chapter for how to run and use Folder windows.

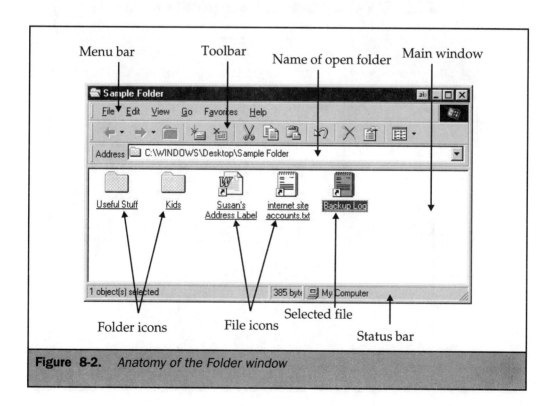

Figure 8-2.   *Anatomy of the Folder window*

What Is Windows Explorer?

Windows Explorer is a file-and-folder-manipulating program that you can launch by selecting Start | Programs | Windows Explorer. As you can see in Figure 8-3, the Windows Explorer window provides a better picture of the large-scale organization of your folders than does a Folder window. The folder tree is displayed in the left pane (the left side of the window), called the Explorer bar, with the open folder highlighted (see "What Is the Explorer Bar?"). The contents of the open folder appear in the right pane.

The rest of the Windows Explorer window is similar to the Folder window: The title bar gives the name of the open folder. Beneath the title bar are the same menu bar and toolbars as in the Folder window. At the bottom of the window lies the status bar.

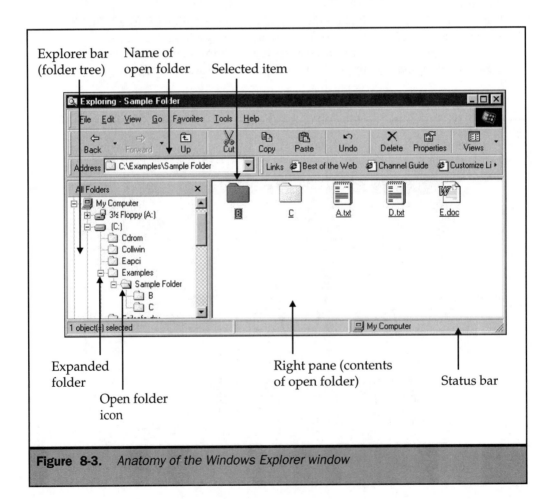

Figure 8-3.   _Anatomy of the Windows Explorer window_

The toolbars and status bar can be made to appear or disappear by toggling the Toolbar or Status Bar commands on the View menu.

You can use the right pane of the Windows Explorer window as if it were a Folder window. However, only one folder is open at a time, and opening a new folder displaces the previously open folder (even in Classic style). The right pane adjusts automatically to display the contents of the selected folder. See "Working with Folder Windows and Windows Explorer Windows" later in this chapter for how to run and use Windows Explorer.

What Toolbars Can Appear in Folder and Windows Explorer Windows?

You can display three toolbars in Folder windows and Windows Explorer windows: the Address Bar toolbar, Standard Buttons toolbar, and the Links toolbar. You can choose which toolbar (if any) to display by choosing View | Toolbars from the menu bar and checking the toolbars in the menu that appears. Among the toolbars you decide to display, you can allocate the space allotted to each toolbar by dragging the boundary line between them. Figure 8-4 includes the Address Bar toolbar, the Standard Buttons toolbar, and the Links toolbar. The Standard Buttons toolbar is expanded to make room for text labels, which you can select by choosing View | Toolbars and making sure that the Text Labels command has a check mark to its left. The Standard Buttons toolbar without text labels is displayed in Figure 8-2.

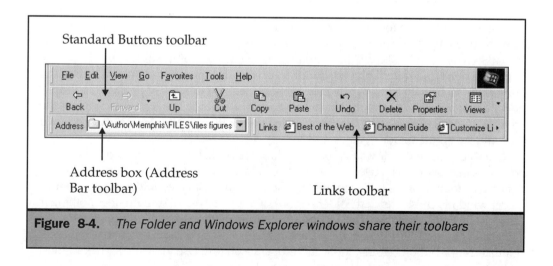

Figure 8-4.   *The Folder and Windows Explorer windows share their toolbars*

WHAT IS THE ADDRESS BOX?   The *Address box*, which appears on the Address Bar toolbar of Folder windows and Windows Explorer windows, displays the name of the open folder. The Address box looks like this:

When you click the arrow at the right end of the Address box, a diagram appears. It displays the top levels of the folder tree, and allows "long-range navigation" by clicking any top-level item you want to open.

Another way to choose which folder to view is to type into the Address box the address of the file or folder you want to open. A major innovation of Windows 98 is that the Address box accepts both file addresses and web addresses (see "What Are Addresses?"). If your computer is online, typing a web address into the Address box opens the corresponding web page. Depending on what options you have chosen elsewhere, your computer may automatically dial up your Internet provider to open the web page (see "Setting Additional Dial-Up Networking Options" in Chapter 22).

WHAT ARE THE BUTTONS ON THE STANDARD BUTTONS TOOLBAR?   The Standard Buttons toolbar can appear on the toolbar of Folder windows and Windows Explorer windows. It looks like this:

The three left-most toolbar buttons are navigation buttons: Back, Forward, and Up. In Web style windows, they behave like the corresponding web-browser buttons (see "What Style Is Your Desktop?" in Chapter 1). The Back button takes the window back to the previous folder it displayed, and the Forward button undoes Back. The Back and Forward buttons have arrows attached to them; clicking the arrow produces a drop-down list of locations to which you can go back or forward. The Up button causes the window to display the folder that contains currently displayed folder; that is, it moves the window up the folder tree.

In a Classic style Windows Explorer window, the Back, Forward, and Up buttons behave as they do in Web style. In Classic style Folder windows, the Forward and Back buttons do nothing. If the folder containing the currently displayed folder has an open Folder window, Up selects that Folder window. Otherwise the Up button does nothing in a Classic style Folder window. The next five buttons are editing tools: Cut, Copy, Paste, Undo, and Delete. They operate on files and folders in much the same way that similar commands in word processing applications operate on text. Use these tools to move files and subfolders from one folder to another (see "Rearranging Files and Folders").

The Properties button brings up the Properties dialog box for the selected object. The Properties dialog box gives you access to much of the information that Windows has stored about a file or folder, and allows you to alter an object's attributes and behaviors (see "What Are Properties of Files and Folders?" in Chapter 9).

The Views button allows you to choose among several options for representing the contents of a folder (see "Changing Views" in Chapter 9). Repeatedly clicking the Views button scrolls through your options. Click the arrow to the right of the Views button to choose one of these options from a list. Right-clicking the Views button allows you to select which toolbars are shown; this menu is the same one that you see by choosing View | Toolbars.

WHAT IS THE LINKS TOOLBAR? The *Links toolbar* contains buttons that connect to various Microsoft web sites. It looks like this:

If you aren't connected to the Internet, don't bother with this toolbar. If you are connected, we recommend that you visit each site once and decide whether you are interested in it. If you are interested in a site, add it to your Favorites menu, so that you can return to it whenever you want (see "What Are Favorites?" in Chapter 25). But don't leave the Links toolbar cluttering up your screen after you've seen all the web sites: Choose View | Toolbar and deselect the Links option.

What Is the Explorer Bar?

The left pane of a Windows Explorer window is called the *Explorer bar*. By default it displays the folder tree, but it has other capabilities as well. Folder windows also can have an Explorer bar, though by default they do not. The Explorer bar of a Folder window cannot display a folder tree, but it has every other capability of a Windows Explorer window's Explorer bar.

To change what you see in the Explorer bar of either a Windows Explorer or Folder window, select an option from the View | Explorer Bar menu. The choices are

- **Search** Lists a number of online search engines for finding information on the World Wide Web, like the Search button in Internet Explorer (see "Using Buttons Common to Both Browsers" in Chapter 24.) If you are online, clicking a link opens the corresponding web site.

- **Favorites** Shows you a list of favorite files, folders, and web sites (see "What Are Favorites?" in Chapter 25). If you are online, clicking an entry for a web site displays the site.

- **History** Displays a day-by-day guide to whatever files or web sites Internet Explorer has opened, either on your computer or on the Internet (see "Examining

History" in Chapter 24). (The History Explorer bar won't keep track of the files or web sites you open with Netscape Navigator or any other web browser.)

■ **Channels**   Shows you the Channel bar. Channels are web sites that you can subscribe to (see "What Are Subscriptions and Channels?" in Chapter 25). If your computer is online, clicking an entry on the Channel bar opens the corresponding web site.

■ **All Folders**   Displays the folder tree. It is the default option for a Windows Explorer window, and is not available in a Folder window.

■ **None**   Makes the Explorer bar disappear, an effect you can achieve more easily by clicking the Close button in the upper right corner of the Explorer bar. This option is the default for a Folder window.

What Is the Web View of a Folder?

The *Web view* of a folder (not to be confused with the Web style for Folder and Windows Explorer windows) displays the folder as if it were a web page. A Folder or Windows Explorer window that is displaying the Web view of a folder includes an additional left pane showing the name of the folder, some facts about whatever file or subfolder might be selected, and maybe a preview of a selected file (described in the next section). If you have customized the folder with HTML, any active content is visible in Web view (see "Customizing a Folder with HTML" in Chapter 9).

Figure 8-5 shows a Folder window in Web view. The same folder with the Web view turned off is shown in Figure 8-2. (The selected file in Figure 8-5 is an earlier version of Figure 8-5 itself.)

Turn Web view on and off by selecting View | As Web Page from the menu of any Folder or Windows Explorer window. If a check appears on the View menu next to As Web Page, then Web view is on.

Using Web view and an Explorer bar at the same time creates a confusing three-pane window whose main window is quite small. We recommend using Explorer bars with Windows Explorer windows and Web view with Folder windows.

What Is a Preview?

When you view a folder as a web page, a small copy of the first page of a selected file appears at the bottom of the left pane of the window (see "What Is the Web View of a Folder?"). These small copies are called *previews*.

Windows 98 does not know how to display previews of every type of file. If you have selected a file of a type that Windows 98 cannot preview, the square where the

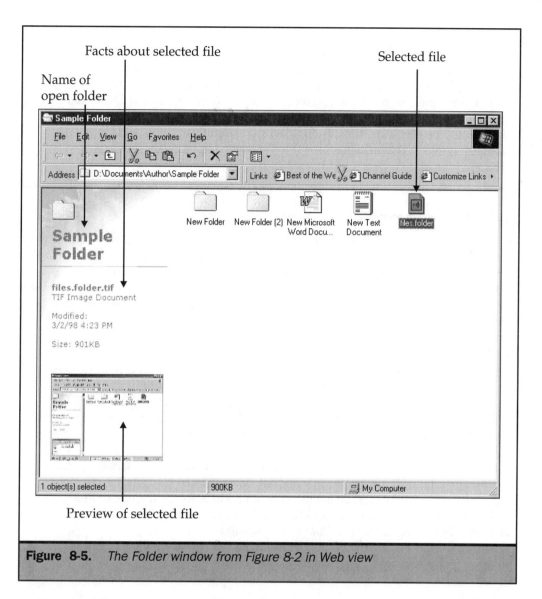

Figure 8-5.   *The Folder window from Figure 8-2 in Web view*

preview would appear is empty. The preview also does not appear if the Folder or Windows Explorer window is not large enough. If you expect to see a preview and don't, try enlarging the window.

Previews in general are not large enough to read, though you may make out a title. The main use of a preview is to help you identify a file—to see whether it is the red picture or the blue picture, the two-column document or the one-column document.

> ## Where Is the Desktop Really?
>
> The Windows 98 interface makes the desktop look as if it contains all hard disks, floppies, CD-ROMs, and other storage devices. But the desktop is only a virtual object, not a piece of hardware; so where is its information stored? The desktop information is stored on your computer's main hard drive, typically the one labeled C. The shortcuts, files, and folders that you move to the desktop are actually stored in the hidden folder C:\Windows\Desktop (see "What Are Hidden Files and Folders?" in Chapter 9).

What Are Filenames?

In order to store a file and retrieve it later, Windows has to give it a *filename*. Often you are asked to invent a name for a file. Good filenames are evocative without being too cumbersome. They also have to obey some rules. Fortunately, the filenaming rules were liberalized when Windows 95 came out, and Windows 98 retains these liberalized rules. You can change a filename using either a Folder window or Windows Explorer window, as well as in the Open and Save As dialog boxes of many applications.

What Filenames Are Legal?

In DOS and Windows systems prior to Windows 95, filenames could be only eight characters long, followed by a three-character extension that told the file's type— Filename.txt, for example. Inventing coherent, easily remembered filenames was an art similar to composing good vanity license plates. Even so, one frequently had to stare at files like jnsdecr.doc for some while before remembering that it was John's December report.

Fortunately, Windows 95 changed all that by introducing long filenames, and Windows 98 retains that advance. File and folder names can be up to 255 characters long, and can include spaces. So jnsdecr.doc can become John's December Report.doc.

Folders, likewise, can have names up to 255 characters long. These names are automatically of type "folder" and have no extension.

In addition to periods and spaces, some characters that were illegal prior to Windows 95 are now legal, including:

+ , ; = [? ?]

But there are still a few characters that you can't use in filenames:

\ / : * ? " < > |

and any character that you make by using the CTRL key.

What Are Extensions and File Types?

File names are still followed by a period and a three-letter *extension*. The extension denotes the *file type*, and, among other things, tells Windows 98 which program to use to open the file and which icon to use to represent the file. Windows 98 handles most file-type issues invisibly. Files that you create with a particular application, for example, are automatically of a type associated with that program (unless you specify otherwise), and the appropriate three-letter extension is added to the name automatically.

You can do a great many things in Windows 98 without paying any attention to file types; therefore, Windows doesn't even show you the extensions unless you ask to see them. If you want to see the extensions:

1. Choose Start | Settings | Folder Options. You see the Folder Options dialog box.

2. Click the View tab.

3. Click the check box next to Hide File Extensions For Known File Types. If the box is checked, the extensions are hidden; if not checked, the extensions are shown.

4. Click OK to make the Folder Options dialog box go away.

When you install a program, the installation program usually tells Windows 98 the file types that the program handles (see "What Happens During Program Installation?" in Chapter 3).

What Are MS-DOS Names?

In addition to its name, each file and folder in Windows 98 has an *MS-DOS name,* an eight-or-fewer-character name that resembles its real name, but that is legal under the pre-Windows 95 file-naming rules. The MS-DOS name exists for the purpose of backward compatibility; programs written for MS-DOS or older versions of Windows might well crash if Windows hands them files with long names and previously illegal characters. So, when dealing with pre-Windows 95 application programs, Windows pretends that nothing has changed, and gives the application the MS-DOS name of a file rather than its real name.

To see a file or folder's MS-DOS name:

1. Select (but don't open) the file or folder in a Folder or Windows Explorer window.

2. Click the Properties button on the toolbar. The file or folder's Properties dialog box appears.

3. If it is not already selected, click the General tab.

4. Look at the top of the third section of the page for the entry MS-DOS Name.

What Are Addresses?

An *address* is information that tells you (and Windows 98) how to find something. The four kinds of addresses are

- **File addresses**, which tell you how to find files on your computer. A typical file address looks something like C:\Windows\Explorer.exe.

- **UNC (Universal Naming Convention) addresses**, which are used when referring to files on some local area networks. UNC addresses are in the format *computername**drive:pathname* or *computername**pathname*, where *computername* is the computer's name on the local area network, *drive* is the disk drive on that computer, and *pathname* is the file address.

- **Internet addresses**, more properly called *URLs*, which specify how to find things on the Web (see "What Is a URL?" in Chapter 24). The URL for Microsoft's home page, for example, is **http://www.microsoft.com**.

- **E-mail addresses**, which tell you how to find the e-mail boxes of the people to whom you want to write. You can comment on this book, for example, by writing to **win98tcr@gurus.com**.

The Address box of Folder and Windows Explorer windows handles every kind of address except e-mail addresses. Typing a file or UNC address into the Address box opens the corresponding file or folder, while typing a URL address opens the corresponding object on the Internet (if your computer is online).

| Note | *E-mail addresses are still handled differently from the other kinds of addresses. You can't send e-mail by typing an e-mail address into the Address box. Chapter 23 describes how to send a message to an e-mail address.* |

File addresses, also called *paths* or *path names*, work in the following way: Files and folders are stored on disks. Each disk drive has a *drive letter* that is its address (see "What Are Drive Letters?" in Chapter 11). Letters A and B typically are reserved for floppy drives, and C denotes your computer's main hard drive. Subsequent letters are used for other hard drives, CD-ROMs, tape drives, removable drives, drives on other computers on your local area network (if any), and other devices. In file addresses, drive letters are always followed by a colon (:).

Each file or folder address begins with the letter of the drive on which the file or folder is stored. The *root folder* (main folder) of each disk is designated by a backslash directly after the drive letter; for example, C:\ is the root folder of drive C. The rest of the address consists of the names of the folders on the folder tree between the given file or folder and the drive that contains it. The folder names are separated by backslashes (\).

For example, the address C:\Windows\ Temp refers to a folder named Temp, which is inside the folder named Windows, which is stored on the C drive. If the file Junk.doc is contained in Temp, Junk.doc's address is C:\Windows\Temp\Junk.doc.

What Is the Recycle Bin?

Files and folders deleted from your hard drives do not go away completely, at least not right away—they live on inside the *Recycle Bin*. From there, they can be either restored to the folder they were in before you deleted them, or moved from the Recycle Bin to any other folder via cut-and-paste or drag-and-drop.

The Recycle Bin icon lives on the desktop and looks like a waste-basket. When you open the icon, a Folder window opens, showing you the files and folders that have been deleted since the Recycle Bin was last emptied.

The Recycle Bin is a hybrid object that behaves like a folder in some ways, but not in others. Like a folder, it contains objects, and can be viewed in either a Folder window or a Windows Explorer window. You can move objects into and out of the Recycle Bin, just as you do with any other folder. Unlike a folder, even an unusual folder like the desktop, the Recycle Bin is not contained on a single drive. Instead, each of your computer's hard drives maintains its own *Recycled folder*, and the contents of all of the Recycled folders are visible whenever you open any of them.

Folders that have been sent to the Recycle Bin are not considered part of the folder tree; they don't appear in a Windows Explorer window's left-pane map, and they can't be opened. If you want to examine the contents of a folder that is in the Recycle Bin, you first must move the folder to another location. Likewise, files in the Recycle Bin cannot be opened, edited, or otherwise worked on.

The intention of the designers is clear: the Recycle Bin is not to be used as a workspace. Instead, it is a last-chance repository. You can put things in the Recycle Bin or take things out—that's all.

Working with the Recycle Bin under the default settings is covered in this chapter (see "Retrieving Files and Folders from the Recycle Bin"). Reconfiguring the Recycle Bin settings is covered in the next chapter in "Managing the Recycle Bin."

Working with Folder Windows and Windows Explorer Windows

Opening the My Computer icon on the desktop causes a Folder window to appear, as in Figure 8-2 or Figure 8-5. Any folder that you open from the desktop creates a new Folder window. In Classic style, opening a folder from within a Folder window opens a new Folder window; in Web style, the newly opened folder takes over the original window (see "Choosing Web Style, Classic Style, or Something in Between").

A Windows Explorer window, shown in Figure 8-3, opens when you run Windows Explorer. You can run Windows Explorer by choosing Start | Programs | Windows

Explorer. Or, you can put a shortcut to Windows Explorer somewhere more convenient, such as the top of the Start menu or on the desktop.

Choosing Web Style, Classic Style, or Something in Between

Folder and Windows Explorer windows can be configured to work in many different ways, which are described in more detail in "Configuring a Folder or Windows Explorer Window" in Chapter 9. But the most fundamental choice is this: Do you want windows to behave the way they did in Windows 95 (and on a Macintosh), or do you want them to behave like web browser windows? Windows 98 calls the former Classic style and the latter Web style. You can also mix the features of the two styles to create your own custom style.

The exact behavior of Web and Classic styles (and how to change from one to the other) is described in "What Style Is Your Desktop?" in Chapter 1. Web style and Classic style each has its own advantages. Classic style is convenient if you want to do a lot of dragging-and-dropping of files between folders. But your desktop can get cluttered, requiring you occasionally to do some housekeeping and close several windows. Single-clicking to open a folder (Web style) results in more frequent inadvertent openings, but double-clicking is an unnatural motion that tends to aggravate carpal-tunnel conditions. Experiment until you know which choice you prefer.

You may decide to take some features from Classic style and others from Web style to create your own custom style. To do this:

1. Select Start | Settings | Folder Options. The Folder Options dialog box appears with the General page on top. Radio buttons at the bottom of the page give three choices of navigation behavior: Web style, Classic style, and Custom.

2. Select Custom.

3. Click the Settings button. The Custom Settings dialog box appears (Figure 8-6).

4. Make your selections by clicking the appropriate radio buttons.

5. Click OK to make the Custom Settings dialog box disappear.

6. Click Close to make the Folder Options dialog box disappear.

Navigating the Folder Tree

Both Folder and Windows Explorer windows allow you to view the contents of any folder on your system. The process of changing your view from one folder to another is referred to as *navigating*. The Folder window provides you with navigation tools that you will recognize if you have used a web browser: You can go up or down in the folder tree, and back or forth along the path you have taken. In addition, you can jump to any folder near the top of the folder tree by clicking its icon on the list that drops

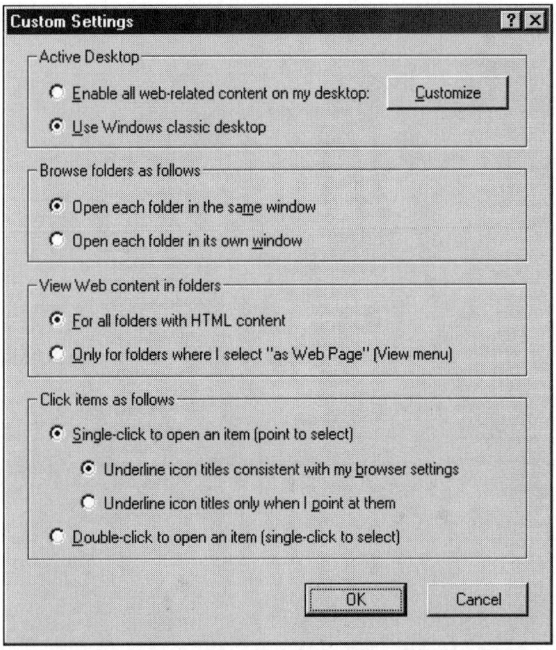

Figure 8-6. *Customize the style of your Folder windows*

down from the Address box on the toolbar. In Web style, all this navigating is done in a single window. In Classic style, you leave behind a trail of windows on the desktop.

The Windows Explorer window provides these same navigation tools, plus the ability to move to any folder by clicking its icon on the folder-tree map in the Windows Explorer window's left pane.

Viewing the Folder Tree with Windows Explorer

The default Explorer bar (left pane) of the Windows Explorer window is a map of the folder tree. You can expand or contract this map to whatever level of detail you find most convenient. In its most condensed form, it looks like Figure 8-7, and shows only the desktop and the objects immediately under it. The dotted lines from the desktop to the other objects show that those objects are contained in the desktop. The Desktop icon is flush left, and each layer of the folder tree is indented a little further to the right of the Desktop icon. The left pane only shows folders; to see files, you must select the appropriate folder and look in the right pane.

Folders that can be expanded (that is, whose subfolders are not shown) have boxes next to them containing small plus signs, called *plus boxes*. In Figure 8-7, the folders My

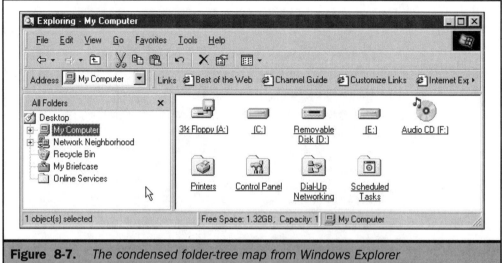

Figure 8-7.   *The condensed folder-tree map from Windows Explorer*

Computer and Network Neighborhood can be expanded. Clicking the boxed plus sign next to a folder expands the tree to include that folder's subfolders. The box remains, but now contains a minus sign to denote that the folder has been expanded. Clicking the minus sign contracts the folder again. When a folder is expanded, it is connected to each of its subfolders by an additional dotted line. If any of the subfolders are expandable, new boxed plus signs appear next to them. Any portion of the folder tree can be expanded as much or as little as you like. A partially expanded folder tree, with both plus and minus signs, is shown in Figure 8-3.

When the folder tree expands beyond the limits of the left pane, scroll bars appear. If you want to see the full width of the folder tree, drag to the right the border between the right and left panes.

Navigating by Using the Address Box

The Address box on the Toolbar displays the name of the folder whose contents appear in the Folder window or in the right pane of a Windows Explorer window. An abbreviated folder-tree diagram drops down from the Address box; it shows only the top layers of the folder tree, together with the folders between the open folder and the drive that contains it. You can use this diagram to jump to a new location in the folder tree by clicking any of the icons shown.

Going Up and Down the Folder Tree

In a Windows Explorer window or a Folder window in Web style, the Up button moves the window up the folder tree. The window then shows the contents of the folder containing the previously viewed folder. For example, if a window displays the contents of the C:\Windows folder and you then click the Up button, a window displays the contents of the C drive. Click Up again, and you see the contents of My Computer. Wherever you begin, if you click Up often enough, you reach My Computer. (In a Windows Explorer window, you can click Up again and reach the desktop. But My Computer is the highest folder you can see in a Folder window. Up is grayed out after you reach My Computer.) Up is also found on the Go menu.

To move the window one step down the folder tree, open a subfolder of the currently open folder.

Going Back and Forth on the Folder Tree

The Forward and Back buttons show the influence of web browsers. In Windows Explorer windows or Folder windows in Web style they move the window back and forth among the folders that have been displayed previously. The Back button returns to the previous open folder. Clicking it again returns to the folder before that, and so on. The Forward button undoes the Back button: Clicking Back and then Forward leaves you where you started. Until you have clicked Back, there is no place to go forward to, so the Forward button is grayed out. Similarly, once you have returned to the first folder you opened, the Back button is grayed out. In a Classic style Folder window, the Back and Forth buttons do nothing.

Lists of folders to which you can go back or forward drop down when you click the arrows that are next to the Back and Forward buttons. Jump to any folder on the list by clicking its name. Back and Forward are also found on the Go menu.

Jumping to Somewhere Else Entirely

The arrow at the right end of the Address box pulls down a diagram showing the path that connects the open folder to the desktop, as well as the layers of the folder tree immediately under the desktop and My Computer. Open any of these folders by clicking its name in the list.

Jumping is particularly easy in a Windows Explorer window. Just find the folder that you want to view on the folder-tree map in the left pane, and click it.

Making and Working with Files and Folders

This section discusses the basic file and folder operations: creating, selecting, naming, and opening.

Creating Files and Folders

New folders and files of certain types can be created either on the desktop, in a Windows Explorer window, or inside any Folder window other than My Computer. On the desktop, right-click any empty area and choose New on the menu that appears. In a Windows Explorer or Folder window, choose File | New. In either case, a submenu appears that lists the new objects you can create: folders, shortcuts, and a variety of types of files. Select an element of this list, and Windows 98 creates the appropriate object. You can also create shortcuts by using this method (see Chapter 9).

You can create files of types other than the types listed from within application programs.

Selecting Files and Folders

Files and folders are represented in Folder and Windows Explorer windows by icons, with the name of the file or folder printed underneath its icon. A *file icon* is a rectangle that looks like a piece of paper. The rectangle bears the design of the default program that opens the file. Icons of a Word document, a Notepad, and a Kodak Imaging document appear in Figure 8-2. A *folder icon* looks like a manila folder.

To select a file or folder in Web style, move the cursor over its icon. When the icon changes color, the corresponding object has been selected. To open the file or folder, single-click the icon. In Classic style, a single-click selects an object and a double-click opens it. You can easily switch from one style to the other, or mix features from the two styles (see "Choosing Web Style, Classic Style, or Something in Between").

To select more than one object, select the first object, and then press the CTRL key while you select others. (If you do not press CTRL, selecting one object deselects all the others.)

If the objects you want to select are close together, move the cursor to an empty spot nearby, hold down the left mouse button, and drag the cursor. A rectangle forms, and any object inside the rectangle is selected. When you release the mouse button, the rectangle disappears, but the objects it contained continue to be selected. You can get the same effect by using the SHIFT key instead of the mouse: Select an object, then hold down the SHIFT key and select another object. All objects in an imaginary rectangle containing the two selected objects are selected as well.

More complicated patterns of objects can be selected by combining the two methods:

1. Drag out a rectangle that contains most of the objects you want to select (and perhaps some others as well). That is, click in one corner of an imaginary rectangle, hold down the mouse button, and drag the mouse pointer to the opposite corner of the rectangle.

2. Release the mouse button and press CTRL.

3. While pressing CTRL, deselect unwanted objects (if any) by passing the cursor over them in Web style, or single-clicking them in Classic style.

4. Keep pressing CTRL, and select any additional objects that you want to select.

To select all the items in a folder, open it in a Folder or Windows Explorer window and choose Edit | Select All from the menu bar or press CTRL-A on the keyboard. To select all but a few objects in a folder, choose Select All, and then hold down CTRL while you deselect those few objects.

Naming and Renaming Files and Folders

Newly created folders and files are given default names, such as New Folder and New Microsoft Word Document. To rename a file or folder, right-click its icon and choose Rename from the menu. A box appears around the current name, and the entire name is selected. Type the new name in the box and press ENTER.

In Classic style, you can also rename by selecting an object, and then clicking the name next to the icon. Again, a box appears around the current name, and you proceed as before. Be sure to pause slightly between the click that selects the object and the click that selects its name—otherwise you double-click and open the object.

If the new name is only a minor change from the old one, edit the old name instead of typing the new one. Click inside the name-box at the place where you want to begin typing or deleting.

Changing a File's Extension

Changing a file's three-letter extension changes its file type. Don't do this unless you know what you are doing. If you assign the file a type that Windows 98 does not recognize, it will not know how to open the file. If you assign the file a type that Windows 98 does recognize, whenever you open the file, Windows 98 uses the application associated with that file type. Unless you have prepared the file in such a way that it is appropriate for that application, the opening fails. (Consider, for example, the Paint program trying to open an audio file.)

When you are renaming a file, be sure you know whether Windows is hiding the file extensions (see "What Are Extensions and File Types?"). If file extensions are hidden, you can't change them when you rename a file. If they are not hidden, you can make changes. When you rename a file whose extension is not hidden, you must include the extension in your renaming, or else the file type is lost. Conversely, if you type in a file extension when the extension is hidden, you wind up with a double extension, like report.doc.doc.

If you change a file's extension (and thus its file type), Windows gives you a warning that the file may become unusable, and asks you to confirm your decision. This feature, although annoying, may save you from making an occasional mistake.

Opening Files and Folders

Any object in a Windows Explorer or Folder window can be opened by single-clicking (in Web style) or double-clicking (in Classic style) its icon. If the object is a folder, it opens in a Folder window or in the right pane of a Windows Explorer window. In Web style, the new Folder window replaces the previous one, while in Classic style, a new Folder window is opened on top of the previous one. If the object is a file of a recognized file type, Windows opens it with the application associated with that file type.

If you open a file in a Windows Explorer or Folder window, and Windows 98 does not recognize its file type, or if that file type has no associated application, an Open With box appears, asking you to identify an application to use in opening the file.

At times, you will want to open a file with an application other than the one associated with its file type. For example, Windows associates HTML files with a web browser (Internet Explorer by default); but if you want to edit an HTML file, you need to open it with FrontPage Express or some other HTML-composing application. You can do this in at least two ways:

- If both the file icon and the application icon (or shortcuts to either) are visible on your screen, drag-and-drop the file icon onto the application icon.

- If the application is open, choose File | Open from the menu bar. The Open window appears and allows you to indicate which file to open (see "Giving Commands" in Chapter 2).

- In a Windows Explorer or Folder window, hold down the SHIFT key while right-clicking the file icon. The shortcut menu that appears always includes the Open With command; select it, then choose the application from the Open With dialog box that appears.

Rearranging Files and Folders

The quest for the perfect system of file organization is endless—you frequently need to move or copy files and folders to somewhere other than where they were originally created. You can rearrange your files and folders by using the following:

- Buttons on the Standard Buttons toolbar
- Commands from the menus
- Drag-and-drop techniques

The commands corresponding to the buttons on the Standard Buttons toolbar are also on the menus, the only difference being how the commands are issued, not what they do. This section examines the toolbar and menu commands first, and then the drag-and-drop techniques.

Cutting, Copying, and Pasting Files and Folders

You can use buttons on the Standard Buttons toolbar to move a file, a folder, or a collection of files and folders from one folder to another (see "What Toolbars Can Appear in Folder and Windows Explorer Windows?"). The relevant buttons are Cut, Copy, and Paste. The Cut button is labeled with a scissors icon, Copy with two document icons, and Paste with a document on a clipboard. You can see the expanded buttons with their text labels in Figure 8-4. The Cut, Copy, and Paste commands can also be issued from the Edit menu.

Cut-and-paste has the effect of moving objects from a source folder to a target folder. The procedure for copy-and-paste is almost identical, but leaves separate copies of the objects in the source folder and the target folder (see "What Is Cut-and-Paste?" in Chapter 7).

Cutting-and-Pasting in Windows Explorer Windows

To cut-and-paste (or copy-and-paste) from a Windows Explorer window:

1. Select the objects to be moved (or copied) from the source folder. You can select them most conveniently in the right pane, but if you are acting on entire folders, you can select them from the left pane, too.

2. Click the Cut (or Copy) button on the toolbar. Ghostly images of the objects remain in their original places until the objects are pasted elsewhere.

3. Select the target folder.

4. Click the Paste button on the toolbar.

Cutting-and-Pasting in Folder Windows

If you can easily navigate from one folder to the other, you can cut-and-paste (or copy-and-paste) by using a single Folder window:

1. Select the objects to be moved.

2. Click the Cut (or Copy) button on the toolbar. Ghostly images of the objects remain in their original places until the objects are pasted elsewhere. (An alternate method is to select the objects with the right mouse button, then choose Cut or Copy from the shortcut menu.)

3. Navigate until the Folder window displays the contents of the folder to which you want to move the objects.

4. Click the Paste button, or right-click an empty spot in the Folder window and choose Paste from the shortcut menu.

If the folders are inconveniently far apart in the folder tree, display each folder in its own window. (Remember that you can always open another Folder window—even in Web style—by opening the My Computer icon on the Desktop. You can open another Windows Explorer window by choosing Start | Program | Windows Explorer.) In this situation:

1. Open the source folder and target folder in different windows.
2. Select the objects to be moved from the source folder.
3. Click the Cut button on the toolbar of the source folder.
4. Click the Paste button on the toolbar of the target folder.

As in the previous instructions, Cut and Paste also can be invoked from the shortcut menu (the menu that appears when you right-click a selection).

Deleting Files and Folders

To delete a file, folder, or collection of files and folders in a single Folder or Windows Explorer window:

1. Select the objects to be deleted.
2. Click the Delete button on the toolbar, choose File | Delete from the menu bar, or press the DELETE key on the keyboard. A dialog box appears that asks whether you really want to send the objects to the Recycle Bin (if they are deleted from your computer's hard drive) or delete the objects (if they are on a removable disk).
3. Click Yes in the dialog box.

Another method for deleting is to select objects with the right mouse button, then choose Delete from the shortcut menu. The dialog box described in step 2 appears, and you click Yes.

Under the default settings objects deleted from your computer's hard drives go to the Recycle Bin, from which they can be recovered. You can reset your preferences so that objects are deleted immediately and do not go to the Recycle Bin (see "Streamlining the Deletion Process" in Chapter 9). Objects deleted from floppy drives or other removable disks do not go to the Recycle Bin, although they may be recoverable by other means (see "Retrieving Files with Third-Party Tools"). For this reason, be especially cautious when deleting objects from floppies or other removable disks.

You can delete files or folders directly, without sending them to the Recycle Bin, if you are very sure that you won't change your mind. To delete a file or folder irrevocably, select it, then press SHIFT-DELETE.

Dragging-and-Dropping Files and Folders

Drag-and-drop is the simplest way to move or copy objects from one drive or folder to another, or between a folder and the desktop (see "What Is Drag-and-Drop? in Chapter 7). You can also delete objects by dragging-and-dropping them onto the Recycle Bin icon.

To drag-and-drop files or folders:

1. Set up the window(s) so that you can see both the source and the target. In a Windows Explorer window, our preference is to have the source folder open in the right-hand window, and the target folder visible in the left-hand folder tree. Drag-and-drop also works with Folder windows, but unless the target is a subfolder of the source, you need two Folder windows. (For drag-and-drop purposes, the desktop itself can be considered a Folder window.) Open the source folder in one window. In the other window, you can either open the target folder, or simply have its icon visible.

2. Select the icons of the objects that you want to drag-and-drop.

3. While holding down the left mouse button, drag the icons to the target. (You can also drag with the right mouse button. This is discussed in the following paragraphs.) If the target is an open window, drag the icons to an open space in the window. If the target is an icon in an open window, drag until the cursor rests over the icon; the target icon changes color when you have the cursor in the right place.

4. Drop by releasing the mouse button.

There is one unfortunate aspect to dragging-and-dropping. If you experiment, you soon notice that it doesn't do the same thing in all circumstances—sometimes it moves an object, sometimes it copies it, and sometimes it makes a shortcut. The reason for this behavior is that the programmers at Microsoft have gone a little bit overboard in trying to be helpful. Windows 98 is doing what it guesses you intend to do, based on the file type of the objects being dragged, the source folder, and the target folder.

Here's what happens when you drag-and-drop:

- If you drag-and-drop a program, Windows 98 makes a shortcut and leaves the program file where it was. This is sensible: Program files tend to be huge, and you wouldn't want multiple copies of them cluttering up your disks. Also, moving them out of the folders they were installed into can create problems in the way they operate. A shortcut to a program is usually as good or better than a copy of the real thing.

■ If you drag-and-drop objects, other than programs, from one folder to another folder on the same disk, the objects are moved. They disappear from the source folder and appear in the target folder. Windows 98 reasons that you are probably just rearranging your files. (Remember: the desktop is a folder on the C drive. Anything else on the C drive is considered to be on the same disk as the desktop.)

■ If you drag-and-drop objects, other than programs, from one folder to another folder on a different disk, the objects are copied. Separate copies exist in both the source and target folders. The rationale is that you are probably making a back-up copy on another disk, or making a copy to give someone else.

Windows 98 at least tells you what it is going to do with the objects you drop. When the object icons are in a droppable position, a tiny + appears next to them if they are going to be copied, while a tiny curved arrow (the same arrow that appears on shortcut icons) appears if a shortcut is going to be created. If nothing appears, the files are going to be moved.

Tip	*If you want to use drag-and-drop, but you neither want to memorize how it works, nor trust Windows 98 to guess your intentions, drag with the right mouse button rather than the left mouse button. When you drop in the target folder, a menu appears. Find the action you intended and select it.*

You can also control drag-and-drop behavior by using the keyboard: If you left-drag with the SHIFT key pressed, the objects are moved when you drop them. Left-dragging with the CTRL key pressed copies the objects when you drop them. You can easily remember this by noting that Copy and CTRL both begin with C.

Using the Send To Menu

Send To is a menu found on the File menu of Folder windows and Windows Explorer windows. Send To enables you to copy files to preselected locations quickly and easily. To use Send To for this purpose:

1. In either a Folder or Windows Explorer window, open a folder that contains files you want to copy.

2. Select the files to copy (see "Selecting Files and Folders").

3. Choose File | Send To from the menu bar, or right-click the item(s) you selected and choose Send To from the shortcut menu that appears. Either way, a menu of possible destinations appears. The Windows 98 installation program creates a default Send To menu that varies according to the resources available to your computer. At the very least, it includes the desktop, a floppy drive, My Briefcase, and Mail Recipient, an option that allows you to e-mail the file to someone. A sample Send To menu looks like this:

4. Choose a destination from the Send To menu. The files are copied to the destination.

Send To is useful only if you want to move files to a destination that is on its menu. To add a new destination to the Send To menu:

1. Open C:\Windows\SendTo in a Windows Explorer window. The right pane of the window displays the shortcuts that make up the current Send To menu.

2. Find the new destination folder or drive on the folder tree in the left pane of the Windows Explorer window.

3. Holding down the right mouse button, drag the destination folder from the left pane to the right pane.

4. Select Create Shortcut(s) Here from the shortcut menu that appears. The new shortcut appears in the right pane.

To delete an item from the Send To menu, delete the corresponding shortcut from C:\Windows\SendTo.

Fixing Your Mistakes

Even the most experienced computer user occasionally clicks the mouse, and then stares at the screen in horror, saying "What did I just do?" Fortunately, the horror need not be lasting—Windows 98 provides tools for recovering from many common errors.

Reversing Your Last Action Using the Undo Button

Toolbars make it easy to do what you want to do, but they also make it easy to do what you don't want to do. Be grateful that the Standard Buttons toolbar in Folder windows or Windows Explorer windows has an Undo button—the button with the counterclockwise arrow on it (see Figure 8-4). If you delete something you want to keep, or cut-and-paste the wrong file, just click Undo and you can pretend the mistake never happened.

Clicking Undo multiple times steps you back through your recent actions. You can also choose Edit | Undo from the menu bar of a Folder window. The keyboard equivalent is CTRL-Z.

Retrieving Files and Folders from the Recycle Bin

If you change your mind about deleting a file or folder, and it's too late to use the Undo button, you can still retrieve it from the Recycle Bin—if it was deleted from a hard drive and you haven't emptied the Recycle Bin in the meantime.

Emptying and configuring the Recycle Bin is discussed in "Managing the Recycle Bin" in Chapter 9.

Opening the Recycle Bin

The easiest place to find the Recycle Bin is on the desktop, where its icon looks like a waste-basket. You can also find the Recycle Bin on the folder tree directly under the desktop after your computer's disk drives and other devices. (Oddly, you will not find it inside C:\Windows\Desktop, but opening the hidden folder C:\Recycled, or similar folders on your other hard drives, also opens the Recycle Bin.)

A Folder window is perfectly adequate for a simple task, like finding a file in the Recycle Bin and putting it back where it was before its deletion. If you want to do something more complicated, open the Recycle Bin with Windows Explorer.

Searching the Recycle Bin

If you know exactly what file or folder you are looking for, any view will do. But if the Recycle Bin is crowded, and you need to do some real detective work to figure out which objects you want to retrieve, the Details view (shown in Figure 8-8) is best. Choose View | Details from the menu bar. The right pane becomes a list with columns showing the following:

- The name and icon of the file or folder
- The address of the folder from which the object was deleted
- The date and time the object was deleted
- The file type
- The size

Clicking the column header sorts the list according to that column's attribute. For example, if you know the date when you deleted the file, click the Date Deleted header to put the objects in the order in which they were deleted. All objects deleted on the

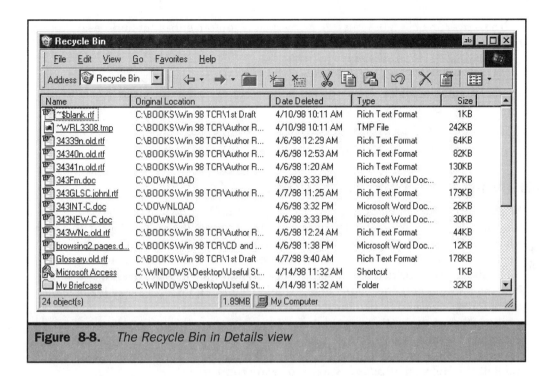

Figure 8-8.   *The Recycle Bin in Details view*

same date that you deleted the file appear together. Or, if you remember the name of the file, but know that you deleted several versions of it, clicking the Name header arranges the list alphabetically by name. All the versions appear next to each other, and you can easily see which is the most recent version.

Recovering Objects from the Recycle Bin

The simplest way to recover an object from the Recycle Bin is to follow these steps:

1. Open the Recycle Bin.

2. Select the object (or collection of objects) you want to recover.

3. Choose File | Restore from the menu bar.

The object returns to the folder it was deleted from—the address given in the Original Location column of the Details view. If the object is a folder, all of its contents return with it. You can use Restore even if the object was deleted from a folder that no longer exists. A folder of the appropriate name will be created to contain the restored object.

To recover an object, but put it in a new place, you can either cut-and-paste from the Recycle Bin to the new location, or:

1. Open the Recycle Bin with Windows Explorer.

2. Expand the folder tree in the left-hand window so that the target folder icon is visible.

3. In the right pane, select the object(s) you want to recover.

4. Drag-and-drop to the target folder in the left-hand window.

Retrieving Files with Third-Party Tools

When a file or folder is emptied from the Recycle Bin, Windows 98 doesn't immediately do anything rash like overwrite the corresponding disk space with zeroes. Windows 98 simply removes the file from its file allocation table, so that the disk space that the file occupied is no longer reserved (see "What Is a File System?" in Chapter 11). If that disk space is needed for something else, Windows will write over it, but until then, the information stays on the disk. (Think of a restaurant with a lazy busboy; the tables don't get cleared until more customers come.)

A number of applications have been written to recover this information and reassemble the file, but none are part of Windows 98. Two of the best known are Norton Utilities by Symantec (on the Internet at **http://www.symantec.com**) and Nuts and Bolts by Helix (at **http://www.helixsoftware.com**).

Chapter 9

Managing Files and Folders

The previous chapter explained what you need to know to start working with files and folders: creating and deleting them, opening them, seeing what's in them, naming them, and moving them from one place to another. This chapter discusses issues that may not come up immediately as you work with files and folders, but that you should know about if you are going to have a long-term relationship with your computer.

To a beginner, having a lot of choices is more of a burden than a convenience, but as users become more familiar with their computers, they develop their own ideas about how things should work. For this reason, Windows 98 has default settings that cause the system to work automatically in the way that the designers believe is simplest for beginners. However, a great many of Windows' behaviors are reconfigurable, so that more advanced users can make their own choices.

The longer you work with your computer, the more files you create. At some point, putting them all in a folder called Jane's Files, or splitting them into two folders called Work and Home, is no longer adequate. You need to come up with a system that organizes your files into smaller, coherently related piles. Discussing organizational systems goes beyond the scope of this book, but you should know about one valuable organizational tool: the shortcut. Shortcuts enable you to access the same file or application from many different points in the folder tree, without the disadvantages that come with having several copies of the same file.

Even the best-organized people occasionally forget where they put something, so you need to know how to use Windows 98's Find command.

Being able to retrieve deleted files from the Recycle Bin (as described in the previous chapter) is a convenience, but in time the bin becomes crowded with long-forgotten files that take up disk space to no purpose. You need to know how to manage the Recycle Bin so that it continues to be useful without unduly burdening your hard drive.

Finally, files and folders have properties (see "What Are Properties?" in Chapter 1). The Properties dialog box for a file or folder contains much useful information, and allows you to make certain choices regarding the object's properties and attributes.

What Is a Shortcut?

Technically, a *shortcut* is a file of type Shortcut, with a .lnk extension. Less technically, a shortcut is a placeholder in your filing system. It has a definite position on the folder tree, but it points to a file or folder that is somewhere else on the folder tree.

The purpose of a shortcut is to allow an object to be, for all practical purposes, in two places at once. For example, you usually should leave a program file inside the folder where it was installed, so that you don't mess up any of the relationships between it and its associated files. At the same time, you might want the program to be on the desktop, so that you can conveniently open files by dragging them to the program's icon. Solution: Leave the program file where it is, but make a shortcut pointing to it, and place the shortcut on the desktop. When you drag a file to the shortcut icon, Windows opens the file with the corresponding program.

Maintaining multiple copies of documents on your system is both wasteful of disk space and potentially confusing—when one copy gets updated, you could easily forget to update the others. And yet, files often belong in many different places in a filing system. If, for example, Paul writes the office's fourth quarter report, the document may belong simultaneously in the Paul's Memos folder and in the Quarterly Reports folder. Putting the document itself in Quarterly Reports and a shortcut to it in Paul's Memos solves the problem, without creating multiple copies of the document. Clicking the shortcut icon opens the associated document, just as if you had clicked the icon of the document itself.

You can recognize a shortcut icon by the curving arrow that appears in its lower-left corner. A shortcut icon otherwise looks just like the icon of the object it points to: a document, folder, or application. A shortcut can be on your desktop or in a folder. On the desktop, a shortcut looks like this:

In a folder, you can see a shortcut in the Folder window or Windows Explorer window: the shortcut looks just a like a file, except that its icon has the telltale shortcut arrow. You can create, delete, move, copy, and rename shortcuts from Folder or Windows Explorer windows (see "Working with Shortcuts").

 Windows 98 also has things called "shortcut keys" and "shortcut menus," which have nothing to do with shortcuts (see Chapter 2).

What Are Properties of Files and Folders?

Like almost everything else in Windows 98, files and folders have *properties*— information about a file or folder that you can access and perhaps change without opening the file or folder.

To view this information and make changes, select the file or folder in a Folder or Windows Explorer window, and then click the Properties button on the toolbar. (Alternately, you can right-click the file or folder and select Properties from the shortcut menu that pops up.) The Properties dialog box appears, with the General tab selected (see Figure 9-1).

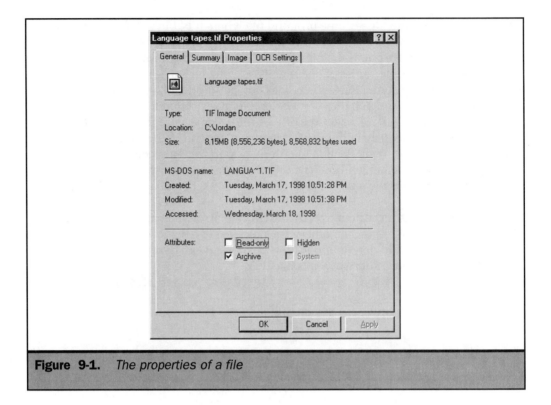

Figure 9-1. *The properties of a file*

The General tab of a file's Properties dialog box displays the file's:

- Name and icon
- File type (see "What Are Extensions and File Types?" in Chapter 8)
- Location in the folder tree (see "What Is the Folder Tree?" in Chapter 8)
- Size (including both the actual size of the file and the slightly larger amount of disk space allocated to the file).
- MS-DOS name (see "What Are MS-DOS Names?" in Chapter 8)
- Date and time of creation, most recent modification, and most recent access
- Attributes (see "What Are Attributes?")

Depending on a file's type, it may have additional tabs of properties, which you can access by clicking them individually. The properties of Word files (with the file extension .doc), for example, include a Summary tab and a Statistics tab. The Summary tab provides room for the author of a file to give keywords and a short summary of the document. The Statistics tab reports the number of pages, paragraphs, lines, words, and characters in the document.

Since a folder is technically a special kind of file, the General tab of its properties contains much of the same information: icon, name, type (Folder), location, size (the number of bytes taken up by the folder and all of its contents, including the contents of subfolders), MS-DOS name, date created, and attributes. The General tab has two additional items: Contains, and Enable Thumbnail View. The Contains line reports the number of files and folders contained in the folder and all of its subfolders. The Enable Thumbnail View check box, when checked, adds thumbnails to the View menu when the folder is opened (see "Thumbnail View").

If your computer is on a local area network, folders also have a Sharing tab, with information about whether the folder (and the files and folders it contains) are shared on the network (see "Sharing Files" in Chapter 29).

To find the total size of a group of files, select all the files, then right-click anywhere in the selected filenames. Choose Properties from the shortcut menu that appears. Windows displays the total number of files and folders, as well as their combined size.

What Are Attributes?

The *attributes* of a file or folder include these settings, which can be selected or unselected for each file or folder:

- **Read-only**   You can read this file or folder, but not accidentally delete or change it. If you try to delete a read-only file or folder, Windows asks if you really want to delete it.

- **Hidden**   File or folder that doesn't usually appear in Folder or Windows Explorer windows (see the next section).

- **Archive**   Depending on which backup program you use, this setting may mean that the file or folder has been changed since the last time it was backed up.

- **System**   This file or folder is part of Windows 98 itself, and does not usually appear in Folder or Windows Explorer windows.

The attributes of a file or folder appear at the bottom of the General tab of the Properties dialog box.

What Are Hidden Files and Folders?

Windows 98 contains a number of files that a beginner might find confusing, and that you don't want to delete or change accidentally. As a safety feature, these files are *hidden*, which means that, by default, they don't show up in Folder or Windows Explorer windows. For example, the desktop is stored in the folder C:\Windows\ Desktop, but if you open My Computer, and then the C disk, and then the Windows folder—you won't find it. If you want to see C:\Windows\Desktop (and all the other hidden files and folders), follow these steps:

1. Choose Start | Settings | Folder Options. The Folder Options dialog box appears.

2. Click the View tab in the Folder Options dialog box. The Hidden Files section contains three radio buttons: Do Not Show Hidden or System Files, Do Not Show Hidden Files, and Show All Files.

3. Click the Show All Files radio button.

4. Click OK.

When hidden files and folders are shown, their icons appear as ghostly images. To hide them again, repeat the preceding procedure, but select the Do Not Show Hidden Or System Files radio button in step 3.

Hidden files and folders usually don't play a significant role in the everyday life of the average computer user. For that reason, we recommend that you leave them hidden whenever you are not working with one. This policy minimizes the chances that you will alter or delete something important by accident.

Non-hidden files and folders contained in a hidden folder have an in-between status: They retain their original attributes, and show up in Folder and Windows Explorer windows if you move them to a non-hidden folder. But they are hidden in practice as long as they stay inside the hidden folder, since the path that connects them to the top of the folder tree includes a hidden link.

 A hidden file or folder should not be considered secure. The Find command finds hidden files and folder (see "Finding Files and Folders"). In fact, anyone who finds your file by using this command can open it directly from the Find window, without knowing that you intended it to be hidden. Also, you can see from the preceding discussion that viewing hidden files is not difficult. If other people use your computer, and you don't want them to find particular files, you should either encrypt those files, or move them to a floppy disk that you keep hidden in a more conventional way. See Chapter 33 for a description of Windows 98's limited security features.

You can hide a file or folder by following this procedure:

1. Select the file or folder.

2. Click the Properties button on the toolbar, or right-click the file or folder and choose Properties from the shortcut menu. The Properties dialog box appears.

3. If it is not already selected, click the General tab. Near the bottom of the General tab is a list of attributes, one of which is Hidden.

4. Click the check box next to Hidden. A check appears in that box.

5. Click OK to make the Properties dialog box disappear.

Configuring a Folder or Windows Explorer Window

You can configure many facets of Folder and Windows Explorer windows to your own taste. At the simplest level, you can resize and move the windows themselves just like any other windows. You can choose Web-style windows or Classic-style windows (see "What Style Is Your Desktop?" in Chapter 1). You can even define a custom style that incorporates your favorite features from each (see "Choosing Web Style, Classic Style, or Something in Between" in Chapter 8).

In addition, you can change the following properties:

- The size of the icons used to represent files and folders
- Whether the files and folders are presented as a list or as icons that you can arrange in two dimensions
- The quantity of information displayed about each file and folder
- The order in which files and folders are displayed

In addition to the changes in the look and behavior of Folder and Windows Explorer windows, you can add features to a folder that will show up in any Folder window that opens it. You can define a background wallpaper for a folder, or create a hypertext template document that opens automatically when the folder is opened, giving the folder all the capabilities of a web page (see "Customizing a Folder with HTML" and "Adding a Background Picture to a Folder Window").

Changing Views

The Views button on the Folder or Windows Explorer window toolbar (or the View menu) gives you a choice of five ways to see icons: Large Icons, Small Icons, List, Details, and Thumbnail. (The Thumbnail view is available for a folder only if you have enabled it; see "Thumbnail View.")

Large Icons and Small Icons are graphical views that allow you to arrange the icons in any two-dimensional pattern you like. List and Details both put the objects into a list. Details includes more information in its list, and enables you to reorder the list according to various criteria. Thumbnail view displays a tiny picture of each file.

Large Icons and Small Icons Views

Large Icons and Small Icons are both graphical ways of presenting the contents of a folder—you can drag-and-drop the files and folders in the window in any way that makes sense to you, just as you might arrange objects on a desktop, piling up some and spreading out others. The only difference between Large Icons and Small Icons (shown in Figure 9-2) is the obvious one: Large Icons (shown on the top part of the figure) gives you larger icons than Small Icons (shown on the bottom). In general, Large Icons

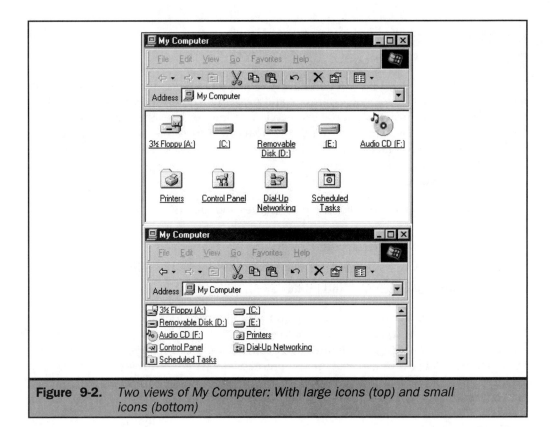

Figure 9-2. *Two views of My Computer: With large icons (top) and small icons (bottom)*

is convenient for folders with a few files, while Small Icons works better for folders with many files.

List and Details Views

List and Details both are ways of putting the contents of a folder into a list. The difference between them is that List gives only a small icon and a name for each file and subfolder. Details, as the name implies, gives a more detailed list that includes four more columns: the size of the file, its file type, when it was last modified, and its attributes (see Figure 9-3).

Details also allows you to sort the list of files and subfolders according to any column by clicking its column head. Clicking Name sorts the contents, putting them in alphabetical order. Clicking a column head twice sorts the contents in reverse order. For example, one click on the Size head sorts from the smallest file to the largest, and a second click on Size re-sorts from the largest file to the smallest. In Figure 9-3, two clicks on the column head Size has sorted the contents of the Windows folder by file size, largest to smallest.

You can adjust the width of the columns in a Details view by dragging-and-dropping the lines between the adjacent column heads.

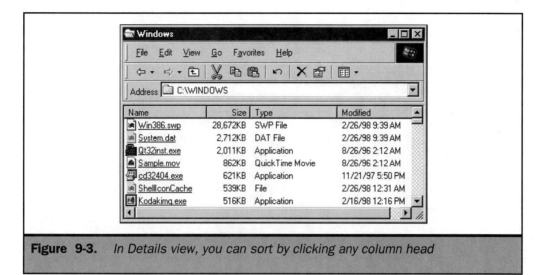

Figure 9-3.   *In Details view, you can sort by clicking any column head*

Thumbnail View

If you can't remember the names of your files, but will know the right document when
you see it, you need Thumbnail view. In Thumbnail view, the icon that represents a file
is a miniature version of its first page, called a *thumbnail*, as in Figure 9-4. Any
normal-sized text is far too small to read, but you can easily tell the difference between,
say, a text document, a spreadsheet, and a picture, or between a three-column
document and a two-column document.

Note *Windows can't seem to decide whether to call this view "Thumbnail" (as in the
Properties dialog box) or "Thumbnails" (as on the View menu). They are the same.*

Unlike the other four views, Thumbnail view requires Windows to set up the folder
in a special way. Consequently, the Thumbnails command only appears on the View
menu if the folder has been thumbnail-enabled. To enable Thumbnail view for a
particular folder:

1. Select the folder's icon in a Folder or Windows Explorer window.
2. Click the Properties button on the toolbar. (Alternatively, you can right-click
   the folder's icon and choose Properties from the menu.) The Properties dialog
   box appears.
3. If it is not already on top, select the General tab.

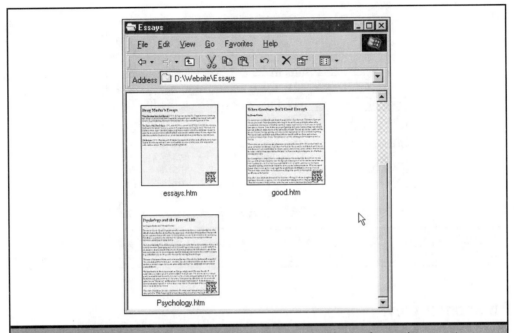

Figure 9-4.   *Thumbnail view shows you miniature versions of your documents*

4. Click the check box Enable Thumbnail View. A check mark appears, telling you that Thumbnail view has been enabled.

5. Click OK to make the Properties dialog box disappear.

Now when you open this folder, the View menu contains the Thumbnails option. To disable Thumbnail view, repeat the preceding procedure, but click the Enable Thumbnail View box again to make the check mark disappear.

Windows 98 enables thumbnails by adding a hidden file, desktop.ini, to the folder. When you switch to Thumbnail view, a second hidden file, Thumbs.db, is created and stored in the folder. Strangely, these files do not vanish when you disable Thumbnail view.

Note   *Displaying a thumbnail of a document is much more work for your computer than displaying an icon. If you have several windows open that show thumbnails, performance may suffer. If you have trouble, disable thumbnails.*

Changing How the View Settings Work

Do you want all your folders to have the same look? Or do you want Windows to display some of them as web pages and others not? Or would you like to work with some folders in Details view and others in Large Icons view? You can control the *view settings*, which specify how folders look, for all of your folders, or for individual folders.

Windows' default view settings are those that Microsoft believes are the easiest for beginners to understand:

- All windows are displayed in Large Icons view.
- The View | As Web Page option is checked in Web style, unchecked in Classic style.

Each folder has its own view settings. If you choose a new view for a given Folder or Windows Explorer window, you change the view for that folder only. Windows remembers the new view the next time you open that folder, but all other folders are unchanged.

Table 9-1 lists the settings on the View tab of the Folder Options dialog box (shown in Figure 9-5). If you change these settings, you can return to the settings that come with Windows 98 by clicking the Restore Defaults button.

Setting	Description
Remember each folder's view settings	Specifies that Windows saves the view settings of each folder when you close the Folder or Windows Explorer window that displays the folder.
Display the full path in title bar	Specifies that the full pathname (file address) of the folder appears in the title bar of the window. Otherwise, only the folder name appears.
Hide file extensions for known file types	Specifies that Windows does not display file extensions for file types that are listed on the File Types tab of the Folder Options dialog box (see "What Are Extensions and File Types?" in Chapter 8).

Table 9-1.   *View Settings on the Folder Options Dialog Box*

Setting	Description
Show Map Network Drive button in toolbar	Displays the Map Drive and Disconnect buttons on the toolbar. These buttons are useful if your computer is on a local area network and you frequently map or unmap drives (see Chapter 32). The buttons perform the same commands as choosing Tools	Map Network Drive and Tools	Disconnect Network Drive.
Show file attributes in Detail View	Displays a column with file and folder attributes when in Detail view.
Show pop-up description for folder and desktop items	Specifies that when you select a file or folder, a small pop-up window appears with information about the file or folder. This pop-up doesn't appear in Web view, since the information already appears in the left side of the window (see "What Is the Web View of a Folder?" in Chapter 8).
Allow all uppercase names	For filenames that are all uppercase, specifies that Windows displays the filename in all uppercase. Otherwise, Windows displays all-uppercase filenames in lowercase with initial capitals.
Do not show hidden or system files	Specifies that neither hidden nor system files appear.
Do not show hidden files	Specifies that hidden files not appear.
Show all files	Specifies that all files appear, including hidden and system files.
Hide icons when desktop is viewed as web page	Specifies that in Web view, Windows does not display icons or names for the items in the folder.
Smooth edges of screen fonts	Specifies that Windows smooths jagged edges of your screen fonts. Unless you have a very large monitor, this option slows down your system's performance for little or no improvement in appearance.

Table 9-1.   *View Settings on the Folder Options Dialog Box* (continued)

Setting	Description
Show window contents while dragging	Specifies that the complete contents of the window appears while you are dragging the window to a new location. Otherwise, only the outline appears during dragging; the complete contents appear at the window's new location.

Table 9-1. *View Settings on the Folder Options Dialog Box* (continued)

Changing the Default View Settings

This behavior is fine if you like the default view most of the time, but only switch to, say, Details view in folders containing a lot of files. On the other hand, you might decide that you like Details (or some other) view, and want to use it for all your folders. Here's how:

1. Configure a folder the way you want all the folders to appear.
2. With that folder open in a Folder or Windows Explorer window, select View | Folder Options. The Folder Options dialog box appears.
3. Click the View tab of the Folder Options dialog box, shown in Figure 9-5.
4. Near the top of this tab is the Folder Views box. Inside this box is the Like Current Folder button. Click it.
5. A confirmation box appears, asking you whether you really mean to change the default view settings. Click Yes.
6. Click OK to close the Folder Options dialog box.

If you want to reset all folders back to the default settings, follow the above instructions except in step 4 click the Restore Defaults button.

Changing the View Settings for a Window

You may also decide that you want the view settings to belong to the window, not to the folder. In other words, when you switch to, say, Small Icons view, you want every folder that you open from that window to come up in Small Icons view until you change to something else. To change window settings:

1. Select Start | Settings | Folder Options. The Folder Options dialog box appears.
2. Click the View tab of the Folder Options dialog box (shown in Figure 9-5). The lower portion of the tab is the Advanced Settings box.

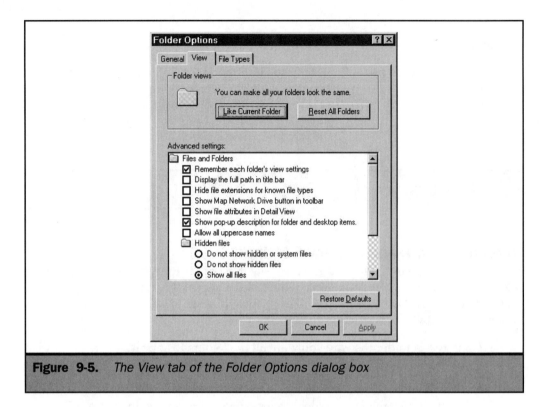

Figure 9-5.   *The View tab of the Folder Options dialog box*

3. In the Advanced Settings box, find the line Remember Each Folder's View Settings. Uncheck the box next to this line.

4. Click OK.

To restore the default behavior, repeat the process, but check the box in step 3.

One thing you can't do is have some Folder windows in Web style and others in Classic, or to have different custom styles for different windows. Whatever decisions you make on the General tab of the Folder Options dialog box are applied automatically to all Folder and Windows Explorer windows.

Sorting and Arranging the Contents of a Folder

The icons in a Folder or Windows Explorer window can be sorted automatically by name (alphabetically), by file type, by size (from smallest to largest), and by date (earliest to most recent). Any of these choices can be made by selecting View | Arrange Icons.

In any of these sortings, folders are listed before files. Thus, in Figure 9-6, the folders B and C come before file A. In Large Icons and Small Icons views, the contents of the folder are sorted in rows. The first element in the order is located in the

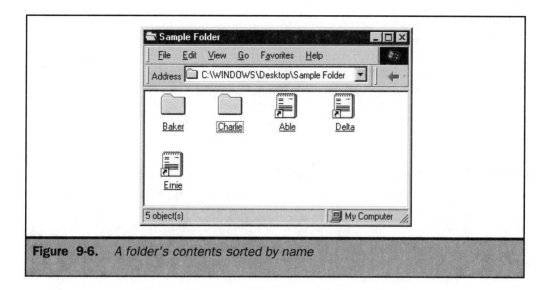

Figure 9-6.   *A folder's contents sorted by name*

window's upper-left corner, the second is to its right, and so on. In List and Details views, the contents are sorted in a list, starting at the top of the window.

In Details view, sorting is particularly easy: Click the column header to sort according to that column. Click it again to sort in reverse order. Only Details view allows this reverse sorting.

In Large Icons or Small Icons views, you can also arrange icons manually, by dragging them. Figure 9-7 shows a folder whose contents have been arranged

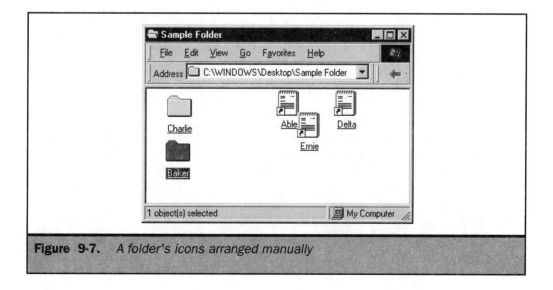

Figure 9-7.   *A folder's icons arranged manually*

manually; notice the irregular spacing, and the overlapping icons. Metaphorically, manual arrangement is more like sorting stacks of paper on a table than sorting items in a filing cabinet. The effect can be similar to having subfolders: You can put work files on the right half of the window and home files on the left, instead of having Work and Home subfolders. Files that all relate to the same project can be grouped together in the folder window, instead of having their own subfolder. If at some point you decide that you want everything in tidy rows again, choose View | Arrange Icons | Auto Arrange.

Adding a Background Picture to a Folder Window

One of the most tempting ways to waste time with a computer is to experiment until you find the absolutely perfect combination of pattern and color for the desktop (see Chapter 13). Windows 98 has multiplied this temptation tenfold (or more) by allowing you to customize the background of each folder independently. When opened in Web style, the customized folder displays its custom background in the Folder or Windows Explorer window. Figure 9-8 shows a folder with a customized background pattern.

Customizing the Appearance of a Folder

We can't think of any compelling reason to give a folder its own background, but it is fun. Follow these steps:

1. Open the folder upon which you want to bestow a custom background.

2. Select View | Customize This Folder. You see the Customize This Folder Wizard with several options for dressing up the folder.

3. Select the Choose A Background Picture radio button.

4. Click Next. You see the window in Figure 9-9. On the right is a list of background patterns that Windows 98 knows about—the same choices you have when choosing a pattern for the desktop (see "Selecting a Background Color and Pattern" in Chapter 13). On the left is a window showing what the selected pattern looks like.

5. Select names from the list and examine the corresponding patterns. If you find one you like, click Next and skip to step 9.

6. If you don't find the pattern you like on this list, and you believe that you have a better pattern somewhere on your system—a scanned-in photo of your two-year-old, for instance—click Browse. An Open window appears.

7. Use the Open window to search out a file containing the image you want. Any .bmp, .jpg, or .gif file will do. (By default, the window is looking for .bmp files. To see other types, select from the pull-down list in the Files Of Type line.)

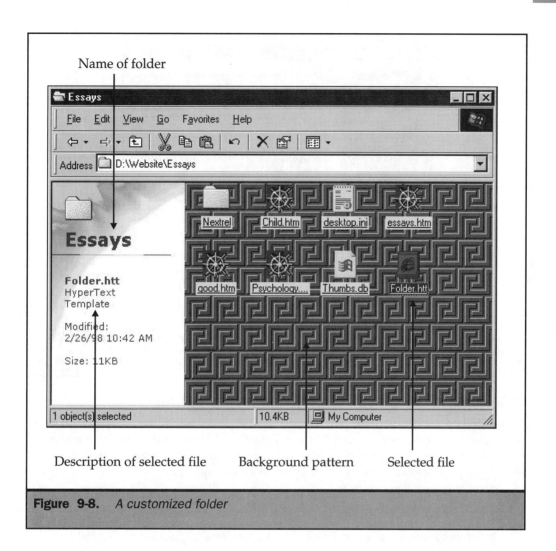

Name of folder

Description of selected file   Background pattern   Selected file

Figure 9-8.   *A customized folder*

8. Click Open. The Open window disappears, returning the window shown in Figure 9-9. Your chosen file has been added to the list and is selected. The image is previewed in the left-hand window. If you like the preview, click Next. Otherwise, click Browse and return to step 7.

9. The confirmation window appears, telling you which changes you have chosen. If this doesn't look like what you want, click Back and return to step 5. If you want to go through with the change, click Finish.

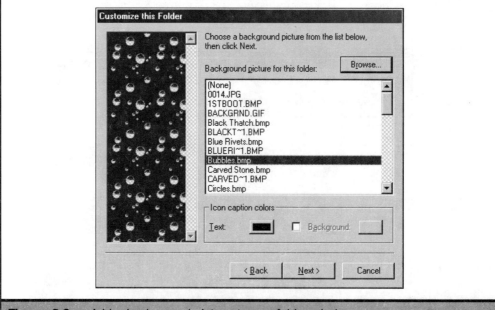

Figure 9-9. *Add a background picture to any folder window*

Removing the Custom Appearance of a Folder

Depending on the background pattern you choose for the folder, you may find that the captions of the icons are hard to read now. This is easily fixed: You can either remove the customization and return to the standard background, or you can get in deeper and change the color or background of the window's icon captions.

To remove the customization:

1. Open the folder.

2. Select View | Customize This Folder to display the Customize This Folder window.

3. Select the Remove Customization radio button.

4. Click Next.

5. Click Finish.

Customizing Icon Captions in a Folder

To change the color or background of the icon captions:

1. Open the folder.

2. Select View | Customize This Folder to display the Customize This Folder window.

3. Select the Choose A Background Picture radio button. The window of Figure 9-9 returns. Find the Icon Caption Colors box.

4. To change the color of the icon captions, click the colored box labeled Text. A box of color choices appears.

5. Select the color you want the text to be by clicking the box of that color.

6. Click OK. The newly chosen color should be on the box labeled Text.

7. To give the icon captions a background field, click the check box next to Background.

8. To choose a color for the background field, click the colored box labeled Background. A box of color choices appears.

9. Proceed as in step 5. Click OK. The newly chosen color should be on the box labeled Background.

10. Click Next. The confirmation window appears.

11. Click Finish.

Customizing a Folder with HTML

Of all the features described in this chapter, by far the least user-friendly is the ability to define and your own HTML documents for display in Folder and Windows Explorer windows. In theory, this feature gives you total control over how to display your folders—if you know how to use it.

When you display a folder in Web view, the default Web view shows a little blue sky graphic in the upper left corner of the window, details about the selected file on the left side, and the folder contents on the right side. (This view is shown in Figure 8-5.) However, you can change the Web view to display other information (see "What Is the Web View of a Folder?" in Chapter 8).

If you customize a folder, Windows creates a hidden file named Folder.htt in the folder to store information about how the Web view of the file should look. Switching to Web view causes Windows to display a customized Web view using information from the Folder.htt file. Folder.htt is no normal web page, though; it is a *hypertext template file* that uses JavaScript programs to allow the web page to change as you select items in the folder and change views.

The Customize This Folder Wizard gives you an insignificant amount of help in creating or modifying the Folder.htt file. The Wizard also opens this file in Notepad to give you a chance to edit it into the form you prefer. This is fine if you understand HTML and JavaScript, skills that go beyond the scope of this book. As far as we can tell, this feature is intended for application developers who want to create folders that behave specially and contain objects that aren't really files, along the lines of the Control Panel folder. Unless you enjoy writing and debugging complex JavaScript code, this feature is useless to end users.

Creating or Modifying the Folder.htt File

You can create, modify, or just take a look at the Folder.htt file as follows:

1. Open the folder you want to customize.

2. Select View | Customize This Folder. The Customize This Folder Wizard starts.

3. Select the Create An HTML Document radio button.

4. Click the Next button.

5. The next screen of the Wizard gives you instructions. It announces that it is about to invoke your default hypertext template editor (Notepad, unless you have chosen another) and create a page. Click Next.

6. At this point, a Notepad (or other hypertext template editor) window opens, displaying the hypertext template file that the wizard has created. If you know HTML and JavaScript, you can edit this file. If you don't know HTML and JavaScript, the contents of this window appear absolutely indecipherable; trust that the Wizard has done its job well. Exit from the editor. The Customize This Folder window reappears, congratulating you for having created the file Folder.htt (even though the Wizard did all the work).

7. Click Finish.

Deleting the Folder.htt File

You can get rid of the customization you've done to a folder, along with the Folder.htt file that contains them. Choose View | Customize This Folder, click Remove Customization, click Next, read what the Wizard is about to do, click Next again, and click Finish.

Working with Shortcuts

Sometimes you'd like a file to be in two places at once: the place where it really belongs, and on the desktop where you can easily get to it. Sometimes your filing system has two logical places to put the same file. Shortcuts allow you to deal with these situations, without the disadvantages that come from having two independent copies of the same file.

Making Shortcuts

Shortcuts are created when you:

- Drag-and-drop an application to a new folder or to the desktop.

- Hold down the right mouse button while you drag any object to a new location, and then select Create Shortcut(s) Here from the menu that appears when you drop the object.

- Invoke the Create Shortcut Wizard either by selecting File | New | Shortcut in a Folder or Windows Explorer window or by right-clicking an open space on the desktop and selecting New | Shortcut from the right-click menu.

In the first two cases, the original file or folder stays in its old location, and a shortcut to that file or folder is created in the drop location. In the third case, the shortcut is created in the folder from which the File | New | Shortcut command was issued.

Windows 98 makes shortcuts automatically in certain circumstances. When you add a web page to your list of Favorites, for example, a shortcut is created and put in the folder C:\Windows\Favorites. Dragging an application icon onto the Start button produces a shortcut in C:\Windows\Start Menu.

We find drag-and-drop techniques to be the easiest way to create shortcuts. But if you prefer, you can use the Create Shortcut Wizard as follows:

1. Open the destination folder, the one in which you want to create the shortcut. If you want the shortcut to be on the desktop, make sure part of the desktop is visible on your screen.

2. Choose File | New | Shortcut in the destination folder's window. Or, if the desktop is the destination, right-click an empty place and select New | Shortcut. Either of these techniques launches the Create Shortcut Wizard.

3. If you know the address of the file or folder to which you want to create a shortcut (the target), you can type it into the Command Line box on the Wizard's first page. If you have the address written in another file, you can cut-and-paste it into the Command Line box by using CTRL-V to paste, then skip to step 7. (If you are creating a shortcut to a folder, entering an address in the Command Line box is the only technique that works. Clicking the Browse button doesn't help.)

4. Click the Browse button. A Browse dialog box appears (see "Open, Save As, and Browse Dialog Boxes" in Chapter 2).

5. Use the Browse dialog box to find the target file.

6. Select the target file or folder, and then click the Open button. The Browse dialog box disappears. The first page of the Create Shortcut Wizard now contains the target's address.

7. Click Next. The second page of the Create Shortcut Wizard appears.

8. If you don't like the suggested name for the shortcut (usually the same as the original object), type a new one in the Select A Name For The Shortcut line.

9. Click Finish.

Shortcuts can also point to web pages on the Internet. These shortcuts are .url files, and they also can be created by the Create Shortcut Wizard. The procedure is the same, except that in step 3, you type the page's Internet address (URL).

Using Shortcuts

For almost all purposes, a shortcut to a file or folder behaves just like the target file or folder: Opening the shortcut, dragging-and-dropping the shortcut, or dragging-and-dropping something onto the shortcut produces the same result as performing the same action with the target file or folder.

The most convenient place to put shortcuts is on the desktop. Documents you are currently working on can reside in the appropriate place in your filing system, yet a shortcut on the desktop can make them instantly available. Programs you use frequently can remain in the folders they were installed into, yet be accessible with a single click.

Tip	*When you frequently use two different applications with a particular file type, set up the file type to open automatically with one application, and put a shortcut to the other application on the desktop. For example, HTML documents open automatically with Internet Explorer, which allows you to read but not edit them. If you also have a shortcut to FrontPage Express on your desktop, you can edit an HTML document by dragging it onto the shortcut icon.*

Internet shortcuts are useful for an additional reason: Attaching them to e-mail is the easiest way to tell another Windows user about a web site. If you make a shortcut file pointing to a particular web site, and then e-mail it to a Windows-using friend, your friend can open that web site with her web browser just by opening the shortcut.

Finding Files and Folders

Even with a well-organized file system, you will occasionally forget where you put a file, or even what its exact name is. Fortunately, Windows provides a Find command that takes care of this situation. By using Find, you can search for a file:

- By name or part of a name
- By date created, modified, or last accessed
- By file type
- By size
- By a string of text contained in the file
- By some combination of all the above

All searches that you do with Find follow the same basic pattern.

Starting the Find Process

Here's how you begin a file or folder search:

1. Select Start | Find | Files Or Folders. Or choose the Tools | Find | Files Or Folders command from a Folder or Windows Explorer window. Either way, the Find dialog box (Figure 9-10) opens.

2. Type the information about the files or folders you want to find into the Name & Location, Date, or Advanced tabs of the Find dialog box. Fill in as many or as few of the lines as you want.

3. Click Find Now to start searching for all files or folders that fit the description you've given. The magnifying glass icon moves in circles while the search continues. As matching files and folders are found, they appear in a window at the bottom of the Find dialog box.

4. If you are not satisfied with the files and folders that Find locates, change the information you entered and search again. When you are done, close the Find dialog box.

The window that appears at the bottom of the Find dialog box resembles a Folder window. From this window you can:

- Open any of the files or folders listed.
- Copy, cut, move, or drag-and-drop any of the files or folders to the desktop or some other window.
- Sort any of the files or folders.

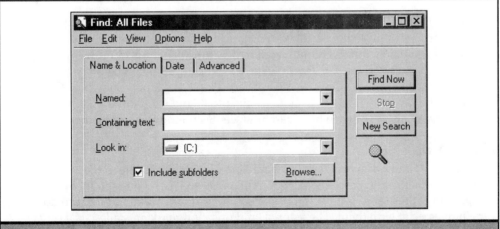

Figure 9-10. *The Find dialog box*

You can also reconfigure the window to show different views. For a complicated search resulting in many files or folders, we recommend Details view.

Searching by Name

The simplest kind of search is when you know the name of the file, but just can't remember where it is located. Just type the name of the file into the Named box of the Name & Location tab of the Find dialog box, then click Find Now.

If you know only part of the name of a file, type that part into the Named box. When you click Find Now, Find lists all the files and folders whose names include that text string. (Even if you type in the full name, Find treats it as a substring and returns all the files and folders whose names contain that text string.) For example, searching for "June" might yield the files june95.doc, Next June.txt, and 97june quarterly report.wks, plus the folders June's Recipes and Juneau Alaska.

If you don't remember much about the name of the file ("It had an 'a' in it somewhere"), the list of files and folders that Find finds is likely to be daunting. You can make your search more specific by combining it with other criteria, or by taking advantage of the following features: location information, case-sensitivity, and wild cards, described in the next three sections.

Location Information

If you know where in the folder tree the desired files or folders are located, search only that portion of the tree. The search does not take so long, and yields fewer false "finds." The Look In pull-down list provides a number of possible limitations to the search; for example, searching only one particular drive rather than all of them. To be even more specific, click Browse; a window opens showing the folder tree. In this window, select a folder to search and click OK; only that folder and its subfolders are searched.

Case Sensitivity

In the preceding "June" example, the search for "June" was not case-sensitive—the capital *J* was not taken into account, which is why june95.doc and 97june quarterly report.wks appeared on the list. If you want your capital letters to be matched only to other capital letters, choose Options | Case Sensitive in the Find dialog box. Case Sensitive is turned on if it has a check mark next to it, and is off otherwise. Case-sensitivity also applies to text searches (see "Searching for Text Strings").

Wild Cards

The asterisk (*) and question mark (?) characters play a special role in filename searches. Neither is allowed to be part of a filename, so when you type them into the Named line of the Name & Location tab, Find knows that you intend for it to do something special with them. The asterisk and question mark are called *wild cards* because (like wild cards in poker) they can stand for any other character.

The question mark stands for any single character, so you can use it when you either don't know or don't want to specify a character in a filename. If, for example, you can't remember whether a file is named Letter to Tim or Letter to Tom, type "Letter to T?m" into the Named line—either Tim or Tom will match T?m. Similarly, you can find both Annual Report 96 and Annual Report 97, by typing "Annual Report 9?" into the Named line.

An asterisk stands for any string of characters. Typing "Letter to T*m" into the Named line would not only find Letter to Tim and Letter to Tom, but also Letter to Travel Management Team.

Searching by Date

The Date tab of the Find dialog box, pictured in Figure 9-11, allows you to input information about when the file or folder was created, modified, or last accessed. If you're thinking "I just looked at the file last week," you can enter that information on the Date tab, and cut down the search considerably.

The default setting on the Date tab is All Files, meaning that no information about the date of the file has been given. To specify date information:

1. Select the Find All Files radio button.

2. Choose Modified, Created, or Last Accessed from the drop-down menu.

3. If you want to specify a range of dates (as in "I worked on this last summer"), click the Between radio button, and specify dates, either by typing them into the boxes in month/day/year format, or by clicking entries on the drop-down

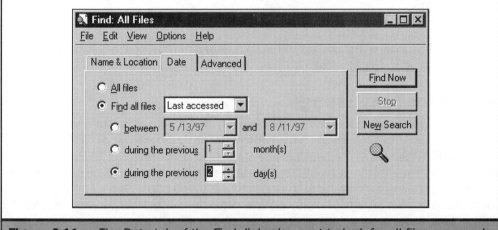

Figure 9-11.   *The Date tab of the Find dialog box, set to look for all files accessed during the previous two days*

calendars. (To change months on the calendars, click the arrows in the upper-left and upper-right corners.)

4. If you want to specify a time period from some time in the past through the present, click either the During The Previous *xx* Months or the During The Previous *xx* Days radio buttons. Then enter a number in the corresponding box.

When you are done, the highlighted radio buttons should make a coherent sentence. The entry in Figure 9-11 would read: Find All Files Accessed During The Previous 2 Days. Click Find Now to search.

Searching by Type

If you know, for example, that the file you want is a Word document, you can limit the search to files with a .doc extension. Click the Advanced tab on the Find dialog box and then select a file type from the drop-down Of Type list.

Searching by Size

If you know the file for which you're looking is several megabytes, don't waste time searching all those 50KB files, or vice versa. You can search large files only or small files only, but you can't search between two sizes. To specify a file size:

1. Click the Advanced tab of the Find dialog box. The Size Is setting consists of two boxes.

2. The left-hand box is a drop-down list that gives you a choice between At Least and At Most. Choose At Least to search for large files, At Most to search for small ones.

3. Type a number into the right-hand box to specify a limiting size.

When you are done, the line should make a coherent (if not particularly poetic) sentence, such as Size Is At Most 50KB.

Searching for Text Strings

The Find process can also search for text strings within documents. This makes for a much more time-consuming search than any of the other criteria, since Find has to look inside the files themselves, rather than just at the files' properties. For this reason, you should avoid using this feature if other criteria are already enough to narrow down the search. But text-string searching may be exactly what you need. For example, you could generate a list of all the letters you've written to your mother by searching for the phrase "Dear Mom".

To add a text string to your search, type it into the Containing Text line of the Name & Location tab of the Find dialog box. Unfortunately, this technique works for contiguous phrases only. Unlike online search engines, you can't search for a series of keywords, such as "Mom" and "Christmas".

Saving and Retrieving a Search

You can save a set of search parameters by selecting File | Save Search in the Find dialog box. The list of files found with that search is not saved. The parameters are saved as a file of type *Saved Search* (with extension .fnd). To perform the search in the future, just open the Saved Search file and click the Find Now button. Once a search has been saved, you can even share it with other people in the same ways that you would share any other file—by copying it to a floppy, or attaching it to e-mail.

Managing the Recycle Bin

Files and folders sent to the Recycle Bin may disappear from the folder tree, but Windows still stores them on your hard drive and keeps track of them. Eventually, one of four things happens:

- You get rid of things in the Recycle Bin, either by emptying it or by deleting some of the files and folders there.
- You retrieve files from the Recycle Bin and put them in some other folder (see "Recovering Objects from the Recycle Bin" in Chapter 8).
- The Recycle Bin gets full.
- You turn off the Recycle Bin so that deleted files aren't put there any more.

This section covers all these possibilities except the second one, which was covered in the previous chapter. In addition, this section tells you how to streamline the deleting process, should you want to do so.

Like most other things in Windows 98, the Recycle Bin has properties. To display them, right-click the Recycle Bin icon on the desktop, and choose Properties from the menu; or, select the Recycle Bin in a Folder or Windows Explorer window and click the Properties button on the toolbar. In either case, the Properties dialog box for the Recycle Bin is displayed, as in Figure 9-12. The Properties dialog box contains a Global tab, plus a tab for each hard drive on your system. Table 9-2 lists the properties of the Recycle Bin.

Emptying the Recycle Bin

Getting rid of old files serves two purposes: It clears useless files away so that you don't confuse them with useful files, and it reclaims the disk space they occupy. The first purpose is served by deleting a file—once it's in the Recycle Bin, you aren't going

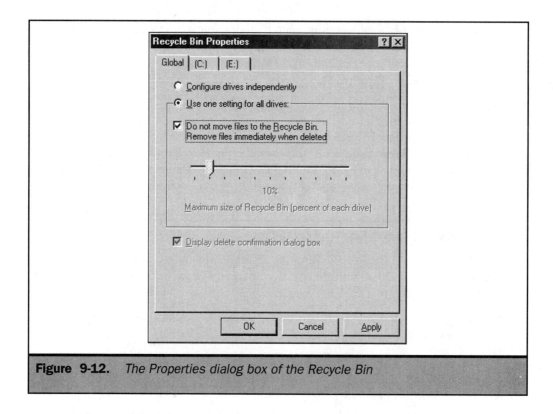

Figure 9-12. *The Properties dialog box of the Recycle Bin*

to open it or work on it by mistake. But a file in the Recycle Bin still takes up disk space: The space isn't reclaimed until the Recycle Bin is emptied.

To empty the Recycle Bin:

1. Open the Recycle Bin in either a Folder or Windows Explorer window.

2. Choose File | Empty Recycle Bin. A dialog box asks you to confirm your choice.

3. Click Yes. Windows empties the Recycle Bin.

4. Close the Recycle Bin.

Another method is to right-click the Recycle Bin and choose Empty Recycle Bin from the menu that appears.

To purge selected files or folders from the Recycle Bin without completely emptying it, open the Recycle Bin folder and delete the files in the usual way (see "Deleting Files and Folders" in Chapter 8). Objects deleted from an ordinary folder on a hard drive are sent to the Recycle Bin, but objects deleted from the Recycle Bin are really deleted.

Setting	Description
Configure drives independently	Allows you to use different settings on the tab for each hard disk.
Use one setting for all drives	Specifies that the settings on the General tab apply to all hard drives.
Do not move files to the Recycle Bin. Remove files immediately when deleted.	Specifies that when you delete files or folders, Windows deletes them directly rather than moving them to the Recycle Bin. The default setting is unselected, so that deleted files move to the Recycle Bin.
Maximum size of Recycle Bin (percent of each drive)	Specifies the maximum amount of disk space that the Recycle Bin can occupy, as a percentage of total disk space.
Display delete confirmation dialog box	Specifies that Windows ask you to confirm whenever you move a file to the Recycle Bin.

Table 9-2. *Properties of the Recycle Bin*

To purge only those objects that have been in the Recycle Bin a long time:

1. Open the Recycle Bin.
2. If the window is not already in Details view, choose View | Details.
3. Click the Date Deleted header to put the objects in order of date.
4. Use the enclosing-rectangle method to select all the objects deleted prior to a certain date (see "Selecting Files and Folders" in Chapter 8).
5. Click the Delete button on the toolbar, or press the DELETE key on the keyboard.
6. When the dialog box appears, asking whether you really want to delete these objects, click Yes.

Resizing the Recycle Bin

By default, the maximum size of the Recycle Bin on any hard drive is 10 percent of the size of the drive itself. For example, a 1GB hard drive has a maximum Recycle Bin size of 100MB. If you delete an object that would cause the Recycle Bin to exceed that size, Windows 98 warns you with an error message.

Having a maximum size for the Recycle Bin forces you not to clutter up your hard drive with useless, deleted files, and 10 percent is as good a maximum size as any. But you may decide to either raise this limit (because you don't want to empty the Recycle Bin right now) or lower it (because disk space is getting tight), either of which you can do by following this procedure:

1. Right-click the Recycle Bin icon on the desktop, and choose Properties from the menu; or, select the Recycle Bin in a Folder or Windows Explorer window and click the Properties button on the toolbar. You see the Properties dialog box of the Recycle Bin (Figure 9-12).

2. The Properties dialog box contains a Global tab, plus a tab for each hard drive on your system. If you want to change the maximum size setting for all the hard drives at once, set the new maximum size of the Recycle Bin (as a percentage of total drive space) by moving the slider on the Global tab. Then click OK. Skip the remaining steps.

3. If you want to reset the maximum Recycle Bin size for only a single drive, leaving the others the same, select the Configure Drives Independently radio button on the Global tab.

4. Click the tab showing the drive you want to change.

5. Set the slider on that tab.

6. Click OK.

Streamlining the Deletion Process

Many times, we've had cause to be thankful that Windows makes it so hard to get rid of a file on a hard drive. Four different actions are usually necessary: Deleting the file in the first place, confirming the deletion in a dialog box, emptying the Recycle Bin (or deleting the file from the Recycle Bin), and then confirming *that* decision in a dialog box. But even though this process can occasionally be a life-saver, it can also be tedious (particularly if you are trying to get rid of sensitive files that you don't want hanging around in the Recycle Bin).

 Even deleting a file from the Recycle Bin doesn't destroy the information right away; Windows makes the file's disk space available for reassignment, but doesn't immediately write over that disk space. People with the proper tools could still read the file. To prevent this, you need software that is not part of Windows 98.

Deleting Selected Files or Folders

If you want certain files and folders gone *right now*, with no shilly-shallying about confirmation dialogs boxes, Recycle Bins, or Undo buttons, hold down the SHIFT key while you drag the files and folders onto the Recycle Bin icon. (Of course, you should be *very sure* you want the files and folders gone, and that you haven't dragged along any extra objects by accident.) Holding down the SHIFT key while you click the Delete button (or press the DELETE key) is almost as quick: You have to click Yes in a confirmation dialog box, but the objects are deleted for real, not just sent to the Recycle Bin. Either method puts the deleted files or folders beyond the power of the Undo button.

Eliminating Confirmation Dialog Boxes

To eliminate the confirmation dialog box when you send something to the Recycle Bin:

1. Right-click the Recycle Bin icon on the desktop, and choose Properties from the menu; or, select the Recycle Bin in a Folder or Windows Explorer window and click the Properties button on the toolbar. You see the Properties dialog box of the Recycle Bin (Figure 9-12).

2. From the Global tab of the Properties dialog box, uncheck the box labeled Display Delete Confirmation Dialog Box.

3. Click OK.

Even after carrying out the preceding procedure, deleting something from the Recycle Bin (that is, getting rid of it for good) still requires a confirmation. If you decide later that you've made the deletion process too easy, you can reinstitute Delete Confirmation Dialog Boxes by repeating the preceding procedure, but checking the box in step 3.

Turning Off the Recycle Bin

If you want to stop sending deleted files to the Recycle Bin:

1. Right-click the Recycle Bin icon on the desktop, and choose Properties from the menu; or, select the Recycle Bin in a Folder or Windows Explorer window and click the Properties button on the toolbar. You see the Properties dialog box of the Recycle Bin (Figure 9-12).

2. On the Global tab of the Properties dialog box (or on the tab corresponding to the particular drive whose Recycle Bin you are turning off, if the Configure Drives Independently option is chosen on the Global tab), check the box labeled Do Not Move Files To The Recycle Bin. Remove Files Immediately On Delete.

3. Click OK.

After you have completed this procedure, files that you delete from your hard drive are gone, just as are files deleted from floppy drives. Files that were already in the Recycle Bin, however, remain there until you empty the Recycle Bin, delete them, restore them, or move them to another folder.

You can turn the Recycle Bin back on by following the same procedure, but unchecking the box in step 3.

 If you turn off the Recycle Bin, don't forget that you did. It remains off until you turn it on again.

Chapter 10

Backing Up Your Files

T he most important thing to say about backing up your files is: Back up your files. You can back up your files onto floppies, tapes, network servers, extra hard drives, recordable CDs, ZIP drives, or whatever you happen to have. How you back up your files is much less important than that you do it. If you have only a few files or folders to back up, you can use Windows Explorer or a Folder window to make the copies.

Windows 98 comes with a Backup program (written by Seagate Software) that makes backing up large numbers of files and folders reasonably painless. Your tape drive or ZIP drive may come with its own backup program. You use Backup to create Backup jobs (descriptions of what and how to backup), then backup them up. If a file is deleted or corrupted, you use Backup to restore the file from your backup.

Note *You might hope that Backup would work with Task Scheduler to do backups automatically, but unfortunately it does not.*

What Is Backing Up?

Backing up means making copies of your files so that you can get the information back should anything happen to the originals.

A great number of unfortunate things can happen to files:

- A physical disaster like fire, flood, or cat hair could destroy your computer.

- A hardware failure could make your disk unreadable.

- A software problem could erase some of your files. For example, installing an upgrade to an application program might accidentally write over the folders in which you stored the previous documents that were created with that application.

- On a business computer system, a disgruntled employee might steal, erase, or corrupt important files.

- A well-meaning roommate, spouse, child, or coworker might delete or alter files without realizing it.

- You might get confused and get rid of files you meant to keep.

Any one of these possibilities might seem remote to you. (We used to think so, until we learned better.) But when you put them all together, it's amazing how often having a recent backup copy of your files turns out to be handy.

What Should You Back Up?

Ideally you would back up everything, but (depending on the speed of your machine, the size of your hard drive, and the type of backup medium you use) a complete backup may take a considerable length of time. Once you have a complete backup to work from, updating that backup takes considerably less time.

A backup of only files that have changed or are new is calleed an *incremental backup*. A complete backup of all files and folders is called a *full backup* or *baseline backup*.

Backing up files is a little like flossing your teeth: We all know it's good for us, but few of us do it as often as we know we should. If it takes you a month or two to get around to doing a complete backup, you should consider backing up the following parts of your system more often.

- **Documents you are working on**   Many applications put new documents in the folder C:\My Documents by default. You may choose to put your documents anywhere you like, but for backing up purposes, it is convenient to have them organized in subfolders of some single, easy-to-find folder.

- **System files**   An early version of Microsoft Backup Help contained a list of the system files that it considered a "minimum backup." We reproduce it for you later in this chapter (see "Backing Up System Files").

- **Databases to which you regularly add data**   For example, if you use Quicken to balance your checkbook once a month, back up the file in which Quicken stores your checkbook data.

- **Correspondence, especially your e-mail files**   Letters and memos that you write are probably already in your documents folder(s). E-mail files, however, are usually stored in whatever folder you set up when you installed your e-mail program. If you use Outlook Express, the default folder is C:\Windows\ Application Data\Microsoft\Outlook Express (see Chapter 23). The Windows Address Book is in the folder C:\Windows\Application Data\Microsoft\Address Book (see Chapter 5).

- **Your Favorites menu**   The World Wide Web would be much less useful if you suddenly lost your list of favorite sites (see Chapter 24). For Internet Explorer, that list is a set of shortcuts in the folder C:\Windows\Favorites. Back up the whole folder. If you use Netscape Navigator, use Find to look for the file bookmark.htm.

If you back up these files frequently, a hard drive disaster is much less of an ordeal. Still, nothing beats the security of knowing that you have backups of *everything*.

Programs are not on the list of important items to back up. We assume that you (or the person who maintains your machine) still have the disks that you used to install the programs in the first place. Make sure you know where they are, and that they are in a safe place. If you lose your hard disk, reinstalling all of your software is a nuisance, but not a disaster. You would, however, lose all the special settings that you have made to personalize the software for yourself. If reselecting all of those settings would be an ordeal, then you need to either back up the program's entire folder, or find out which specific files contain those settings.

How Often Should You Back Up?

Different sources will tell you to back up your files daily or weekly or monthly, but the real answer is that you should back up your files as soon as you have created or changed something that you don't want to lose. You need to balance the regular nuisance of backing up your files against the possible ordeal of regenerating your creative work.

A document that you are working on changes daily, and a single day's work can be a lot to lose. System files change when you reconfigure the settings of your system, or when you install new hardware or software. Only you know how frequently your databases change, or how much e-mail you are willing to lose in an accident. Backing up these frequently updated files need not be as involved as a full system backup (see "What Should You Back Up?").

If your machine is part of a larger network, such as an office-wide local area network, check with the network administrator to see whether your hard drive is backed up automatically, and if so, how often. If it isn't, you might consider nagging an appropriate person. Programs exist that allow a network administrator to back up all the hard drives on the network automatically. Many offices do this every night, relieving the individuals of the need to worry about backups at all.

What Should You Do with Your Backup Disks or Tapes?

Put your backup disks or tapes in a safe place, preferably as far from your computer as practical. Backups that sit right next to your computer may be handy in a hardware or software crash—but they don't protect you at all in case of fire, theft, or sabotage.

What Is Microsoft Backup?

Microsoft Backup is a program that is included with Windows 98. Its purpose is to allow you to back up and recover files quickly and efficiently. Backup uses file compression techniques to use as little disk space as possible in storing your backups. It also is able to spread your backup files across many floppy disks or other removable media without confusing itself.

Run Backup selecting Start | Programs | Accessories | System Tools | Backup. If you do not find Backup there, you probably need to install it from the Windows 98 CD (see Chapter 3).

 *Microsoft Backup was written by Seagate Software, which sells a more full-featured version (see their web site at **http://www.seagatesoftware.com**).*

What Is a Backup Job?

Backing up files requires you to make a series of decisions: what files to back up, what device to store the backup files on, plus a number of more technical decisions, like whether to use compression. Ideally, you would make these decisions once for each type of backup that you regularly do (complete backup, document backup, mail backup, system backup, and so on), and then have the computer remember those decisions so that you don't have to go through them again every time you back up.

Microsoft Backup handles this situation by maintaining a list of *Backup jobs*. Its Backup Wizard helps you define a Backup job by leading you through all the necessary decisions (see "Using Microsoft Backup"). In the course of that process, you give the job a name. The next time you want to back up those same files and/or folders, you need only tell Backup the name of the job. When you perform a Backup job, the set of files that it creates is called a *backup set*.

Backing Up a Few Files or Folders

Even if you can't get around to a complete backup, you can protect yourself against the worst, without too much effort, by backing up your most valuable files and folders each day that you work on them.

Copying Files onto a Floppy Disk

Even on a slow system, it usually takes only a minute or two at the end of each day to pop in a floppy and copy the files you worked on that day. It's a good habit to develop.

If you typically work on only a few files each day, just find them in the right pane of a Windows Explorer window, and drag-and-drop them onto the floppy drive icon in the left pane. You can save yourself some clicks and drags by using the Send To menu (see "Using the Send To Menu" and "Dragging-and-Dropping Files and Folders" in Chapter 8). When you find a file you want to back up, select it in Windows Explorer or a Folder window, and then choose File | Send To (or right-click the file and choose Send To from the menu that appears). Your floppy drive should appear on the list of Send To destinations—choose it, and the file is copied to the floppy.

If you work on a larger number of files, look at the Start | Documents menu to make sure you remember them all. If you want to make sure you don't miss any, use Find to search for all files modified in the last day (see "Searching by Date" in Chapter 9). You can drag-and-drop files directly out of the Find All Files window onto a floppy icon in Windows Explorer or a Folder window. Or you can right-click any file in the Find All Files window and choose Send To from the menu.

Tip *If you use Find to list the files you've worked on today, construct your search in such a way as to avoid finding all the temporary files that Windows 98 creates in the course of a day. (If you do a lot of web browsing, there can be hundreds of them.) These files are contained in subfolders of the C:\Windows folder. Either use the Look In box of Find to constrain your search within a folder that doesn't contain C:\Windows, or specify a file type.*

Copying Files onto Larger Drives

Anything you can copy onto a floppy, you can copy onto a recordable CD, a ZIP drive or other removable disk, a second hard drive, or another machine on your local area network. The drag-and-drop techniques work in exactly the same way. If the drive (or folder) that you use for storing backup copies isn't already available on the Send To menu, you can add it (see "Using the Send To Menu" in Chapter 8).

A larger backup drive makes it less important to be selective about what you copy. A ZIP disk is approximately seventy times larger than a floppy, and a backup hard drive may be dozens of times larger yet. You probably can copy, without too much time or trouble, your entire documents folder (whether it is C:\My Documents or some other folder that you have chosen) at the end of each day. You probably can copy your entire e-mail folder, as well (see "What Should You Back Up?").

Using Microsoft Backup

Microsoft Backup has several advantages over a more informal system of copying key files onto floppies or other storage media:

- Backup copies files in a compressed form, so that they take up less disk space.

- Backup can spread a single backup job over several floppies or removable disks. This feature makes it possible to backup larger jobs.

- When you define a backup job, you decide once and for all what folders you want the job to back up. You don't have to go through the decision process again every time you do a backup.

- Backup is thorough. It doesn't lose its place when the phone rings.

- Backup is automated. Once the job starts, all you need to do is feed it a new disk if it asks for one. If you are backing up onto a tape drive, or some other medium with sufficient size, you don't need to do anything at all.

Backup is a system tool that you run by selecting Start | Programs | Accessories | System Tools | Backup. If you don't find Backup on the Start | Programs | Accessories | System Tools menu, you probably need to install it from your Windows 98 CD (see "Installing and Uninstalling Programs That Come with Windows 98" in Chapter 3). Open the Control Panel, open Add/Remove Programs, click the Windows Setup tab, choose the System Tools group of components, click Details, and choose Backup.

When you start Backup, the startup dialog box, shown in Figure 10-1, asks whether you want to create a new Backup job, run an existing job, or restore files from a previous Backup job. Click the appropriate radio button, and then click OK.

Note *If someone has configured Backup not to display the startup dialog box, you see the main backup window instead.*

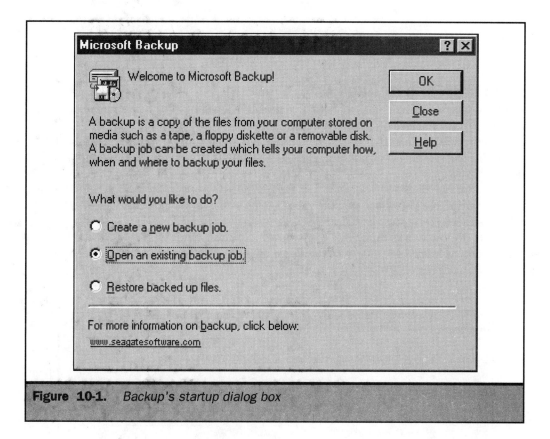

Figure 10-1.   *Backup's startup dialog box*

Creating a Backup Job with the Backup Wizard

Selecting Create A New Backup Job from Backup's startup dialog box (Figure 10-1)
starts the Backup Wizard, which takes you through the following decisions that you
need to make to create a new Backup job:

- Which files to back up
- Whether to back up all the selected files, or just the ones that have changed
  since the previous backup
- Where to store the backup data
- Whether to verify the backup
- Whether to use compression to make the backup file smaller
- What name to give the Backup job

You can also start the Backup Wizard by clicking the Backup Wizard button on the toolbar in the main Backup window (which will be shown later in Figure 10-3).

Selecting Files to Back Up

The first decision you need to make is whether this job should be a complete backup or a backup only of selected files. Selecting the Back Up My Computer radio button defines this job as a complete backup—it backs up everything under My Computer on the folder tree. If this is your choice, click Next, and you are ready to move on to the next section.

Selecting the Back Up Selected Files, Folders, And Drives radio button defines this job as a partial backup. Click Next to move to the screen shown in Figure 10-2, which is where you select the specific files, folders, and drives to back up.

This window works much like a Windows Explorer window: Each of your computer's disk drives (other than the floppy drive) are listed in the left pane (see

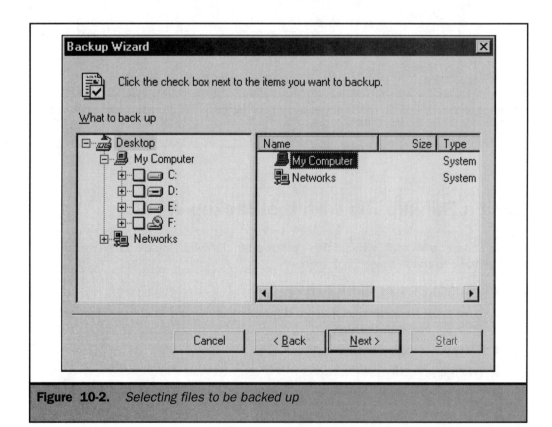

Figure 10-2. *Selecting files to be backed up*

"What Is Windows Explorer?" in Chapter 8). When a folder in the left pane is selected, its contents appear in the right pane. The boxes with plus or minus signs denote whether a folder is expanded. Click a plus sign to see the next level of the folder tree under a given folder.

The difference between this window and a Windows Explorer window is that each folder has a second check box next to it. Clicking this second check box puts a blue check mark in the box, indicating that the entire folder (and all its subfolders) have been added to the list of files and folders to be backed up. For example, clicking the check box next to the C drive icon adds the entire contents of the C drive to the Backup job.

If you want to back up some of the files on a drive, but not all of them, click the plus sign to expand the folder tree underneath that drive. This gives you an opportunity to decide to back up some of its subfolders but not others. Continue this process until you have selected only those files and folders that you want to be part of this Backup job. A gray check mark appears in the box next to a folder from which you have chosen to back up some, but not all, of its contents.

 Documents on your desktop are stored in the folder C:\Windows\Desktop. That's where they show up on Backup's folder tree.

Choosing a Baseline or an Incremental Backup

After you have chosen which files to back up, whether you have chosen all or only a few, the next screen of the Backup Wizard asks whether to back up all the files you selected, or only files that are new or changed since the previous backup. If this is the first time you have backed up these files, you should choose All Selected Files. Otherwise, you have a judgment call: If you choose New And Changed Files, the job runs faster, but you have to keep both the original full backup file and the incremental backup. Click one of the two radio buttons, and then click Next.

Choosing a Destination for the Backup File

The next screen of the Backup Wizard allows you to tell the Wizard where to store the backed-up files. The Where To Back Up box asks you to choose the backup medium: either a file on one of your computer's disk drives, or a backup medium, such as a cartridge tape drive. If you have no backup media on your system, File is the only choice on the pull-down menu.

If you choose File in the Where to Back Up box, a second box appears, asking for an address for the backup file. The Wizard may suggest a location, or the box may be blank. In either case, you can either type an address into the box, or click the button next to it—the Backup Wizard's version of a Browse button. Clicking the button opens a Browse window. Find a folder for the backup file, and then type a name for the file into the File Name box. Click Open to return to the Backup Wizard. The address of the backup file should be in the second box. Click Next.

In our tests, Backup gets confused when we try to back up onto a series of compressed disks, whether floppies, ZIP disks, or other removable media. It reaches the end of the disk unexpectedly, and the job terminates. The same jobs with uncompressed disks complete successfully.

If you choose a tape drive in the Where To Back Up box, no second box appears, because tapes don't allow you to select locations on the tape. Just click Next.

Choosing How to Back Up

The Backup Wizard's next screen consists of two check boxes:

- Compare original and backup files to verify data was successfully backed up.
- Compress the backup data to save space.

Both of these options cost you a little time, but they're worth it. Verifying that the backup was successful takes only a little less time than the backup itself, and it may seem unnecessary, but remember: Paranoia is what backing up is all about. If you had faith that things always work properly, you wouldn't be backing up at all.

Compression makes the backup file roughly half the size of the original files (less if the files you're backing up are already compressed). (See "What Is Disk Compression?" in Chapter 35.) When you're talking gigabytes, that's space worth saving. And for smaller jobs, compression can make the difference of being able to back up onto a single removable disk.

Naming and Starting a Backup Job

The final screen of the Backup Wizard asks for a name for the Backup job. Once you have given the job a name, check over the summary of the choices you have made. Since this is the last screen, the Next button is grayed out. You can either Cancel the job, back up to change some of your choices, or start backing up by clicking the Start button in the Backup Wizard's windows.

Choosing a Media Name

One more question pops up after you click Start: Backup asks you to provide a unique media name, and also suggests one—the job name followed by a number. This is intended to be the label that you put on the disks, tapes, or other media on which you store the backup. It allows you to tell the difference between this week's backup and last week's, as well as the difference between the second disk in the backup set and the fourth.

If you are reusing disks or tapes that you have used on this job before, replace Backup's suggested name with the media name on the disk label. Otherwise, accept Backup's suggestion (by clicking OK) and copy the new media name onto the disk or tape label.

Modifying an Existing Backup Job

Choosing Open An Existing Backup Job in Backup's startup dialog box (Figure 10-1) takes you to the Open Backup Job dialog box. This box contains a list of your previously defined Backup jobs. Click one of the jobs, and then click Open. You arrive at Backup's main window, shown in Figure 10-3. The main Backup window has two tabs: Backup and Restore. Modifying an existing Backup job is done on the Backup tab.

Note   *If you are already looking at the main Backup window, just click the Backup Job box and choose from the list which Backup job you want to modify.*

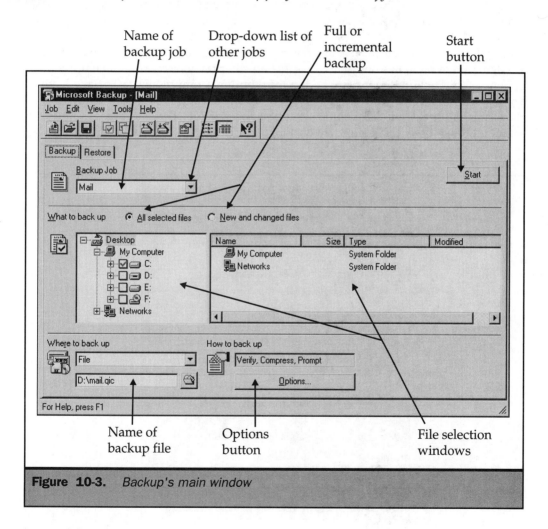

Figure 10-3.   *Backup's main window*

Revising Your Choices

The pieces of the Backup tab of the main Backup window should be familiar if you
have created a Backup job with the Backup Wizard: The Wizard's questions correspond
to the parts of this window (see "Creating a Backup Job with the Backup Wizard").
From here, you can change any of the decisions you made when you created the job:
the name of the job, the files to back up, whether to do a baseline or incremental
backup, and where to store the backup file. When you finish your editing, you can
either save the changes to this job, save the revised job under a new name, or not
save at all.

Decisions about verification and compression can be modified by clicking the
Options button. The Options dialog box appears with the General tab selected, as in
Figure 10-4. The check box corresponds to the verify/don't verify decision made
during the creation of the job (see "Choosing How to Back Up"). The When Backing Up
To Media set of radio buttons gives the same no-compression/maximum-compression
options as the Backup Wizard, but adds a third option, Compress Data To Save Time.
This option means exactly what it says: The resulting backup file is larger than if you
choose maximum compression, but running the Backup job takes less time. Table 10-1
shows all the options available when backing up files.

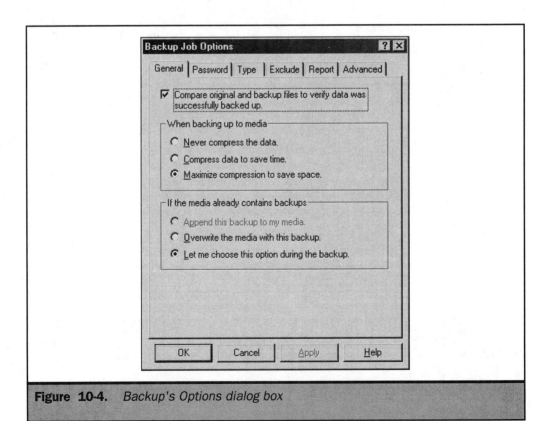

Figure 10-4.   *Backup's Options dialog box*

Tab	Setting	Description
General	Compare original and backup files to verify data was successfully backed up	Specifies that after backing up the files, Backup compares the backed-up copies to the original files.
General	Never compress the data	Turns off compression during backups.
General	Compress data to save time	Compresses the backed-up copies of the files without sacrificing for speed.
General	Maximize compression to save space	Compresses the backed-up copies of the files as much as possible, even if doing so slows down the backup operation.
General	Append this backup to my media	Specifies that Backup store this backup set after any existing information on the backup media.
General	Overwrite the media with this backup	Specifies that Backup delete the current contents of the backup media and replace it with the new backup set.
General	Let me choose this option during the backup	Specifies that when you perform a backup, Backup displays a dialog box that lets you choose whether to append the new backup set to the media or overwrite the existing data.
Password	Protect this backup with a password	Specifies that a password be necessary to restore files from backups. Type the same password in the Password and Confirm password boxes.

Table 10-1.   *Backup Job Options*

Tab	Setting	Description
Type	All selected files	Specifies that Backup include all the files you select in the backup.
Type	New and changed files only	Specifies that Backup include only files that are either new or that have changed since the last backup.
Type	Differential backup type	Specifies that Backup include only the files that have changed since the last backup for which the All Selected Files setting was selected.
Type	Incremental backup type	Specifies that Backup include only the files that have changed since the last backup for which the All Selected Files setting or the Incremental Backup Type setting was selected.
Exclude	Do not back up these file types	Specifies the list of file types to skip when backing up (for example, temporary and backup files). Click Add to add a file type to the list.
Report	List all files that were backed up	Specifies that the backup report include filenames of all files that were backed up.
Report	List files that were not backed up	Specifies that the backup report include files that were not backed up.
Report	List errors reported while backing up files	Specifies that the backup report include error messages.
Report	List warnings reported while backing up files	Specifies that the restore report include warning messages.

Table 10-1.   *Backup Job Options* (continued)

Tab	Setting	Description
Report	List unattended messages and prompts	Specifies that the backup report include all the messages that were responded to on your behalf during an unattended backup.
Report	Show report summary	Specifies that the backup report include a summary of the numbers of files backed up and other statistics.
Report	Perform an unattended backup	Specifies that Backup not prompt for any information during the backup operation.
Advanced	Back up Windows Registry	Specifies that when you back up the Windows program folder (usually C:\Windows), you back up the Windows Registry, too (see Chapter 40).

Table 10-1. *Backup Job Options* (continued)

Overwriting Backup Files

When you run a Backup job that has been run before, Backup creates a file of the same name as a file that already exists. The bottom set of radio buttons on the General tab of the Options dialog box addresses this situation. You have three options: Append This Backup To My Media (available only if the destination is a backup device such as a tape drive), Overwrite The Media With This Backup, and Let Me Choose This Option During The Backup.

Each of the three choices has its advantages. Overwriting takes the least space. Appending means that the old backup is still there, in case the new backup is deficient in some way. Choosing during the backup preserves your options, but because Backup will wait for you to make the decision before continuing, you must be present and paying attention during the backup.

Establishing a Password

Stealing a backup tape or disk is an easy way to get all of a person's important files. Moreover, since backups are needed in case of emergency only, you may not notice a stolen backup tape for some time. For these reasons, you may want to protect your backup with a password.

 If you forget the password on a Backup job, there is no one you can call to get it. Make sure you have a record of your password—somewhere other than in one of the files you are backing up. The best passwords are ones that are memorable to you, but not obvious to anyone else.

From Backup's main window, you can establish a password for a Backup job as follows:

1. Select the job name from the Backup Job drop-down list.
2. Click the Options button. The Options dialog box appears, as in Figure 10-4.
3. Click the Password tab.
4. Click the Protect This Backup With A Password check box.
5. Enter a password into the Password box.
6. Enter the same password into the Confirm Password box.
7. Click OK.

To remove a password from a Backup job, repeat these steps, but uncheck the check box in step 4. Then click OK.

Eliminating the Startup Dialog Box

You can set up Backup so that it opens directly into its main window (Figure 10-3), skipping the startup dialog box (Figure 10-1). First you need to get to the main window, which you can do by starting Backup, then clicking the Close button on the first screen of the Backup Wizard. From the main window:

1. Start Backup. The Backup Wizard starts.
2. Click Close to get out of the Backup Wizard, revealing Backup's main window.
3. Select Tools | Preferences.
4. Uncheck the Show Startup Dialog When Microsoft Backup Is Started check box.
5. Click OK.

You can still access the Backup Wizard and the Restore Wizard from the toolbar or from the Tools menu.

Running a Backup Job

Once you have created and named a Backup job, you can run it without going through the Backup Wizard.

Running a Backup Job from the Startup Dialog Box

To run an existing Backup job from the startup dialog box (Figure 10-1), select Open An Existing Backup Job. Backup presents you with a list of existing Backup jobs: Choose one by clicking its name, and then click Open. The main window appears, with the job already selected. Follow the instructions in the next section for running a Backup job from the main window.

Running a Backup Job from the Main Backup Window

To run an existing Backup job from the main Backup window (Figure 10-3):

1. Select the name of the job from the Backup job drop-down menu.

2. Check over the information about the job presented in the rest of the main window.

3. Click the Start button.

4. Answer any questions Backup asks (such as whether to overwrite previous Backup files). The Backup Progress box appears, as shown in Figure 10-5.

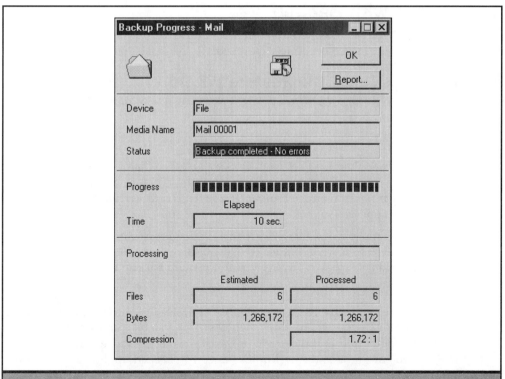

Figure 10-5. *The Backup Progress box*

5. If you are backing up onto floppies or other removable media, Backup may ask for additional disks from time to time. Insert the disks and deal with Backup's questions about media names (see "Choosing a Media Name").

6. At some point, the status line of this box announces that the job is complete, and tells you (if verification is part of the job) whether or not there were errors. If you want to look at the report on this job—which is worth doing if the verification showed errors—click the Report button. A text box appears. Close it when you are done reading it. The report is stored in the folder C:\Program Files\Accessories\Backup\Reports.

7. Click OK in the Backup Progress box.

You Can't Run a Backup Job Automatically

This lack is one of the biggest disappointments in Windows 98. When Backup opens, it waits for someone to tell it what job to run. There appears to be no way to tell it to just go ahead and run Job X if Task Scheduler wakes it up in the middle of the night. If you want the capability to have your files backed up automatically on a schedule, you'll have to find a different backup program.

Restoring Files with Backup

To restore files that you have backed up with Microsoft Backup, you can use the Restore Wizard, or you can select options yourself.

Restoring Files Using the Restore Wizard

To run the Restore Wizard to walk you through restoring one or more files, follow these steps:

1. Start Backup.

2. Select Restore Backed Up Files from Backup's startup dialog box (Figure 10-1), or, if Backup opens with the main Backup window (Figure 10-3), click the Restore Wizard button on the toolbar (the seventh button from the left). A list of Backup jobs appears.

3. Choose a Backup job, and then click Open to start the Restore Wizard, whose opening screen is shown in Figure 10-6. (You can exit the Restore Wizard at any point by clicking Cancel, returning you to the main Backup window, shown in Figure 10-3.)

4. The two boxes in Figure 10-6 show where the Restore Wizard thinks the backup data is stored: The upper box shows whether it is on a backup medium or in a file on the folder tree, and the lower box shows what the address of the file is. Unless you have moved the backup file since you backed up, this information should be correct. If it is correct, click Next. If it isn't correct, click the Browse

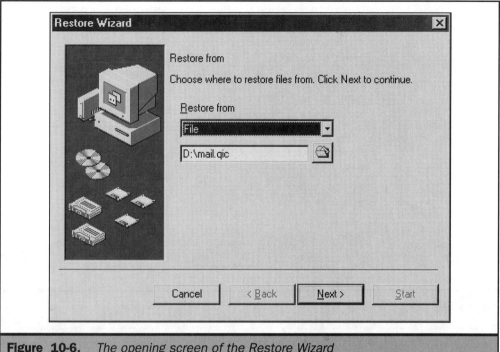

Figure 10-6. *The opening screen of the Restore Wizard*

button (the one with the folder icon on it), and find the backup file's current location. Then click Next. The Select Backup Sets box appears, shown in Figure 10-7.

5. If more than one backup set is in the box, select which sets you want to restore by clicking the check box next to their names. Selected sets have blue check marks in the boxes next to their names. Click OK.

6. A dialog box appears, allowing you to select which files to restore. This box works just like the box in the Backup Wizard in which you selected files to back up (see "Selecting Files to Back Up"). When you have chosen the files you want to restore, click Next.

7. A dialog box asks where to restore the files to, giving the choices Original Location and Alternate Location. If you choose Alternate Location, a second line appears inside of which you can type an address of a folder in which to put the restored files. Or you can click the Browse button next to this line and browse for a location. When you are done choosing a location for the restored files, click Next.

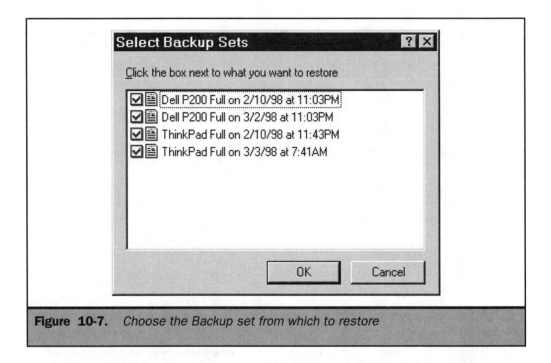

Figure 10-7.   *Choose the Backup set from which to restore*

8. A dialog box asks what to do if the destination folder already contains a file of the same name. Your options are to never overwrite, to choose whichever version of the file is newer, or to always overwrite. Pick one and click Start.

9. A dialog box asks whether the appropriate media is available. Make sure appropriate disks or tapes are inserted, and then click Yes. If the job has a password, Backup asks for it now. The restoring process begins.

10. A Restore Progress box appears, resembling the Backup Progress box shown in Figure 10-5. It asks for additional disks or tapes as needed, and announces when the job is complete.

11. If you want to read a report on the job (as you should if errors are reported), click the Report button. When you are done with the report, close it, returning to the Backup Progress box.

12. Click OK to end the restoration.

Restoring Files Using the Restore Tab

Alternatively, you can use the Restore tab on the main Backup window to select what to restore. Follow these steps:

1. Click the Restore tab in the main Backup window (Figure 10-3). Backup asks if you'd like to refresh the current view (that is, update the Backup window to display the information from your backup device.)

2. Click Yes. Backup displays a list of backup sets on the current backup device (each backup set is the result of running a Backup job). The list (Figure 10-7) shows the time and date that each backup set was made.

3. Choose the Backup set from which you want to restore files, and click OK. Backup displays the folders and files in that Backup set in the main Backup window, with the Restore tab selected (see Figure 10-8). If you are restoring from a tape, this can take a few minutes. Backup isn't restoring any files yet; it's just displaying filenames so you can choose what to restore.

4. Use the What To Restore section of the window to choose which files to restore. Click the plus sign to the left of drives or folders to see their contents, or click

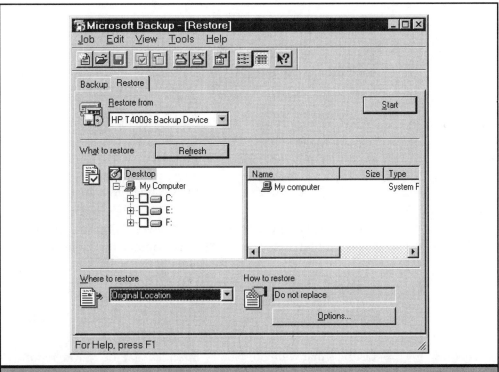

Figure 10-8.   *The Restore tab of the main backup window*

the folder icon. Click in the check box to the left of drives, folders, or files to select them for restoration.

5. The Where To Restore box is normally set to Original Location, to restore the file to the location from which it was backed up. Change this setting to Alternate Location if you want to specify a different folder to store the restored copy of the file. A box appears below the Where To Restore box in which you can specify the folder (click the little yellow folder button to the right of the box to choose a folder from the folder tree).

6. Click the Options button to choose other options for restoring files. Table 10-2 shows the options available when restoring files.

7. When you have selected the file(s) to restore, click the Start button in the main Backup window. If you are restoring from a tape or other removable media, Backup prompts you to put in the necessary tape or disk; do so and click OK. Then Backup restores the file or files.

Tab	Setting	Description
General	Do not replace the file on my computer (recommended)	Specifies that if a file with the same name in the same location already exists, Backup doesn't overwrite the existing file with the backed-up file.
General	Replace the file on my computer only if the file is older	Specifies that if a file with the same name in the same location already exists, Backup overwrites the existing file only if it is older than the backed-up file.
General	Always replace the file on my computer	Specifies that if a file with the same name in the same location already exists, Backup always overwrites the existing file.
Report	List all files that were restored	Specifies that the restore report include filenames of all files that were restored.
Report	List files that were not restored	Specifies that the restore report include files that were not restored.

Table 10-2.   *Restore Options*

Tab	Setting	Description
Report	List errors reported while restoring files	Specifies that the restore report include error messages.
Report	List warnings reported while restoring files	Specifies that the restore report include warning messages.
Report	List unattended messages and prompts	Specifies that the restore report include all the messages that were responded to on your behalf during an unattended restore.
Report	Show report summary	Specifies that the restore report include a summary of the numbers of files restored and other statistics.
Report	Perform an unattended restore	Specifies that Backup not prompt for any information during the restore operation.
Advanced	Restore Windows registry	Specifies that when Backup restores files, it restores the Windows registry, too.

Table 10-3. *Restore Options (continued)*

Backing Up System Files

An earlier version of Backup's Help recommended creating a "minimum backup set" consisting of the following:

- **The Windows Registry** The Registry is not an ordinary file appearing on the folder tree (see Chapter 40). Backup has a special way to add the Registry to a Backup job: Choose Job | Option from the Backup menu bar, or click the Options button on the Backup tab. When the Backup Job Options dialog box opens, choose the Advanced tab. Then check Back Up Windows Registry.

- **From the C folder** The files Autoexec.bat, Command.com, Config.sys, Io.sys, and Msdos.*

- **From the C:\Windows folder** All files of type .dat or .dao, Command.com, Dblbuff.sys, Emm386.exe, Explorer.exe, Himem.sys, Ifshlp.sys, Setver.exe, System.ini, Win.com, Win.ini, and Winver.exe.

■ **The following folders in their entirety**   C:\Windows\System, C:\Windows\Fonts, C:\Windows\Temp, C:\Windows\Start Menu, and C:\Program Files\Accessories\Backup.

This minimum backup set contains all the files you need to boot Windows and run the Backup program. In addition to being a good list of system files worth backing up, the minimal backup set serves a bootstrapping function: In the event of a complete loss of your files, recovering and reinstalling these files allows you to run Backup and restore the rest of the files you have backed up.

Chapter 11

Formatting and Partitioning
Disks

Before Windows 98 can use a hard disk or removable disk, the disk has to be prepared for use. Hard disks have to be *partitioned*, divided into one or more logical sections, using the FDISK program. Both hard disks and removable disks have to be formatted with a *file system*, the information that keeps track of which files are stored where on the disk. Windows 98 supports two file systems, FAT16 (the file system used in Windows 95) and the new FAT32. If you have a large disk (larger than 500MB), you may want to consider converting to FAT32.

On computers with Windows 98 pre-installed, the hard disk has already been partitioned (into a single large partition) and formatted, but if you install an additional hard disk or replace the original hard disk, you have to partition and format the new disk. Some disks (both hard disks and removable disks) come preformatted and some don't. Regardless of whether a disk is preformatted, you can reformat it to remove any existing files and make it a "clean" empty disk.

Each disk drive, including diskette and CD drives, has a drive letter assigned by Windows, but you can change these letters, or assign drive letters to folders, if you need to. You can also check how much free space is on any disk, and look at the properties of a disk.

This chapter describes how to partition and format hard disks, how to decide whether to use FAT32 (and how to convert to FAT32 if you decide to use it), how to assign drive letters to disk drives, how to check for free space, and how to control the way in which Windows 98 uses CD-ROMs.

What Are Partitions, File Systems, and Drive Letters?

Partitions and files systems determine how and where Windows 98 stores information on your disk. Drive letters determine how to refer to the disks on your computer.

What Is a Partition?

A *partition* is a section of a hard disk. Every hard disk must be partitioned before Windows 98 can use it. Normally a disk is set up as a single large partition spanning the entire disk, but there are some circumstances where it makes sense to use more than one partition. When you partition a disk, you allocate a fixed amount of space to each partition.

Each partition on a disk is marked with an operating system type. For historical reasons, the types for Windows 98 partitions are *Primary DOS partition* and *Extended DOS partition*. If you run more than one operating system on your computer, such as Windows 98 and UNIX or OS/2, you can create a partition for each operating system, and then start the computer from either of the partitions, depending on which operating system you want to use. (Unfortunately, you can't easily use multiple partitions to switch between Windows 98 and earlier versions of DOS or Windows, since they all start from the Primary DOS partition.)

What Is a File System?

A *file system* is the information that keeps track of which files and folders are stored where on the disk, and what disk space is free. Windows' file system includes a *FAT*, or *File Allocation Table*, which stores information about each *sector*, or physical block of storage space, on the disk.

Microsoft supports two different file system types: the older FAT16 (with a File Allocation Table that can store 16-bit entries) and the newer FAT32 (which stores 32-bit entries).

What Are the FAT16 and FAT32 File Systems?

FAT16 dates back to DOS 3.0, while *FAT32* was introduced with the OSR2 update to Windows 95. Each partition on a hard disk and each removable disk must be formatted with either a FAT16 or FAT32 file system, but it's possible (and often desirable) to have on the same system some disks with one format and some with the other format.

FAT32 is designed for large partitions and disks, larger than 500MB, and offers no significant benefits when used on smaller disks. FAT32 offers these advantages on large disks:

- Nearly unlimited partition sizes. A single FAT16 partition can be no larger than 2GB, while a FAT32 partition can be thousands of gigabytes, larger than any disk likely to be available in the near future.

- More efficient use of space. FAT32 allocates disk space in 2K chunks, while FAT16 on a large disk allocates space in 32K chunks, wasting a lot of space on small files.

FAT16 offers these advantages on smaller disks:

- Backwards compatibility. Disks can be read and written by earlier versions of DOS and Windows, back to DOS 3.0 and Windows 2.0.

- Disks and partitions can be compressed (see Chapter 35).

- DOS and 16-bit Windows programs can access FAT16 file systems somewhat faster than FAT32.

Tip *Disks and partitions less than 500MB have to be FAT16. Partitions larger than 2GB have to be FAT32. Partitions between 500MB and 2GB can be either FAT16 or FAT32, but should be FAT32, unless you plan to use disk compression or expect to use the disk with an older version of DOS or Windows. If you're not sure whether to use FAT16 or FAT32, use FAT16, since Microsoft provides a utility to convert existing FAT16 file systems to FAT32, if you change your mind later.*

How Big Should You Make Partitions?

Most often, you allocate all the space on a hard disk to the Primary DOS partition, which Windows treats as a single logical disk drive using a single drive letter (drive C for the first hard disk). You can also allocate some of the space to the Primary DOS partition and some to an Extended DOS partition, which can, in turn, be subdivided into multiple logical disks.

Earlier versions of DOS and Windows had limits on the size of a single logical disk: 32MB for the obsolete FAT12 file system used by DOS 1.x and 2.x, and 2GB for FAT16. Therefore, disks larger than these size limits had to be partitioned into multiple logical drives. (One of the authors used a 500MB disk on a DOS 2.0 server, which was partitioned into logical drives D through O.) FAT32 removes the size limit for the foreseeable future, but in some cases, it still makes sense to have more than one DOS partition.

If you want to use disk compression (described in Chapter 35), you have to make each compressed partition less than 2GB, since compression works only on FAT16 file systems. If you want a disk to be usable from earlier versions of Windows and DOS, you also need to use FAT16 and make each partition less than 2GB. In some cases, it's useful to have a separate partition to use as a scratch area that you can reformat to quickly wipe out its contents and start afresh.

What Are Drive Letters?

Every partition, logical drive, and removable disk available to Windows has a *drive letter*. Drive A is the diskette drive, and drive B is reserved for a second diskette. Hard disk partitions are assigned letters in order. Drive C is the Primary DOS partition on your first hard disk. If there are logical drives in an Extended DOS partition, they are assigned letters next. If you have more than one hard disk, the partitions on those disks are assigned letters next. Finally, each removable disk, such as a CD-ROM or ZIP disk, is assigned a letter, with the order of the letters being arbitrary. Any remaining letters can be used for network drives.

On a typical simple system, the diskette is A, the hard disk is C, and the CD-ROM is D.

Although not recommended, you can add your own drive letters to the ones that Windows assigns to each drive, using the DOS SUBST command to assign letters to folders (see "Choosing Your Own Drive Letters").

What Are the Properties of Disk Drives, Partitions, and Logical Drives?

Windows 98 stores a set of properties for each installed disk drive. To see the Properties dialog box for a disk drive, choose Start | Settings | Control Panel, open the

System icon, click the Device Manager tab, and click View Devices By Type (see "Using the Device Manager" in Chapter 15). If the Disk Drives entry does not already show a list of drives, double-click the Disk Drives icon to get the list. Click a drive and click the Properties button.

The Properties dialog box for a disk drive includes three tabs—General, Settings, and Driver, as shown in Figure 11-1. Table 11-1 lists the properties of a disk drive.

Each item on your system that has a drive letter—each hard disk, floppy disk, removable disk, and logical drive—also has properties. You can display these properties from a Folder window or Windows Explorer window: right-click the drive and choose Properties from the menu that appears. You see the Properties dialog box shown in Figure 11-2. Table 11-2 lists the settings on the General and Tools tabs. The Tools tab doesn't appear for disks you can't write on, such as CD-ROM drives. The Compression tab doesn't appear for disks you can't compress, such as FAT32 partitions (see Chapter 35). If you use a local area network, the Sharing tab appears (see "Sharing Disk Drives" in Chapter 32). If you have installed a hard-disk housekeeping program like Norton Utilities, additional tabs may appear.

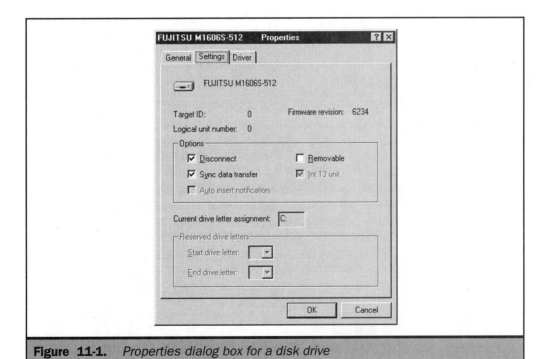

Figure 11-1. *Properties dialog box for a disk drive*

Tab	Setting	Description
General	Device type	Set to "Disk drives" by Windows.
General	Manufacturer	Specifies the manufacturer of the disk drive, if known.
General	Hardware version	Specifies the version number of the disk drive hardware, if known.
General	Device status	Shows the current status of the disk drive.
Settings	Target ID	For SCSI disks, the SCSI device number (see "SCSI Device Numbers" in Chapter 15).
Settings	Firmware revision	For SCSI disks, specifies the version number of the firmware on the disk.
Settings	Local unit number	For SCSI disks, always zero. (Used for tape and CD-ROM changers.)
Settings	Disconnect	For SCSI disks, whether the disk can continue working while the SCSI controller manages a different device. This setting is usually selected.
Settings	Sync data transfer	For SCSI disks, whether the disk can handle fast synchronous data transfer. This setting should be selected for all disks except CD-ROMs unless the disk is acting unreliable.
Settings	Auto insert notification	For CD-ROM drives, specifies that the drive notify Windows when you insert a CD.
Settings	Removable	Specifies whether you can remove the disk from this drive. For example, floppy disks, ZIP disks, and Jazz disks are *removable disks*, while hard disks are not.
Settings	Int 13 unit	Specifies that this disk drive is compatible with the antiquated real-mode BIOS calls for disk access (almost all disks are). If the disk is compatible, you can't change this setting.
Settings	DMA	Specifies that this disk drive uses Direct Memory Access to communicate with the computer (see "DMA Channels" in Chapter 15).

Table 11-1. *Properties of a Disk Drive*

Tab	Setting	Description
Settings	Current drive letter assignment	Specifies the drive letter assigned to this disk drive.
Settings	Start drive letter/End drive letter	Specifies the starting and ending letters for the range of drive letters than can be used for the partitions on partitioned removable disks.
Driver	Provider/Date	Specifies the source and date of the driver used for this disk drive. Many drivers come with Windows 98.
Driver	Update Driver	Runs the Update Device Driver Wizard to look for a more recent driver for your disk drive. The Wizard can look on the Windows CD (or floppies) or can connect to the Internet to look for a driver.

Table 11-1.   *Properties of a Disk Drive* (continued)

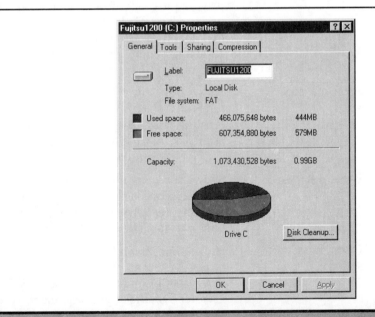

Figure 11-2.   *Properties dialog box for a disk, partition, or logical disk*

Tab	Setting	Description
General	Label	Specifies the name of the disk, which you can edit.
General	Type	Specifies whether this disk is a *local disk* (disk connected to your own computer), *network disk* (hard disk connected to a computer you can access over a network), floppy disk, CD-ROM drive, *RAM drive* (memory that simulates a disk drive), or removable disk drive.
General	File system	Specifies the file system used on the disk: FAT16 or FAT32.
General	Used space	Specifies how much disk space is occupied by files (including files in the Recycle Bin).
General	Free space	Specifies how much disk space is available for use.
General	Capacity	Specifies the total capacity of the disk drive; a pie chart shows how much is in use. Click the Disk Cleanup button to look for and delete unneeded files (see "Deleting Temporary Files Using Disk Cleanup" in Chapter 34).
Tools	Error-checking status	Shows how long it has been since you ran ScanDisk on this disk drive (see "Testing Your Disk Structure with ScanDisk" in Chapter 34). Click the Check Now button to run Scan Disk.
Tools	Backup status	Shows how long it has been since you ran Microsoft Backup on this disk drive (see Chapter 10). Click the Backup Now button to run Microsoft Backup.
Tools	Defragmentation status	Shows how long it has been since you ran Disk Defragmenter on this disk drive (see "Defragmenting Your Disk" in Chapter 34). Click the Defragment Now button to run Disk Defragmenter.

Table 11-2.   *Properties of a Disk, Partition, or Logical Disk*

Partitioning a Disk with the FDISK Program

When you buy a new computer or hard disk, you receive it ready for use—already partitioned and formatted. If, however, you are adding new disk drives, or if you want to create a computer system that can run one of several operating systems—such as switching between Windows 98 and UNIX—you may need to partition a disk yourself.

To partition a hard disk, you use the FDISK program, a DOS-mode program that survives nearly unchanged from the early 1980s. To start FDISK, select Run | Start, type **fdisk**, and then press ENTER.

If your disk is larger than 500MB, FDISK first asks whether you want to use FAT32. Press Y, unless you need to use FAT16 (see "What Are the FAT16 and FAT32 File Systems?"). If you have more than one physical hard disk, FDISK asks which disk you want to work on. You then should see the main FDISK screen, as Figure 11-3 shows.

To create a new partition for Windows, select 1. FDISK "knows" what combinations of partitions are valid, and suggests creating a new Primary DOS partition if none exists, and otherwise (rarely) suggests an Extended partition. FDISK then suggests allocating all available space on the disk to the partition, which usually is the right thing to do, unless you want to reserve space for other partitions or deliberately limit the size of a partition. Note that the Extended partition will be subpartitioned into

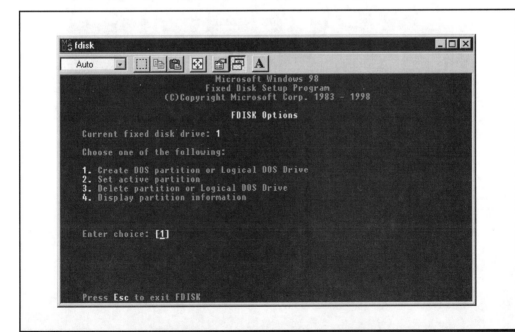

Figure 11-3. *The FDISK program*

logical drives. Thus, if you have a 2GB disk and want four 500MB partitions, for example, you should assign 500MB to the Primary DOS partition and the remaining 1.5GB to the Extended partition. After creating each partition, press ESC to return to the main FDISK menu.

If you create an Extended partition, you have to create logical drives in that partition. In the main FDISK menu, press 1 and then 3 to create logical drives. Again, FDISK suggests creating a single large logical drive, which is usually the best idea, unless you need more than one logical disk or need smaller partitions for compatibility with earlier versions of DOS and Windows. Continuing with the preceding example, to create three 500MB logical drives, tell Windows to create a 500MB logical drive, and then return to the logical-drive creation screen two more times to create the other two drives. (Due to rounding, the last drive may be a little more or less than 500MB. That's normal and creates no problems.)

After you create your partitions, press 4 on the main FDISK menu to look at a list of the partitions. Figure 11-4 shows the arrangement on one of our computers. We divided the disk in half: half for Windows 98 and half for UNIX. There's a 403MB Primary DOS partition for Windows 98 (1/4 of the Windows half), and a 1596MB

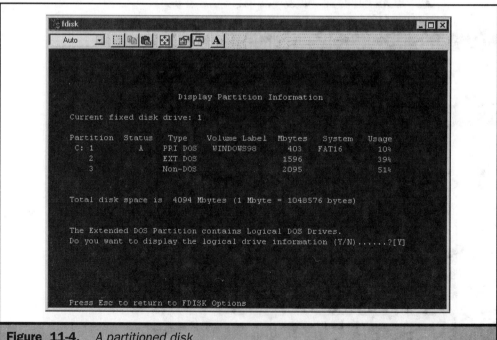

Figure 11-4. *A partitioned disk*

Extended DOS partition. The 2095MB non-DOS partition contains a UNIX system. Press Y to see the logical drives in the Extended DOS partition (not shown here, but it's a single large drive).

Press ESC at the main FDISK menu to exit. If you've created new partitions or logical drives, FDISK reboots your computer so that Windows notices what you've done.

Selecting the Active Partition

If you partition your disk among multiple operating systems, one of the partitions is the *active partition*, which is the partition from which your computer starts. If you run Windows only, the Primary DOS partition is always active.

To switch to another operating system in a different partition, run FDISK, press 2 to change the active partition, set that system's partition as active, and then reboot. To return to having Windows start when you reboot the computer, use the other system's equivalent of FDISK to make the Primary DOS partition active, and then reboot.

If you switch systems frequently, you'll probably want to install a *boot manager* program, which lets you select which partition to start from each time you restart your computer. Nearly every operating system other than Windows provides a boot manager.

Repartitioning a Disk

Repartitioning a disk is unpleasant at best. First, back up all the useful data in the partitions that you want to change. Then run FDISK and select 2 to delete partitions or logical drives. FDISK is very reluctant to delete them, since files in those partitions are lost, so you'll have to confirm about six times that you really want to do so. (This is not a bad idea: FDISK's skepticism has saved us from some serious mistakes.) If you want to delete the Extended DOS partition, you first have to delete all the logical drives in the partition.

Once the old partitions or logical drives are deleted, you create new ones, as previously described, and then reload the backed up data.

Third-party disk utilities, such as Partition Magic, make this process somewhat easier and permit a few kinds of changes, without backing up and reloading everything, but we still recommend that you avoid repartitioning whenever possible.

Choosing Your Own Drive Letters

Whenever possible, we recommend that you use the drive letters that Windows assigns (see "What Are Drive Letters?"). If you can't use the letters that Windows assigns by default (for example, you are using an antiquated program that expects files to be on certain drives), you have two options: change the letters in Windows, or use the DOS SUBST command to create new letters.

Changing the Drive Letters that Windows Uses

In some cases, you can persuade Windows to assign different drive letters to your drives. The process is lengthy but straightforward:

1. Choose Start | Settings | Control Panel.
2. In the Control Panel window, open the System icon.
3. Click the Device Manager tab, then click the View Devices By Type radio button.
4. One of the icons in the window is labeled Disk Drives. If it's not already showing a list of your drives, double-click the Disk Drives icon to get the list.
5. In that list, select the drive whose letter(s) you want to change, and then click the Properties button at the bottom of the window. This opens the properties dialog box for your disk.
6. In the Properties dialog box, click the Settings tab (see Figure 11-1). You see Current Drive Letter Assignment with a box listing the current drive letter(s).
7. If the box is white, you can enter new drive letters to take effect the next time you reboot. If the box is gray, as it is more often than not, you can't immediately change the letters for this disk, because the software driver for your disk doesn't support it. However, you can set the Reserved drive letters at the bottom of the window to give a range of letters from which you'd like the system to select the disk's drive letter.
8. Either way, click OK when you're done.

Assigning Drive Letters to Folders

You can use the DOS SUBST command to assign new drive letters that correspond to folders on existing disks. Open an MS-DOS window and type the SUBST command in the following format (press ENTER after typing the command):

SUBST N: C:\MYAPP

This command makes the drive letter N a synonym for the folder C:\Myapp. You can use any unused drive letter and the address (pathname) of any folder. The new substituted drive letter is available immediately. If the path of your folder uses long names, then in the SUBST command, you have to use the MS-DOS name equivalent, as shown by the DOS DIR command (see "What Are MS-DOS Names?" in Chapter 8). To disconnect a SUBSTed drive letter, type the following:

SUBST N: /D

If you use a SUBSTed drive on a regular basis, put the SUBST command in your Autoexec.bat file so that it's available every time you start Windows (see Chapter 39).

Formatting a Disk

Every disk must be formatted before you can use it. Formatting a disk writes the file system, the low-level structure information needed to track where files and folders will be located on the disk (see "What Is a File System?").

Formatting a Hard Disk

To format a hard disk, follow these steps:

1. Run Windows Explorer or open a Folder window that displays the drive you want to format.

2. Right-click the icon for the drive, and then choose Format in the menu that pops up. You see the Format dialog box (Figure 11-5). Almost none of the fields in the window, except for the volume label, are applicable to hard disks.

3. Type a drive label in the Label box (if the box is blank, or if you want to change the existing label), and then click the Start button in the Format dialog box.

4. If the drive contains files or folders, Windows asks whether you really want to reformat the disk, since existing files will be lost. Assuming you want to format

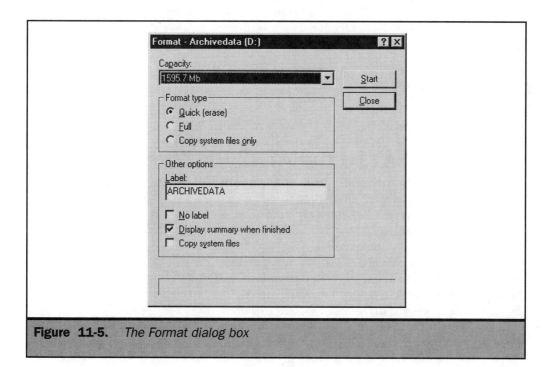

Figure 11-5. *The Format dialog box*

the disk, choose Yes to do so. Formatting can take several minutes, because the process involves reading the entire disk to check for bad spots.

You can't format the disk from which you are running Windows; Windows displays an error message saying that the disk contains files that Windows is using. You can't format a compressed drive or CD-ROM either (see Chapter 35).

Formatting a Removable Disk

Formatting a removable disk is just like formatting a hard disk, except that more of the format options are available. If you just want to erase the files on a previously formatted disk without rechecking for bad spots, select Quick Format or Quick (Erase) on the Format dialog box. If you want to be able to boot from the disk, choose Copy System Files. (We don't recommend this choice; make an emergency boot disk instead, as described in Chapter 37.) Then click the Start button in the Format dialog box.

Checking Free Space

You can easily see how much free space is available on any drive. Run Windows Explorer or open a Folder window, right-click the drive, and then select Properties from the menu that appears. You see a Properties dialog box with a pie chart like the one in Figure 11-2 (if the General tab isn't selected, click it). On regular disk partitions, the amount of free space shown is computed exactly, while on compressed drives the amount is an estimate.

Click the Disk Cleanup button to look for and delete unneeded files (see "Deleting Temporary Files Using Disk Cleanup" in Chapter 34).

Converting FAT16 to FAT32 Partitions

If you have an existing hard disk partition larger than 500MB that uses the older FAT16 file system, you can convert it in place to FAT32 (see "What Are the FAT16 and FAT32 File Systems?"). Conversion is a one-way process, so keep in mind that once you convert it, you can neither use the disk with older versions of Windows and DOS, nor create compressed drives on that disk.

If you do want to convert, run the FAT32 converter. Choose Start | Programs | Accessories | System Tools | FAT32 Converter. The Converter guides you through the process of conversion, telling you which drives you can convert, doing the conversion on a selected drive, and rebooting when done.

If you regret having done the conversion, you have to repartition: back up the data, delete the partition, recreate a FAT16 partition, and reload the data (see "Repartitioning a Disk"). Alternatively, some third-party programs, such as Partition Magic, can do a reverse FAT32-to-FAT16 conversion in place (for information about Partition Magic, see the web page at **http://www.powerquest.com**).

Using CD-ROMs and Audio CDs

Since CD-ROMs and audio CDs are prerecorded at the factory, no preparation is needed to use them. Just stick them in the drive, and Windows recognizes them. If a CD-ROM contains an AutoRun program (that is, a file named Autorun.inf in the root folder of the CD-ROM, containing instructions for what program to run), Windows runs it. On audio CDs, Windows runs the CD Player application automatically, turning your $2,000 computer into a so-so imitation of a $199 CD player (see "Playing Audio CDs with CD Player" in Chapter 17).

Tip   *If you don't want the Autorun program on a specific CD-ROM to run, or you don't want Windows to start playing an audio CD, open the drive, insert the disk, and hold down the SHIFT key while closing the drive—keep the SHIFT key down until you are sure that no program has started.*

You can turn off Windows' autorun feature, so that CD-ROM programs don't run and audio CDs don't play automatically:

1. Choose Start | Settings | Control Panel. In the Control Panel, open the System icon and click the Device Manager tab.

2. Click the View Devices By Type radio button, click the plus sign next to CDROM, click the CD-ROM drive, and click Properties. You see the properties dialog box for your CD-ROM drive.

3. Click the Settings tab and then click the Auto Insert Notification check box until it doesn't contain a check mark.

4. Click the OK button on both dialog boxes.

The Complete Reference

Part III

Configuring Windows for Your Computer

Chapter 12

Setting Up Your Start Menu and Taskbar

You probably learned to use the Start menu and the Taskbar almost as soon as Windows 98 was installed on your computer. The Start menu is usually the first method you learn how to use to start programs (see "Starting Programs from the Start Menu" in Chapter 2). For programs you run often, you might create shortcuts on your desktop to avoid having to use the Start menu (see "Using Shortcuts" in Chapter 9). But chances are good that you continue to use the Start menu—at least for programs that you don't use often, since it's not worth cluttering up the desktop with shortcuts that you hardly ever use.

The Start menu can contain so many submenus and commands that you can lose programs in it; luckily, you can search the Start menu for the program you want. To make the Start menu easier to use, you may want to reorganize it, putting frequently used programs on the Programs menu and demoting other programs to submenus. You can also add or reorganize the items on your Favorites menu. Windows 98 has added features that make the Windows 98 Start menu easier to edit than the Windows 95 Start menu was. You can change the size of the icons on the Start menu, too.

The Task Manager section of the Taskbar shows you which programs you're already running. You can customize the Taskbar, too. The Taskbar normally appears at the bottom of the screen, but you can move it, expand it, shrink it, or even make it disappear. You can also include toolbars on the Taskbar—you can display any number or none at all of the four predefined toolbars, display toolbars on the desktop, and even define your own toolbars.

What Is the Start Menu?

The *Start menu* appears when you click the Start button on the Taskbar. These are the items that are usually on the Start menu:

- **Windows Update**   Connects to Microsoft's web site to find out about, download, and install updates to Windows 98 (see "Updating Your Computer with Windows Update" in Chapter 38). Choose this command if you want to see whether updates to Windows 98 are available for download.

- **Programs**   Displays the *Programs menu*, a menu of programs you can run. This menu is defined by the contents of the C:\Windows\Start Menu\Programs folder, which you can change (see "Reorganizing the Start Menu"). Choose the Programs menu when you want to run a program.

- **Favorites**   Displays the *Favorites menu*, a list of the documents and files that are in the Favorites folder, at C:\Windows\Favorites. You can change the contents of this folder to change the items on the Favorites menu. Choose the Favorites menu when you want to open one of the files that you've put in your Favorites folder. (See the next section for more information about Favorites.)

■ **Documents**   Displays the _Documents menu_, a list of the documents that you have opened recently. To open one of the documents, choose it from the list. Windows 98 runs the program that handles that type of file, and then opens the document in that program.

■ **Settings**   Displays a menu of commands you can use to control how Windows 98, your desktop, and your printers work. The Control Panel command helps you install software and change your Windows 98 settings (see "What Is the Control Panel?" in Chapter 1). The Printers command helps you see the status of your printers (see Chapter 16). The Taskbar & Start Menu command helps you customize the Taskbar and the commands that appear on the Start menu. The Folder Options command helps you customize your desktop, Folder windows, and Windows Explorer windows (see "Changing How the View Settings Work" in Chapter 9). The Active Desktop command helps you display web pages on your desktop (see "What Is Active Desktop?" in Chapter 13). The Windows Update command allows you to update Windows from the Internet (it's the same as the Windows Update command that appears on the Start menu, described earlier in this section). Applications or utility programs may add other commands to the Settings menu.

■ **Find**   Displays a menu of the types of things that Windows 98 can help you find. The Files or Folders command searches your disks for files and folders (see "Finding Files and Folders" in Chapter 9). The Computer command searches for computers by name if your computer is part of a local area network (see "Finding Computers on the Network" in Chapter 31). The On the Internet command runs your web browser to search the Internet for information (see "Finding What You Want on the Web" in Chapter 25). The People command can search for people's addresses by using your own Windows Address Book or various Internet address search pages (see "Storing Addresses in the Address Book" in Chapter 5). Applications or utility programs may also add other commands to the Find menu.

■ **Help**   Displays online help (see Chapter 6).

■ **Run**   Lets you run a program by typing the name of the file that contains it (see "Starting Programs from the Run Dialog Box" in Chapter 2).

■ **Log Off**   If your computer is on a local area network, this command appears, allowing you to log off from one user name and log on as another (see "Logging In and Out" in Chapter 30 for peer-to-peer networks, or Chapter 31 for NetWare or Windows NT networks).

■ **Suspend**   If your computer has a suspend mode, the command Suspend appears on the Start menu, allowing you to put your computer in a state of suspended animation that uses less power than when it's fully turned on (see "Suspending Windows 98" in Chapter 1).

■ **Shut Down** Displays the Shut Down Windows dialog box. Choose Shut Down if you are ready to turn off your computer (see "Shutting Down Windows 98" in Chapter 1). Choose Restart to restart your computer (see "Restarting Windows 98" in Chapter 1). Choose Restart in MS-DOS Mode to shut down Windows 98 and run MS-DOS (see "Starting DOS Programs" in Chapter 41).

What Is the Programs Menu?

The Programs menu, which you display by choosing Start | Programs, shows a list of the programs you can run. It's the most commonly used part of the Start menu, and it's the part that you can customize to the greatest extent. The Start and Programs menus are hierarchical: that is, you can add menus and submenus to them. The Start menu includes the Program command, which displays the Programs menu, which can contain commands which in turn display other menus and submenus.

Figure 12-1 shows a Start menu, the Programs menu that appears when you choose Programs from the Start menu, the Accessories menu that appears when you choose Accessories from the Programs menu, and the Games menu that appears when you chose Games from the Accessories menu.

When you install new programs, the installation program is likely to add a folder or item to the Start menu or (more likely) to the Programs menu. You may prefer to put these new items in a submenu of the Programs menu, or perhaps eliminate them from the Start menu completely. The Start menu in Figure 12-1 has been customized with the addition of three choices: New Office Document, Open Office Document, and WinZip. Several commands have been added to the Programs menu, too. You can control what appears on the Programs menu (and its submenus) by editing the contents of the C:\Windows\Start Menu\Programs folder.

What Are Favorites and the Favorites Menu?

You can add frequently used files, folders, web pages, and programs to the *Favorites menu*. The Favorites menu (which you display by choosing Start | Favorites) displays the contents of the Favorites folder (C:\Windows\Favorites). The Favorites menu is easy to access, not only from the Start menu, but also from Folder windows, Windows Explorer windows, and most Open and Save As dialog boxes. The Favorites folder is usually used to store shortcuts to frequently used files, folders, and programs, but you can also store files there (just like any other folder).

You can edit and organize the items that appear on the Favorites menu by organizing the shortcuts in the C:\Windows\Favorites folder.

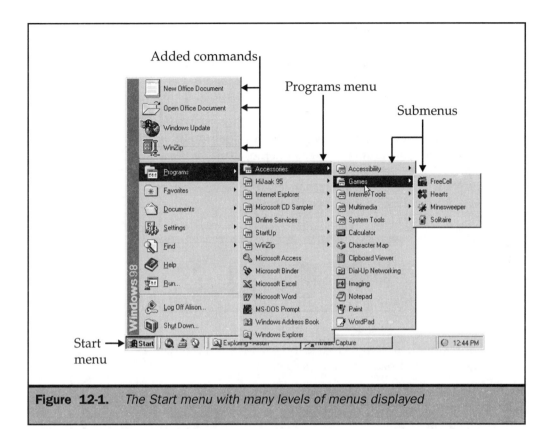

Figure 12-1.   *The Start menu with many levels of menus displayed*

What Is the Document Menu?

Choosing Start | Documents displays a list of recently used files. You can use the *Documents menu* to open a file—just click the file, and the file's application opens to display it. You may find that a recently used file does not appear on the Documents menu—that's because not all applications update the Documents menu.

    If you want to delete the contents of the Documents menu, choose Start | Settings | Taskbar & Start Menu and click the Clear button on the Start Menu Programs tab of the Taskbar Properties dialog box.

What Is the Taskbar?

The Taskbar is a row of buttons and icons that usually appears at the bottom of the Windows desktop. The Taskbar has four parts: the Start button, the toolbar(s), the

Task Manager (with a button for each open window on the desktop), and the system tray. You can customize your Taskbar by moving it, changing its size, and changing what appears on it (see "What Is the Taskbar?" in Chapter 1).

Toolbars on the Taskbar and desktop are a new feature in Windows 98. Four toolbars come with Windows 98 (actually, with Internet Explorer 4.0, which is included with Windows 98):

■ **Quick Launch toolbar**   Usually contains four buttons, as shown left to right in the following illustration: Launch Internet Explorer Browser, Launch Outlook Express, Show Desktop (minimizes all open windows to reveal the desktop), and View Channels. You can change which buttons appear on this toolbar (see "Editing the Quick Launch Toolbar").

■ **Address toolbar**   Contains a text box where you can type a URL to open a web page. A drop-down list contains recently used URLs.

■ **Links toolbar**   Displays a button for each of the web pages that Microsoft would like you to visit. This toolbar also appears in Internet Explorer. Click a button to open the web page.

■ **Desktop toolbar**   Displays a button for each icon on the desktop.

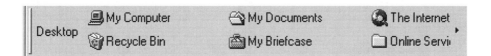

Windows 98 usually displays the Quick Launch toolbar on the Taskbar immediately to the right of the Start button. You can remove that toolbar from the Taskbar or move it onto the desktop (see "Adding and Removing Toolbars from the Taskbar"). You can also display other toolbars on the Taskbar or on the desktop.

Searching the Start Menu

If you can't find the program you want in the Start menu, you can search the menu to find what you're looking for by using the Find dialog box (see "Finding Files and Folders" in Chapter 9). To search the Start menu, follow these steps:

1. Right-click the Start button and choose Find from the shortcut menu that appears.

2. Type the name of the program you're looking for in the Named box.

   Notice that the contents of the Look In text box is the C:\Windows\Start Menu folder, where the shortcuts used to create the Start menu are stored.

3. Click the Find Now button.

The files that match the text you typed are displayed at the bottom of the dialog box. Notice that the full path name is displayed—this information can be used to find the item in the Start menu. If you can't see the full path, you may want to increase the width of the In Folder column by clicking-and-dragging its right border to the right.

Figure 12-2 shows the Find dialog box with the settings used to find the HiJaak Capture program in the Start menu. The shortcut for HiJaak 95 Capture is in C:\Windows\Start Menu\Programs\Hijaak 95. That translates to choosing Start | Programs | Hijaak 95 | HiJaak 95 Capture to start the program.

Editing the Start Menu

Most of the Start menu is customizable. The exceptions to this are most of the options that appear on the first level of the Start menu—they cannot be removed or reorganized.

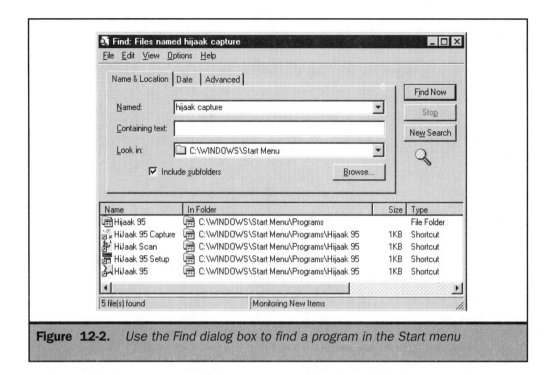

Figure 12-2. Use the Find dialog box to find a program in the Start menu

These options are the Shut Down, Log Off, Suspend, Run, Help, Find, and Settings items. You can, however, add items to the first level of the Start menu, and you have total control over the Programs menu and submenus.

If your Program menu has lots of submenus, getting to the choice you want may take longer than you would like. If you find that the Start menu is cumbersome, you may want to explore the other methods of starting programs, covered in Chapter 2.

Reorganizing the Start Menu

You can add a program to the first level of the Start menu by dragging the program's shortcut to the Start button. You organize existing shortcuts by dragging items within the Start menu itself. However, if you want to reorganize the whole Start menu, delete parts of it, rename menu items, or add submenus, you need to go a little (but only a little) further into Windows' innards. There are three ways to organize those parts of the Start menu that you are allowed to edit—you can drag-and-drop items on the Start menu, use Folder windows and Windows Exploring windows on the C:\Windows\Start Menu folders, or use the Taskbar Properties dialog box.

Dragging Start Menu Items

The easiest way to add items to the Start menu, Programs menu, and their submenus, and to reorganize items already in the menus, is to drag-and-drop the shortcuts where you want them. To add an item to the Start menu, drag the file, folder, or program (the .exe file for the program, that is) from a Folder window or Windows Explorer window and drop it on the Start button. Windows creates a new shortcut and the new command appears in the top part of the Start menu (where WinZip, New Office Document, Windows Update, and Open Office Document appear as displayed in Figure 12-1). If you don't want the item at the top of the Start menu, drag the item within the Start menu to move it to a new position.

You can also reorganize the Start menu by dragging menu items when the menu is open, as follows:

1. Display the Start menu by clicking the Start button.

2. Display the menu containing the item you want to move (for instance, you may need to click the Programs command to see the Microsoft Word option, which you want to move to a submenu called Microsoft Applications).

3. Click the item you want to move and hold the mouse button down.

4. While holding the mouse button down, move the pointer in the menu until you see a black bar appear in the position where you want the item to appear. You can open submenus by highlighting them, using the same method as when you are not moving a menu item.

5. Let go of the mouse button to drop the item in its new position.

Editing the Start Menu Folder

In our opinion, the next easiest way to edit the Start menu is to use a Folder window or Windows Explorer window to add, remove, move, and rename shortcuts. A Folder window or Windows Explorer window (described in Chapters 8 and 9) gives you a familiar tool for editing the Start menu. You can also rename submenus and menu items and create new submenus by using this method, which can't be done using the drag-and-drop method described in the previous section.

The Start menu displays shortcuts that are stored in the C:\Windows\Start Menu folder and its subfolders. Adding, removing, and reorganizing the Start menu is as simple as adding, deleting, and moving shortcuts within the C:\Windows\Start Menu folder and subfolders. Menu items can be renamed by renaming the shortcuts.

You can display the Start Menu folder in a Folder window or Windows Explorer easily by right-clicking the Start button and choosing Open or Explore from the menu (Open displays the C:\Windows\Start Menu folder in a Folder window; Explore displays it using Windows Explorer). Figure 12-3 shows the Start menu folder in Windows Explorer. Notice that all the customizable choices that appear on the Start menu in Figure 12-1 also appear in the Start Menu folder: the Programs folder, the

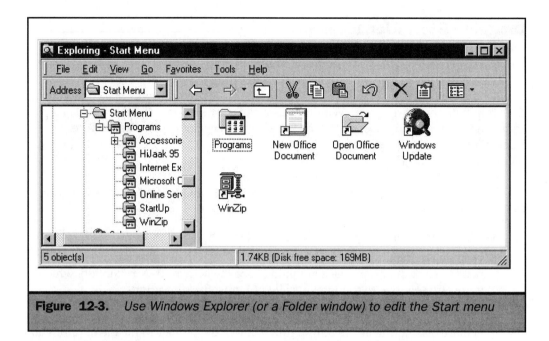

Figure 12-3. *Use Windows Explorer (or a Folder window) to edit the Start menu*

New Office Document shortcut, the Open Office Document shortcut, the Windows Update shortcut, and the WinZip shortcut. Commands you can change (like Help and Run) don't appear.

To display the contents of the Programs menu, open the Programs folder in the Start Menu folder (click or double-click, depending on whether you have configured Windows 98 to use Web style or Classic style—see "Choosing the Style of Your Desktop" in Chapter 1). The shortcuts and folders in the Programs folder are the same as the commands and submenus on the Programs menu. You can continue to explore the Start Menu folders by using the same methods that you use to explore all folders on your computer.

Since the Start menu is stored as shortcuts within folders, it can be edited in the same way that you edit folders and files:

- You can move an item from one menu group to another by dragging or cutting-and-pasting the shortcut to another folder.

- You can create a new menu group by creating a new folder: Select the folder where the new submenu will be stored, and then choose File | New | Folder.

- You can rename a shortcut by selecting it and clicking the name (or right-clicking the name and choosing Rename from the shortcut menu that appears). Windows highlights the name and shows a box around it. Type a new name, or use the cursor to edit the name. Press ENTER when you finish (or press ESC if you change your mind).

Although you can edit the Start menu by changing the contents of the Start Menu folder and its subfolders, the Start Menu folder and Programs folders are more than just regular folders. For instance, you can move the Programs folder out of the C:\Windows\Start Menu folder, and you still see the Programs option on the Start menu (this can lead to complications that are hard to fix, though, so don't try it).

Editing the Start Menu by Using the Taskbar Properties Dialog Box

If you are not comfortable using a Folder window or Windows Explorer to edit the Start menu, you may prefer to use the Taskbar Properties dialog box.

Display the Taskbar Properties dialog box, shown in Figure 12-4, by using one of these methods:

- Choose Start | Settings | Taskbar & Start Menu.
- Right-click an unoccupied part of the Taskbar and choose Properties from the shortcut menu.

Click the Start Menu Programs tab to edit the Start menu, using the three buttons on the dialog box: Add, Remove, and Advanced. The Add and Remove buttons are self-explanatory—they allow you to add items to, or remove items from, the Start menu. The Advanced button opens Windows Explorer so that you can edit the Start menu there, as described in the previous section.

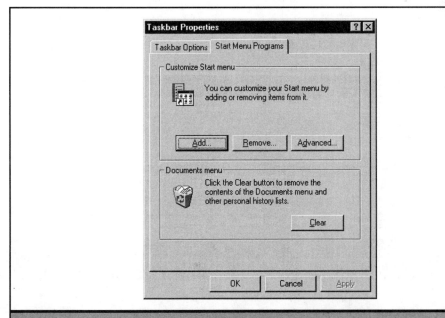

Figure 12-4.   *The Start Menu Programs tab of the Taskbar Properties dialog box allows you to change the choices that appear on the Start menu*

ADDING A SHORTCUT TO THE START MENU   You can add a shortcut to the Start menu by using the Add button on the Taskbar Properties dialog box. You see the Create Shortcut dialog box, shown in Figure 12-5. This is a Wizard that guides you through adding an item to the Start menu (see "What Is a Wizard?" in Chapter 1). Its three steps ask you for the following:

- **The file to which you are creating the shortcut**   You can type the full path name or use the Browse button to find the file in the Browse dialog box.

- **Where you want the shortcut to appear in the Start menu**   Select a folder from the folder structure diagram or create a new folder. To create a new folder, select the folder that the new folder will appear under, and then click the New Folder button. The new folder can be renamed by typing a new name as soon as it is created—notice that the new folder appears highlighted with a box around it.

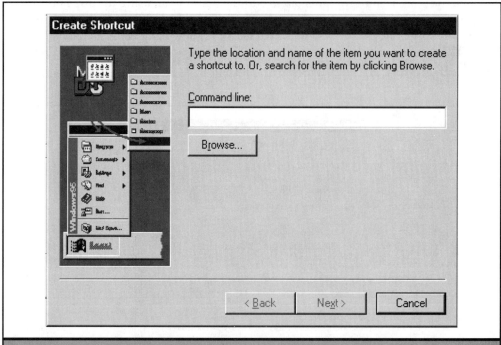

Figure 12-5.   *Click the Browse button to find the file you want to add to the Start menu*

■ **The name of the shortcut**   You can provide any name you want for the shortcut by editing the name that appears or by typing a new name.

REMOVING ITEMS FROM THE START MENU   The Remove button displays the Remove Shortcuts/Folders dialog box, shown in Figure 12-6. You can remove any item in the Start menu (except those noted earlier that cannot be edited) by selecting the item and clicking the Remove button. Any folder that contains menu items or other folders appears with a plus sign next to it—click the plus sign to see the contents of the folder. If you remove a folder, you also remove its contents—a dialog box asks you to confirm that you want to delete the folder and its contents. A menu item that is not a folder will be deleted without any confirmation.

Removed menu items are available in the Recycle Bin, if you make a mistake and remove an item that you'd rather keep (see "Managing the Recycle Bin" in Chapter 9).

EDITING THE START MENU   The Advanced button displays the Start Menu folder in Windows Explorer, where you can use the file management techniques detailed in the last section to edit the Start menu. There is a difference between using the Advanced button on the Taskbar Properties dialog box, and right-clicking the Start

Figure 12-6.   *Removing an item or subfolder from the Start menu*

button and choosing Explore to edit the Start menu in Windows Explorer. The Advanced button allows you to use Windows Explorer only to edit the Start menu folders, whereas right-clicking the Start button and choosing Explorer opens a regular version of Windows Explorer that you can use to display any folder on any drive.

Changing Start Menu Icon Sizes

The default size of icons on the first level of the Start menu is large—you can see the large icons in Figure 12-1. If you prefer the smaller icons, an example of which are shown next, turn on the Show Small Icons In Start Menu option on the Taskbar Options tab of the Taskbar Properties dialog box. Display the Taskbar Properties dialog box by choosing Start | Settings | Taskbar & Start Menu, or by right-clicking an unoccupied part of the Taskbar.

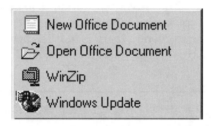

Adding and Editing Favorites

Making frequently used files and folders "favorites" makes them easy to access from the Start menu, Folder windows, and programs. Favorites are usually shortcuts stored in the C:\Windows\Favorites folder. Occasionally, you may want to store an actual file in that folder, and not a shortcut. The items in your Favorites folder appear on the Start menu's Favorites menu, just as the shortcuts in the C:\Windows\Start Menu\Programs folder appear in the Start | Programs menu.

Windows 98 comes preprogrammed with some favorites. The Favorites menu, shown next, comes with both preprogrammed favorites and one item added by the computer's user. The Channels, Links, Software Updates, and Windows Update items all are preprogrammed and lead to web sites. The Shortcut to Books item opens the C:\Windows\My Documents folder, where the computer's user stores manuscript files (this shortcut was added by the user).

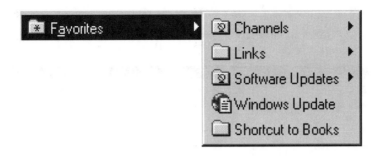

You can easily access the shortcuts in the Favorites folder from any dialog box that has the Look In Favorites button. The Microsoft Word 97 Open dialog box (shown in Figure 12-7), like many others, has two buttons that make finding and creating Favorites easy:

- The Look In Favorites button displays the contents of the C:\Windows\ Favorites folder. In many applications, the Look In Favorites button is a toggle button—when the Favorites folder is displayed, the name of the button changes to Return To *previous folder*. Click it again to display the contents folder you were looking at before you displayed the contents of the Favorites folder.

- The Add To Favorites button adds to the Favorites folder a shortcut to the highlighted file or folder.

To edit the Favorites folder, thereby also editing the Favorites menu, make changes to the C:\Windows\Favorites folder in the same way that you make changes to the C:\Windows\Start Menu folder to change the contents of the Start menu. You can create new folders in the Favorites folder to create a hierarchical Favorites menu. You can also edit the Favorites menu by using the same drag-and-drop techniques used to edit the rest of the Start menu. You can drag a menu item from the Programs menu to the Favorites menu to move it; if you hold down the CTRL key while you drag, you can *copy* the item to the Favorites menu.

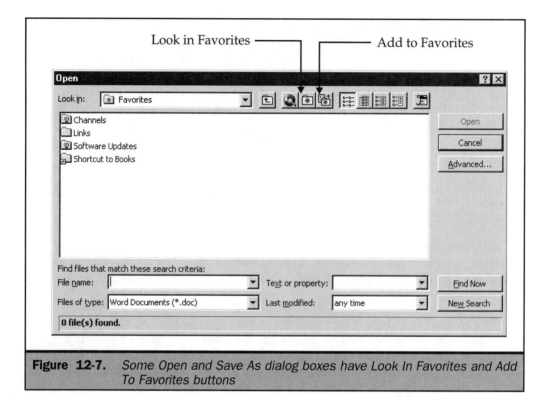

Figure 12-7. *Some Open and Save As dialog boxes have Look In Favorites and Add To Favorites buttons*

Customizing the Taskbar

Although many Windows 98 users find no reason to customize the Taskbar, others do. You can move the Taskbar around the desktop, and you can control its size and whether it is visible all the time. The Taskbar is shown in Figure 12-8.

Moving the Taskbar

Move the Taskbar to any edge of the desktop by clicking-and-dragging it to the desired position. You see no indication that the Taskbar is being moved until the pointer is near an edge of the desktop—the Taskbar then suddenly moves to that position. You have to click an unoccupied area of the Taskbar to drag it—not the Start button, or a Task Manager program button. There is always an unoccupied piece of Taskbar at the right end of the Task Manager.

When the Taskbar appears on the left or right side of the desktop, it looks a little different (see Figure 12-9), but it still has the same parts. The Taskbar does not cover icons on the desktop when it is moved—the icons shift to slightly new positions. (The exception to this "icon shifting" rule is when Auto Hide is turned on. Then the icons don't move, but the Taskbar disappears so that you can see them.)

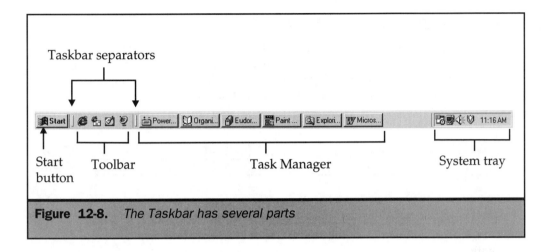

Figure 12-8.   *The Taskbar has several parts*

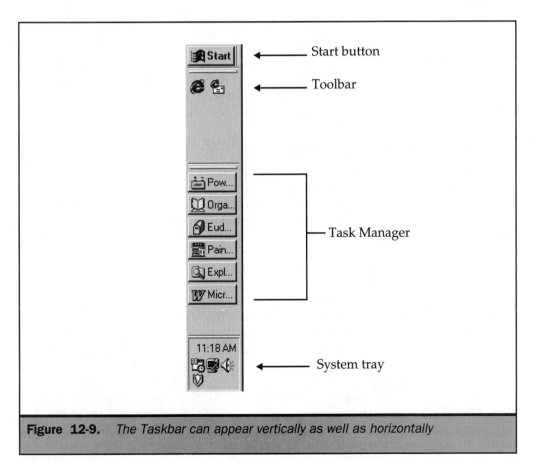

Figure 12-9.   *The Taskbar can appear vertically as well as horizontally*

Changing the Size of the Taskbar

You can change the size of the Taskbar by clicking-and-dragging its inside edge—that is, the edge that borders the desktop. If the Taskbar appears at the bottom of the screen, then change its size by clicking-and-dragging its top edge. The following illustration shows a Taskbar made taller to display two rows of buttons:

A larger Taskbar displays more information on each button in the Task Manager; however, it also claims more of the screen that could be used to display other information.

You can size the Taskbar back down by clicking-and-dragging the inside edge back toward the edge of the screen—make sure to release the mouse button when the Taskbar is the desired size.

It is possible to decrease the size of the Taskbar to a very thin stripe along one edge of the screen by using this method. If this has been done to your Taskbar, you can find the Taskbar by putting the pointer on each edge of the screen. When the pointer turns into a double-headed arrow, click-and-drag to increase the size of the Taskbar.

Changing Taskbar Properties

The Taskbar Options tab of the Taskbar Properties dialog box provides you with some options to change how the Taskbar works. To display the Taskbar Properties dialog box, choose Start | Settings | Taskbar & Start Menu, or right-click an unoccupied portion of the Taskbar and choose Properties from the shortcut menu that appears. You see the Taskbar Properties dialog box, shown in Figure 12-10. Click the Taskbar Options tab if it's not selected.

Hiding the Taskbar

You can hide the Taskbar in two different ways: by decreasing its size and by using the Auto Hide option. Changing the size of the Taskbar is covered in the previous section—click-and-drag the inside edge of the Taskbar to the screen's closest edge. The Taskbar becomes a thin gray line on one edge of the screen. The other option is to use the Auto Hide feature to hide the Taskbar. Auto Hide tries to figure out when you need the Taskbar and when you don't, and display it only when you need it.

To turn on Auto Hide, display the Taskbar Options tab of the Taskbar Properties dialog box, and then click the Auto Hide option so that a check appears in the box.

When Auto Hide is on, the Taskbar disappears when it is not being used. To display it, just point at the edge of the screen where it last appeared. Alternatively,

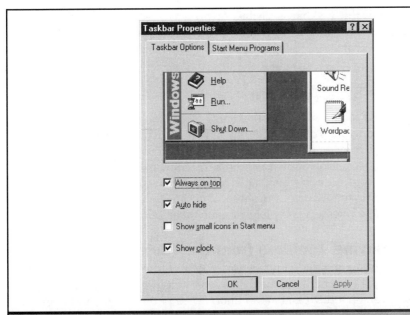

Figure 12-10.   *The Auto Hide option (as well as some others) can be found on the Taskbar Options tab of the Taskbar Properties dialog box*

you can press CTRL-ESC or the Windows key (some keyboards have a key with the Windows symbol that displays the Start menu) to display the Taskbar and open the Start menu all at the same time.

If you can't find your Taskbar, try this: point the pointer at each edge of the screen. If Auto hide is on, the Taskbar will appear. If the Taskbar is shrunk, the pointer will turn into a double-headed arrow—click-and-drag to increase the Taskbar's size.

Hiding the Clock on the Taskbar

You can choose to display or hide the clock that usually appears in the system tray section of the Taskbar. Display the Taskbar Properties dialog box, click the Taskbar Options tab, and then click the Show Clock option to clear the check from the check box.

Allowing the Taskbar to Be Covered by a Window

You can choose whether you want the Taskbar to be covered by other windows by using the Always On Top setting on the Taskbar Options tab of the Taskbar Properties dialog box. When the option is on, the Taskbar always appears over any other windows. When the option is off, windows may cover the Taskbar. To use the Taskbar when the Always On Top option is turned off, you can move or minimize windows until the Taskbar is visible, or press CTRL-ESC or the Windows key to both display the Taskbar and open the Start menu (press ESC once if you want to use just the Taskbar).

Adding Toolbars to the Taskbar

Windows 98 lets you add toolbars to your Taskbar. Taskbar toolbars give you easy access to frequently used icons: You no longer have to minimize all open programs to display a desktop icon to open a program. Instead you can use a toolbar button. Or, you can use the toolbar button Show Desktop to minimize all open programs with one click. You can configure the Taskbar to include these toolbars, or you can display these toolbars elsewhere on your desktop. You can even edit the buttons that appear on a toolbar, or create a completely new toolbar.

Adding and Removing Toolbars from the Taskbar

Use the Taskbar shortcut menu to add and remove toolbars from the Taskbar. The Taskbar shortcut menu, shown here, can be displayed by right-clicking an unoccupied part of the Taskbar (even on a full Taskbar, an unoccupied part can be found at the far right of the Task Manager).

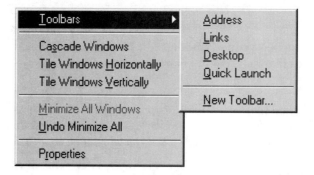

The Toolbars option on the Taskbar shortcut menu displays a menu with the four toolbars. To display a toolbar, click its name. The next time you display the shortcut menu, that toolbar has a check mark next to it. To remove a displayed toolbar, follow the same procedure, but this time remove the check mark.

Moving a Toolbar to the Desktop

You have the option of displaying toolbars on the desktop rather than on the Taskbar. To move a toolbar to the desktop, click-and-drag the toolbar's handle, which looks like a raised vertical bar on the left end of the toolbar.

Toolbar handle ⟶

Drag-and-drop the toolbar onto the desktop. Each toolbar looks different on the desktop, but they all appear with a title bar, a Close button, and their tools, something like this:

Once the toolbar is on the desktop, you can no longer make it disappear by using the Taskbar shortcut menu—instead, you can use its Close button to get rid of it. You can move and change the size of the toolbar by using the same techniques you use on any window (see Chapter 2).

You can move a toolbar from the desktop back to the Taskbar, or to any edge of the desktop, by clicking-and-dragging the title bar—when the toolbar reaches any edge of the desktop, it changes shape to occupy the whole edge. If you move it to the edge with the Taskbar, the toolbar is integrated back into the Taskbar. If you move it to an empty edge, the toolbar takes up the whole edge of the desktop.

Controlling the Look of a Toolbar

You can control the way a toolbar works by using the toolbar shortcut menu, shown here:

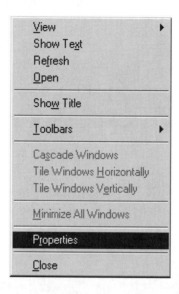

Display the toolbar shortcut menu by right-clicking an unoccupied part of the toolbar (if you have trouble finding an unoccupied part of the toolbar, right-click the toolbar handle).

The following choices on the toolbar shortcut menu control your toolbar (the rest of the choices that appear affect the whole Taskbar—see "Adding and Removing Toolbars from the Taskbar").

- **View** Allows you to display either large or small icons. The default setting is Small.

- **Show Text** Displays text on each button. Choose this option again to display icons with no text. Turning off this option makes a toolbar take up less space.

- **Refresh** Refreshes the toolbar display. This is particularly useful if you create a new toolbar to display the contents of a disk or folder.

- **Open** Displays the shortcuts that make up the toolbar in a Folder window.

- **Show Title** Turns off or on the display of the name of the toolbar.

■ **Toolbars**   Allows you to display a new toolbar, remove an existing toolbar, or create a new toolbar. This option is the same as the Toolbars option on the Taskbar shortcut menu.

■ **Close**   Removes the toolbar from the screen.

When the toolbar is attached to an edge of the desktop, but not in the Taskbar, you see two additional choices:

■ **Always On Top**   The toolbar cannot be covered by a window.

■ **Auto Hide**   The toolbar disappears when not in use. Move the pointer to the edge of the screen where the toolbar is located to display it.

These additional two options work the same as the Always On Top and Auto Hide options for the Taskbar.

Moving the Toolbar on the Taskbar

You can control how the Taskbar is partitioned between the Task Manager and the toolbars by dragging the divider between the two. When the Task Manager gets small, scroll buttons appear, allowing you to view all the buttons for open applications. By moving the divider all the way to the opposite end of the Taskbar, you can move the toolbar from one side of the Taskbar to the other.

Editing the Quick Launch Toolbar

You can edit the buttons on the Quick Launch toolbar in the same way that you edit the Start menu—by editing the folder that contains the shortcuts. The shortcuts for the Quick Launch toolbar are buried in the folder structure—you can find them in C:\Windows\Application Data\Microsoft\Internet Explorer\Quick Launch. You can add new shortcuts and delete the shortcuts that appear in this folder to change the buttons displayed on the Quick Launch toolbar.

Creating a New Toolbar

In addition to the four existing toolbars, you can create your own toolbar to display the contents of a drive or folder or Internet address. Depending on the options you choose for your new toolbar, it may look something like the one shown next, which displays the contents of a folder called Consult. The Consult folder contains three other folders and numerous files. On the toolbar, you can see the three folders—you can display the files by clicking the scroll arrow at the right end of the toolbar.

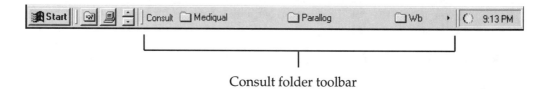

Consult folder toolbar

Clicking a folder button opens a Folder window for that folder; clicking a file button opens the file.

To create a new toolbar, right click the Taskbar or a toolbar and choose Toolbars | New Toolbar from the shortcut menu that appears. You see the New Toolbar dialog box (shown in Figure 12-11), which allows you to browse available drives and folders. Click the plus sign next to a folder name to expand that branch of the folder tree. You can open any folder or drive available to you in Windows Explorer or a Folder window—these may include drives and folders on the Internet. Select the folder you want to use to create a toolbar and click OK on the New Toolbar dialog box.

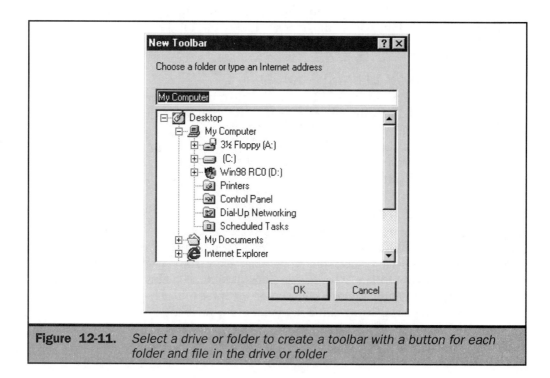

Figure 12-11. *Select a drive or folder to create a toolbar with a button for each folder and file in the drive or folder*

The
Complete
Reference

Chapter 13

Setting Up Your Desktop

273

Whe your desktop is set up in a way that is right for you, everything flows more smoothly. Files and programs are where you expect them to be. The screen is attractive and doesn't hurt your eyes. Your wallpaper, color scheme, and screensaver are different from everyone else's, giving your computer a familiar, homey feel. You use Windows' display properties to configure your desktop and monitor. If you really want to dress up your desktop, you can change the size, color, or font of the individual elements that make up the desktop, or install a desktop theme to give your screen an artistic look.

But Windows 98 allows you to do more than just a little interior decorating. Two features new to Windows 98 create additional possibilities for your desktop. *Active Desktop* turns your desktop into a web page, fully interactive with live content from whatever networks you have access to, including the Internet. And Windows 98 supports multiple displays and multiple graphics adapters, greatly increasing your display options.

What Are Display Properties?

The command center for anything having to do with your monitor or desktop is the Display Properties dialog box, shown in Figure 13-1. You can access it from the Control

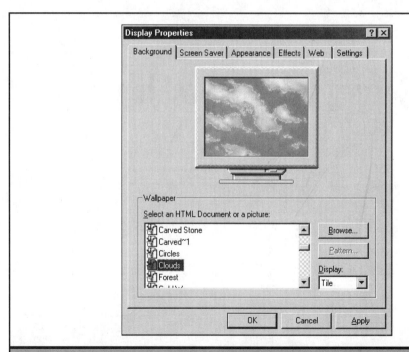

Figure 13-1. *The Display Properties dialog box. The preview box in the center lets you see the effect of proposed changes before you apply them*

Panel, or by right-clicking any unoccupied spot on the desktop and choosing Properties from the menu.

This Display Properties dialog box has six tabs (possibly more if your system has any special display software). Table 13-1 lists the tabs and the purpose of each tab. You can change the settings on most of these tabs to change the way your desktop looks and acts (see "Designing and Decorating Your Desktop").

What Is Active Desktop?

Active Desktop turns your desktop into a web page. Your desktop can contain pictures, text, animation, sounds, links, weather maps, stock tickers, or anything else that can appear on a web page. Information can be brought in automatically from the Internet or a local network by subscribing to the corresponding sites, or you can display files from your own computer.

Some people find Active Desktop a useful way to get up-to-date information automatically; others find it little more than animated advertisements cluttering up the screen. Try Active Desktop for a little while to see which camp you fall into.

Microsoft maintains an online gallery of items that you can add to your Active Desktop (see "Adding an Active Desktop Item"). To try Active Desktop, see the section "Activating Your Desktop" later in this chapter.

Tab	What It Controls
Background	Wallpaper and background patterns
Screen Saver	Screen savers and automatic settings for turning off your monitor
Appearance	Color, size, and font of every standard type of object Windows uses
Effects	Customization of icons and visual effects
Web	Active Desktop
Settings	Size of desktop (in pixels), number of colors displayed, and monitor performance

Table 13-1. *Tabs of the Display Properties Dialog Box, and What They Control*

What Is Wallpaper?

Putting wallpaper on your desktop is a bit of a mixed metaphor—perhaps contact paper would be better. *Wallpaper* is the background pattern behind all the windows, icons, and menus on your desktop. Any image file can be used as wallpaper. The image can be centered on the screen, or it can fill the screen by being repeated as tiles. If you choose not to have wallpaper, the desktop can have either a solid background color or a two-tone repeating pattern.

To choose wallpaper from the images that ship with Windows 98, or any other image, see the section "Wallpapering Your Desktop" later in this chapter.

What Is a Screen Saver?

If you walk away from your computer and leave the monitor on, the same image might be on your screen for hours at a time. Years ago, this would tend to "burn in" the image permanently on the screen, and so people created *screen savers*—programs that kick in when the display hasn't changed in a while. A good screen saver contains some kind of moving image, so that no section of the screen is consistently bright or dark.

Monitor technology eventually improved to the point that burn-in is not such a serious concern. In addition, many monitors now have an energy-saving feature that allows a monitor to turn off automatically if its display hasn't changed for some period of time (see "Saving Energy Automatically").

But even though screen savers are no longer needed for their original purpose, many people continue to use them just because they are pleasant to look at. (They also discourage random passers-by from reading the document you're working on when you step out for coffee.) Screen savers like "Mystify Your Mind" or "Curves and Colors" make attractive geometric patterns that can be soothing to watch, while others like "3D Maze" create a more active mood. In offices with multiple networked computers, the screen saver can display the computer's name, suitably colorized and animated.

To select and activate a screen saver, see "Setting Up a Screen Saver" later in this chapter.

What Is a Desktop Scheme?

The ability to select any conceivable color, size, or font for every single type of object on the desktop is more power than most of us need or want. We'd like to be able to change things around every now and then, but we don't want to spend all day figuring out exactly what shade of dark green frame to put around windows with a light green background.

Fortunately, Windows 98 comes with a large number of preconfigured *desktop schemes*. Making a single choice on the Appearance tab of the Display Properties dialog box simultaneously adjusts active windows, inactive windows, window backgrounds, title bars, message boxes, and all the other configurable desktop objects. It's so simple that you can have one favorite desktop scheme for sunny days, another for cloudy days, and a third for nighttime—something you would never do if you had to make all the adjustments individually (see "Choosing Sizes, Colors, and Fonts of Desktop Elements").

What is a Desktop Theme?

A theme is like a scheme, only more so. A *desktop scheme* is a system of colors and fonts designed to look attractive together (see the preceding section). A *desktop theme* takes this idea a little farther, adding a screen saver, desktop background, mouse pointer, sounds, and icons all customized around a central idea.

For example, the Leonardo da Vinci theme (our favorite) has a reddish-brown color scheme and a desktop background that looks like a weathered parchment covered with Leonardo's drawings. The My Computer icon is a notebook, Network Neighborhood is a jar of drawing tools, and the Recycle Bin is a wicker basket. The icon signifying that Windows is busy changes from an hour glass to a paint brush putting blobs of color in a notebook. The screen saver includes several da Vinci sketches. The system noises are more musical than the Windows default noises.

Desktop themes are not part of the default installation of Windows 98, and for a good reason: they're a space hog. Installing all 17 desktop themes on your system takes up 30MB on your hard drive. If you want them, you must install them from the Windows CD. From the Control Panel, open Add/Remove Programs, click the Windows Setup tab, and choose Desktop Themes (see "Installing and Uninstalling Programs That Come with Windows 98" in Chapter 3).

Given that desktop themes add no functionality other than cuteness to your system, you may decide to forego them. If you do install desktop themes from the Windows CD-ROM or floppies, we recommend you play with the themes for a while, then pick one or two favorites and uninstall the rest.

Selecting and editing desktop themes is discussed in the section "Choosing a Desktop Theme" later in this chapter.

Designing and Decorating Your Desktop

You can customize the appearance of almost everything on the desktop from the Display Properties dialog box, shown in Figure 13-1.

Changing the Background

When you decorate the walls of a room, is your first choice paint or wallpaper? You have a similar choice about the background of your desktop: Do you want a solid color background, or do you want to use a more complex pattern as wallpaper?

Wallpapering Your Desktop

You can cover your desktop with any image, from a straw mat to the Mona Lisa. Use either an image file of your own or one of the many wallpapers that come with Windows 98.

Windows 98 doesn't install all of the wallpapers that come with it. To install the rest of the wallpaper files, open the Add/Remove Programs icon on the Control Panel, click the Windows Setup tab, choose Accessories from the list of components, click Details, and click Desktop Wallpaper (see "Installing and Uninstalling Programs That Come with Windows 98" in Chapter 3).

SELECTING WALLPAPER FROM THE WALLPAPER LIST Select your wallpaper from the Background tab of the Display Properties dialog box, shown in Figure 13-2. The Wallpaper window of that tab lists all the available wallpapers. Click a name in this list to see the wallpaper pattern displayed on the Desktop Preview—the monitor-like graphic just above the list.

A wallpaper is just a file in an image format (with extension .bmp, .jpg, .gif, or .tif). That image has a size, which may or may not match the dimensions of your display. If the image is smaller than the display, the Display drop-down list (to the right of the Wallpaper list) gives you three choices:

- **Center** the image on the display, letting the background color of the desktop form a frame around the wallpaper. This is your best choice for photographs that are just slightly smaller than the display.

- **Tile** the display with the image. This works particularly well with wallpapers such as Black Thatch or Houndstooth, which are small images designed to create intricate patterns when tiled.

- **Stretch** the image to fill the display. Photographs end up looking like fun house mirrors, but many abstract patterns stretch well.

Tile and Stretch fill the display with the wallpaper, but Center may leave a border, which you can fill with either a solid color or a pattern (see "Selecting a Background Color and Pattern").

If the wallpaper you choose is larger than your display, Center and Tile both give you a single copy of the image, with the edges of the image off the screen. If this isn't satisfactory, you can use Paint to crop the image, or you can redefine the dimensions of your display (see "Changing Resolution and Color Refinement").

BROWSING FOR WALLPAPER You aren't limited to the wallpapers that come with Windows 98. Any image file can be used as wallpaper. To make wallpaper out of any other image file, click the Browse button on the Background tab of the Display Properties dialog box, shown in Figure 13-2. Use the Browse window that appears to find the file you want (see "Open, Save As, and Browse Dialog Boxes" in Chapter 2).

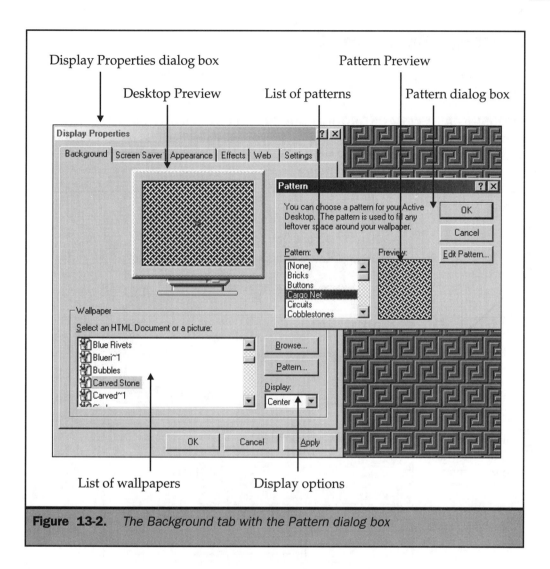

Display Properties dialog box

Desktop Preview

List of patterns

Pattern Preview

Pattern dialog box

List of wallpapers

Display options

Figure 13-2.   *The Background tab with the Pattern dialog box*

Then click Open. The file you select should now appear in the Wallpaper list. Proceed as in the previous section.

ADDING TO THE WALLPAPER LIST PERMANENTLY   Browsing for wallpaper adds the selected image file to the Wallpaper list only temporarily. The next time you open the Display Properties dialog box, the browsed-for file will not be on the Wallpaper list. The Wallpaper list is actually a list of the image files in the C:\Windows folder. So, to add an image to this list permanently, move or copy its file to the C:\Windows folder.

Selecting a Background Color and Pattern

Wallpaper covers paint, so you see the background color and pattern of your desktop only if your wallpaper choice is either None or centered with the background visible around the edges.

CHOOSING A NEW BACKGROUND COLOR   The background color of your desktop is set on the Appearance tab of the Display Properties dialog box (not on the Background tab, as you might have thought). The Appearance tab is shown in Figure 13-3.

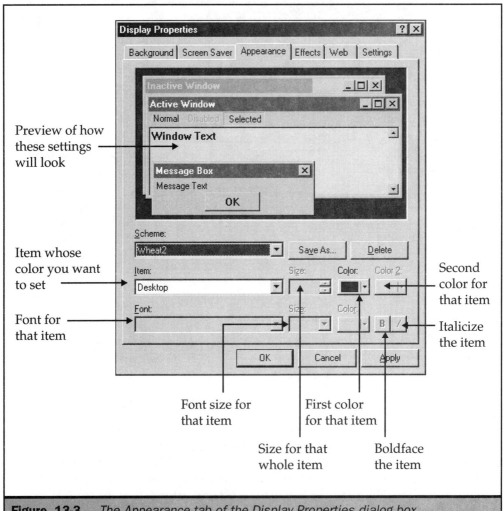

Figure 13-3.   *The Appearance tab of the Display Properties dialog box*

To select a new background color:

1. Click the Appearance tab of the Display Properties dialog box.

2. Select Desktop from the Item drop-down list. The current background color is shown in the Color box to the right of the Item box.

3. Click the current background color. A palette of colors appears.

4. If one of the colors on the palette is what you want, click it. The background of the Preview window changes to the new color.

5. If you don't like any of the colors on the palette, click Other, and follow the directions in "Finding the Perfect Color."

6. Click Apply to change the desktop color, or OK to change the color and make the Display Properties dialog box disappear.

You can change the colors and sizes of other elements on the desktop, too (see "Choosing Sizes, Colors, and Fonts of Desktop Elements").

FINDING THE PERFECT COLOR   When you start trying to change the color of the desktop, the title bars, or any of the other basic objects, Windows offers a simple palette of 16 basic colors plus the four additional colors that you have used most recently. If this is not enough choice for you, click Other to display the Color dialog box, shown in woefully inadequate black-and-white in Figure 13-4.

The number of basic colors has now tripled to 48, shown in a palette of little boxes on the left side of the Color dialog box. If the color you want is on this palette, click it, click OK, and then continue just as you would have if one of the original 16 colors had been satisfactory. But if even the 48 colors are not enough for you, you can use the right-hand side of the Color dialog box to get any color you want.

The currently selected color is shown in the Color | Solid box. To the right of the Color | Solid box are two different numerical systems of describing the current color: its hue, saturation, and luminescence (known as HSV coordinates), and its red, green, and blue components (known as RGB coordinates). Above the Color | Solid box and the coordinates is a graphical representation of the current color's HSV coordinates. The horizontal position of the cross-hairs in the large square represents the hue, and the vertical position of the cross-hairs represents the saturation. The position of the vertical slider next to the square represents the luminescence.

Thus, the same color is represented three ways: as RGB, as HSV, and as a position of the cross-hairs and slider. You can select a new color by manipulating any of the three descriptions—move the cross-hairs and slider with the mouse, or type new numbers (from 0 to 255) into the HSV or RGB coordinate boxes. However you specify the color, the other two descriptions (and the Color | Solid box) change automatically to match.

If you think you will want to use this color again in the future, click Add To Custom Colors rather than OK. The new color appears in one of the boxes in the Custom colors palette on the left side of the Color dialog box. If you like, you can

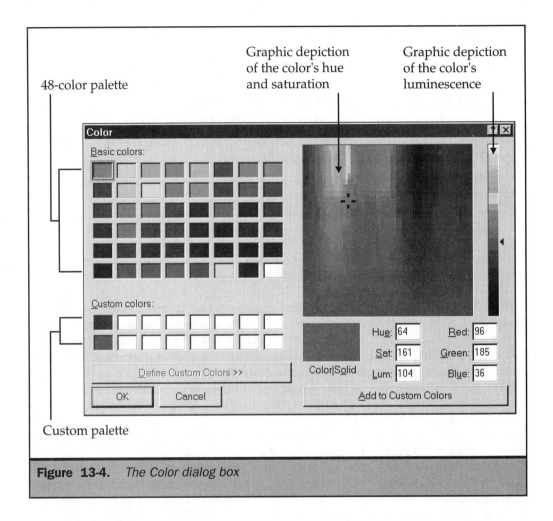

48-color palette

Graphic depiction
of the color's hue
and saturation

Graphic depiction
of the color's
luminescence

Custom palette

Figure 13-4.   *The Color dialog box*

define several custom colors, one at a time. Custom colors can be selected just like basic colors, by clicking them.

When you have created all the colors you want, select the one you want to use, and click OK. The color is applied and the Color dialog box vanishes.

CHOOSING A BACKGROUND PATTERN   Patterns are simple 64-pixel, two-color images that interlock to give your background a textured appearance. The two colors are the background color and black (see "Choosing a New Background Color"). To choose or change your background pattern, follow these steps:

1. Click the Background tab of the Display Properties dialog box, which is shown (along with the Pattern dialog box) in Figure 13-2.

2. If the Pattern button is grayed out, your current wallpaper covers the entire background, making a background pattern irrelevant. The current wallpaper is probably stretched or tiled. Either choose Center from the Display list or set your wallpaper choice to None to reactivate the Pattern button.

3. Click the Pattern button. The Pattern dialog box appears, as shown in Figure 13-2.

4. Click the name of a pattern on the Pattern list to see what it looks like in the Pattern Preview window.

5. When you find a pattern you like, click OK. Then close the Display Properties dialog box.

EDITING A BACKGROUND PATTERN   When none of the listed patterns is exactly what you want, you can create a new pattern by editing an existing one. Follow the instructions from the previous section until the Pattern dialog box appears in step 4. Then follow these steps:

5. Select the pattern you want to edit by clicking its name on the drop-down list.

6. Click the Edit Pattern button. The Pattern Editor dialog box appears, as shown in Figure 13-5. The box labeled Pattern is an 8x8 grid of pixels, each of which is either black or the background color.

7. Click any pixel to change it from one color to the other. As you change the pattern, the Sample box changes to preview how the new pattern will look on your screen.

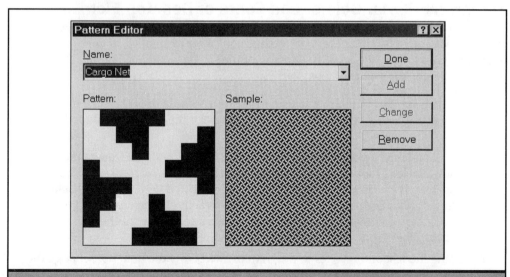

Figure 13-5.   *You can edit patterns*

8. When you have the pattern the way you want it, click Done, and then OK in the confirmation dialog box. The edited pattern is saved under the original name. If, instead, you decide you prefer the original pattern, click No in the confirmation dialog box. The original pattern is retained and you return to the Pattern dialog box.

Choosing Sizes, Colors, and Fonts of Desktop Elements

You can choose much more than just the color of your background. In Windows 98, the color and font of almost anything is configurable—title bars, active windows, inactive windows, message boxes, you name it. You can make all these choices one-by-one, choose a scheme preselected by Microsoft's desktop decorators, or start with one of Microsoft's schemes and redefine one or two things.

The locus of all this power is the Appearance tab of the Display Properties dialog box, shown in Figure 13-3.

Selecting a Predefined Desktop Scheme

To select a desktop scheme (a group of preselected settings), click the scheme's name on the Scheme list of the Appearance tab of the Display Properties dialog box. The Preview window changes immediately to show you how the various components are displayed in this desktop scheme. Previewing a scheme by itself changes nothing, so feel free to check out as many schemes as you want. When you find one that you like, click either Apply or OK to change your display settings to match the scheme.

Editing the Sizes, Colors, and Fonts of Desktop Elements

You can change the size, color, or font of elements individually. For example, you can make the Minimize, Maximize, and Close buttons larger or smaller, or change the color of the text on window title bars. To edit any of the screen elements that make up a desktop scheme, follow these steps:

1. Click its name on the Scheme list of the Appearance tab of the Display Properties dialog box. To change the settings for the way the desktop looks now, skip this step.

2. Select an item to alter from the Item list (or click it in the Preview window). The Font, Size, or Color boxes become active to show what is configurable about this item. For example, when Desktop is the selected item, only the background color is configurable, so only the Color box is active. When Active Title Bar is selected, by contrast, you can select two colors and a size for the bar, as well as the size, color, font, and style of the text on the bar.

3. Using the rest of the boxes to the right of and below the Item box, change the way that item looks. (See the various settings you can use in Figure 13-3.)

4. When you alter anything in a desktop scheme, the scheme name vanishes from the Scheme window, indicating that the altered desktop scheme has not been given a name and saved. To save your new scheme, click Save As and choose a name for it. You may give it the same name as the desktop scheme you altered (displacing that scheme in the Scheme list), or you can give it a new name.

5. To apply your changes, click Apply. To apply your changes and exit the Display Properties dialog box, click OK. To forget about the changes you made, click Cancel.

Choosing a Desktop Theme

A desktop theme provides not just a system of colors and fonts, but sounds, icons, mouse pointers, a desktop background, and a screen saver as well (see "What is a Desktop Theme?").

Desktop themes are not part of the default installation of Windows 98, but is simple to add from the Windows 98 CD-ROM or floppies (see "Installing and Uninstalling Programs That Come with Windows 98" in Chapter 3). If desktop themes have been installed on your computer, a Desktop Themes icon appears on your Control Panel.

Selecting a Desktop Theme

To select a desktop theme:

1. Select Start | Settings | Control Panel. The Control Panel appears. If Desktop Themes is installed on your computer, you see a Desktop Themes icon.

2. Open the Desktop Themes icon on the Control Panel. Click the icon once or twice, depending on whether your desktop is configured to use Web style or Classic style (see "Choosing the Style of Your Desktop" in Chapter 1). The Desktop Themes dialog box opens, as shown in Figure 13-6.

3. Select the name of a theme from the Theme drop-down list. A preview of the theme appears in the Preview window below the Theme list. The theme's desktop background is the background of the Preview window. The colors and fonts of various kinds of windows and message boxes are shown in the lower right of the Preview window. The scheme's custom icons are displayed on the left side of the Preview screen.

4. To preview the screen saver, click the Screen Saver button in the upper right corner of the dialog box. To end the preview of the screen saver, move the mouse.

5. To preview the other aspects of the theme, click the Pointers, Sounds, Etc. button. The Preview Current Window Settings dialog box appears. The box has three tabs: Pointers, Sounds, and Visuals. Each tab contains a list of custom items. To preview a pointer or visual, click its name on the list and look at the preview window in the lower portion of the Preview Current Window Settings dialog box. To try out a sound, click its name in the list and then click the arrow

Figure 13-6.   *The Desktop Themes dialog box*

in the lower portion of the dialog box. Click Close to make the Preview Current Window Settings dialog box disappear.

6. When you are convinced that you want to use a particular theme, examine the Settings portion of the Desktop Themes dialog box. Uncheck any of the boxes that you do not want to apply. For example, if you like everything about a scheme except its sounds, uncheck the Sound Events box and leave the other Settings boxes checked.

7. Click OK. The Desktop Themes dialog box disappears and Windows applies the theme to your desktop.

If you decide you don't like the theme you've applied, return to the Desktop Themes dialog box and choose either the Windows 98 or Windows Default theme.

Editing a Desktop Theme

The Desktop Themes dialog box does not allow you to edit a theme directly. However, you can edit any of the aspects of the theme (sounds, color scheme, icons, screen saver, background, and other elements) in the usual ways. When you have everything the way you want it, open Desktop Themes from the Control Panel. Select Current Windows Settings from the drop-down Theme list, then click Save As to give your custom theme a name. Ever after, that theme will appear on the Theme list.

Setting Up a Screen Saver

When you are not working on your computer, a screen saver can display something far more engaging and attractive than your desktop or your unfinished documents.

To choose a screen saver:

1. Click the Screen Saver tab of the Display Properties dialog box, shown in Figure 13-7.

2. Select a screen saver from the drop-down list. The previewer shows you a miniaturized version of what the screen saver displays. Or you can click the Preview button and see a full-size preview.

3. When you find a screen saver you like, click either the Apply or OK button.

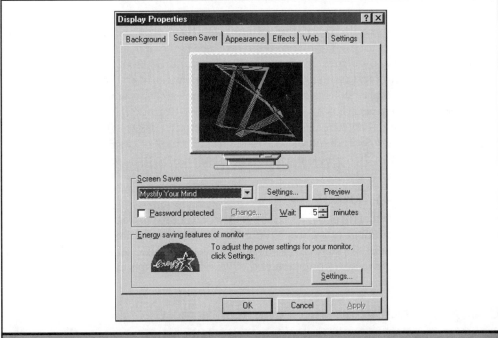

Figure 13-7.   *Choosing and configuring a screen saver*

While you have the Screen Saver tab selected, you can make a number of choices about how your screen saver functions:

- **Change the settings** by clicking the Settings button. Each screen saver has its own list of settings; some let you change a handful of parameters, while some have an entire screen full of choices for you to make. In general, the settings of your screen saver control how fast the screen saver cycles, the colors it uses, the thickness of the lines it draws, and so forth.

- **Change the wait time** for your screen saver by entering a new number of minutes into the Wait box. The *wait time* is the length of time that your system must be inactive before the screen saver starts up. Windows waits this long for keyboard or mouse input before starting the screen saver.

- **Add a password** to your screen saver by checking the Password Protected box. Remove password protection by unchecking the box. Change your password by clicking the Change button. If you have never established a screen saver password before, click Change to choose one.

Note   *Windows considers your screen saver password to be different from your login password. Changing one password does not automatically change the other.*

Windows 98 comes with a choice of several screen savers. Additional screen savers are available over the Internet, many of them for free. You can begin your search at Yahoo (**http://www.yahoo.com**) by choosing Business and Economy, then Companies, then Software, then Entertainment, and finally Screen Savers from the Yahoo web site. Or, look at the web site of your favorite TV show or movie to see whether there is a promotional screen saver. (Fox's *Millennium* has one, for example.)

To install a new screen saver, put the corresponding file of type screen saver (.scr) into the C:\Windows\System folder. The next time you look at the Screen Saver tab of the Display Properties dialog box, the new screen saver is on the drop-down list.

Changing Display Settings

Windows 98 gives you control over the dimensions of your desktop (in pixels, naturally, since the number of inches on your monitor is fixed), the color resolution of your display, the size of the standard fonts and icons, and many other properties. Most of this power resides on the Settings tab of the Display Properties dialog box, shown in Figure 13-8.

Changing Resolution and Color Refinement

Resolution is controlled by the Screen Area slider on the Settings tab of the Display Properties dialog box. Your current desktop's dimensions (in *pixels*, or colored dots on the screen) are stated under the slider. Naturally, the size of your monitor doesn't change, so when you increase the number of pixels on your desktop, each pixel gets

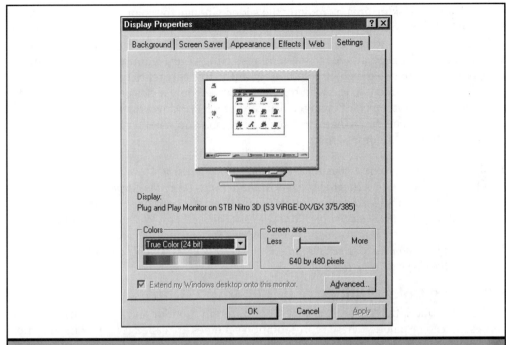

Figure 13-8. *The Settings tab of the Display Properties dialog box*

correspondingly smaller, increasing resolution. Icons and fonts shrink as well. As you increase desktop area, you may want to increase font and icon size to compensate (see "Changing Font Size"). The range of resolutions depends on what type of monitor you use. For a 14-inch monitor, your choices may range only from 640x480, to 800x600. For a 17-inch monitor, you can increase the resolution up to 1024x768.

The Settings tab also controls the number of colors you display. The Colors drop-down list gives you choices that also depend on the quality of your monitor: your choices may include 16 colors, 256 colors, high color (16-bit, or 65,536 colors), and true color (24-bit, or 16,777,216 colors). Below the list is a color bar showing the spectrum under the selected color palette.

The choice to be made is a speed versus beauty tradeoff. Displaying fewer colors or pixels is less work for your computer and may help it run faster. More colors and pixels provide a richer viewing experience, particularly if you are looking at photographs. Colors and pixels also trade off against each other, since increasing either one puts a strain on the portion of RAM that your system devotes to the display. Windows 98 accounts for this automatically; if you increase the desktop area beyond the capabilities of your RAM, it decreases the color palette to compensate. Likewise, if you increase the color palette beyond what your RAM can handle, Windows decreases the desktop size.

Change the desktop area by moving the slider. Change the color palette by making a new choice from the drop-down list. Apply your changes by clicking the Apply button.

A few programs don't work properly with the new color palette until you restart your computer. In general, we recommend restarting your computer to be completely safe, but if you change the color palette frequently, this can get to be a nuisance. You may want to experiment to see whether the software you use has any problems when you don't restart after a color change. You can set up Windows to either restart automatically when you change the color palette, ask you whether to restart, or not restart (see "Other Monitor Settings").

> **Tip** *If you change screen resolution or color palette often, you can add a Display Properties icon to your system tray. On the Settings tab of the Display Properties dialog box, click the Advanced button. On the General tab of the new dialog box that appears, click the Show Settings Icon On Task Bar check box. When you click OK, a Display Properties icon appears in the system tray on your Taskbar. Click the icon once to see a menu of screen resolutions and color palettes. Double-click the icon to see the Display Properties dialog box.*

Changing Color Profiles

There are subtle differences in the ways that different monitor and printer drivers represent a color palette. These representation schemes are called *color profiles*. For most purposes, the difference between color profiles doesn't matter, but if you need to be sure that the colors you see on your monitor are exactly the colors you will get when you print, you can set the color profiles of your monitor and printer to reflect the exact way that your monitor and printer render colors.

Windows comes with profiles for many popular monitors, and a default profile called the *sRGB Color Space Profile* that matches most monitors reasonably well. Unless you are a graphic artist, you probably won't notice the difference between the default profile and a perfectly tuned one. We recommend that 99% of users leave their color profiles alone.

To change the color profile of your monitor, click the Settings tab of the Display Properties dialog box and click the Advanced button. In the new window that opens, click the Color Management tab. Any profiles you have previously used are listed in the large window, with the current default profile in the box above the large window. To change to a new default color profile, select a new profile from the list and click the Set As Default button. To add a profile to the list, click the Add button and select from all the color profiles that Windows is aware of. To remove a profile from the list, select it and click the Remove button.

As on all the other tabs of the Display Properties dialog box, no changes are actually made until you click Apply or OK.

Changing Font Size

If the print in a book is too small to read, you can address the situation in two fundamentally different ways: Get a large-type book, or use a magnifying glass. Similarly, the fonts on your screen can be made larger or smaller in two fundamentally different ways: By changing point size, or by changing the *magnification*. There are two major differences between these two ways of changing fonts:

- Changing point size is more specific—you can enlarge or shrink the text of title bars or menu bars, for example, and leave everything else alone. Changing font magnification changes the appearance of all fonts.

- Changing magnification doesn't affect the printout of your documents, while changing point size does.

CHANGING POINT SIZE   The point size of the fonts used in any particular document is changed from within the applications that edit that document. The size of the fonts that Windows uses in menus, title bars, and so forth, is controlled from the Appearance tab of the Display Properties dialog box. Just click a text item in the Preview window, and then enter a larger number into the Size box next to the Font box.

CHANGING MAGNIFICATION   Font magnification is controlled by displaying the Settings tab of the Display Properties dialog box, shown in Figure 13-8, and then clicking the Advanced button. You see a dialog box that displays settings that your display driver lets you change. For most display drivers, these settings include font size. A drop-down list gives you three choices: Small Fonts (defined as "normal" or 100 percent magnification), Large Fonts (125 percent magnification), and Other. Choosing Other opens a new dialog box, Custom Font Size. From this dialog box, you can type in whatever size you want, or change the size by using the ruler as a slider. However you do it, click OK to return to the display driver's dialog box, where your chosen size is displayed under the Font Size box. If you like it, click Apply. If Windows doesn't restart your computer automatically, restart it yourself.

Changing Icons

You can change the size or arrangement of the icons on your desktop. You can even define new icons for the various types of desktop objects.

CHANGING ICON SIZE   The Use Large Icons check box on the Effects tab of the Display Properties dialog box controls whether you use regular icons (32 points) or large icons (48 points). Icon size is also controllable from the Appearance tab (see Figure 13-3); but rather than choosing Large or Small, you can insert any point-size between 16 and 72. Just choose Icon from the drop-down Item list, and then type a number into the Size box. (The next row of boxes controls the font and size of the labels underneath your icons.) In either case, you have made an across-the-board change; you can't have some large icons and some small ones.

ARRANGING ICONS ON THE DESKTOP   You can arrange your desktop icons manually by dragging-and-dropping them. If your system is set up for single-click opening, however, you may open the corresponding objects by mistake when you try to drag-and-drop icons. If you're having this problem, use right-click drag-and-drop. Select Move Here from the menu that appears when you drop the icon.

Arrange your desktop icons automatically by choosing Arrange Icons from the menu that appears when you right-click any open spot on the desktop. Windows arranges the icons in columns, starting on the left side of the desktop. The Arrange Icons menu gives you the option of arranging by name, type, size, or date. Make sure you really want the icons arranged in columns, however, because there is no "undo" selection on the Arrange Icons menu.

The final option on the Arrange Icons menu is Auto Arrange. If Auto Arrange is checked, the icons are arranged in rows and columns, and any new item is automatically ushered to the next open spot in the pattern. Auto Arrange prevents you from arranging your icons manually; any icon is whisked to the appropriate row or column as soon as you set it down.

You can control the spacing between icons in this automatic arrangement, as follows:

1. Click the Appearance tab of the Display Properties dialog box.

2. From the drop-down Item list, choose Icon Spacing (Horizontal) or Icon Spacing (Vertical).

3. Type a number (of points) into the Size box. Larger numbers create bigger spaces.

4. Click OK.

Changing the icon spacing affects the icon arrangement of Windows Explorer and Folder windows as well as the desktop.

ASSIGNING NEW ICONS   You can choose new icons for any of the standard desktop objects. Open the Effects tab of the Display Properties dialog box and find the type of icon you want to change in the Desktop Icons list. Just click an object from the list and select Change Icon, and then choose a new icon from the list, or browse for an icon file anywhere on your system. To change back, select the item again and click the Default Icon button. Having your own system of icons makes your computer substantially harder to use, so we recommend that you leave the default icons alone. To change all the standard Windows icons, you can use a desktop theme (see "What is a Desktop Theme?").

DELETING DESKTOP ICONS   Most items on your desktop represent some kind of file or folder, and you can move or delete them just as you would move or delete any file or folder (see "Rearranging Files and Folders" in Chapter 8). My Computer, Network Neighborhood, and Recycle Bin, however, represent capabilities of your system, and Windows will not let you delete them.

Activating Your Desktop

Active Desktop lets your desktop do anything a web page can do: contain pictures, text, links to other web pages, sound, animation, or 3-D effects.

Central to Microsoft's vision of the Active Desktop is *push technology*—desktop items that are "subscribed" to information sources on the Internet (see "What Are

Subscriptions and Channels?" in Chapter 25). With push technology, information comes to your desktop on its own rather than because you looked for it and requested it. For example, rather than having to ask for specific stock quotes or news headlines, you can have a ticker continuously scrolling across the bottom of your desktop.

In general, the early users of Windows 98 (and Internet Explorer 4.0, where Microsoft introduced Active Desktop) have been less excited by Active Desktop—and by push technology as a whole—than Microsoft had hoped. For the most part, the early users tended to be people who enjoy looking for information on the Web, and appreciate the freedom of seeing only the information they ask for, when they ask for it. Whether the larger public will agree with them or with Microsoft remains to be seen.

The Channel Bar

The Channel Bar is the only Active Desktop item that is automatically installed when you set up Windows 98. It consists of a column of buttons corresponding to various "channels" to which you can subscribe, such as ESPN Sportzone or MSNBC News, as shown here:

Clicking any of the buttons connects you (if you are online) to the corresponding web site, and gives you the option to subscribe to that site (see "What Are Subscriptions and Channels?" in Chapter 25). Don't be afraid to experiment—"subscribe" in this context does not mean "pay money"; you're safe until someone asks you for a credit card number.

Adding an Active Desktop Item

To add an item to your Active Desktop, follow these steps:

1. Go to the Web tab of the Display Properties dialog box (shown in Figure 13-9) and click the New button. A dialog box asks whether you want to visit Microsoft's online gallery of Active Desktop items.

2. If you are online, you can click Yes. (It's worth checking out at least once to see what is available.) The online instructions guide you through the downloading and installation process.

3. If you want to add an item from somewhere other than the Microsoft gallery, click No.

4. Answer the questions posed by the New Active Desktop Item Wizard.

5. When you are done, the new item appears in the list in the Web tab of the Display Properties dialog box. You can use the check box to toggle the item on or off. A box appears in the monitor-like picture at the top of the Display Properties dialog box, showing where the item will appear (see Figure 13-9).

6. Click OK to exit the dialog box.

The Folder Options button at the bottom of the Web tab of the Display Properties dialog box doesn't actually control display or desktop settings. Instead, it displays the Folder Options dialog box, which controls how your folders look and act on the desktop (see "Changing How the View Settings Work" in Chapter 9).

One useful thing you can do with Active Desktop is to maintain a "hot" to-do list. Using FrontPage Express or some other HTML-writing application, create a to-do list in which each action item is hot-linked to the appropriate documents and/or web sites (see Chapter 26). When you add this HTML document to your Active Desktop, it sits in the background of everything you do, and provides more context than just a lot of shortcuts scattered around your desktop.

Arranging Active Desktop Items

When you select an Active Desktop item, a bar appears above it. You can use that bar as you use a title bar to drag the window wherever you want it.

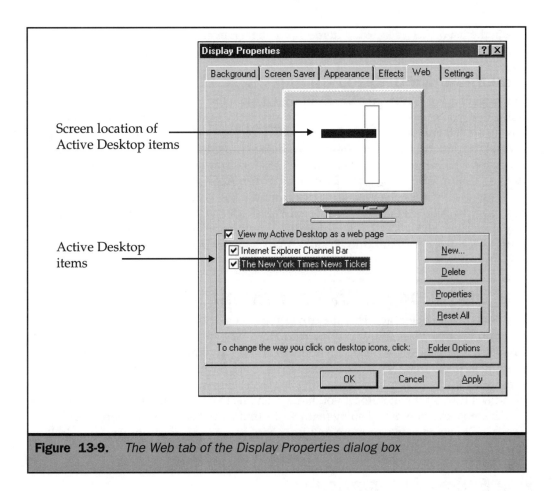

Screen location of
Active Desktop items

Active Desktop
items

Figure 13-9.   *The Web tab of the Display Properties dialog box*

Updating Your Active Desktop Items

To update your Active Desktop items, right-click an empty spot on the desktop, and select Update Now from the Active Desktop menu. When you update an item, it checks the Web for any new information. For example, if a headline ticker is one of the items on your Active Desktop, it updates itself by checking the Web for new headlines.

Removing Active Desktop Items

When you select an Active Desktop item, a bar appears above it. Click the X on that bar to close the window and make the item inactive. Restore it by going to the Web tab of the Display Properties dialog box, shown in Figure 13-9. Click the corresponding check box in the list of Active Desktop items. If you never, ever want to see the item again, select it in the list of Active Desktop items and click the Delete button.

Turning Active Desktop On and Off

You can get rid of all the active items on your desktop by turning Active Desktop off. By doing this, you reserve the possibility of turning Active Desktop back on again and having everything just as it was. To turn Active Desktop on or off, right-click any empty spot on the desktop and select View As Web Page from the Active Desktop menu. This is a toggle-switch; when it is checked, Active Desktop is on, and when it is not checked, Active Desktop is off. Follow the same steps to turn Active Desktop back on.

Equivalently, both the Web and Background tabs of the Display Properties dialog box have check boxes that say Disable All Web-Related Content In My Desktop. If this box is checked, all the stock tickers, headline-scrolling teletypes, weather maps, and so forth vanish from your desktop. Restore them again by unchecking the box.

Getting Along with Your Monitor(s)

Windows 98 can detect and install a driver for a plug-and-play monitor with very little effort on your part (see "How Do You Add Hardware to a Windows Computer?" in Chapter 15). Moreover, it makes a variety of choices automatically, without you even needing to know that there was a choice to be made. In addition, many recent monitors comply with Energy Star power saving standards, allowing you to choose to have Windows turn off the monitor if you have been inactive for a sufficiently long time.

The most exciting new display feature of Windows 98 is that it supports multiple displays. If you have two or more monitors hooked up to your computer, your desktop can stretch across all of them, and each can have its own settings.

Saving Energy Automatically

The most power-hungry component of your computer system is the monitor. Turning it off when you aren't going to be using it for several hours saves energy, in exchange for the relatively minor inconvenience of waiting a few seconds for the monitor to come on again when you're ready to go back to work.

Even more convenient is to have your computer notice when it isn't being used and turn off the monitor on its own. This is possible if your monitor and video card support the Energy Star standards (most new ones do). Set this up from the Power Management Properties dialog box, as follows:

1. Choose Start | Settings | Control Panel, then open the Power Management icon to display the Power Management Properties dialog box.

2. Select a wait time from the Turn Off Monitor drop-down list.

3. Click OK.

To check whether your monitor is Energy Star compliant:

1. Click the Settings tab of the Display Properties dialog box (see Figure 13-8).

2. Click the Advanced button. A display driver dialog box opens; the title of the box varies, depending on your display driver.

3. Click the Monitor tab.

4. Look at the Monitor Is Energy Star Compliant check box. If it is checked, your monitor is compliant. If it is grayed out, your monitor is not compliant. If it is not checked, but not grayed out, check it.

5. Click OK.

Using Multiple Displays

Windows 98 introduces the ability to use two screens on a single system. The system displays a single desktop that spans both screens. A pair of 15-inch monitors have considerably more screen area than a single 17-inch monitor, and can be a very cost-effective alternative to a single larger screen. (Similarly, a pair of 17-inch monitors provide more area than a 20-inch monitor, at far lower cost.)

Configuring a second screen is straightforward once you've installed the new hardware (see "How Do You Add Hardware to a Windows Computer?" in Chapter 15). Open the Settings tab of the Display Properties window, which now looks like Figure 13-10 if two displays are installed.

To configure the second display:

1. Click the picture of monitor number 2 to highlight it. Windows displays a box warning you that some programs may not work correctly with two monitors. Take a chance and click OK.

2. Drag the two pictures of monitors so that they agree with the physical arrangement of your two screens.

3. Configure the second display. If possible, configure the two displays to have the same number of colors and the same screen area, to avoid confusion when you move a window from one screen to another.

4. Click OK.

Windows configures the new display.

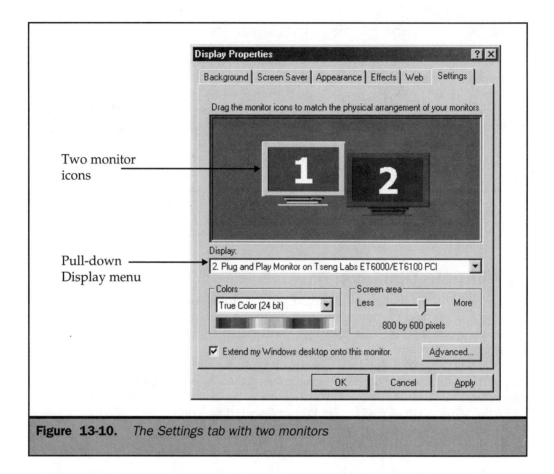

Two monitor icons

Pull-down Display menu

Figure 13-10. *The Settings tab with two monitors*

Once configured, the second display becomes part of the Windows desktop, and you can drag windows back and forth between the two displays. You can even have a single window that spans both screens, which can be convenient for looking at spreadsheets with very wide rows.

Other Monitor Settings

Depending on the capabilities of your monitor, some other configuration settings are available. When you click the Advanced button on the Settings tab of the Display Properties window, you see a dialog box with a title based on the type of monitor you use (see Figure 13-11). Table 13-2 lists the settings in this dialog box.

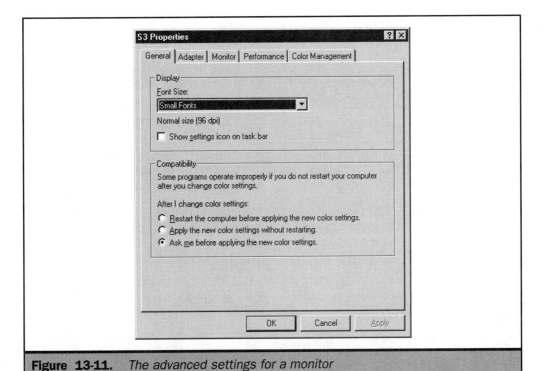

Figure 13-11. *The advanced settings for a monitor*

Tab	Setting	Description
General	Font Size	Specifies the screen font magnification (see "Changing Magnification"). Choosing Other displays the Custom Font Size dialog box, in which you can choose the magnification as a percentage of the normal Windows screen font size.
General	Show settings icon on task bar	Displays a Display Properties icon in the system tray on the Taskbar, from which you can choose screen resolution and color palette.

Table 13-2. *Advanced Display Settings*

Tab	Setting	Description
General	Restart the computer before applying the new color settings	Specifies that after you change the screen resolution or color palette on the Settings tab of the Display Properties dialog box, Windows restarts automatically.
General	Apply the new color settings without restarting	Specifies that after you change the screen resolution or color palette, Windows does not restart.
General	Ask me before applying the new color settings	Specifies that after you change the screen resolution or color palette, Windows prompts you to decide whether to restart.
Adapter	(various)	The settings on this tab depend on the display device driver. Clicking the Change button runs the Update Device Driver Wizard.
Monitor	Monitor is Energy Star Compliant	Specifies that this monitor can power down automatically after a period of inactivity.
Monitor	Automatically detect Plug & Play monitors	Specifies that Windows automatically detects which monitor driver to use. If this detection process causes your monitor to flash, unselect this option.
Monitor	Reset display on suspend/resume	Specifies that Windows reset the display once you resume using a computer (usually a laptop) that has been in suspend mode.
Performance	Hardware acceleration	Specifies how fast Windows updates your screen.
Color Management	(Listing of color profiles)	Specifies the color profiles you have defined.

Table 13-2.   *Advanced Display Settings* (continued)

Chapter 14

Configuring Your Keyboard and Mouse

Windows 98, like all operating systems, sits between the programs you run and the computer you run them on. Whenever a program accepts input from the keyboard, mouse, or a game controller, or sends output to the screen or printer, Windows gets involved. As a result, when you configure Windows to work with your keyboard, mouse, or game controller, the settings you choose affect all the programs you run. You can choose the keyboard layout you want to use and set the sensitivity of the mouse.

Windows has a built-in calendar that all programs can use. It knows the current date and time (which is usually displayed at the right end of the Taskbar), and understands time zones, U.S. daylight saving time, and leap years. You can set the date, time, and the time zone in which you are located, so the Windows calendar will be accurate.

Different countries use different currencies and formats for writing numbers, monetary amounts, dates, and times. Amazingly, Windows has regional settings that let it know about the formats used in most countries in the world (at least most of the ones where people are likely to use computers). By telling Windows which country you live in, you can cause Windows and most programs to use the date, time, and numeric formats you are comfortable with.

You can change most of these settings by using the Keyboard, Mouse, and Regional Settings icons on the Control Panel (see "What Is the Control Panel?" in Chapter 1). If you have installed a game controller or joystick, you can check or change its settings, too.

Configuring Your Keyboard

For the keyboard, you can control the keyboard layout and how keys repeat. (You can also control how fast the cursor blinks, which is not actually a characteristic of the keyboard).

What Are Keyboard Settings?

These settings, which appear on the Speed tab of the Keyboard Properties dialog box (shown in Figure 14-1), control how your keyboard works:

Setting	Description
Repeat delay	Delay between starting to hold down a key and when the key begins repeating.
Repeat rate	How fast the key repeats once it starts repeating.
Cursor blink rate	How fast the cursor blinks.

You can also control which language layout the keyboard uses; different languages use different letters and assign the letters different locations on the keyboard. If you use more than one language, you can choose a key combination that switches between two keyboard layouts.

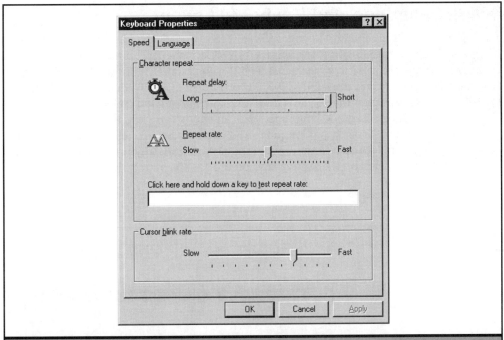

Figure 14-1.   *The Keyboard Properties dialog box contains settings for the keyboard and cursor*

For some languages, Windows 98 offers a selection of *keyboard layouts*, which define the physical organization of the keys on the keyboard. For example, if you choose U.S. English as your language, you can choose among layouts that include the standard 101-key layout, the Dvorak keyboard, and even the left-handed Dvorak keyboard.

To see or change the settings of your keyboard, choose Start | Settings | Control Panel. In the Control Panel window, run the Keyboard program. If the icons are underlined, click the icon once. If they are not underlined, double-click the icon. (You can control whether you need to single- or double-click icons to run programs; see "What Style Is Your Desktop?" in Chapter 1.) You see the Keyboard Properties dialog box shown in Figure 14-1.

   For those who have trouble using the keyboard, see "Setting Keyboard Accessibility Options" in Chapter 20.

Setting the Repeat Delay, Repeat Rate, and Cursor Blink Rate

Click the Speed tab of the Keyboard Properties dialog box to set the repeat delay, repeat rate, or cursor blink rate. You can test how your keys repeat by clicking in the text box and holding down a key.

Installing Language and Keyboard Layouts

To choose which language and keyboard layout to use, click the Language tab of the Keyboard Properties dialog box (see Figure 14-2). Click the Add button to install additional layouts; if you have never installed this keyboard layout on this system, you may have to insert the Windows 98 CD-ROM or floppy disks. To delete a language layout you no longer plan to use, click that language and click the Delete button.

If you install more than one language, you can choose one language to be the default for Windows 98; click that language and click the Set As Default button. Each language on the list has a two-letter abbreviation. When this keyboard layout is in use, the abbreviation appears on the system tray on the Taskbar.

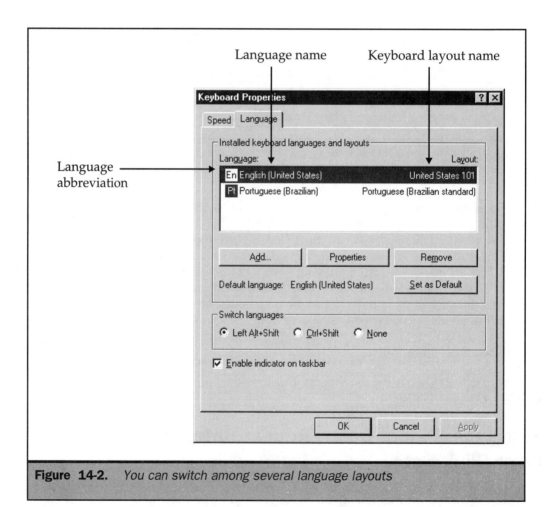

Figure 14-2.   *You can switch among several language layouts*

Tip   *If you don't want the language abbreviation to appear on the system tray, click the*
Enable Indicator On Taskbar box to clear the check mark.

You can also set a key combination for switching among keyboard layouts. Your
options are LEFT ALT-SHIFT (that is, the left-hand ALT key plus the SHIFT key), CTRL-SHIFT,
or none. Another way to switch among the installed keyboard layouts is to click the
language abbreviation on the Taskbar, and then choose a language from the menu
that appears.

Choosing a Keyboard Layout

Even if you don't use a second language, you can use the Language tab of the
Keyboard Properties dialog box to change your keyboard layout. You choose among a
number of predefined layouts, including the standard 101-key layout and the Dvorak
layout. In the Keyboard Properties dialog box, click the Language tab, click the
language you use, and then click the Properties button. On the Language Properties
dialog box that appears, choose a keyboard layout.

Configuring Your Mouse

For the mouse, you can control what the mouse looks like, what its buttons do, and
how fast the *mouse pointer* (the screen object that moves when you move the mouse)
moves. You can define the shape of the mouse pointer, but not the *cursor* (the blinking
element that shows where what you type will be inserted).

What Settings Control the Mouse?

These settings, which appear on the Mouse Properties dialog box, control how your
mouse or trackball works:

Setting	Description
Button configuration	Right-handed (the default), in which the left button is for normal clicking-and-dragging and the right button is for displaying shortcut menus; or left-handed, in which the buttons' functions are reversed.
Double-click speed	Time between double-clicks. If Windows frequently doesn't recognize your double-clicks, set this speed slower.
Pointer speed	How fast the mouse pointer moves when you move the mouse.

Setting	Description
Pointer trail	Whether the mouse pointer leaves a shadowy trail behind it as it moves, and how long the trail should be. If you have trouble finding the mouse pointer, try giving it a trail.

You can also choose the shape that the mouse pointer assumes when used for pointing, when Windows is busy (the hourglass), when you are typing, when selecting text, when clicking a web link, when dragging window borders, and other functions. If you choose shapes other than the Windows default shapes, you can save the set of shapes that you like to use as a *pointer scheme*; Windows 98 comes with more than a dozen predefined pointer schemes you can choose from. Here are some pointers from the 3-D Pointers scheme:

To see or change your mouse settings, choose Start | Settings | Control Panel. In the Control Panel window, run the Mouse program. You see the Mouse Properties dialog box, shown in Figure 14-3.

 For additional settings for those who have trouble using a mouse, see "Setting Mouse Accessibility Options" in Chapter 20.

Defining the Mouse Buttons

Normally, you click or double-click the left mouse button to select, open, or run items on the screen. You click the right mouse button to display the shortcut menu of commands about the item you clicked (see "Choosing Commands from Shortcut Menus" in Chapter 2). Some programs use the right mouse button for other purposes.

If you are left-handed, you can reverse the meanings of the two buttons. On the Mouse Properties dialog box, click the Buttons tab, and click Left-handed. To switch back to the normal meanings, click Right-handed.

Defining Your Double-Click Speed

Windows defines a double-click as two clicks within a specified time period, with no mouse motion during that period. You can set the time period that Windows uses. If you have trouble clicking fast enough for Windows to realize that you want to double-click, make this time period longer.

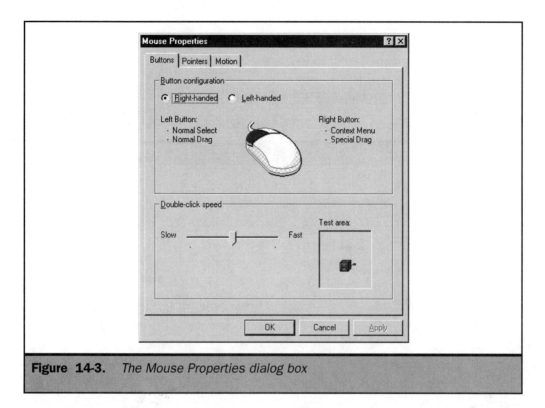

Figure 14-3.   *The Mouse Properties dialog box*

On the Mouse Properties dialog box, click the Buttons tab, and drag the Double-Click Speed slider to adjust the time period. To test the setting, double-click in the Test Area box.

Configuring the Appearance of the Mouse Pointer

The mouse pointer changes shape depending on the context: for example, it appears as an arrow when you are selecting items, or as an I when you are editing text. You can choose the shape that your mouse pointer assumes. On the Mouse Properties dialog box, click the Pointers tab to display a list of the current pointer shapes (see Figure 14-4). To choose a different set of pointer shapes (mouse pointer scheme), click in the Scheme box and choose one from the list. The list of pointer shapes shows the scheme that you selected.

You can also control whether the mouse pointer has a "trail" as it moves, making the pointer easier to see. To turn the pointer trail on or off and to set the length of the trail, click the Motion tab. Click the Show Pointer Trails box to turn the trail on or off, and drag the Pointer Trail slider to the length you want.

To see how the new pointer scheme or pointer trails look, click the Apply button.

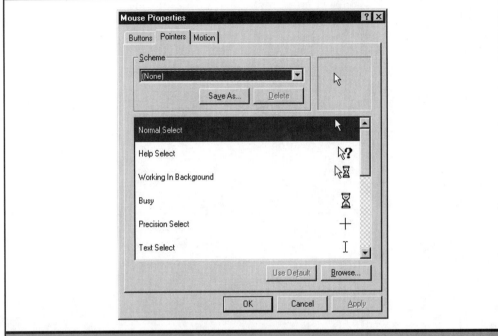

Figure 14-4. *Windows comes with predefined mouse pointer schemes*

Setting the Mouse Speed

You can adjust how far the mouse pointer moves when you move the mouse. For example, if you move the mouse in a small area of your desk, you can adjust Windows to make the mouse very sensitive, so that moving the mouse one inch (2.5 cm) moves the pointer halfway across the screen. If you have shaky hands, you can make the mouse less sensitive, so that small motions of the mouse result in small motions of the pointer.

On the Mouse Properties dialog box, click the Motion tab and drag the Pointer Speed slider to adjust the mouse speed. To try out the new setting, click the Apply button.

Configuring Your Game Controller

Game controllers and *joysticks*—devices that allow you to play arcade-style games on your computer—come in many sizes and shapes. Windows includes drivers for many game controllers (see "What Are Drivers?" in Chapter 15).

To install a game controller, follow the instructions that come with it. Usually, you just shut down Windows, turn off the computer, plug the game controller or joystick into the game port on your computer, and turn your computer back on. Windows 98 should recognize the new device and install it.

To find out whether Windows has recognized your game controller, or to change the settings for a game controller, choose Start | Settings | Control Panel. In the Control Panel window, run the Game Controllers program. You see the Game Controllers dialog box, shown in Figure 14-5.

Checking Whether Your Game Controller Is Installed

If no devices are listed, Windows didn't recognize your game controller. Click the Add button on the Game Controllers dialog box to see the Add Game Controller dialog box, shown in Figure 14-6.

To specify the manufacturer and modem of your game controller, click the Add Other button, choose the manufacturer from the list, and then choose the device from the list. If your game controller came with a floppy disk, click the Have Disk button and follow the instructions for installing the driver from the floppy disk. Otherwise, just

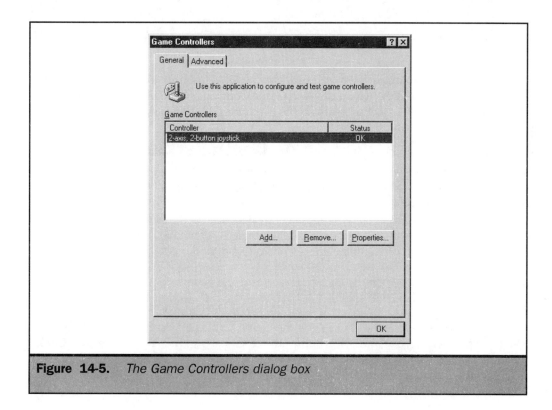

Figure 14-5. *The Game Controllers dialog box*

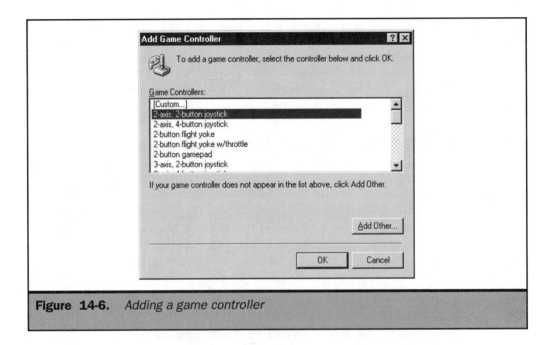

Figure 14-6. *Adding a game controller*

choose the type of game controller you have (the number of buttons and axes that the joystick can move) from the list on the Add Game Controller dialog box, and then click OK. Now the game controller appears on the list in the Game Controllers dialog box.

Displaying and Changing Game Controller Settings

To see the settings for your game controller, select it from the list in the Game Controllers dialog box and click Properties. You see the Game Controller Properties dialog box, shown in Figure 14-7.

One computer can have several game controllers attached. Each controller has an ID number, starting with 1. You can see and change the controller ID numbers by clicking the Advanced tab on the Games Controllers dialog box.

Testing Your Game Controller

To test your game controller, select it from the list on the Game Controllers dialog box, click Properties, and click the Test tab on the Game Controller Properties dialog box. Move the joystick or yoke and see whether the cross-hairs in the Axes box move. Click the buttons on the game controller and see whether the button indicators light up. If not, calibrate the game controller by clicking the Settings tab, clicking the Calibrate button, and following the instructions.

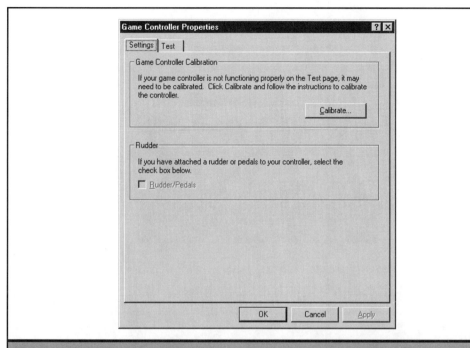

Figure 14-7. *You can calibrate and test your game controller from the Game Controller Properties dialog box*

Windows' Regional Settings

Windows comes with predefined regional settings for most of the countries in the world. *Regional settings* affect the format of numbers, currency, dates, and times. For example, if you choose the regional settings for Germany, Windows knows to display numbers with dots between the thousands and a comma as the decimal point, to use Deutschmarks as the currency, and to display dates with the day preceding the month.

To see or change your settings, choose Start | Settings | Control Panel. In the Control Panel window, run the Regional Settings program. You see the Regional Settings Properties dialog box, shown in Figure 14-8.

Telling Windows Where You Live

Windows has predefined sets of regional settings, so that you don't have to select numeric, currency, date, and time formats separately. Click the Regional Settings tab on the Regional Settings Properties dialog box, click in the box, and choose the

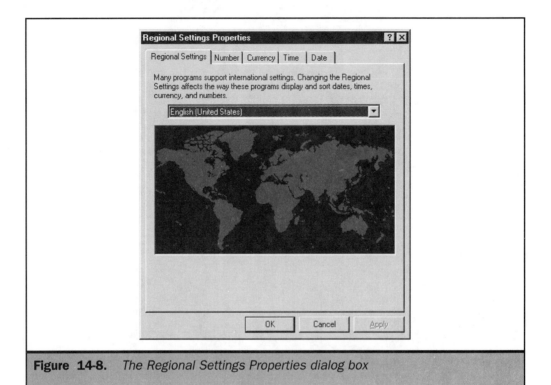

Figure 14-8.   *The Regional Settings Properties dialog box*

language you speak; for languages commonly spoken in more than one country, choose the country where you live.

You can also tell Windows in which time zone you live (see "Setting the Current Date and Time").

   The map is just for decoration; clicking it does nothing!

Setting Number, Currency, Time, and Date Formats

After telling Windows which language you speak and where you live, you can see and change the individual settings that control how Windows displays numbers, currency, times, and dates. Click the Number, Currency, Time, and Date tabs on the Regional Settings Properties dialog box to see or change these settings.

Numbers

The following table shows the settings that tell Windows how you write numbers:

Setting	Description
Decimal symbol	Which character appears as the decimal point, separating the whole from the fractional portion of numbers. (In the U.S., this is a dot.)
No. of digits after decimal	How many digits usually appear to the right of the decimal symbol.
Digit grouping symbol	Which character appears to group digits into groups in large numbers. (In the U.S., this is a comma.)
No. of digits in group	For large numbers, the number of digits in a group between digit grouping symbols. (In the U.S., this is 3.)
Negative sign symbol	Which character indicates negative numbers. (In the U.S., this is −.)
Negative number format	Where the negative sign symbol appears. (In the U.S., the negative sign symbol appears to the left of the number.)
Display leading zeros	For numbers between −1 and 1, whether to display a zero before the decimal symbol. (In the U.S., a zero is displayed; for example, 0.4.)
Measurement system	Whether you use the U.S. or metric system of measurements.
List separator	Which character to use to separate items in lists, for entering lists in Windows text boxes. (The Windows default for the U.S. is a comma.)

Currency

The following settings control how Windows displays currency (money):

Setting	Description
Currency symbol	Symbol that indicates which currency is in use for amounts of money. (In the U.S., this is $.)
Position of currency symbol	Where the currency symbol appears with respect to the number. In the list of options for this setting, a special symbol represents the currency symbol. (In the U.S., the currency symbol $ appears to the left of the amount.)

Setting	Description
Negative number format	How Windows formats negative amounts of money. (In the U.S., accountants usually enclose negative amounts of money in parentheses.)
Decimal symbol	Which character appears as the decimal point in amounts of money, separating the whole from the fractional portion of numbers. (In the U.S., this is a dot.)
No. of digits after decimal	How many digits appear to the right of the decimal symbol in amounts of money. (In the U.S., this is 2, so that dollars and cents are displayed.)
Digit grouping symbol	Which character appears to group digits into groups in large amounts of money. (In the U.S., this is a comma.)
Number of digits in group	For large amounts of money, the number of digits in a group between digit grouping symbols. (In the U.S., this is 3.)

Time and Date Formats

This table shows your options for displaying the time and date:

Setting	Description
Time style	Format for displaying times. In the sample, *h* represents the hour, *hh* the hour with leading zeros, *H* the hour using the 24-hour clock, *HH* the hour using the 24-hour clock and leading zeros, *mm* the minutes, *ss* the seconds, and *tt* the AM/PM symbol. (In the U.S., the format is *h:mm:ss tt*, for example, 2:45:03 PM.)
Time separator	Which character separates the hours, minutes, and seconds. (In the U.S., this is :.)
AM symbol	Which characters or symbols indicate times before noon. (In the U.S., this is AM.)
PM symbol	Which characters or symbols indicate times after noon. (In the U.S., this is PM.)

Setting	Description
Calendar type	Which calendar your computer uses (usually the Gregorian Calendar, and not editable).
Short date style	Short format for displaying dates. In the sample, *M* represents the month number with no leading zeros, *MM* the month number with leading zeros displayed, *MMM* the three-letter abbreviation for the month name, *d* the day with no leading zeros, *dd* the day with leading zeros displayed, *yy* the two-digit year, and *yyyy* the four-digit year. (In the U.S., this is *M/d/yy*, for example, 12/25/98.)
Date separator	Which character separates the month, day, and year. (In the U.S., this is /.)
Long date style	Long format for displaying dates. In the sample, *dddd* represents the name of the day of the week, *MMMM* the name of the month, *dd* the day number, and *yyyy* the four-digit year.

Setting the Current Date and Time

Windows is good at keeping its clock and calendar correct. It knows about U.S. daylight saving time and leap years. But depending on where you live, and the accuracy of your computer's internal clock, you may need to reset Windows' clock or calendar from time to time.

To display the Date/Time Properties dialog box, shown in Figure 14-9, double-click the time on the Taskbar (usually displayed at the right end of the Taskbar). Alternatively, you can choose Start | Settings | Control Panel. In the Control Panel window, run the Date/Time program.

To set the date or time:

- **Year** Click the year, and then type a new year or click the up and down arrow buttons to move the year forward or backward.

- **Month** Click the month and choose the correct month from the list that appears.

- **Day** Click the day number on the calendar.

- **Hour, minute, or second** Click the hour, minute, or second section of the digital clock, and then type a new value or click the up or down arrows.

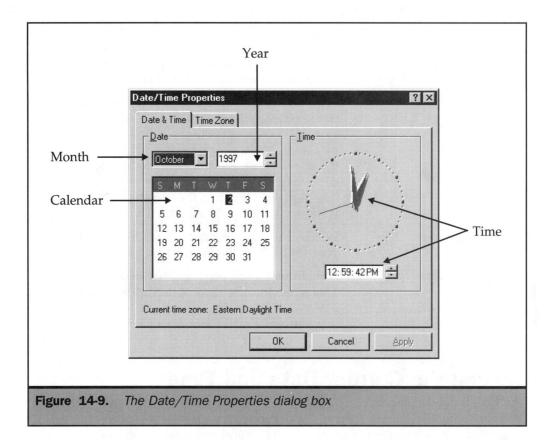

Figure 14-9.   *The Date/Time Properties dialog box*

- **AM or PM**   Click the AM or PM indicator, and then type the new value or click the up or down arrow.

- **Time zone**   Click the Time Zone tab, click in the box that shows the time zone, and then choose a new time zone. (Clicking the map does nothing.) If you want Windows to adjust the clock an hour for daylight saving time in the spring and fall, click the box at the bottom of the window so that a check appears in the box.

Chapter 15

Adding and Removing Hardware

One of the ways that Windows 98 is better than its predecessors is that it lets you add new hardware to your computer relatively easily. But you still have a lot of details to get right. This chapter describes the general steps for installing hardware, the types of hardware you may want to install, how to configure Windows to work with new hardware, troubleshooting hardware, and adding memory.

How Do You Add Hardware to a Windows Computer?

Most Windows computers let you add extra hardware to extend your computer's capabilities. Some hardware fits inside your computer, some plugs into existing connectors on the back of the computer, and some requires adding a card inside your computer, into which you plug external equipment. After you add the device, you need to configure Windows to use your new hardware.

Adding hardware is a three-step process:

1. Set any switches and jumpers on the new equipment, as needed.

2. Turn off and unplug the computer, open it up and install internal cards, if needed, plug in external equipment, and put the computer back together.

3. Turn on the computer and tell Windows about the new equipment.

What Types of Hardware Can You Install?

IBM-compatible computers, having evolved for over 15 years, offer far too many ways to attach new kinds of equipment. The details of PC hardware are beyond the scope of this book, but this section describes the basics of PC hardware that you need to know to get a recalcitrant Windows driver installed. See Chapter 11 for more information about configuring hard disks.

Integrated versus Separate Peripherals

The original IBM Personal Computer contained nothing built into the computer beyond the central processing unit (*CPU*), memory, and keyboard. Everything else, including screens, floppy disk drives, hard disk drives, printers, modems, and serial ports, were provided by separate extra-cost add-in cards. (Hardware you add to your computer, other than processors and memory, is called a *peripheral*.) Over the years, manufacturers have found that, as the functions of the computer were combined into fewer and fewer chips, it is cheaper to build the most common peripherals into the computer's *motherboard* or *system board*, the printed circuit board that carries the CPU and memory. Modern computers typically include a parallel port for a printer, two serial ports, a mouse, controllers for up to two floppy disk drives and two hard disk drives, and, sometimes, the screen adapter on the motherboard. Windows usually can't tell whether these items are built-in or on separate cards, so Windows treats them all as though they are on separate cards.

Connectors

The back of your PC is bristling with connectors for various sorts of devices (see Figure 15-1). If your computer has internal *expansion slots* (slots into which you insert an adapter card), each card in an expansion slot may have a connector or two, as well. Connectors to which you connect cables are also called *ports*.

Serial Ports

Most PCs have one or two *serial ports* or *comm ports*, which are D-shaped connectors with 9 or 25 pins:

Most commonly, you plug an external modem into a serial port, but serial ports are also used for serial mice, computer-to-computer cabling for "poor man's networking," and, occasionally, for printers.

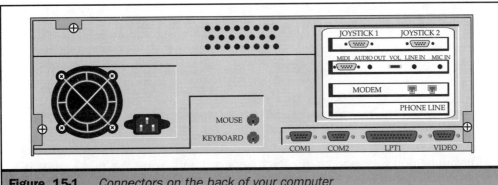

Figure 15-1.   *Connectors on the back of your computer*

Telephone Plugs

If your computer has an *internal modem*, it installs inside your computer. If you have an *external modem*, it is a separate box that connects to one of your computer's serial ports, as well as getting power from a wall plug. Either way, your modem has one or two *RJ-11* telephone plugs that are identical to the plugs on the back of a U.S. telephone.

If there are two plugs, one is for the incoming phone line plugged into the wall, and the other is for a phone that shares the line with the modem. (The advantage to plugging the phone in via the modem is that, while the modem is on-line, the phone is disconnected, so you won't mess up your modem call if you pick up the phone by mistake.)

Parallel Ports

Most PCs have a *parallel port*, a D-shaped socket with holes for 25 pins. Parallel ports are used for printers, and sometimes for other devices, such as a low-performance CD-ROM, tapes, and network adapters.

The 25-pin serial port is mechanically identical to the parallel port, except that the serial port is "male" and the parallel port is "female." Despite the similar connectors, you can't plug a device intended for one port into the other port.

Keyboard/Mouse Ports

All PCs have a connector for the keyboard, and nearly all PCs have a connector for a mouse. There are two kinds of keyboard connectors: the older, larger AT connector and the newer, smaller PS/2 connector. (These types of round connectors are also called *DIN connectors*, for the German standard-setting agency that named them.)

The mouse port is identical to the PS/2 keyboard port. You can plug a keyboard with an AT connector into a PS/2 keyboard port, or vice versa, using an inexpensive adapter plug. On computers with identical PS/2 and keyboard connectors, it's not supposed to matter which one you plug into which port, although on a few computers, it does matter nonetheless.

A few computers use a 9-pin connector for the mouse and provide a 9-pin-to-round-mouse connector adapter. Although the 9-pin connector is physically identical to a serial port, it's electrically different.

VGA Ports

VGA and Super VGA screens use a 15-pin connector that is similar in size to the 9-pin serial connector.

All VGA and Super VGA screens made in recent years use the same plug and are compatible with all screen controllers, at least at lower resolutions such as 640x480.

Universal Serial Bus (USB)

The *Universal Serial Bus* (*USB*) is a new connector for which Microsoft introduced support in Windows 98. It is intended to be a faster and simpler replacement for serial and parallel ports, as well as for low- to moderate-speed devices such as modems, printers, sound cards, and backup tapes.

The USB uses a small rectangular connector. Unlike most other connection schemes, USB lets you *daisy chain* devices, so that your first device plugs into the computer, the second device plugs into the first device, and so forth, so that you can have a desk full of USB devices, even though there's only a single USB connector on your computer.

Audio Jacks

Multimedia PCs have connectors for speakers or headphones and sometimes a microphone. The speaker connector is a standard mini-audio jack. The microphone connector is usually also a mini-audio jack, so you have to be careful not to confuse the two.

If your computer doesn't have speaker connectors, you can add an internal sound board. Many CD-ROM drives have headphone jacks so you can listen to audio CDs even if your computer has no speakers.

PC Cards

Laptop computers usually have one or two *PC card* slots (formerly known as *PCMCIA* slots). A few desktop computers have them, too. These take credit-card sized adapter cards of many varieties, including modems, networks, and disk and tape controllers.

PC cards, unlike other adapter cards, can be added to, and removed from, your computer while it's running. To add a PC card, press it firmly into the slot until it seats. To remove a PC card, press the button next to the PC card to eject the card slightly, and then pull out the card.

Before removing a PC card, you should first tell Windows, so that it can stop sending data to, or receiving data from, the card.

Internal Adapter Cards

If you add a device to your computer that can't be plugged into one of the existing connectors on your computer, you have to add an *adapter card* that plugs into a slot inside the computer.

As the PC has evolved over the past 15 years, the slots into which you can plug adapter cards have evolved as well.

ISA Cards

The original IBM PC and PC/AT defined what now are known as *Industry Standard Architecture (ISA)* slots, into which you plug ISA cards. An ISA slot has a two-part connector. The oldest 8-bit cards plug into the front part only, while newer 16-bit cards plug into both parts. Most ISA cards are configured manually; that is, you have to set the hardware parameters for the card by flipping little switches on the card, or by plugging and unplugging little jumpers on the card. This manual configuration is, by far, the most tedious and error-prone part of hardware installation, and usually requires considerable manual trial-and-error to make it work.

PCI Cards

PCI (Personal Computer Interface) slots are a modern replacement for ISA, and accept PCI cards. They are better than ISA in every way—smaller, faster, cheaper to manufacture, more reliable, and much easier to set up. A PCI connector is about half the size of an ISA connector, due to a much more advanced design. Whenever possible, use PCI cards rather than any other kind in your PC, because they're a lot easier to set up and they work better.

Other Kinds of Cards

The IBM PS/2 series computers introduced, in the 1980s, the *Microchannel (MCA)* slots, an alternative to ISA slots that never caught on. If your computer has MCA slots, you need MCA cards, which are now very hard to get. Around the same time, other PC manufacturers introduced EISA (Enhanced or Extended ISA) slots, an improved version of ISA slots that have now been superseded by PCI.

Most computers have a few specialized slots and connectors for specific devices. There are usually four small slots for memory, and a connector or two for IDE or EIDE expansion disks. Your computer's manual should list the available slots and connectors.

Hardware Parameters

Every card in your PC needs a variety of hardware parameters to be set, so that the CPU can communicate with the card reliably and without interfering with other cards. With the newer kinds of connections, such as PCI and USB, most—if not all—of these parameters are set automatically, but older ISA cards and some PCI cards require manual tweaking.

To see a list of your computer's hardware, choose Start | Settings | Control Panel to display the Control Panel, open the System icon, click the Device Manager tab, click the first entry (Computer), and click the Properties button. You see the Computer Properties dialog box, shown in Figure 15-2. You can click the radio buttons at the top of the dialog box to see a listing of the interrupts (IRQs), I/O addresses, DMA channels, or memory addresses.

 Keep a logbook for your computer, listing all the cards installed in your computer and the hardware parameters you've set on them. This makes troubleshooting a lot easier.

I/O Address

Every device attached to a PC has at least one *I/O address*, a hexadecimal number that the CPU uses to communicate with the device. All I/O addresses on a given computer

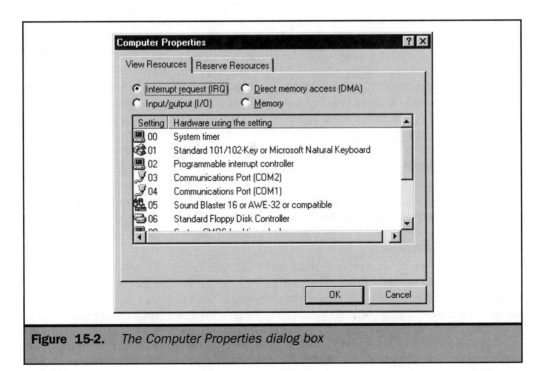

Figure 15-2. *The Computer Properties dialog box*

must be unique; address "collisions" are the most common reason that a new I/O device doesn't work.

Devices on the motherboard have I/O addresses that either are permanently assigned or can be changed in the setup menus built into your motherboard (see the documentation that came with your computer). Devices on ISA cards have addresses that generally can be changed by moving jumpers on the card, while PCI cards have addresses that are set by software when you start your computer.

All traditional PC devices have well known fixed addresses. These include up to four serial ports, a parallel port, floppy and hard disk controllers, and internal devices such as the clock and keyboard controller. Other add-in devices have more-or-less fixed addresses, depending on how popular the device is and how long it's been around. PCI cards automatically get unique addresses, but ISA cards often need jumpers to be reset.

See the troubleshooting section later in this chapter for advice on getting I/O addresses unscrambled.

Interrupts

The PC architecture provides 15 *interrupts*, channels that a device can use to alert the CPU that the device needs attention. The interrupts are numbered 0, 1, and 3 through 15. (For historical reasons, interrupt 2 isn't available, and the few devices that used interrupt 2 on early PCs use interrupt 9 instead.) PCI devices all can, and usually do, share a single interrupt, but nearly every ISA device that uses an interrupt needs a separate unique interrupt number. Motherboard devices use interrupts 0 and 1, built-in serial ports usually use 3 and 4, the floppy disk uses 6, the parallel port uses 7, the clock uses 8, a built-in mouse uses 12, the floating-point unit uses 13 (even if you don't do any floating-point calculations), and the hard disk controller uses 15, leaving 5, 9, 10, 11, and 14 for other devices. Assigning interrupts correctly on ISA cards is one of the most troublesome and error-prone parts of hardware configuration. A few ISA cards can have their interrupt number set in software, in which case Windows sets the interrupt automatically, but most have jumpers you have to change.

DMA Channels

DMA, which stands for *Direct Memory Access*, is a motherboard facility used by a few medium-speed devices. There are six DMA channels, of which the floppy disk always takes DMA 2. Some sound cards need a DMA channel, usually DMA 1.

Memory Addresses

A few devices, notably screen controllers and some network cards, use a shared memory region to transfer data between the CPU and the device. Those devices need a range of memory addresses for their shared memory. Screen cards generally use the ranges (expressed in hexidecimal numbers, or hex) 0xA0000 through 0xAFFFF, 0xB0000 through 0xBFFFF, and sometimes 0xC0000 through 0xCFFFF. The range from the end of the screen controller's memory to about 0xE0000 is available for other devices. Some ISA cards have their memory addresses set in software, in which case Windows sets the addresses automatically, but others have jumpers you have to change. PCI cards always have their addresses set in software.

IDE and SCSI Devices

IDE and SCSI disk controllers present an extra challenge, because you can attach more than one device to a single controller. See Chapter 11 for more information about configuring hard disks.

IDE Device Numbers

IDE (which stands for Integrated Drive Electronics) disk controllers support up to two devices, the first of which is usually a hard disk, and the second of which can be either a hard disk or CD-ROM drive. The controller has two connectors into which drive cables are plugged, and which device is which depends on which connector each is plugged into. The first device is called the *primary* device, and the second the *secondary* device.

Some motherboards contain two IDE controllers, each of which can have a primary and secondary device, for a system total of four devices.

SCSI Device Numbers

Each *SCSI* (Small Computer Systems Interface) controller can connect up to 7 devices for older controllers, or 15 devices for more recent controllers. To identify devices attached to one SCSI controller, each device has a device number from 0 to 7, or 15.

The SCSI controller itself has a device number, usually the highest possible number, 7 or 15. The first disk is invariably device 0, but other numbers can be assigned arbitrarily, as long as each device has a separate number. A few devices have sub-units, such as tape or CD-ROM jukebox drives that can contain several different tapes or disks.

The Many Flavors of SCSI

Since SCSI has evolved over the years to support bigger and faster devices, several varieties have appeared: regular, wide, fast/wide, and ultra. The differences are mostly invisible to Windows, so your main concern is that your devices are compatible with the controller. If their cables use compatible connectors, the devices are almost certainly compatible.

On PCs there are also internal and external SCSI devices, depending on whether the device is housed inside the PC or in a separate cabinet. An external device is merely an internal device installed in a separate cabinet. The important difference is that internal and external SCSI cables are different: Internal cables are simple ribbon cables and external cables are thick round cables with a variety of connectors. Again, so long as the connectors match, the devices should be compatible.

Due to some extremely bad planning in the early 1980s, older external SCSI devices use connectors that are physically identical to the DB-25 and Centronics connectors used on modems and printers on parallel and serial ports. Even if they fit physically, don't try connecting a SCSI device to a non-SCSI controller, or vice versa, because it won't work and you may well cause expensive damage to the electronics.

Memory (RAM)

Memory, or RAM (random access memory), is the temporary storage your computer uses for the programs that you are running and the files you currently have open. Most PCs have four special memory slots, and usually the computer is shipped with one or two of the four slots already containing memory. There are many different sizes, speeds, and types of memory, so you must ensure that the memory you add is compatible with your particular computer. Memory chips are extremely sensitive to static electricity, so be sure to understand and follow the procedures needed to avoid static damage. (Most memory ships with an anti-static wrist strap and instructions on how to use it.) See "Adding Memory" later in this chapter.

What Are Drivers?

Many hardware devices—whether they come as part of your computer or are added later—require a *driver*, a program that translates between your operating system (Windows 98) and the hardware. For example, a printer driver translates printing requests from Windows (and through it, your applications) to commands that your printer can understand.

Windows 98 comes with standard drivers for a wide range of monitors, printers, modems, and other devices. When you buy hardware, you may receive a floppy disk or CD-ROM that contains the driver for the device, which you need to install during the configuring process to get the device to work with Windows.

Configuring Windows for New Hardware

One of the biggest improvements in Windows 95, compared to DOS and Windows 3.1, is its automatic device configuration. Windows 98 uses basically the same system as Windows 95, but with support added for many more-recent devices. In most cases, Windows can identify and configure new hardware automatically.

Follow these steps to install new hardware and configure Windows to use it:

1. Shut down your computer, turn it off, unplug it, and install your new hardware. This may involve opening up the computer and installing a card, or

inserting a card into a PC Card slot, or just plugging a new external device into a SCSI adapter or USB plug.

2. Turn on the device (if external), and turn on and start up your computer. PCI and SCSI devices usually have a BIOS setup routine that you have to enter when you turn on the computer and run one time to do low-level configuration of your new device.

3. If you're lucky, Windows notices the new device as it starts and automatically configures it for you.

4. If you're less lucky, Windows just starts up. Run the Add New Hardware Wizard, described in the next section.

5. If you're very unlucky, Windows doesn't start at all. Use Safe Mode to figure out what's wrong (see "Booting in Safe Mode").

Using the Add New Hardware Wizard

Windows' Add New Hardware Wizard does a good job handling the details of installing new device drivers. After you've installed a new device, run the Wizard by following these steps.

1. Choose Start | Control Panel, and then open the Add New Hardware icon. Click or double-click depending on whether your desktop uses Web or Classic style (see "Choosing the Style of Your Desktop" in Chapter 1). The Add New Hardware Wizard starts. The first thing the Wizard does is search for new *Plug and Play* devices, devices which can communicate with Windows to provide their own configuration information. Even if you know you don't have any new Plug and Play devices, you have to wait while Windows checks for them. If the Wizard finds new devices (or old but unused devices), it shows you a list, as in Figure 15-3. (The list in Figure 15-3 includes unused motherboard IDE disk and PS/2 mouse devices, because the computer in this example has a SCSI disk controller and a serial port mouse.)

2. If one of the devices in the list is the one you want to install, check Yes, click the correct device, and then click Next.

3. If Windows didn't find your new device, click No and Next to proceed to the next screen, where Windows offers to search for non-Plug and Play devices. Searching for non-Plug and Play is slower and riskier than searching for Plug and Play, and sometimes crashes the computer. If you know what you just installed, you can click No and select the driver yourself. If you click Yes, Windows attempts to find any new devices, which takes a while. When it finishes, click the Details button to see a list of what it found (Figure 15-4).

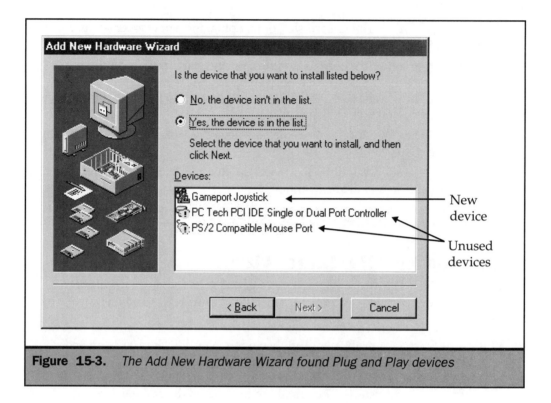

New device

Unused devices

Figure 15-3.   *The Add New Hardware Wizard found Plug and Play devices*

4. If you click No and Next, you see a list of hardware types (Figure 15-5).

5. Pick your hardware type from the list, and click Next to see a list of manufacturers and models (Figure 15-6). It's often difficult to guess what category a device falls into, so you may have to pick one category, look there, and then click Back and try another category or two before you find your device.

6. Choose the manufacturer, and then the model of your device. If your device came with a driver on a floppy disk and you want to use that driver, click Have Disk and tell Windows which drive contains the disk, which usually is drive A.

Tip   *Windows 98 contains up-to-date drivers for an enormous number of devices. If you have a driver disk, check the dates of the files on the disk. If they're older than mid-1997 and Windows has a driver for your device, the standard Windows driver is probably better than the one on the disk.*

7. Click Next, and Windows finishes installing your device. You may have to insert your Windows 98 CD-ROM or floppy disks if the device needs drivers that haven't been used before, and you may have to reboot Windows.

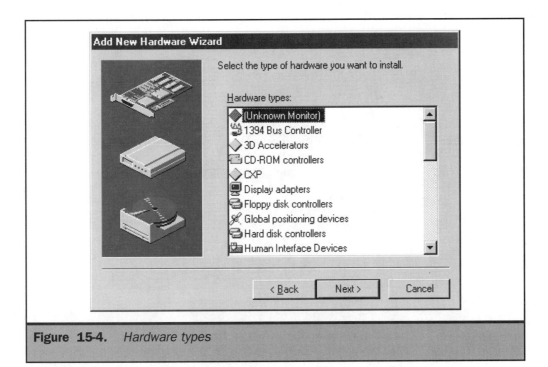

Figure 15-4. *Hardware types*

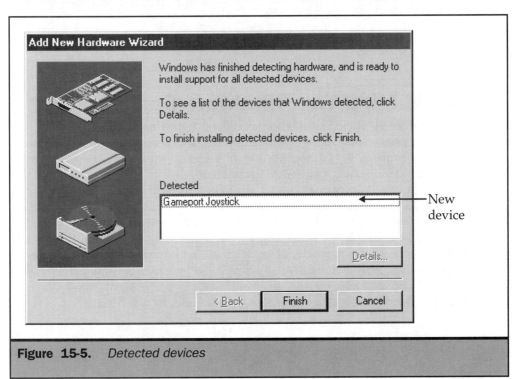

Figure 15-5. *Detected devices*

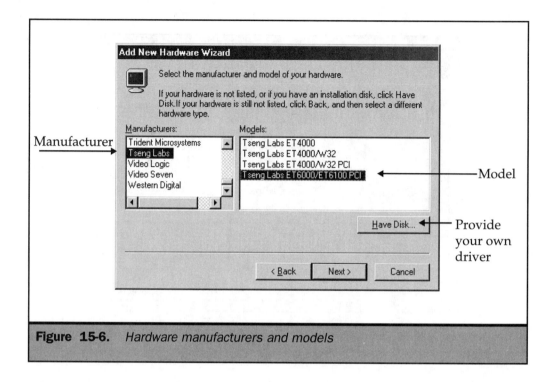

Figure 15-6.   *Hardware manufacturers and models*

At this point, unless Windows has reported a configuration problem, your device should be ready to use.

Troubleshooting Your Hardware Configuration

In a perfect world, every device installation would work the first time. In the real world, something goes wrong about one time in three, and you have to fix it. The most common problem is that an I/O device address or interrupt used by the new device conflicts with an older one (see "Hardware Parameters").

In the worst case, Windows doesn't boot at all after you add your new device. If you installed an ISA card, this invariably means that the settings on the card conflict with an existing device. Turn off the computer, take out the new device, turn on the computer, and reboot. Use the Device Manger to see what addresses and interrupts are currently in use, and use the card's documentation to find out how to change jumpers to addresses and interrupts that are available (see "Using the Device Manager"). Then reinstall the card and try again.

If you can't tell what the conflicts are, boot the computer in Safe Mode.

Booting in Safe Mode

Safe Mode provides minimal Windows functions by disabling all devices except the keyboard, screen, and disk. To boot in Safe Mode, start your computer normally, but watch the screen carefully. As soon as you see the Starting Windows 98 message, press F8. You should see a menu of startup options, one of which is Safe Mode. (Other options include Safe Mode With Network Support, which you can use if you're 100 percent sure that the problem isn't a network device, nor any other device that might be conflicting with the hardware resources used by a network device.)

Once you've booted in Safe Mode, you can use the Device Manager and other Windows facilities to figure out what's wrong.

To leave Safe Mode, reboot the computer normally.

Using the Device Manager

The *Device Manager* lists all the devices that make up your computer and lets you see and modify their configuration. If the Add New Hardware Wizard detects a device conflict, it starts the Device Manager automatically. To start it yourself, open the System icon in the Control Panel, and then click the Device Manager tab, as shown in Figure 15-7. You can view devices by type or by connection; by connection is usually better for driver debugging, since it displays each connected device separately. (On

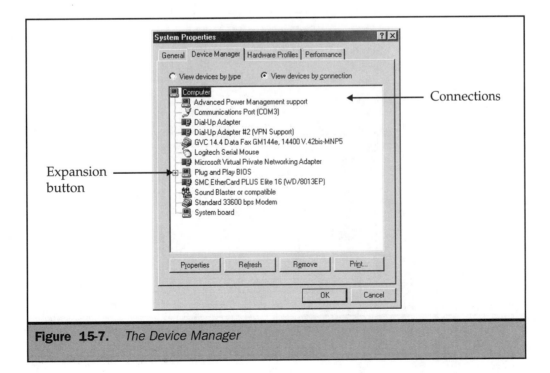

Figure 15-7. *The Device Manager*

most computers, the majority of devices are under the Plug and Play BIOS, so click its expansion button to see the Plug and Play devices.)

To deal with a configuration problem, follow these steps:

1. Display the Device Manager by choosing Start | Settings | Control Panel, opening the System icon, and then clicking the Device Manager tab.

2. To see a particular device, click that device, click the Properties button, and then the Resource tab. If a device has resource conflicts, Windows displays them, as in Figure 15-8. In this case, the conflict is the interrupt number.

3. To resolve a conflict, uncheck Use Automatic Settings (if it's checked), click the conflicting resource, and then click Change Setting. Windows lets you adjust the resource used, telling you at each step what conflicts still exist.

4. Once you've found a setting with no conflicts, write it down on a piece of paper and click OK. Windows will offer to shut down the computer to let you adjust the device to agree with the setting you just changed.

5. Do so, and then turn off the computer, change the jumpers as needed, reinstall the card, and restart Windows.

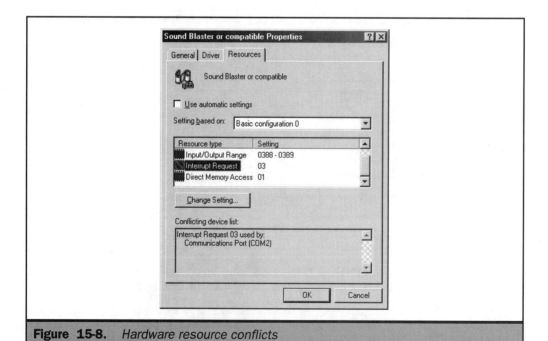

Figure 15-8.   *Hardware resource conflicts*

Adding Memory

Adding memory to a Windows PC is simple, because no drivers are required. To add memory, follow these steps:

1. Shut down Windows, turn off and unplug the computer, open up the computer, and add the memory to available memory slots.

2. Close up the computer, plug it back in, and start it up. Most PCs do an internal memory test, notice that the amount of memory has changed, and complain before Windows starts.

3. If your computer complains, enter the computer's low-level configuration setup (also called BIOS or CMOS setup) and adjust the configured amount of memory to reflect the total now installed. Then reboot. When Windows starts, it automatically takes advantage of all memory installed in your computer.

Chapter 16

Setting Up Printers and Fonts

Windows 98 has a sophisticated and powerful printer management system. Setting up your printers can be painful, but once they're configured, you can quickly and easily print from your programs by using any local or network printer accessible to your computer, and be confident that your printouts will look the way you want.

After your printer is installed, you can manage your print jobs, holding or canceling documents you print. You can change the printer configuration, including settings such as paper size and default fonts. If you run into printer trouble, you can use the Print Troubleshooter to find the problem.

Windows 98 handles the fonts that appear on the screen and on your printed pages. Windows itself comes with fonts, as do many application programs, and you can buy and install additional fonts.

How Does Windows Handle Printers?

Each printer installed on your system has an entry in the Windows 98 *Printers folder*. When you print something from an application, a Windows *printer driver* (printer control program) for the current printer formats the material for that particular printer. As far as printer limitations permit, documents look the same regardless of what printer they're printed on.

You can have several printers defined on your system. They may be different physical printers or different modes on the same printer. For example, a few printers handle both Hewlett Packard's PCL printer control language and the Adobe Postscript language. You can have two printer drivers installed, one for PCL and one for Postscript. If your printer can print on both sides of the paper, you can have two drivers installed, one for single-sided printing and one for double-sided printing. To see the installed printers, open your Printers folder by choosing Start | Settings | Printers.

You can print on a *local printer* (a printer that is connected directly to your computer) or to a *network printer* (a printer that your computer can access over a local area network). Once you have configured Windows to use either a local or network printer, printing works exactly the same for either type.

At any particular moment, one of the printers is marked as the *default printer*. Anything you print goes to the default printer unless you specifically tell your program to use a different printer. In the Printers folder, you can make any of your printers the default.

Windows also provides *spooling*, a service that stores document data on disk until the printer can accept it. When you print a document from an application, the information to be printed (the *print job*) is stored temporarily in the *queue* (storage for print jobs) until it can be printed. If you print a long document to a slow printer, spooling lets you continue working with your application while the printer works. (Many years ago, "spool" stood for Simultaneous Printer Operation On-Line, but nobody remembers that any more.)

Windows also treats a fax modem as a kind of printer. Unlike Windows 95, Windows 98 doesn't come with a built-in fax facility. (If you install Microsoft Exchange or Microsoft Outlook, but not Outlook Express, you get Microsoft Fax as part of the package.)

What Are Fonts?

Modern computer screens and printers can display text in a variety of *typefaces* and sizes, as illustrated in Figure 16-1. In *fixed pitch* typefaces, all the characters are the same width, like on a typewriter. In *proportionally spaced* typefaces, different characters are different widths. (The relative widths vary from one typeface to another.) Most typefaces are available in different sizes, with the sizes measured in printer's points, 1/72 inch. The most common sizes are 10-point and 12-point, roughly corresponding to sizes of elite and pica typewriter type. Fonts are often provided in several variations, such as normal, bold, italic, and bold-italic.

Typographers refer to the collection of all the characters in a typeface of a given size and variation as a *font*. For example, Arial italic 12-point is a font, although in the computer field, the terms *font* and *typeface* (or face) are often (incorrectly) used interchangeably.

Windows comes with a small but adequate set of fonts, but many programs and printer drivers include fonts of their own. Once a font is installed, any program can use it, regardless of where the font came from. Thus, a typical Windows installation may have 50 to 100 fonts available. Entire books have been written on typeface design and usage, so we won't attempt to say anything about the topic other than to note that documents that use many different typefaces are usually harder to read than those that use only one or two.

Note *In addition to fonts that contain letters and numbers, Windows comes with several fonts of special characters. You can use the Character Map program to look at them and add them to your documents (see "Using Special Characters with Character Map" in Chapter 5).*

This is a sample of 12-point Times, a proportionally spaced typeface.
This is a sample of 12-point Arial, another proportionally spaced typeface.
`This is a sample of 12-point Courier, a fixed-pitch typeface.`
This is very small 6-point type.
This is rather large 18-point type.

Figure 16-1.   *Sample typefaces and sizes*

What Is TrueType?

Computer printers and screens print and display characters by printing or displaying patterns of black and white dots. The size of the dots depends on the resolution of the device, ranging from 72 to 100 dots-per-inch on screens, to 300, 600, or even 1200 dots-per-inch on laser printers. In early versions of Windows, each typeface was provided as a bitmap of the actual black and white dots for each character, with separate bitmaps for each size. The bitmaps were available only in a small variety of sizes, such as Courier 10-, 12-, and 15-point.

This scheme does not produce very good-looking documents, because the dot resolution of printers is rarely the same as that for a screen. In the process of printing, Windows had to rescale each character's bitmap to the printer's resolution, producing odd-looking characters with unattractive jagged corners. Even worse, if you used a font in a size other than one of the sizes provided, the system had to do a second level of rescaling, producing even worse-looking characters.

TrueType solves both of these problems by storing each typeface not as a set of bitmaps, but essentially as a set of formulas the system can use to *render* (draw) each character at any desired size and resolution. This means that TrueType fonts look consistent on all devices, and that you can use them in any size.

 Use only TrueType fonts in documents that you plan to print, to make your documents look their best.

How Do Printers Handle Fonts?

Older printers had one or two fonts built in, and when you printed a document, those were the fonts you got. Modern printers can print any image that the resolution of the printer prints, so they can print all the fonts that are installed on your system.

Printers handle fonts in three different ways. Most printers have a reasonable set of built-in general-purpose fonts, and some can accept font cartridges with added fonts. If you use fonts other than the built-in ones, then on lower performance printers, Windows reverts to printing graphics, in effect turning your document into a full-page bitmap image that Windows can send (slowly) to the printer. Some printers, notably laser printers that use the Postscript and PCL5 printer control languages, can handle downloaded fonts, so Windows can send the printer all the fonts that a particular document needs.

To speed up printing, Windows uses *font substitution*, using built-in printer fonts where possible for similar TrueType fonts. For example, Microsoft's Arial font is nearly identical to the Helvetica font found in Postscript printers, so when Windows prints Arial text, it tells the printer to use Helvetica instead. This process of font substitution normally works without trouble, although occasionally, on clone printers, the built-in fonts aren't exactly what Windows expects and the results can look a little off. (You can tell Windows to turn off font substitution if you suspect that's a problem.)

Adding and Deleting Printers

Windows has almost entirely automated the process of adding a new printer. Whether you are installing a new printer attached to your computer (a local printer) or configuring Windows to use a printer on your local area network, you use the Add Printer Wizard.

Adding a New Local Printer

Be sure your printer is connected to your PC and is turned on. If the printer came with floppy disks or a CD-ROM, have them in hand. Then, follow these steps:

1. Open the Printers folder from a Folder window (open the My Computer icon on the desktop and open the Printers item), from Windows Explorer (where the Printers folder appears on the folder tree after all the disk drives), or by choosing Start | Settings | Printers. Figure 16-2 shows the Printers window, which displays an icon for every printer on your system.

2. Open Add Printer. Click the Add Printer either once or twice, depending on whether you have configured Windows to use Web style or Classic style (see "Choosing the Style of Your Desktop" in Chapter 1). The Add Printer Wizard walks you through the process of adding a new printer.

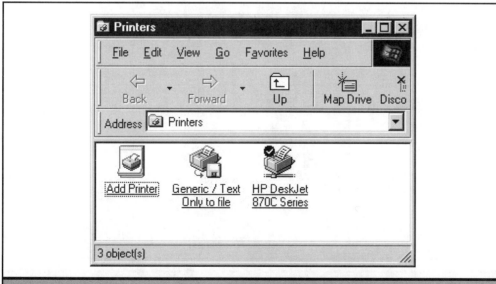

Figure 16-2.   *The Printers window*

3. The Wizard asks whether you're adding a local or network printer. Then it asks what kind of printer you're installing, showing the list of printers for which it has drivers (see Figure 16-3). Windows 98 has drivers for a huge variety of printers, so your printer will most likely be in the list. Some printers have more than one driver—for example, separate PCL and Postscript drivers for printers that can handle both, in which case you can choose any of the drivers for your printer. If your printer doesn't appear in the list, you probably can use the driver for another similar printer. Most PCL printers are similar to one of the HP Laserjet series, and most Postscript printers are similar to one of the Apple Laserwriters. If your printer comes with a diskette containing a printer driver, or you know there's a printer driver available on a network to which you are connected, you can click Have Disk, and enter the location of the driver.

If you have a disk, but your printer appears in the Windows list, use the Windows driver, unless your disk is dated 1997 or later. Older disks contain less up-to-date drivers than the ones that come with Windows.

4. The Wizard asks which port your printer is attached to. Select the appropriate port, usually LPT1.

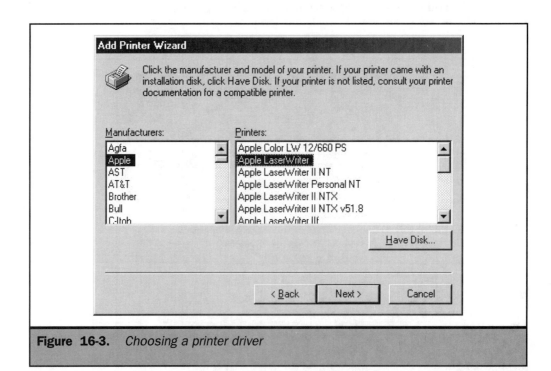

Figure 16-3.   *Choosing a printer driver*

5. The Wizard asks whether you want to change the name you use for this printer (which you probably don't), and whether to use this printer as the default printer. (You can later change the default at any time if you want.)

6. Finally, the Wizard asks whether it should print a test page. At this point, Windows installs the printer driver. Be sure the Windows CD-ROM is in the drive, unless you specified a printer driver located somewhere else.

Windows prints a test page with a Windows logo and a description of the printer. If the test page prints and looks correct, your printer is installed.

Adding a New Network Printer

Installing a new printer on a local area network is very similar to installing a new local printer.

1. Open the Add Printer icon, as previously described, to start the Add Printer Wizard, but click Network printer instead. The Wizard asks for the network path or queue name of the printer.

2. If you know the path, type it in; otherwise, click the Browse button to see a map of your network (see Figure 16-4). In that map, if the printer doesn't appear, double-click the computer to which the printer is connected to display the printers on that computer, select the printer you want to use, and then click OK.

3. You also have to specify whether you plan to print from MS-DOS programs to the network printer. MS-DOS provides no standard technique for programs to print via a network, so Windows can "capture" output sent to one of the standard printer ports and redirect it to the network printer. If you don't plan to print from MS-DOS programs, there's no need to capture a port, so click No. You can later change which ports are or are not captured (see "Configuring Printers").

4. To arrange to capture a printer port, click Yes where the Add Printer Wizard asks whether you print from MS-DOS programs, and then click Capture Printer Port on the window that follows. Windows asks you to select the printer port to capture. Choose LPT1, unless there is a local printer on that port, in which case you should choose an unused port, and then click OK.

5. Windows then asks you to choose a printer driver. From this point on, installing a network printer is exactly the same as installing a local printer, as described in the previous section. See Chapter 32 for more information on sharing resources (including printers) on a network.

Deleting a Printer

If you want to remove an installed printer, just drag the printer's icon from the Printer window into the Recycle Bin.

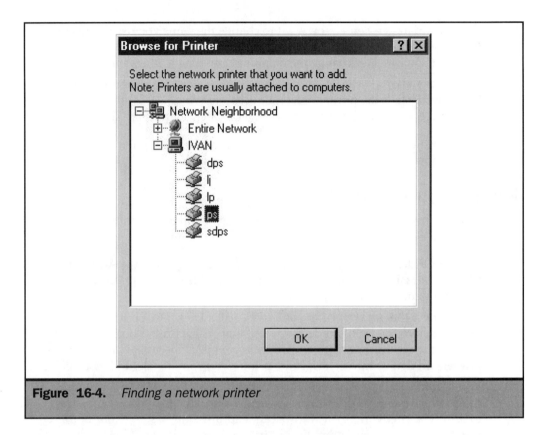

Figure 16-4. *Finding a network printer*

Troubleshooting Your Printer

Microsoft provides a somewhat useful troubleshooting feature for getting printers to work correctly. Follow these steps:

1. Choose Start | Help to display the Windows Help window (see Chapter 6).

2. Click the Contents tab, open the Troubleshooting entry in the list of topics, open the Windows 98 Troubleshooters entry to see the list of troubles that can be shot, and then click Print in that list. The Windows 98 Print Troubleshooter appears in the right pane of the Windows Help window.

3. The Troubleshooter asks you questions about your printer problem, so that it can identify the problem, and then it makes suggestions to fix the most common printer problems, such as no printing at all, slow or garbled printing, and distorted graphics. Click the radio button that describes your problem and

click the Next button to find out what Windows recommends. With luck, your problem will be one that the Troubleshooter addresses.

Configuring Printers

After you install your printer or printers, you configure the driver to match your printer's setup. Some simple printers have little or no setup, while laser printers have a variety of hardware and software options.

To configure a printer, open the Printers folder by choosing Start | Settings | Printers. Right-click the printer of interest and select Properties from the menu that appears. You see the Properties dialog box for the printer, as shown in Figure 16-5. Some of the properties are the same for all printers, while others are printer-specific.

The settings for the printer are organized into groups, which you can display by clicking the appropriate tab along the top of the window. Commonly used tabs include:

- **General** Comments about the printer, and a button to print a test page.

- **Details** Select the network connection or printer port, start or end MS-DOS port capture, and change spooler settings.

- **Paper** Change the size of paper the printer is using, handle options such as double-sided, portrait or landscape print orientation, and the number of copies of each page to print.

- **Graphics** Change the dots-per-inch resolution of printed graphics (higher looks better, but prints slower), change dithering, half-toning, and screening (techniques used to approximate shades of gray on black-and-white printers).

- **Fonts** Change which font cartridges are in use, control font substitution, control whether TrueType fonts are downloaded to the printer as fonts or graphics (can be useful to work around flaky print position problems).

- **Device Options or Setup** Change what optional equipment the printer has, such as extra memory, envelope feeders, and other paper handling equipment, change among various print quality modes on ink-jet printers.

- **Postscript** On Postscript-compatible printers, select Postscript suboptions, control whether Postscript header information is sent with each print job (important on printers shared with other computers) or only once per session.

- **Sharing** If your computer is on a local area network, change whether other people on the network can share this printer (see Chapter 32).

- **Services** Some printer drivers include procedures for maintenance, like cleaning print cartridges or aligning print heads.

After you have the properties for your printer set to your liking, you'll find that you seldom need to change the properties.

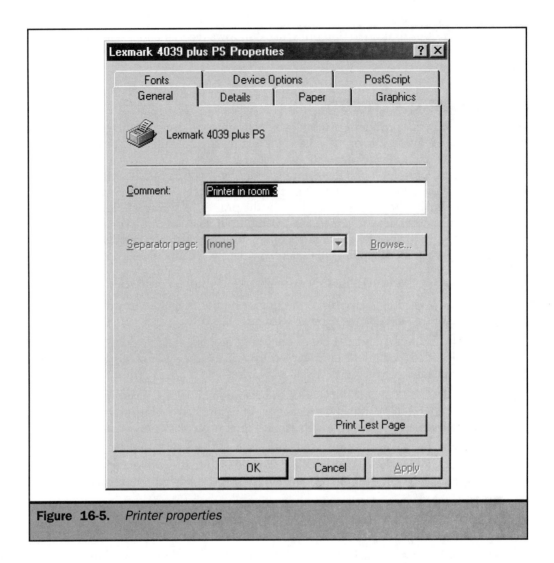

Figure 16-5. *Printer properties*

> **Tip**
> *If you find that you frequently switch between two different sets of properties, such as single- and double-sided printing, install the printer twice, and configure one installation for single-sided and one for double-sided printing. Windows lets you configure single- versus double-sided printing on a dialog box, but switching "printers" is a lot easier.*

Table 16-1 lists the settings that appear in most printer Properties dialog boxes. For information on the Sharing tab of the printer Properties dialog box, see Chapter 32.

Tab	Setting	Description
General	Comment	Allows you to type a description of the printer; the command appears when others on a network connect to the printer.
General	Separator page	Specifies whether Windows prints a *separator page* between print jobs, which can be useful for network printers. Click Browse to specify what to print on the separator page.
Details	Print to the following port	Specifies how a local printer is connected to the computer. Click Add Port to specify the address of a network printer or to add a new type of port. Click Delete Port to delete a port from the list.
Details	Print using the following driver	Specifies the printer driver. Click New Driver to choose a different printer driver.
Details	Capture Printer Port	Displays the Capture Printer Port dialog box, which allows you to assign a network printer to receive all output that applications try to send to a printer port.
Details	End Capture	Cancels the network printer connection you create using the Capture Printer Port button.
Details	Not selected: *xx* seconds	Specifies how many seconds Windows waits before reporting that a printer is offline.
Details	Transmission retry: *xx* seconds	Specifies how many seconds Windows waits before reporting a printer error.
Details	Spool Settings	Displays the Spool Settings dialog box, which allows you to control whether Windows stores waiting print jobs by using the spooler, the format in which print jobs are stored, and when Windows starts printing information from the spooler.
Details	Port Settings	Displays the Configure Port dialog box, which allows you to configure the port to which the printer is connected.

Table 16-1. *Printer Properties*

Tab	Setting	Description
Paper	Copies	Specifies the number of copies of the job to print.
Paper	Orientation	Specifies whether to print using *portrait orientation* (lines of print are parallel to the short side of the paper) or *landscape orientation* (lines of print are parallel to the long side of the paper).
Paper	Paper Size	Specifies the size of paper to print on. Your options depend on the printer's capabilities.

Table 16-1. *Printer Properties* (continued)

Managing Printer Activity

If you have a local printer that only you use now and then, you'll find that it hardly needs any management at all. When you print something from one of your programs, the printer prints it. But if you share a network printer, or you use your printer heavily and spool multiple print jobs to it, some printer management is necessary.

Managing Print Jobs

Each printer has a window that shows the activity for that printer (see Figure 16-6). The printer control window lists the print jobs waiting to be printed, and the one that is currently printing. Open the Printers folder by choosing Start | Settings | Printers, and then open the printer's icon in the Printers window. To open the local printer, click the small printer icon on the Taskbar.

You can pause and resume printing by choosing Printer | Pause Printing from the menu. To pause or delete a particular print job, highlight the job, and then choose Document | Pause Printing or Document | Cancel Printing. To get rid of everything waiting for that printer, choose Printer | Purge Print Jobs. To change the order in which jobs are printed, you can drag print jobs up or down the list.

Setting the Default Printer

In the Printers window, the current default printer is identified with a check mark. You can make any printer the default printer by opening the printer's control window and choosing Printer | Set As Default.

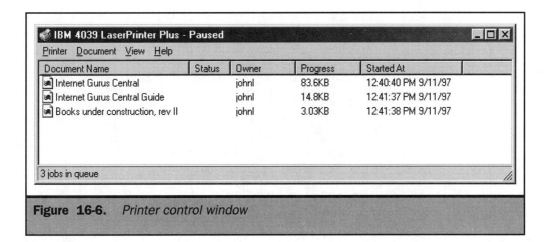

Figure 16-6. *Printer control window*

Printing to a File

Sometimes, you may want to send printer output to a file, either to print later, or to transport on diskette to a printer not connected to your computer. To do so, open the Printers window and open the Add Printer icon to install the printer you want to use as a local printer, choosing FILE as the port to which it is attached.

Whenever a program prints to that printer, Windows pops up a dialog box asking you to specify which file to use.

You can temporarily arrange to print documents for one of your installed printers to a file by opening the printer's Properties dialog box, clicking the Details tab, and choosing FILE: as the port. When done, change the port back to the actual port or network connection.

Installing and Using Fonts

Windows provides a straightforward way to install and use fonts. To see which fonts you have installed, open the folder C:\Windows\Fonts in a Folder window or in Windows Explorer, as in Figure 16-7. TrueType fonts have a TT icon, older fonts have an A icon. You can open any font to see a description and samples of the font in a variety of sizes. If you have a lot of fonts installed, then choose View | Hide Variations to omit the icons for fonts that are bold or italic versions of other fonts.

Installing Fonts

To install new fonts from a diskette or network, follow these steps:

1. View the C:\Windows\Fonts folder in a Folder window or in Windows Explorer.

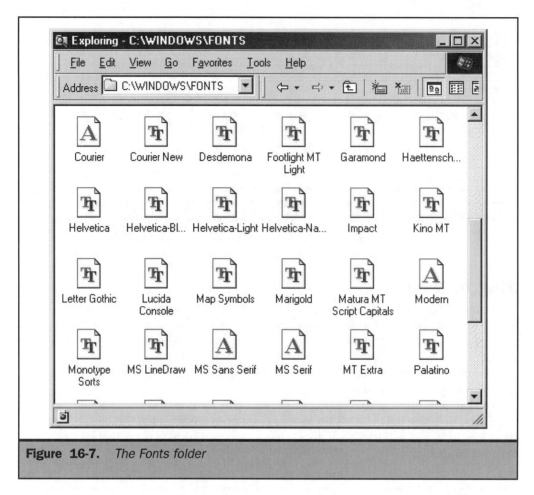

Figure 16-7.   *The Fonts folder*

2. Choose File | Install New Font, and the Add Fonts dialog box, shown in Figure 16-8, appears.

3. In the Drives and Folders boxes, select the drive and folder where the files are located for the new font or fonts. Click the Network button if the font files are on a network drive that is not mapped to a drive letter on your computer. Windows displays the fonts it finds.

4. In the List Of Fonts box, select the font(s) you want to install.

5. Normally, Windows copies the font files into its font folder (C:\Windows\Fonts). If you are installing fonts from a networked folder, you can uncheck Copy Fonts To Fonts Folder to use the fonts where they are located, which saves space in exchange for some loss in speed.

6. Click OK, and Windows installs the fonts you want.

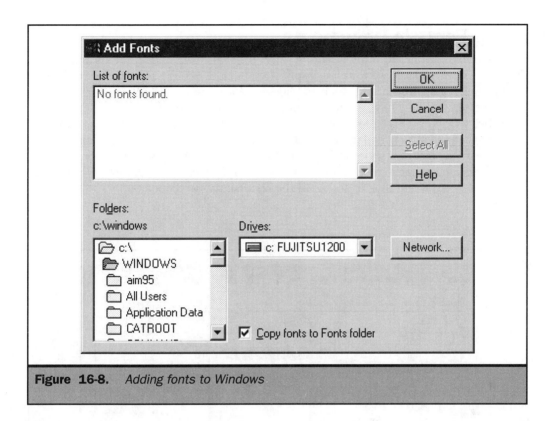

Figure 16-8. *Adding fonts to Windows*

 Alternatively, you can just drag font files from the install disk or folder to the C:\Windows\Fonts folder.

Deleting Fonts

To delete a font or fonts, display the C:\Windows\Fonts folder in a Folder window or Windows Explorer window. Then select the fonts you want to get rid of and choose File | Delete.

Finding Similar Fonts

Windows offers an occasionally useful "font similarity" feature that lets you look for fonts that are similar to a particular font. When viewing your list of fonts, choose View | List Fonts By Similarity, and then choose the target font at the top of the Fonts window. The font similarity feature depends on special information in the font files, so older fonts without this information aren't ranked for similarity.

Choosing Fonts in Documents

Most windows applications allow you to select the fonts used in documents and screen displays. When you select a font, the application usually opens a Font dialog box, like Figure 16-9. Some applications, such as Microsoft Word and Microsoft PowerPoint, use fonts so often that they have a font selection button on the toolbar.

Either way, you select a font in three steps: the name of the font (really the name of the typeface), the style (regular, bold, italic), and the point size. TrueType fonts are available in any size and style, and are identified by the TT logo before the font name. Older fonts are available in only a few fixed sizes and styles. You can force Windows to use an older font in any size or style, but the results invariably look bad.

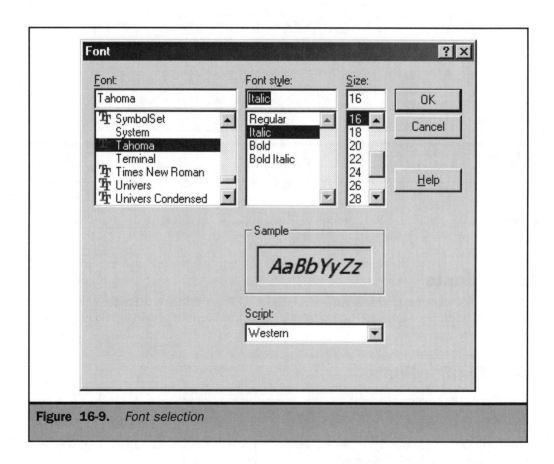

Figure 16-9.   *Font selection*

Chapter 17

Working with Sound and Graphics

W indows 98 contains better support for multimedia devices—hardware that enables your computer to play sounds and show and take photos and video. In addition to better built-in drivers for multimedia devices, Windows 98 comes with a number of programs that let you record or play multimedia files or disks, including Sound Recorder, CD Player, Media Player, NetShow, ActiveMovie, and DVD Player.

This chapter provides an introduction to multimedia hardware and file formats, with instructions for using the graphics and sound programs that come with Windows 98. Chapter 18 describes Windows 98's video features. (Chapter 15 describes how to install hardware, including multimedia hardware; this chapter explains how to configure and use the devices.)

What Is Multimedia?

Multimedia is information other than plain text. Multimedia includes pictures (graphics), sound (audio), and movies (video). Multimedia information—pictures, sounds, and video—is captured and digitized by *input devices* to get the information into your computer; for example, to get a picture into your computer, you can scan it. Your computer stores multimedia information in a variety of standard file formats. You can display or play multimedia information on *output devices*; for example, to play a sound file, you need speakers or headphones. In some cases, your computer needs special hardware to connect to the output device; for example, to connect a speaker to a PC, you need a sound card (which comes standard with most new computers). Table 17-1 shows input devices, output devices, and some standard file formats for the major types of multimedia.

Medium	Input Device	Output Device	File Extensions for Popular File Formats
Graphics	Scanner, digital camera, paint program	Printer, display	BMP, PCX, GIF, JPG, TIF, and others
Audio	Microphone, MIDI keyboard, synthesizers	Speakers, headphones	WAV

Table 17-1. *Multimedia Devices and File Formats*

Medium	Input Device	Output Device	File Extensions for Popular File Formats
Streaming audio	Same as regular audio	Speakers, headphones	RAM, RA (for RealAudio files), ASF, ASX (for Active Streaming Format files)
Video	Digital camera, virtual reality software	Display, speakers, headphones	AVI, MPG, QT (for QuickTime files)
MIDI	MIDI-compatible instrument	MIDI-compatible instrument, speakers, headphones	MID or RMI
Streaming video	Generated from regular video	Display, speakers, headphones	RV (for RealVideo files), ASF, ASX (for Active Streaming Format files)

Table 17-1. *Multimedia Devices and File Formats* (continued)

What Is MIDI?

A specialized type of audio data is called *MIDI* (Musical Instrument Digital Interface), a format for transmitting and storing musical notes. MIDI devices are musical instruments that have digital inputs and outputs and can transmit, store, and play music using the MIDI language. For example, if you connect a MIDI keyboard to your computer, you can view the music you play on the MIDI keyboard on your computer screen and hear it on your speakers. Data from MIDI devices is stored in MIDI-format files. Windows includes software that can "play" MIDI files; that is, software that can translate the musical notes in the files into sound that can be played through speakers or headphones.

See "Working with MIDI" later in this chapter for how to record and play MIDI files.

What Are Streaming Audio and Video?

Streaming audio and *streaming video* are audio and video files stored in a format for use over the Internet. When you want to play a streaming audio or video file over the

Internet, your computer can start playing the file after downloading only the beginning of the file, and can continue to play the audio or video while the rest of the file downloads—downloading stays a step ahead of the player. To play streaming audio or video files from the Internet, run Microsoft NetShow (see "Playing Streaming Video Files with NetShow" in Chapter 18).

Tip *RealAudio Player, a standard program for playing streaming audio files from the Internet, is included on the Windows 98 CD-ROM. To install RealAudio, open the Add/Remove Programs icon on the Control Panel, click the Windows Setup tab, choose Internet Tools from the list of components, click Details, and choose Real Audio Player (see "Installing and Uninstalling Programs That Come with Windows 98" in Chapter 3).*

Working with Multimedia Devices and Files

For your computer to use a multimedia input or output device, Windows 98 has to know about the device. Information about how to send and receive information from devices is stored in *drivers* (see "What Are Drivers?" in Chapter 15). When you buy a scanner, camera, or other multimedia device, a floppy disk or CD-ROM may come in the package, containing the drivers Windows 98 needs to work with the device. Windows 98 comes with drivers for many standard devices, including many displays and sound cards.

You use the Multimedia Properties dialog box (Figure 17-1) to tell Windows 98 what drivers to use for audio, video, and MIDI input and output, as well as how to play music CDs in your CD-ROM drive. To display this dialog box, choose Start | Settings | Control Panel and open the Multimedia icon. Click or double-click the icon depending on whether you have configured your desktop as Web style or Classic style (see "Choosing the Style of Your Desktop" in Chapter 1).

Controlling Multimedia Devices from the Multimedia Properties Dialog Box

The Multimedia Properties dialog box has five tabs:

- **Audio** Controls which driver Windows 98 uses to play and record sound (see "Configuring Windows to Work with Sound" later in this chapter).

- **Video** Controls how Windows 98 displays video on your display (see "Configuring Windows 98 to Work with Video" in the following chapter).

- **MIDI** Controls which driver Windows 98 uses for MIDI input and output, and how these instruments are configured (see "Working with MIDI" later in this chapter).

- **CD Music** Controls how Windows 98 plays music CDs in your CD-ROM drive (see "Playing Audio CDs with CD Player" later in this chapter).

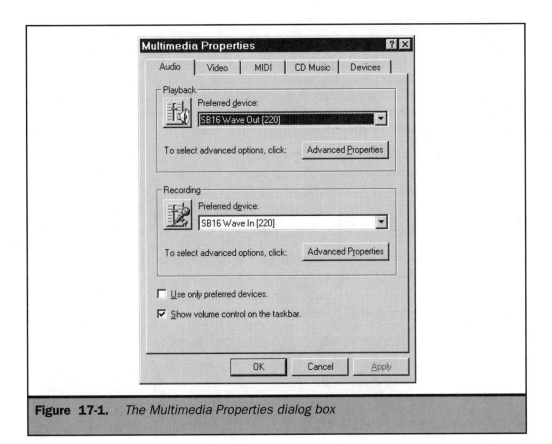

Figure 17-1.   *The Multimedia Properties dialog box*

- **Devices**   Lists all the multimedia devices installed on your system, as well as game controllers and joysticks (see "Configuring Your Game Controller" in Chapter 14). To see or change the settings for some devices, you can click the category of device (for example, Audio Devices for a microphone), click the device, and then click the Properties button. Many of the devices are software only, notably the audio and video codecs (compressing and decompressing schemes) that determine the scheme used to encode sounds in audio and video files (see "What Is Video Data?" in Chapter 18).

Displaying and Changing the Properties of Multimedia Devices

Windows shows a list of all the multimedia devices installed on your computer on the Devices tab of the Multimedia Properties dialog box. You see the list shown in Figure

17-2. This list is organized by type. If there are devices of a specified type, a plus box appears to the left of the type; click the plus box to see a list of devices of that type.

To see the properties of a device, click it and then click the Properties button. Figure 17-3 shows the Properties dialog box for a sound board. The Properties dialog box for a device shows the status of the device. The settings you see depend on the driver for that device, but most Properties dialog boxes (whether the device handles graphics, audio, or video) contain the following settings and buttons:

- **Use features on this device**   Allows programs to use this device. (This setting is usually selected.)

- **Do not use features on this device**   Does not allow programs to use this device. Although the driver for this device remains on your hard disk, Windows does not load it into memory. If you are not using an installed device, this option lets you free up the memory that its driver would take up. You might also want to choose this setting if you think that the driver for this device is causing a conflict with some other device.

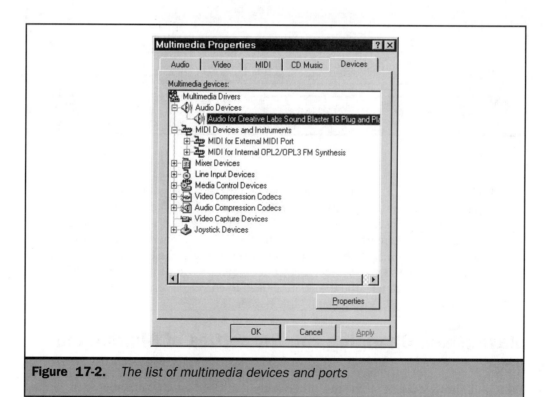

Figure 17-2.   *The list of multimedia devices and ports*

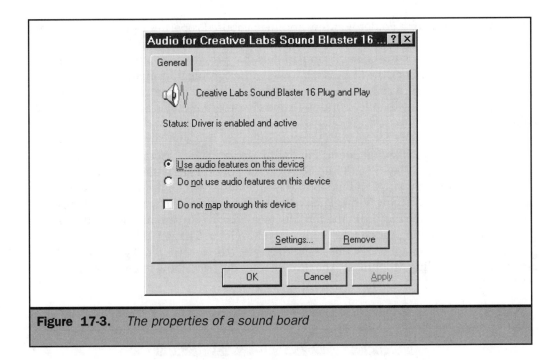

Figure 17-3.   *The properties of a sound board*

- **Do not map through this device**   Does not allow programs to route information via this device. Windows loads the driver for this device, but programs can't use it unless they specifically request this device.

- **Settings button**   Displays additional settings for this device, if any exist. If there are no other settings, this button may be gray and unclickable.

- **Remove button**   Deletes the driver for this device from your hard disk. Choose this setting if you have removed a multimedia device from your system but its device driver still loads.

- **Apply button**   Saves all the changes made to the settings in this dialog box, but doesn't close the dialog box. (OK saves and closes, and Cancel closes without saving.)

Displaying and Playing Multimedia Files

Many applications, particularly games, have built-in multimedia features. Those programs automatically take advantage of any devices you have, once those devices are configured into your system.

Multimedia information is stored in multimedia files in a variety of formats (see Table 17-1). To see the properties of any multimedia file, right-click the filename in

Windows Explorer or a Folder window and then choose Properties from the menu that appears. You see a Properties dialog box like the one shown in Figure 17-4.

The information on the General tab parallels that provided for almost any file: type, size, and attributes. Click the Details tab to see more specific information about the contents of the file, such as its copyright holder, length, and format. If a Preview tab appears, click it to play the file. Windows runs the program that is associated with that file type, if any.

Media Player, which comes with Windows 98, can play a wide variety of multimedia files (see "Playing Sound Files with Media Player"). Sound Recorder can play audio files (see "Playing and Recording WAV Sound Files with Sound Recorder"). ActiveMovie can play MIDI and video files (see "Playing MIDI Files with ActiveMovie" in this chapter and "Playing Video Files with ActiveMovie" in Chapter 18). NetShow plays audio and video files from the Internet (see "Playing Streaming Video Files with NetShow" and "Playing Video Files with ActiveMovie" in Chapter 18).

The rest of this chapter describes how to create and view (or play) graphics and sound files (including MIDI files). The next chapter describes how to create and play video files.

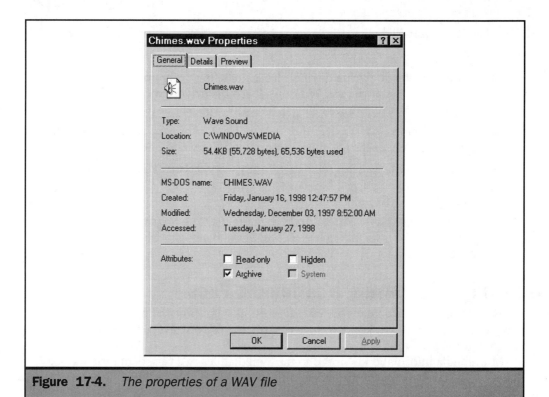

Figure 17-4.   *The properties of a WAV file*

Working with Graphics

A *scanner* digitizes pictures or other visual information for storage in your computer. A *digital camera* does the same thing, using a camera lens instead of the flat glass panel on a scanner. Your scanner or digital camera should come with drivers that allow it to work with Windows 98. (Windows 95-compatible drivers should work fine.) To view pictures, you use your monitor or printer.

Configuring a Scanner or Digital Camera

To install or configure a scanner or digital camera, you can use the Scanners And Cameras Properties dialog box. In the Control Panel, open the Scanners And Cameras icon. If the Scanners And Cameras icon doesn't appear (it usually doesn't if no scanner or digital camera is installed), you can see the dialog box by searching for **scanner** in Windows Help and displaying the help information about installing scanners; the Help text contains a link to the program (see Chapter 6).

If your scanner or digital camera doesn't appear in the list of installed devices, click the Add button in the dialog box to run the Scanner And Cameras Installation Wizard. Unless you are installing one of a short list of devices for which Windows 98 has drivers, you'll need the floppy disk or CD-ROM that came with the device. Click the Have Disk button to tell the Wizard to find the device driver on the floppy disk or CD-ROM that you've inserted. After installing the drivers, the Wizard may suggest that you restart Windows so that the new drivers can take effect.

You can test your scanner or digital camera by clicking its entry on the Scanners And Cameras dialog box, clicking the Properties button, and then clicking the Test Scanner Or Camera button.

Note | *Even after you install your scanner or digital camera and it works fine, the Scanners And Cameras icon may not appear in the Control Panel. If you open the Scanners And Cameras Properties dialog box, your scanner or camera may not appear in the list of installed devices, either. The device should appear, however, in your System Properties dialog box: Open the System icon in the Control Panel, click the Device Manager tab, and look down the list of all installed devices (see "Using the Device Manager" in Chapter 15).*

Scanning, Editing, and Printing Digitized Pictures

Most scanners are compatible with TWAIN (a standard scanner interface), which means that most graphics programs can accept data from them. For example, you can use the Kodak Imaging program that comes with Windows 98 to receive, edit, and store a scanned image from the scanner (see "Annotating Images with Kodak Imaging" in Chapter 5). Microsoft Paint can display, edit, and print graphics files (see "Drawing Pictures Using Microsoft Paint" in Chapter 5). For more advanced editing, as well as for converting files to different graphics formats, we like Paint Shop Pro, a shareware program you can download from the Internet at **http://www.jasc.com/ psp.html**. Other graphics editing and conversion programs are available from the Consummate Winsock Applications web page at **http://www.stroud.com**.

Linking Your Scanner or Digital Camera to a Program

In addition to graphics programs, some other types of programs accept digital graphic information directly from a scanner or camera. For example, a database program may accept a digital picture of a person for storage in a personnel database. If both your scanner or camera and your program support this feature, you can tell Windows to run a program whenever you scan an image or take a digital picture. Follow these steps:

1. Display the Scanners And Cameras Properties dialog box (see "Configuring a Scanner or Digital Camera").

2. Click the device and then click the Properties button to display the Properties dialog box for that scanner or camera. Click the Events tab. (If the Events tab does not appear, your scanner or digital camera does not support linking to programs.)

3. In the Scanner Or Camera Events box, click an event.

4. In the Send To This Application box, click the name of the program that will receive the image from the scanner or camera. Only programs that can accept digital images appear on the list.

5. Click OK.

Configuring Windows to Work with Sound

Most new computers come with a *sound board*, an adapter inside the computer that lets you connect a microphone and either speakers or headphones to your computer for audio input and output. Many programs use sound to alert you to events, like the lovely musical snippets that you may hear when Windows 98 starts or shuts down. You need sound capabilities to participate in Internet phone and voice chats and to listed to sound clips on the Web.

Windows 98 plays sounds when certain events occur. You can associate a sound with a new event, or change which sounds Windows plays (as described in the next few sections of this chapter). You can also play and record sounds by using the Sound Recorder or Media Player programs, and play an audio CD in your CD-ROM by using the CD Player program. If you plan to use MIDI devices with Windows 98, see "Working with MIDI" later in this chapter.

Choosing and Configuring Audio Input and Output Drivers

To tell Windows which sound drivers to use and to choose settings for your audio devices, follow these steps:

1. Choose Start | Settings | Control Panel, and then open the Multimedia icon. You see the Multimedia Properties dialog box.

2. Click the Audio tab if it's not already selected (shown in Figure 17-1).

3. Choose the driver used to play sounds by clicking in the Preferred Device box in the Playback section of the dialog box and then choosing a driver from the list that appears. The default sound driver, used with standard speakers and headphone, is called SB16 Wave Out.

4. Tell Windows more about your speakers or headphones by clicking the Advanced Properties button in the Playback section of the dialog box. You see the Advanced Audio Properties dialog box, shown in Figure 17-5.

5. Click the Speakers tab if it's not already selected. Click the Speaker Setup box and choose your computer's arrangement of speakers (or headphones).

6. To set the amount of computing power your computer devotes to playing audio, click the Performance tab. Then set the Audio Playback Hardware Acceleration slider and Sample Rate Conversion Quality slider. Click OK.

7. To control the volume of your speakers or headphones, click the button on the left side of the Playback section of the Multimedia Properties dialog box. You see the Volume Control window (see "Controlling the Volume, Balance, and Tone").

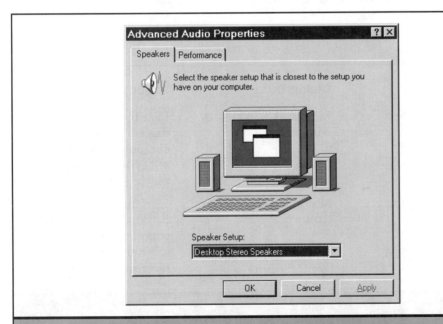

Figure 17-5.   *Setting the properties of your speakers or headphones*

8. Choose the driver used to record sounds by clicking in the Preferred Device box in the Recording section of the Multimedia Properties dialog box and then choosing a driver from the list that appears. The default recording driver, used with standard microphones, is called SB16 Wave In.

9. To set the amount of computing power your computer devotes to recording audio, click the Advanced Properties button in the Recording section of the Multimedia Properties dialog box. Then set the Audio Recording Hardware Acceleration slider and Sample Rate Conversion Quality slider. Click OK.

10. To control the volume when recording, click the button on the left side of the Recording section of the Multimedia Properties dialog box. You see the Recording Control window (see "Playing and Recording Sound Files").

11. You can control whether the Volume icon appears in the system tray on the Taskbar by checking or not checking the Show Volume Control On The Taskbar check box.

12. Click OK to exit the Multimedia Properties dialog box.

Table 17-2 lists the settings in various dialog boxes that control audio input and output.

 If you have trouble getting sounds to play, try Windows 98's Sound Troubleshooter (see "Diagnosing Problems Using Troubleshooter" in Chapter 37).

Setting	Dialog Box	Description
Playback Preferred Device	Multimedia Properties, Audio tab	Lists the audio output drivers installed on your computer, and lets you select the one to use when playing sounds.
Recording Preferred Device	Multimedia Properties, Audio tab	Lists the audio input drivers installed on your computer, and lets you select the one to use when recording sounds.

Table 17-2. *Settings That Control Sound Playback and Recording*

Setting	Dialog Box	Description
Use Only Preferred Devices	Multimedia Properties, Audio tab	When checked, specifies that programs that require specific types of sound cards are limited to using those supported sound cards. The default is unselected.
Show Volume Control On The Taskbar	Multimedia Properties, Audio tab	Specifies whether the Volume icon appears in the system tray. The default is selected.
Speaker Setup	Advanced Audio Properties (Playback version), Speakers tab	Specifies your arrangement of speakers for audio playback.
Audio Playback Hardware Acceleration	Advanced Audio Properties (Playback version), Performance tab	Specifies how much processing power is used when playing audio. The default is Full.
Audio Playback Sample Rate Conversion Quality	Advanced Audio Properties (Playback version), Performance tab	Specifies how much processing power is used when converting audio files to signals you can play on speakers. The default is Good.
Audio Recording Hardware Acceleration	Advanced Audio Properties (Recording version), Performance tab	Specifies how much processing power is used when recording audio. The default is Full.
Audio Recording Sample Rate Conversion Quality	Advanced Audio Properties (Recording version), Performance tab	Specifies how much processing power is used when converting signals from your microphone to digital audio files. The default is Good.

Table 17-3. *Settings That Control Sound Playback and Recording* (continued)

Setting	Dialog Box	Description
Volume, Balance, and Mute	Volume Control	Specifies the volume, balance between left and right, and whether the device is muted (suppressed). (See "Adjusting the Volume and Balance.")
Bass and Treble	Advanced Controls for Microphone	Controls the balance between high (treble) and low (bass) tones when recording (see "Adjusting the Tone").

Table 17-4. *Settings That Control Sound Playback and Recording* (continued)

Controlling the Volume, Balance, and Tone

You can control the volume and balance of the sound that comes out of your computer's speakers or headphones and goes into your microphones. You can also choose to mute (suppress) the sound for any audio device. You use the Volume icon (the little yellow loudspeaker icon) in the system tray on your Taskbar.

 If the icon doesn't appear, choose Start | Settings | Control Panel, open the Multimedia icon, click the Audio tab (if it's not already selected), and then click the Show Volume Control On The Taskbar check box until a check appears. Then click OK.

Adjusting the Volume and Balance

To adjust the volume of your speakers, click the Volume icon once; you see a Volume slider and a Mute check box. Drag the Volume slider up for louder volume or down for softer volume. Select the Mute check box to suppress audio output. Click outside the window to make it disappear.

To adjust the volume and balance of any audio device, double-click the Volume icon. You see the Volume Control window, shown in Figure 17-6. Another way to display this window is by clicking the button to the left of the Preferred Device box in either the Playback or Recording section of the Multimedia Properties dialog box.

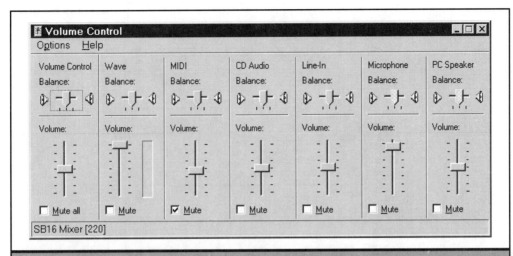

Figure 17-6.   *Controlling volume and balance for audio output*

The Volume Control window can display a volume, balance, and mute setting for each audio input and output device on your computer. To choose which audio devices are included in the window, choose Options | Properties from its menu bar to display the Properties dialog box (see Figure 17-7). Click the Playback setting to include audio output devices, the Recording setting to include audio input devices, or the Other setting to include other audio devices; the only other audio device is Voice Commands, which allows you to use software that interprets your voice input as commands to control programs. You can also click check boxes for individual audio devices in the Show The Following Volume Controls list. Then click OK to return to the Volume Control window.

When you display volume controls for playback devices, the window is called Volume Control, when you display recording devices, it's called Recording Control, and when you display voice command devices, it's called Voice Commands.

If your speakers or headphones have a physical volume control knob, it's generally simpler to leave the Windows volume set fairly high and just turn the knob to change the volume.

Adjusting the Tone

When you display either recording or voice command devices in the Volume Control window, you can also display an Advanced button (if it doesn't appear, choose Options | Advanced Controls from the window's menu bar). Click the Advanced

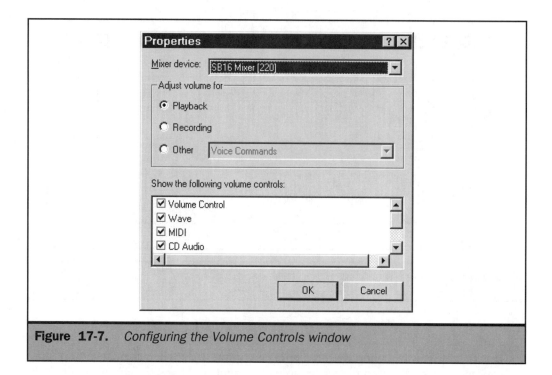

Figure 17-7.   *Configuring the Volume Controls window*

button to display the Advanced Controls For Microphone dialog box, shown in Figure 17-8. Use the Bass and Treble sliders to adjust the mix of high and low tones when recording with your microphone or using it for voice control. The Other Controls section of the dialog box may contain other settings, depending on the type of microphone you use.

Choosing What Sounds Windows Makes

Windows 98 comes with an array of sounds that it makes when certain *events* (Windows operations) occur. When you start Windows, for example, a rich, welcoming sound occurs, but you might prefer the sound of a friend yelling "Hello!" You can control which sounds Windows plays when specified events occur by opening the Sounds icon in the Control Panel. You see the Sounds Properties dialog box, shown in Figure 17-9.

The Events box lists all the events that you can associate with a sound, including events that happen in Windows and other programs that use sound. Select an event, click in the Name box, and then choose a sound. To test out the sound, click the right-pointing triangle button to the right of the yellow speaker icon (clicking the yellow speaker itself does nothing). If an event has no yellow speaker icon to its left, no sound is current assigned to the event.

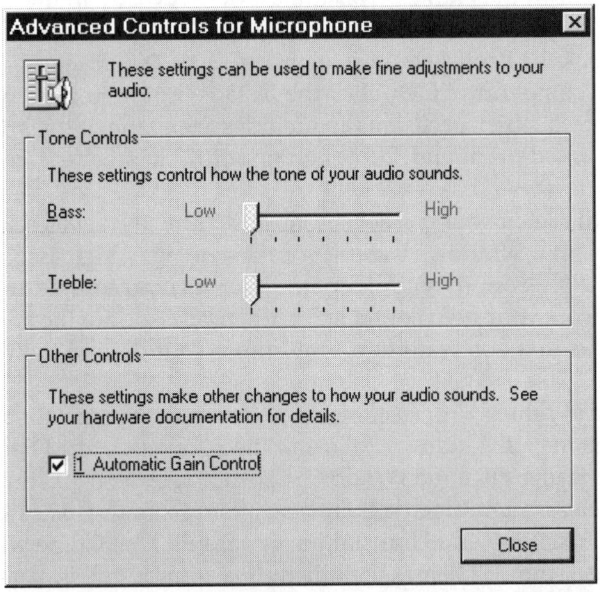

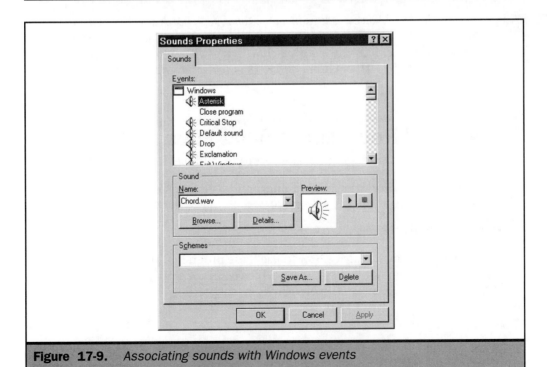

Figure 17-8.   *Controlling the tone of audio inputs*

Figure 17-9.   *Associating sounds with Windows events*

The list of sounds in the Name box is the list of WAV files in the C:\Windows\ Media folder (files with the extension .wav). You can use WAV files in any folder on your computer; click the Browse button to choose a file. You can also get more information about some sound files; click the Details button to display the sound file's Properties dialog box, which occasionally includes the name of the artists who made, designed, and recorded the sound. To assign no sound to an event, choose (None) from the Name list.

You can save the set of sound associations and name the set as a *sound scheme*. Windows comes with a Windows Default sound scheme, which associates sounds with many events, and a No Sounds sound scheme, in which no sounds are associated with events. You can create your own sound schemes, too; associate the sounds you want to hear with the events that you want to prompt those sounds, and then click the Save As button.

Windows 98 also comes with a set of sound schemes that are not automatically installed when you install Windows; to install them, open Control Panel, open Add/Remove Programs, click the Windows Setup tab, choose Multimedia, click Details, and then choose Multimedia Sound Schemes from the list of Multimedia components (see "Installing and Uninstalling Programs That Come with Windows 98" in Chapter 3). These sound schemes include jungle sounds, musical snippets, and robot-like sounds. The desktop themes that you can install from the Windows 98 CD-ROM or floppies also include sound schemes (see "Choosing a Desktop Theme" in Chapter 13).

| Note | *Some PC Cards (add-on cards used in laptop computers) use drivers that generate sounds; to turn them off, open the PC Card Properties icon on the Control Panel, click the Global Settings tab, and then click Disable PC Card Sound Effects to uncheck its check box. If the PC Card Wizard runs, follow the Wizard's instructions and then try again.* |

Playing and Recording Sound Files

Windows comes with several programs for recording and playing sound files:

- Sound Recorder for recording, editing, and playing WAV files
- Media Player for playing WAV files
- CD Player for playing audio CDs

The following sections describe how to use these programs. To play streaming audio files from the Internet, run NetShow, which comes with Windows 98 (see "Playing Streaming Video Files with NetShow" in Chapter 18).

Playing and Recording WAV Sound Files with Sound Recorder

To play or record WAV files (with the extension .wav), you can use the built-in Sound Recorder program. Run it by choosing Start | Programs | Accessories | Entertainment | Sound Recorder. You see the Sound Recorder window, shown in Figure 17-10.

Playing Sounds

To play a sound file, choose File | Open, choose the filename, and then click Open. Sound Recorder opens the file, displays the filename on the title bar, the waveform of the first part of the sound file, and the length of the sound in seconds. Next, click the Play button. You can use the Stop button to stop playback.

The Position slider tracks your current position in the sound—it's similar to your cursor in the file. To change your current position, drag the Position slider left or right to move forward or backward in the sound file. For example, to hear the second half of the sound, drag the Position slider to the middle and then click the Play button.

To discover other interesting ways that you can play back a sound (like slow, or backwards), see "Editing Sounds" later in this chapter.

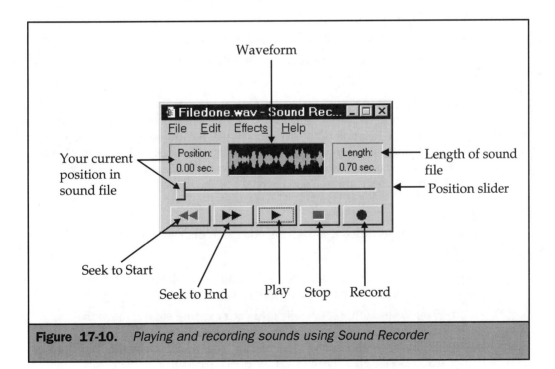

Figure 17-10.   *Playing and recording sounds using Sound Recorder*

Some sound files come with information about who created the sound; choose File | Properties to see the properties of the file.

Windows 98 comes with lots of sounds in WAV files; some are in your C:\Windows\Media folder, and others are on the Windows 98 CD-ROM, in the \Cdsample\Sounds folder. To play these sounds, you can also use Media Player (see "Playing Sound Files with Media Player").

Recording Sounds

If your computer has a microphone, you can record sounds and store them in WAV files. Follow these steps:

1. Choose File | New to begin a new sound file. If you are editing a sound file and haven't saved your changes, Sound Recorder asks whether you want to save them now.

2. Arrange the microphone so that you are ready to record.

3. Click the Record button in the Sound Recorder window.

4. Start the sound you want to record (for example, start talking).

5. When the sound you want to record is over, click the Stop button.

6. Play back the sound by clicking the Play button.

7. Edit the sound, as necessary (see "Editing Sounds").

8. If you want to save your recording, choose File | Save As, type a filename, and click Save.

If a file is already open in Sound Recorder when you record a sound, the recorded sound records over part of the existing sound or is added to the end of the existing sound, depending on the location of the Position slider. To add on to the end of a sound, move the Position slider to the right end (or click the Seek To End button), and then record. To replace part of any existing sound, move the Position slider to the beginning of the sound you want to record over, and then record.

Editing Sounds

Once you've opened or recorded a sound file, you can fool around with it in the following ways:

- **Copy**   To copy the entire sound to the Windows Clipboard so that you can paste it later, choose Edit | Copy or press CTRL-C.

- **Insert**   To insert another sound file into your existing sound, move the Position slider to the point where you want to insert the file, choose Edit | Insert File, and then choose the filename. To insert a copy from the Windows Clipboard, choose Edit | Paste Insert (or press CTRL-V).

- **Mix**   To mix another sound file with your existing sound, move the Position slider to the point where you want to mix the other sound, choose Edit | Mix With File, and then choose the filename. To mix a sound from the Windows Clipboard, choose Edit | Paste Mix. Sound Recorder mixes the two sounds together, so you hear both at the same time. For example, you can record your voice several times and then mix the sounds together to sound like a crowd.

- **Cut**   You can omit parts of the sound, from the beginning of the sound to your current position or from your current position to the end of the sound. Move the Position slider to the point before or after which you want to delete and then choose Edit | Delete Before Current Position or Edit | Delete After Current Position. Click OK to confirm that you want to delete part of the sound.

- **Speed up or slow down**   To speed up the sound, choose Effects | Increase Speed. Sound Recorder plays the sound in half the time, raising the pitch at the same time. To slow down the sound, choose Effects | Decreases Speed; the sound plays in twice the time at a lower pitch.

- **Change volume**   To make the sound 25 percent louder, choose Effects | Increase Volume. To make the sound softer, choose Effects | Decrease Volume.

- **Add special effects**   To play the sound backwards, choose Effects | Reverse. To add an echo, choose Effects | Add Echo.

Note   *You can't edit a sound if it is stored in compressed format. You can tell that a sound is stored in a compressed format, because no green waveform appears in the Sound Recorder window.*

Editing a sound changes the sound in memory but doesn't affect the sound file; to save your changes, choose File | Save or File | Save As. Until you save a sound, you can choose File | Revert to return to the previously saved version of the sound.

Converting Sounds to Other Formats

WAV files can use one of many different standard audio formats. Different formats offer trade-offs between audio fidelity and disk space, and are designed for different kinds of sounds, such as music or voice. You can also change the attributes of the sound, such as the sampling speed in Hz, the number of bits used to store each sample, and whether the sound is stereo or mono. Some formats are considered to be compressed; if you convert a sound to a compressed format, you can't edit the sound in Sound Recorder.

To change the format of your WAV file, choose File | Properties to display the Properties For Sound dialog box, shown in Figure 17-11. The top half of the dialog box shows information about the sound, including its format. (In Figure 17-11, the format is PCM, the format that Sound Recorder uses when recording sounds from your microphone.)

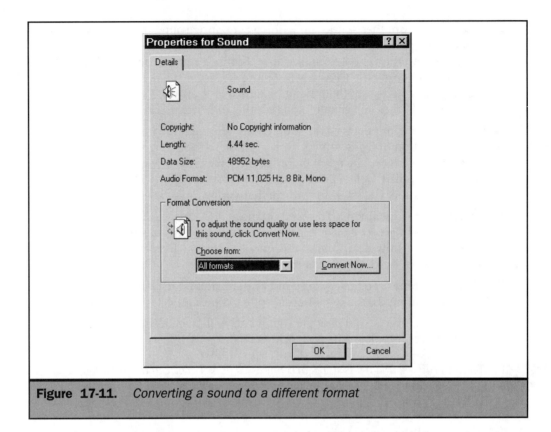

Figure 17-11.   *Converting a sound to a different format*

The Format Conversion section of the Properties For Sound dialog box lets you convert the sound to a different format; however, all the available formats are still stored as WAV files. Click the Convert Now button to see the Sound Selection dialog box, shown here:

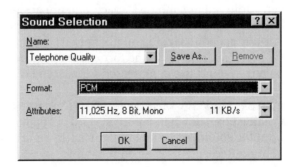

You can choose the format and the attributes you want to use by clicking in the Format and Attributes boxes and making a selection in each. The list of Attributes changes based on the Format you choose. Some widely used combinations of formats and attributes have been named to make them easier to select; click in the Name box to choose a named combination of format and attributes. Then click OK twice to convert the sound. Choose File | Save or File | Save As to save the converted sound in a file.

You can also change the format when saving a file. Choose File | Save or File | Save As and type or select the filename. Click the Change button to display the Sound Selection dialog box and then perform the conversion as described in this section.

Playing Sound Files with Media Player

Another program that can play sound files is Media Player. Start Media Player by choosing Start | Programs | Accessories | Entertainment | Media Player. To play a sound file, choose File | Open, set the Files Of Type box to Sound, choose a WAV file, and then click Open. Next, click the Play button in the lower-left corner of the Media Player window to play the sound. See "Playing Video Files with Media Player" in the next chapter for details about the Media Player program.

Playing Audio CDs with CD Player

Windows 98 comes with CD Player, a program that can play audio CDs in your CD-ROM drive. (If you work in an office and your CD-ROM drive has a headphone jack, you can use your computer as your own personal sound system.) When you put an audio CD in your computer's CD-ROM drive, Windows 98 detects that the CD contains sound, runs the CD Player program automatically, and starts playing the CD. If you want to run CD Player yourself, choose Start | Programs | Accessories | Entertainment | CD Player. You see the CD Player window, shown in Figure 17-12.

If you have turned off the autorun feature for your CD-ROM drive, neither CD-ROMs nor audio CDs play automatically (see "Using CD-ROMs and Audio CDs" in Chapter 11).

To stop play, click the Stop or Pause buttons, and the Play button to start play. You can also click the other small buttons to skip forward or backward, or seek to the next or previous track on the CD. To change the volume or balance, choose View | Volume Control, move the sliders in the CD Audio section of the Volume Control window, and then close the window.

If no CD-ROM is in the drive when you run CD Player, or if the CD-ROM contains data rather than music, CD Player displays the message "Data or no disc loaded" in the Artist box. After you insert a CD, it may take as long as ten seconds for your CD drive to get up to speed and for CD Player to clear the error message; just wait!

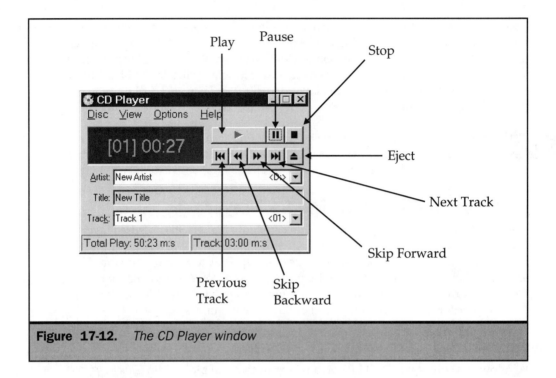

Figure 17-12. *The CD Player window*

CD Player Options

Table 17-3 describes the settings in the Multimedia Properties dialog box that control how CD Player works. The settings are on the CD Music tab, shown in Figure 17-13.

Setting	Description
Default CD-ROM Driver For Playing CD Music	Specifies the drive letter of the CD-ROM drive you use for playing audio CDs.
CD Music Volume	Controls the volume when playing audio CDs in your CD-ROM drive.
Whenever Possible, Use Digital Playback On This Device	Specifies digital rather than analog playback for playing audio CDs. When this setting is selected, you can't use headphones. The default is unselected.

Table 17-5. *Audio CD Settings on the Multimedia Properties CD Music Tab*

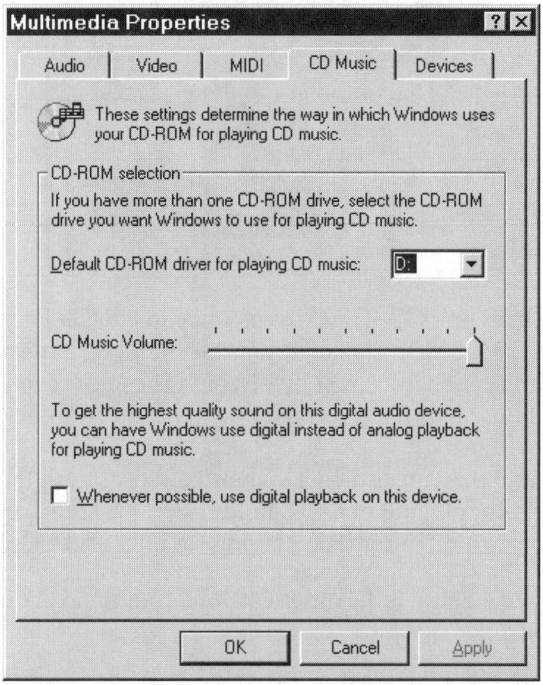

Figure 17-13.   *The CD Music tab of the Multimedia Properties dialog box*

Normally, CD Player plays all the tracks on the CD in order, and then stops. However, you have these other options:

- Choose Options | Random Order from the CD Player menu bar to play the tracks in an order chosen randomly by CD Player.
- Choose Options | Continuous Play to start over at the beginning track after playing the last track.
- Choose Options | Intro Play to play only the first few sections of each track.

To control what information appears in the CD Player window, choose the View command and select the items you want to appear; those options with check marks to their left appear in the CD Player window. You can further configure the program by choosing Options | Preferences to display the Preferences dialog box, shown in the following illustration.

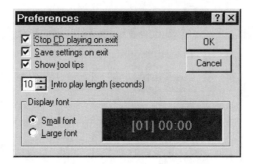

If you have more than one CD-ROM drive, you can tell CD Player about it by choosing the Options | Multidisc Play command. When you have audio CDs in more than one CD-ROM drive, click the Artist box (which chose the drive letter at the right end of the box) and choose a different artist name (and drive letter) from the list that appears.

You may not want to play an audio CD when you insert it in the CD-ROM drive. To suppress automatically playing one CD, hold down the SHIFT key while you insert the CD. If you want to turn off automatic playing for all audio CDs, follow these steps:

1. Choose the Start | Settings | Folder Options command. You see the Folder Options dialog box.

2. Click the File Types tab. You see the list of the types of files that Windows 98 knows how to deal with.

3. Click the AudioCD entry on the Registered File Types list. Information about that type of file (or CD, in this case) appears in the lower part of the dialog box.

4. Click Edit to change what Windows 98 does when it encounters this type of file. You see the Edit File Type dialog box.

5. Click Play in the Actions list and then click Set Default. The Play entry in the Actions list switches from boldface to regular type, indicating that Windows won't play this type of "file" automatically. Then click Close on both dialog boxes.

If you want to turn auto-play back on for audio CDs, repeat the same steps. The Play entry in the Actions list in the Edit File Type dialog box switches back to boldface. Alternatively, you can turn off the autorun feature entirely, so that neither CD-ROMs nor audio CDs play automatically (see "Using CD-ROMs and Audio CDs" in Chapter 11).

Creating a Play List

You can tell CD Player exactly which tracks you want to play and in which order. A *play list* is a list of the tracks that you want to play, in the order specified. Normally, the Artist and Title boxes show only the messages New Artist and New Title, and the

Track box shows the track number. You can type in the list of tracks and their titles, as well as a title for the CD. Then you can create a play list for the CD; Windows 98 stores the play list for you (in the file C:\Windows\Cdplayer.ini). Follow these steps:

1. Choose Disc | Edit Play List from the menu. You see the CD Player: Disc Settings window, shown in Figure 17-14.

2. Referring to the cover of the CD-ROM, fill in the Artist and Title boxes. The Play List box on the left side of the window shows the tracks that you've chosen to play. The Available Tracks box on the right side of the box shows all the tracks on the CD.

3. Click the first unnamed track in the Available Tracks list (that is, the first track that is named something like Track 1). Click in the Track box at the bottom of the window, delete the current entry, and then type the title of the track. Next, click the Set Name button. CD Player records the name of the track, which now appears in both the Play List and Available Tracks boxes.

4. Repeat step 3 for all the tracks on the album. You don't absolutely have to name all the tracks to create a play list, but having the titles on the screen makes them easier to identify. To correct mistakes in track names, click the track in the

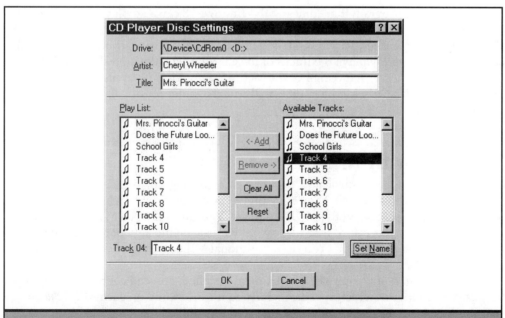

Figure 17-14. *Entering a play list for an audio CD*

Available Tracks list, edit the name in the Track box at the bottom of the window, and then click the Set Name button again.

5. Create a play list. Delete tracks from the Play List box by selecting the track in the Play List box and clicking the Remove button. Move tracks to a position earlier or later in the play list by using the mouse to drag tracks up and down the list. If you'd rather start from scratch than from a list of the tracks in the order in which they appear on the CD, click the Clear All button to empty the Play List box, and then add tracks to the play list by clicking the track in the Available Tracks box and clicking the Add button (or by clicking a track, releasing the mouse button, and dragging the track from the Available Tracks box to the Play List box).

6. When you are done, click OK. Now when you play the CD, CD Player follows your play list.

    Some audio CDs come with computer-readable information about the music, including the title and list of tracks. The information appears in the lower half of the CD Player window. When you swap CDs, the CD Player window displays information about the CD you just put in.

Playing Audio CDs with Media Player

The Media Player program that comes with Windows 98 can also play audio CDs. Start Media Player by choosing Start | Programs | Accessories | Entertainment | Media Player. To play an audio CD that is already in the CD-ROM drive, choose Device | CD Audio. Media Player displays the tracks of the CD along the Position slider. Click the Play button in the lower-left corner of the Media Player window to play the CD. See "Playing Video Files with Media Player" in the next chapter for details about the Media Player program.

Working with MIDI

MIDI devices are usually musical instruments or recording devices (see "What Is MIDI?" earlier in this chapter). They have digital inputs and outputs and can transmit and understand music using the MIDI language. You can connect a MIDI instrument, like a keyboard to your PC, so that you can play music on the keyboard and record and listen to the music on your PC. You need additional MIDI software to play, edit, and mix MIDI inputs.

If you have more than one MIDI instrument installed, you can configure Windows 98 with a *MIDI scheme*, which specifies which inputs are stored on each *MIDI channel*, so that instruments can be edited separately and then mixed together later. You can use MIDI editing programs to edit and mix the MIDI inputs channel by channel.

Windows 98 comes with two programs that work with MIDI: ActiveMovie and Media Player. This section describes how to install a MIDI device, configure Windows to use it, and play MIDI files.

Installing a MIDI Device

To install a MIDI device, you connect a cable from the instrument to a MIDI port on your computer's sound card. Then follow these steps:

1. Choose Start | Settings | Control Panel and open the Multimedia icon.

2. Click the MIDI tab (see Figure 17-15). The box just below the Single Instrument setting shows the driver that Windows plans to use for MIDI output. The box below that lists the MIDI ports to which you can connect MIDI devices. If any MIDI instruments are installed, each appears under the port to which it is connected.

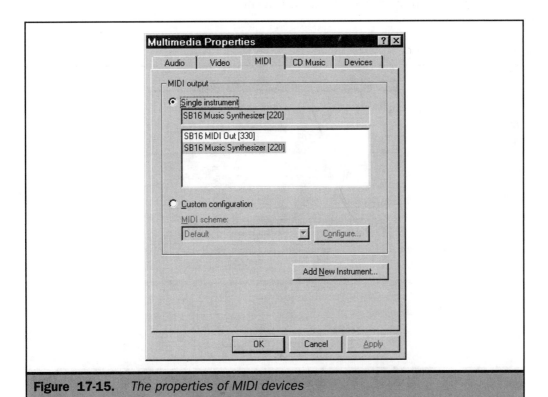

Figure 17-15. *The properties of MIDI devices*

3. Click the Add New Instrument button. The MIDI Instrument Installation Wizard runs and asks for the MIDI port to which the instrument is connected, the definition of the instrument, and the name you plan to use for this instrument. Click Next after answering each question and Finish after the last question. The new instrument appears in the Multimedia Properties dialog box, just below the MIDI port to which the instrument is connected.

4. Click the Single Instrument setting, and then the instrument you just installed. Click OK.

Creating a MIDI Scheme

If you have one MIDI instrument, choose the Single Instrument setting in the Multimedia Properties dialog box. If you have more than one MIDI device and you want to be able to mix together sounds from the devices, choose the Custom Configuration setting to create or edit a MIDI scheme. Click the Configure button to display the MIDI Configuration dialog box, shown in Figure 17-16.

You can assign MIDI instruments to one of the sixteen MIDI channels. One channel may accept input from more than one instrument.

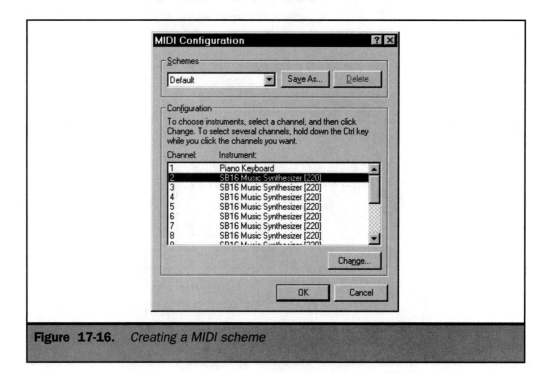

Figure 17-16. *Creating a MIDI scheme*

To assign an instrument to a channel, select the channel and then click the Change button. On the Change MIDI Instrument dialog box that appears, choose an instrument and click OK. To assign the same instrument to several channels, select several channels before clicking the Change button. Click one channel and then SHIFT-click another channel to select all the channels in between. Or CTRL-click another channel to add that one channel to your selection.

Once you have assigned your instruments to channels, you can save the set of assignments as a MIDI scheme. For example, you might have one MIDI scheme to use when your four friends with MIDI-compatible saxophones come by, and another scheme to use when you and another friend are jamming with two MIDI keyboards. To save your set of channel assignments as a new MIDI scheme, click the Save As button and type a new name for the scheme.

Playing MIDI Files with ActiveMovie

To play a MIDI sound file, click or double-click its filename in a Folder window or Windows Explorer window. Windows starts the ActiveMovie program and begins playing the MIDI file, as shown here:

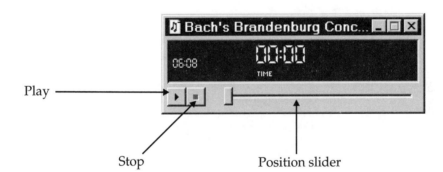

You can click the Stop button to stop the music, the Run button to start playing again, or the Pause button (which appears only when the music is playing) to pause. You can also drag the Position slider left and right to change which part of the file plays. See "Playing Video Files with ActiveMovie" in Chapter 18 for more about how ActiveMovie works.

Windows 98 comes with some sample MIDI files that are not automatically installed when you install Windows; to install them, open Control Panel, open Add/Remove Programs, click the Windows Setup tab, choose Multimedia, click Details, and then choose Sample Sounds from the list of Multimedia components (see "Installing and Uninstalling Programs That Come with Windows 98" in Chapter 3).

Windows stores the MIDI files in the C:\Windows\Media folder, in files with the .rmi extension.

Playing MIDI Files with Media Player

The Media Player program can also play MIDI files. Start Media Player by choosing Start | Programs | Accessories | Entertainment | Media Player. To play a MIDI file, choose File | Open, set the Files Of Type box to MIDI Sequencer, choose a MIDI file, and then click Open. Next, click the Play button in the lower-left corner of the Media Player window. See "Playing Video Files with Media Player" in the next chapter for details about the Media Player program.

Chapter 18

Working with Video

It's natural for computers to handle video data—after all, when you use a computer you are already sitting in front of a video screen. Windows 98 supports video, both input and output, if you add the necessary hardware to your computer. This chapter describes what formats video data is stored in, how to configure Windows to display video, and how to play video files using ActiveMovie, Media Player, and NetShow. You can also use the DVD Player to play digital video disks, and WebTV for Windows to watch broadcast television.

What Is Video Data?

You can use various *video capture devices* to get video information into your computer, such as digital video cameras. See Chapter 15 for instructions on how to install video capture devices. To display video, Windows uses your screen, and to play the accompanying audio, it uses your sound board and speakers.

Because the amount of data coming from a digital video camera is so immense, your computer can't process and store it fast enough. Instead, video data is compressed on its way into the computer from the camera and is then stored in a compressed format. The compression is done by a very fast DSP (digital signal processor, a kind of specialized computer) chip in your video capture hardware. Windows 98 comes with a number of *codecs*, programs for video compression and decompression, so that Windows can decompress and recompress video data when you want to display or edit it. Windows also includes DirectX, a feature that improves video playback. Windows stores most video in *AVI files*, files with the filename extension .avi. Other popular formats for video files are QuickTime (.qt) and MPEG (.mpg).

To see a list of your installed video capture devices, along with a list of the available codecs, choose Start | Settings | Control Panel, open the Multimedia icon, and then click the Devices tab. You see the list that was shown in the previous chapter in Figure 17-2. To see a list of video capture devices, click the plus box to the left of the Video Capture Devices entry. If no plus box appears, no devices are installed. To see a list of codecs that are available, click the plus box to the left of the Video Compression Codecs entry.

To experiment with playing video, you can use some video clips on the Windows 98 CD-ROM, in the \Cdsample\Videos folder. The video clips are all ads, but they are useful for testing.

Configuring Windows to Work with Video

When Windows plays video, it determines the size of the window in which the video appears based on settings on the Video tab of the Multimedia Properties dialog box. To see or change the size at which video plays on your screen, choose Start | Settings | Control Panel, open the Multimedia icon, and then click the Video tab (Figure 18-1). To open the Multimedia icon, click or double-click the icon depending on whether you have configured your desktop as Web style or Classic style (see "Choosing the Style of Your Desktop" in Chapter 1).

The picture of a computer screen shows the currently selected size at which Windows 98 plays video files. To change size, click the Full Screen setting, or click the Window box and choose a size. We recommend leaving the Window setting selected and set to Original Size. Playing video at sizes different from the original size usually results in fuzzier or distorted figures—but you can try various settings for yourself on your system.

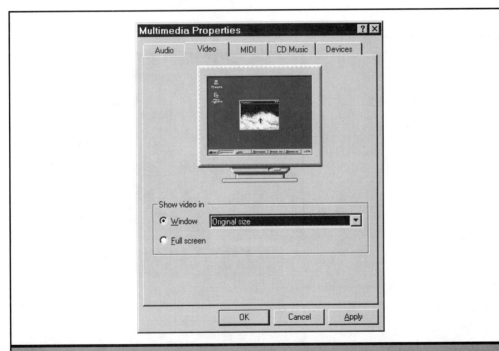

Figure 18-1. *Setting the size at which video plays onscreen*

Playing Video Files

Windows 98 comes with several programs for playing AVI video files: ActiveMovie, Media Player, and NetShow.

Playing Video Files with ActiveMovie

If you click the name of an AVI file in Windows Explorer or a Folder window, Windows runs the ActiveMovie program (see Figure 18-2). ActiveMovie can also play MPEG (with extension .mpg), QuickTime (.qt), and other video formats, as well as MIDI audio files (see "Playing MIDI Files with ActiveMovie" in Chapter 17). Alternatively, you can choose Start | Programs | Accessories | Entertainment | ActiveMovie Control; ActiveMovie displays an Open dialog box from which you must select the movie file you want to play. (Try one of the ads on the Windows 98 CD-ROM, in the \Cdsample\Videos folder.)

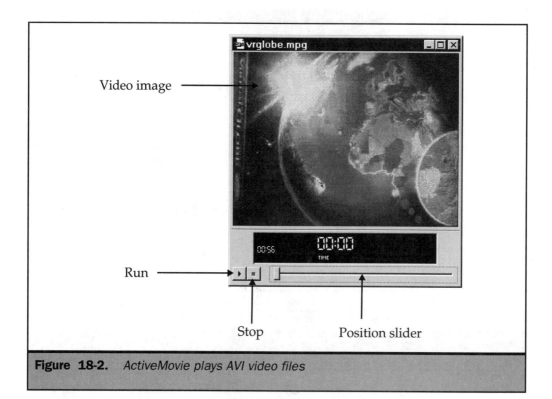

Figure 18-2. *ActiveMovie plays AVI video files*

ActiveMovie begins playing the movie as soon as it loads. You can click the Stop button (or press CTRL-S) to stop the video, click the Run button (or press CTRL-R) to start playing it again, or click the Pause button (which appears only when the video is playing) to pause it (or press CTRL-P). You can also drag the Position slider left and right to change which part of the video file ActiveMovie plays.

You can switch the display in the lower part of the window from time (in hours and minutes) to frames, or back again. Right-click anywhere in the ActiveMovie window (even in the video image) and choose Frames or Time from the menu that appears. You can also hide the time or frame display by right-clicking and choosing Display. If you want to hide the controls for stopping and starting the video, too, you can right-click and choose Controls. When the controls are hidden, you can still start and stop the video by right-clicking and choosing Run, Pause, or Stop.

To set other properties of the ActiveMovie program, right-click in the ActiveMovie window and choose Properties. You see the ActiveMovie Control Properties dialog box, shown in Figure 18-3. Table 18-1 lists the properties you can set on the ActiveMovie Control Properties dialog box.

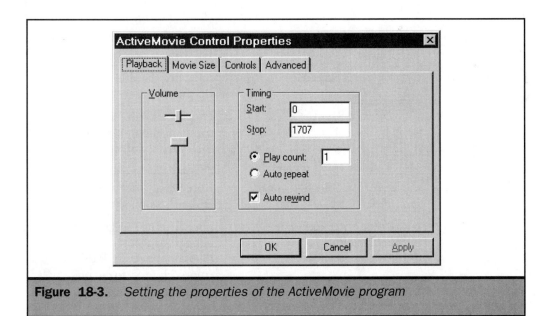

Figure 18-3. *Setting the properties of the ActiveMovie program*

Tab	Setting	Description
Playback	Volume	Sets the volume and balance for playing sound.
Playback	Timing Start and Stop	Specifies the starting and stopping frame of the video. Initially, Start contains 0 and Stop contains the number of the last frame of the video.
Playback	Play Count	Specifies the number of times the video plays when you click Run.
Playback	Auto Repeat	Specifies whether the video starts over at the beginning when you reach the end.
Playback	Auto Rewind	Specifies whether the video "rewinds" when you reach the end, so that the Position slider returns to the left end.
Movie Size	Select the Movie Size	Specifies the size of the video window.
Movie Size	Run Full Screen	Specifies that the video take up the whole screen.
Controls	Display Panel	Displays a panel with the frame number or time below the video window.
Controls	Control Panel (Position controls, Selection controls, and Trackbar)	Displays a control panel with Run, Stop, and Pause buttons, and a Position slider.
Controls	Color Foreground and Background	Specifies the foreground and background color in the display panel. Click the colored button to change the color.

Table 18-1.   *The Properties of the ActiveMovie Program*

Tab	Setting	Description
Advanced	Filter Properties box and Properties button	Selecting an audio or video filter and clicking the Properties button displays the advanced settings for that filter.

Table 18-1.   *The Properties of the ActiveMovie Program* (continued)

Playing Video Files with Media Player

Media Player is a program that can play a number of different types of multimedia files, including audio, MIDI, and video files. To start Media Player, choose Start | Programs | Accessories | Entertainment | Media Player.

Playing a File

To play a video file, choose File | Open, set the Files Of Type box to ActiveMovie or Video for Windows or All Files, choose a video file, and click Open. You can also drag the filename of a video file (or any multimedia file) from Windows Explorer or a Folder window into the Media Player window. Media Player loads the video file and displays a separate window to play it in. Click the Play button to start the video (see Figure 18-4).

If a video file has been compressed using a compression technique for which you do not have a codec that can process the file, you see an error message when you try to play the file. If Media Player can't figure out how to process a video file, try playing it with ActiveMovie instead; that is, click the video filename in Windows Explorer or a Folder window and see what happens.

Another way to open a file is to choose one of the following commands from the Device menu:

- ActiveMovie for MPG and other video formats.
- Video for Windows for AVI video files.

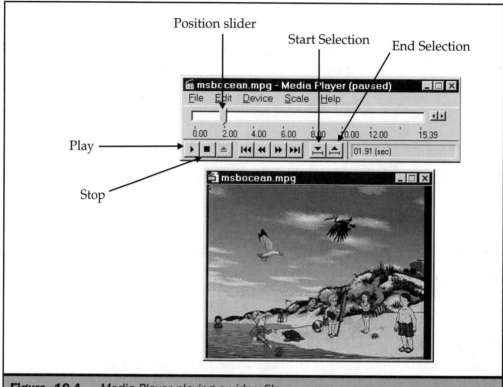

Figure 18-4.   *Media Player playing a video file*

■ Sound for WAV audio files (see "Playing Sound Files with Media Player" in Chapter 17).

■ MIDI Sequencer for MIDI audio files (see "Playing MIDI Files with Media Player" Chapter 17).

■ CD Audio to play an audio CD in your CD-ROM drive (see "Playing Audio CDs with Media Player" in Chapter 17).

While you are playing a file, you can also perform these actions:

■ Stop the video by clicking the Stop button.

■ Go to the beginning or end of the file by clicking the Previous Mark or Next Mark button.

■ Move forward or backward in the file by clicking the Scroll Forward, Scroll Backward, Fast Forward, or Rewind buttons, or by dragging the Position slider.

- Adjust the volume by choosing Device | Volume from the Media Player menu bar to display the Volume Control window (see "Controlling the Volume, Balance, and Tone" in Chapter 17).

- Change the display between time and frames along the Position slider by choosing Scale | Time or Scale | Frames from the Media Player menu bar. If the type of file you are playing has tracks (like an audio CD), you can display rack numbers on the Position slider by choosing Scale | Tracks.

Setting Media Player Options

You can set the options by choosing Edit | Options from the Media Player menu to display the Options dialog box, shown here:

These options are listed in Table 18-2.

Setting	Description
Auto Rewind	Rewinds the file when Media Player reaches the end.
Auto Repeat	Repeats the file when Media Player reaches the end (continuous play).
OLE Object Control Bar On Playback	Specifies that a control bar (with Play and Stop buttons) is inserted when you insert a multimedia file into a document, and that the OLE Object Caption is also inserted.
OLE Object Caption	Specifies the caption to appear when you insert a multimedia file into a document.

Table 18-2. *Media Player Options*

Setting	Description
Border Around Object	Specifies that a border appear around the icon that appears when you insert a multimedia file into a document.
Play In Client Document	Specifies that after you insert a multimedia file into a document, double-clicking the resulting icon plays the file.
Dither Picture To VGA Colors	Adjusts the colors of a video file to use the standard VGA display colors, to provide approximate colors on low-performance display cards.

Table 18-2. *Media Player Option* (continued)

Copying All or Part of a File

You can copy all of a multimedia file into another file by using Media Player. For example, you can copy a section of a video into a WordPerfect document; viewers of the document can then play the video clip by clicking the icon that appears. Follow these steps to copy all or a selected part of a file to the Windows Clipboard, for insertion into another file:

1. Open the file in Media Player by using the File | Open command.

2. Play the file until you decide which section you want to copy (or that you want to copy the whole file).

3. Select the part you want to copy by using one of these methods (the selected part of the file appears in dark blue along the Position slider):

   ■ Move the Position slider to the beginning of the part you want to copy and click the Start Selection button. Then, move the Position slider to the end of the part you want to copy and click the End Selection button.

   ■ Move the Position slider to one end of the part you want to copy and then hold down the SHIFT key while you drag the slider to the other end.

   ■ Choose Scale | Time or Scale | Frames to set the way you want to specify positions in the file. Then choose Edit | Selection from the menu bar to display the Set Selection dialog box, shown here:

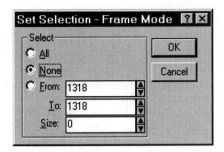

Enter the starting time or frame in the From box and the ending time or frame in the To box; click OK.

■ If you want to copy the entire file, choose Edit | Selection, click All, and then click OK.

4. Once you have selected the part of the file you want to copy, choose Edit | Copy Object or press CTRL-C to copy the selected section to the Windows Clipboard.

If nothing is selected (which you can achieve by choosing Edit | Selection and clicking None), Media Player copies the current video frame to the Clipboard. Once you have copied part or all of the file to the Windows Clipboard, switch to the application into which you want to copy the video clip, and then use that program's command (usually Edit | Paste or CTRL-V) to paste the multimedia data into the document.

Playing Streaming Video Files with NetShow

Video files tend to be huge, because each frame of a video requires many thousands of bytes of information. Viewing video over the Internet can involve long waits for video files to arrive. The invention of streaming video improved matters: You can begin playing a streaming video file after only the first section of the file has arrived (see "What Are Streaming Audio and Video?" in Chapter 17). The streaming video player continues to receive later sections of the file at the same time that it is playing earlier sections. As long as the program can receive information at least as fast as it can play it, you see uninterrupted video. Streaming audio files and players work the same way.

The most popular streaming audio and video formats are RealAudio (with file extension .ra) and RealVideo (with extension .rv). You can download the RealPlayer program for free from the web site **http://www.real.com**; this program works with your web browser to play RealAudio and RealVideo files from the Internet. The RealAudio Player is on the Windows 98 CD-ROM, if you are interested only in audio, not in video.

Microsoft has come up with its own streaming video format, called *Active Streaming Format*, or *ASF*. Files in this format have the extension .asf or .asx. *ASF files* with the .asf extension contain the actual streaming video data. *ASX files* with the .asx extension contain a single line of text, with the URL of a continuously updating video newsfeed. To play ASF or ASX files, you use NetShow, which comes with Windows 98. This section describes NetShow versions 2.0 and 2.1.

NetShow is not automatically installed with Windows 98. Even when Windows installs NetShow, Windows doesn't add a command to your Start or Programs menu for NewShow. To determine whether NetShow is installed, use Windows Explorer or a Folder window to look for a folder named C:\Program Files\Microsoft NetShow\ Player. If it's not there, you can install NetShow from the Windows 98 CD-ROM or floppy disks by opening Control Panel, opening the Add/Remove Programs icon, clicking the Windows Setup tab, choosing Multimedia from the list of components, clicking Details, and then choosing NetShow from the Multimedia components (see "Installing and Uninstalling Programs That Come with Windows 98" in Chapter 3).

> **Tip**   *You can get more information about NetShow from Microsoft's web site, including free updates to the software. Choose Go | NetShow Home Page to go to the home page for the program at* **http://www.microsoft.com/netshow**. *Choose Go | NetShow Software Updates to go to the web page from which you can download new versions of NetShow and related tools, at* **http://www.microsoft.com/netshow/ download.htm**.

Running NetShow

Normally, NetShow runs automatically when you start to download an ASF or ASX file from the Internet. You can also run NetShow by opening a Windows Explorer or Folder window, displaying the contents of the C:\Program Files\Microsoft NetShow\Player folder, and then running the Nsplayer.exe file.

When you see a link on a web page for a NetShow (ASF) file or newsfeed (ASX file), click the link. Depending on how your browser is configured, you may see a message asking whether to open the file or save it; choose to open the file. Your browser downloads the first section of the file, runs the NetShow program, and begins to play the file (Figure 18-5).

You can use the Stop and Play buttons to stop and start the video. How the other buttons and the Position slider work depends on whether you are playing an ASF file or an ASX file:

■ Since ASX files are continuously generated, usually by a live video camera, the file has no beginning or end. The Position slider doesn't move, and you can't use any of the four buttons in the lower-right part of the NetShow window to change position in the file.

■ When you play an ASF file, you can use the Rewind button, Fast Forward button, and Position slider to move around the file. If the author of the file stored markers (like bookmarks) in the file, you can also use the Previous Marker and Next Marker buttons to move around.

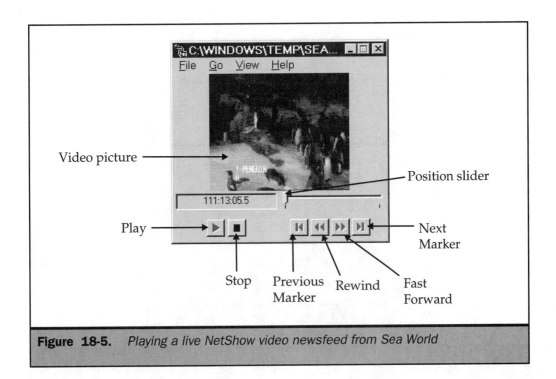

Figure 18-5.   *Playing a live NetShow video newsfeed from Sea World*

When you are done playing the video, close the NetShow window. If you started NetShow by clicking a link in your web browser, the browser window is probably still open where you left it.

If you have an ASF or ASX file on your computer, you can open it from NetShow by choosing File | Open.

Looking at the Properties of a NetShow File

You can find out more about the ASF or ASX file that you are viewing by choosing File | Properties from the NetShow menu. You see the Microsoft NetShow Player Properties dialog box (Figure 18-6). Four tabs on this dialog box contain information about the file you are playing:

- **General**   If information about the ASF file is included with the file, you see title, author, copyright, rating, and description information.

- **Details**   This tab shows more technical information about the ASF or ASX file.

- **Statistics**   You can also see how well your computer has been receiving the ASF or ASX file. This tab shows a pie chart of how well the information in the file has been received.

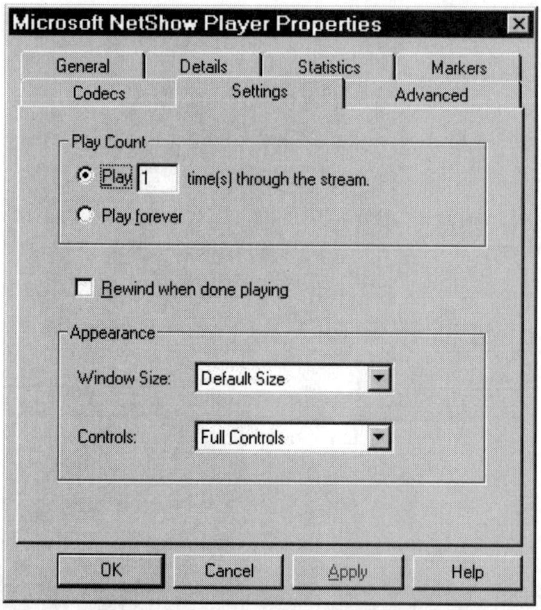

Figure 18-6. *Configuring the NetShow program*

- **Markers** If you are playing an ASF file that contains markers (bookmarks), this tab lists the markers by number, position in the file (time), and description. If the file doesn't contain markers, the tab doesn't appear.

See the next section for information about what's on the rest of the tabs in this dialog box.

Configuring NetShow

For settings that control how NetShow works, choose File | Properties or View | Play Settings. Either way, you see the Microsoft NetShow Player Properties dialog box (Figure 18-6). The General, Details, Statistics, and Markers tabs show information about the file you are playing; see the preceding section. Table 18-3 shows the settings on the Settings and Advanced tabs, which control the program rather than one specific file.

The Codecs tab of the Microsoft NetShow Player Properties dialog box lists the codecs that NetShow can use when playing ASF and ASX files, along with the URL of the web page you can consult for more information (see "What Is Video Data?").

Tab	Setting	Description
Settings	Play *xx* time(s) through the stream	Specifies how many times to play the ASF file.
Settings	Play forever	Tells NetShow to start again at the beginning when it reaches the end of the file.
Settings	Rewind when done playing	Tells NetShow to move the Position slider to the beginning of the file after playing the file.
Settings	Window Size	Specifies the size of the NetShow window: your options are Default Size, Half Size, and Double Size.
Settings	Controls	Specifies whether controls (Play, Stop, and other buttons) appear in the NetShow window: your options are Full Controls, Simple Controls, and No Controls.
Advanced	Use default buffering	Specifies that NetShow use the standard amount of buffering (storage of incoming ASF data before displaying the data as video).
Advanced	Buffer *xx* seconds of data	Specifies the amount in seconds of ASF data to store in a buffer.
Advanced	Multicast	Enables NetShow to accept ASF data using the Multicast protocol.
Advanced	UDP/Use port *xx* to receive UDP data	Enables NetShow to accept ASF data using UDP (User Datagram Protocol), and specifies the Internet port from which to receive the data.

Table 18-3. *Configuration Settings on the Microsoft NetShow Player Properties Dialog Box*

Tab	Setting	Description
Advanced	TCP	Enables NetShow to accept ASF data using TCP (Transmission Control Protocol), the standard protocol used on the Internet.
Advanced	HTTP	Enables NetShow to accept ASF data using the HTTP (Hypertext Transport Protocol), the protocol with which web browsers and web servers communicate.
Advanced	No proxy/Use browse proxy settings/Use proxy *xx* port *xx*	For HTTP connections, specifies whether to use a proxy server (intermediate server for connecting a private LAN to the Internet), and if so, the name and port of the proxy server.

Table 18-3. *Configuration Settings on the Microsoft NetShow Player Properties Dialog Box (continued)*

Viewing TV by Using Your Computer

Windows 98 comes with an application called WebTV for Windows, which allows you to watch broadcast television channels on your computer screen. To use the WebTV for Windows program to watch TV, you need a TV tuner card installed in your computer. Even without a TV tuner card, you can see a program guide.

Note *WebTV for Windows has nothing to do with WebTV. WebTV is a box you can buy to attach to your television and phone line to convert the television into a computer capable of browsing the Web and sending and receiving e-mail. WebTV turns your television into a computer; WebTV for Windows turns your computer into a television. Actually, WebTV for Windows has one thing in common with WebTV: They are both owned by Microsoft.*

Since most computers don't have TV tuner cards, WebTV for Windows is not installed automatically when you install Windows 98. To install WebTV for Windows, open the Control Panel, open the Add/Remove Programs icon, click the Windows Setup tab, and choose WebTV for Windows from the list of components (see "Installing and Uninstalling Programs That Come with Windows 98" in Chapter 3). You have to restart Windows twice in the process of configuring WebTV for Windows.

To run WebTV for Windows, choose Start | Programs | Accessories | Entertainment | WebTV for Windows. The first time you run, a Wizard walks you through configuring the program. Once you see the WebTV for Windows window (Figure 18-7), which takes up the entire screen, double-click the TV Configuration channel (usually 96) to use the Wizard to change your configuration again.

If you don't have a TV tuner card installed in your computer, you can run WebTV for Windows, but no channels appear. Even without a TV tuner card you can display television listings in the Program Guide window. To configure WebTV for Windows to display listings, restart the configuration program by double-clicking the TV Configuration channel, and then click the GUIDE PLUS+ link. Windows connects to the Internet, asks you for your location and cable company (choose Broadcast if you

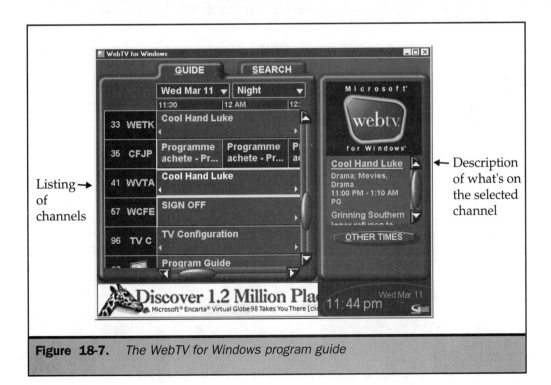

Figure 18-7.   *The WebTV for Windows program guide*

don't have cable), and configures WebTV for Windows to display television listings for your area.

Here are some things you can do with the WebTV for Windows:

■ Watch a channel by clicking a channel and clicking the Watch button.

■ Display the TV Toolbar by pressing ALT or F10. Use buttons on the TV Toolbar to display the program guide (click Display) or change your selection of favorite channels (click Settings).

■ Change channels by clicking one of your favorite channels on the TV Toolbar, changing the channel number on the TV Toolbar, or choosing a channel from the program guide.

■ Search for a program based on its title, category, actors, or movie ratings. Display the program guide and click the Search tab.

■ Display the WebTV for Windows in a window (instead of full-screen) by clicking the Minimize button on the TV Toolbar. Unless you have a huge monitor, the resulting television image is too small to be useful.

■ Get help by pressing F1 or by clicking Help on the TV Toolbar. WebTV for Windows displays a Help system that works like Windows Help (see Chapter 6).

■ Exit by clicking the Close button on the TV Toolbar.

Unless your computer came with a built-in TV tuner, a regular color television probably provides a better picture at a lower cost than a TV tuner card for your computer.

Playing Video Disks with DVD Player

A *DVD (Digital Versatile Disk* or *Digital Video Disk)* is like a large CD—it's a digital disk that can contain video material. If you buy movies on DVDs and you have a DVD drive connected to your computer, you can play DVDs on your computer by using the DVD Player program that comes with Windows 98. Before you try this, make sure that your DVD drive has the appropriate decoder card and software drivers to play DVDs.

DVD Player is not installed automatically when you install Windows 98. To install it, open the Control Panel, open the Add/Remove Programs icon, click the Windows Setup tab, choose Multimedia from the Components list, click Details, and then choose DVD Player from the list of Multimedia components (see "Installing and Uninstalling Programs That Come with Windows 98" in Chapter 3).

To run DVD Player, insert the DVD in your DVD drive and then choose Start | Programs | Accessories | Entertainment | DVD Player.

Chapter 19

Running Windows 98 on
Laptops

Many computer users use laptops—it is convenient to be able to pick up your computer, with all its data and software, and take it anywhere. But laptops have disadvantages, too, many of which are addressed by Windows 98. This chapter is full of suggestions about how to make the most of your laptop, including these suggestions:

- You can coordinate files with those on a desktop computer by using the Windows 98 Briefcase.

- You can print a document, even when you aren't attached to a printer, by deferring printing until a printer is available.

- You can use power management to make your battery last longer.

- If you use a docking station to connect your laptop to desktop devices, you should know about docking and undocking, and hardware profiles.

- You can connect to a network or another computer to use its resources when you don't have a network card by using Direct Cable Connection or Dial-Up Networking.

Coordinating Your Laptop with Your Desktop by Using the Windows Briefcase

If you use more than one computer on a regular basis, you should try the Windows Briefcase, a program that coordinates files that you work on, so that you always use the most up-to-date version. Windows Briefcase is especially useful if you use a laptop when you're on the road and a desktop machine in the office, but Briefcase is useful for anyone who uses several computers.

The Windows Briefcase program creates and maintains *Briefcases*, which are folders containing files and subfolders that you can move between your laptop and another computer. Your default Briefcase is called My Briefcase, but you can rename it or create additional Briefcases (see "Using Multiple Briefcases").

The easiest way to use Briefcase to coordinate files on different computers is to have the two computers connected by a network or another connection. However, you can also use Briefcase with a floppy disk, although that limits the total size of the files you can move from computer to computer.

The My Briefcase icon appears on the desktop: open the icon to see its contents. Click or double-click the My Briefcase icon depending on whether you use Web style or Classic style for your desktop (see "Choosing the Style of Your Desktop" in Chapter 1). If you don't see it, you may need to install the Windows 98 Briefcase from your Windows 98 CD-ROM or floppy disks by using the Windows Setup program (see "Installing and Uninstalling Programs That Come with Windows 98" in Chapter 3). Open Control Panel, open the Add/Remove Programs icon, click the Windows Setup tab, choose Accessories from the groups of components, click Details, and then choose Briefcase.

 If you think My Briefcase is installed, but it doesn't appear on the desktop, right-click the desktop and choose New | Briefcase from the menu that appears.

The first time you open the My Briefcase window, you see the Welcome To The Windows Briefcase window, with tips for using the program. Click Finish when you have read the tips.

Using Briefcase to Synchronize Files

The most common use of a Briefcase is for transferring files from a desktop to a laptop for use while away from the office, and then transferring the updated files back to the desktop when you return. Using Briefcase to transfer files has four steps:

1. Move files to the Briefcase. Choose only the files that you will use and update while you're away from your desktop computer.

2. Copy the Briefcase to the laptop.

3. Use files from the Briefcase while you are on the road using the laptop.

4. When you are ready to work at your desktop again, tell Briefcase to synchronize the files on the two computers, so that both computers contain the latest version of each file in the Briefcase.

Note *Briefcase uses the system time and date to synchronize files—make sure that the time and date on each computer is correct.*

These steps are somewhat different depending on whether you have a network connecting the laptop and desktop computers. When you don't have a network, you have to use a floppy disk (or disks) to move the Briefcase to the laptop. When you do have a network, you can sit at the laptop and drag files from the desktop to the laptop's Briefcase.

Moving Files to the Briefcase

The first step is to find the files you want to have on the road, and drag them to your Briefcase. The easiest way to do this is to select files in a Folder window or Windows Explorer and drag them to the Briefcase icon or window. You can do this in several steps as you select files in different folders on your hard disk. You can also right-click a file and choose Send To | My Briefcase from the shortcut menu.

You move files differently if the laptop and the desktop are connected by a network. If you have a network, sit at the laptop and drag files from a drive located on the desktop computer to the laptop's Briefcase.

If you don't have a network, you need to complete a few extra steps:

1. Sit at the desktop and drag the files you need to the Briefcase icon on the desktop, or the Briefcase window, if it's open.

2. Drag the Briefcase to a floppy drive or right-click the Briefcase and choose Send To | Floppy (choosing the drive where you want to move the Briefcase).

 Make sure to drag actual files to the Briefcase, not shortcuts to files.

Copying the Briefcase to the Laptop

If you have a network, you don't have to do this step, because the Briefcase with the files you need is already on the laptop. However, if you don't have a network, the Briefcase with the files you need is still on the desktop computer, where it will do you no good when you leave the office.

You also don't have to complete this step if you want to use the Briefcase files from the floppy. However, using a floppy instead of the hard disk will slow you down noticeably if you are using large files.

So, to copy the Briefcase with its files to the laptop's hard drive, follow these steps:

1. Take the disk to which you copied the Briefcase, insert it in the floppy drive of the laptop, and view the contents of the drive. You see the Briefcase icon.

2. Drag the Briefcase from the floppy drive to the laptop's desktop.

 If the laptop already has an icon on the Desktop called My Briefcase, and that is the name of the Briefcase that you are copying, rename the old My Briefcase, so that the two do not have the same name.

Using Files in a Briefcase

While you're on the road (or just not using your desktop computer), make sure to use the files from the Briefcase. To do so, simply open the Briefcase window (shown in Figure 19-1) and double-click a file that you want to use, just like you would a file in any other folder. You can use the usual Folder window commands to control how files in the Briefcase window appear (see "Changing Views" in Chapter 9).

If you need to use an application's File | Open command, display the files in the Briefcase by clicking the Up One Level button in the Open dialog box until you can't go up any more levels—the Briefcase is on your computer's desktop. Open the Briefcase to see the files it contains.

When you save a file from the Briefcase, use the Save button to make sure that you save it back to the Briefcase. If you don't save the file back to the Briefcase, the Briefcase won't be able to synchronize files for you.

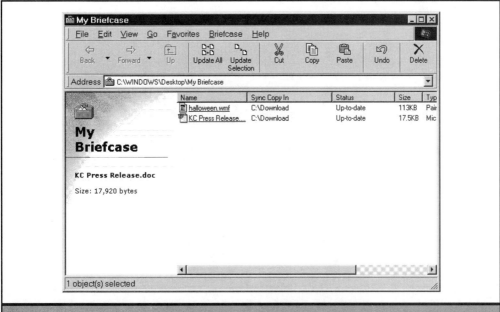

Figure 19-1. *You can open files from the Briefcase window*

Note *You should edit a file on only one computer before you synchronize the files with Briefcase. If you edit a particular file while you're on the road, and someone at the office edits the same file, you won't be able to keep all the changes, unless the program the file uses can show you what they are—Briefcase gives you the option to keep only one of the two files. However, if someone at the office edits a file that you took with you in your Briefcase but didn't edit, you can keep the most up-to-date version of the file.*

Here are other things you can do in the Briefcase window:

■ You can check the status of a file in the Briefcase by selecting it in the Briefcase window and choosing File | Properties from the menu bar. Or right-click the file and choose Properties from the menu that appears. When you see the Properties dialog box for the file, click the Update Status tab (see Figure 19-2).

■ If you drag a file from another location into the Briefcase, you can find the original copy of this file: In the Properties dialog box for the file, click the Find Original button. Windows displays the folder containing the original file in a Folder window.

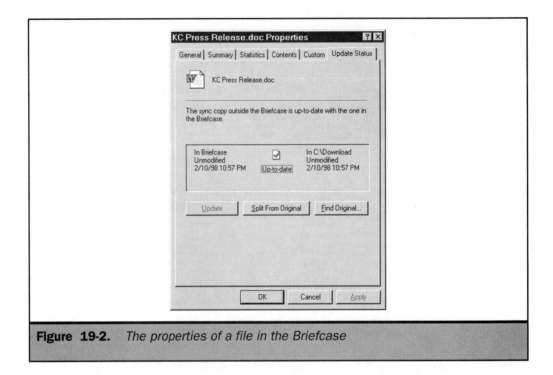

Figure 19-2.   *The properties of a file in the Briefcase*

■ You can sever the connection between the original file and the copy of the file in the Briefcase—for example, if the copy in the Briefcase has changed sufficiently that you want to keep the original copy, too. Select the file in the Briefcase window and choose Briefcase I Split From Original from the menu bar. Alternatively, right-click the filename, choose Properties from the menu that appears, click the Update Status tab, and then click the Split From Original button.

Synchronizing the Edited Files in a Briefcase

When you return and want to use your desktop PC again, you need to synchronize the files on your laptop and on your desktop. Follow these steps to synchronize the files:

1. If you have a network, reestablish the connection between the two computers. If you have a docking station that supports hot docking (installing or removing the computer in the docking station without turning the computer off), the Briefcase may open automatically (see "Using a Docking Station"). If you don't have a network, you need to move Briefcase from the laptop's desktop back to the floppy disk, take the floppy disk to the original computer, and then move the Briefcase back to the original computer's desktop.

2. Open the Briefcase window. You see the status of each file in the Status column, as shown in Figure 19-1. (Choose View | Details if this column doesn't appear.) A file's status can be one of the following three:

■ **Orphan**   The file exists only in the Briefcase and not on the source computer (in this example, the desktop computer is the source computer).

■ **Up-to-date**   The file has not changed on either computer.

■ **Needs Updating**   The file has changed on either the desktop or the laptop (or both).

3. Click the Update All button on the Briefcase toolbar. The Update My Briefcase dialog box appears, showing how each file needs to be updated, as shown in Figure 19-3. A file can be updated in one of the following ways:

■ **Replace, and an arrow pointing to the right**   This is the most common action. It means that the file in the Briefcase will replace the file of the same name on the desktop computer.

■ **Replace, and an arrow pointing to the left**   This means that the file on the desktop computer is the most recent—it will replace the file of the same name in the Briefcase.

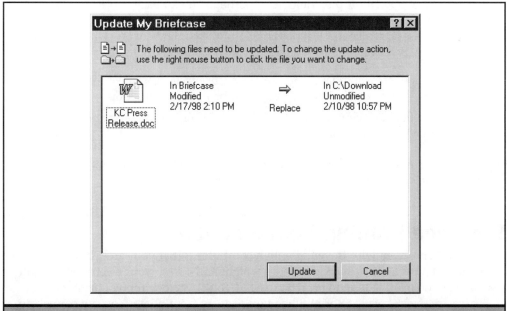

Figure 19-3.   *Briefcase tells you how files have changed, and what needs to be done to synchronize the files in the Briefcase with the files on the desktop*

■ **Skip (both changed)**   This means that both files (the one on the desktop and the one on the laptop) have been changed and Briefcase can't determine which file should be used. You need to figure out which version of the file you want to use.

4. If you don't want a file updated as shown, right-click the file and choose how to update the file from this shortcut menu:

5. Click the Update button to update the files.

Using Multiple Briefcases

You may want to have multiple briefcases—perhaps one for each project that you are working on. Multiple briefcases allow you to take with you only the files that you need. Multiple briefcases can also make it possible to fit the contents of one whole briefcase onto one floppy disk. Follow these steps to create additional briefcases:

1. Right-click the desktop and choose New | Briefcase from the menu that appears. An icon called New Briefcase appears on the desktop.

2. Rename the new icon to reflect the files it will contain (see "Naming and Renaming Files and Folders" in Chapter 8).

   You can create a Briefcase in a folder as well as on the desktop (in Windows Explorer or a Folder window, choose File | New | Briefcase).

Deferring Printing from a Laptop

One frequent problem with traveling with a computer is that you rarely have access to a printer. Even portable printers add more weight and cost to your electronic carryall than most people are willing to bear. So instead you survive without a printer.

There are several ways to print when you're away from home: You can connect to someone else's computer (using a network card, direct cable connection, or Dial-Up Networking) and print on its printer; you can fax your document to the nearest fax machine (assuming you have fax software and a fax/modem); or you can just go ahead and give the command to print the document, taking advantage of Windows 98's deferred printing feature.

See Chapter 16 for more information about printing from Windows 98.

Printing in Offline Mode

When a printer is set up, but not currently attached to your computer, you can still give the command to print a document. You see a message telling you that the printer isn't available and telling you that the printer will be put into *offline mode*, which means that files intended for the printer will be stored on your disk, instead. When you next connect to the printer, you see a message that print jobs are waiting—you can then print or cancel the documents.

If you don't see the message asking whether you want to print, when you are reconnected to a printer, follow these steps:

1. Open the Printers folder by choosing Start | Settings | Printers.

2. Right-click the offline printer (grayed out printers are offline). You see a check mark next to the Use Printer Offline option on the menu.

3. Choose Use Printer Offline to remove the check mark from the menu option and put the printer online. The print jobs waiting in the print queue start to print.

Printing on a Different Printer

If you want to print your queued documents using a printer other than the one you usually use, you can change the description of the printer temporarily. The problem with this approach is that you will probably be asked to insert your Windows 98 CD-ROM—and you may not have it if you and your laptop are on the road. (The driver you need may be available on the Internet, if you want to print that badly.)

If you use a wide variety of printers, you may want to install the Generic printer driver on your laptop to give you a basic printing option, no matter what kind of printer you're using.

Follow these steps to change the description of a printer temporarily:

1. Open the Printers folder by choosing Start | Settings | Printers.

2. Open the printer that you printed to (the printer appears grayed out to indicate that it is offline). You see the Printer window with all your print jobs listed.

3. Right-click the printer and choose Properties from the menu that appears. You see the Properties dialog box for the printer.

4. Click the Details tab to see the options shown in Figure 19-4.

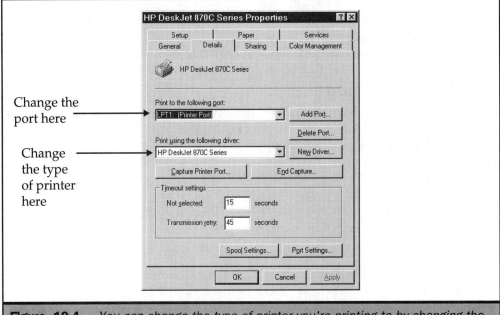

Change the
port here

Change
the type
of printer
here

Figure 19-4.   *You can change the type of printer you're printing to by changing the
printer's properties*

5. If necessary, change the port in the Print To The Following Port box. If you
usually print to a network printer, you definitely need to choose another port.
If you print to a local printer, and you've hooked the printer to the parallel port,
you don't need to change the port.

6. Use the Print Using The Following Driver box to choose the type of printer you
have available. If the printer you have available isn't listed (because you haven't
used it before), click the New Driver button to choose the kind of printer you do
have.

7. Close all the dialog boxes. You may be asked for your Windows 98 CD-ROM.

If you change the driver for the printer, you'll need to repeat the preceding steps to
change it back when you return to the office and connect to your regular printer.

*Windows 98 uses a single driver for a variety of similar printers. If you already have
a printer defined that is similar to the one you want to use, you'll probably find that
you can define the new printer, and Windows won't need any extra files.*

Managing Your Computer's Power

If you often use your laptop when it's not plugged in, you have run into the problem of a battery that doesn't last until you've finished your work. Windows 98 and some applications support power management, which eases this problem without actually solving it. Windows 98 supports two power management standards: *APM* (Advanced Power Management) and *ACPI* (Advanced Configuration and Power Interface). However, in order to take advantage of Windows 98's power management features, you must have a computer with hardware that supports one of these standards. (The computer doesn't have to be a laptop.)

Power management is handled from the Power Management Properties dialog box, displayed in Figure 19-5. To display the Power Management Properties dialog box, open the Power Management icon on the Control Panel. The options displayed on your Power Management Properties dialog box may differ, depending on what type of power management your hardware supports.

Many laptop manufacturers add extra power management drivers to take advantage of special power-saving features, such as running the CPU slower when the computer is working on batteries than when it's plugged in, or turning off serial and parallel ports when you're not planning to use them. Consult your laptop's documentation to see whether your computer has any extra features you can enable.

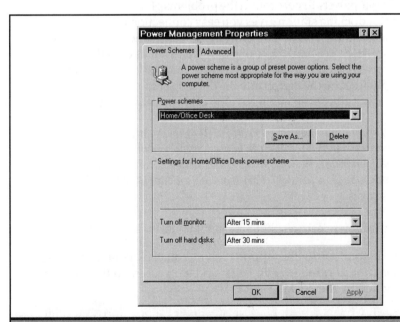

Figure 19-5.   *Manage how your laptop (or desktop) uses power by using these settings*

You can choose a *power scheme*, which is a group of settings that define when and if Windows should turn off the power to parts of your computer. Power schemes allow you to create and use different power management profiles for use under different circumstances.

Click the Power Schemes tab in the Power Management Properties dialog box, and then click the Power Schemes box (the topmost setting). Choose the power scheme that reflects the type of hardware you're using: Home/Office Desk or Portable/Laptop. Then make changes to the rest of the settings in the dialog box. Once you choose all the power settings you want to use, you can save them as a new power scheme by clicking the Save As button, typing a new name for the power scheme, and clicking OK.

You can display the Power Meter in the system tray section of the Windows 98 Taskbar. Click the Advanced tab on the Power Management Properties dialog box and click the Show Power Meter On Taskbar check box until a check appears. The Power Meter shows whether the computer is connected to AC power or running on batteries. Double-clicking the Power Meter on the system tray displays the Power Management Properties dialog box.

Using a Docking Station

Docking stations allow laptop users to get around the problems of the limited resources that most laptops have. A docking station gives you easy connection to a better monitor, a real mouse and full-sized keyboard, and possibly a network. Some docking stations put additional hardware, such as a hard drive or CD-ROM drive, at your disposal. In addition to giving you access to additional resources, docking stations give you convenience—by simply clicking the laptop into the docking station, you gain access to the additional resources, rather than having to plug cables into the laptop.

Port replicators *are a kind of simple docking station that contain no resources except additional ports. A port replicator can be used to give you immediate access to a full-sized screen, keyboard, mouse, printer, and network connection, without having to plug each cable in separately. Port replicators do not have hard drives or other internal resources.*

Windows 98 provides some features that are useful to users of docking stations:

■ **Hot docking**   If your hardware supports it, you can click your laptop into its docking station *without turning off the laptop* and gain access to the additional resources provided by the docking station.

■ **Hardware profiles**   Allows you to create profiles so that your laptop will work properly regardless of whether it is connected to the docking station.

Docking and Undocking

If your laptop supports hot docking, you can usually undock it by choosing Start | Eject PC. Windows 98 automatically adjusts to the change in hardware, notifying you of open files, and loading or unloading any necessary drivers. When you're ready to dock the laptop again, simply put it in the docking station. Windows 98 will again adjust automatically to the change in hardware.

If your laptop does not support hot docking, you need to shut down Windows and turn the laptop off before docking or undocking. When your laptop doesn't support hot docking, you'll benefit from creating two hardware profiles—one for use when connected to the docking station and one for use when the laptop is being used away from the docking station. Multiple hardware profiles can save you time. When you undock your laptop, you don't have to change each hardware setting that needs to be changed; instead, you can choose the correct hardware profile when the machine boots.

Creating and Using Hardware Profiles

A *hardware profile* is a description of your computer's hardware resources. Creating multiple hardware profiles gives you an easy way to tell Windows 98 what hardware the computer is connected to. If the laptop is attached to a network, you want to be able to use the network printer. If it's in a docking station, you want to be able to use the docking station hardware—extra drives or sound card—and you may want to change your screen resolution to take advantage of a regular monitor. Hardware profiles can save information about the hardware that's available and the drivers used by the hardware. You create one hardware profile for each hardware configuration you use.

Hardware profiles store information about printers, monitors, video controllers, disk controllers, keyboards, modems, sound cards, network cards, pointing devices, and ports.

Hardware profiles are useful when you have more than one way that you commonly use a computer. Your computer may sometimes be connected to a network and use shared drives and printers, and at other times be disconnected from the network without have access to the network's shared resources. Or you may have a laptop that you sometimes use with a docking station and sometimes use without it. Hardware profiles allow you to easily load and unload the drivers needed for the resources to which your computer has access.

Creating a New Hardware Profile

The following are the steps for creating a new hardware profile. This example creates two additional profiles—one with a network card, called *Networked*, and one without the network card, called *No Network*—so that there are three profiles in all. The steps are almost exactly the same, no matter what hardware you're disabling in a second profile. You can make profiles with other hardware enabled or disabled, and you may want to use different names, depending on the profiles you are creating.

Follow these steps to create new hardware profiles:

1. Configure your hardware the way that you will usually use your computer (see Chapter 15). Make sure to get all your peripherals working—printers, modems, sound cards, and extra drives. If your computer is on a local area network, configure the computer to use the network card (see Chapter 29).

2. Open the System Properties dialog box by choosing Start | Settings | Control Panel and opening the System icon.

3. Click the Hardware Profiles tab to see the options shown in Figure 19-6.

4. Select the hardware profile Original Configuration.

5. Click the Copy button to display the Copy Profile dialog box.

6. Type **Networked** in the To box as the name of the profile you'll use when your computer is in the same configuration as you are in now (in this example, the computer is currently connected to a LAN). This configuration includes all the hardware that you are using now. Click OK.

7. Click the Copy button a second time to display the Copy Profile dialog box again. You will make a copy of the Original Profile for use in case something goes wrong.

8. Type a profile name in the To box, such as **Copy of Original**, and click OK. This profile will remain identical to the Networked profile.

Note   *It's a good idea to make a copy of the Original Configuration profile and leave it as is, in case you have problems with the other profiles.*

9. Select the Original Configuration and click the Rename button to see the Rename Profile dialog box.

10. Type **No Network** as the name of this profile and click OK. You will edit this profile to disable the network card. The current profile is now called No Network.

11. Click the Device Manager tab of the System Properties dialog box to see the tab shown in Figure 19-7.

12. Expand the Network Adapters category to display the network adapter that you want to disable in the No Network profile. Look for the hardware device(s) you want to disable when your computer is not connected to the network.

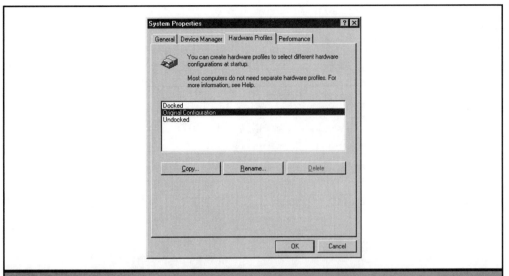

Figure 19-6.   *Creating additional hardware configurations for your computer*

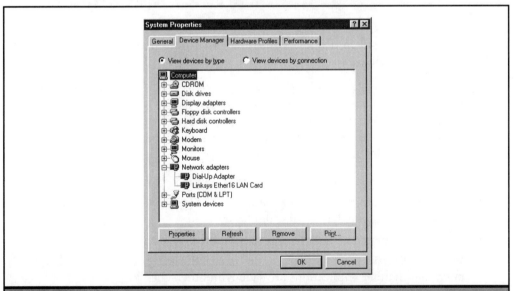

Figure 19-7.   *The Device Manager tab shows hardware components of your computer*

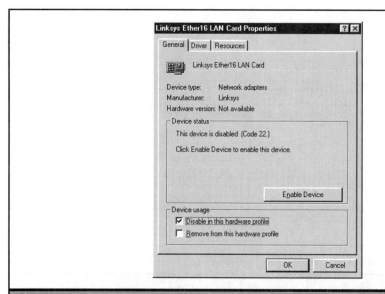

Figure 19-8. *Disabling hardware in the current profile in the Properties dialog box*

13. Select the network card and click the Properties button to see the properties for the card. The dialog box you see looks like the one displayed in Figure 19-8.

14. Select either the Disable In This Hardware Profile check box or the Remove From This Hardware Profile check box. When Disable is selected, the device appears with a red X in Device Manager, the driver is not loaded, and the hardware device is unavailable. (Figure 19-8 shows how the Device Manager appears when the network card is disabled.)

15. When Remove is selected, the hardware is removed from Device Manager.

16. Click OK to return to the Device Manager tab. Repeat steps 13 and 14 to disable or remove additional hardware from this profile.

17. Click OK to close the System Properties dialog box.

18. Windows 98 asks whether you want to restart the computer. Make sure that all open files in other applications are saved, and then click Yes.

Switching Hardware Profiles

When the computer reboots—and whenever it starts from now on—you see a menu similar to the following:

```
    Windows cannot determine what configuration your computer
is in.
Select one of the following:
1. Original profile
2. Networked
3. No Network
4. None of the above
```

The menu lists the hardware profiles you created. Pick the configuration you want to use.

Modifying and Deleting Hardware Profiles

If you decide not to use a hardware profile any more, you can delete it by selecting it on the Hardware Profile tab of the System Profiles dialog box and clicking Delete.

To re-enable a hardware device in a hardware profile, start the computer using the hardware profile. Then open the Add New Hardware icon in the Control Panel to add the drivers for this device to the hardware profile.

Connecting Two Computers with Direct Cable Connection

While a LAN is the best way to use resources on another computer, you may find yourself in a situation where you want to share resources, but you don't have a network card. A *direct cable connection* (or *DCC*) allows you to create a slow but usable network between two computers by using a cable between the serial or parallel ports of the two computers—you don't need a network card. All you need is the Windows 98 Direct Cable Connection program.

If you need a continuous connection, you really should invest in the hardware and time needed to set up a LAN—the hardware isn't expensive, the setup is not that onerous, and the performance and reliability are far better than a DCC (see Chapter 29). While a DCC isn't a good long-term solution to your network needs, it can be extremely useful when you need to transfer files between two computers. One particularly convenient use of a DCC is to hook up a laptop without a CD-ROM drive to a desktop machine, in order to install new software using the desktop computer's CD-ROM drive, or to copy files to or from the laptop. A DCC can even allow you to access the network to which the host computer is attached.

When you attach two computers by using DCC, one computer is the *host computer*, the computer that has the resources you want to use (usually a desktop computer). The other computer is the *guest computer*, the computer that needs to make use of the resources (such as reading from the CD-ROM drive or printing to the printer). The guest computer is frequently a laptop. A DCC is one-way: The guest computer can see and use any shared resources on the host computer, and can access any shared network resources the host can access. However, the host computer cannot see the guest computer.

 We had trouble getting the Direct Cable Connection program to work, as have many other Windows 98 users.

Getting Your Cable

The only piece of hardware you need for a DCC is a cable. However, you need the right kind of cable with the right kind of connectors on the ends. The cable should be called a *null-modem cable*, but may also be called a LapLink cable, Serial PC-to-PC File Transfer cable, or InterLink cable. Before you go shopping, check for available ports on the two computers you want to connect. You can use parallel ports, but serial ports are preferable—they are probably labeled Serial, Com1, or Com2. (Serial ports are usually used for a mouse or modem; parallel ports are usually used for a printer.)

Serial ports come in 9 pin and 25 pin varieties—see what you have available on the computers you want to connect and get the cable with the appropriate connectors (see "Serial Ports" in Chapter 15). If you're connecting a 25-pin serial port and a 9-pin serial port, try to get a cable with a 25-pin plug on one end and a 9-pin plug on the other. If you think you may create a DCC often, and with different computers, try to find an "octopus" cable that has both kinds of plugs on both ends. Check also whether there are pins on the port (male), in which case you need a female plug on the cable, or whether the plug on the cable needs to have pins (male). You can buy gender changers for the plugs, if necessary.

Once you have the correct cable, you're ready to create the DCC. There are four steps to creating the connection:

1. Connect the cable to the computers.
2. Install Network Neighborhood, other networking components, and the Direct Cable Connection program on both computers.
3. Configure the Direct Cable Connection program on the host computer.
4. Configure the Direct Cable Connection on the guest computer.

Then you are ready to use your new connection.

Connecting the Cable

The first step is to connect the cable to the computers. It's safer, but not absolutely required, to turn off both computers before connecting the cables. Note which port the cable is attached to—you'll need to know when you configure the Direct Cable Connection program. If you're using the parallel port, you must use the parallel port on both computers. If you're using serial ports, you can use either serial port: COM1 on one computer and COM2 on the other will work fine.

When the cable is firmly connected to both ends, power up the two computers.

Networking Software Needed for Direct Cable Connection

For Direct Cable Connection to work, you must install and configure networking options first. Both computers must have the following networking components installed:

- Network Neighborhood
- IPX/SPX-compatible Protocol
- NetBEUI Protocol
- Dial-Up Adapter
- Client for Microsoft Networks
- A unique computer name
- A workgroup name in common

If you use a local area network, some of these components may already be installed, and thus do not need to be reinstalled. The Direct Cable Connection Wizard can install the Dial-Up Adapter for you, but additional networking components must be installed too.

Installing Network Neighborhood and Networking Components

You need to have Network Neighborhood installed on both computers in order to use the Direct Cable Connection program. Skip this section if you see this Network Neighborhood icon on the desktop on each computer:

Network
Neighborhood

(Refer to Chapter 30 for more information about installing networking components.)

You need your Windows CD-ROM (or floppy disks) before you begin. Follow these steps on both the host and guest computers:

1. Choose Start | Settings | Control Panel to display the Control Panel.

2. Click or double-click the Network icon to display the Network dialog box. If network components are installed, you don't need to complete these steps. You may have missed the Network Neighborhood icon, or it may be hidden. Open Windows Explorer and look for Network Neighborhood in the folder tree (usually near the bottom).

3. Click the Add button to display the Select Network Component Type dialog box.

4. Select Protocol and click Add to display the Select Network Adapters dialog box.

5. Select Microsoft as the Manufacturer and IPX/SPX-compatible Protocol as the protocol, and then click OK. You may need to have your Windows 98 CD-ROM available so that the needed files can be copied. When the files are copied, you see the Network dialog box again. The installed components now include, Dial-Up Adapter and IPX/SPX-compatible Protocol. (The Dial-Up Adapter is installed automatically when IPX/SPX is installed, and it is necessary to make Direct Cable Connection work.)

6. If you want to gain access to a network through Direct Cable Connection, you also need to install NetBEUI. Click the Add button to display the Select Network Component Type dialog box.

7. Select Protocol and click Add to display the Select Network Protocol dialog box.

8. Select Microsoft as the Manufacturer and NetBEUI as the Network Protocol, and then click OK. You see the Network dialog box with NetBEUI included as an installed component.

9. If you want to share resources (you can share resources only on the host computer), you need to install the Client For Microsoft Networks: Click the Add button to display the Select Network Component Type dialog box.

10. Select Client and click Add to see the Select Network Client dialog box.

11. Select Microsoft as the Manufacturer and Client For Microsoft Networks as the Network Client, and then click OK. The Network dialog box now has three tabs: Configuration (the one you've been using), Identification, and Access Control. The Primary Network Logon box should now be set to Client For Microsoft Networks.

12. The next step is to identify the computer: Click the Identification tab and provide a computer name and workgroup. If the host computer is already part of a workgroup, you should use the same workgroup name for the guest computer.

13. If you want to share resources owned by the computer you're working at, click the File And Print Sharing button on the Configuration tab of the Network dialog box.

14. Choose what you want to share—most users usually select the first two options. Click OK to close the dialog box. Windows may ask for the Windows 98 CD-ROM or floppy disks. You may also have to reboot—Windows tells you if you do. When the process is complete, you see the Network Neighborhood icon on the desktop, and you have installed all the components necessary for Direct Cable Connection.

Installing Direct Cable Connection

You use the Start | Programs | Accessories | Communications | Direct Cable Connection command on both the host and guest computers to configure and use Direct Cable Connection. If the command doesn't appear on each computer, you need to install it. To install this program, follow the instructions for adding a component of Windows 98 in Chapter 3: Open the Control Panel, open the Add/Remove Programs icon, click the Windows Setup tab, choose Communications from the list of components, click Details, and then choose Direct Cable Connection.

Configuring the Host Computer

To configure a computer as either a host or a guest, you run the Direct Cable Connection Wizard. Complete these steps on the host computer—the computer with the resources that you want to access from a second computer:

1. Choose Start | Programs | Accessories | Communications | Direct Cable Connection to start the Direct Cable Connection Wizard, shown in Figure 19-9.

2. Choose Host to configure the host computer. Click Next.

3. Choose from the list of ports the port you are using for the cable on this computer. If the port you are using doesn't appear, it may be because of interrupt (IRQ) conflicts (see "Hardware Parameters" in Chapter 15). Click Next.

4. If you want to password-protect the host computer (a prudent idea), select the Use Password Protection option and then click the Set Password button to set the password. A password requires the user of the guest computer to know the password before using resources on the host computer. In the Direct Cable Connection Password dialog box, type the password twice, once in the Password box and again in the Confirm Password box. Then click OK.

5. Click Finish to complete configuring the connection.

Configuring the Guest Computer

Follow these steps configure the guest computer:

1. Choose Start | Programs | Accessories | Communications | Direct Cable Connection to start the Direct Cable Connection Wizard, shown in Figure 19-9.

2. Choose Guest to configure the guest computer. Click Next.

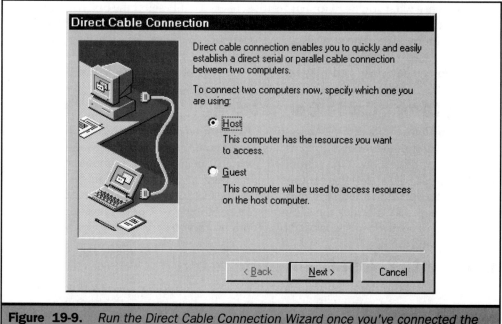

Figure 19-9.   *Run the Direct Cable Connection Wizard once you've connected the cable between the two computers*

3. Choose from the list of ports the port you are using for the cable on this computer.

4. Click Next to see the final screen and then click Finish.

You are now ready to connect the two computers.

Using Direct Cable Connection

After you complete the configuration in the Network dialog box, connect the cable to both computers, and run the Direct Cable Connection Wizard on both the host and guest computers, you're ready to try your connection.

Follow these steps to connect the two computers:

1. On the host computer, choose Start | Programs | Accessories | Communication | Direct Cable Connection to see the Direct Cable Connection dialog box, shown in Figure 19-10.

2. If Direct Cable Connection displays the wrong port in the Settings box, click the Change button to use the Direct Cable Connection Wizard to change the port to which the cable should be connected. When you are done, you again see the dialog box shown in Figure 19-10.

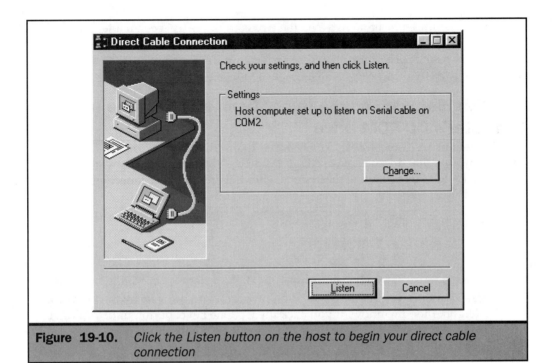

Figure 19-10.   *Click the Listen button on the host to begin your direct cable connection*

3. Click the Listen button. You see a dialog box telling you that the host is waiting for a guest computer to connect. If you change your mind at this point, you can click Close to cancel the connection.

4. On the guest computer, choose Start | Programs | Accessories | Communication | Direct Cable Connection to see the Direct Cable Connection dialog box, shown in Figure 19-10. Instead of a Listen button, the dialog box on the guest computer has a Connect button.

5. Click the Connect button. When the two computers are connected, a small Direct Cable Connection dialog box appears on both computers, to tell you that there is a connection.

Using the Host Computer's Resources from the Guest Computer

Remember that a direct cable connection is one-way: The guest computer can see and use any shared resources on the host computer, but the host computer cannot see the guest computer. If you need to copy files from or to the host computer, do it while you're sitting at the guest computer.

To access the shared resources on the host computer from the guest computer, click the View Host button in the Direct Cable Connection dialog box on the guest computer, after the connection between the two computers has been made. You see a Folder window showing the shared resources on the host computer (to find out how to share resources and use shared resources, see Chapter 32). You can also view shared resources by using Network Neighborhood.

Installing Software on the Guest Computer from the Host Computer's CD-ROM Drive

One frequent use of Direct Cable Connection is to install software from a CD-ROM onto a computer that doesn't have a CD-ROM drive. You can install software from a shared CD-ROM by following these steps, after the direct cable connection is established:

1. Share the CD-ROM drive on the host.

2. Put the software CD-ROM in the drive.

3. On the guest computer, install the software according to the instructions. Usually this procedure consists of running the Install.exe or Setup.exe file on the CD-ROM. To find the installation program, you can display the Network Neighborhood window (if you click the Up One Level button until you can't go up any more levels, you'll see the Network Neighborhood icon).

4. Open the host computer's icon in the Network Neighborhood window to see the shared drives.

5. Open the shared drive's icon and find the file you need.

6. Proceed as instructed by the software's documentation.

See Chapter 3 for more information about how to install programs.

Closing the Connection

To close Direct Cable Connection, click the Close button on the Direct Cable Connection dialog box on either computer.

Troubleshooting Direct Cable Connection

If you have trouble getting Direct Cable Connection to work, Windows 98 has a troubleshooter for Direct Cable Connection that you should use to solve the problem. Start the troubleshooter by following these steps:

1. Choose Start | Help.

2. Click the Contents tab.

3. Open the Troubleshooting topic.

4. Open the Windows 98 Troubleshooters topic.

5. Open the Direct Cable Connection topic.

The troubleshooter asks you to check the following:

- Each end of the cable is securely connected.

- The Dial Up Networking adapter is bound to IPX/SPX-compatible Protocol.

- Both computers have a protocol in common.

- File and printer sharing is enabled, and the specific resources are shared (at least one resource must be shared at the time of connection).

- Each computer has a unique computer name and the same workgroup name.

- Each port used has the same settings (bits/second, data bits, parity, stop bits, flow control). Baud rate should be 115200 to maximize the speed of transfers.

Note *If you find yourself setting up a direct cable connection frequently, and between the same two computers, please build yourself a LAN: It's slightly more expensive in the short run, but more reliable and easier to work with, and much, much, faster in the long run (see Chapter 29).*

Connecting Two Computers by Using Dial-Up Networking

Dial-Up Networking is most frequently used to attach your computer to the Internet through a SLIP or PPP connection (see "What Is Dial-Up Networking?" in Chapter 22). However, it can also be used to attach your computer to another computer through a modem. For example:

- If you have a desktop computer and a laptop computer, both with modems, you can use Dial-Up Networking to call your desktop from your laptop. Your laptop can share the resources (hard disks and printers) on your desktop.

- If you have a laptop computer that is usually connected to a LAN at your office, and another computer on the LAN has a modem, you can use Dial-Up Networking when you're away from your office to call that computer from your laptop and use facilities on the LAN. Dial-Up Networking is a slow way to access a LAN's resources, but in some cases it is exactly what you need.

The computer you call using Dial-Up Networking is called the *dial-up server*. The computer that makes the call is called the *dial-up client*. The dial-up server is usually the desktop back at the office. It has resources, such as files or a printer, that you want to use from the dial-up client computer, which is usually a laptop. Those resources must be shared. Chapter 32 discusses sharing disks and printers over a network. You cannot configure the resources for sharing from a remote location, so make sure that you've shared all the necessary resources before you hit the road. You may even want to spend a day working on the laptop to discover what resources you might need to have configured for sharing while you're on the road.

When the dial-up server computer is attached to a LAN, the client computer that is dialing in becomes a *remote node* on the network, meaning that the client computer's connection to the network works exactly as it would if you were in the building and attached to the LAN—from the client computer, you can use resources on the network, and other computers on the network can see the shared resources on your computer. Of course, access from a remote node through phone lines is much slower than access from a computer that is connected to the network using cables.

Hardware and Software Needed on the Client and Server Computers

Here's a summary of what you need to connect two computers using Dial-Up Networking:

■ Both the server and client computers must have a modem attached to a phone line (and yes, you do need two different phone lines). Neither computer needs a network card. See Chapter 21 for instructions on how to configure Windows to work with your modem.

■ Both computers must have Dial-Up Networking installed, as described in the next section. The following section describes how to configure Dial-Up Networking on the client computer.

■ The server computer needs server software that allows it to handle incoming Dial-Up Networking calls from the client computer. Windows 98 comes with server software called Dial-Up Server. The section "Installing and Configuring Dial-Up Server on the Server Computer," later in this chapter, describes how to install and configure Dial-Up Server.

Tip

You don't have to use Windows 98 Dial-Up Server in order to connect a remote computer to your LAN. Instead, you can use other remote server products—some only work with particular kinds of networks. For instance, Windows NT has RAS (Remote Access Server), which allows remote computers to call in. You may also want to use a remote control product that allows you to take control of a computer on a LAN when you are not actually within a cable's reach of the LAN. Popular remote control products are ReachOut Remote and PCAnywhere.

Installing Dial-Up Networking on Both Computers

Check whether Dial-Up Networking is installed on both the client and server computer by choosing Start | Programs | Accessories | Communications on each computer. If you don't see Dial-Up Networking on the menu that appears, you need to install it from the Windows CD-ROM or floppy disks (see "Installing and Uninstalling Programs That Come with Windows 98" in Chapter 3). Open the Control Panel, open the Add/Remove Programs icon, click the Windows Setup tab, choose Communications from the list of components, click the Details button, and then choose Dial-Up Networking. You may need to restart Windows before you can configure Dial-Up Networking.

Once Dial-Up Networking is installed, you need to configure it on the client computer, as described in the next section.

Configuring Dial-Up Networking on the Client Computer

Follow these steps:

1. Open Dial-Up Networking by choosing Start | Programs | Accessories | Communications | Dial-Up Networking. You see the Dial-Up Networking window, shown in Figure 19-11.

2. Open the Make New Connection icon to start the Make New Connection Wizard, shown in Figure 19-12. (This Wizard is also described in Chapter 22.)

3. In the first box, type a name for your connection: You can use the name of the computer you are calling, or a more general name, such as the location of the network.

4. Choose your modem in the Select A Device box and then click Next. The Wizard displays a window in which you enter the details about the phone number to call to connect to the network.

5. Type the area code and telephone number of the server computer's modem. If necessary, chose a country code from the drop-down list. Don't get fancy here with extra codes to dial an outside line or turn off call waiting—you have a chance to enter that information later.

6. Click Next and then click Finish to create a new icon in the Dial-Up Networking window.

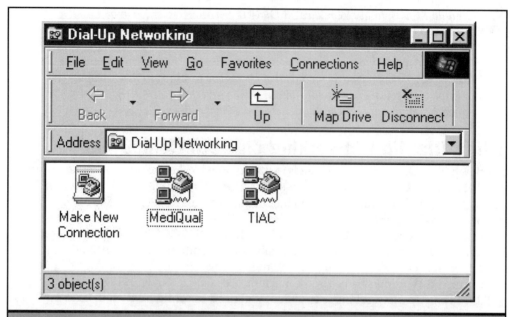

Figure 19-11. *Define a new dial-up connection from the Dial-Up Networking window*

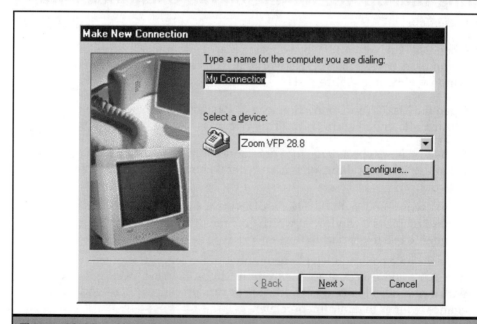

Figure 19-12. *Name your Dial-Up Networking connection and select your modem*

7. Right-click the new icon and choose Properties from the menu that appears. You see the Properties dialog box for the connection.

8. Click the Server Types tab to see the options shown in Figure 19-13.

9. Set the Type Of Dial-Up Server to PPP, and set the other options so that the Server Types tab looks like Figure 19-13. (Log On To Network and Enable Software Compression are selected, as are all three network protocols.)

If you plan to call more than one dial-up server, you can create additional Dial-Up Networking connections by repeating steps 2 through 9. If you need to change the phone number or modem, right-click the new icon and choose Properties from the shortcut menu.

Installing and Configuring Dial-Up Server on the Server Computer

To configure a computer as a dial-up server, you need to install Dial-Up Server. If it's not already installed on the server computer, install it from the Windows CD-ROM or floppy disks (see "Installing and Uninstalling Programs That Come with Windows 98" in Chapter 3). Open the Control Panel, open the Add/Remove Programs icon, click the Windows Setup tab, choose Communications from the list of components, click the

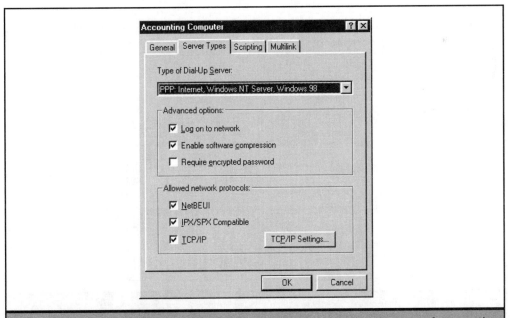

Figure 19-13. *Set properties for the dial-up server, including the type of connection*

Details button, and then choose Dial-Up Server. You may need to insert the Windows 98 CD-ROM or floppy disks, or restart Windows.

To configure Dial-Up Server on the server computer, follow these steps:

1. Choose Start | Programs | Accessories | Communications | Dial-Up Networking to display the Dial-Up Networking window, like the one shown in Figure 19-11.

2. Choose Connections | Dial-Up Server from the window's menu bar. (If you don't see the Dial-Up Server option on the Connections menu, you haven't installed the Dial-Up Server component of Windows 98.) You see the Dial-Up Server dialog box, shown in Figure 19-14.

3. Choose the Allow Caller Access option.

4. Click the Change Password button to display the dialog box in which you type a password for the server.

5. Type the password twice (once in each box). It's very important to protect your computer with a password—otherwise, anyone with Windows can dial in and do whatever they like to your shared resources. Then click OK to return to the Dial-Up Server dialog box.

6. Click the Server Type button to see the Server Types dialog box.

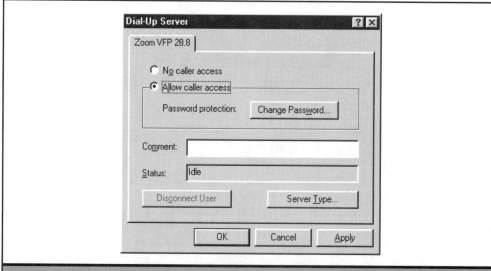

Figure 19-14.   *When you choose Allow Caller Access, you enable networking via a dial-up connection*

7. Select PPP as the Type Of Dial-Up Server and select both the Enable Software Compression and Require Encrypted Password check boxes on the dialog box.

8. Click OK to close all open dialog boxes.

Once you've configured a computer as a dial-up server, be sure to read the section "Dial-Up Networking Security Issues" later in this chapter.

Before you leave your server computer, make sure that it picks up the phone when the remote computer calls in. Since this seemingly small glitch can totally ruin your plans to access network resources remotely, you might want to make a trial run before you go very far, following the steps in the next section.

Connecting via Dial-Up Networking

Once you have configured both the client and the server computers, you can use Dial-Up Networking to connect the two computers. If your client computer is sometimes connected to a LAN, the easiest way to initiate Dial-Up Networking is to request a LAN resource from the client computer. When Windows cannot find the resource through a LAN, it suggests finding it by using Dial-Up Networking.

You can also establish a Dial-Up Networking connection manually by following these steps on the client computer:

1. Open the Dial-Up Networking window by choosing Start | Programs | Accessories | Communications | Dial-Up Networking.

2. Open the connection icon you created when you configured Dial-Up Networking. You see the Connect To dialog box, shown in Figure 19-15.

3. Click the Dialing Properties button to display the Dialing Properties dialog box, shown in Figure 19-16.

4. You can use the Dialing Properties dialog box to set properties for the different places that you dial in from (see "Configuring Windows for Dialing Locations" in Chapter 21). To create a new dialing profile, change all the options that need to be changed, type a new name in the I Am Dialing From box, and click the New button. For instance, you may create different profiles depending on whether you're calling in from the office, home, or a hotel.

5. Click OK to close the Dialing Properties dialog box. Check that the correct location is chosen in the Dialing From setting on the Connect To dialog box.

6. Type the password needed to access the dial-up server in the Password box. Use the password you used in step 6 of the section "Installing and Configuring Dial-Up Server on the Server Computer," earlier in this chapter.

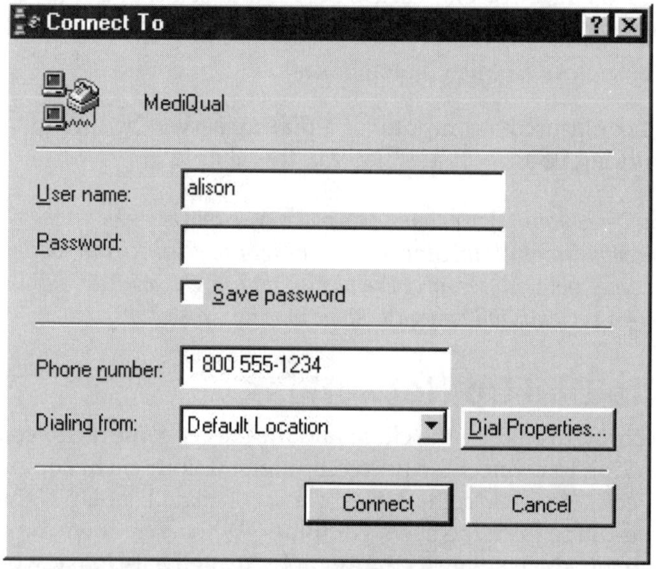

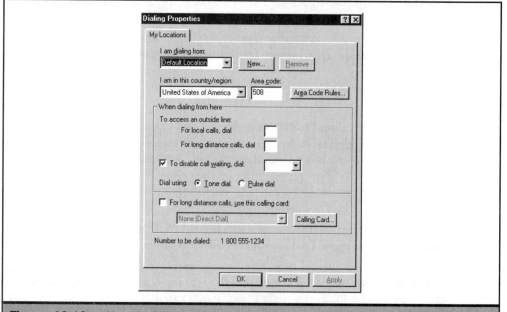

Figure 19-15. You see the Connect To dialog box when you open your new Dial-Up Networking connection

Figure 19-16. Use the Dialing Properties dialog box to add additional numbers to dial

7. Click Connect to make the connection to the dial-up server. Establishing the connection takes a few seconds. When the connection is made, you see a dialog box telling you that you are connected.

Note *When you want to close the connection, click the Disconnect button on the dialog box.*

Once you have established the connection, you can use Network Neighborhood on the client computer to use resources on the dial-up server.

Dial-Up Networking Security Issues

When a computer is configured as a dial-up server, anyone with a computer and a modem can dial in to it and use its shared resources. That includes reading and destroying files on shared drives, as well as introducing viruses. So it is a good idea to disable Dial-Up Networking when you won't be using it. Here's how:

1. Open the Dial-Up Networking window by choosing Start | Programs | Accessories | Communications | Dial-Up Networking.
2. Choose Connections | Dial-Up Server from the menu.
3. Click the No Caller Access option.

Repeat the same steps, but choose Allow Caller Access to turn Dial-Up Networking back on when you plan to use your computer as a dial-up server. Since Dial-Up Networking does you no good when it's turned off, you should take some additional measures for the times that you need it enabled. Additional prudent security measures include:

- Keep your modem's phone number a closely guarded secret.

- Implement passwords and change them regularly.

- Consider using the callback feature.

- Use a third-party security device or software.

- Monitor network activity for abnormalities.

Chapter 20

Accessibility Options

Microsoft has built into Windows 98 a number of options to help people who have disabilities that make using a computer difficult. In some cases, people without disabilities may also find the accessibility options useful. The options include settings for your keyboard, sound, display, and mouse.

To set your accessibility options, you can use the Windows Accessibility Wizard, described in this chapter. (You may need to install the options from your Windows 98 CD-ROM or floppy disks first.) After you set your options, you can turn them on and off by using the Accessibility Properties dialog box, or the icons that appear in the system tray on your Taskbar.

What Accessibility Options Are Available in Windows 98?

Windows 98 includes the accessibility options for people who have difficulty typing, reading the screen, hearing noises the computer makes, or using a mouse.

Keyboard aids for those who have difficulty typing include:

- **StickyKeys** Lets you avoid pressing multiple keys by making keys like the CTRL, SHIFT, and ALT keys "sticky"—they stay in effect even after they have been released.

- **FilterKeys** "Filters out" repeated keystrokes. Good for typists who have trouble pressing a key once briefly.

- **ToggleKeys** Sounds a tone when the CAPS LOCK, SCROLL LOCK, and NUM LOCK keys are activated.

Visual translation of sounds for those who have difficulty hearing include:

- **SoundSentry** Displays a visual warning when the computer makes a sound.
- **ShowSounds** Displays a caption when the computer makes a sound.

Display options for those who have trouble reading the screen include:

- **High Contrast** Uses a high-contrast color scheme, and increases legibility wherever possible.
- **Magnifier** Displays a window magnifying part of the screen.

Mouse options for those who dislike or have trouble using a mouse or trackball include:

- **MouseKeys** Allows you to use the numeric keypad to control the pointer.
- **SerialKey** Turns on support for alternate input devices attached to the serial port.

All these Accessibility options are found on the Accessibility Properties dialog box. Choose Start | Settings | Control Panel to display the Control Panel. Then, open the dialog box by opening the Accessibility Options icon on the Control Panel. Click or double-click the Accessibility Options icon, depending on whether you are using the Web style or Classic style desktop (see "Choosing the Style of Your Desktop" in Chapter 1).

Installing Accessibility Options

Although accessibility options are packaged with Windows 98, they may not have been installed on your computer. If you don't see the Accessibility Options icon on the Control Panel, you need to install the Accessibility Options by opening the Add/Remove Software icon on the Control Panel (see "Installing and Uninstalling Programs that come with Windows 98" in Chapter 3). Click the Windows Setup tab and choose Accessibility from the list of components.

Do Applications Use the Windows 98 Accessibility Settings?

Although accessibility options are built into the Windows 98 operating system, software applications must be designed to work with them. Microsoft maintains standards, including standards for accessibility, that developers must meet to put the Designed for Windows logo on their product. As of this writing, the standards are the following:

- Support for the Control Panel's size, color, mouse, and keyboard settings.
- Support for High Contrast mode.
- Provide and document keyboard access to all features (required with Windows 98).
- Expose the location of the keyboard focus (required with Windows 98). This option helps Microsoft Magnifier determine which part of the screen to magnify.

Future requirements include:

- Allow other software to identify and manipulate all screen elements that the user interacts with.
- Avoid fonts smaller than 10 points.
- Allow the user to choose font names and font sizes wherever appropriate.
- Support scaleable system fonts.

Do Applications Use the Windows 98 Accessibility Settings? (continued)

■ Use system colors wherever appropriate and allow the user to customize all other colors.

■ Allow the user to customize user interface timings.

■ Allow the user to explore with the mouse and keyboard without triggering unexpected changes.

■ Do not convey important information by sound alone.

If you need to use accessibility options with new software, make sure the software supports Windows 98's accessibility options before you buy.

Microsoft maintains an accessibility web site at **http://www.microsoft.com/enable**.

Configuring Windows by Using the Accessibility Wizard

Accessibility has been deemed important by Microsoft—important enough to get its own menu. Choose Start | Programs | Accessories | Accessibility to see the two accessibility options: the Accessibility Wizard and Microsoft Magnifier (see "Magnifying the Screen").

The Accessibility Wizard is new in Windows 98, and gives you easy access to the accessibility options in Windows 98. The Accessibility Wizard (shown in Figure 20-1) steps you through the settings for the accessibility options that will make using a computer easier for you. All the accessibility options that are changed by the Accessibility Wizard appear on the Accessibility Properties dialog box, and are covered in detail in the rest of this chapter.

Setting Keyboard Accessibility Options

The options to change the way the keyboard accepts input are found on the Keyboard tab of the Accessibility Properties dialog box, shown in Figure 20-2. Choose Start | Settings | Control Panel, run the Accessibility Options program, and click the Keyboard tab if it's not selected.

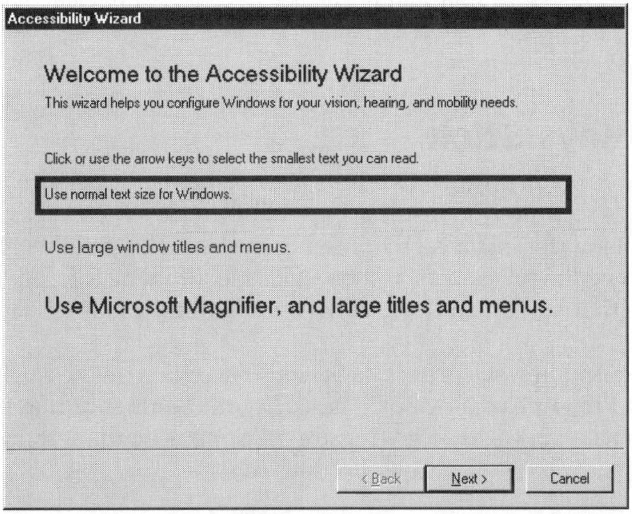

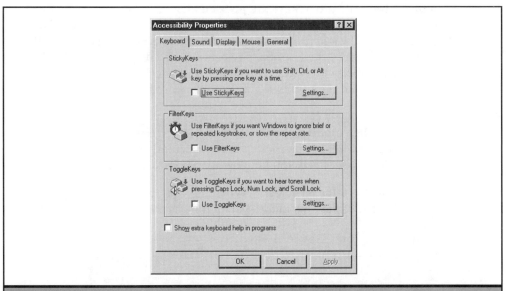

Figure 20-1. *The Accessibility Wizard steps you through Windows 98's accessibility options*

Figure 20-2. *Use the Keyboard tab of the Accessibility Properties dialog box to turn on the keyboard accessibility options*

Other keyboard settings, including character repeat settings and language, are available on the Keyboard Properties dialog box (see "Configuring Your Keyboard" in Chapter 14).

Making Your Keys Stick

If you have trouble holding down two keys at once, activate StickyKeys so that you can press the keys separately and still get the same effect. When StickyKeys is on, you can save a document (for instance) by pressing the CTRL key and then pressing the S key—you don't need to press them at the same time. Pressing a second key turns off (or unsticks) the first key. StickyKeys works only with the modifier keys: SHIFT, CTRL, and ALT.

To turn on StickyKeys, select the Use StickyKeys option on the Keyboard tab of the Accessibility Properties dialog box. Then, click the Settings button to define exactly how StickyKeys will work. The following are the options on the Settings For StickyKeys dialog box:

- **Use Shortcut**   Use this check box to enable you to turn on StickyKeys by pressing SHIFT five times.

- **Press modifier key twice to lock**   Use this check box to allow you to lock on a modifier key when you press it twice. Turn off the key by pressing it once again.

- **Turn StickyKeys off if two keys are pressed at once**   This option does just what it says—if two keys are pressed at once, StickyKeys is turned off. To make a modifier key sticky again, StickyKeys must be turned back on by using the shortcut (if the Use Shortcut option is selected), or by displaying the Keyboard tab of the Accessibility Properties dialog box and selecting the Use StickyKeys option. This option can be annoying if you ever want to press two keys at the same time.

- **Make sounds when modifier key is pressed**   When this option is on, you hear a beep when a modifier key is stuck. This is particularly useful when the previous option is on—it lets you know when StickyKeys is turned off.

- **Show StickyKeys status on screen**   When this option is on, a small graphic appears to the left of the time in the system tray, as shown here:

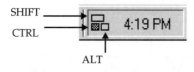

The three blocks represent the three modifier keys: SHIFT at the top, CTRL at the bottom left, and ALT at the bottom right. When a modifier key is stuck, its block is shaded on the diagram. When StickyKeys is off, the diagram is removed from the system tray.

Filtering Out Extra Keystrokes

If you have trouble typing each letter only once, you may want to turn on FilterKeys rather than spending time editing out extra keystrokes. FilterKeys can be configured to ignore repeated keystrokes that are repeated too quickly, and to slow down the repeat rate (the rate at which a character is repeated when a key is held down).

To turn on FilterKeys, select the Use FilterKeys option on the Keyboard tab of the Accessibility Properties dialog box. Then, click the Settings button to define exactly how FilterKeys will work. The following are the options on the Settings For FilterKeys dialog box:

- **Use shortcut** Use this check box to enable you to turn on FilterKeys by holding down the right SHIFT key for eight seconds.

- **Ignore repeated keystrokes** This option is sometimes called BounceKeys—it allows you to configure FilterKeys to ignore keys that are repeated without a sufficient pause. When you choose this option, click the Settings button next to it, and then define the interval within which repeated keys should be ignored. Getting the right interval is crucial to avoiding frustration, so use the Test area to type words with repeated letters to see whether the setting works for you.

- **Ignore quick keystrokes and slow down the repeat rate** These options are also called RepeatKeys and SlowKeys. RepeatKeys allows you to change the way that keys are repeated—normally, if you hold down a key, it repeats at a certain rate after it has been held down for a certain interval (see "What Are Keyboard Settings?" in Chapter 14). SlowKeys allows you to filter out keys that are pressed only briefly. When SlowKeys is on, typing must be more methodical, but keys touched lightly or quickly are ignored. When you choose this option, click the Settings button next to it, and define the RepeatKeys and SlowKeys settings: Whether holding down a key should cause it to repeat; if so, after what interval and at what rate should it repeat; and how long a key should be held down to register.

- **Beep when keys pressed or accepted** When this option is on, Windows beeps when a key is pressed, and Windows beeps again when a key is accepted.

- **Show FilterKey status on screen** When this option is on, a small graphic appears to the left of the time on the system tray, as shown here:

Hearing When a Toggled Key Is Pressed

ToggleKeys is the last option on the Keyboard tab of the Accessibility Properties dialog box. ToggleKeys is useful if you accidentally press keys that change the behavior of the keyboard. When ToggleKeys is on, a tone sounds when CAPS LOCK, NUM LOCK, or SCROLL LOCK are toggled on or off.

To turn on ToggleKeys, select the Use ToggleKeys option on the Keyboard tab of the Accessibility Properties dialog box. Click the Settings button to turn on the Use Shortcut setting, which enables you to turn on ToggleKeys by holding down the NUM LOCK key for five seconds.

 We had trouble getting ToggleKeys to work consistently on all Windows 98 systems.

Setting Sound Accessibility Options

Windows 98 includes options to help translate the sounds that programs make for people who have difficulty hearing. The sound accessibility options don't work for all sounds, but they do work for most sounds generated by Windows and for some sounds generated by applications. The options are found on the Sound tab of the Accessibility Properties dialog box, shown in Figure 20-3. Choose Start | Settings | Control Panel, run the Accessibility Options program, and click the Sound tab.

The two sound options are SoundSentry and ShowSounds. SoundSentry tells Windows to use a flashing element on the screen to tell the user that a sound has been made. Click the Settings button next to the Use SoundSentry option to choose a screen element to flash. It is a good idea to use either the Flash Active Caption Bar or the Flash Active Window option—otherwise, it is impossible to figure out which application caused the sound. The ShowSounds option displays a caption on the screen each time Windows (and some other programs) makes a sound.

Setting Display Accessibility Options

Windows 98 has two features that make the screen easier to read: One option is to use a high-contrast color scheme, and the other option is to enable Microsoft Magnifier in order to magnify part of the screen.

 Other display settings—including colors and fonts—are available on the Display Properties dialog box (see "What Are Display Properties?" in Chapter 13).

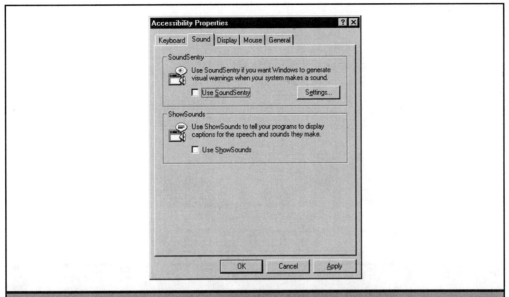

Figure 20-3. *Use the Sound tab of the Accessibility Properties dialog box to turn on the accessibility options for the hearing-impaired*

Displaying in High Contrast

The High Contrast feature is controlled from the Display tab of the Accessibility Properties dialog box, shown in Figure 20-4. Choose Start | Settings | Control Panel, run the Accessibility Options program, and click the Display tab.

High Contrast changes the Windows 98 color scheme and increases legibility wherever possible, often by increasing font sizes. Turn on the High Contrast feature by clicking the Use High Contrast check box; control the way High Contrast is implemented by clicking the Settings button. Also, use the Settings button to display the Use Shortcut check box. The shortcut for High Contrast is LEFT ALT-LEFT SHIFT-PRINT SCREEN (that is, hold down the ALT and SHIFT keys that appear on the left side of the keyboard near the X and Z keys, and also press the PRINT SCREEN button).

The result of turning on High Contrast is a screen that looks like Figure 20-5 (the black-on-white color scheme is shown). Using bigger fonts results in less information fitting on the screen, so you'll see more scroll bars than usual. Also, the different color scheme may take some getting used to—it's a lot different than the default color scheme, and can be confusing.

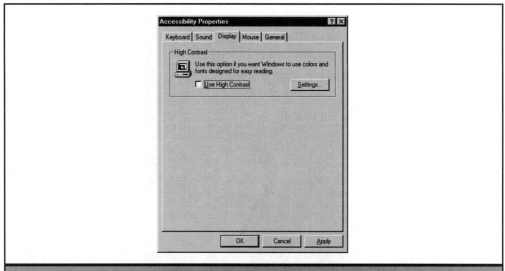

Figure 20-4.   *Turn on the High Contrast option by using the Display tab of the Accessibility Properties dialog box*

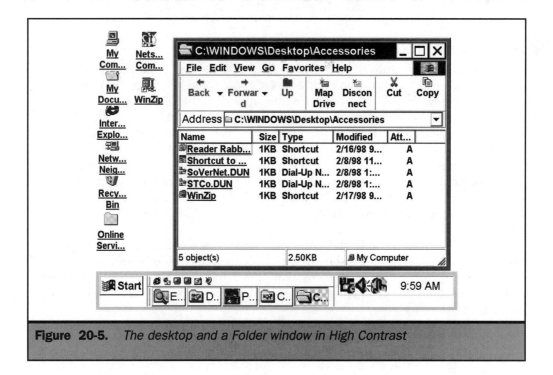

Figure 20-5.   *The desktop and a Folder window in High Contrast*

Magnifying the Screen

A new feature in Windows 98 is the Microsoft Magnifier. The Magnifier is an alternative to High Contrast mode—it allows you to magnify only a part of the screen at a time. Turn on Microsoft Magnifier by choosing Start | Programs | Accessories | Accessibility | Microsoft Magnifier. Once you give the command, you see the magnification window on your screen, and the Microsoft Magnifier dialog box, as shown in Figure 20-6.

You can control which part of the screen is displayed in the magnification window, its magnification level, its location on the screen, and its color scheme.

The part of the screen shown in the magnification window is determined by the tracking options selected on the Microsoft Magnifier dialog box. You can choose to Follow Mouse Cursor, Follow Keyboard Focus, and Follow Text Editing. These three options are not mutually exclusive—if you select all three, the display in the magnification window is determined by what you are currently doing—in other words, Windows does its best to display in the magnification window the part of the screen you're working with.

You can change the magnification level by using the Magnification Level option on the Microsoft Magnifier dialog box. The larger the level, the more the contents of the magnification window are magnified. You can also change the magnification level

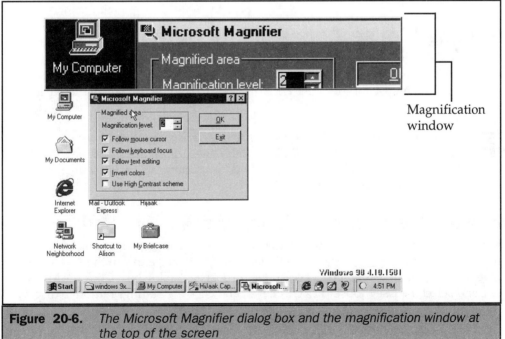

Magnification window

Figure 20-6.   *The Microsoft Magnifier dialog box and the magnification window at the top of the screen*

without displaying the Microsoft Magnifier dialog box—hold down the Windows key (the key with the Windows logo, if you have one on your keyboard), and press the up arrow to increase magnification, and the down arrow to decrease magnification.

You can change the size of the magnification window by dragging the window border up or down. You can change the position of the window by clicking inside the window and dragging. You can "dock" the window along any edge of the desktop, or put it somewhere in the middle of the screen. If the magnification window appears as a window rather than a wide border, you can control its size and position in the same way that you change the size and position of any window. Your ideal magnification window may be a small square near one corner of the screen. The magnification window always appears on top—it cannot be covered by another window.

You have two choices for the colors you see in the magnification window—it can have the same colors as whatever it's magnifying, or it can have inverted colors. Inverted colors may make it easier to see that the magnification window is a special part of the screen—on the other hand, inverted colors may make the display more confusing. Use the setting you prefer. The Use High Contrast Scheme option changes the color scheme for the whole screen (not just the magnification windows) to the high contrast scheme selected on the Settings For High Contrast dialog box.

You can redisplay the Microsoft Magnifier dialog box by right-clicking the magnification window and choosing Options from the shortcut menu. Close the magnification window by right-clicking the magnification window and choosing Exit.

Setting Mouse Accessibility Options

If you have difficulty using a mouse or other pointing devices, if your pointing device is broken, or if you don't like to use it, turn on MouseKeys. If you have trouble using a keyboard and mouse for input, let Windows know that you use an alternative input device.

Other mouse settings—including button configuration, double-click speed, and mouse pointer speed—are available on the Mouse Properties dialog box (see "Configuring Your Mouse" in Chapter 14). See Chapter 15 for information on installing other pointing devices.

Controlling the Pointer by Using the Number Pad

MouseKeys allows you to control the mouse pointer by using the numeric keypad. To turn on MouseKeys, choose Start | Settings | Control Panel, and run the Accessibility Options program to display the Accessibility Properties dialog box. Click the Mouse tab, and select the Use MouseKeys check box, and click the Settings button to display the Settings For MouseKeys dialog box, shown in Figure 20-7.

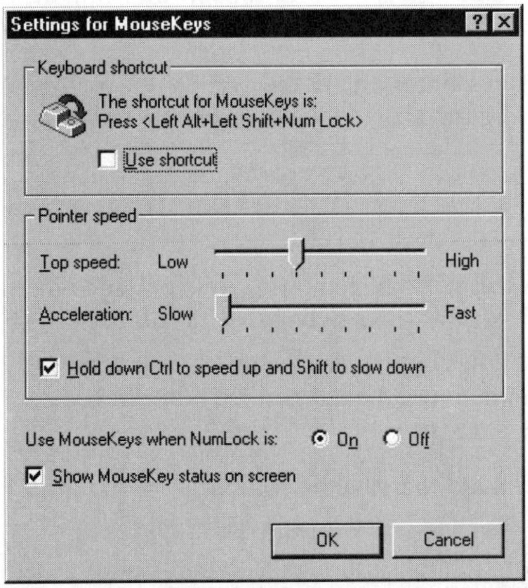

Figure 20-7. *The Settings For MouseKeys dialog box*

The following are the options on the Settings For MouseKeys dialog box:

- **Use Shortcut**   Enables you to turn on MouseKeys by pressing LEFT ALT-LEFT SHIFT-NUM LOCK (hold down the ALT and SHIFT keys that appear on the left side of the keyboard near the X and Z keys, and also press the NUM LOCK key).

- **Top Speed**   Changes the pointer's top speed when you hold down keys to move it.

- **Acceleration**   Changes the speed at which the pointer accelerates when you hold down a key to move it. A faster rate of acceleration means that the pointer reaches its top speed sooner.

- **Hold down Ctrl to speed up and Shift to slow down**   Gives you more ways to control the speed of the mouse pointer. When this option is selected, you can hold down CTRL when you want the pointer to move in big jumps across the screen, and hold down SHIFT when you want the pointer to move in smaller than usual increments.

- **Use MouseKeys when NumLock is: On/Off**   Determines when the number pad keys move the mouse pointer—when NUM LOCK is on or off. If you choose the Off setting, then you can enter numbers by using the number pad when NUM LOCK is on. However, you need another set of arrows to move the cursor.

■ **Show MouseKeys status on screen** When this option is on, a small graphic appears in the system tray to the left of the time, as shown here:

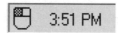

The shaded key shows which mouse key is pressed when you press the 5 key on the numeric keypad. Switch between the mouse keys by pressing the – key.

The following list shows how to use the number pad to control the pointer when MouseKeys is on (be sure to use the keys on the numeric keys, not the equivalent keys elsewhere on your keyboard):

■ Press the arrow keys to move the pointer.

■ Press the 5 key to click whatever the pointer is on.

■ Press the + key to double-click whatever the pointer is on.

■ Press the INSERT key to begin dragging (the equivalent of holding down the mouse button). Move the item by pressing the arrow keys on the number pad. Drop the item (release the mouse button) by pressing DELETE.

■ Press the – key to right-click the item the pointer is on (we had trouble getting this to work).

■ Press the – key, and then the Insert key, to right-click-and-drag something. Drop the item by pressing DELETE.

■ Press the * key to click both mouse buttons.

Configuring an Alternative Input Device

If you are using an alternative input device (something other than the keyboard and a mouse), and you want to connect that device to a serial port, turn on the Support SerialKey Devices option on the General tab of the Accessibility Properties dialog box. Use the Settings button to choose the serial port and baud rate for the device.

Turning Accessibility Options Off and On

In general, you'll probably want to turn on whichever accessibility options you find useful, and leave them on. However, if you share your computer, you may want the ability to turn them on and off easily. The General tab of the Accessibility Properties dialog box has some options for turning accessibility options off and on: Choose Start | Settings | Control Panel, run the Accessibility Options program, and click the General tab.

If more than one person uses the computer, you may want the accessibility options turned off when it has been idle for a certain interval. The Automatic Reset option on the General tab allows you to choose how long the computer must be idle before all accessibility options are turned off. If you want accessibility options to remain on always, make sure that the Automatic Reset option is not selected.

You may also want notification when accessibility options are turned on or off. The Notification options on the General tab allow you to see a message when an accessibility feature is turned on, and hear a sound when an accessibility option is turned on or off.

After you have activated an accessibility option and enabled its shortcut by using the Accessibility Properties dialog box, you can turn the option on and off by using the keys in Table 20-1.

Setting	How to Toggle On and Off
FilterKeys	Hold down SHIFT for eight seconds
High Contrast mode	Press LEFT ALT-LEFT SHIFT-PRINT SCREEN
MouseKeys	Press LEFT ALT-LEFT SHIFT-NUM LOCK
StickyKeys	Press SHIFT five times
ToggleKeys	Hold down NUM LOCK for five seconds

Table 20-1. *Accessibility Option Shortcut Keys*

Using the Accessibility Icons

If you choose to display the status of your accessibility options in the system tray (StickyKeys, FilterKeys, and MouseKeys give you that option), there are a number of things you can do with those icons:

- You can either double-click an icon, or right-click it and choose Adjust Settings on the shortcut menu, to change the settings for the accessibility option it represents (this works for icons in the Accessibility Status window, too, as described later in this section).

- You can right-click the icon and choose Show Status Window to display the accessibility options in their own small window—the Accessibility Status window.

The Accessibility Status window displays icons for accessibility options, similar to the icons that can appear in the system tray, like this:

The advantage to the Accessibility Status window is that you can easily spot the status of your accessibility options—you don't have to sift through the many icons that may appear in the system tray. Right-click the Accessibility Status window's title bar to change how the window works. You can choose to have the window Always On Top, so that it won't get covered by other windows. You can also turn on small icons (small icons are about the size of the icons in the system tray); otherwise, the icons are slightly larger. You can move and size the Accessibility Status window in the same way that you move and size other windows.

Part IV

Windows 98 on the Internet

Chapter 21

Configuring Windows to Work
with Your Modem

Before you connect to the Internet (or any other computer) using a modem, you must install your modem, whether you use a conventional modem and phone line, or a high-speed ISDN line (see Chapter 15).

This chapter describes how to configure your modem, set up a dialing location for each telephone line from which you dial, tell Windows how your phone company requires you to dial 1 and area codes, and configure Windows to dial using your telephone calling card. If you use an ISDN phone line, you need to configure its connection, too. Once your modem is up and running, you're ready to read Chapter 22 to choose an account with which to connect to the Internet and sign up for a new Internet account, or set up Windows 98 to connect to an existing account.

Note   *If you connect to the Internet over a local area network rather than by using a modem, contact your LAN system administrator.*

Configuring Windows to Use Your Modem

Each model of modem is programmed to respond to a set of commands that tell it to pick up the phone, dial, and hang up, as well as a set of configuration commands. Windows 98 needs to know exactly which make of modem you have, so that it can send the appropriate commands. You can also tell Windows from which area code you usually dial, from what other locations you make calls (if you have a portable computer), and to which calling cards you want to charge your phone calls.

What Does Windows Know About Your Modem?

When you install a modem, Windows either determines what kind of modem it is or it will ask you what kind it is (see Chapter 15). Windows installs a modem driver that includes information about the commands that the modem understands. You can look at or change your modem configuration settings by using choosing Start | Settings | Control Panel, and then running the Modems program. Click or double-click the Modems icon depending whether your desktop is configured as Web style or Classic style (see "Choosing the Style of Your Desktop" in Chapter 1). (If Windows doesn't know that you have a modem, the Install New Modem Wizard runs; make sure your modem is on—if it is external—and follow the Wizard's instructions to set up the modem.) You see the Modems Properties dialog box shown in Figure 21-1.

Select the modem from the list of installed modems on the Modems Properties dialog box, and then click the Properties button to see another Properties dialog box, shown in Figure 21-2. (The exact appearance of this dialog box depends on the modem driver.)

Table 21-1 lists the modem properties that appear on the General and Connection tabs of the Properties dialog box for most modems, as well as those on the Advanced Connection Settings dialog box (accessible by clicking the Connection tab on the modem's Properties dialog box, and then clicking the Advanced Settings button).

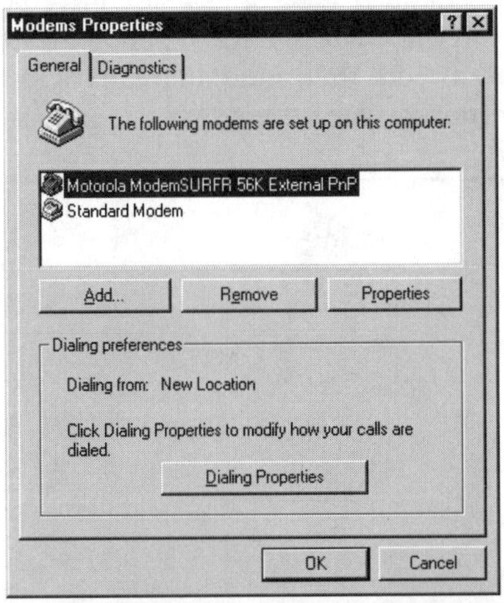

Figure 21-1. *The Modems Properties dialog box*

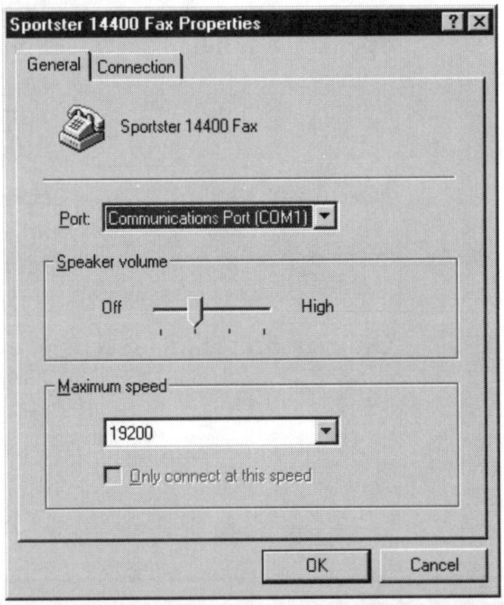

Figure 21-2. *The properties of a modem*

Except where noted, do not change the settings listed in Table 21-1 unless you are sure that your modem is configured incorrectly. Most people never have to mess with the settings except in consultation with their modem manufacturer, communications software publisher, or Internet service provider.

Dialog Box Tab	Setting	Description
General	Port	Specifies how your modem is connected to your computer. PCs have serial communications ports named COM1, COM2, COM3, and COM4 (most PCs come with only COM1 and COM2). Even if your modem is internal (installed inside the computer), it is assigned a port. If you connect your modem to a different port, update this setting.
General	Speaker volume	Specifies how loud the modem's speaker is set. Adjust this setting if your officemates complain.
General	Maximum speed	Specifies the maximum speed at which your modem can communicate, in *bps* (bits per second).
General	Only connect at this speed	Prevents the modem from connecting at a slower speed than the maximum speed you specified (not all modems support this option).

Table 21-1.   *Modem Properties*

Dialog Box Tab	Setting	Description
Connection	Data bits	Specifies the number of *data bits*, the number of bits of information that are included in each byte sent (must be 8 bits).
Connection	Parity	Specifies whether the modem uses *parity*, which means that the modem sends an error-detection bit as the eighth bit of each byte; if so, which type of parity bit (must be None).
Connection	Stop bits	Specifies how many extra *stop bits* are sent after each byte (must be 1 bit).
Connection	Wait for dial tone before dialing	Specifies whether to wait for the modem to detect a dial tone before sending commands to dial; if the modem can't detect a dial tone, this should be unselected. Many non-U.S. modems require this to be unselected.
Connection	Cancel the call if not connected within *xx* secs	Specifies whether to time-out after the specified number of seconds if no connection occurs (usually selected, with a time-out period of 60 seconds).

Table 21-1. *Modem Properties (continued)*

Dialog Box Tab	Setting	Description
Connection	Disconnect a call if idle for more than *xx* mins	Specifies whether to hang up the phone connection if no data is transmitted for a specified number of minutes (usually not selected). Choose this setting if you want to avoid leaving the phone off the hook when you remain online by accident.
Advanced Connection Settings	Use error control	Whether to use error control (usually selected). Not all modems support error control.
Advanced Connection Settings	Required to connect	Whether to allow a connection without error control (usually not selected). If selected, the modem won't connect unless error control works.
Advanced Connection Settings	Compress data	Whether to compress data before transmitting it (usually selected). Not all modems support data compression, and the modem to which it is communicating must support it, too.
Advanced Connection Settings	Use cellular protocol	Whether to use the cellular protocol, which is used in cellular phones and modems. Most modems don't support the cellular protocol. Set only if your modem is connected to a cellular phone.

Table 21-1. *Modem Properties* (continued)

Dialog Box Tab	Setting	Description
Advanced Connection Settings	Use flow control	Whether to use a system of *flow control* to control the flow of data between your modem and your computer. If selected, you have two options: XON/XOFF or RTS/CTS (preferred).
Advanced Connection Settings	Modulation type	Specifies the *modulation*, which is how your modem converts the digital information from your computer into analog "sound" information for transmission over the phone. Usually set to Standard.
Advanced Connection Settings	Extra settings	Additional commands to send to your modem after Windows sends the standard initialization commands. Consult your modem's manual for a list of commands your modem understands.
Advanced Connection Settings	Append to log	Whether to store information sent to and from the modem in a log file, C:\Windows\ Modemlog.txt (usually not selected). The log file is useful for trouble-shooting; to see the log file, click View Log.

Table 21-1.   *Modem Properties* (continued)

Note *If you display the modem's Properties dialog box from the properties dialog box for a Dial-Up Networking connection, an Options tab appears with settings for dialing an Internet connection (see "Changing the Settings for a Dial-Up Networking Connection" in Chapter 22). If you display it from the Device Manager, Windows displays additional modem settings.*

To see additional technical information about your modem, click the Diagnostics tab on the Modems Properties dialog box, select the port to which your modem is attached, and then click the More Info button. The More Info dialog box that appears (Figure 21-3) shows a lot of information about your modem, including its response to a series of configuration commands sent by Windows 98 and date of its firmware (program stored on a chip inside the modem).

To communicate with your modem, Windows uses a *modem driver*, a small program that usually comes with the modem (Windows 98 comes with modem drivers built in for many popular modems). To see which modem driver Windows uses for your modem, click the Diagnostics tab on the Modems Properties dialog box, select the modem, and then click the Driver button. Windows displays a small window showing the name, size, and date of the modem driver file.

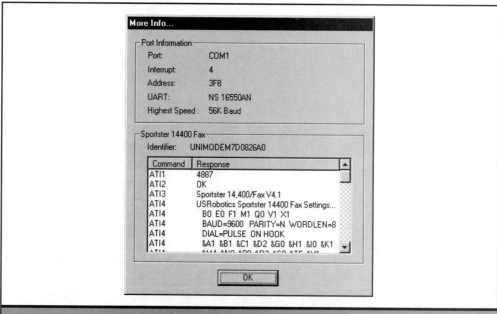

Figure 21-3.   *More information about your modem*

Does Your Modem Use the Fastest UART?

Top-quality computers use a 16550A-compatible *UART* (Universal Asynchronous Receiver/Transmitter) chip in their serial communication ports rather than the older 8250 or 16450. This chip provides buffering in the serial port, so that it can communicate more reliably at high speeds. If your modem is connected to a serial port with a 16550A UART chip, you can configure your modem to transmit faster.

To find out whether your computer's serial port uses a 16550A-compatible chip, click the Diagnostics tab on the Modems Properties dialog box, select the port to which your modem is attached, and then click the More Info button. The More Info dialog box that appears (Figure 21-3) shows the type of UART the serial port uses; 16550A-compatible UARTS have the characters "16550A" in the part number.

If your serial port does have a 16550A UART, you can configure your modem to use FIFO (first in, first out) buffers, which speed up data rates. Select the modem from the list of installed modems on the Modems Properties dialog box, and then click the Properties button. Click the Connection tab, and then the Port Settings button. You see the Advanced Port Settings dialog box for the port to which the modem is attached (Figure 21-4). Make sure that a check mark appears in the Use FIFO Buffers box.

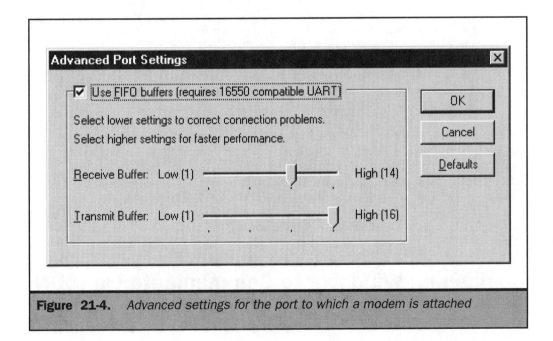

Figure 21-4.   *Advanced settings for the port to which a modem is attached*

Troubleshooting Your Modem

If you have trouble getting your modem to connect, here are some things to check:

■ **Make sure that the right modem driver is installed.** Look on the General tab of the Modems Properties dialog box to make sure that the correct modem is listed. Remove any modem drivers that are no longer installed. If the wrong modem is listed, click Add to run the Install New Modem Wizard. If your modem doesn't appear on the Wizard's lists of models, choose Standard Modem Types for the manufacturer and choose the modem speed from the list of models.

■ **Make sure that the modem driver is enabled.** Choose Start | Settings | Control Panel, run the System program, and click the Device Manager tab. Click View Devices By Type and then click the plus sign next to the Modems entry on the list of devices. Your modem should appear. Click it and click the Properties button (this version of the properties dialog box for the modem contains additional settings). On the General tab make sure that neither check box is selected.

■ **Make sure the modem is connected to the right port.** Display the properties dialog box for the modem as described in the preceding paragraph. On the Modem or General tab, check that you see the port to which the modem is connected. See "Connectors" in Chapter 15.

■ **Make sure that the modem speed is right.** On the Modem or General tab on the Properties dialog box for the modem, check the Maximum Speed setting. Choosing a lower speed may solve your problem.

You can also use the Windows 98 Modem Troubleshooter (Figure 21-5) to help pinpoint the problem. To start the troubleshooter, click the Diagnostics tab on the Modems Properties dialog box, and then click the Help button. Then, follow the instructions in the Internet Explorer window that appears. (The web pages that make up the Modem Troubleshooter are stored on your own hard disk.)

 If you have an external modem, be sure that the modem is turned on.

Configuring Windows to Communicate via ISDN

Rather than communicating using a regular phone line, your computer can communicate much faster using an ISDN phone line.

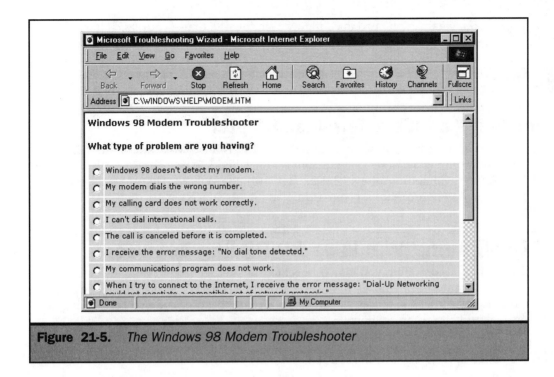

Figure 21-5. *The Windows 98 Modem Troubleshooter*

What Is ISDN?

ISDN (Integrated Services Digital Network) is a special type of phone line that lets your computer connect to another computer faster than with a normal phone line, and enables your computer to transfer data more quickly. An ISDN line is all digital; with a normal phone line, your modem converts the digital information from your computer into an analog signal for transmission. At the other end, another modem converts the analog signal back into digital information. Along the way, your phone company may perform additional conversions. With an ISDN line, your digital information never has to be converted.

You can order an ISDN line from your local telephone company. ISDN lines are more expensive than normal phone lines, and not all phone companies can provide them. Even companies that do provide ISDN lines often have trouble installing them correctly. You also need an *ISDN terminal adapter*, rather than a modem, to connect your computer's serial port to the ISDN phone line. Better yet, get an ISDN adapter card that installs inside your computer for faster communications. Your Internet service provider (or whatever computer you are connecting to) must have ISDN phone numbers for you to connect to (see "Internet PPP and SLIP Accounts" in

Chapter 22). Finally, you need to configure Windows 98 to use your ISDN line; you can use the ISDN Configuration Wizard.

 *Microsoft provides information at their web site about how to sign up for an ISDN account: Go to the web page **http://www.microsoft.com/windows/getisdn**.*

Configuring an ISDN Terminal Adapter

Once you have an ISDN line and terminal adapter installed, you can run the ISDN Configuration Wizard to set up your connection. Choose Start | Programs | Accessories | Communications | ISDN Configuration Wizard. The Wizard steps you through the procedure for configuring an ISDN connection.

Configuring Windows for Dialing Locations

If you a laptop computer, you may connect to the Internet or your online service from different locations using different phone numbers. Windows 98 lets you define one or more *dialing locations* so that Windows knows from what area code you are calling and can dial numbers appropriately.

What Is a Dialing Location?

A dialing location defines a location from which you use your modem. Windows 98 stores information about the area code and phone system from which you are dialing, including whether to dial extra digits to get an outside line. It also remembers whether the phone line at that location uses *call waiting*, a phone line feature that beeps when another call is coming in on the line. The call waiting beep disrupts most modem connections, so you should tell Windows 98 to turn off call waiting before dialing the phone if you don't want your online session interrupted.

You can use dialing locations when connecting to Internet accounts via Dial-Up Networking (explained in the next chapter), or when placing voice phone calls via Phone Dialer (see "Using Phone Dialer" in Chapter 5).

Displaying Your Dialing Locations

To define or change your dialing locations, choose Start | Settings | Control Panel, run the Telephony program, and then click the My Locations tab if it's not already selected. You see the Dialing Properties dialog box, shown in Figure 21-6. (You can also display this dialog box from the Modems Properties dialog box, by clicking the Dialing Properties button on the General tab.)

The Dialing Properties dialog box also lets you create area code rules to tell Windows when to dial 1, and calling cards to tell Windows the access number, account number, and PIN you use when charging phone calls to a calling card.

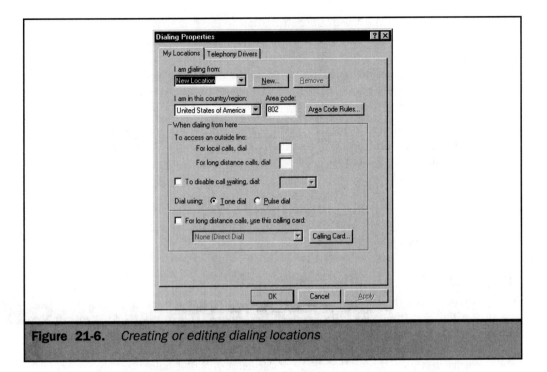

Figure 21-6.   *Creating or editing dialing locations*

Note   *The Telephony Drivers tab on the Dialing Properties dialog box displays the installed telephony drivers, which will eventually be used by Windows with software for making phone calls over the Internet.*

Creating a Dialing Location

To make a new dialing location, follow these steps:

1. Click the New button on the Dialing Properties dialog box. Windows creates a new dialing location named New Location. (If this is the first dialing location you create, you can skip this step and edit the New Location dialing location that already appears.)

2. Type a name for the dialing location in the I Am Dialing From box, choose the country from list, and type the area code or city code from which you are dialing.

3. If you have to dial 1 and the area code for some exchanges in this area code, or if you have to dial 1 and the area code for all exchanges, even in your own area code, click the Area Code Rules button to tell Windows exactly what to dial (see "Setting Up Area Code Rules").

4. If you need to dial extra digits before dialing the phone number, type the digits into the For Local Calls Dial and For Long Distance Calls Dial boxes.

5. If the phone line has call waiting (that is, if incoming calls cause a beep on the phone line), select the check box to disable call waiting and select the number to disable it. (Check with your phone number if you are not sure.) If your phone doesn't accept tone dialing, click Pulse Dial.

6. If you use a calling card to charge the calls made from this phone line, select the For Long Distance Calls, Use This Calling Card check box and then click the Calling Card button to select a card (see "Configuring Windows to Use Calling Cards").

7. Click OK.

To delete a dialing location, choose the dialing location from the list (using the I Am Dialing From box), and then click Remove.

Setting a Default Dialing Location

Before you exit from the Dialing Properties dialog box, select the dialing location you use most often, and then click OK to exit the dialog box. Windows displays this dialing location in Dial-Up Networking and Phone Dialer as the default dialing location.

> **Tip** *When you go on a trip and arrive at your destination, create a dialing location for the phone from which your computer will be dialing. Select this dialing location before exiting the Dialing Properties box to make this location the default. When you return from your trip, display the Dialing Properties dialog box again, select the dialing location for your home or office, and click OK. This resets the default to your usual dialing location.*

Using Dialing Locations

In the Dial-Up Networking dialog box, you select your dialing location by clicking the Dialing From box and choosing another location (see "What Is Dial-Up Networking?" in Chapter 22). To make changes to the settings for a dialing location, you can click the Dial Properties button to display the Dialing Properties dialog box.

In the Phone Dialer, you select your dialing location by choosing Tools | Dialing Properties from the menu bar and then choosing a location on the Dialing Properties dialog box (see "Using Phone Dialer" in Chapter 5).

Setting Up Area Code Rules

You can configure Windows to dial 1 and the area code automatically when necessary, but not to dial it for local calls.

What Are Area Code Rules?

In the old days, you probably had to dial 1 and the area code only for numbers outside your own area code. Now, you may have to dial 1 and the area code for some or all of the phone numbers, even within your own area code. In other areas, you dial a 1 only for calls to other area codes. You can tell Windows exactly when it has to dial what numbers, so that when you type a phone number to dial, Windows can dial the correct sequence of digits. Windows stores this information as *area code rules*.

Creating Area Code Rules

To tell Windows the dialing rules for an area code, choose Start | Settings | Control Panel, run the Telephony program, and then click the My Locations tab if it's not already selected. (Alternatively, you can click the Dialing Properties button on the General tab of the Modems Properties dialog box.) In the I Am Dialing From box, choose the dialing location for which you want to create area code rules, and then click the Area Code Rules button. You see the Area Code Rules dialog box, shown in Figure 21-7.

If you must dial 1 and the area code for all calls (this is true for area codes that overlap another area code), click the Always Dial The Area Code (10-Digit Dialing) box.

If you have to dial 1 plus the area code for some exchanges within your area code for in-area toll calls, you can tell Windows which exchanges require the 1. For each exchange that requires a 1, click the New button in the When Calling Within My Area

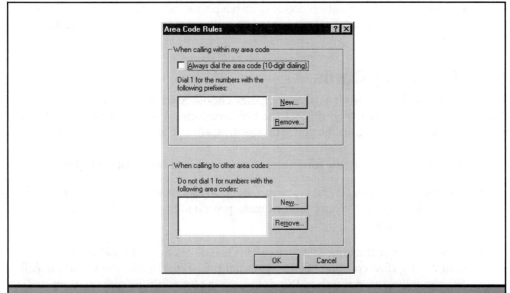

Figure 21-7. *The Area Code Rules dialog box tells Windows when to dial 1 and the area code*

Code section of the dialog box, type the prefix (three-digit exchange) in the box on the New Area Code And Prefix dialog box that appears, and then click OK. The exchange appears on the list of prefixes. To delete an exchange that doesn't require dialing 1, click the exchange on the list, and then click the Remove button.

If you don't have to dial 1 when calling certain other area codes, because you're in an area where local calls to other area codes are dialed with ten digits (notably Texas, metro Washington D.C., and all of Maryland), you can tell Windows which area codes these include. For each area code for which you do not have to dial 1, click the New button in the When Calling To Other Area Codes section of the dialog box, type the area code in the New Area Code dialog box that appears, and then click OK. The area code appears on the list of area codes. To delete an area code that does require dialing 1, click the area code on the list, and then click the Remove button.

Configuring Windows to Use Calling Cards

If you use a telephone calling card to charge your phone calls, especially when you are away from your home or office, Windows 98 can dial all the extra digits for you.

What Is a Calling Card?

A *calling card* is a telephone credit card to which you charge toll calls. To use a calling card, you dial several series of digits in addition to the phone number you want to call, usually including some digits to identify your calling card account. Windows 98, like Windows 95, can store information about your telephone calling cards so that when you need to connect to an Internet account via a calling card, Windows can dial the special digits for you.

Setting Up Calling Cards

To create, edit, or delete your list of calling cards, choose Start and | Settings | Control Panel, run the Telephony program, click the My Locations tab if it's not already selected, and then click the Calling Card button. You see the Calling Card dialog box, shown in Figure 21-8.

Windows needs to know the following in order to place calls using a calling card:

- **Personal ID Number (PIN)**   The number that identifies you to the calling card company, frequently your phone number preceded or followed by four additional digits.

- **Access number for long distance calls**   The digits that you dial to connect to your calling card company before you dial the phone number you want to call or your calling card number. Windows doesn't let you type punctuation, such as dashes—just the digits to dial. For example, to use AT&T from most locations in the U.S., you dial 10288, followed by 0, so you would type 102880.

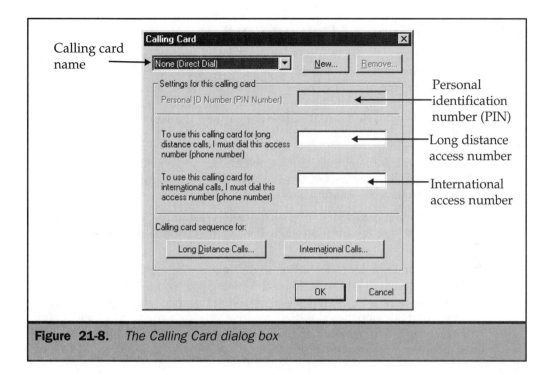

Figure 21-8.   *The Calling Card dialog box*

- **Access number for international calls**   The digits that you dial to connect to your calling card company when you want to place an international call. For example, to dial an international call using AT&T from most locations in the U.S., you dial 10288, followed by 01, so you would type 1028801.

- **Calling card sequence**   The sequence of steps you follow when you place a call using the calling card, including what you dial and how long you have to wait before the next step.

Creating a Standard Calling Card

Windows already knows about dozens of widely used calling cards, including their access numbers and the sequence of numbers to dial when placing a call. To set up a calling card that Windows already knows about, choose the type of card from the list in the unnamed pull-down menu box in the upper-left corner of the Calling Card dialog box. Windows displays the default properties for that type of calling card. Only the Personal ID Number (PIN Number) box is blank; you must type this number before Windows can use the calling card.

Type your PIN into the Personal ID Number (PIN Number) box, and review the rest of the settings to make sure that they match the way you use your calling card.

Creating a New Type of Calling Card

If your type of calling card doesn't appear on the list that appears when you click in the unnamed pull-down menu box in the upper-left corner of the Calling Card dialog box, you can create a new type of calling card by entering all the settings for the card. First make a note of what you dial and what you wait for when you place a call by hand. Then follow these steps to configure Windows to perform the same sequence of steps automatically:

1. Click the New button on the Calling Card dialog box, type the name of the calling card, and then click OK twice. The settings for a new calling card are blank, so you have to enter all of them.

2. Type your calling card's PIN, long distance access number, and international access number into the three boxes on the Calling Card dialog box (see Figure 21-8).

3. Click the Long Distance Calls button to display the Calling Card Sequence dialog box, shown in Figure 21-9. On this dialog box, you tell Windows the sequence of steps to follow when dialing a long distance number by using the calling card. Each step includes dialing something, or switching to tone dialing. After each step, you can tell Windows to wait a specified amount of time, or until it detects a tone on the phone line.

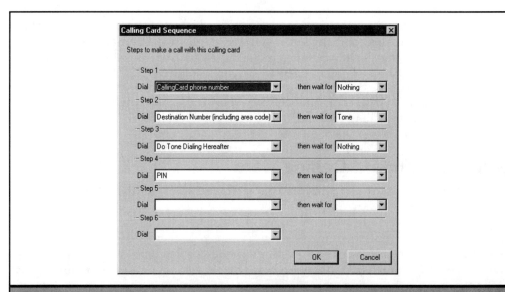

Figure 21-9. On the Calling Card Sequence dialog box, you specify the series of steps for dialing a phone number by using a calling card

4. In the Step 1 section of the dialog box, click the Dial box and choose the number to dial by choosing it from the list that appears (see Table 21-2). For most calling cards, the number to dial in Step 1 is the calling card's access number (choose Calling Card Phone Number from the list).

5. Click in the right-hand box in the Step 1 section, and then choose what Windows should do after dialing the number. You can choose to wait for a tone, wait a specified number of seconds, or not wait at all (wait for nothing).

6. Select the settings in the Step 2 and following sections of the dialog box until you have completed the series of numbers that Windows must dial to use the calling card. Refer to Table 21-2 for descriptions of the numbers you can dial. For the last step, choose Done in the right-hand box.

7. Click OK to save the sequence of steps for dialing long distance numbers.

8. Click the International Calls button. Repeat steps 4 through 7 to tell Windows the sequence of steps for dialing international calls.

Tip   *To test your calling card, run the Phone Dialer and try dialing a call.*

Number to Dial	Description
CallingCard phone number	Access number for this calling card. You enter this long distance access number (used when you are specifying the steps for long distance calls) or international access number (used when you are specifying the steps for international calls) on the Calling Card dialog box.
Destination Number (without area code)	Number you want to call. This number comes from the program that is placing the call—Dial-Up Networking or Phone Dialer. This option omits the area code (rarely useful).
Destination Number (including area code)	Number you want to call. This option dials the area code (usually correct for U.S. calls).
Destination Country/Region	Country code for the country or region you are calling.

Table 21-2. *Numbers to Dial in the Calling Card Sequence Dialog Box*

Number to Dial	Description
PIN	Personal Identification Number for this calling card. This PIN may be your phone number preceded or followed by some additional digits.
Specified digits	Digits that you type. If you choose this option, a Digits To Dial dialog box appears in which you type in the digits to dial, and then click OK.

Table 21-2.   *Numbers to Dial in the Calling Card Sequence Dialog Box (continued)*

Deleting a Calling Card

To delete a calling card, choose the calling card that you no longer want to use from the Calling Card dialog box, and then click Remove.

 Don't delete any of the standard calling cards that come with Windows. You might want to use one again later, and it would be a shame to lose all the specifications of that type of calling card. To avoid using the calling card, just erase the entry for its PIN.

Using Calling Cards

When placing calls using Phone Dialer, choose Tools | Dialing Properties to display the Dialing Properties dialog box (see "Using Phone Dialer" in Chapter 5). Click the For Long Distance Calls, Use This Calling Card check box, and then click the Calling Card button to choose the calling card you want to use. When you click OK, Phone Dialer stores this information and dials all subsequent long distance calls with the calling card that you chose.

When placing calls using Dial-Up Networking, click the Dial Location button to display the Dialing Properties dialog box, and then click the Calling Card button to choose or configure the calling card you want to use (see "What Is Dial-Up Networking?" in Chapter 22).

Chapter 22

Connecting to PPP
and SLIP Accounts

Once your modem is installed, you need to decide (or find out) what kind of account you'll be using: an online service, a UNIX shell account, a bulletin board, or an Internet account. The next step is to set up an account, if you don't already have one; Windows 98 comes with sign-up software for several online services and large Internet service providers.

 If you connect to the Internet via your local area network, see your LAN system administrator.

If you choose an Internet account, you'll have to configure the Internet connection programs which come with Windows 98—Dial-Up Networking and Dial-Up Adapter—to work with the account. Luckily, the Internet Connection Wizard makes this process relatively easy, assuming that you'd rather not type a lot of Internet parameters by hand. Then you use Dial-Up Networking to connect to and disconnect from the Internet. You can configure Windows to connect automatically when you request information from the Internet. The built-in Ping, Tracert, and Netstat programs can help you test your connection.

Getting connected to the Internet can be harrowing, but it's worth it. Once you know how to get online, you can read Chapter 23 for how to send and receive e-mail by using Outlook Express, Chapters 24 and 25 for how to browse the World Wide Web using Internet Explorer or Netscape Navigator, Chapter 26 for how to create your own web pages, Chapter 27 for how to chat over the Internet, and Chapter 28 for how to use the other Internet programs that come with Windows 98.

This chapter describes how to choose, sign up for, test, and use an Internet PPP or SLIP account from an Internet service provider or an online service account. If you use a UNIX shell account, bulletin-board system, or other text-based system, you can connect to the Internet by using HyperTerminal, Windows 98's terminal program (see "Logging in to Text-Based Systems Using HyperTerminal" in Chapter 28).

 No matter what kind of account you select, if you connect to the account by phone, you can tell Windows to either dial direct or use a telephone calling card, and you can specify whether to dial the area code (see Chapter 21).

To What Types of Internet Accounts Can Windows 98 Connect?

To connect to the Internet, you can use one of several types of accounts: SLIP and PPP accounts, UNIX shell accounts, bulletin board systems, or online services.

Internet PPP and SLIP Accounts

A *PPP* (Point-to-Point Protocol) or *SLIP* (Serial Line Internet Protocol) account is an Internet account that uses PPP or SLIP communications protocols. These are the most popular accounts, because the most popular software—Internet Explorer, Netscape Navigator, Eudora, and other programs—are designed to work with PPP and SLIP accounts. PPP is a more modern communications protocol than SLIP, so choose PPP if you have a choice when opening an account. Occasionally, you may run into a *CSLIP* account (compressed SLIP), which is a more efficient version of SLIP, but still not as good as PPP. This book refers to PPP, SLIP, and CSLIP accounts as *Internet accounts*.

An *Internet service provider* (*ISP*) is an organization that provides dial-in Internet accounts, usually PPP, CSLIP, or SLIP accounts, but sometimes UNIX shell accounts. U.S. versions of Windows 98 come with the following sign-up programs for two ISPs that provide PPP accounts:

- **AT&T WorldNet**   A large ISP owned by a large telephone company.
- **Prodigy Internet**   The ISP successor to the outdated Prodigy Classic online service.

To use a PPP, CSLIP, or SLIP account, you need a PPP-, CSLIP-, or SLIP-compatible communications program, such as Windows 98's Dial-Up Networking program (see "What Is Dial-Up Networking?"). This program dials the phone by using your modem, connects to your Internet service provider, logs into your account by using your user name and password, and then establishes a PPP, CSLIP, or SLIP connection, so that your computer is on the Internet. While connected, you can use a variety of Winsock-compatible programs to read your e-mail, browse the Web, and access other information from the Internet. When you are done, you use Dial-Up Networking to disconnect from your Internet account.

To sign up for a PPP account with one of the services listed above, or to set up your computer to use an account you already have with one of those services, see the section "Signing Up for a New Account." To connect to an existing account with another Internet provider, you configure Dial-Up Networking by using the Windows 98 Internet Configuration Wizard (see "Creating a Dial-Up Networking Connection Using the Internet Connection Wizard"). You can also create and edit Dial-Up Networking configurations manually (see "What Is Dial-Up Networking?").

UNIX Shell Accounts and Bulletin Board Systems

Before the advent of PPP and SLIP accounts, most Internet accounts were text-only *UNIX shell accounts*. You run a *terminal-emulation program* (a program that pretends that your PC is a computer terminal) on your PC to connect to an Internet host computer. Most Internet hosts run UNIX, a powerful but frequently confusing operating system, and you have to type UNIX commands to use a UNIX shell account. To send and receive e-mail or browse the Web, you run text-only programs, such as Pine (the most popular UNIX e-mail program) and Lynx (the most widely used UNIX web browser). UNIX shell accounts don't let you see graphics, use a mouse, or easily store information on your own computer.

Some Internet service providers still let you sign up for a UNIX shell account. Some providers give you both a PPP account and a UNIX shell account; you use the PPP account for your regular Internet work, and the UNIX shell account only when you need to change your account's password.

A *bulletin board system* (BBS) is another type of text-based account. Like UNIX shell accounts, you usually connect to BBSs with a terminal emulator.

Windows 98 comes with a terminal-emulator program that you can use to connect to UNIX shell accounts and BBSs: HyperTerminal (see "Logging in to Text-Based Systems Using HyperTerminal" in Chapter 28).

Online Services

An *online service* is a commercial service that allows you to connect and access its proprietary information system. Most online services also provide an Internet connection, e-mail, the World Wide Web, and, sometimes, other Internet services. Online services usually require special programs to connect to and use your account.

U.S. versions of Windows 98 come with sign-up programs for three online services:

- **America Online (AOL)** The world's most popular online service, with a wide range of AOL-only chat rooms.

- **CompuServe** One of the oldest online services, with an excellent selection of proprietary technical- and business-oriented discussion groups. CompuServe was purchased by America Online, so the two services may merge. CompuServe has access phone numbers in dozens of countries.

- **Microsoft Network (MSN)** Microsoft's online service.

Versions of Windows 98 for other countries may come with signup programs for online services or ISPs with local access numbers for that country.

Some online services—including AOL, CompuServe, and MSN—let you use some Winsock-compatible programs while you are connected to the account. For example, you can use the Internet Explorer or Netscape Navigator web browsers with any of these accounts.

You can also use Windows 98 to connect to Prodigy Classic and other online services, but you have to get the proprietary connection software for these services from the online service.

To sign up for an online service, see the section "Signing Up for a New Account," later in this chapter.

What Are Dial-Up Networking, the Dial-Up Adapter, and Winsock?

To use a PPP, CSLIP, or SLIP account, you use Dial-Up Networking and the Dial-Up Adapter to connect to the account, and Winsock software to send and receive information.

What Is Dial-Up Networking?

You use the Dial-Up Networking program to connect to an Internet PPP, CSLIP, or SLIP account. Dial-Up Networking uses the Windows 98 Dial-Up Adapter to communicate with Internet accounts by using TCP/IP, the communication protocol used on the Internet. You don't have to use Dial-Up Networking to connect to your PPP, CSLIP, or SLIP account—you can use another compatible communications program, like Trumpet Winsock, instead—but Dial-Up Networking works well, and comes with a Wizard to set it up.

Note *Dial-Up Networking provides only the communication link needed by Internet services; you use Winsock-compatible applications to read e-mail, browse the Web, and transmit and receive other information on the Internet.*

To use Dial-Up Networking, you create a *Dial-Up Networking connection*, which is an icon with all the settings required to connect to an Internet account. You can have several Dial-Up Networking connections on one computer. For example, your laptop might have one connection for the local ISP you use every day, and another connection for the national Internet provider you use when you are away from home.

To create a new connection, connect to the Internet by using a connection, edit the settings for an existing connection, or get rid of a connection, choose Start | Programs | Accessories | Dial-Up Networking. You see the Dial-Up Networking window, shown in Figure 22-1. (You can also see the contents of the Dial-Up Networking window using Windows Explorer. At the bottom of the folder tree, Dial-Up Networking is listed as a subfolder of My Computer.)

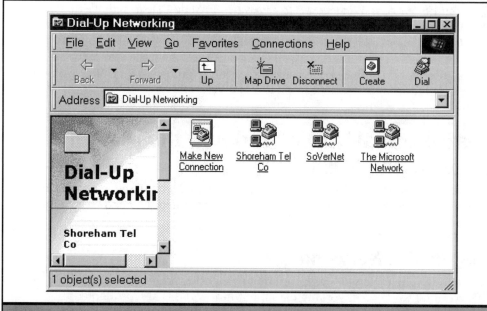

Figure 22-1. *The Dial-Up Networking window shows icons for your Dial-Up Networking connections, as well as the Make New Connection icon*

What Is TCP/IP?

TCP/IP stands for Transmission Control Protocol/Internet Protocol, the way that computers communicate with each other on the Internet. Both PPP and SLIP accounts use TCP/IP. Windows 98 comes with a *TCP/IP stack*, a communications program with which programs (including Dial-Up Networking and Direct Cable Connection) communicate with the Internet.

What Is the Dial-Up Adapter?

The *Dial-Up Adapter* is a Windows 98 network driver that Dial-Up Networking uses to connect to the Internet with a modem or ISDN line. To use the Dial-Up Adapter with an Internet PPP, CSLIP, or SLIP account, you configure it to communicate via TCP/IP (see "Setting Up Dial-Up Networking Manually"). The Dial-Up Adapter can also be used with protocols other than TCP/IP, if your computer communicates with other computers that use a NetWare network.

To check whether the Dial-Up Adapter is installed on your computer and configured to communicate using TCP/IP, see the section "Installing and Configuring the Dial-Up Adapter and TCP/IP" later in this chapter.

What Is Winsock?

Winsock (short for *Windows Sock*ets) is a standard way for Windows programs to work with Internet connection software. Any Winsock-compatible program can work with any Winsock-compatible connection software. Dial-Up Networking is Winsock-compatible; if you use Dial-Up Networking to connect to your Internet account, you can use almost any Winsock-compatible program with your account. Most popular Internet programs are compatible with the Winsock standard.

The key file for Winsock is named Winsock.dll. Dial-Up Networking comes with a Winsock.dll file in the C:\Windows folder. The connection software for some online services (such as America Online) also provide Winsock.dll files, so that you can use Winsock-compatible software with their services.

Windows 98 comes with a bunch of Winsock-compatible programs, including Internet Explorer (see Chapter 24) and Outlook Express (see Chapter 23). See Chapter 28 for descriptions of other Winsock programs.

Signing Up for a New Account

U.S. versions of Windows 98 come with automated sign-up programs for three online services (America Online, CompuServe, and The Microsoft Network) and two Internet service providers (AT&T WorldNet and Prodigy Internet). Non-U.S. versions may come with sign-up programs for other ISPs and online services, varying country by country.

To sign up for one of these online services or ISPs, or to set up your computer to use an existing account with one of these providers, choose Start I Programs I Online Services, and then choose a provider. Or, open the Online Services folder on your desktop and open the icon for the provider. Click or double-click the icon depending on whether you have configured your Windows desktop to use Web style or Classic style (see "Choosing the Style of Your Desktop" in Chapter 1). Then, follow the instructions that the sign-up program displays.

Note   *You'll need a credit card so that the online service or ISP can bill you.*

During the sign-up process, the provider may display information about your account, including your account name, password, e-mail password, support phone numbers, and other information. Write down all the information you see! You may need it.

Before using your account, find out whether the number your modem will be dialing to connect to the account is a local call for you. If not, you should probably cancel the account, because the long distance charges for using the account will be many times the cost of the account itself. Instead, find a local ISP with a local phone number and configure Dial-Up Networking to connect to the account.

Signing Up for America Online (AOL)

America Online, an online service geared toward individual rather than business users, requires its own proprietary connection software, also called America Online. You can't use Dial-Up Networking to connect to your AOL account, but once you are connected, you can use many Winsock-compatible programs, such as Netscape Navigator and Internet Explorer (see Chapter 24). One exception is e-mail—the only way to send and receive mail on your AOL account is to use the AOL software, not Outlook Express or any other mail program. (This restriction may be lifted if AOL adds support for standard Internet e-mail programs.)

AOL is available in the U.S., Canada, and the U.K., with other countries being added. The latest version of the America Online software (as of 1998) is 4.0.

To install the America Online software and either sign up for a new AOL account or connect to an existing account, choose Start | Programs | Online Services | AOL. The AOL Setup program runs; follow its instructions. You'll need your Windows 98 CD-ROM or floppy disks along with the following information:

- If you want to connect to an existing AOL account, you'll need your account name and password.

- If you are signing up for a new account, you need to choose a "screen name" (user name), which can be up to ten characters long. Because AOL already has over 9 million members, many of whom have several different screen names, all the good ones are long since taken, so be creative.

When the Setup program is done, you have an AOL icon on your desktop and a menu command under Start | Programs. The America Online window is shown in Figure 22-2.

Signing Up for CompuServe

CompuServe, a business-oriented online service owned by AOL, comes with its own proprietary connection software. (You can use HyperTerminal to connect to CompuServe in text-only mode, but we don't recommend it.) CompuServe is available in the U.S., Canada, most of Western Europe, and many other countries. The latest version of the CompuServe software (as of 1998) is 4.0. You can use almost any Winsock-compatible software with CompuServe, including e-mail programs.

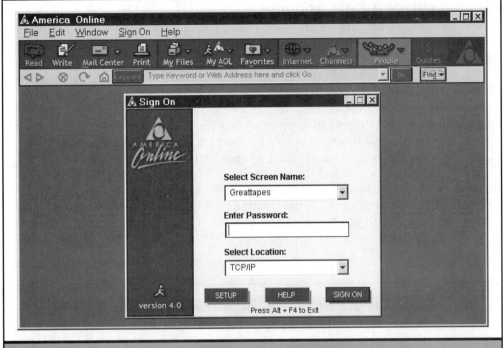

Figure 22-2.   *America Online is waiting for you to sign on*

Installing the CompuServe Program

To install the CompuServe software, choose Start | Programs | Online Services | CompuServe. The CompuServe installation program runs; follow its instructions. If you didn't install the CompuServe installation program when you installed Windows 98, it asks you to insert your Windows 98 CD-ROM or installation diskettes.

The installation program asks you to create a *Virtual Keyword,* a word that it can use whenever you are accessing a World Wide Web or other Internet site that is password-protected. This must be different from your password. CompuServe displays your Virtual Keyword in the title bar of the dialog box that asks for your CompuServe password; this key proves to you that the dialog box is a valid CompuServe dialog box, and not the result of a thief trying to get you to reveal your password. The Virtual Keyword can be up to 16 characters long.

When the installation is done, you have a CompuServe 4.0 command on your Start menu (look above the Programs menu or in the Start | Programs | Online Services | CompuServe menu), a CompuServe icon on your desktop, or both, based on what you choose during the installation.

Signing Up for a New Account

When you run the CompuServe program, it asks whether you want to sign up for a new account or use an existing account. If you want to sign up for a new account, click the Signup icon.

Using an Existing Account

If you want to connect to an existing account or change your CompuServe configuration, run the CompuServe program and click Setup. (If the Setup icon doesn't appear, choose Access | Preferences.) You see the Preferences dialog box, shown in Figure 22-3. The Connection tab contains settings for how you connect to your CompuServe account and how to log in. Type your name, CompuServe member ID (a number with a comma in it), and password in the appropriate boxes.

You can choose whether to use the CompuServe Internet Dialer to connect to your CompuServe account. If you already have an account with an ISP and would like to access CompuServe through that account, you can do so. If you live in an area where

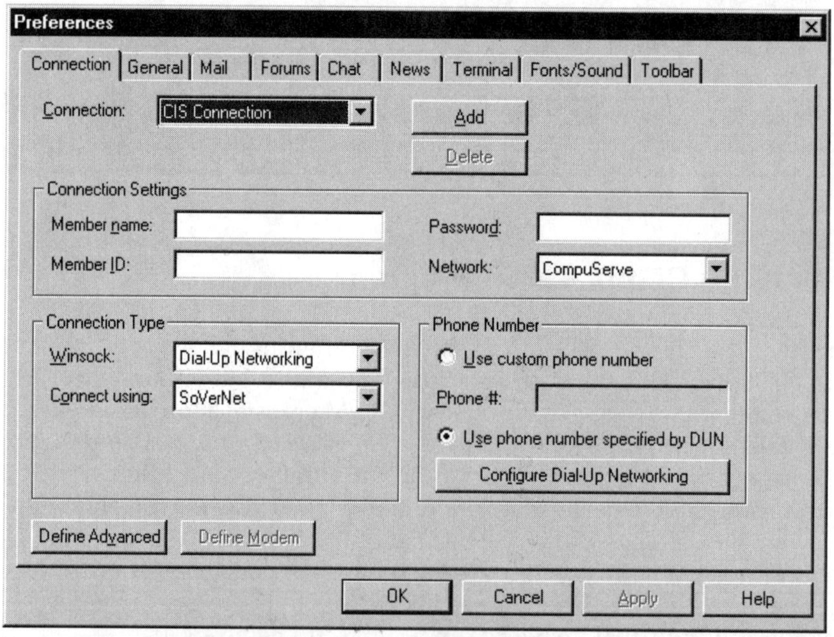

Figure 22-3. *CompuServe's Preferences dialog box*

the nearest call to CompuServe is long distance, and you have an account with a local ISP, the cheapest way to use CompuServe may be to connect to your ISP and use that Internet connection to access CompuServe. Choose one of these two options:

- **To connect to CompuServe through an existing Internet account**   In the Connection Type box, set Winsock to Dial-Up Networking (if you use it) or Default WINSOCK (if you connect over a LAN or by using other connection software). Also set Connect Using to the name of the Dial-Up Networking connection you want to use. To look at or change the settings for that connection, click the Configure Dial-Up Networking button in the Phone Number box.

- **To connect to CompuServe directly**   Set the Connect Using box to CS3 Connection on the Connection tab of the Preferences dialog box. Click the Configure Dial-Up Networking button to display the CS3 Connection dialog box, which shows the settings for CompuServe's Dial-Up Networking connection. The General tab shows CompuServe's U.S. 800 number, which you use to connect to CompuServe from anywhere in the U.S. until you find out a local phone number. Set the Connect Using box to your modem. Click the Server Types tab and make sure that the Type of Dial-Up Server is set to CISPPP: PPP Connection Using CompuServe Network. Of the check boxes on this tab of the dialog box, only Enable Software Compression and TCP/IP should be checked. Click OK to save these connection settings.

Caution   *If you connect to CompuServe directly rather than through an ISP, it's important to find out what the closest access phone number is and configure your CompuServe program to use it. Until you tell it otherwise, CompuServe dials their 800 number, which costs extra. To find out whether CompuServe has a local access number in your area, click in the Page box, type **phone**, press ENTER, and follow the instructions on-screen. When you find a CompuServe access number you want to use, disconnect from CompuServe, choose Access | Preferences, click the General tab, click the Configure Dial-Up Networking button, and type the area code and phone number in the dialog box that appears.*

Click OK to exit the Preferences dialog box and save your settings. You see the CompuServe window. You are ready to connect to CompuServe by choosing commands or clicking icons in the CompuServe window. For example, click the Mail Center button and then the Get Mail icon to check your e-mail.

Tip   *For help signing up for an account or connecting to an existing account, you can see a list of technical support phone numbers by clicking the Help button in the opening screen, or by choosing Help | Contents | CompuServe Customer Service.*

Signing Up for Microsoft Network (MSN)

Microsoft Network (MSN) is Microsoft's entrant in the world of online services. Although it's gained a lot of users because of the easy-to-click icon on the Windows 95 desktop, it's never been as highly-rated as AOL or CompuServe. Microsoft has been slowly changing MSN from an online service to a regular Internet account since the service was introduced in 1995. You use Dial-Up Networking to connect to MSN, and Winsock programs to access its services.

Configuring Windows for MSN

To configure Dial-Up Networking for MSN and either sign up for a new account or connect to an existing account, choose Start | Programs | Online Services | The Microsoft Network. The MSN Setup program runs; follow its instructions. If you haven't previously installed the MSN software, you'll need to insert your Windows 98 CD-ROM or diskettes when requested.

You can choose to connect to MSN as your ISP. Or, if you already have an account with an ISP and want to access MSN through that account, you can do so. If you live in an area where the nearest call to MSN is long distance, and you have an account with a local ISP, the cheapest way to use MSN may be to connect to your ISP and use that Internet connection to access MSN.

Creating a New Account or Using an Existing Account

To finish the process of signing up for a new account or connecting to an existing one, run the MSN program. To use an existing account, type your user name and password in the MSN Sign-In window. To sign up for a new account, click the New button and follow the instructions.

If you are connecting directly to MSN, the Setup program also needs to know what phone number to call. Click the Settings button to see the Connection Settings dialog box, shown in Figure 22-4. Next, click the Phone Book button to the right of the Phone Number box. Set the Service Type box to Modem (for a regular modem), ISDN, or other type of phone connection. Set the Country and State or Region boxes to your location. Then, choose the access number closest to you and click OK. (This number may be long distance; call your phone company to find out. If it is long distance, connect to a local ISP rather than MSN, to avoid huge phone bills!) Finally, click OK to dismiss the Connection Settings dialog box.

Click Connect to connect to MSN. Windows connects to MSN using Dial-Up Networking and displays the MSN home page using your default browser (see "What Is the Default Web Browser?" in Chapter 24). If you haven't configured Outlook Express or another e-mail program, MSN prompts you to do so now and steps you through the process. MSN also asks you whether you'd like to use Content Advisor, Microsoft's Web censorship system, to protect family members that might use this computer (see "Avoiding What You Don't Want on the Web with Content Advisor" in

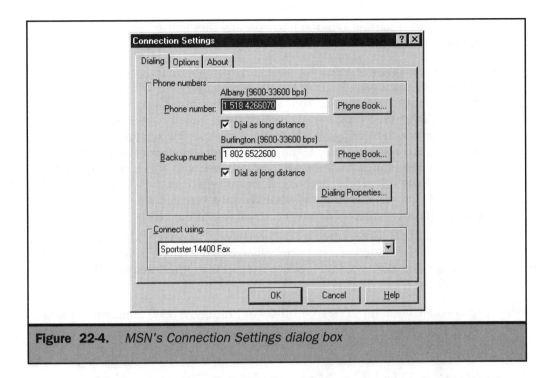

Figure 22-4. *MSN's Connection Settings dialog box*

Chapter 25). To hang up, double-click the Dial-Up Networking icon in the system tray (the icon of two green computer screens). When you see the Connected To MSN dialog box, click Disconnect.

To connect to MSN in the future, choose Start | Programs | Online Services | The Microsoft Network or run the MSN icon on the desktop. Your Dial-Up Networking folder now contains an MSN connection, which you can also use to connect to your MSN account (see "Communicating Using Dial-Up Networking").

Signing Up for AT&T WorldNet or Prodigy Internet

AT&T WorldNet is one of the largest Internet service providers in the U.S., and is also available in Canada and some other countries. Prodigy Internet is the new incarnation of Prodigy, one of the older online services. (The old version of Prodigy, renamed Prodigy Classic, still exists, but the sign-up software for it doesn't come with Windows 98.) AT&T WorldNet and Prodigy Internet both give you a standard PPP account to which you can connect by using Dial-Up Networking.

To either sign up for a new AT&T WorldNet or Prodigy Internet account or connect to an existing account, choose Start | Programs | Online Services | AT&T WorldNet Service, or Prodigy Internet. The ISP's set-up program runs; follow its instructions. The process may involve restarting Windows, so save any files you are editing and exit all other programs. You'll need the following information:

- AT&T WorldNet can create a file named Account.txt that records all the information about your Internet account. If you lose your settings, or if you want to connect to WorldNet from a different computer, you use this file. The WorldNet setup program suggests that you have a blank, formatted diskette on which to store this file. If you want to connect to an existing WorldNet account, you'll need your account name, password, e-mail password, and the last eight digits of the credit card number with which you pay for your account. (Note that capitalization does matter when you type your e-mail password.) Or, you'll need the file that WorldNet created when you set up the account. (Prodigy Internet doesn't create an Account.txt file.)

- AT&T WorldNet uses its own AT&T WorldNet Connection Manager to connect to WorldNet, although you can manually configure Dial-Up Networking to do the same thing, if you prefer. Prodigy Internet uses Windows 98's Dial-Up Networking.

When you are done installing AT&T WorldNet or Prodigy, a new command appears under Start | Programs.

Creating a Dial-Up Networking Connection Using the Internet Connection Wizard

To create a new Dial-Up Networking connection to an Internet provider, you can use the *Internet Connection Wizard*. The Wizard can help you sign up for a new Internet account, or configure your computer to work with an existing account. The Wizard doesn't always do all the configuration needed to get your Windows 98 system on the Internet; you may need to do further configuration. This Wizard does a lot more than the Make New Connection program whose icon appears in the Dial-Up Networking window; Make New Connection only creates a Dial-Up Networking connection, while the Internet Connection Wizard both creates a connection and configures it (see "Making a New Dial-Up Networking Connection").

You can start the Wizard by choosing Start | Programs | Internet Explorer | Connection Wizard or open the Connect To The Internet icon on the desktop. The Internet Connection Wizard gives you three choices:

- Sign up for a new Internet account and configure Dial-Up Networking to connect to it.

- Configure Dial-Up Networking to connect to an existing account.

- Do nothing, and don't run this Wizard in the future.

If you want to create a new Dial-Up Networking connection without any help from a Wizard, run the Make New Connection program in the Dial-Up Networking window (see "Making a New Dial-Up Networking Connection").

Creating a New Account Using the Wizard

If you choose to set up a new account by using the Internet Connection Wizard, the Wizard asks you for your phone number, and then (if you are in the U.S.) connects to the Microsoft Internet Referral server, using a toll-free number. After a delay, you see a window that lists its suggested ISPs. You can read about each ISP by clicking the document icon to the right of its name, or you can decide to sign up with a provider by clicking the check mark to the right of its name. The sign-up procedure varies by provider.

 Microsoft's list of providers doesn't include local providers, only a few of the large national ones. In fact, Microsoft may choose to make a deal with one or two big ISPs and recommend only those ISPs to everyone. The providers listed don't necessarily have local numbers in your area, even though you told Microsoft your area code and exchange. Before you choose an ISP, look for ads in the business section of your local newspaper to see what local providers are available. A small local ISP may give better service and support than a large one, along with having a better selection of local numbers.

If you choose to create a new account by using one of the providers that Microsoft lists, the Wizard asks you to provide information about yourself, including a credit card to which you want to charge your account. During the sign-up, be sure to write down all the information that the sign-up program displays, including technical support phone numbers, account numbers, and passwords.

Creating a Connection to an Existing Account Using the Wizard

If you choose to create a connection to an existing account, the Internet Connection Wizard asks you to enter the following information about your Internet account:

- Whether your connection is via a local area network or a phone line.
- Whether to use an existing Dial-Up Networking connection or create a new one.
- The phone number you dial to connect to the account.
- The user name and password for the account.
- The name that you want to use for the connection (this name appears under the Dial-Up Networking icon that the Wizard creates).

- Whether you want to set up Microsoft Outlook Express to handle e-mail for this account (see Chapter 23). The Wizard can create a new mail account on your computer into which mail from your Internet account is downloaded. (Outlook Express can handle mail from multiple accounts.) If you choose to configure Outlook Express to get your mail, you need to provide your e-mail address, your account name if it is different from your e-mail address, which type of mail server your account provides (usually either a POP3 or IMAP server), the name of your ISP's POP server (which handles incoming mail), the name of your ISP's SMTP server (which handles outgoing mail), and your e-mail password (usually the same as your account password).

- Whether you want to set up Outlook Express to enable you to read Usenet newsgroups. If you do, you must provide the e-mail address that you want included in your newsgroup postings, and the name of your ISP's NNTP server (which handles newsgroup postings). (See Chapter 23 for a description of Usenet newsgroups.)

- Whether you want to set up a "white pages" directory service (LDAP, or Lightweight Directory Assistance Protocol) for this account. Some accounts, include an LDAP server that acts as a centralized directory of names and e-mail addresses. If your account provider hasn't told you about an LDAP server, answer No to this question.

When the Wizard is done running, it creates a Dial-Up Networking connection with an icon in the Dial-Up Networking window, and it configures Outlook Express for the account.

| **Note** | *When you installed Windows 98, you may not have installed all the program files that the Internet Connection Wizard needs. If not, the Wizard prompts you to insert your Windows 98 CD-ROM or diskettes so that it can load the program files it needs. It may also require that you restart Windows before it can proceed.* |

Setting Up Dial-Up Networking Manually

You don't have to use the Internet Connection Wizard to create a Dial-Up Networking connection and to configure your Windows 98 system to use it. You can install and configure a Dial-Up Networking connection yourself. It's not a bad idea to know how to do this, because the Internet Connection Wizard can't create every connection you might need, and occasionally you'll want to change the details of an account that the Wizard set up. The Wizard doesn't know how to create a connection for most small ISPs, for example.

Before you make a new Dial-Up Networking connection, you need to make sure that the Dial-Up Adapter is installed and configured to work with TCP/IP.

Installing and Configuring the Dial-Up Adapter and TCP/IP

The Dial-Up Adapter and TCP/IP may not have been installed when you installed Windows 98.

Displaying Your Network Adapters and Protocols

To check whether the Dial-Up Adapter and TCP/IP are installed, choose Start | Settings | Control Panel and then run the Network program to display the Network dialog box, shown in Figure 22-5; click the Configuration tab, if it is not already selected. If networking has been installed you can also right-click the Network Neighborhood on the desktop and select Properties from the shortcut menu that appears. (See Chapter 29 for more information about Network Neighborhood.)

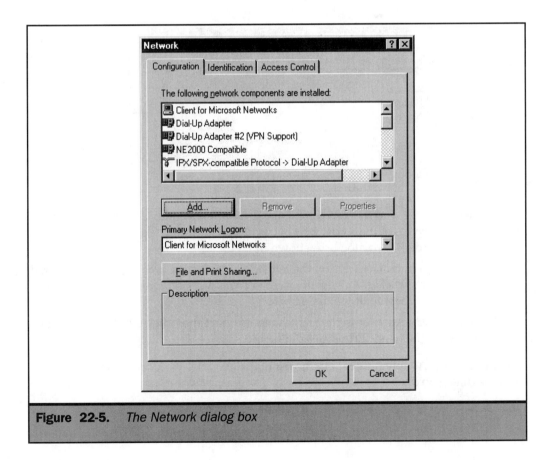

Figure 22-5.   *The Network dialog box*

Check whether the list of network components includes these items:

- Dial-Up Adapter
- TCP/IP -> Dial-Up Adapter

This second item indicates that the Dial-Up Adapter is configured to communicate using TCP/IP. (The Dial-Up Adapter can also work with other network protocols, such as NetBEUI and IPX/SPX, if your computer is connected to a local area network.)

Installing the Dial-Up Adapter

If the Dial-Up Adapter doesn't appear on your list, follow these steps:

1. In the Network dialog box, click the Add button. You see the Select Network Component Type dialog box, shown here, which lists the types of network software you might need to install.

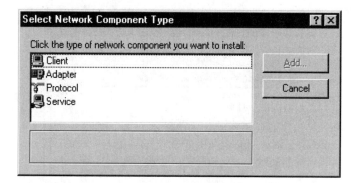

2. Select Adapter, and then click Add again. Windows builds a database of the network drivers of that type, which may take a minute. Next, you see the Select Network Adapters dialog box, shown in Figure 22-6.

3. In the list of manufacturers on the left side of the dialog box, scroll down to find Microsoft and click it. The list of Microsoft's network adapters appears in the box on the right side of the dialog box.

4. Click Dial-Up Adapter in the right-hand box, and then click OK. Click OK again to close the Network Properties dialog box.

Now the Dial-Up Adapter appears in the list of installed network components in the Network dialog box.

Installing TCP/IP

If the TCP/IP -> Dial-Up Adapter entry doesn't appear on your list, follow these steps:

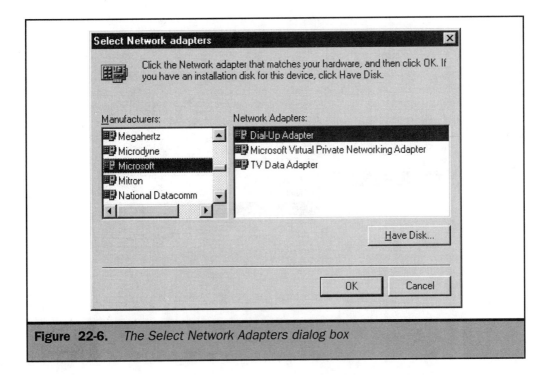

Figure 22-6. *The Select Network Adapters dialog box*

1. In the Network dialog box, click the Add button. You see the Select Network Component Type dialog box (shown in the previous section).

2. Select Protocol, and then click Add again. You see the Select Network Protocol dialog box, shown in Figure 22-7.

3. In the list of manufacturers on the left side of the dialog box, scroll down to find Microsoft and click it. The list of Microsoft's network protocols appears in the box on the right side of the dialog box.

4. Click TCP/IP in the right-hand box, and then click OK to install the protocol and return to the Network dialog box.

TCP/IP -> Dial-Up Adapter now appears on the list of installed network components. Now you can use the Dial-Up Adapter with TCP/IP to communicate with the Internet. Click OK to close the Network dialog box. Windows prompts you to restart Windows in order for the new network settings to take effect.

Note   *If you use networking only to dial into an Internet account, you can delete all of the protocols except TCP/IP. To delete NetBEUI and IPX/SPX, select the entries for them from the list of components in the Network dialog box and click Remove.*

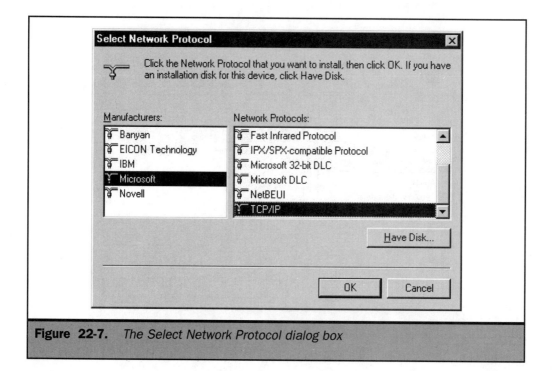

Figure 22-7.   *The Select Network Protocol dialog box*

Don't Configure Your Dial-Up Adapter

The Dial-Up Adapter has many settings that control how it connects to other computers. You can configure these TCP/IP settings by using the Properties button on the Network dialog box, but it's better not to. Instead, configure each of your Dial-Up Networking connections with the appropriate settings for the account to which it connects.

Making a New Dial-Up Networking Connection

To make a new Dial-Up Networking connection, choose Start | Programs | Accessories | Dial-Up Networking to see the Dial-Up Networking window, shown in Figure 22-1. Run the Make New Connection icon.

The Make New Connection Wizard asks what you want to call the connection and what phone number to dial to connect to the account. Next, the Wizard creates a new icon in your Dial-Up Networking window. This connection lacks most of the configuration required; see the next section for how to enter the rest of the settings yourself.

Changing the Settings for a Dial-Up Networking Connection

To configure a Dial-Up Networking connection or to change an existing connection's configuration, right-click the icon for the connection in the Dial-Up Networking window, and then choose Properties from the menu that appears. Alternatively, select the connection icon and choose File | Properties. Either way, you see the Properties dialog box for the Dial-Up Networking connection (see Figure 22-8); the name of the dialog box depends on the name you gave the connection. Table 22-1 lists the properties for a Dial-Up Networking connection. It includes settings that appear on the Options tab of the modem Properties dialog box that you see when you click the Configure button on the General tab of the Properties dialog box for the connection.

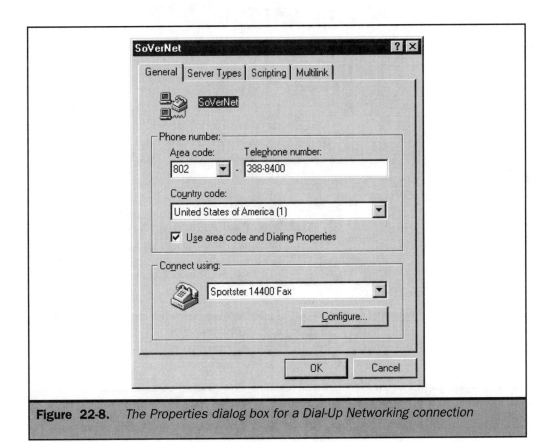

Figure 22-8.   *The Properties dialog box for a Dial-Up Networking connection*

Configuring a TCP/IP Connection

For a connection to an Internet account, you must also configure the TCP/IP protocol. On the Properties dialog box for the connection, click the Server Types tab, select

Tab in Properties Window	Setting	Description
General	Phone Number	Specifies the phone number that your computer dials to connect to the account. Composed of the area code, telephone number, and country code (you choose from a list of countries).
General	Connecting Using	Specifies which modem to use to connect. Click the Configure button by this setting to check or change the configuration of the modem. (See Chapter 21 for how to configure your modem.) You can choose VPN (Virtual Private Networking) if you have installed it (see "Connecting to Your Organization's Network Using Virtual Private Networking" in Chapter 28).
Server Types	Type Of Dial-Up Server	Specifies the type of account; all ISPs provide PPP. Choice of SLIP, CSLIP, PPP (three standard types of accounts available from ISPs), NRN (NetWare Connect for NetWare-based local area networks), or Windows for Workgroups and Windows NT 3.1 (for Windows-based local area networks).
Server Types	Log On To Network	Tells Dial-Up Networking to log onto the account by using your Windows 98 user name and password. Usually not selected for Internet accounts.

Table 22-1.   *Settings for a Dial-Up Networking Connection*

Tab in Properties Window	Setting	Description
Server Types	Enable Software Compression	Compresses information sent between this computer and the account; your Internet account must also support compression (PPP and CSLIP accounts do).
Server Types	Require Encrypted Password	Encrypts your password before sending it to your Internet account when logging on. Your Internet account must support password encryption (most don't).
Server Types	Allowed Network Protocols	Specifies how to communicate over the network. You can select any of these: NetBEUI, IPX/SPX, and TCP/IP (see "Installing the Protocol" in Chapter 30). Select TCP/IP for Internet accounts and unselect NetBEUI and IPX/SPX. To set options for TCP/IP accounts, click the TCP/IP Settings button (see Table 22-2).
Scripting	Script File Name	Specifies the name of the file containing the logon script for this connection (see "Creating and Using Logon Scripts"). Click Edit to edit a script file, or Browse to select an existing file.
Scripting	Step Through Script	Runs the logon script for this connection (see "Creating and Using Logon Scripts").
Scripting	Start Terminal Screen Minimized	Minimizes the terminal window that shows the interaction between the Dial-Up Networking connection and the account while the logon script is running (see "Creating and Using Logon Scripts"). During debugging, deselect this setting so that you can see the terminal window.

Table 22-1. *Settings for a Dial-Up Networking Connection (continued)*

Tab in Properties Window	Setting	Description
Multilink	Do Not Use Additional Devices	Specifies that this connection uses only one device to connect (see "Creating Multilink Connections").
Multilink	Use Additional Devices	Specifies that this connection uses more than one device to connect (for example, two modems and two phone lines). The large box below this setting lists the additional devices used by this connection, and the Add, Remove, and Edit buttons let you add, delete, or change devices on the list. (See "Creating Multilink Connections.")
Options	Bring up terminal window before dialing	Displays a terminal window, before dialing, that you can use to type modem commands and see the results (see "Creating and Using Logon Scripts"). (Refer to your modem's manual for the commands that it understands.)
Options	Bring up terminal window after dialing	Displays a terminal window after dialing that you can use to type commands as see the results.
Options	Operator assisted or manual dial	Prompts you to dial the phone yourself, for situations where you need to speak to an operator. When you are connected, click the Connect button and hang up your phone.
Options	Wait for credit card tone: *xx* seconds	Specifies the number of seconds to wait for a tone when you are using a telephone credit card.
Options	Display Modem Status	Displays a status window indicating the progress of your phone connection.

Table 22-1. *Settings for a Dial-Up Networking Connection (continued)*

TCP/IP as an allowed network protocol, and then click the TCP/IP Settings button. You see the TCP/IP Settings dialog box, shown in Figure 22-9. Table 22-2 shows the settings on this dialog box. Contact your ISP for the settings and addresses to enter.

When your computer is connected to the Internet using TCP/IP, it has its own *IP address* (*IP* stands for Internet Protocol). An IP address is in the format

xxx.xxx.xxx.xxx

where each xxx is a number from 0 to 255. (That is, an IP address consists of four eight-bit numbers.) For example, a computer's IP address might be 204.71.16.253.

A few ISPs assign you a permanent IP address. If you have been assigned a permanent IP address, select Specify An IP Address on the TCP/IP Settings dialog box, and then type the IP address. Most ISPs assign you a temporary IP address when you log on. If you have been assigned a temporary IP address, select Server Assigned IP Address.

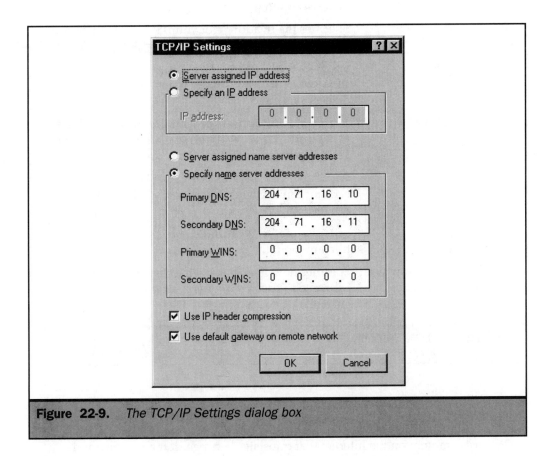

Figure 22-9.   *The TCP/IP Settings dialog box*

Setting	Description
Server Assigned IP Address	Specifies that your ISP assigns your computer an IP address when you log on (most ISP accounts do this).
Specify An IP Address	Indicates that your computer has a permanently assigned IP address, which you specify in the IP Address setting.
IP Address	Specifies your permanently assigned IP address.
Server Assigned Name Server Addresses	Specifies that your ISP assigns your computer domain name servers when you log on (most ISP accounts do this).
Specify Name Server Addresses	Indicates that you have entered Primary and Secondary domain name server IP addresses in the next two settings.
Primary DNS	Specifies the IP address of your ISP's domain name server.
Secondary DNS	Specifies the IP address of another domain name server your account can use when the primary DNS does not respond.
Primary WINS	Specifies the IP address of your organization's *WINS* (Microsoft's Windows Internet Naming Service) server. For dial-up accounts, leave this blank.
Secondary WINS	Specifies the IP address of another WINS server your account can use when the primary WINS server does not respond.
Use IP Header Compression	Specifies that packet headers be compressed for faster transmission (the default is on).
Use Default Gateway On Remote Network	Specifies how IP packets to the rest of the Internet are routed (leave on, unless your ISP tells you to change it).

Table 22-2. *TCP/IP Settings*

In addition to IP addresses, computers on the Internet have *domain names*, alphanumeric names like **www.microsoft.com** or **net.gurus.com**. A *domain name server* or *DNS* is a computer on the Internet that translates between domain names and numeric IP addresses. Your ISP provides you at least one domain name server to do these translations. Some ISPs assign the domain name server when you log in; if so, select Server Assigned Name Server Addresses. Most ISPs give you the IP address of two domain name servers that your computer can use. If so, select Specify Name Server Addresses and enter the IP addresses in the Primary DNS and Secondary DNS settings. Some ISPs (not many) also provide *WINS* (Microsoft's Windows Internet Naming Service) servers, which provide other name lookups.

If your computer is connected to a large corporate system via a LAN or by dialing in, your connection may use WINS to automatically manage network parameters. Your computer contacts the WINS server at boot time (if you connect via a LAN) or when you dial up to get its own configuration information.

Creating and Using Logon Scripts

Dial-Up Networking tries to log onto your account automatically. Most accounts follow a standard series of steps: They transmit your user name, and your account's password, and then receive confirmation that you are logged in and that communications can begin.

If your account uses a nonstandard dialog for logging in, Dial-Up Networking can't log in automatically. You can automate logging in by creating a *logon script*, a text file that contains a small program that tells Dial-Up Networking what prompts to wait for and what to type in response. For example, if your Internet provider's computer uses a nonstandard prompt to ask for your password, or requires you to type a command to begin a PPP session, you can write a script to log on for you.

To use a logon script, follow these steps:

1. Log on manually, making notes about which prompts you see and what you must type in response to those prompts. To log on manually, you can use your Dial-Up Networking connection with a *terminal window,* which allows you to see the session and type commands to your Internet provider. To tell Windows to open a terminal window while connecting, click the Configure button on the General tab of the Properties dialog box for the connection, to see the Properties dialog box for your modem (see "What Does Windows Know About Your Modem?" in Chapter 21). Then, click the Options tab and select the Bring Up Terminal Window After Dialing check box. Or you can use HyperTerminal to connect to your Internet provider (see "Logging in to Text-Based Systems Using HyperTerminal" in Chapter 28).

2. Create a logon script by using a text editor, such as Notepad (see "Reading Text Files with Notepad" in Chapter 4). Windows 98 comes with a short manual about writing logon scripts, in the file C:\Windows\Script.doc.

3. Tell Windows 98 about the logon script by typing the filename in the Script File Name box on the Scripting tab of the Properties dialog box for the Dial-Up Networking connection. (See Table 22-1.)

4. Test the script, editing it with your text editor and viewing the results in a terminal window.

Dial-up Networking comes with a set of well-commented sample scripts. Usually, it's easier to customize one of the sample scripts than it is to write your own from scratch.

Creating Multilink Connections

Multilink is a new Dial-Up Networking feature that allows you to use multiple modems and phone lines (usually two modems and two phone lines) for a single Internet connection, to increase the effective connection speed (throughput). For example, you could use two 56Kb modems together to simulate a 112Kb connection to the Internet. Data flows through both modems and both phone lines for a single connection.

Your ISP must support multilink connections in order for you to use such a connection, because the ISP's hardware and software must be able to combine the packets of information from the two phone lines into one Internet connection. Multilink connections, where they are available, usually cost more than a regular dial-up Internet account; contact your ISP for details.

When you create a multilink connection, you specify one device—usually a modem—on the General tab of the connection's Properties dialog box. Then you list the other device(s)—usually one other modem—on the Multilink tab. Click the Use Additional Devices setting to tell Windows that this is a multilink connection. Then add the additional devices. To add a device, click the Add button, and then in the window that appears, select the name of the device to use (usually a second modem) and the phone number to dial. (The Add button doesn't work unless you have two modems installed.) When you are done, the device name appears in the large box in the Multilink tab of the Properties dialog box for the connection.

To change the configuration of a device, select it and click the Edit button. To remove a device from the list, select it and click Remove.

Once you've set up a multilink connection, it works just like a regular Internet connection, but faster.

Setting Additional Dial-Up Networking Options

You might think that all the properties of a Dial-Up Networking connection would appear on the connection's Properties dialog box (shown in Figure 22-8), but you'd be wrong. A few additional settings appear on the Internet Properties and Dial-Up Settings dialog boxes. The Internet Properties dialog box has miscellaneous settings, including those that control the default mail, e-mail, and other Internet application programs. The Dial-Up Settings dialog box contains settings that control how often Dial-Up Networking redials if the line is busy, and how long a connection can remain inactive before Dial-Up Networking hangs up.

To display the Internet Properties dialog box, choose Start | Settings | Control Panel and run the Internet program. Figure 22-10 shows the Connection tab of the Internet Properties dialog box. Most of the settings on the various tabs of this dialog box apply to using a web browser, and are covered in Chapter 25. However, most of

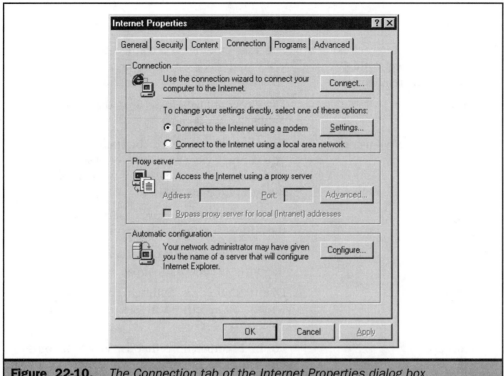

Figure 22-10. *The Connection tab of the Internet Properties dialog box*

the settings on the Connection tab control your Internet connection; those settings that do are listed in Table 22-3.

Assuming that the Connect To The Internet Using a Modem setting is selected on the Connection tab of the Internet Properties dialog box, click the Settings button to display the Dial-Up Settings dialog box shown in Figure 22-11. Table 22-4 lists the settings and buttons on this dialog box.

Deleting a Dial-Up Networking Connection

If you don't expect to connect to a particular account in the future, delete its connection from the Dial-Up Networking window by selecting the icon for the connection and pressing the DEL key. Be sure to delete any shortcuts to the connection, too.

Setting	Description
Connect to the Internet using a modem/Connect to the Internet using a local area network	Specifies whether you connect to the Internet via a modem or via a local area network (see "Dialing the Internet Automatically").
Settings	Displays the Dial-Up Settings dialog box (see Table 22-4 for details).
Access the Internet using a proxy server	For connections via a LAN, specifies whether you connect via a proxy server (a server that acts as a gatekeeper between your LAN and the rest of the Internet).
Address	For connections via a proxy server, specifies the address of the proxy server.
Port	For connections via a proxy server, specifies the port number of the proxy server.
Advanced	Displays the Proxy Settings dialog box, in which you specify addresses for use with your proxy server.
Configure	For LAN connections that use WINS or some other automated configuration system, displays a dialog box in which you can specify the URL of the configuration information for your Internet Explorer program (see Chapter 24).

Table 22-3. *Connection-Related Settings on the Internet Properties Dialog Box*

Communicating Using Dial-Up Networking

When you want to connect to an account by using Dial-Up Networking, follow these steps:

1. Choose Start | Programs | Accessories | Dial-Up Networking to display the Dial-Up Networking window. Then run the connection icon. If a connection

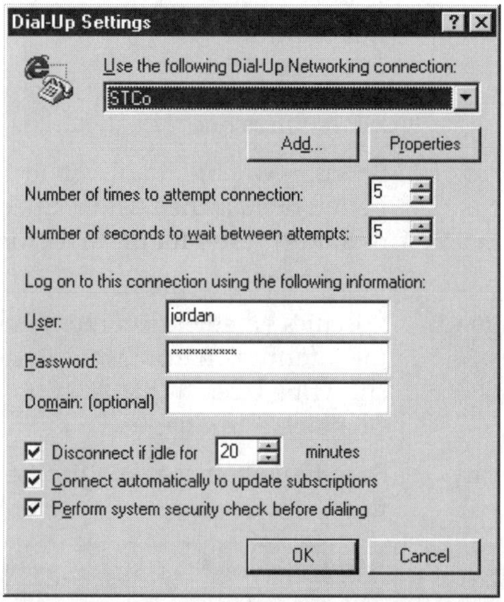

Figure 22-11.   *The Dial-Up Settings dialog box*

Setting or Button	Description
Add	Runs the Make New Connection Wizard.
Properties	Displays the properties of the Dial-Up Networking connection.
Number of times to attempt connection	Specifies how many times Dial-Up Networking dials the connection. The default is five times.
Number of seconds to wait between attempts	Specifies how long to wait after one attempt to connect failed before trying again. The default is five seconds.
User	Specifies the user name to use when logging in.
Password	Specifies the password to use when logging in.

Table 22-4.   *Settings on the Dial-Up Settings Dialog Box*

Setting or Button	Description
Domain	Specifies the domain name for your account, if your ISP requires one. The default is blank.
Disconnect if idle for *xx* minutes	Specifies whether to disconnect automatically after a period of inactivity. The blank contains the number of minutes after which to disconnect. The default is 20 minutes.
Connect automatically to update subscriptions.	Specifies whether to connect automatically to update the information from web sites to which you have subscribed (see "What Are Subscriptions and Channels?" in Chapter 25).
Perform system security check before dialing.	Specifies whether to require a password each time the system dials out.

Table 22-4.   *Settings on the Dial-Up Settings Dialog Box* (continued)

icon appears on your desktop, you can run it instead. You see the Connect To dialog box, shown in Figure 22-12.

2. Unless you are worried about someone else using your computer to connect to your account, select the Save Password check box so that you don't have to type your password each time you connect.

3. Click the Connect button. Dial-Up Networking dials your account, logs in, and starts the type of connection that you set in the Type of Dial-Up Server setting in the Properties dialog box for the connection. You see a window telling you that you are connected to the account (Figure 22-13).

Click the Do Not Show This Dialog Box In The Future check box, so you don't have to see this confirmation dialog box each time you connect to the Internet.

4. Click the Close button.

To make it easier to start Dial-Up Networking, copy the icon for your connection from the Dial-Up Networking window to your desktop. Right-click the connection's icon and choose Create Shortcut from the menu that appears. Windows asks whether to put the shortcut on your desktop. Click Yes. You may also want to add the connection to your Start menu or Programs menu (see Chapter 12).

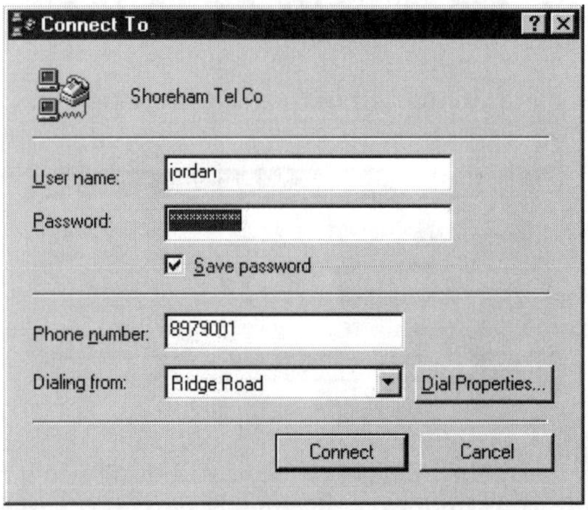

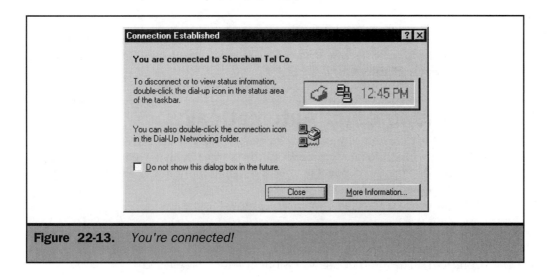

Figure 22-12. *Connecting using Dial-Up Networking*

While you are connected, the Dial-Up Networking icon appears in the system tray on the Taskbar. Move the mouse pointer to it (without clicking) to see how many bytes have been sent and received and your connection speed. Double-click the icon to see more details.

Figure 22-13. *You're connected!*

Disconnecting from Your Account

To disconnect your Internet connection, double-click the Dial-Up Networking icon in the system tray. You see the Connected dialog box, shown here. Click Disconnect.

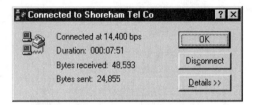

If you are connected to your Internet account and don't use it for a while (usually 20 minutes), Windows or your ISP may disconnect you automatically. You may see this dialog box asking whether you'd like to disconnect:

Or you may see a dialog box saying that you have been disconnected and asking whether you'd like to reconnect. See the next section for how to configure Windows to connect and disconnect automatically.

Dialing the Internet Automatically

What happens if you are not connected to the Internet and you tell your e-mail program to fetch your mail, or ask your web browser to display a web page? Dial-Up Networking can dial up and connect to your Internet account automatically when you request Internet-based information.

To set Windows to connect automatically, follow these steps:

1. Choose Start | Settings | Control Panel and run the Internet program. Click the Connection tab on the Internet Properties dialog box and make sure that the Connect To The Internet Using A Modem setting is selected.

2. Click the Settings button to display the Dial-Up Settings dialog box, shown in Figure 22-11.

3. In the first box, choose the Dial-Up Networking connection you want to use when connecting automatically to the Internet.

4. Set the other options to tell Windows how many times to try and how long to wait between attempts (if your ISP's line is busy, for example). Also type your username and password. If you want Windows to disconnect automatically after a period of inactivity, chose the Disconnect If Idle For *xx* Minutes check box, and type the number of minutes.

5. Click OK to dismiss the Dial-Up Settings dialog box, then click OK again to dismiss the Internet Properties dialog box.

When you use an Internet program and Windows detects that you are asking for information from the Internet, you see the Dialing Progress dialog box shown in Figure 22-14. The dialog box displays messages as it dials, connects, and logs in to your Internet account using the information in the Dial-Up Settings dialog box.

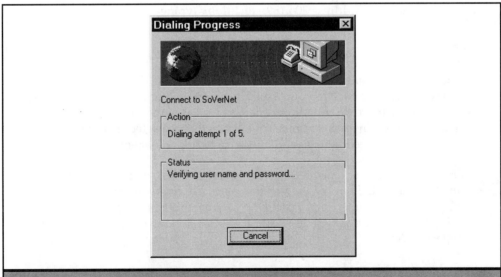

Figure 22-14.   *Dial-Up Networking can dial the Internet automatically*

Testing Your Connection

After dialing up a Dial-Up Networking connection, you can use Windows 98's Ping program to test whether packets of information can make the round trip from your computer, out over the Internet to another computer, and back to your computer. You can use the Tracert program to check what route packets take to get from your computer to another computer. And you can use the Netstat program to find out which computers your computer is talking to.

Pinging Another Computer

Sending a small text packet on a round trip is called *pinging*, and you can use Windows 98's built-in Ping program to send one.

To run Ping, open a DOS window by choosing Start | Programs | MS-DOS Prompt (see Chapter 41). Then, type the Ping command:

ping *system*

Replace *system* with either the numeric IP address or the Internet name of the computer you want to ping. Choose any Internet host computer that you are sure is up and running, such as your ISP's mail server. Then press ENTER.

For example, you can ping the web server at InterNIC (the Internet Information Center), which has the IP address 204.159.111.101, by typing

ping 204.159.111.101

Ping sends out four test packets (pings) and reports how long the packets take to get to InterNIC's computer and back to yours (see Figure 22-15). For each packet, you see how long the round-trip takes in milliseconds, as well as summary information about all four packets' trips. Ping has a number of options that are listed in Table 22-5. Ping has other options, not listed here, useful only to network managers.

*First try Ping with a numeric IP address, to see whether packets get out to the Internet and back. Then try Ping with a name, like **www.internic.net**, to see whether you successfully contact your DNS to convert the name into an IP address. If the first test works and the second doesn't, your connection isn't set up properly to contact a DNS.*

Tracing Packets over the Internet

Packets of information don't usually go directly from one computer to another computer over the Internet. Instead, they are involved in a huge game of "whisper-down-the-lane," in which packets are passed from computer to computer until they reach their destination. If your data seems to be moving slowly, you can use the Tracert (short for *trace route*) program to follow your packets across the Internet,

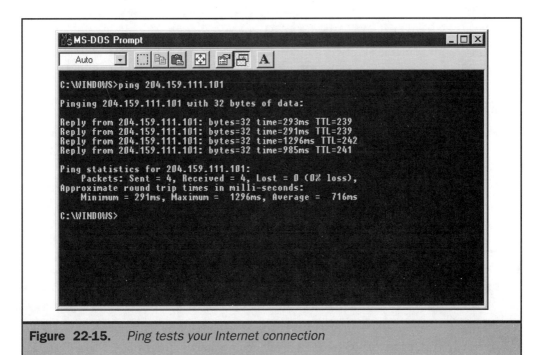

Figure 22-15. *Ping tests your Internet connection*

from your computer to an Internet host you frequently use. The technique that Tracert uses doesn't always work, so it's quite possible that running Tracert to a remote computer can fail even though the computer is working and accessible.

Option	Description
-a	Reports numeric addresses rather than host names.
-f	Specifies that packets contain a Do Not Fragment flag, so that packets are not fragmented on route. (Useful to test very slow dial-up connections.)
-i *ttl*	Specifies the *Time To Live* for the packets (how many times the packet can be passed from one computer to another while in transit on the network).

Table 22-5. *Options for the Ping Program*

Option	Description
-l *length*	Specifies the length of the packets to send. The default length is 64 bytes. The maximum length is 8192 (8K).
-n *n*	Specifies to send *n* pings. (The default is four.)
-r *n*	Specifies that the outgoing and returning packets should record the first *n* hosts on the route they take, using the Return Route field. *N* is a number from 1 to 9.
-t	Specifies to continue pinging until you interrupt it. (Otherwise, it pings four times.)
-w *n*	Specifies a time-out of *n* milliseconds for each packet.

Table 22-5. *Options for the Ping Program (continued)*

To run Tracert, open a DOS window by choosing Start | Programs | MS-DOS Prompt (see Chapter 41). Then type the Tracert command:

tracert *system*

Replace *system* with either the numeric IP address or the Internet name of the computer to which you want to trace the route. Then press ENTER.

For example, you can trace the route of packets from your computer to the Yahoo! Web directory at **www.yahoo.com** by typing:

tracert www.yahoo.com

You see a listing like the one in Figure 22-16, showing the route that the packets took from your computer to the specified host (sometimes Tracert reports a different host name from the one you specified, which means that the host has more than one name). For each *hop* (stage of the route), Tracert sends out three packets, and reports the time that each packet took to reach that far. It also reports the name and numeric IP address of the host.

Table 22-6 shows the options you can use with the Tracert program. A few other options, not listed here, are useful only to network managers.

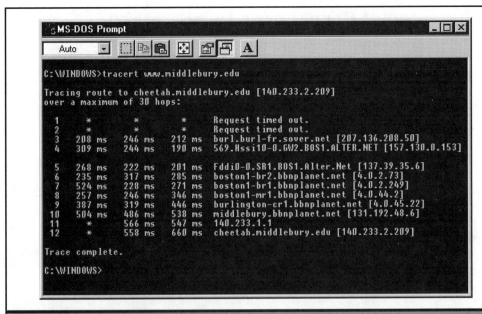

```
MS-DOS Prompt                                            _ □ ✕
Auto      ▼   □ 🖻 🖺 💠 🖾 🖾 A

C:\WINDOWS>tracert www.middlebury.edu

Tracing route to cheetah.middlebury.edu [140.233.2.209]
over a maximum of 30 hops:

  1     *        *        *     Request timed out.
  2     *        *        *     Request timed out.
  3   208 ms   246 ms   212 ms  bur1.burl-fr.sover.net [207.136.208.50]
  4   309 ms   244 ms   190 ms  569.Hssi10-0.GW2.BOS1.ALTER.NET [157.130.0.153]

  5   268 ms   222 ms   201 ms  Fddi0-0.SR1.BOS1.Alter.Net [137.39.35.6]
  6   235 ms   317 ms   285 ms  boston1-br2.bbnplanet.net [4.0.2.73]
  7   524 ms   228 ms   271 ms  boston1-br1.bbnplanet.net [4.0.2.249]
  8   257 ms   246 ms   346 ms  boston1-mr1.bbnplanet.net [4.0.44.2]
  9   387 ms   319 ms   446 ms  burlington-cr1.bbnplanet.net [4.0.45.22]
 10   504 ms   486 ms   538 ms  middlebury.bbnplanet.net [131.192.48.6]
 11     *      566 ms   547 ms  140.233.1.1
 12     *      558 ms   660 ms  cheetah.middlebury.edu [140.233.2.209]

Trace complete.

C:\WINDOWS>
```

Figure 22-16. *Tracert shows the route that packets take from your computer to an Internet host*

Option	Description
-d	Specifies not to resolve addresses to host names, so that the resulting list of hosts consists only of numeric IP addresses.
-h *n*	Specifies a maximum number of *n* hops to trace before giving up.
-w *n*	Specifies that the program wait *n* milliseconds for each reply before giving up.

Table 22-6. *Options for the Tracert Program*

Displaying Internet Connections Using Netstat

Netstat is a network diagnostic program that you can use for any TCP/IP connection—Internet connections or LANs. You can run Netstat to see which computers your computer is connected to over the Internet—not the ISP to which you dial in, but other Internet hosts to or from which you are transferring information.

To run Netstat, open a DOS window by choosing Start | Programs | MS-DOS Prompt (see Chapter 41). Then type:

    netstat

When you press ENTER, you see a listing of the Internet connections that are currently running. Figure 22-17 shows that the computer is connected to the host ivan.iecc.com for FTP file transfer (see "Transferring Files Using Ftp" in Chapter 28). The computer is also connected to several computers at the Yahoo! Web directory, probably for receiving web pages (the "80" at the end of the address signifies the port commonly used for web page retrieval).

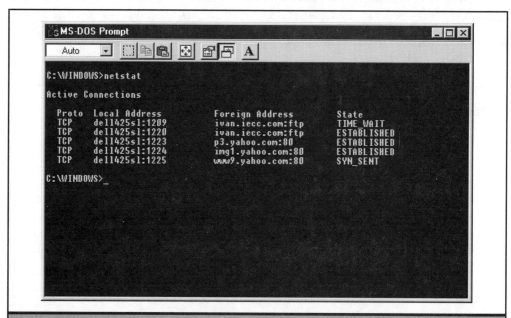

Figure 22-17. *The Netstat program lists Internet hosts you are using*

The
Complete
Reference

Chapter 23

E-Mail and Newsgroups Using
Outlook Express

The most popular use of the Internet is to send and receive messages from other Internet users. Windows 98 comes with Outlook Express, an e-mail and news reading program that Microsoft introduced with Internet Explorer 4.0. You can also install and use any number of mail and news reading applications, whether they are Microsoft products or not. If you've upgraded from Windows 95, you can also use the old Microsoft Exchange program included with Windows 95.

Our summary recommendation is that Outlook Express is a fine program, and that if you are looking for a mail or news reading program, you should try it. (In particular, we prefer it over Exchange.) However, nothing about Outlook Express puts it in the "gotta-have" category. If you're happy with whatever applications you are using, stick with them.

> **Tip** *If you use Netscape Navigator as your web browser, you may want to use its e-mail program, Netscape Messenger, which comes as part of the Netscape Communicator set of programs. See Netscape's web site at **http://home.netscape.com/products**. Another excellent e-mail program, Eudora, is available at **http://www.eudora.com/**.*

This chapter describes how to use Outlook Express to send and receive e-mail messages, organize the messages you decide to keep, and read and post articles to Usenet newsgroups. If you correspond with people whose software can read messages written in HTML (the language in which web pages are written), you can compose them using Outlook Express. Whatever program you use for e-mail or newsreading, you should learn *netiquette* to avoid getting into trouble.

> **Tip** *If you'd like to test your e-mail program, get news about updates to this book, or just say "Hi" to the authors, send a message to **win98tcr@gurus.com** (our mail robot will send an automatic response, and we read all our messages).*

What Is E-Mail?

E-mail, short for *electronic mail*, is a way to send messages over the Internet (or a local area network or other network) to people who may not be logged in right now. (To send messages right away to people who are logged in at the same time you are, and receive answers in seconds, use a chat program—see Chapter 27). Oversimplifying somewhat, the process works like this:

1. Using an e-mail program, such as Outlook Express, the sender creates a message and decides who the recipients should be.

2. At a designated place at the beginning of the message, the sender lists the e-mail addresses of all the recipients. (There can be as many recipients as the sender wants, but for simplicity, we'll pretend there is only one.) An *e-mail address* specifies two things: a computer on the Internet where a recipient

receives mail (called a *mail server*), and the name that the mail server uses to designate the mailbox of the recipient. So, for example, the e-mail address president@whitehouse.gov specifies the mail server whitehouse.gov and a mailbox on whitehouse.gov called president.

3. The sender connects to a *mail gateway*, a computer connected to the Internet (usually a computer owned by the sender's Internet service provider) that runs a mail-handling program that supports *SMTP* (the Simple Mail Transfer Protocol used for Internet mail). The message is sent from the sender's computer to the mail gateway.

4. From the mail gateway, the message is passed across the Internet to the recipient's mail server.

5. The recipient's mail server files the message in the recipient's *mailbox*, a file or folder containing all the messages that the recipient hasn't downloaded to her own computer yet.

6. Using an e-mail program (which need not be the same as the one the sender used to create and send the message), the recipient looks for new mail by logging into the mail server. The mail server runs a program that supports *POP3* (Post Office Protocol 3) or *IMAP* (Internet Message Access Protocol) to deliver the message, along with any other messages that may have arrived since the recipient last checked, to the recipient's computer.

7. The recipient uses the e-mail program to read the message.

Every e-mail message consists of a *header* (lines containing the address, the return address, the date, and other information about the message) and a *body* (the text of the message).

What Are Newsgroups?

Newsgroups are another way to use your computer and the Internet to communicate with the outside world. Unlike e-mail, however, a newsgroup is a public medium. When you send a message to a newsgroup, the message is available to anyone who wants to look at it—it's as if you have posted an article on a public bulletin board. You'll never know who—if anyone—reads your article. The Internet-based system of newsgroups is called *Usenet* or *netnews*.

Newsgroups are organized by topic. Since there are tens of thousands of newsgroups, topics can be very specific. When you have something to say about the topic of a newsgroup, you can use a *newsreading program*, such as Outlook Express, to compose an *article* (which may be many pages or only one line) and send it to your *news server*, a computer on the Internet that supports *NNTP* (Net News Transfer Protocol), which makes your article available to other news servers. People who want to read the recent contributions to this newsgroup (including your article) can use a newsreading program (not necessarily the same as yours) to download articles from their own news servers.

What Is Netiquette?

A contraction of "net etiquette," *netiquette* is the informal system of courtesies that people expect from you when you trade e-mail with them or participate in newsgroups. Much of netiquette is common sense, and has to do with not wasting people's time or resources, giving people credit when you quote them, and not forwarding messages to a wider audience than the author would want.

The purpose of most netiquette is to compensate for the peculiarities of the medium. For example, the Internet unfortunately is the ideal medium for chain letters and mass mailings. With a few easy clicks, you can forward a chain letter to 100 people, or send your get-rich-quick scheme to every newsgroup in the world. If social convention did not restrain people, such messages would choke the whole Internet. The Internet is also an ideal medium for destructive gossip. If Bill told Mary in person what John told Bill about her, she might take it with a grain of salt. But if Bill forwards John's exact e-mail message to Mary, or if a chain of 15 people forward John's message (eventually reaching Mary), a more difficult situation emerges.

A good online reference for netiquette is Brad Templeton's satirical "Emily Postnews" web page at **http://www.clari.net/brad/emily.html**, or check our site at **http://net.gurus.com/win98tcr**.

Getting Started with Outlook Express

To begin using Outlook Express, click the Outlook Express icon on the Quick Launch toolbar, or choose Outlook Express from Start | Program | Internet Explorer. If you have never used Outlook Express before, the Internet Connection Wizard starts (see "Creating a Dial-Up Networking Connection Using the Internet Connection Wizard" in Chapter 22). After you complete or cancel the Wizard, the Outlook Express opening screen appears, as shown in Figure 23-1.

Working with the Outlook Express Window

The Outlook Express window, shown in Figure 23-1, resembles a Windows Explorer window. At the top is a menu bar, with a toolbar underneath it. Below the toolbar, the window is cut into two panes. The right pane is fairly self-explanatory: Click any of the six icons to begin the activity or examine the object mentioned in the label. The left pane is a folder list, similar to the left pane in a Windows Explorer window. Outlook Express is at the top of the list and is highlighted, indicating that it corresponds to what is currently shown in the right pane.

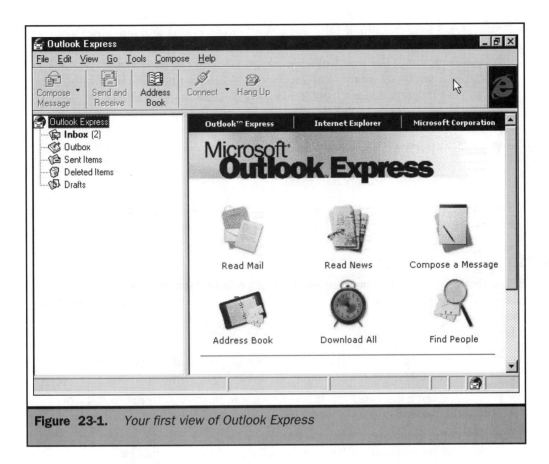

Figure 23-1. *Your first view of Outlook Express*

The folders immediately beneath Outlook Express on the folder list are necessary parts of the mail system:

- **Inbox** Where Outlook Express puts the incoming messages that it downloads from your e-mail server. The messages remain there until you delete them or move them to another folder.

- **Outbox** Contains the outgoing messages that you have completed and chosen to send, but which have not yet been sent. For example, you might complete and choose to send several messages while you are offline. Those messages wait in the Outbox folder until the next time your computer is connected to your mail server.

- **Sent Items** Contains messages that you have sent. They remain in this folder until you delete or move them.

■ **Deleted Items** Contains the messages (both incoming and outgoing) that you have deleted. Like the Recycle Bin, it is a last-chance folder that gets unwanted messages out of the way, but from which they still can be retrieved. Outlook Express can be set up to clean out the Deleted Items folder automatically, or you can delete messages from it manually (see "Saving and Deleting Messages"). Messages deleted from the Deleted Items folder are beyond Outlook Express's power to retrieve.

■ **Draft** Contains unfinished messages that you have chosen to save and work on later. Any time you are composing a message, you can choose File | Save to save the message in the Draft folder.

As you begin sending and receiving messages, you will set up other folders to keep track of your correspondence (see "Organizing Your Correspondence").

Setting Up Your Accounts

Before Outlook Express can send or receive mail, or allow you to interact with newsgroups, you need to tell the Internet Connection Wizard what accounts you have and how it can access them. Before you start the Wizard, make sure you have the following information handy:

■ The name you want attached to any message you send. Do you want to be known as Johnny Public, Jonathan Q. Public, or by some nickname?

■ Your return e-mail address. If people want to reply to your messages, where should the replies go?

■ The name of the servers your account deals with. For a *news account* (which lets you read newsgroups), this is an NNTP server with a name like news.serviceprovider.com. For an e-mail account, you provide two names: One server for incoming mail (a POP3 or IMAP server), and one server for outgoing mail (an SMTP server). Your Internet provider should have given you this information—if you don't have it, call them.

■ A "friendly name" to give the account. Outlook Express puts this account name on its menus, so that you recognize which account it is.

■ How to connect to the account. Do you connect through a modem or a LAN? Have you already defined a Dial-Up Connection for this account?

■ What directory you want to store Outlook Express messages in. The Wizard suggests a directory; accept it unless it conflicts with your own ideas about organizing your files.

Once you have assembled this information:

1. Choose Tools | Accounts. The Internet Accounts dialog box opens.

2. Click the Add button and select the type of account you want to define: mail, news, or directory service. The appropriate Internet Connection Wizard begins.

3. Insert the information the Wizard asks for.

You have to go through this process once for each account you want to establish.

Importing Messages from Other Mail Programs

If you've been using e-mail for a while, your message files are an important asset. Continuity can be an important reason to stick with whatever mail program you've been using. Outlook Express lets you convert your message files from these other mail programs:

■ Eudora Pro or Light, versions 1 through 3

■ Microsoft Exchange, Outlook, Internet Mail for Windows 3.1, or Windows Messaging

■ Netscape Mail or Communicator

To import messages from one of these mail applications:

1. Select File | Import | Messages from the menu.

2. Answer the questions asked by the Outlook Express Import Wizard. It needs to know from which application it is importing, and where the files are located.

Folders of imported messages show up in the Outlook Express folder list, from which you can move them into whatever folders you like (see "Organizing Your Correspondence"). The imported folders retain their names and structure. If, for example, you import the People At Work folder from Eudora, when it arrives in Outlook Express, it should still have the subfolders Bob and Jenny, and those subfolders should contain all the messages they had in Eudora.

 Early versions of these importation programs didn't always work perfectly. In the conversion from Eudora Light, for example, filed outgoing messages were given the date of the conversion rather than keeping the date on which they were originally sent. Microsoft will eventually get this right, but don't throw away your old files until you're satisfied that the conversion really worked.

Importing Addresses from Other Mail Programs

Outlook Express can import addresses from these programs:

■ Eudora Pro or Light, versions 1 through 3

■ LDIF-LDAP data interchange format

- Microsoft Exchange or Internet Mail for Windows
- Netscape Address Book or Communicator
- Text files

To import addresses from one of these mail applications:

1. Select File | Import | Messages from the menu.
2. Answer the questions asked by the Outlook Express Import Wizard.

If all goes well, the addresses wind up in the Windows Address Book (see "Storing Addresses in the Address Book" in Chapter 5).

Setting Your Mail and News Reading Programs

You can tell Windows 98 which mail and news reading programs to run with Internet Explorer; these are the programs that Internet Explorer runs when you click a mail or news link (see Chapter 24). Choose Start | Settings | Control Panel. In the Control Panel window, open the Internet icon. On the Programs tab in the Messaging section, the Mail and News boxes show the default programs that Internet Explorer runs; both are set to Outlook Express when you install Windows 98.

You can also configure Outlook Express by choosing Tools | Options to display the Options dialog box. Table 23-1 lists the most commonly-used settings on the tabs of the Options dialog box. To find out about the rest of the settings, display the Options dialog box and use the question mark help button in the upper right corner of the dialog box (see "Finding Out What an Onscreen Object Is" in Chapter 6).

Tab	Setting	Description
General	Check for new messages every *xx* minutes	Specifies how often Outlook Express connects automatically to the mail server to download incoming messages and upload outgoing messages.
General	Make Outlook Express my default e-mail program	Specifies that when another program (for example, a web browser) gets a request to compose an e-mail message, Windows should run Outlook Express to compose the message.

Table 23-1. *Some Settings on the Options Dialog Box*

Tab	Setting	Description
General	Make Outlook Express my default news reader	Specifies that when another program gets a request to read or post newsgroup messages, Windows should run Outlook Express.
Send	Mail sending format/News sending format: HTML/Plain text	Specifies whether your e-mail messages and newsgroup postings are sent as HTML or as plain text (see "Turning HTML On and Off").
Send	Include message in reply	Specifies that replies contain the text of the original message (see "Including the Original Message in Your Reply").
Send	Send messages immediately	Specifies that Outlook Express connect to your mail server and send messages whenever a message is in your Outbox (see "Sending Messages Automatically (or Not)").
Spelling	Always check spelling before sending	Specifies that Outlook Express automatically run its spell-checking when you send each message.
Security	Digitally sign all outgoing messages	Adds a digital signature to all messages that proves that you sent the messages. Click Advanced Settings to specify the type of digital signature.
Security	Encrypt contents and attachments for all outgoing messages	Encrypts (encodes) all outgoing messages so that they cannot be read unless the recipient has the encryption key. Click Advanced Settings to specify the type of encryption.
Security	Get Digital ID	Click to install a *digital ID*, a file that Outlook Express uses for digital signatures and encryption (see **http://www.verisign.com** on the Web).

Table 23-1.   *Some Settings on the Options Dialog Box (continued)*

Tab	Setting	Description
Dial Up	Do not dial a connection/ Dial this connection/Ask me if I would like to dial a connection	Specifies what Outlook Express does when you start the program.
Dial Up	Hang up when finished sending, receiving, or downloading	Specifies whether Windows stays online with your Internet account after transferring messages.
Dial Up	Automatically dial when checking for new messages	Specifies whether Windows connects automatically to your Internet account when checking for incoming mail.

Table 23-1.   *Some Settings on the Options Dialog Box* (continued)

Sending and Receiving E-Mail

After you set up one or more mail accounts (see "Setting Up Your Accounts"), you can check your mail by clicking the Send and Receive button on the toolbar. If you have more than one mail account, Send and Receive displays a drop-down list so that you can access any or all of your accounts. Once you have clicked Send and Receive, Outlook Express then goes through the following process automatically.

1. Connects to your mail server. If you are on a local area network, this part of the process may happen so quickly that it is almost invisible to you. If you connect to the Internet over a modem, however, and are not already online for some other reason, Outlook Express runs Dial-Up Networking to dial up your Internet provider and establish a connection. Once an Internet connection is established, Outlook Express contacts your mail servers over the Internet.

2. Sends all the messages in your Outbox. Messages you aren't ready to send should be stored in the Draft folder, not in the Outbox.

3. Downloads all the incoming messages from the server into your Inbox.

After your messages are downloaded, you may decide to disconnect from the Internet. Choose File | Hang Up from the menu bar.

Receiving Mail

New mail accumulates in your Inbox, staying there until you decide to move it to another folder. To look at it, click Inbox in the left pane of the Outlook Express window (see "Organizing Your Correspondence"). The window now has three panes, as it does when you look at any mail folder. You can drag the boundaries of these three panes to reallocate the space occupied by each. The three panes are the following:

- **The folder list view in the left pane** The selected folder is highlighted. In Figure 23-2, Inbox is the selected folder.

- **The selected folder's message list in the upper-right pane** Each message receives one line in the list. The line tells who is the author of the message, what the subject line says, and when the message was received (or sent, if the message is outgoing). If the author rated the message as Urgent, an exclamation point (!) appears on the left side of its entry on the list. If the message has an *attachment* (a file attached to the message), a paper clip appears to the left of its entry. The currently selected message is highlighted. Unread messages have a closed-envelope icon next to them; read messages have an open-envelope icon.

- **A preview of the selected message in the lower-right pane** The bar at the top of the lower-right pane lists the sender and receiver of the message, together with its subject line. Below this bar is a scrollable window containing the full text of the message.

Sorting the Messages in a Folder

You can sort the messages in a folder according to any of the columns in the message list—just click the label above any of the columns. Click once to sort in ascending order, twice for descending order.

For example, clicking the From column label sorts the messages according to whom they are from. The various senders appear in alphabetical order. Click From again to sort in reverse alphabetical order.

Reading the Messages in a Folder

To read the messages in any folder:

1. Click the name of the folder in the folder list of the Outlook Express window. If the folder you want is not visible, it is either off the screen or contained in another folder. Use the left pane scrollbar to look up or down in the folder list. Click the plus box next to a folder's name to see the list of folders contained inside it.

2. Find the message you want to read in the message list in the upper-right pane.

3. Double-click to read the message in its own window, or single-click to read the message in the preview pane of the Outlook Express window.

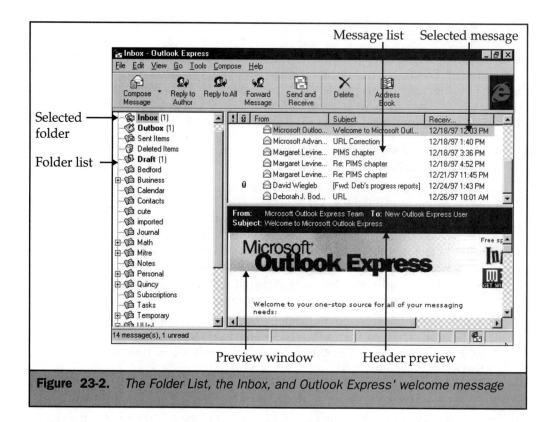

Message list   Selected message

Selected folder

Folder list

Preview window   Header preview

Figure 23-2.   *The Folder List, the Inbox, and Outlook Express' welcome message*

Opening Attached Files

Messages with attached files are denoted with a paper clip icon in the message list of the Outlook Express window. When the message is selected, a larger paper clip icon appears in the title bar of the preview pane. When the message is opened, the attached files appear as icons at the bottom of the message window.

Clicking the large paper clip icon produces a list of the attached files; selecting one of the files from this list opens the file. Similarly, selecting an attached-file icon from the bottom of the message window opens the file.

Caution   *When an attached file opens, it uses whichever application is associated with its file type—you are no longer dealing with Outlook Express. For this reason, we recommend that you do not open unsolicited file attachments from strangers, unless you're sure you know what the files are. It's safe to read e-mail messages from strangers—they're just text, and they can't change how your system works. However, attached executable (.exe) files can make changes to your system. Other attached files may be less dangerous, depending on the file type. If you have doubts, either delete the message or save it to a disk and run a virus-checking program on it.*

Composing Messages to Send

You create messages in three ways:

- **Compose a new message from scratch**   Click the Compose Message button on the Outlook Express toolbar.

- **Reply to a message you have received**   Select a message from an Outlook Express folder (such as Inbox) and click either the Reply To Author button or the Reply To All button on the Outlook Express toolbar.

- **Forward a message you have received**   Select a message from an Outlook Express folder and click the Forward Message button on the Outlook Express toolbar.

Any of these three actions opens a message window, as shown in Figure 23-3. The message window has two main parts: a header and a body. The body is the window into which you enter the text of your message. Use it as you would use a word processor. If you are composing a message from scratch, the body of the message window has nothing in it other than what you type. If you are forwarding a message, the text of the original message is included automatically. If you are replying, Outlook

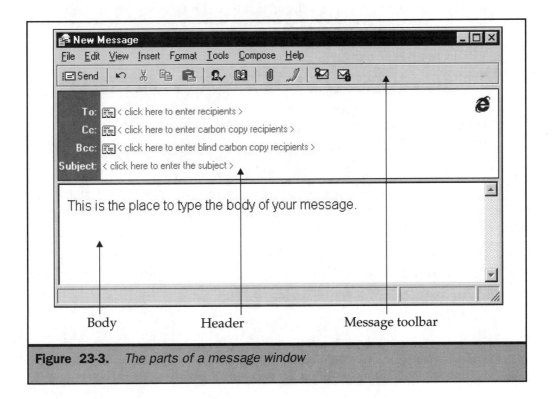

Figure 23-3.   *The parts of a message window*

Express can be set up to either include or not include the original text (see "Including the Original Message in Your Reply")

Completing the Header

The header section of the message window consists of four lines:

- **To**   Type the e-mail addresses of the primary recipient(s) of your message. If there is more than one recipient, separate the e-mail addresses with commas. Click the index card icon to look up addresses in the Address Book (see "Storing Addresses in the Address Book" in Chapter 5). This is the only line of the header that cannot be left blank. If you generate the message window by choosing Reply To Author, Outlook Express puts the address of the author of the original message on this line. If you use Reply To All, Outlook Express lists the addresses of the author and the other primary recipients of the original message. You may add more addresses or delete some of them if you want to.

- **Cc**   (Carbon Copy) Type the e-mail addresses of secondary recipients (if any). If you are Replying To All, Outlook Express uses the same Cc list as the original message. You may add to or delete from the list if you want to.

- **Bcc**   (Blind Carbon Copy) Type the e-mail addresses of other secondary recipients, if any. The recipients listed in the To and Cc boxes can see the list of other recipients listed in the To and Cc boxes, but not those listed in the Bcc box. If one of the To or Cc recipients Replies To All, someone on your Bcc list will not receive the reply.

- **Subject**   Enter a word or short phrase to describe the subject of your message. The subject line helps both you and your recipients keep track of the message in your files. If you are replying to another message, Outlook Express automatically uses the original subject line, preceded by Re. If you are forwarding, Outlook Express uses the original subject line, preceded by Fw.

Including the Original Message in Your Reply

One advantage e-mail has over paper mail is that you can indicate exactly what part of an e-mail message you are responding to. To make Outlook Express automatically include the original message in any reply:

1. Select Tools | Options to open the Options dialog box.
2. Select the Send tab.
3. Check the Include Message In Reply check box.
4. Click OK.

Now whenever you click the Reply To Author or Reply To All buttons, the body of the message window contains a divider, with the original message below the divider. The text of the original message is indented, with a > at the beginning of each line.

To remove the indentation or change the indentation character:

1. Open the Send tab of the Options dialog box, as just explained.

2. If Plain Text is selected as the Mail Sending Format, click the Settings button to open the Plain Text Settings dialog box. (If HTML is selected, see "Composing HTML Messages" later in this chapter.)

3. Unchecking the Indent The Original Text With check box at the bottom of the Plain Text Settings dialog box causes the original text to not be indented. The drop-down list next to the Indent The Original Text With check box lets you choose a different indentation character.

You can use the original text in two different ways. You can type your message at the beginning of the message window body, leaving the original message at the end for reference. Or you can edit the original message to delete all but the parts relevant to your reply, and then type your reply in parts, each immediately below the portions of the message to which you are responding, as in Figure 23-4. The second method creates

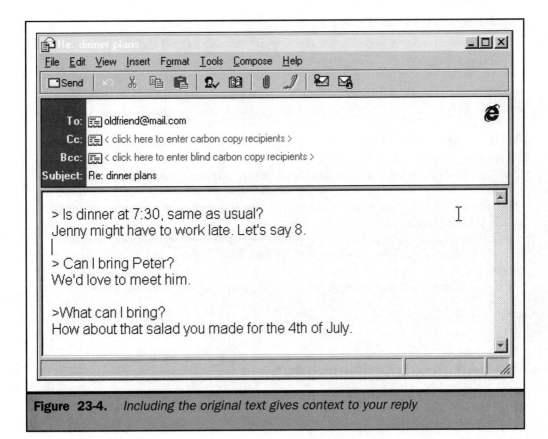

Figure 23-4. *Including the original text gives context to your reply*

the appearance of a dialog, and is especially useful if you are answering a series of questions. Given the proper context from the original message, a reply like "Yes. Yes. No. Not until Thursday," can actually make sense.

 Pay attention to whether the original message is making your reply wastefully long. You probably shouldn't include an entire three-page original message in your three-word reply. And if a topic goes back and forth many times, with both authors including the original message, the entire history of the correspondence is sent with each message—usually a waste.

Inserting Text Files into a Message

If what you want to say is already contained in a text file, you don't have to retype the text or even cut-and-paste the text out of the file. Just follow these steps to incorporate the text into your message:

1. Move the insertion point to the place in the text of your message where you want the text file inserted.

2. Select Insert | Text From File.

3. When the Insert Text File window opens, browse to find the text file you want.

4. Click Open.

The complete text of the text file is now inserted into the spot where the insertion point is located.

Attaching a File to a Message

You can use e-mail to send more than just text. Any file—a picture, a spreadsheet, a formatted text document—can be sent along with your message as an attachment. To attach a file to a message, click the paper clip icon on its message window toolbar. When the Insert Attachment window appears, browse to find the file you want to attach, and then click OK.

Outlook Express uses *MIME*, the most widely used method of attaching files to messages. Most e-mail programs, including Netscape, Eudora, and AOL's mail program, can deal with MIME attachments. But some e-mail programs can't, especially LAN e-mail programs that weren't originally designed to work with the Internet.

 Don't send attached files to people who don't have the software to read them. Ask first before sending an attachment.

Saving and Deleting Messages

Outlook Express hangs on to the messages that you send and receive until you tell it to forget them. Messages that you receive are stored in your Inbox folder. Messages that you send wind up in your Sent Items folder. They remain there until you either delete them or move them to another folder (see "Organizing Your Correspondence").

Saving Messages

Even though Outlook Express saves your messages automatically, you need to pay attention to three issues:

- **Outlook Express folders and the messages in them are separate from the overall filing system of your computer**   You may have a folder called Mom in Outlook Express, but no Mom folder exists on the folder tree you see in Windows Explorer. If you want a message to be a file in your computer's filing system, you have to save it as a file: Select the message in Outlook Express' message list window, and then select File | Save As. Give the file a name, and it will be saved with the extension .eml.

- **Unfinished messages are lost when you close Outlook Express unless you save them**   You don't have to start and finish a message in one sitting. If you want to put the message away and work on it later, select File | Save to save the message in your Draft folder. If you want the unfinished message to be in an Outlook Express folder other than Draft, save it to Draft first, and then drag it to another folder.

- **Your mail files should be backed up as often as (perhaps more often than) any other files on your system**   Defining a special Backup job for your mail folders is just a little tricky, given that your Outlook Express folders don't correspond to folders in the usual sense (see "Creating a Backup Job with the Backup Wizard" in Chapter 10). The simplest method is to back up the entire folder in which you told Outlook Express to store your messages.

Deleting and Recovering Messages

Delete a message by selecting it in the message list and pressing DELETE. The message is sent to the Deleted Items folder, which functions within the Outlook Express filing system as a kind of Recycle Bin.

You can examine messages from the Deleted Items folder by opening them, and you can move them to another folder if you change your mind about deleting them. If you delete an item from the Deleted Items folder, it is gone permanently.

Outlook Express can be set up to empty the Deleted Items folder automatically when you exit the program:

1. Select Tools | Options. The Options dialog box appears.

2. From the General tab of the Options dialog box, check Empty Messages From The 'Deleted Items' Folder On Exit.

3. Click OK. The Options dialog box closes, returning you to the Outlook Express main window.

Naturally, you can undo this at any time by unchecking the Empty Messages From The 'Deleted Items' Folder On Exit check box.

Sending Messages

Once you are satisfied with the message you've composed, click the Send button in its message window. The message is moved to your Outbox folder, where it stays until the next time your computer is connected to your mail server. To send the contents of your Outbox immediately, click the Send And Receive button on the Outlook Express toolbar. Outlook Express connects to your Internet provider and then finds your mail server automatically.

Sending Messages Automatically (or Not)

If you decide it's a waste of time for messages to sit in your Outbox until you get around to clicking Send And Receive, you can tell Outlook Express to automatically connect to your e-mail server whenever there is a message in your Outbox:

1. Open the Options dialog box by selecting Tools | Options.

2. Select the Send tab.

3. Check the Send Messages Immediately check box.

4. Click OK.

You can undo this decision at any time by returning to the Send tab of the Options dialog box and unchecking Send Messages Immediately.

Even if Send Messages Immediately is checked, you can move a message to your Outbox without sending it immediately to your mail server by selecting File | Send Later. In particular, this is handy if you are temporarily unable to connect to the Internet—if you are on the road, for example, and your computer is not currently connected to a phone line.

Canceling Messages

So long as the message is sitting in your Outbox, you can still intercept it:

1. Select the Outbox folder from the folder list of the Outlook Express window.

2. Select the message from the Outbox message list.

3. Press the DELETE key or select Edit | Delete to get rid of the message completely. To put the message away to edit later, drag-and-drop the message from the upper-right pane into the Draft folder in the left pane. Or select Edit | Move To Folder and choose a folder in which to move the message. Alternatively, you can right-click the message and select Move To from the shortcut menu.

Organizing Your Correspondence

A mail program is more than just a way to read and write messages, it is also a filing system. Over time, the records of your correspondence may become a valuable asset. Although you can leave all of your mail in your Inbox, it's a lot easier to find messages if you file messages by sender or topic.

Outlook Express allows you to create folders and move messages from one folder to another. It also provides an Inbox Assistant utility to allow you to perform some secretarial actions automatically.

Working with Folders

The Outlook Express filing system resembles the filing system that Windows itself uses (see Chapter 8). But the Outlook Express files and folders can't be seen by Windows Explorer—you must use Outlook Express to manipulate them.

Creating and Deleting Folders

To create a new folder in Outlook Express:

1. Select File | Folder | New Folder. The Create Folder window opens.

2. Type the name of your folder into the Folder Name line.

3. In the bottom half of the Create Folder window, select the folder into which you want to place the new folder.

4. Click OK.

To delete a folder, select it in the folder list of the Outlook Express window, and then select File | Folder | Delete.

Moving and Copying

To move or copy a message from one folder to another:

1. Select the folder that contains the message in the folder list of the Outlook Express window. You may need to expand some folders (by clicking the plus boxes in the margin) to find it.

2. Find the message in the message list and right-click it.

3. Select either Move To Folder or Copy To Folder from the right-click menu. A window appears displaying a folder list.

4. Select the folder into which you want the message moved or copied.

5. Click OK.

You can also move a message by dragging it from the message list and dropping it onto the icon of the target folder in the folder list.

To move a folder, drag-and-drop its icon on the folder list to the location you want it to be located.

Finding Messages in Your Files

A filing system isn't worth much unless you can find what you put there, when you want to retrieve it. Outlook Express gives you a search tool that lets you search for messages based on:

- The sender
- The recipient
- The subject
- A word or phrase in the message body
- Whether the message has attachments
- The date received
- A folder containing the message

Begin your search by selecting Edit | Find Message. The Find Message dialog box appears, as shown in Figure 23-5. Enter as much information as you know about the message, and then click the Find Now button. Outlook Express lists at the bottom of the window all the messages that fit the description you've given. Open any message on this list by double-clicking.

Type any string of characters into the From, Sent To, Subject, or Message Body lines of the Find Message dialog box. This restricts your search to messages whose corresponding parts contain those character strings.

To specify the date of a message, check either the Before or After check box in the Received box. Enter a date in MM/DD/YY format into the corresponding line, or click the drop-down arrow to locate the date you want on a calendar. (Change months on the calendar by clicking the left or right arrows at the top of the calendar.) You can use Before and After together to specify a range of dates.

The Look In drop-down list specifies a folder in which to search. The Include Subfolders check box does just what it says—if the box is checked, the search includes all the subfolders of the specified folder; if it is not checked, the subfolders are not included.

Filtering Your Correspondence with Inbox Assistant

Outlook Express can do a little secretarial work for you automatically. It can:

- File messages to the appropriate folders, rather than letting them pile up in the Inbox.

- Forward messages to another e-mail address.

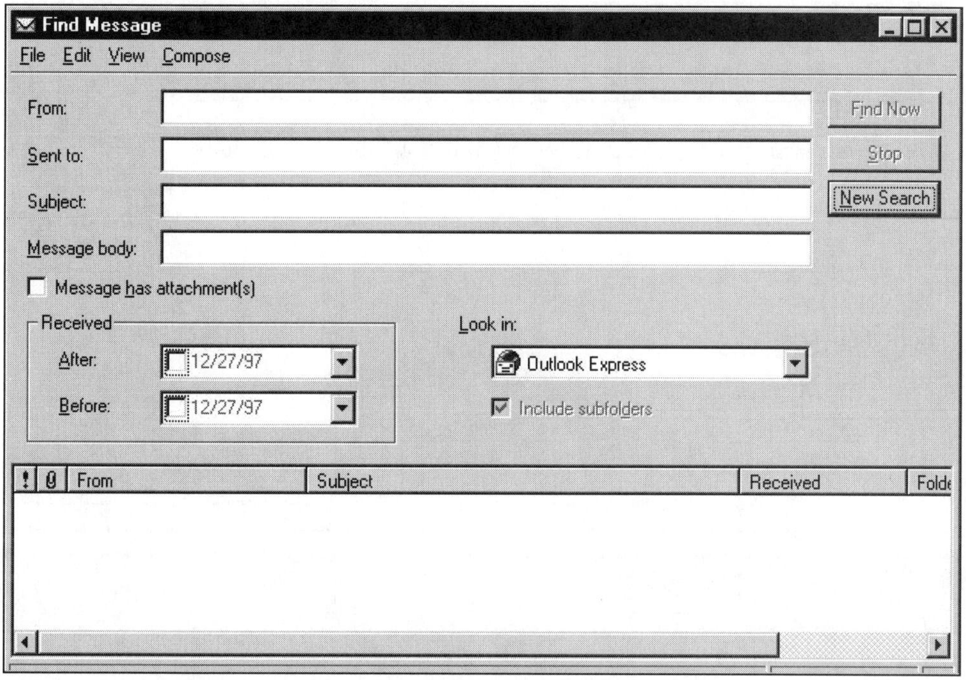

Figure 23-5. *The Find Message window*

■ Send a stock reply message.

■ Delete messages so that you never have to look at them.

The part of Outlook Express that handles these duties is Inbox Assistant. Get started with Inbox Assistant by selecting Tools | Inbox Assistant. This opens the Inbox Assistant dialog box, as Figure 23-6 shows. The Description window of this box lists the mail filters that you have defined so far. The active ones have checks in their check boxes, and the inactive ones do not. The first time you open Inbox Assistant, this window is empty.

Inbox Assistant lets you create *filters* to specify what mail you want Outlook Express to deal with automatically and what actions you want Outlook Express to take. To define a new filter, click the Add button. This opens the Inbox Assistant Properties dialog box, shown in Figure 23-7. This box is divided into two halves. The top half defines a type of message that you want Inbox Assistant to handle, and the bottom half tells Inbox Assistant what to do with such messages.

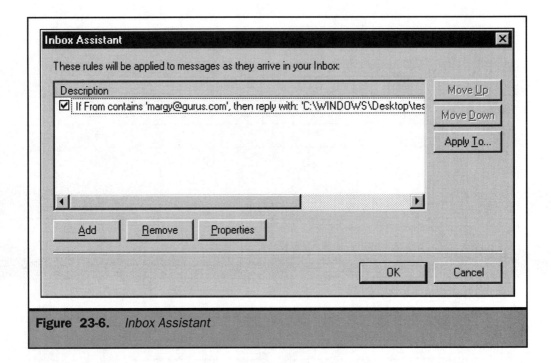

Figure 23-6.   *Inbox Assistant*

Using the Filtering Criteria

If you want Inbox Assistant to do the same thing for every message that comes in, you can check the All Messages box on the Inbox Assistant Properties dialog box, and ignore the other criteria. You might do this, for example, if you want to reply automatically to every message with "Thanks for writing, but I won't respond until I get back from Tibet in June."

If you want Inbox Assistant to do something special with a particular class of messages, you need to use the six filtering criteria to describe those messages. There are three kinds of criteria: header information, account, and length.

When you list several criteria at once, Outlook Express puts them together with a logical AND operator. The action defined in the lower half of the Inbox Assistant Properties dialog box is performed only on messages that meet *all* the criteria simultaneously. If you want to put criteria together with a logical OR operator, define separate filters with the same action.

FILTERING BASED ON HEADER INFORMATION   The To, Cc, From, and Subject lines of the Inbox Assistant Properties dialog box correspond to the lines in the header of a mail message. ("From" does not appear in the New Message window of messages you create with Outlook Express, because Outlook Express assumes that you are the sender.) Any string of characters that you type on one of these lines filters out any

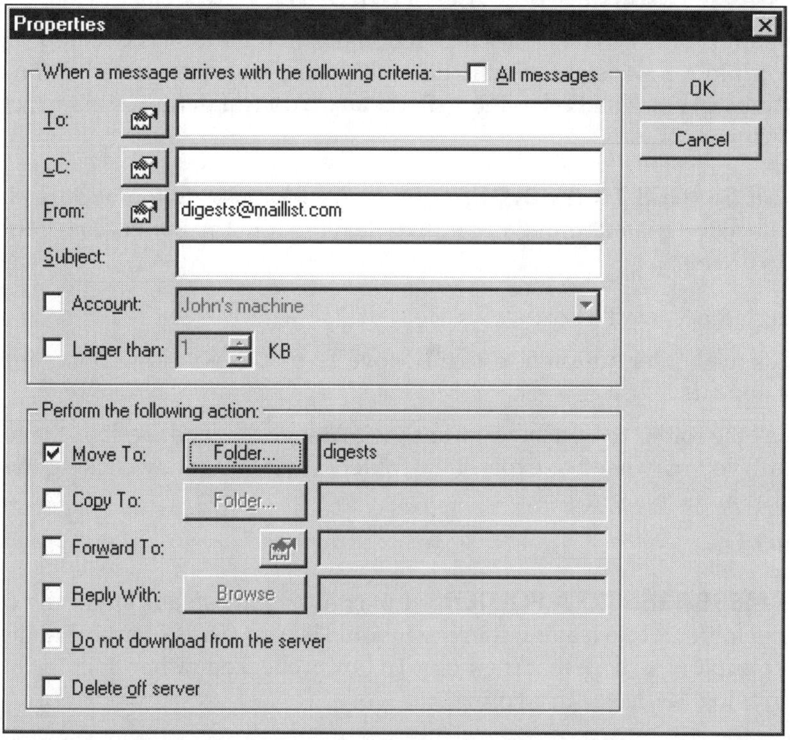

Figure 23-7. *Defining a new action for Inbox Assistant*

message that does not contain that string on the corresponding line of its header. For example, typing "apple" into the Subject line (and leaving the other criteria blank) selects all messages that have "apple" in their subject lines.

To enter an address from the Address Book on the To, Cc, or From lines, click the index card icon next to the corresponding line.

FILTERING BASED ON ACCOUNT   If you have several mail accounts, you can define a filter to apply to only one of them by checking the Account box and choosing one of your accounts from the drop-down list. If the Account box is not checked, the filter applies to all of your mail accounts. If you want the filter to apply to two or more accounts, but not all accounts, define separate filters for each account.

FILTERING BASED ON LENGTH   If you want to select only messages larger than a given size, check the Larger Than box and type a number into the box next to it.

Telling Inbox Assistant what Action to Take

The items in the Perform The Following Action box in the Inbox Assistant Properties dialog box tell Inbox Assistant what to do with the messages described in the When A Message Arrives With The Following Criteria box. You can define as many actions as you want with one filter.

MOVING MESSAGES TO A FOLDER   Inbox Assistant can automatically place a new message into a designated folder, rather than leaving it in the Inbox. To tell Inbox Assistant to do this:

1. Check the Move To box.
2. Click the Folder button next to the Move To box. A window containing a folder list appears.
3. Click the folder to which you want the messages moved. To find the folder you want, you may need to expand the folders containing it by clicking the plus boxes in the margin.
4. Click OK.

COPYING MESSAGES TO A FOLDER   Inbox Assistant can automatically copy a message to a folder while leaving it in the Inbox. The process is identical to moving messages to a folder, except that the Copy To box is checked rather than the Move To box (see "Moving Messages to a Folder").

FORWARDING MESSAGES TO ANOTHER E-MAIL ADDRESS   You can tell Inbox Assistant to forward messages automatically to another e-mail address by following these steps:

1. Check the Forward To box.
2. Type an e-mail address into the line to the right of the Forward To box, or click the index card icon and choose an address from the Address Book.

GENERATING AUTOMATIC REPLIES   If the filtering criteria at the top of the Inbox Assistant Properties dialog box are identifying orders for your business, for example, you might want to generate an automatic response assuring the customer that its order has been received and is being processed. In order to do this:

1. Create the message you want to use as a response (see "Composing Messages to Send").
2. From either the message window or the Outlook Express window (with the message selected), save the message with the .eml extension by using File | Save As. Remember what folder you saved it in.
3. Open Inbox Assistant by selecting Tools | Inbox Assistant. The Inbox Assistant dialog box opens.

4. Click the Add button in the Inbox Assistant dialog box. The Properties dialog box opens.

5. Use the filtering criteria in the top half of the Properties dialog box to define which messages should receive the automatic response (see "Using the Filtering Criteria").

6. Check the Reply With box.

7. Click the Browse button next to the Reply With box. An Open dialog box opens.

8. Use the Open dialog box to find and select the file you saved in step 2. The Open dialog box closes. The Properties dialog box now contains the file address of the message you want to send as an automatic response.

9. Click OK. The Properties dialog box closes. A description of the action you've defined is now in the Description window of the Inbox Assistant dialog box.

10. Click OK. The Inbox Assistant dialog box closes, returning you to the Outlook Express window.

DEALING WITH THE MAIL SERVER   The last two check boxes in the Perform The Following Action box of the Inbox Assistant Properties dialog box have to do with the mail server. Checking Do Not Download From The Server causes messages that fit the filtering criteria to be held up at the mail server—Outlook Express never takes possession of them. When this filter is deactivated, the held-up messages will be downloaded.

Checking Delete Off Server causes Outlook Express to tell the mail server not to hold the message. Checking both boxes simultaneously means that you never see the message at all—Outlook Express doesn't take possession of the message, but tells the server not to hold it either.

Managing Your Filters

Any Inbox Assistant filter that you define is described in the Description window of the Inbox Assistant dialog box. If the check box next to the description is checked, the filter is active. You can turn a filter on or off by checking or unchecking its check box.

To edit a filter, select it in the Description window and click the Properties button. The Properties dialog box appears—the same dialog box you used to define the filter. Change any of your choices and click OK.

Reading and Posting to Newsgroups

Before you can read and post to newsgroups with Outlook Express, you must set up a news account (see "Setting Up Your Accounts"). Once your account is set up, its folder appears in the folder list of the Outlook Express window, just below your mail folders. To begin using your news account, click its icon.

You can read and post to newsgroups using a web browser rather than a newsreader. The web site **http://www.dejanews.com** *gives you access to a large number of newsgroups.*

Notice that a news folder has a different icon than a mail folder, and that selecting a news folder rather than a mail folder changes the Outlook Express toolbar. Many of the news buttons resemble the mail buttons in name and function, but some do not. Left to right, the news buttons are as follows: Compose Message, Reply to Group, Reply to Author, Forward Message, Newsgroups, Connect, Hang Up, and Stop.

Subscribing to Newsgroups

The main thing that a newsreading application does is look at the list of newsgroups to which you subscribe and then check its news server to see whether those newsgroups have any new messages. The first step, then, in learning to use Outlook Express as a newsreader is to find some interesting newsgroups and subscribe to them.

Downloading the List of Available Newsgroups

The first time that you click your news account icon, Outlook Express informs you that you are not subscribed to any newsgroups, and asks whether you want to download a list of available newsgroups from your news server. Be aware that there are thousands and thousands of newsgroups on most servers, so downloading the whole list takes some time. Fortunately, you have to do this only once for each news account you establish. From time to time you will want to update this list, but updating does not take nearly as long.

Searching for Interesting Newsgroups

Once you have a list of available newsgroups, you can view it by:

1. Selecting a news account in the left pane of the Outlook Express window.

2. Clicking the Newgroups button on the toolbar. The Newsgroups window appears, as shown in Figure 23-8.

In the early days of the Internet, you could choose the newsgroups to which you wanted to subscribe just by scanning the list of available groups. By now, the number of groups has grown so large that this is a little like wandering through the stacks of a poorly organized library. Scrolling down this list can be an entertaining way to give yourself an idea of the kinds of things that are available, but it is not an efficient way to look for interesting newsgroups.

Fortunately, the Newsgroups window gives you a few tools to aid in your search. This window has three tabs:

■ **All**, showing the complete list of newsgroups available on this server.

- **Subscribed**, listing the (much smaller) list of newsgroups to which you have chosen to subscribe.

- **New**, showing the newsgroups that your server has added since the previous time you updated the newsgroup list.

Above each of these tabs is the Display Newsgroups Which Contain line. When this line is blank, a tab lists all the newsgroups appropriate to it. (That is, All lists all newsgroups.) Typing something onto this line restricts the list to newsgroups containing what you have typed. In Figure 23-8, for example, the All tab lists all newsgroups that have chicago somewhere in their names.

So, for example, if you want to know whether there is a newsgroup devoted to your favorite author or entertainer, go to the All tab of the Newsgroups window and type his or her last name into Display Newsgroups Which Contain. If you had already done that search last week, but want to know whether there are any new newsgroups you should look at, do the same thing with the New tab.

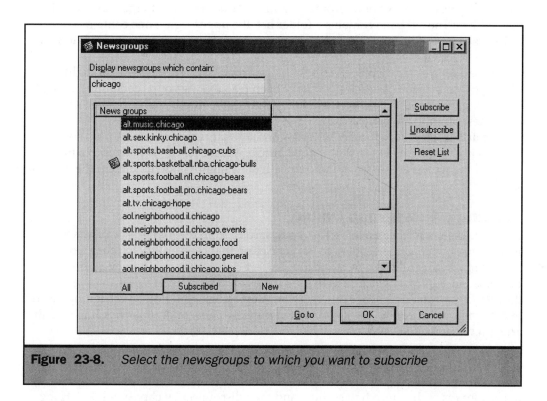

Figure 23-8. *Select the newsgroups to which you want to subscribe*

Subscribing to a Newsgroup (or Not)

Once you have found a newsgroup you want to try out:

1. Select its name in the Newsgroups window. (In Figure 23-8, alt.music.chicago is selected.)
2. Click the Subscribe button.

The newsgroup is now listed on the Subscribed tab of the Newsgroups window, and a folder corresponding to the newsgroup is automatically created as a subfolder of the news account folder. Whenever the newsgroup appears in the Newsgroups window, it has a newspaper icon next to it. For example, in Figure 23-8, alt.sports.basketball.nba.chicago-bulls has been subscribed to.

You can examine a newsgroup without subscribing to it by selecting it in the Newsgroups window and clicking the Go To button rather than the Subscribe button. Outlook Express downloads the headers of recent articles on a one-time-only basis.

Reading a Newsgroup

Outlook Express displays newsgroups in a format that is similar to the way it displays mail folders: The left pane contains a folder list, the upper-right pane contains an article list for the currently selected newsgroup, and the lower-right pane previews the currently selected article.

Unread articles are displayed in bold in the article list, and their icon is slightly different than the icon of articles that have been read. Newsgroups containing unread articles are displayed in bold on the folder list, with the number of unread articles in parentheses next to the name.

The article list groups articles with any articles that reply to them. A plus box appears in the margin next to the original article; when clicked, it changes to a minus sign and the replies are displayed underneath (and slightly indented from) the original article.

Reading a Newsgroup Online

If you are online, selecting a subscribed newsgroup from the folder list causes Outlook Express to download the headers of the articles on that newsgroup. In other words, the article list window fills up automatically. The articles themselves, however, are not downloaded until you select them in the article list. (The point of this is to save both download time and disk space on your computer.) When you find an intriguing header in the article list, click it to see its text in the preview pane, or double-click it to give the article a window of its own.

Reading a Newsgroup Offline

To read a newsgroup while spending the minimum amount of time online, download the headers as in the preceding section, and then disconnect by choosing File | Hang

Up. You can examine the headers of articles offline. When you find one you want, select it in the article window and then choose Tools | Mark For Retrieval | Mark Message. (If you want to read the entire thread or newsgroup, choose Mark Thread or Mark All Messages.) The next time you get online, Outlook Express downloads all the marked messages, which you can then read either online or offline.

Filtering a Newsgroup

After you've been reading a newsgroup for a while, you may notice that you are never interested in certain kinds of articles, or even that you find them irritating. Outlook Express allows you to filter a newsgroup so that you never even see these articles or their headers. Filtering a newsgroup gives you a more focused list of headers from which to choose, and saves download time.

You can filter out articles based on the following:

- **Who wrote them**   Almost any newsgroup has one or two regular contributors who rub you the wrong way. You need never see their articles.

- **The subject line**   Sometimes a subject drags on interminably, with one article answering another long after everything useful has already been said. You can stop paying attention.

- **Length**   If you know you're not interested in ten-page essays, you can tell Outlook Express not to download them.

- **How old they are**   Some newsgroups discuss timeless truths, and others consist of timely announcements. If you know that messages more than three days old are useless to you, you don't have to download them.

SETTING UP A NEWSGROUP FILTER   To set up a newsgroup filter:

1. Select a news folder or account in the folder list of the Outlook Express window.

2. Select Tools | Newsgroup Filters. The Newsgroup Filters dialog box appears. The Description window lists all the filtering criteria that you have previously set up. These criteria are on or off, depending on whether or not the boxes next to them are checked.

3. If you want to turn on (or off) a filter that you have previously established, click the box next to its description. Then click OK to close the dialog box.

4. If the filter you want is not listed in the Description window, click Add. The Newsgroup Filters Properties dialog box appears, as shown in Figure 23-9.

5. Select the newsgroup(s) you want to filter from the Group(s) drop-down list.

6. Fill out as many lines of the Do Not Show Messages That Meet The Following Criteria box as you want to (see "Working with the Filter Criteria").

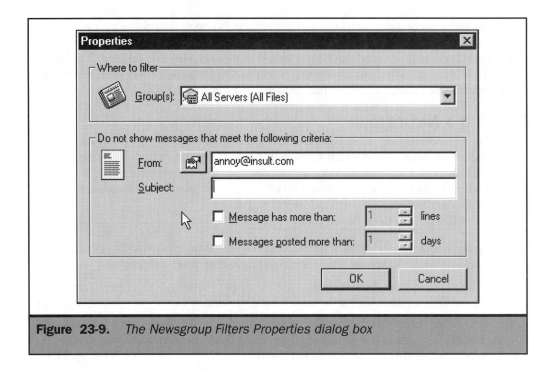

Figure 23-9. *The Newsgroup Filters Properties dialog box*

7. Click OK. The Properties dialog box closes, and the new filter is listed in the Description window of the Newsgroup Filters dialog box.

8. Click OK.

To edit a filter that you have already defined, select its description (not its check box) in the Newsgroup Filters dialog box, and then click the Properties button. The Properties dialog box opens, displaying the current criteria that define the filter. Change anything you want, and click OK.

WORKING WITH THE FILTER CRITERIA   Typing a string of characters into the From or Subject lines of the Newsgroup Filters Properties dialog box defines a criterion that eliminates anything containing that character string. For example, typing "King" (without the quote marks) into the From line eliminates not only any article written by King, but also by King Kong or Nanking. Similarly, typing "back" into Subject eliminates not only that boring discussion about back pains, but also the discussion of backgammon.

The lines Message Has More Than *xx* Lines and Message Posted More Than *xx* Days both work the same way. Click the check box, and then enter a number.

When you list several criteria in a single filter, Outlook Express puts them together with a logical AND operator. In other words, if you put "King" on the From line and "back" on the Subject line, you eliminate only those messages that satisfy both criteria. You won't see the articles that King Kong writes about back pain, but you will see King Kong's articles about bananas, and Dr. Scholl's articles about back pain.

If you want to put criteria together with a logical OR operator, use separate filters. For example, one filter could eliminate anything written by King, and another could eliminate anything with "back" in the subject line.

Saving Articles

Outlook Express saves the text of downloaded articles only until the end of the current session. When you close Outlook Express, the articles downloaded during that session are thrown away, unless you save them by selecting File | Save As. Articles are saved with the .nws extension.

Participating in a Newsgroup

Many people read a newsgroup for years and never respond to it in any way, neither writing e-mail messages to the authors of the articles they read, nor posting articles of their own. This is called *lurking*, and is a widely accepted practice. In fact, even if you do intend to post your own messages to a group eventually, we recommend that you lurk for a while first to learn the social norms of the group.

One alternative to lurking is to examine the archives of the newsgroup. Many newsgroups are archived at the web site **http://starbase.neosoft.com/~claird /news.lists/newsgroup_archives.html**.

Reading the FAQ

One use of a newsgroup is to ask questions about a subject, in the hope that someone more experienced can answer them for you. If, for example, you have just bought a gadget that is supposed to slice and dice, but you have only been able to make it slice, you might find that there is a newsgroup devoted to this product, to which you can address the question "How do I make it dice?" Unfortunately, the regular readers of this newsgroup (who are mainly interested in discussing the existential implications of slicing and dicing in this postmodern world) are probably sick to death of newbies interrupting their discussion to ask "How do you make it dice?" and are likely to make unpleasant and unhelpful suggestions.

To avoid problems like this, many newsgroups maintain a list of common answers to *Frequently Asked Questions* (*FAQ*). As a courtesy to the other readers of the newsgroup, you should check whether the FAQ answers your question, before you post it to the group. Typically, the FAQ is re-posted at regular intervals (usually monthly), so if you look at a month's worth of postings, you should find it. If that sounds like too much work, several web sites maintain archives of newsgroup FAQs. One such site is the International FAQ Consortium at **http://www.faqs.org/faqs**. A search engine at this web site will help you find the FAQ you are looking for.

Replying to Authors

Replying to the author of a newsgroup article is no different from replying to the author of a mail message. Just select the article and click the Reply To Author button on the toolbar. Outlook Express opens a mail message window with the author's e-mail address entered automatically in the recipient list. You can create and edit this message just as you would any other mail message.

Posting an Article to a Newsgroup

To begin creating a newsgroup article, select a newsgroup from the folder list of the Outlook Express window, so that the Outlook Express News toolbar replaces the Mail toolbar. You may then create an article in any of the following three ways:

- **Compose a new message from scratch**   Click the Compose Message button on the Outlook Express toolbar.

- **Reply to an article**   Select an article from the article list of a newsgroup and click the Reply To Group button on the toolbar. (Clicking the Reply To Author button creates a mail message addressed to the author of the selected article, and does not create an article to the newsgroup.)

- **Forward an article from one newsgroup to another**   Select an article from the article list of a newsgroup and click the Forward Message button on the toolbar.

Any of these actions creates a New Message window. Like an e-mail message window, it has a header and a body, as shown in Figure 23-10.

A news message header has three lines:

- **Newsgroups**   List the newsgroup(s) to which the article is to be posted. If you are replying to an article, Outlook Express inserts the newsgroup of the original article automatically. If you are composing a new message, Outlook Express inserts the currently selected newsgroup. If you are forwarding, this line is initially blank.

  To add newsgroups to the list, click the newspaper icon on the Newsgroups line of the header. The Pick Newsgroups dialog box appears. Its right pane lists the newsgroup(s) the article is currently addressed to, while its left pane lists the newsgroups you subscribe to. Clicking the button below the left pane causes the left pane to list all newsgroups, not just the ones you subscribe to. The line at the upper-left of the Pick Newsgroups window is labeled Type Name Or Select From List, which is what you do. When this line contains the name of a newsgroup you want to add to the Newsgroups To Post To list in the right pane, click the Add button. Repeat this process until the right pane lists all the newsgroups to which you want to post your article.

  If you change your mind about any of the newsgroups you have selected, select those newsgroups in the right pane and click the Remove button. When you are

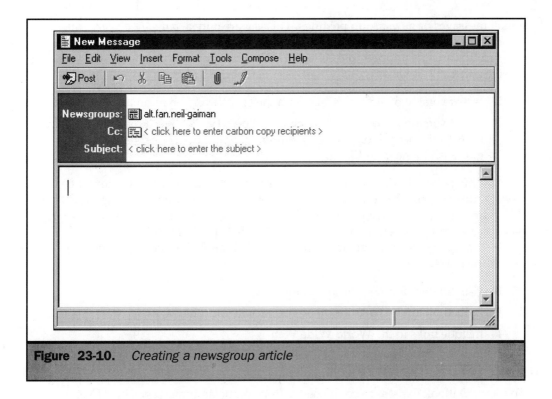

Figure 23-10.   *Creating a newsgroup article*

satisfied that you have just the right list of newsgroups, click OK to make the
Pick Newsgroups window vanish.

- **Cc**   If you want your article sent (as e-mail) to anyone, list their e-mail
  addresses in the Cc line of the header. Click the index card icon if you want to
  choose an address from the Address Book.

- **Subject**   Give your article a title. If you are replying or forwarding, the subject
  line is automatically the same as the original article, preceded by Re or Fwd.

After you have completed the header of your article, type the text into the body of
the New Message window, and then click the Post button. The article is then sent to
your Outbox, where it is treated the same as your outgoing mail messages (see
"Sending Messages").

Composing in HTML

Hypertext Markup Language (HTML) is the language that web pages are written in
(see "What Is HTML?" in Chapter 26). Outlook Express allows you to send HTML

e-mail messages or newsgroup postings. This is a great idea, *but only if your recipients are set up to receive HTML messages.* At the moment, most e-mail programs and newsgroups aren't equipped to receive HTML messages. Your recipients will probably receive either:

- A text version of your message with the HTML version as an attachment.
- A text version of your message either followed or preceded by a version in raw HTML—it sort of looks like text, but includes control codes that look like gibberish to the uninitiated.

At some point, HTML may well take over as the dominant language for e-mail and newsgroups, just as it has for web sites. But for now, we recommend using HTML *only* if you are sure that your recipient uses Outlook Express or some other e-mail program (such as Netscape Messenger or Eudora Pro 4.0) that speaks HTML.

Assuming that your recipient can read HTML, though, it opens up some very cool possibilities. You can:

- Use different fonts, sizes, and colors of text.
- Embed pictures, charts, or other graphics in your messages.
- Include links to the World Wide Web.

Turning HTML On and Off

To set up Outlook Express to compose (or stop composing) messages in HTML:

1. Select Tools | Options to open the Options dialog box.
2. Select the Send tab of the Options dialog box.
3. Choose either the Plain Text or HTML radio button in the Mail Sending Format box (for e-mail) and the News Sending Format Box (for newsgroups).

Composing HTML Messages

When Outlook Express is composing in HTML rather than plain text, the message box contains another toolbar (called the *formatting toolbar*) just below the header, as shown in Figure 23-11.

Most of the tools on the formatting toolbar are familiar if you have used a word processor. All of them are used by FrontPage Express, though the dialog boxes that appear may be slightly different (see Chapter 26). From left to right, the tools are the following:

- **Font Name**   Choose another font from the drop-down list.
- **Font Size**   Choose from the drop-down list.
- **Style Tag**   The drop-down list shows the choices of paragraph style.

- **Bold, Italic, Underline**
- **Font Color**   Click to see the palette.
- **Formatting Numbers**   For making numbered lists.
- **Formatting Bullets**   For making bulleted lists.
- **Increase/Decrease Indentation**
- **Align Left/Center/Right**
- **Insert Horizontal Lline**   Draws a dividing line across your message.
- **Insert Hyperlink**   Links text in your message to web addresses (see "Linking to the Web").
- **Insert Picture**   Inserts any image file into your message (see "Inserting Pictures").

Linking to the Web

If your message mentions a web page, or if a web page reference would back up the point you are making, why not link to it? If your recipients have HTML-reading e-mail

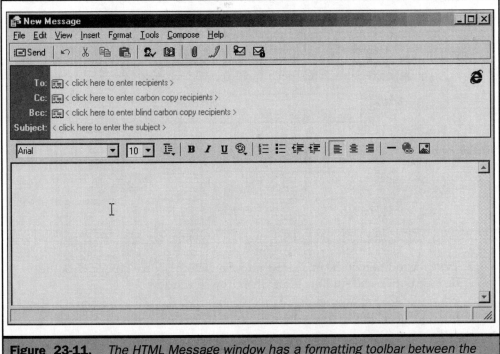

Figure 23-11.   *The HTML Message window has a formatting toolbar between the header and the body*

programs, they'll be able to open the page with their web browsers just by clicking the hyperlink in your message.

To insert a hyperlink into a message you are writing in HTML:

1. Select the text you want to link to the web.

2. Click the Insert Hyperlink button on the formatting toolbar, located below the header. The Hyperlink dialog box opens.

3. Select the web address prefix from the drop-down list of the Hyperlink dialog box.

4. Type the web address into the URL box of the Hyperlink dialog box.

5. Click OK. The selected text should now appear in a different color from the rest of the message.

Inserting Pictures

You can insert photographs, diagrams, charts, or any other image file into any message you compose in HTML.

1. Move the insertion point to the place in your message where you want the picture to be located.

2. Click the Insert Picture button on the formatting toolbar, below the header. The Picture dialog box appears, as shown here:

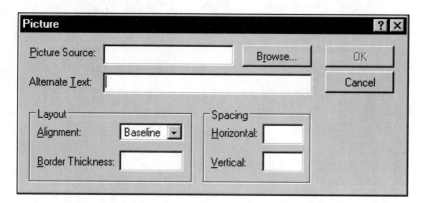

3. Type the location of the image file into the Picture Source box, or click the Browse button and find the file with a Browse window.

4. Type into the Alternate Text box the text that recipients will see if the picture (for whatever reason) is not displayed.

5. Choose the alignment from the drop-down list. This controls where the picture appears relative to the text.

6. Type a number into the Border Thickness box. This defines the width (in points) of a border surrounding the image.

7. Type numbers into the horizontal and vertical spacing boxes. These numbers define the width (in points) of a region of empty space surrounding the image.

8. Click OK. You see the image inserted into the message window.

If you want to change any of these decisions before you send the message, select the image in the message window and click Insert Picture on the formatting toolbar. The Picture dialog box opens with all your current choices. Change anything you want to change and click OK.

Using Stationery

To get you into the spirit of overformatted HTML, Outlook Express provides a choice of *stationery* for your e-mail messages. The Balloon Birthday stationery is shown in Figure 23-12.

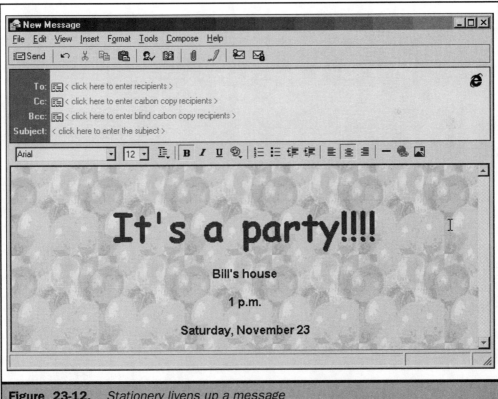

Figure 23-12. *Stationery livens up a message*

To choose stationery for your message:

1. Open a message window by either replying, forwarding, or composing a new message.

2. Choose a stationery from Format | Apply Stationery.

 Stationery makes your message about five times as large as it would be otherwise, and will not endear you to recipients who have to download their mail over a slow phone line. Also remember that recipients who don't have an HTML mail program will see your message as a very large message filled with meaningless binary data.

The
Complete
Reference

Chapter 24

Browsing the World Wide Web

The World Wide Web is (with e-mail) one of the two most popular Internet services. This chapter describes the concepts behind the Web, including HTML, URLs, browsers, the default web browser, and plug-ins. When you want to use the World Wide Web, this chapter describes how to set up your web browser and configure it, along with how to use the various buttons and menus that your browser displays.

The next chapter describes how to configure your browser, use web subscriptions and channels, find what you are looking for by using web guides and search engines, and control what your web browser can display.

What Is the World Wide Web?

The *World Wide Web* (usually just referred to as "the Web") is a collection of millions of files stored on thousands of computers (called *web servers*) all over the world. These files represent text documents, pictures, video, sounds, programs, interactive environments, and just about any other kind of information that has ever been recorded in computer files. It is probably the largest and most diverse collection of information ever assembled.

What unites these files is a system for linking one file to another and transmitting them across the Internet. HTML codes allow a file to contain links to related files (see "What Is HTML?"). Such a *link* (also called a *hyperlink*) contains the information necessary to locate the related file on the Internet. When you connect to the Internet and use a web browser program (see "What Is a Web Browser?"), you can read, view, hear, or otherwise interact with the Web without paying attention to whether the information you are accessing is stored on a computer down the hall or on the other side of the world. A news story stored on a computer in Singapore may link to a stock quote stored in New York, a picture stored in Frankfurt, and an audio file stored in Tokyo. The combination of the web servers, the Internet, and your web browser assembles this information seamlessly and presents it to you as a unified whole. This system of interlinked text, called *hypertext*, was first described in the 1960s by Ted Nelson, but it took thirty years for it to be widely used in the form of the World Wide Web.

By following links, you can get from almost any web document to almost any other web document. For this reason, some people like to think of the entire Web as being one big document. In this view, the links just take you from one part of the document to another.

An *intranet* is an internal network that uses the same communication protocols as the Internet, but is limited to a specific group, usually the employees in one company. Some organizations create private versions of the World Wide Web on their intranets, so that access to the web pages is limited to employees of that organization.

What Is HTML?

The *Hypertext Markup Language* (*HTML*) is the universal language of the Web. It is a language for laying out pages that are capable of displaying all the diverse kinds of information that the Web contains.

This chapter and the next discuss web browsers, which are programs that read and interpret HTML (see "What Is a Web Browser?"). Chapter 26 discusses programs that allow you to write your own web pages using HTML.

While various software companies own and sell HTML-reading and HTML-writing programs, no one owns the language HTML itself. It is an international standard, maintained and updated by a complicated political process that so far has worked remarkably well. The World Wide Web Consortium (W3C), at **http://www.w3c.org**, manages the HTML standard.

What Is a URL?

When the pieces of a document are scattered all over the world, but you want to display them seamlessly to a viewer who could be anywhere else in the world, you need a very good addressing system. Each file on the Internet has an address, called a *Uniform Resource Locator* (*URL*), also sometimes called an *Internet address* or *web address*. For example, the URL of the ESPN Sportzone web site is **http://espnet.sportzone.com**.

The first part of a URL specifies the *transfer protocol*, the method that a computer needs to use to access this file. Most web pages are accessed with the *Hypertext Transfer Protocol* (HTTP, the language of Web communication), which is why web addresses typically begin with http (or its secure versions, https or shttp). The http:// at the beginning of a web page's URL is so common that it often goes without saying; if you simply type **espnet.sportzone.com** into the address window of Internet Explorer or Netscape Navigator, the browser fills in the http:// for itself. In common usage, the http:// at the beginning of a URL is left out.

The rest of the address denotes the web page, but doesn't tell you where its files actually are located. Whether ESPN's web server is in Los Angeles or Bangkok is invisible from the URL. Information about which web server is responsible for answering requests for which URLs is contained in a huge database that the web servers themselves are constantly updating. As users, we don't need to deal with this level of detail, and that's a good thing. The World Wide Web would be much less usable if sports fans had to learn a new set of URLs every time ESPN got a new computer.

What Are Web Pages and Web Sites?

A *web page* is an HTML document that is stored on a web server and that has a URL so that it can be accessed via the Web.

A *web site* is a collection of web pages belonging to a particular person or organization. Typically, the URLs of these pages share a common prefix, which is the address of the *home page* of the site. The home page is the "front door" of the site, and is set up to help viewers find whatever is of interest to them on that site. The URL of the home page also serves as the URL of the web site.

For example, the URL of *TV Guide*'s home page is **http://www.tvguide.com**. From the home page, you can get to *TV Guide*'s gossip column, *The Daily Dish*, at **http://www.tvguide.com/dish**. A specific story in *The Daily Dish* is at **http://www.tvguide.com/dish/0122b.htm**.

What Is a Web Browser?

A *web browser* is a program that your computer runs to communicate with web servers on the Internet, so that it can download the documents you ask for and display them. At a bare minimum, a web browser has to be able to understand HTML and display text. In recent years, however, Internet users have come to expect a lot more. A state-of-the-art web browser provides a full multimedia experience, complete with pictures, sound, video, and even 3-D imaging.

The most popular browsers, by far, are Netscape Navigator and Microsoft Internet Explorer. Both are state-of-the-art browsers, and the competition between them is fierce. Both are regularly upgraded, so it is worthwhile to keep an eye on the Netscape and Microsoft web sites to see when new versions are available. Both are available over the Internet at no charge.

What Is Internet Explorer?

Internet Explorer is the web browser that comes with most versions of Windows 98 and is available for free from the Internet (from **http://www.microsoft.com/ie**). If your version of Windows 98 comes with Internet Explorer, it is ready to go as soon as you install Windows 98 and set up an Internet connection.

The Internet Explorer window that you see when you browse the Web is similar, but not identical, to the Folder window that you see when you look at folders on your own system (see "What Are Folder Windows and Windows Explorer Windows?" in Chapter 8). Technically, both are Internet Explorer windows, but the toolbar is *context sensitive*, which means that you get different toolbar buttons, depending on what you are looking at. Figure 24-1 gives two views of the Internet Explorer toolbar.

What Are Netscape Navigator and Netscape Communicator?

Netscape Navigator is the web browser that dominated the market prior to Microsoft's aggressive push of Internet Explorer (by bundling it with Windows 95, among other

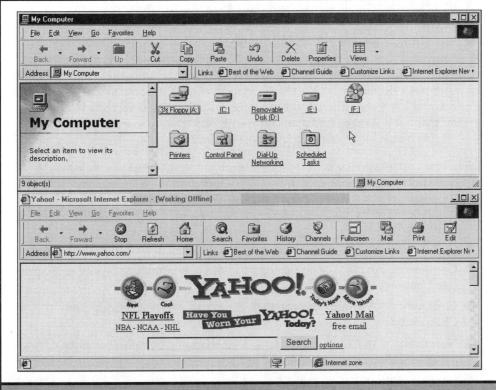

Figure 24-1.   *Internet Explorer's context-sensitive toolbar has one set of buttons (top) for folders, and another (bottom) for the Web*

tactics whose legitimacy is being decided in court). Though no longer as dominant, Navigator is a state-of-the-art browser that remains popular. You can acquire it in four ways:

- **Download it free from Netscape's web site at http://home.netscape.com.**   In January 1998, Netscape reversed its policy and made downloading Navigator and Communicator Standard Edition free. There is a small charge if you want Netscape to ship you the software on CD.

- **Get it free from your Internet service provider.**   The great majority of ISPs used to offer Navigator, but by now, Microsoft has induced most ISPs to favor Internet Explorer instead (by offering to mention the ISPs in Windows' Internet Connection Wizard, another tactic with antitrust implications for the courts to decide). To find an ISP in your area that still offers Navigator, your best bet is to search through Netscape's web site at **http://ispselect.netscape.com**.

- **Buy it at a store**.   This is the only way to get Netscape Navigator's printed manual.

- **Buy a computer that has it pre-installed**.   This is the main issue in a current court case. Compaq offered Netscape Navigator, and not Internet Explorer, pre-installed on some of its machines. Microsoft allegedly threatened to revoke Compaq's license to use Windows on its machines if Compaq did not pre-install Internet Explorer rather than Navigator, and Compaq reversed itself. At the moment, it is hard to find a machine with Navigator pre-installed, but this might change, depending on the court's rulings.

Netscape Communicator is Netscape's complete Internet package, of which Navigator is only one component. The other components are the following:

- **Messenger**   An e-mail and news client that is comparable to Outlook Express (see Chapter 23).

- **Collabra**   A tool for collaborative discussions in a newsgroup-like format.

- **Composer**   An HTML composing program comparable to FrontPage Express (see Chapter 26).

- **Conference**   A groupware product, comparable to NetMeeting (see Chapter 27).

- **Netcaster**   A tool for subscribing to web channels, comparable to the Channel bar (see "Subscribing to Channels" in Chapter 25).

What Is the Default Web Browser?

If you have web browsers on your system in addition to Internet Explorer, which one is used when you open a web shortcut or select a web page from the Favorites menu? At any given time, one of the browsers on your system is defined to be the *default web browser*, the one that Windows uses when you don't specify a particular browser. For example, if you open a web page by clicking or double-clicking its filename in Windows Explorer or a Folder window, Windows runs the default web browser to display the web page.

Your Internet shortcuts and HTML documents bear the icon of the current default web browser. You can easily check which browser is the default by looking at these icons, and then change the default browser if you prefer to use another browser as the default (see "Defining a Default Browser").

What Is a Browser's Home Page?

Your browser's home page (also called a *start page*) is the web page that the browser loads when you open the browser without requesting a specific page. You can also see the browser's home page by clicking the Home button on the toolbar of either Internet

Explorer or Navigator. (Don't confuse this use of "home page" with the home page of a web site—see "What Are Web Pages and Web Sites?".)

A good home page for your browser is one that loads quickly (so that you don't sit forever waiting for the first page to come up), contains information you want to check regularly (like headlines in your area of interest, or a local weather forecast), and links to a wide variety of other pages (so that you can go where you want quickly). Each browser has a default home page on its company's web site. In general, these are not bad home pages, and many people never change them. (Microsoft and Netscape count on that; the Internet Explorer and Navigator default home pages are some of the most valuable real estate in cyberspace.) But you can select any web page or file that you want to be your browser's home page (see "Choosing and Customizing Your Browser's Home Page").

What Are Plug-Ins?

Plug-ins are programs that are independent of your web browser, but that "plug in" to it in a seamless way, so that you may not even be aware that you are using software that is not part of Internet Explorer or Navigator. Typically, plug-ins arise when a software company develops a way to display a new type of data over the Web—3-D animation, for example. Rather than create a whole new browser with this additional capability, the software company writes a plug-in for Navigator or Internet Explorer. Users who want to extend the capabilities of their browser in this particular way can install the plug-in, which then operates as if it is part of the web browser.

A number of plug-ins (such as RealAudio for receiving streaming audio, or QuickTime for downloading video) have become standard accessories for Internet Explorer or Navigator, and are installed automatically when you install the web browser. To install other plug-ins, download them from the Internet (the web site at **http://www.tucows.com** has a wide variety), and then follow the directions that come with the plug-in (see "Downloading, Installing, and Running Other Internet Programs" in Chapter 28).

As with any kind of software, downloading and installing a plug-in requires faith in whoever created and distributed the plug-in. A plug-in theoretically could introduce viruses into your system, or modify files without your consent, or transmit data from your machine without your knowledge. Plug-ins from reputable software companies are as safe as any other kind of Internet software, but you should be cautious about downloading plug-ins from web sites that you know nothing about.

Setting Up a Web Browser

If Internet Explorer comes with your copy of Windows 98, it is installed automatically when you install Windows 98. If Netscape Navigator or Communicator comes with your Internet service provider account, it may be installed automatically when you set up your Internet account. If not, you can install Navigator or Communicator either from the CD-ROM that you get by purchasing the software in a store, or by opening the file that you download from the Netscape web site. In either case, once you start the process, a Wizard guides you through the installation.

To run Internet Explorer, choose Start | Programs | Internet Explorer | Internet Explorer. To run Navigator (if it is installed), choose Start | Programs | Netscape Communicator | Netscape Navigator or click the Internet Explorer icon on the Taskbar.

Uninstalling Internet Explorer—Don't Try

One difference between Windows 98 and any previous version of Windows is that uninstalling Internet Explorer is no longer a simple matter, and we recommend that you not try it. (This is one of many subjects in a complex legal battle, and Microsoft may be forced to make a last-minute change to Windows 98 after this book is printed.) By making Internet Explorer an integral part of the operating system, Microsoft has eliminated one of Netscape's selling points. Navigator takes up less disk space than Internet Explorer, but to take advantage of this feature you would have to install Navigator *in place of* Internet Explorer, not *in addition to* it. If you can't uninstall Internet Explorer, Navigator's compactness is of little value.

Defining a Default Browser

When you install a new browser on your system, the installation wizard usually asks whether this should be your default browser. If you click Yes, then any HTML document or Internet shortcut on your system carries the icon of the new browser, and opening that document or shortcut opens the new browser. (Even when another browser is open, its links should bear the icon of the default browser. For example, the Internet Explorer links on the Links toolbar in Figure 24-5, later in this chapter, display the Communicator icon.)

Even if Internet Explorer is not the default browser, it is still used to display Folder windows. You can open any browser by choosing Start | Programs or by opening its icon on the desktop, regardless of whether it is the default. Once a browser is running, you can use it to open any web page.

When you run a browser that is not currently the default browser, it typically asks whether you want to make it the default browser—unless you have clicked the box telling it to stop asking you that question. You can define Internet Explorer to be the default browser even if it no longer asks. In Internet Explorer, choose View | Internet Options. When the Internet Options dialog box appears, go to the Programs tab. Click the check box labeled Internet Explorer Should Check To See Whether It Is The Default Browser.

Defining User Profiles

Internet Explorer inherits its user profiles from Windows (see "What Is a User Profile?" in Chapter 33). Anyone who has a Windows user name has his or her own Favorites list, History folder, and preferences in Internet Explorer.

Navigator does not inherit user profiles from Windows. If more than one person uses Navigator on your computer, and if you want each user to be able to have a Bookmarks file, a History list, and preferences that are independent of the other users', each person must define a user profile within Navigator.

 Because Navigator has its own user profiles, your Navigator user name may be different from your Windows user name, although we recommend that you make the names the same.

To set up, remove, or rename a Netscape user profile, follow these steps:

1. If Navigator is running, exit by selecting File | Exit.

2. Choose Start | Programs | Netscape Communicator | Utilities | User Profile Manager. The Profile Manager dialog box opens.

3. To remove or rename an existing user profile, select it from the list and click the Remove or Rename button. If you are renaming the profile, enter the new name in the dialog box that appears.

4. To create a new user profile, click the New button. The Profile Setup Wizard starts.

5. Enter the information the Wizard requests. You need to know the names of the new user's mail and news servers, and the new user's e-mail address.

Setting Your Preferences

You see Internet Explorer preferences on the Internet Properties dialog box (shown in Figure 24-2), which you access by opening the Internet icon on the Control Panel. From the name, and from its appearance on the Control Panel, you might expect the Internet Properties dialog box to set properties for any web browser on your system, but it does not. You can access the same dialog box from within Internet Explorer by selecting View | Internet Options. You set Navigator preferences on its own Preferences dialog box (shown in Figure 24-3), which you access by selecting Edit | Preferences from Navigator's menu bar.

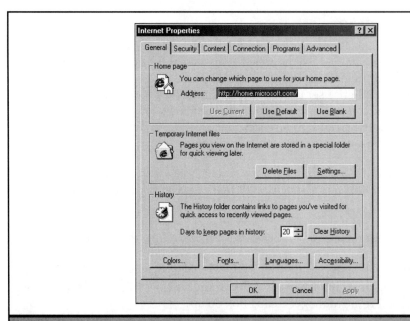

Figure 24-2. The Internet Properties (or Internet Options) dialog box is used for Internet Explorer, not Navigator

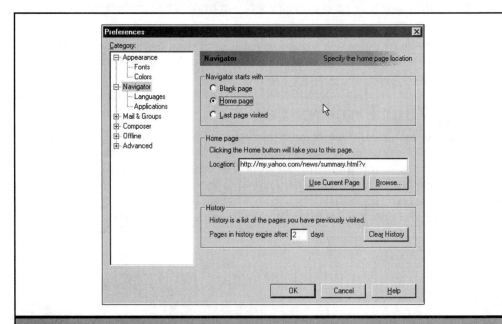

Figure 24-3. Control how Navigator looks and acts from its Preferences dialog box

Inexplicably, Microsoft has given the same dialog box two different names. When you access the Internet Properties dialog box from within Internet Explorer by selecting View | Internet Options, it's titled the Internet Options dialog box. It's the same dialog box—only the title bar is different. We kept expecting Microsoft to pick one name or the other, but in the most recent version of Windows 98 we could lay our hands on, the dialog box still had two names.

The Navigator Preferences dialog box has two panes. The left pane is a list of the categories of preferences. Click the plus box to the left of a category to see its sub-categories. One category is highlighted, and the controls for that preference category are shown in the right pane. To access any of the preference controls, click the category in the left pane, and then express your preferences in the right pane.

Choosing Fonts

Navigator has a very simple way to expand or shrink the size of the text on a web page, without making any permanent changes to the way it displays text: select View | Increase Font or View | Decrease Font. Internet Explorer gives you a similar capability, using either View | Fonts or the Font button on the toolbar. To make this button appear, go to the Advanced tab of the Internet Properties dialog box and check the Show Font Button check box. For each browser, the changed font size applies to the current session only, and is forgotten when you exit.

Navigator and Internet Explorer have similar dialog boxes for making longer-lasting changes in the fonts they use to display text. Control the fonts Internet Explorer uses by clicking the Fonts button on the General tab of the Internet Properties dialog box. The Fonts dialog box opens, shown in Figure 24-4. In Navigator, click Fonts in the Categories window of the Preferences dialog box.

Each of these dialog boxes contains the same basic elements:

- **A list of character sets, or alphabets** In Internet Explorer this list is in a window labeled Character Sets, and the selected character set is highlighted. Navigator has a drop-down list labeled For The Encoding, and the selected character set is the one visible when the list is retracted. In English-language versions of these browsers, the default character set is Western.

- **Drop-down lists specifying the proportional (or variable-width) font and the fixed-width font for the selected character set** Change the font by picking a new one from the list. Change the font size in Navigator by typing a point size into the boxes next to the font names. Change the font size in Internet Explorer by choosing from a drop-down list that goes from smallest to largest. The default proportional font for the Western character set is Times New Roman (12 point), and the default fixed-width font is Courier New (10 point). Internet Explorer lists both of these default sizes as Medium.

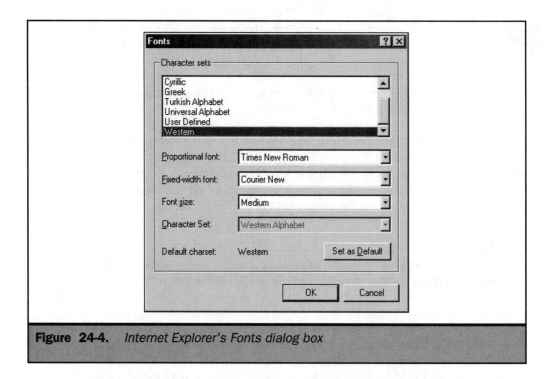

Figure 24-4.   *Internet Explorer's Fonts dialog box*

Navigator's Fonts page also contains a set of radio buttons that let you decide whether your font choices should override those of the web page author, in case the web page specifies a font. To find these choices in Internet Explorer, click the Accessibility button on the General tab of the Internet Properties dialog box.

Choosing Colors

You can change the colors your browser uses to display text, backgrounds, and links. To change the color of the text and background in Internet Explorer, click the Colors button on the General tab of the Internet Properties dialog box. In Navigator, click Colors in the Categories window of the Preferences dialog box. The two dialog boxes are almost identical.

In each case, the default is to use Windows colors—that is, the colors defined on the Appearance tab of the Display Properties dialog box (see "Designing and Decorating Your Desktop" in Chapter 13).

If you don't want to use the Windows colors:

1. Remove the check from the Use Windows Colors check box.

2. Click the colored button next to the Text or Background labels. A palette of colors appears.

3. Click the color you want for the Text or Background, and then click OK to make the palette disappear. The button next to Text or Background should now be the color you selected.

4. Click OK to make the Colors dialog box go away.

Changing the colors used for links is a similar process, except that you don't need to remove the check from Use Windows Colors. The Internet Explorer Colors dialog box also allows you to define a *hover color*, a color that links change to when the cursor is over them.

Internet Explorer has other accessibility features for the visually impaired (see Chapter 20).

 We suggest you leave the colors alone, except perhaps for making the background color white (if it's not white already).

Changing Language Preferences

Some web pages are available in multiple languages, and your web browser picks the one that matches your preferences. To define or change your language preferences in Internet Explorer, click the Languages button near the bottom of the General tab of the Internet Properties dialog box to open the Language Preferences dialog box. In Navigator, open the Preferences dialog box and click Languages in the Category list. The Internet Explorer and Navigator dialog boxes are quite similar.

The purpose of each of these dialog boxes is to maintain a list of favored languages, in order, with your preferred language on top. Add a language to the list by clicking the Add button and selecting a language from the list that appears. Remove a language from the Language list by selecting it and clicking the Remove button. Reorder the Languages list by selecting a language on the list and clicking the Move Up or Move Down buttons in Internet Explorer, or the up and down arrow buttons in Navigator. When you are satisfied with the list of languages, click OK.

Choosing Whether to Download Images, Audio, and Video

Many web pages have pictures or other graphics on them. These are more time-consuming to download than text, so if your connection is slow, you may decide not to bother downloading graphics. Many web pages also have multimedia content, such as audio, video, or animation. These are even slower to download, and you can tell Internet Explorer to ignore them, too. To do this, go to the Advanced tab of the Internet Properties dialog box. Scroll down until you see the Multimedia heading. Remove the check from each box next to any type of content that you want to ignore.

To control image downloading in Navigator, click Advanced on the Category list of the Preferences dialog box. If the Automatically Load Images check box is not checked, Navigator does not download the images on a web page. If you are viewing a page whose images are not being displayed, you can display them (for this page only, without changing the policy) by selecting View | Show Images.

Choosing and Customizing Your Browser's Home Page

The home page or start page is the page that your browser looks up when you start your browser without choosing a specific page.

Customizing Internet Explorer's Home Page

Choose a new home page for Internet Explorer from the Internet Properties dialog box. You can open this box either by choosing View | Internet Options from Internet Explorer's menu bar, or by opening the Internet icon on the Control Panel. The Internet Properties dialog box opens with the General tab on top. You can type the URL of the new home page into the Home Page box on this tab, or you can click one of the following buttons:

- **Use Current**   The page currently displayed by Internet Explorer becomes the home page. (If Internet Explorer is not open, this button is grayed out.) This can be any page on the Web, or even an HTML document on your hard drive.

- **Use Default**   The home page becomes **http://www.microsoft.com**.

- **Use Blank**   The home page is blank. This is handy if you want Internet Explorer to start up as quickly as possible, and don't necessarily want to invoke your Internet connection.

Microsoft allows you to customize the default home page so that it reflects your preferences. For example, you can include a local weather forecast or a link to your local city guide. You can see an example of a customized Microsoft home page in Figure 24-5. Clicking the Personalize link at the top of the default home page takes you to a questionnaire about your preferences.

Customizing Navigator's Home Page

Navigator regards the home page (which you reach by clicking the Home button on the toolbar) as different from the start page (which opens when Navigator starts up). Change either page by choosing Edit | Preferences. Then select Navigator in the Category box.

The Navigator Starts With box gives you three choices for your start page: It can be the same as the home page, a blank page, or the last page that you visited in your previous session.

Change the home page by entering a URL into the Location line, or by clicking the Use Current Page button (to make the page Navigator is currently displaying the home page) or the Browse button (if you want the home page to be a page on your system).

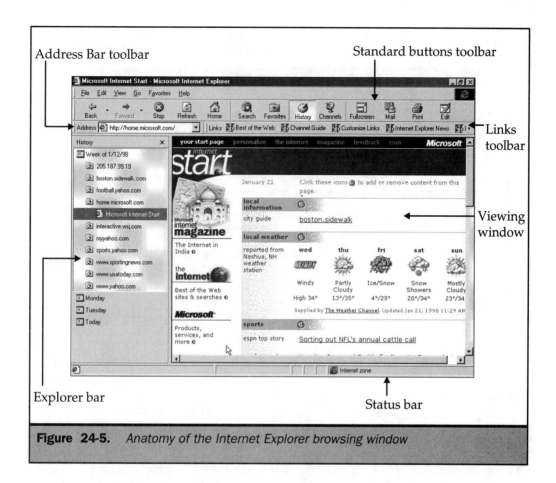

Figure 24-5. *Anatomy of the Internet Explorer browsing window*

Choosing a Different Home Page

Lots of web sites would like to be your home page, because they can sell advertising based on the number of viewers they get. Many allow you to customize the page to get local weather, headlines in your areas of interest, scores for your favorite teams, quotes for the stocks you own, and so on. The competition is intense, and all the competitors add features as fast as they can think of them. None of them charge a fee for this service. Some of the industry leaders are Yahoo! (**http://my.yahoo.com**), Excite (**http://my.excite.com**), and C I net (**http://www.snap.com**). A customized Yahoo! home page is shown in Figure 24-6.

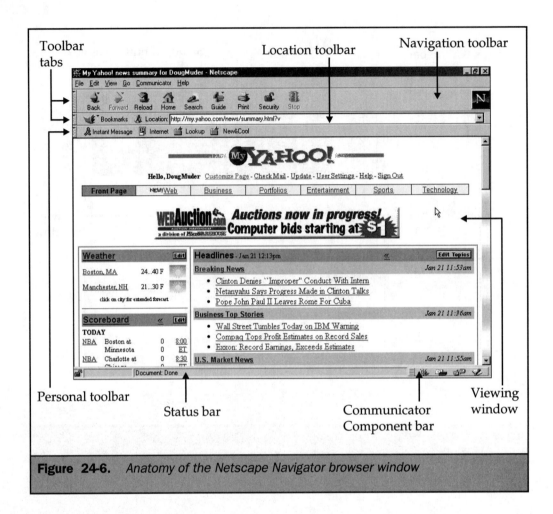

Figure 24-6.   *Anatomy of the Netscape Navigator browser window*

Making Your Own Start Page

Your browser's start page can be a file on your own computer. This lets you control what's on the page, and provides very fast browser startup. Often, a simple page with links to your favorite web sites is more useful than any outside page.

You can create a simple web page by using FrontPage Express or any other web page editor (see Chapter 26). Then, view the file containing the page in your browser, and tell your browser to make that your home or start page.

If you use Netscape, your bookmarks are stored in a file called Bookmark.htm, usually stored in C:\Program Files\Netscape\Users*yourname*. If you make that file your start page, your browser will start up displaying links to all of your bookmarks. We find this very convenient.

Working with the Browsing Window

The main window of Internet Explorer or Navigator provides you with an array of menus, buttons, labels, and information displays. Depending on what you are trying to do, and how familiar you are with the workings of the browser, these elements may be either useful tools or distracting clutter. Fortunately, most of what you see can be customized, so that you can display exactly what you find worthwhile.

Configuring the Internet Explorer Browsing Window

When all of its components are made visible, the Internet Explorer browsing window looks like Figure 24-5. From top to bottom, it contains:

- **Menu bar** Visible at all times, not configurable.

- **Standard buttons toolbar** The same toolbar you see in Folder windows (see "What Are the Buttons on the Standard Buttons Toolbar?" in Chapter 8). This is the toolbar we are referring to if we don't specify which toolbar we mean. It can be hidden, or displayed in a variety of ways. To hide this toolbar, uncheck View | Toolbars | Standard Buttons. Remove the labels from the buttons (and consequently shrink the amount of space needed) by unchecking View | Toolbars | Text Labels. Make the icons smaller by checking the Small Icons box on the Advanced tab of the Internet Properties box. Add a Fonts button by checking the Add Fonts Button box on the Advanced tab of the Internet Properties box. Any of these decisions can be reversed with the same check box or toggle.

- **Address Bar toolbar** Displays the URL of the currently displayed web page, or the Windows address of the currently displayed local file. Hide the Address Bar by unchecking View | Toolbars | Address Bar. Expand or shrink the Address Bar by dragging the right boundary.

- **Links toolbar** A row of icons linked to web pages that Microsoft would like you to keep in mind. The Links toolbar doesn't usually have a line to itself—it takes the right side of whatever bar sits above the viewing window. Hide Links by unchecking View | Toolbars | Links. Expand or shrink this toolbar by dragging the left boundary.

- **Explorer bar** Displays Search, History, Favorites, or Channels (see "What Is the Explorer Bar?" in Chapter 8) in a pane down the left side of the Internet Explorer window. Choose which of these to display from the View | Explorer Bar menu. Hide these by selecting View | Explorer Bar | None, or by clicking the X in the upper-right corner of the Explorer bar. You can drag the border between the Explorer bar and the Viewing window.

- **Viewing window** Displays web pages. It can't be hidden, since otherwise there would be no point in running a browser. Maximize the viewing window by clicking the Fullscreen button on the toolbar. Return to the previous (unmaximized) state by clicking Fullscreen again.

- **Status bar** Displays a variety of useful information. When the cursor passes over a link in the viewing window, the URL of the link is displayed in the status bar. When Internet Explorer is looking for or downloading a web page, the status bar keeps you apprised of its progress. Hide the status bar by unchecking View | Status Bar.

Configuring the Navigator Browsing Window

When all of its components are made visible, Navigator's browsing window looks like Figure 24-6. From top to bottom, it contains:

- **Menu bar** Visible at all times, not configurable.
- **Toolbar tabs** Each visible toolbar has a vertical tab on its left edge. Clicking the tab makes the toolbar disappear. The tab then turns horizontal and moves to a narrow bar just above the Viewing window, as if the toolbar has been folded up. Clicking the horizontal tab makes the toolbar reappear. The tab disappears completely if you choose the View | Hide command for that toolbar.
- **Navigation toolbar** We usually just refer to this as the toolbar. Hide or restore the toolbar by clicking its toolbar tab, or from the View menu. Configure the toolbar by opening the Preferences dialog box and clicking Appearance in the Category list. The Show Toolbar As box gives you three choices: Pictures And Text, Pictures Only, and Text Only. Choose one and click OK.
- **Location toolbar** This contains the Bookmarks menu, a draggable bookmark for the current page, and the Location box, which shows either the URL of the currently displayed page or the Windows address of the currently displayed local file. Hide or restore the Location toolbar by clicking its toolbar tab, or from the View menu.
- **Personal toolbar** Similar to the Links toolbar in Internet Explorer, the Personal toolbar contains links to various Netscape web sites. It may also contain an icon for AOL Instant Messenger, a free service that allows you to send immediate messages to other AOL Instant Messenger users who are online. Hide or restore this toolbar with its toolbar tab, or from the View menu.
- **Viewing window** Displays web pages.
- **Status bar** Similar to the Status bar in Internet Explorer.
- **Communicator Component bar** Clicking an icon opens the corresponding component of Communicator. Clicking the tab on the left of this bar turns it into a movable toolbar with text labels.

Working with Browser Toolbars

Navigator and Internet Explorer have very similar toolbars. If you are familiar with one, the other is easy to learn.

Using Buttons Common to Both Browsers

Several buttons are common to the toolbars of both browsers: Back, Forward, Print, Stop, Home, Search, and Refresh/Reload.

- The Back, Forward, and Print buttons are just like those on the Folder window Standard Buttons toolbar (see "What Are the Buttons on the Standard Buttons Toolbar?" in Chapter 8). Back and Forward have drop-down menus that let you choose from the most recently visited web pages. In Internet Explorer, these are accessed just as they would be in a Folder window—by clicking the arrow to the right of the button. In Navigator, access these menus by right-clicking the button.

- The Stop button is active only when the browser is in the process of downloading a page from the Web; clicking it stops this process.

- The Home button is linked to the browser's home or start page. To redefine the home page, see "Choosing and Customizing Your Browser's Home Page," earlier in this chapter.

- The Navigator Search button sends you to Netscape's Net Search page, which contains links to most of the major search engines, web guides, online white and yellow pages, as well as more-specialized search tools. The Internet Explorer Search button opens one of the major search engines in the Explorer bar.

- The Internet Explorer Refresh button and the Navigator Reload button do approximately the same thing—ask the server to send the most recent version of the page currently being viewed. When a page is updated on the server, the new version is not automatically sent out to anyone who might be viewing an older version. Pushing Refresh/Reload makes sure you have the latest version. Clicking Reload causes Navigator to check whether the server has a more recent version of the web page you are viewing. If there is a more recent version, it is downloaded; if not, the page is reloaded from Navigator's cache. Pressing the SHIFT key while you click Reload downloads the page from the server whether there is a new version or not.

- The Print button does the obvious thing—sends the current web page to the printer.

Using Buttons Specific to Internet Explorer

Several buttons on the Internet Explorer toolbar don't correspond to anything on the Navigator toolbar: Favorites, History, Channels, Fullscreen, Mail, Edit, and Fonts.

■ The Favorites, History, and Channels buttons display the Favorites, History, or Channels folder trees on the Explorer Bar.

■ The Fullscreen button shrinks all icons and toolbars to maximize the viewing area. If the browser window is already in full-screen mode, clicking the Fullscreen button again returns the browser window to its previous state.

■ The Mail button opens your designated e-mail client. By default, this is Outlook Express, but if you have named another client such as Eudora on the Programs tab of the Internet Properties dialog box, that program opens instead.

■ The Edit button opens the currently displayed page in your designated HTML composing application. By default, this is FrontPage Express, but if you have named another HTML composing application on the Programs tab of the Internet Properties dialog box, that program opens instead.

■ The Fonts button lets you increase or decrease the size of all the fonts on the web pages you view, without changing Internet Explorer's default settings. This button is optional. To put it on your toolbar, check the Show Font Button icon on the Advanced tab of the Internet Properties dialog box.

Using Buttons Specific to Navigator

The Guide and Security buttons on the Navigator toolbar do not match up with any buttons on the Internet Explorer toolbar.

■ Guide links to Netscape Guide, a site developed for Netscape by Yahoo!. It resembles the personalizable start page that Yahoo! offers for free on its own site.

■ Clicking the Security button takes you to the Netscape security information screen. This screen lets you review and reset your policies for accepting Java applets, using encryption, passwords, and other security issues.

Understanding Browser Display Conventions

On a standard web page, text phrases that are linked to other web pages are displayed in underlined blue type. If you have recently displayed the web page to which the text is linked, the text is displayed in maroon. When you are exploring a web site, this feature lets you know where you've been and keeps you from going in circles. In Internet Explorer you can also define the color a link turns when the cursor is above it (the default is red). You can change these colors (see "Choosing Colors").

When you pass the mouse pointer over a linked object (including a linked text phrase), the pointer changes from an arrow to a hand, and the URL of the web page that the object is linked to is displayed in the status bar of the browser window (if you have the status bar enabled). Not all links on a page are obvious; a small picture, for example, might just be an illustration, or it might be linked to a larger version of the same picture. Passing the mouse pointer over an object is the easiest way to tell whether it is linked.

While files are being downloaded to your web browser, the mouse pointer changes to an hourglass. However, it is still functional—you can push buttons or scroll the window with an hourglass pointer. Most importantly, you can use it to click the Stop button if a link is taking longer to download than you're willing to wait.

Chapter 25

Working with Your Browser

Y our web browser is one of the most powerful programs in your computer. Although basic browsing is extremely easy, many facilities exist to make the browsing experience faster, richer, and easier, including favorites (also called bookmarks), subscriptions (or channels), cookies, various types of applets, and Microsoft Wallet.

Your browser displays various buttons and menus (many of which you can configure) in addition to the web page you are looking at. Unlike web pages that wait for you to display them using your browser, subscriptions and channels come to you, using the Channel bar or Netscape's Netcaster.

Once you start to browse the Web, finding what you are looking for can be hard, so this chapter describes web guides and search engines, as well as ways to control what your web browser can display. You can get more information about both Internet Explorer and Netscape Navigator from—where else?—the Web.

What Are Internet Shortcuts, Favorites, and Bookmarks?

Even though URLs are a step up from needing to know the exact computer that contains the information you want, they are still not very easy to remember, and mistyping one can take you someplace totally unexpected. Favorites, bookmarks, and Internet shortcuts are all ways to get your computer to remember URLs, so that you don't have to.

What Are Internet Shortcuts?

Shortcuts are files that you can put on your desktop (or anywhere you like) as placeholders for other files on your system (see "What Is a Shortcut?" in Chapter 9). Internet shortcuts work the same way, except that they have a different file extension (.url) and point to pages on the Web rather than files on your system.

If, for example, you have an online brokerage account, you can define an Internet shortcut called My Broker.url and put its icon on your desktop (see "Creating Internet Shortcuts" later in this chapter). The URL is contained in the shortcut file, so you don't need to remember it. When you open the shortcut, Windows connects to your Internet account, starts your default web browser, and displays the web page of your broker.

What Are Favorites?

Favorites are entries in a folder of shortcuts and Internet shortcuts, accessible by choosing Start | Favorites (see "What Are Favorites and the Favorites Menu?" in Chapter 12). Choosing an entry on the Favorites menu has the same effect as opening the corresponding shortcut or Internet shortcut. Internet Explorer uses the Favorites folder to keep track of the web sites to which you want to return.

The location of the active Favorites folder depends on whether or not your computer has user profiles (see "What Is a User Profile?" in Chapter 33). If the user profiles feature is off, the entries you see when you choose Start | Favorites are those stored in the folder C:\Windows\Favorites. If the user profiles feature is on, it shows the entries in C:\Windows\Profiles*your user name*\Favorites.

What Are Bookmarks?

The Bookmarks menu is Navigator's version of a Favorites menu. Clicking the Bookmarks button on Navigator's toolbar displays a menu of favorite web pages. Choosing an entry from that menu tells Navigator to display the corresponding web page.

Although bookmarks work like favorites, bookmarks technically are quite different. While favorites are stored in a folder of shortcuts, bookmarks are stored in an HTML file of links. The location of this file is C:\Program Files\Netscape\Users*your Netscape user name*\bookmark.htm. The user name, in this case, is the one that you defined while installing Communicator or created later in Navigator or another one of Communicator's components. It could be different from your Windows user name, although normally the two names are the same.

What Are Subscriptions and Channels?

A *subscription* is an automatic process for checking a web site for new content, and possibly downloading it to your hard drive for examination offline. For example, rather than connecting to your favorite newspaper's web site just before leaving for work (when everyone else does), and dealing with the delays involved in downloading the stories you want, you can tell Internet Explorer or Netscape's Netcaster to subscribe to the newspaper's web site. You can set up the subscription so that your computer connects to the Internet automatically at some low-traffic hour (like 3 a.m.) and downloads any new web pages from the newspaper's site. Then, when you are ready to read the morning paper, the web pages are already on your hard drive, so you can read them offline without any transmission delays. If your computer is portable, you can read the web pages anywhere, whether you have access to a phone line or not.

A second type of subscription automatically keeps track of the new or revised web pages at a site, but does not download them. This provides a simple way to keep track of a web site, without taking the time to browse through it on a regular basis.

A *channel* is a method of organizing a web site according to a subscription model. In addition to HTML files, a channel contains files in *channel definition format* (*CDF*, with extension .cdf). While an HTML file contains only information about how to display content, CDF files also allow tags that say something about the content itself. This feature makes it easier for a browser to make automatic decisions about what to download based on your preferences.

A random sampling of the channels available at the time of this writing, however, is not particularly impressive. Most channels automatically download little more than headlines or a table of contents and some ads. To see the stories or features to which the headlines refer, you must go online, just as you do when accessing a web site in the usual way. For now, you may find little practical difference between subscribing to a channel and having a comparable web site on your Favorites or Bookmarks menu of your web browser.

Both subscriptions and channels are examples of what has become known as *push technology*. In ordinary web browsing, you search for and "pull" in the information you want. In a "push" model of the Web, by contrast, you don't request each page your browser receives. Instead, you subscribe to a web site or a channel, and your browser receives whatever pages that web site or channel "pushes."

For directions on how to use either Internet Explorer or Netscape Netcaster to subscribe to web sites or channels, see "Subscribing to Web Sites and Channels," later in this chapter.

What Are Cookies?

A *cookie* is a small (at most 4K) file that a web server can store on your machine. Its purpose is to allow a web server to personalize a web page, depending on whether you have been to that web site before, and what you may have told it during previous sessions. For example, when you establish an account with an online retailer, or subscribe to an online magazine, you may be asked to fill out a form that includes some information about yourself and your preferences. The web server may store that information (along with information about when you visit the site) in a cookie on your machine. When you return to that web site in the future, the retailer's web server can read its cookie, recall this information, and structure its web pages accordingly.

Much has been written about whether cookies create a security or privacy hazard for you. If your web browser is working properly, the security hazard is minimal. It is, at first glance, unsettling to think that web servers are storing information on your hard drive without your knowledge. But cookies are not executable programs. They cannot, for example, search for and accumulate information from elsewhere on your system. They simply record information that you have already given to the web server.

Cookies do make it easier for advertising companies to gather information about your browsing habits. For example, a company that advertises on a large number of web sites can use cookies to keep track of where you have seen its ads before, and which ads (if any) you clicked on. If this possibility bothers you, both Navigator and Internet Explorer let you control their use of cookies, including the option to disable the storage of all cookies (see "Managing Cookies" later in this chapter).

Unfortunately, none of the Internet Explorer options for avoiding cookies is really satisfactory. Disabling all cookies blows away the utility of personalized web sites; for example, we were unable to log on to My Yahoo!, or access any other site that requires a password. You can require Internet Explorer ask you whether to accept each cookie that a web site offers, but you will spend more time answering questions than browsing the web. In addition to these options, Navigator lets you accept only those cookies that get sent back to the originating server—a good compromise.

What Are Java, JavaScript, VBScript, and ActiveX?

Java is a language for sending small applications (called *applets*) over the Web, so that they can be executed by your computer. *JavaScript* is a language for extending HTML to embed small programs called *scripts* in web pages. The main purpose of applets and scripts is to speed up the interactivity of web pages; rather than interacting with a distant web server, you interact with an applet or script that the web server runs on your machine. Java and JavaScript are also used for animation; rather than transmitting the frames of an animation over the Internet, the web server sends an animation-constructing applet or script that runs on your computer. Typically, this process is invisible to the user—the interaction or the animation just happens, without calling your attention to how it happens.

VBScript, a language that resembles Microsoft's Visual Basic, can be used to add scripts to pages that are displayed by Internet Explorer. Anything that VBScript can do, JavaScript (which Microsoft calls JScript) can do, too, and vice versa.

ActiveX controls, like Java, are a way to embed executable programs into a web page. Unlike Java and JavaScript, but like VBScript, ActiveX is a Microsoft system that is not used by Navigator. When Internet Explorer encounters a web page that uses ActiveX controls, it checks to see whether that particular control is already installed, and if it is not, Internet Explorer installs the control on your machine.

Some people are squeamish about the idea of a strange web server running applications on their machine without their knowledge, and their concerns are not entirely unjustified. These programming systems have security safeguards, but from time to time, bugs are found either in the programming languages themselves or in the way that they have been implemented by a particular browser or on a particular machine. These bugs involve some security risk. You can disable all three systems (see "Managing Your Web Browser").

 ActiveX controls are considerably more dangerous than JavaScript or VBScript scripts or Java applets. The latter three are run in a "sandbox" inside your web browser, which limits the accidental or deliberate damage they can do, while ActiveX controls are programs with full access to your computer's resources.

Netscape and Microsoft have a strong interest in reacting quickly to fix the security holes that people discover in their browsers, which is a good reason to check their web sites (at **http://home.netscape.com** and **http://www.microsoft.com**) periodically to make sure that you are running the most recent versions of Navigator or Internet Explorer. See "What Security Do Web Browsers Offer?" in Chapter 33 for details about the security features of Internet Explorer and Navigator.

What Is Microsoft Wallet?

Microsoft Wallet is Windows 98's Internet commerce tool. Up until now, the process of paying for things over the Internet has been a little clunky. Each web site has its own form for gathering your credit card information, and it's inconvenient to type those long credit card numbers every time you want to buy something. And it would also be nice if you could tell the merchant your shipping address just by pushing a button.

Wallet is an attempt to standardize this process. It works like this: You type your credit card information into your computer once, and Wallet stores it on your computer in an encrypted, password-protected form. When you are ready to pay for something that you want to buy from participating online merchants, you tell Wallet which credit card to use, and give it that card's password. You also tell it which address you want the product shipped to. Wallet then relays all this information to the merchant.

Microsoft plans for Wallet to eventually interact with electronic cash systems, Internet bank accounts, and whatever other payment schemes people come up with. Right now, it is set up to handle the major credit cards: American Express, Discover, Master Card, and Visa.

Whether Wallet will take off or not is anyone's guess. It's a chicken-and-egg situation: Wallet is useless to you until merchants set up their web sites to interact with it. But Internet merchants may not be motivated to accommodate Wallet until they see whether consumers use it. Microsoft has a lot of marketing muscle, though, and if they push hard Wallet might get over the hump. At press time, the list of participating merchants was a little slim. (Check it out at **http://www.microsoft.com/wallet**.) Popular retailers like Amazon.com Books weren't on the list, and the first time we tried to use Wallet with a merchant that was on the list, we ended up having to type in our credit card number anyway.

Whether or not you feel secure letting Windows handle your credit cards is another question. The nightmare is that some devilishly clever web site will be able to trick your credit card numbers out of Wallet without your knowledge, or that someone with access to your computer (either directly or over a network) will be able to break the encryption and get your credit card information that way. Microsoft obviously believes it has these problems solved, and we're in no position to say that they're wrong. But personally, though we did test Wallet, we're not tempted to be the first ones on our block to use it regularly. Let the hackers try to steal someone else's credit card numbers for six months or so.

Once you have credit card information and addresses in Wallet, using it is easy: Just buy things on a web site in the usual way. If that web site is set up for Wallet, when the time comes to pay for your purchases you will be asked whether you want to type your information into their online form, or input it directly from Wallet. If you choose Wallet, you'll be shown a list of the credit cards Wallet knows about. Select one and give the password.

To enter information into Wallet follow these steps:

1. Open the Internet Properties dialog box either by clicking the Internet icon on the Control Panel, or by choosing View | Internet Options from Internet Explorer's menu bar. You click or double-click the Internet icon depending on whether you use Web style or Classic style for your desktop (see "Choosing the Style of Your Desktop" in Chapter 1).

2. Click the Content tab of the Internet Properties dialog box. At the bottom of the page are two buttons: Addresses and Payments.

3. To add, edit, or delete a credit card from Wallet, click the Payments button. To add, edit, or delete an address, click the Addresses button. In either case a dialog box appears containing a list of the credit cards (or addresses) that Wallet knows about.

4. If you want to delete one of the current entries, select it on the list and click the Delete button. Then click OK.

5. If you want to edit one of the current entries, select it on the list and click Edit. A window appears containing the current information about the entry. Edit it and click OK.

6. To add an entry, click the Add button. If you are adding a credit card, a Wizard guides you through the process. If you are adding an address, fill out the form that appears, or click the Address Book button to choose an entry from the Windows Address Book.

7. When you are done, click OK to close the Internet Properties dialog box.

Viewing Web Pages

The main purpose of a web browser is to display web pages. Those pages may actually be on the Web, or they may be on your own computer.

Before you can display web pages, though, you need to find them. The Web itself provides search engines and web guides for finding your way around. Once you have found a web site that you like, you need to be able to mark it so that you can go back to it easily. Internet Explorer and Navigator provide a variety of tools to help you do this—Internet shortcuts, favorites, bookmarks, history files, and lists that drop down from the Address or Location box.

Since some content on the Web may be offensive to you, you may decide to avoid it or limit your children's access to it. To help you create and implement such a policy, Internet Explorer provides a Content Advisor that is based on a web site rating system called *PICS* (Platform for Internet Content Selection; see the web site **http://www.w3.org/PICS**). PICS lets you use ratings from any number of ratings bureaus, but the only bureau that Internet Explorer knows about (unless you add others) is the Recreational Software Advisory Council for the Internet (RSACi).

Finally, having found content that you want to examine at leisure or share with those who aren't connected to the Internet, you may decide to print it out. Internet Explorer and Navigator give you several options for doing this.

Opening Files on Your System

You can use either Navigator or Internet Explorer to view HTML files that are stored on your hard drive or elsewhere on your system. You can also view images stored in several different image formats, such as JPEG, GIF, or BMP:

1. Select File | Open in Internet Explorer or File | Open Page in Navigator. An Open or Open Page dialog box appears.

2. If you know the file address of the file you want to open, type it into the dialog box and click OK (in Internet Explorer) or Open (in Navigator). Then skip to step 8.

3. If you don't know the file address or don't want to type it, click Browse (Internet Explorer) or Choose File (Navigator). An Open window appears.

4. Makes sure that the Files Of Type line of the Open window contains the type of file you want to open. Web pages are of type HTM, and pictures are of type JPG, GIF, or BMP, depending on picture format. If the Files Of Type line doesn't contain the file type you want to open, choose another type from the drop-down menu. If you can't find the right type, choose All Files.

5. Browse until you find the file you want to open.

6. Select the file by clicking its name. Its name then appears in the File Name line.

7. Click Open. You are returned to the Open or Open Page dialog box, with the web address of the file entered.

8. Click OK (Internet Explorer) or Open (Navigator). You see the file in your browser window.

Getting Around on the Web

You can open a web page by using any of the following methods:

- **Entering its URL into the Address or Location box of a web browser** The most direct way is to type the URL, but if you have the URL in a file or a mail message, you can cut-and-paste it. The Paste command on the Edit menu may not work when the cursor is in the Address window, but you can always paste by pressing CTRL-V. Both Internet Explorer and Navigator have an auto-complete feature—the browser tries to guess what URL you are typing and finishes it for you, by guessing similar URLs that you've visited before.

■ **Selecting it from the list that drops down from the Address or Location box** Both Internet Explorer and Navigator remember the last 25 URLs that you have typed into the Address or Location box.

■ **Linking to it from another web page** The reason it's called a "web" is that pages are linked to each other in a tangled, unpredictable way. Click a link (usually underlined, blue text or icons) to see the web page it refers to.

■ **Linking to it from a mail message or newsgroup article** If Outlook Express or Netscape Messenger notices that a URL appears in a mail message, it automatically links it to the corresponding web page (see Chapter 23). Clicking the URL opens a web browser, which displays the web page.

■ **Selecting it from History** Both Internet Explorer and Navigator maintain records of the web pages you have viewed in the past several days. You can display these records and return to any of the web pages with a click (see "Examining History").

■ **Selecting it from the Favorites menu or (in Navigator) from the Bookmarks list** Accessing a Favorite from the Start | Favorite menu opens the target web page in the default browser. Accessing a Favorite from the Internet Explorer Favorites menu (usually) opens it in Internet Explorer, no matter what the default browser is.

■ **Opening an Internet shortcut** An Internet shortcut displays the icon of the default browser. Opening it starts the default browser (even if another browser is already running), connects to the Internet, and displays the web page to which the shortcut points.

Finding What You Want on the Web

No one designed the content of the Web—it's a collection of whatever various people and businesses have decided to put there. It also changes quickly, as web sites come and go, or get reworked. Consequently, finding your way around is a bit of an art. The Web provides two main tools for you to work with: web guides and search engines.

Using Web Guides

Web guides or *web directories* take a top-down approach to finding your way on the Web. Various companies have taken on the job of trying to be the librarians of the Web, and have created classification systems. The Web is divided into a list of categories, each of which categories is subdivided into categories, and so on. If you have a vague idea of what you want to find, you can start at the top and work your way down through the levels of categories and subcategories until you find what you want. Yahoo! (at **http://www.yahoo.com**) was one of the first web guides.

For example, if you hear that United Airlines has a web site that allows you to check whether the flight you are meeting has been delayed, you might start at the top of Yahoo!'s classification system and zero in on the site with the following series of clicks: Recreation | Travel | Air Travel | Airlines | United Airlines. The United Airlines listing is linked to United's web site.

Some of the top web guides are:

- Yahoo! (**http://www.yahoo.com**)
- Excite (**http://www.excite.com**)
- Lycos (**http://www.lycos.com**)
- Infoseek (**http://www.infoseek.com**)

Using Search Engines

Search engines are a bottom-up approach to finding your way on the Web. You give a search engine a list of keywords or phrases (called a *query*), and it returns to you a list of web pages that contain those words or phrases.

Given the vast number of web pages, a query that is too general may yield tens of thousands of web pages, most of them useless to you. If, for example, you are looking for the text of the novel *Robinson Crusoe*, using "Robinson" and "Crusoe" as keywords would produce search results that include pages that mention Al Robinson and Bill Crusoe. Using "Robinson Crusoe" as a phrase would narrow the list down a little, but would still include any article in which some person is compared to Robinson Crusoe. Using "Robinson Crusoe" and "Daniel Defoe" would restrict the list mostly to pages that talk about the novel. Using the first line of the novel, "I was born in the year 1632," when we tried it in AltaVista, yielded a single web page.

Some search engines search only the titles of web pages, while others search every word. (This takes much less time than you might think.) Each search engine has its own way of deciding which of the web pages on its list is most likely to be one that you are looking for. Some allow more complicated queries than others. It's worthwhile to try a few search engines to decide which one best suits you.

Each of the web guides previously listed has a search engine associated with it. Other popular search engines are AltaVista (**http://altavista.digital.com**) and Metacrawler (**http://www.metacrawler.com**).

A particularly easy way to search the Web with Internet Explorer is to type your search into the Address box. Just type:

> ?<space>*key word or phrase*

Internet Explorer uses the Autosearch service of Yahoo! to come up with a list of web pages corresponding to your key word(s).

*Our web site at **http://net.gurus.com/search** has links to the web guides and search engines that we recommend.*

Avoiding What You Don't Want on the Web with Content Advisor

Almost anything that people want to see, hear, or read is on the Web somewhere. You may decide that you want to block your web browser's access to certain kinds of content, either because you find it offensive yourself, you don't want your children to see it, or you don't want your workers to waste their time on it. Content Advisor gives you some measure of control over the content that Internet Explorer displays. Future versions of Navigator may have a similar feature, but the most recent version available at this writing (4.04) does not.

Rating Web Sites: How the System Works

The Recreational Software Advisory Council for the Internet (RSACi) is a non-profit corporation that has developed a questionnaire for rating the content of web sites in several areas that people might find offensive—language, nudity, sex, and violence. The questionnaire is a series of yes/no questions about what the web site displays, and is intended to be as objective as possible. Web site managers who want their sites rated fill out the questionnaire and submit it to RSACi, which grades it by computer and issues numerical ratings in each of the four categories. The web sites are then allowed to tag their pages with the RSACi ratings.

When you set up Content Advisor, you choose a password and indicate what language, nudity, sex, and violence ratings you consider acceptable. When you (or anyone using your copy of Internet Explorer) try to access a rated web page, Internet Explorer reads the page's RSACi tags, compares them to your choices, and refuses to display the page if its ratings exceed the maximum rating you considered acceptable.

Only someone who knows the Content Advisor password can authorize Internet Explorer to display an unacceptable web page, or change the acceptability ratings.

Enabling and Disabling Content Advisor

To set up Content Advisor for the first time:

1. Open the Internet icon on the Control Panel. The Internet Properties dialog box appears.

2. Go to the Content tab of the Internet Properties dialog box.

3. Click the Enable button in the Content Advisor box of the Content tab. A Create Supervisor Password dialog box opens.

4. Choose a password for Content Advisor. Type the password twice, once in the Password box and once in the Confirm Password box.

5. Click OK. The Content Advisor dialog box opens.

6. At this point, Content Advisor has been enabled with the most restrictive settings. If this is what you want, click OK. Otherwise, you can use the Content Advisor dialog box to change the settings (see "Setting and Changing Your Content Advisor Preferences").

To disable Content Advisor:

1. Open the Content tab of the Internet Properties dialog box, as you did when you enabled Content Advisor.

2. Click the Disable button. A Supervisor Password Required box appears.

3. Type the Content Advisor supervisor password into the Supervisor Password Required box and click OK.

4. A confirmation box tells you that Content Advisor has been turned off. Click OK in this box.

5. Click OK to close the Internet Properties box.

Enabling Content Advisor again (after disabling it) is simpler than setting it up the first time: Click the Enable button on the Content tab of the Internet Properties dialog box, and then give the supervisor password when asked. Content Advisor remembers the settings you were using before you disabled it.

Setting and Changing Your Content Advisor Preferences

Content Advisor's default settings are its most restrictive. To change these settings:

1. Open the Content tab of the Internet Properties dialog box, as you did when you set up Content Advisor (see "Enabling and Disabling Content Advisor").

2. Click the Settings button. A Supervisor Password Required box appears.

3. Type the supervisor password into the box and click OK. The Content Advisor dialog box appears.

4. Click the category (Language, Nudity, Sex, or Violence) whose rating you want to change. A rating slider appears.

5. Move the slider to the desired setting. The slider moves from 0 (least offensive) to 4 (most offensive). A description of the currently selected level appears in the Description box below the slider. The More Info button takes you to the web page at **http://www.rsac.org/ratingsv01.html**, which contains a table of more complete descriptions of the rating levels.

6. Click Apply. When you have changed all the settings you want to change, click OK.

To change the supervisor password or other policies, open the Content Advisor dialog box, as previously explained, and click the General tab. One check box on this tab makes it possible for users to view unrated web sites, the other disables the supervisor password override. To change the supervisor password:

1. Click the Change Password button on the General tab of the Content Advisor dialog box. A Change Supervisor Password box opens.

2. Type the old password into the first line of the Change Supervisor Password box.

3. Type the new password into the second and third lines of the Change Supervisor Password box.

4. Click OK. You may be prompted to restart Windows.

Browsing with Content Advisor Enabled

So long as you are viewing rated web pages whose rating is within your acceptability criteria, Content Advisor is invisible. When a user attempts to access a web site that is unrated or that violates your criteria, Content Advisor displays a dialog box like the one in Figure 25-1. The dialog box lists the areas in which the site's ratings exceed the

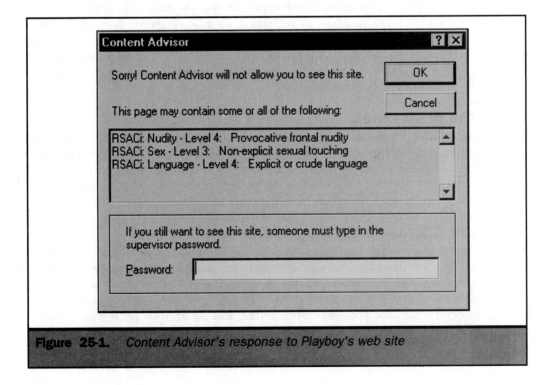

Figure 25-1. *Content Advisor's response to Playboy's web site*

criteria, and requests the supervisor password before continuing. To allow Internet Explorer to display the requested page, type the supervisor password into the Password box and click OK. Otherwise, click Cancel to return to the previously displayed page.

As of this writing, the main difficulty with Content Advisor is that most sites remain unrated—including Yahoo!, *The USA Today*, and *The Wall Street Journal*, just to name some of the first web sites we tried. For this reason, blocking unrated sites is currently a very restrictive policy, especially for older children. Most of the useful content of the Web is filtered out along with the potentially offensive content. On the other hand, since the rating system is voluntary, if you don't block unrated sites, you're only protecting your family from those pornographers who are responsible enough to bother with the rating system. RSACi anticipates that the number of rated sites will increase—until it does, Content Advisor is not very useful.

If your older children are computer-savvy and determined to defeat the system, they probably will. For example, they could install Navigator in some obscure directory and hope you don't notice, or they could, if technically savvy, circumvent the Content Advisor password.

Remembering Where You've Been on the Web

Navigator and Internet Explorer provide a variety of ways to remember which web sites you've already visited, and how to get back to them, if you want. Both browsers have a Back menu that keeps track of the last few web pages you've viewed, and a drop-down list from the Address (or Location) box that shows the most recent URLs that you've typed in. And there's a History feature you can check when you find yourself saying "I know I saw that last week."

Using the Back Menu

Both Navigator and Internet Explorer have a Back button on the toolbar. These buttons each have a drop-down menu of the last several web pages you have looked at during the current session. To access the Back menu in Internet Explorer, click the arrow on the right side of the Back button. To access the Back menu in Navigator, right-click the Back button. Then choose a web page from the list that appears.

Using the Address or Location List

Both Navigator and Internet Explorer have a box on the toolbar into which URLs can be typed; Navigator calls its box Location while Internet Explorer uses Address. Both work the same way. As you type a URL into the box, the browser attempts to finish the URL for you, based on what you have typed so far and your viewing history. If the browser generates the URL you want, press ENTER, and the browser fetches the corresponding web page.

In addition, each browser maintains a drop-down list of the last 25 URLs that you have typed into the Address/Location box. Select an entry off the drop-down list, and the browser fetches the corresponding web page.

Clearing the History list also clears the Address/Location drop-down list and insures that the browser does not auto-complete a URL that you have visited many times.

Examining History

Both Internet Explorer and Navigator maintain a list of web pages that you have accessed recently. Internet Explorer stores this information in the form of Internet shortcuts that are arranged into a hierarchy of folders inside the History folder. Navigator maintains a history database that can be accessed or edited only from within Navigator. Both browsers allow you to return to a web page with a single click.

If other people use your computer, you need to be aware of the privacy implications of having a History list. A History list is a trail that someone else can follow to see what you've been viewing on the Web. Conversely, you may use the History list to see what other people (your children, for example) have been viewing on the Web.

Both Navigator and Internet Explorer allow you to turn off the History list, or wipe clean the History list. Internet Explorer allows you (or someone else) to selectively edit the History folder, removing only the web pages you (or they) don't want recorded.

 Clearing the History list in either Internet Explorer or Navigator does not clear either the Back menu or the drop-down list under the Location box in Navigator. If you want to be sure to cover your tracks, exit the browser after you clear History—when it restarts, the Back menu is empty as well. In Navigator, clear the Location drop-down list by deleting the file Prefs.js in the C:\Program Files\Netscape\Users\your user name folder.

In both Navigator and Internet Explorer, History is subject to user profiles: Each user has his/her own History list, with its own settings. Navigator has its own user profiles (see "Defining User Profiles" in Chapter 24). Internet Explorer applies the Windows user profiles (see "What Is a User Profile?" in Chapter 33).

USING INTERNET EXPLORER'S HISTORY FOLDER   Clicking the History button on the Internet Explorer toolbar opens a new Explorer Bar in the Internet Explorer window. This pane (shown in Figure 25-2) is similar to the left pane of a Windows Explorer window, and it displays the contents of the History folder in a folder-tree view. Selecting a closed folder expands the tree to show its contents; selecting an open folder compresses the tree to hide its contents. Clicking the History button again causes the History pane to disappear.

The History folder is organized into subfolders—one for each day of the current week, and one for each previous week, going back 20 days. (You can use the steps

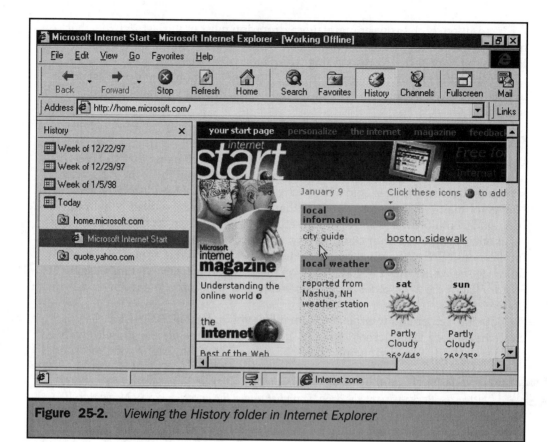

Figure 25-2. *Viewing the History folder in Internet Explorer*

listed below to change the number of days History remembers.) Each day's folder contains one subfolder for each web site visited with Internet Explorer. Inside the web site folders are Internet shortcuts to each of the pages viewed on that web site.

Return to a web page by opening its shortcut. Selecting a shortcut (either by resting the cursor on it in web view or single-clicking it in classic view) displays its title and address in a tool tip window. When you are offline, a symbol having a circle with a line through it appears next to the cursor, if the page is not cached. You can look up the exact time when the page was accessed by choosing Properties from the right-click menu.

Delete a shortcut or a subfolder from the History folder by selecting Delete from the right-click menu.

To change the History settings:

1. Open the Internet Options dialog box either by choosing View | Internet Options from within Internet Explorer or by opening the Internet icon on the

Control Panel. The dialog box opens with the General tab on top. The History box is near the bottom of the General tab.

2. If you want to delete all the entries in the History folder, click the Clear History button in the History box of the General tab.

3. If you want to change the number of days that the History folder remembers a web page, enter a new number into the Days To Keep Pages In History box.

4. Click OK.

The History folder can also be viewed and edited in a Folder window or in Windows Explorer. If your system is not using user profiles, there is a single History folder, C:\Windows\History (see "What Is a User Profile?" in Chapter 33). If your system is set up for user profiles, your history folder is C:\Windows\Profiles*your user name*\History.

USING NAVIGATOR'S HISTORY LIST   Access the Navigator History list by selecting Communicator | History. The History list appears in its own window, organized into six columns: page title, location, when the page was first visited, when the page was last visited, the date when this page is scheduled to be removed from the History list, and the number of times the page has been visited. Double-clicking a line in the History list accesses the corresponding web page.

Navigator does not organize its History list into folders and subfolders as Internet Explorer does, but it gives more information about the web pages, which lets you sort and search the list in more ways than Internet Explorer allows.

Clicking a column head sorts the list according to that column; clicking it again sorts the list in descending order. Search the History list as follows:

1. Open the History list by selecting Communicator | History.

2. From the History list menu bar, select Edit | Search History List. A Search History List dialog box opens, as shown here:

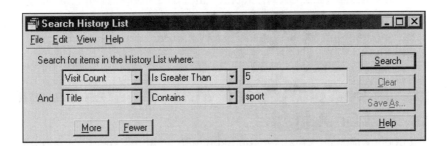

3. Define a condition of the search. In our example, two conditions are defined. A condition is defined by filling out three boxes on a horizontal line. In the first box, you choose (from a drop-down list) to which column of the History list the

condition applies. In the second box, you choose from a drop-down list of verbs that go with that column. And in the third box, you type something to compare the column entries against. When you are done, the condition should describe what you are looking for. In our example, the first condition reads Visit Count Is Greater Than 5.

4. If you want to enter another condition, click the More button. A second condition-definition line appears. Continue defining conditions until you are satisfied. If you change your mind about the number of conditions you want, click the Fewer button to make the bottommost condition-definition line go away.

5. Click the Search button. A list of the entries on the History list that satisfy the condition appears at the bottom of the Search History List dialog box.

6. If the list is still too long, refine your search by defining more conditions or tightening the ones you have. Then click Search again.

7. If what you want is not on the list, refine your search by eliminating conditions (using the Fewer button) or by loosening conditions. Click Search again.

8. If you find what you are looking for on the list presented, you can go to that page by double-clicking its entry on the list.

9. If you want to save the results of a search, click the Save As button. A Save As window appears, giving you the option of saving the resulting list as a text file or as an HTML file. If you save as an HTML file, each line of the list is linked to the corresponding web page.

To change the History settings:

1. Choose Edit | Preferences. The Preferences box opens.

2. Select Navigator in the Category window.

3. If you want to delete all entries on the History list, click the Clear History button, and then click OK when Navigator asks you to verify the decision.

4. If you want to change the length of time that entries remain on the History list, type a number into the Pages In History Expire After *xx* Days box.

5. Click OK.

Revisiting Where You've Been with Favorites, Internet Shortcuts, and Bookmarks

When you find a web page you like, you likely will want to look at it again sometime. Favorites, Internet shortcuts, and bookmarks allow you to return easily to a web page, without having to write down or remember the page's URL (see "What Are Internet Shortcuts, Favorites, and Bookmarks?").

Using Favorites, Internet Shortcuts, and Bookmarks

Opening an Internet shortcut causes Windows to connect to your Internet provider (if necessary), open your default web browser, and display the web page that the shortcut points to.

Favorites is a folder of Internet shortcuts, so choosing Start | Favorites and selecting a web page has the same effect as opening an Internet shortcut that points to that web page.

The Bookmarks menu is a part of Navigator. To use it, click the Bookmarks button on the Navigator toolbar and select a bookmark from the menu that appears. Navigator then opens the web page that the bookmark points to.

Adding Favorites

To add favorites in Internet Explorer:

1. Display the page you want to add in Internet Explorer.

2. Select Favorites | Add to Favorites. An Add Favorite dialog box opens, as shown here:

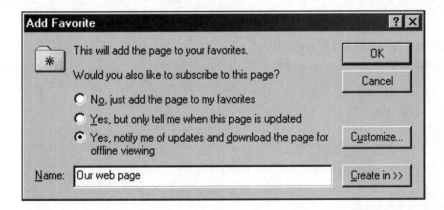

Three radio buttons ask whether you want to subscribe to this page. In this section, we assume the answer is No. We discuss subscriptions later in this chapter.

3. Select a name to appear on the Favorites menu. The dialog box suggests the name that the page's creator has given it. If some other name would do a better job of reminding you which web page this is, type it into the Name line.

4. If you organize your Favorites menu into folders (a good idea if you have a lot of favorites), click the Create In button to choose a folder in which to put this new favorite. The dialog box enlarges to include a folder tree showing the subfolders of the Favorites folder.

5. Select a folder in which to create the new favorite. If you want to define a new folder for the favorite, select a folder in which to put the new folder and then click New Folder. The new folder appears on the folder tree.

6. Click OK to create the new favorite in the selected folder.

To add favorites in Navigator: In between the words Bookmarks and Location on the Location toolbar is a bookmark icon. This icon represents a bookmark or shortcut pointing to whatever page is currently displayed.

1. Display the page you want to add in Navigator.

2. In a separate Windows Explorer window, display the Favorites folder. It's called C:\Windows\Favorites if you don't have personal profiles on your system, or C:\Windows\Profiles*your user name*\Favorites, if you do.

3. Switch to the Navigator window and then drag the bookmark icon into the Favorites folder. This creates the Favorites entry.

4. The new Favorites entry will be named Shortcut To *title of web page*. To change the name to something snappier, right-click the new entry, select rename, and change the name. You can also change the icon it displays. Right-click the entry, select Properties, and in the Properties window, click Change Icon.

Creating Internet Shortcuts

To create shortcuts in Internet Explorer:

1. Open the page to which you want to create a shortcut.

2. Choose File | Send | Shortcut To Desktop.

To create shortcuts in Navigator:

1. Open the page to which you want to create a shortcut.

2. Drag the bookmark icon to the desktop or into a folder displayed in a Windows Explorer window.

From the desktop, Windows Explorer, or a Folder window:

1. Choose File | New | Shortcut in Windows Explorer or a Folder window. From the desktop, right-click, and then choose New | Shortcut. A Create Shortcut box opens.

2. Type the URL of the web page into the Create Shortcut box. Or, if you have copied the command line from some other document, paste it into Create Shortcut by pressing CTRL-V. Click Next.

3. Give the shortcut a name. Click Finish.

Adding Bookmarks in Navigator

If you drag the bookmark icon to the left, onto the Bookmarks button, the Bookmarks menu appears. Drag the icon into whichever menu or submenu of Bookmarks you want this page's bookmark to be located. Alternatively, you can click the Bookmarks button and choose Add Bookmark from the menu that appears. Choosing File Bookmark from this menu displays an expanding menu of folders into which the bookmark can be filed.

Organizing Favorites and Bookmarks

If you have picked out only a few web pages, your favorites and bookmarks don't have to be well organized. But as time goes by, favorites and bookmarks accumulate like knick-knacks. It saves time to reorganize them once in a while and toss out the ones that are obsolete. Both Internet Explorer and Navigator let you create a folder system to organize your list of favorite sites.

The Favorites list is actually a folder (C:\Windows\Favorites if you haven't established user profiles on your computer; C:\Windows\Profiles*your user name*\Favorites if you have), and each of the entries on the Favorites list is a shortcut pointing to the URL of the corresponding web page. Consequently, one way to organize Favorites is to use the same techniques you would use to organize any other folder in a Folder window or in Windows Explorer. Or you can choose Favorites | Organize Favorites from Internet Explorer's menu bar. An Organize Favorites box opens. Move, rename, or delete entries on your Favorites list by selecting the entries and clicking the corresponding buttons in the Organize Favorites box.

To reorganize your Navigator bookmarks, click the Bookmarks button and select Edit Bookmarks. A bookmark editing window opens, allowing you to delete, cut, paste, and drag bookmarks. New folders and separators (which go between classes of folders) are created from the File menu of this window.

Subscribing to Web Sites and Channels

Internet Explorer allows you to subscribe to web sites and channels. Netscape Communicator has a similar capability, but not in its Navigator web browser. Instead, Communicator has a separate component, Netcaster, for handling subscriptions. To get a better idea of what subscriptions and channels are, see "What Are Subscriptions and Channels?" earlier in this chapter.

Subscribing to Web Sites

The subscription process in Internet Explorer is handled by a Subscription Wizard, which does a good job of guiding you through the process. Netscape Netcaster requires you to fill out a dialog box. In either case, you need to make decisions about the following issues:

- Do you want to download web pages for viewing offline, or do you just want to be informed that the web site has changed, so that you can browse it on your own?

- If you are downloading content, how do you want to handle links? Do you want to download all the pages that the subscribed page links to? If so, how many layers of links do you want to download? Internet Explorer allows you to specify that you want to download only linked pages that stay within the subscribed web site—this is a good way to avoid downloading the advertisements attached to a web page.

- How do you want to be informed about updates? When a subscribed web page has been updated, Internet Explorer adds a red gleam to the icon that denotes it on the Subscription list. If this seems insufficient, you can instruct Internet Explorer to automatically send you e-mail.

- Do you want the subscription to be updated automatically on a schedule, or do you want updates to take place only when you click an Update Now button? If you want a schedule, how frequently should the web site be checked for new material? What would be a good time? (The best time for updating subscriptions is when your computer is on, but not being used for anything else.)

- Does the web site require a user name and password?

Subscribing to Web Sites with Internet Explorer

Internet Explorer handles subscriptions through the Add Favorites dialog box. To subscribe to a web site from Internet Explorer, follow these steps:

1. Select Favorites | Add To Favorites from the menu bar. An Add Favorites dialog box appears, which gives you three choices: You can add the site to your Favorites menu without subscribing (which is covered in "Adding Favorites," earlier in this chapter), you can have the browser notify you when the site has new content, or you can schedule regular downloads of the site for offline viewing. Click the appropriate radio button.

2. Click the Customize button. This starts the Subscription Wizard, which guides you through the choices available to you.

Tip   *If you want to subscribe to a web site that is already one of your favorites, you don't need to be online. Just right-click the Internet shortcut in your Favorites folder and choose Subscribe from the menu.*

Subscribing to Web Sites with Netscape's Netcaster

To add a web site to Netcaster's My Channels list, you must know the URL. Follow these steps:

1. Click the New button on Netcaster's toolbar. A Channel Properties dialog box opens, as in Figure 25-3. The General tab is on top.

2. On the Name line of the Channel Properties dialog box, type in the name you want to appear in the My Channels menu.

3. In the Location line, enter the URL.

4. Use the check box and drop-down list at the bottom of the General tab to set up an updating schedule, if you want one.

5. Click the Cache tab.

6. Fill in the boxes on the Cache tab to establish how links are dealt with, and how much disk space the subscription can use.

7. Click OK.

Figure 25-3.   *The Netscape Channel Properties box*

Subscribing to Channels

Because channels are designed for subscriptions, subscribing to channels tends to be even easier than subscribing to web sites. Most channels have some kind of preview screen for you to examine; it usually contains an Add Channel button that starts the Subscription Wizard.

The easiest way to subscribe to a channel is to click one of the entries on the Channel bar and then click its Add Channel button. However, what you can see on the Channel bar is only the tip of the iceberg. When you click the Channel Guide button on the Channel bar (or select Start | Favorites | Channels | Microsoft Channel Guide), Internet Explorer goes online to find the latest listing of channels. The last time we tried this, there were hundreds of channels. (Many, such as the Roanoke County Police Channel, are probably not of general interest.)

Netcaster's Channel Finder bar, which resembles Internet Explorer's Channel bar, appears automatically when you select Start | Programs | Netscape Communicator | Netcaster. Clicking the Channel Finder button on this bar sends Navigator online to find the latest listing of channels. In general, Microsoft's channel listings are larger than Netscape's.

When you find a channel that looks interesting, either on Microsoft's Channel Guide or Netscape's Channel Finder, you can add it to your current channel subscriptions by clicking a single button. A Wizard takes you through the process.

You can see to which channels you have subscribed by choosing Favorites | Manage Subscriptions from the Internet Explorer menu bar, or by clicking the My Channels button on the Netcaster Channel bar.

Editing Subscriptions and Unsubscribing

None of the decisions you make when you set up a subscription is etched in stone. Your Internet Explorer subscriptions (both web sites and channels) are contained in the folder C:\Windows\Subscriptions (if you have no user profiles on your computer) or C:\Windows\Profiles*your user name*\Subscriptions (if you have user profiles). You can open this folder from Internet Explorer by selecting Favorites | Manage Subscriptions.

Once the Subscriptions folder is open, right-click any icon in it and choose Properties. When the Properties dialog box opens, you can change any of the choices you made. To unsubscribe from a channel or web site, delete its icon from the Subscriptions folder.

To edit a subscription in Netcaster, click the Options button. When the Options dialog box appears, select the channel whose subscription you want to edit from the list on the Channels tab. Then click the Properties button. The Channel Properties dialog box opens. This is exactly the same dialog box in which you established the channel in the first place. Change anything you want, and then click OK.

To unsubscribe a channel or web site in Netcaster, right-click it on the My Channels list and choose Delete from the menu.

Updating Subscribed Web Sites and Channels

Internet Explorer and Netcaster can check and download your subscribed web sites and channels automatically on a schedule. For this to happen:

- In Internet Explorer, the Scheduled radio button must be selected on the Schedule tab of the Properties dialog box for each subscription. This is set up by the Subscription Wizard when you create the subscription, or you can change it later by editing the Properties dialog box.

- In Netcaster, the Update This Channel box must be checked on the General tab of the Channel Properties dialog box.

- Your Internet connection must be set up to connect automatically. In particular, you need to have saved any passwords that are needed to establish your connection.

- Your computer must be running at the scheduled time.

You can update Internet Explorer subscriptions manually by choosing Favorites | Update All Subscriptions from Internet Explorer's menu. If you want to update some subscriptions but not others, select Favorites | Manage Subscriptions. A Folder window opens with icons corresponding to each of your subscriptions. To update a specific subscription, select its icon and click the Update button on the toolbar.

To manually update a Netcaster subscription, right-click its name in the My Channels list, and choose Update from the menu.

Reading a Subscribed Site or Channel Offline

To read a subscribed channel or web site offline in Netcaster, click its name on the My Channels list. In Internet Explorer, choose File | Work Offline, and then open the channel or web site from the Favorites menu, or in any of the standard ways of opening a web page.

Managing Your Web Browser

Web browsers are intended to be simple enough for novice users. For this reason, most of what the browser does is invisible. Some choices that your browser makes for you, however, have implications for your system's use of disk space or its security—implications that more-advanced users may want to consider. Internet Explorer and Navigator allow you some limited opportunities to "get under the hood" and make choices for yourself about caching web pages, accepting cookies, and running applets in Java or ActiveX.

Managing Caches of Web Pages

Web browsers store some of the pages that you view, so that they can be redisplayed quickly if you return to them. In general, this speeds up the browsing experience, but if you are running short of disk space, you may decide to limit or eliminate these caches. Navigator stores web pages in the folder C:\Program Files\Netscape\Users*your Navigator user name*\Cache, while Internet Explorer uses C:\Windows\Temporary Internet Files or C:\Windows\Profiles*your user name*\Temporary Internet Files.

You control Internet Explorer's cache of web pages from the General tab of the Internet Properties dialog box. Delete all these web pages by clicking the Delete Files button. To set limits on the amount of disk space that can be devoted to temporary Internet files, click the Settings button to open the Settings dialog box. Move the slider to raise or lower the percentage of your hard drive that the Temporary Internet Files folder is allowed to use. Click OK to apply your changes.

Navigator has two caches for web pages: a small but extremely fast cache in your computer's memory (RAM), and a larger but slower one on your hard disk. To empty or change the size of either one:

1. Select Edit | Preferences to open the Preferences dialog box.

2. Expand the Advanced category by clicking the plus box next to Advanced in the Category list.

3. Select Cache in the Category list. The Cache controls appear in the right pane of the Preferences dialog box.

4. Empty either cache by clicking the corresponding Clear button.

5. Change the size of either cache by entering a new size into the Memory Cache or Disk Cache box.

6. Click OK.

Managing Cookies

Both Internet Explorer and Navigator let you control how they use cookies (see "What Are Cookies?"). In each case, the default option is to accept all cookies. You also have the option to refuse all cookies, or to be asked whether to accept or refuse cookies on a case-by-case basis. Navigator gives you the additional option of accepting only cookies that get sent back to the originating server.

In Internet Explorer, go to the Advanced tab of the Internet Properties dialog box. Scroll down until you see Cookies. The three options are presented as radio buttons. Click the button next to the policy you prefer, and then click either Apply or OK.

In Navigator, select Edit | Preferences to open the Preferences dialog box, and then click Advanced in the Category list. The bottom portion of the right pane controls your cookie policy. The options to accept all cookies, accept only those that get sent back to the originating server, and disable all cookies, are given as radio buttons. Click the radio button corresponding to your chosen policy. In addition, a check box controls whether Navigator should warn you before accepting a cookie. The warning includes the option to refuse the cookie.

Navigator lists the cookies it is currently storing in a text file, cookies.txt. In the default installation, this file is in the folder C:\Program Files\Netscape\Users*your Navigator user name*.

Internet Explorer cookies are stored as text files either in the folder C:\Windows\Cookies (if user profiles are not being used on your system) or in C:\Windows\Profiles*your user name*\Cookies. Some cookies may also be in C:\Windows\Temporary Internet Files (or one of its subfolders) or C:\Windows\Profiles*your user name*\Temporary Internet Files (or one of its subfolders).

Reading a cookie in WordPad or some other text program probably will not tell you much, though it may set your mind at ease to realize just how little information is there (see "Taking Advantage of Free Word Processing with WordPad" in Chapter 4). Delete cookies from your system by deleting the corresponding text files.

Managing Java and JavaScript

Java and JavaScript are programming languages that are used to give some web pages advanced features. If you want to deactivate Java and JavaScript in your web browser, you can. In Navigator, select Edit | Preferences and click Advanced in the Categories window of the Preferences dialog box. The check boxes, Enable Java and Enable JavaScript, turn Java and JavaScript on or off. In Internet Explorer, open the Internet Preferences dialog box from the Control Panel, and then go to the Advanced tab. The Java Console Enabled, Java JIT Compiler Enabled, and Java Logging Enabled check boxes control Internet Explorer's use of Java.

Managing ActiveX Controls

ActiveX controls are stored in the folder C:\Windows\Downloaded Program Files. If you use Internet Explorer, you should check this file periodically to see what applications Internet Explorer has downloaded. Deleting files from this folder uninstalls the associated applications.

Getting Help

Internet Explorer Help is part of the overall Windows Help (see Chapter 6). To get help in Navigator, select Help | Help Contents from the Navigator menu bar. This opens the Communicator NetHelp screen, shown in Figure 25-4. If you have installed Navigator by itself, without the other components of Communicator, NetHelp goes straight to the Navigator Help files.

The NetHelp window has two main components: a large display window and a panel of links to its left. At the top of the display window are Communicator's component icons. Clicking any of these icons takes you to the Help files of the

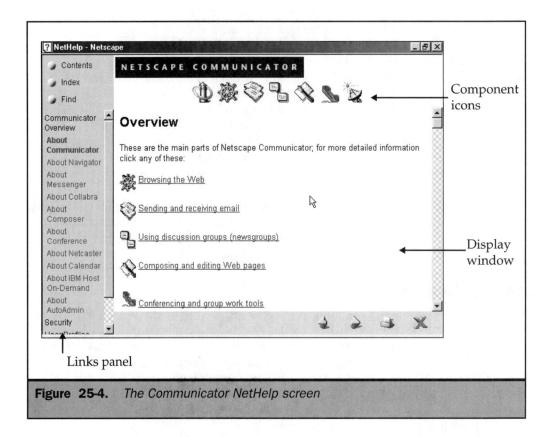

Figure 25-4.   *The Communicator NetHelp screen*

corresponding Communicator component. From left to right, the icons represent Communicator itself, Navigator, Messenger, Collabra, Composer, Conference, and Netcaster. Below the component icons is Help's text display. This is an HTML document with links. You can read it top to bottom, or you can expand one of the links by clicking it.

The links panel has three modes, denoted by the three circular buttons at the top of the panel. The button corresponding to the active mode is enclosed in a square. Change modes by clicking a button. The buttons are the following:

- **Contents**   The panel contains links corresponding to the different sections of the document shown in the display window. Reading the column is like looking at a table of contents for the document. Click a link to jump to that portion of the document.

- **Index**   The panel contains a Look For box just below the buttons, followed by a list of Help topics. These topics are not limited to the currently displayed document. When you first click the Index button, wait a few seconds for the list of topics to be assembled. (It is done when the box in the scroll bar stops shrinking.) When the list is complete, type a word or phrase into the Look For box. The list of Help topics changes so that only those topic titles are shown that contain the word or phrase you typed. If any Help topic sounds like the one you are looking for, click it to display the text of the topic in the display window.

■ **Find**   Clicking Find opens a Find window that searches for text in the current document. Type the word or phrase into the Find window; decide whether you want to find the next occurrence or the previous occurrence of the word or phrase, and click the Up or Down radio button; then click Find Next.

The
Complete
Reference

Chapter 26

Building Web Pages with
FrontPage Express

Y ou've browsed around the World Wide Web, noting page designs you like and thinking about the kinds of information you'd like to share on the Web. Now it's time to create your own web pages and publish them on the Web.

This chapter describes how to create web pages in the FrontPage Express program, which comes with Windows 98. With FrontPage Express, you don't have to know the HTML codes necessary to create a simple web page. The codes are available as menu options and buttons on the toolbar—all you need to do is enter text and select the graphics, choose a menu option or button, and let FrontPage Express do the rest. You can create a new web page, edit your existing pages, add pictures to your pages, and even make web pages with forms for other people to fill out. Once you create web pages, you can test them, and then publish them on the World Wide Web.

What Is HTML?

Hypertext Markup Language (HTML) is a set of commands that have been defined to code web pages. The HTML codes are called *tags* and they control how the text is formatted, where you go when you click a link, and how graphics are displayed on the page by your web browser (see Chapter 24). HTML is an application of SGML (Standard Generalized Markup Language), a standard general-purpose document-description language.

HTML tags are enclosed in angle brackets. Most tags require a beginning tag and an ending tag. When it comes to formatting text, you can think of tags as similar to the style codes used in word processing programs. Figure 26-1 shows HTML tags for a typical heading and paragraph on a page.

New HTML tags are being proposed and added all the time. A governing body called the *World Wide Web Consortium* (W3C) receives and manages the requests for new HTML capabilities, and publishes a list of accepted HTML tags. To keep HTML tags organized, different version numbers are assigned as new specifications are released. As of this writing, HTML 4.0 is the latest available version of the HTML standard.

Tip *For more information on the specifications included in each version of HTML, visit the consortium's web site at **http://www.w3.org**. The consortium is headed by the inventor of the World Wide Web, Tim Berners-Lee.*

When you create web pages, remember that older browsers may not support the newest HTML tags. If your pages are going to be published on the World Wide Web, test the pages in as many browsers as you can, to make sure the content and layout looks the way you want. If you are creating pages for your company's intranet and you know everyone uses the same browser, you can be more confident about which set of tags to use.

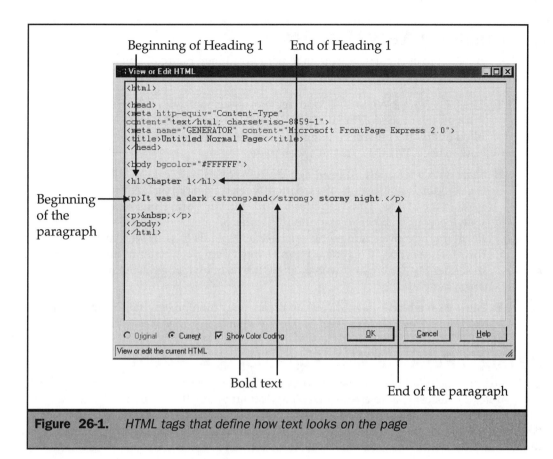

Figure 26-1.   *HTML tags that define how text looks on the page*

What Is FrontPage Express?

FrontPage Express, which comes with Windows 98, is a *web page editor*, a program that helps you add HTML tags to your web pages. Creating a web page in FrontPage Express is as easy as creating a document in your favorite word processing program. You don't need to learn or memorize HTML tags. The tags you need to format text, add graphics, and insert hyperlinks are listed on the toolbar. You can view the HTML tags if you want to, or you can work solely on the WYSIWYG (what-you-see-is-what-you-get) FrontPage Express screen. If you want to go beyond the HTML codes offered on menu options or toolbars, you can also add HTML tags manually in FrontPage Express.

To run FrontPage Express, choose Start | Programs | Internet Explorer | FrontPage Express.

Creating a New Web Page

When you want to create a new web page with FrontPage Express, you have three options:

- **Get help from a Wizard**   FrontPage Express comes with Wizards to step you through the process of creating a personal home page and creating a form to be filled out by the person viewing the web page. The following section describes how to use a Wizard to make a web page.

- **Start with a template**   FrontPage Express comes with *templates* that contain all the standard components of a frequently used type of page. All you have to do is fill in the blanks. The templates include Survey Form (for asking someone viewing your web site to respond to a series of questions) and Confirmation Form (for acknowledging when someone responds to your web site using a form). The section "Creating a Form Using a Template," later in this chapter, describes how to create a web page with a form by using the Survey Form template.

- **Start with a blank page**   You can create your own page with no suggestions from FrontPage Express (see "Starting with a Blank Page").

Creating a Personal Web Page Using a Wizard

Wizards are included in FrontPage Express to help you create a web page quickly. For example, the fastest way to create a web page about yourself is to use the Personal Home Page Wizard. When you use this Wizard, you are asked to define categories, such as Employee Information or Biographical Information, that you want to include on your page. After you create the page with a Wizard, you can revise the page any way you want. For example, you might want to add more text or graphics, or change the colors used on the page. A Wizard is a convenient way to get off to a quick start, but you don't have to keep the selections you make when you fill out the Wizard screens.

To create a personal home page, follow these steps:

1. Choose File | New.

2. In the New Page dialog box, select Personal Home Page Wizard, and click OK. The first Wizard screen appears.

3. Select the major sections you want to include on your page. Figure 26-2 shows the selections for a page that includes five major sections.

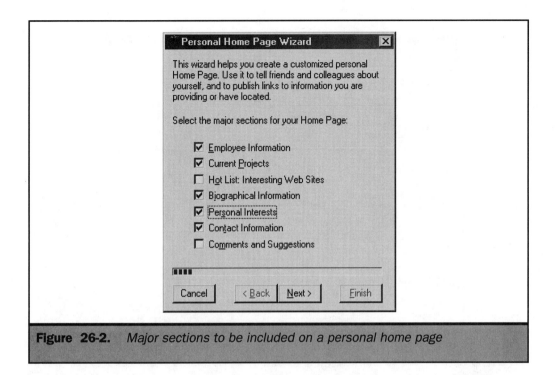

Figure 26-2.   *Major sections to be included on a personal home page*

4. Click Next to advance to the next screen. Continue filling in answers on the screens. At the final screen, click Finish. The Wizard generates your page, which looks something like the employee profile page shown in Figure 26-3.

The Wizard creates links for each major section you selected. You should fill in more text under each section. In some cases, the beginning of the sentence is supplied for you and you need only fill in the remainder of the sentence. When you are done editing the web page, be sure to save your work (see "Revising Web Pages"). Then test the result (see "Testing Web Pages").

Creating a Form Using a Template

Using a form on a web page is a handy way to gather information from people who view your web site. On the Web, *forms* are used as questionnaires, surveys, or even to order products online. FrontPage Express comes with templates that help you format

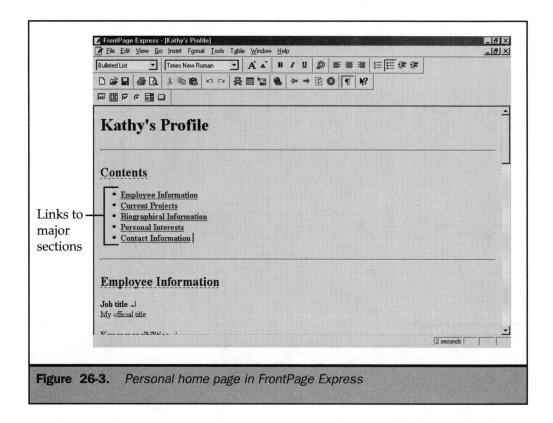

Figure 26-3. *Personal home page in FrontPage Express*

forms quickly. If you've used templates in Microsoft Word or in other programs, you are familiar with the role templates play in FrontPage Express.

To create a form or other web page from a template, choose File | New. In the New Page dialog box, select the template you want to use, in this case Survey Form, and click OK. FrontPage Express displays a preformatted form, ready for you to customize. You can replace the headings and text with your own information by typing over the existing text. As you scroll down the form, you see the question areas where respondents will fill in text boxes and choose options, as shown in Figure 26-4. Each text box or selection option is called a *form field*.

You can add, modify, and delete the form fields in FrontPage Express. However, you cannot choose a selection or enter a response while you're displaying the form in FrontPage Express. Form fields are accessible only in a browser, such as Internet Explorer.

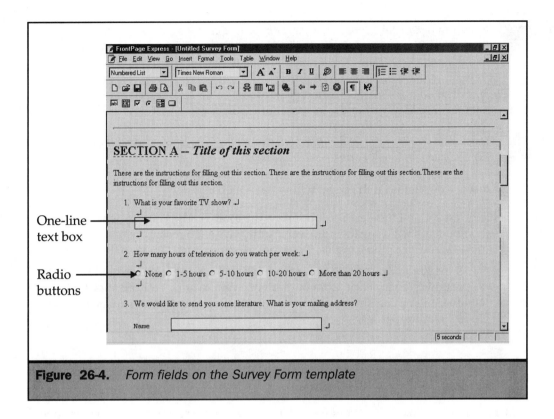

Figure 26-4.   *Form fields on the Survey Form template*

If you want to modify your form and add your own form fields, select one of the buttons on the Forms toolbar:

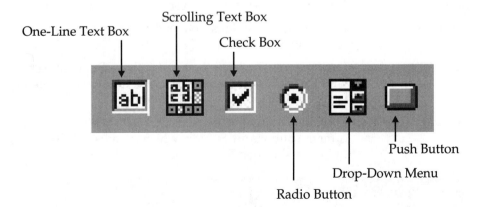

Be sure to replace the words that come with the template. As you can see in Figure 26-4, the words are intended only as placeholders or to provide instructions on how to use the template. They are not meant to be published on your page.

Each form field has a slightly different purpose. Table 26-1 describes the best ways to use each form field to gather the information you need.

 If you don't see the form field buttons on your toolbar, choose View from the menu bar and make sure that Forms Toolbar is selected.

To insert form fields on the page, follow these steps:

1. Click the One-Line Text Box button on the toolbar. The text box where respondents will type their answers is displayed. To resize the box, right-click the box and drag the handles. Type the question or label next to the text box.

2. Click the Radio Button button on the toolbar. Type the label next to the button. Repeat this step for each radio button you want to add. You can specify whether the button should appear by right-clicking the button and selecting Form Field Properties.

Form Field	Description
One-Line Text Box	Provides a blank space where respondents can enter one line of information.
Scrolling Text Box	Provides a blank space where respondents can enter many lines of information.
Check Box	Let respondents select or not select an option (yes/no).
Radio Button	Lists a group of options from which respondents can select only one.
Drop-Down Menu	Lists options in a drop-down menu the respondents see when they click a down-arrow. Using a drop-down menu is a good way to save space on a form.
Push Button	Provides a button respondents can click. The most common buttons are Submit, which submits the answers for processing, and Reset, which clears the form.

Table 26-1.   *Using Form Fields to Gather Information*

3. Click the Drop-Down Menu button on the toolbar. To add options to the drop-down menu, right-click the drop-down menu box, and select Form Field Properties. Click the Add button, type the first menu item, and then click OK. Click the Add button again, and add the next menu item. Continue using the Add button until all the options are added to your menu.

4. Click the Push Button button on the toolbar. The Submit button is added to the page automatically. If you want to change it, right-click the Submit button, select Form Field Properties, type the new label, and then indicate what type of button it should be.

Tip *You can also choose Insert | Form Field to add all of the form fields.*

When you're finished with the form, choose File | Save As, select a location on your local computer or network, type a filename, and then click Save. This saves your form to a local file, and you are ready to test it in a browser.

Open a browser window, enter the local filename on the Address bar, and view your form in the browser. Review the form's layout to be sure it is easy to follow. Test the form fields to make sure all the options you want are displayed, and to verify the text boxes are large enough to enter information in them. If you need to revise the form, go to FrontPage Express and make the changes. To resize a text box, select the box and drag the handles until the box is the size you want.

Creating the form is the first step in getting the form published. After you create your form, you need to get it posted on the Web, so that respondents can use it. To publish your form on the Web, contact your web server administrator or your Internet service provider (ISP) to determine their requirements for processing forms. You've created the form, but your administrator or ISP needs to set up the processing that takes places when respondents click the Submit button. In most cases, a short program, or script, is required to process the information submitted on the form, and your administrator or ISP can either give you instructions on how to create the script, or set up the script for you.

Starting with a Blank Page

Suppose a Wizard doesn't include the information you want, and a template doesn't match the design you had in mind. You can always just start from a blank page and add your own formatting by using the menu options and the buttons on the toolbar.

A blank page is displayed whenever you open FrontPage Express. You can start typing text at the first blank line. If you have a page open in FrontPage Express and you want to create a new blank page, choose File | New, select Normal Page in the New Page dialog box, and click OK. Your blank page is ready for your input.

Revising Web Pages

Building a web page is like constructing a house. You start with a basic framework, add the details that you want, and apply a design that brings it all together.

- The framework is the basic structure supplied by a Wizard, template, or your own ideas.
- The details are components, like the blocks of text you enter or the graphic files you insert, that make up the bulk of the page.
- The design is the colors and backgrounds you select to set a mood or convey an image.

Web pages are put together by combining different components. The finished web page you see in a browser is actually a text file that contains the text and HTML tags, along with separate graphic, sound, or video files. The HTML file you save contains the overall structure of the page, the text, and tags pointing to the filenames of the graphic, sound, or video files you've included on the page.

The components on your page should work together to make your page a pleasant place to visit and to relay the information you want readers to have. You can do several things to achieve these goals:

- Add pictures to help break up long passages of text, and to illustrate what you're saying in the text.
- Include links that lead to the next page or related subjects, to help guide readers through your web site.
- Place horizontal lines in the text to mark the beginning of a new topic.
- Present text in different formats to add visual interest to the page and avoid long narratives.
- Break up long pages into several shorter ones, both to make them faster to load, and to let users zoom in more quickly on the material they want.

Formatting Text

Formatting text in FrontPage Express is similar to formatting text in other text editors. You type text, select the word or phrase you want to format, and choose a formatting option. When you format text, the appropriate HTML tags are added automatically.

The formats you apply on web pages are not as exact as the formats you apply to printed pages. Some browsers interpret styles differently; for example, a Heading 1 style might be 14-point bold font in one browser, and 16-point regular font in another. HTML was not designed to give web page creators lots of control over the fonts, colors, and layout of the page; instead, HTML was designed to make it easy to create simple, readable pages that browsers can lay out using the screen area and fonts available on any computer.

Text formatting buttons are displayed on the Format toolbar:

The text formatting options available in FrontPage Express (from left to right) are

- **Change Style**   The styles available in FrontPage Express correspond to HTML standard formats for text. You cannot create your own styles. The Headings styles are used in almost all documents you see on the Web.

- **Change Font**   A variety of fonts are available in FrontPage Express. You can also add your own fonts. Be sure the font you select is easy to read online, and keep in mind that users reading your web page probably won't have exactly the same set of fonts available that you have available.

- **Increase Text Size**   Increases the text size each time you click the button.

- **Decrease Text Size**   Decreases the text size each time you click the button.

- **Bold**   Applies bold highlighting to selected text.

- **Italic**   Changes the selected text to italic print.

- **Underline**   Underlines the selected text.

- **Text Color**   Allows you to choose a different color for the selected text.

- **Align Left**   Aligns text on the left side of the screen.

- **Center**   Aligns text in the center of the screen.

- **Align Right**.   Aligns text on the right side of the screen.

- **Decrease Indent**   Moves the selected text to the left.

- **Increase Indent**   Moves the selected text to the right.

   To place horizontal lines between blocks of text, choose Insert | Horizontal Line.

Arranging Information in Lists

If you're looking for information on a web page, you probably get annoyed if the author has written all the text in long, narrative paragraphs. That structure is great for fiction, but it makes it difficult to locate quickly the information you need.

HTML provides several different kinds of lists that you can use to give information to your readers. Figure 26-5 shows the lists used most often on web pages.

The bulleted list is useful when you have a number of options to present, and you don't care in which order they are presented. To start a bulleted list, click the Bulleted List button on the toolbar. As you enter text, the bullet is added to the next line automatically when you press ENTER. To return to regular text, click the Change Style item on the toolbar and select Normal.

If steps must be performed in an exact sequence, or if you want your options ordered, use the numbered list. Click the Numbered List button on the toolbar to start the list, and select the Normal style to stop the list.

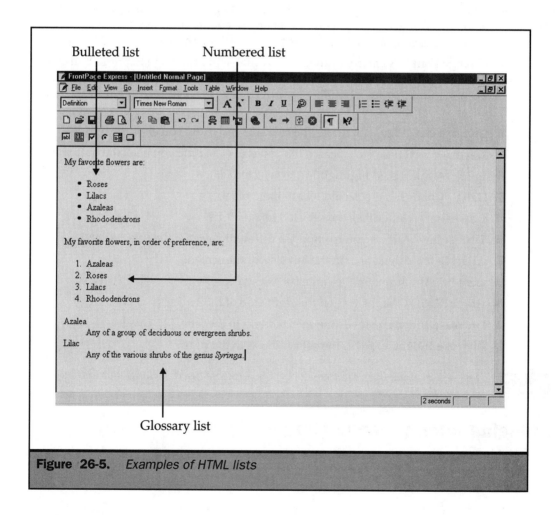

Figure 26-5. *Examples of HTML lists*

The glossary list was designed to look like a glossary or dictionary entry, with the term on a line by itself, and the definition below the term. To start a glossary list, click the Change Style down-arrow and select Defined Term. Type the term and press ENTER. The Definition style is applied to the line automatically. When you are finished with the list, click the Change Style item on the toolbar and select Normal.

Two other types of lists are available in HTML that are not used very much any more: Menu lists and Directory lists. Menu lists were intended for short lists of single items. Directory lists were intended for even shorter lists, such as a DOS directory of files. Both of these lists are included in the Style box in FrontPage Express.

Presenting Information in Tables

Using a table is a good way to provide a lot of information in a small space. In your travels around the Web, you've probably viewed pages that were formatted in tables, even though the formatting was not apparent.

Tables are not just for statistical information. You can use tables to present all types of information, including

- Price lists
- Online catalogs with graphics
- Quick reference sheets
- News bulletins
- Weather maps and conditions
- Anything else that can be displayed in a grid format

To add a table to your page, follow these steps:

1. Click the Insert Table button on the toolbar. (You can also choose Table | Insert Table.) You see the Insert Table dialog box, shown in Figure 26-6.

2. Select the number of rows and columns you want to include on your table. In the Alignment box, select whether you want the table placed on the Left, Right, or Center of the page. If you do not want a visible border around each cell, select 0 in the Border Size box. To set the table at a specific size, select the Specify Width option and indicate the size.

3. When you click OK, the table is displayed, and you are ready to enter text or graphics in the table cells. If you want to change any of the table settings, choose Table | Table Properties. Make your changes in the Table Properties dialog box, as shown in Figure 26-7.

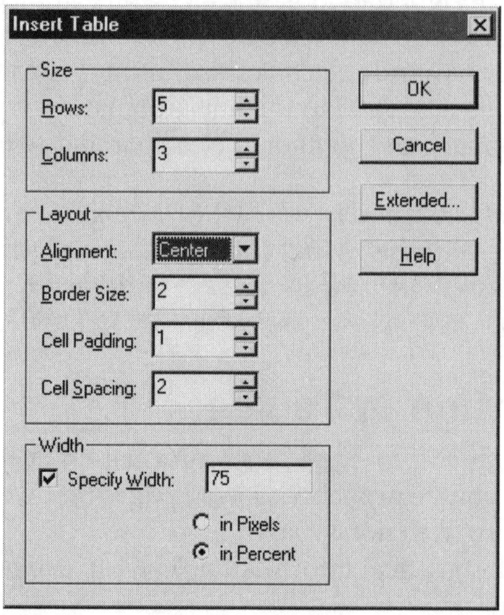

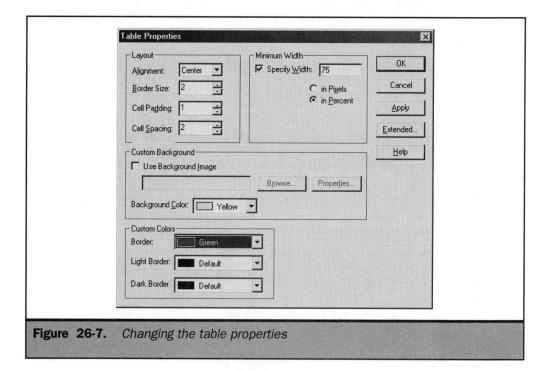

Figure 26-6. *Inserting a new table on a web page*

Figure 26-7. *Changing the table properties*

Tip   *The table cells adjust to accommodate the contents of the cell. To control the format of a single cell, choose Table | Cell Properties, or right-click the table and select Cell Properties.*

4. To insert a graphic, click the Insert Image button on the toolbar and select the file. Figure 26-8 shows a table containing text and graphics.

Adding Graphics

Graphics are the pictures, buttons, arrows, or other art that you add to web pages to illustrate the text or provide quick ways to navigate around the site.

Two graphic formats are usually used in web pages:

■ *GIF*, or Graphics Interchange Format, is the most widely used format and can be read by most browsers. GIF is good to use for buttons, icons, line art, and other simple images.

■ *JPEG*, or Joint Photographic Experts Group, was designed for more intricate graphics, and it's a good choice to use for photographs.

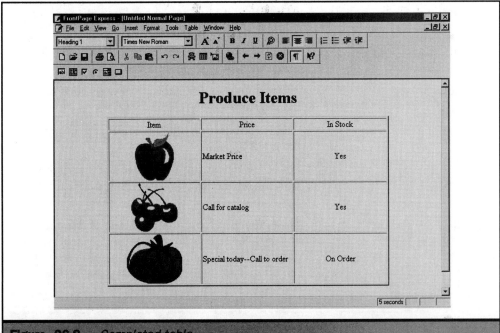

Figure 26-8.   *Completed table*

Where can you get graphic files to add to your web page? You can buy clip-art packages with files in GIF or JPEG format, you can download graphics files from the Web, you can use a scanner to digitize existing artwork, or you can create your own artwork with a graphics editor and save it as a GIF or JPEG file.

No matter which source you use, you want the graphics to fit in with the page design and flow with your text. To help control the way text and graphics are arranged on the page, HTML includes alignment options. Table 26-2 describes the alignment options that are available.

There are subtle differences among these alignment options. Sometimes it's hard to tell which option was used.

Alignment Option	Description
Bottom	Aligns the baseline of the text with the bottom of the graphic.
Middle	Aligns the baseline of the text with the middle of the graphic.
Top	Aligns the topmost item on the line with the top of the graphic.
Absbottom	Aligns the lowest item on the line with the bottom of the graphic.
Absmiddle	Aligns the middle of the largest item on the line with the middle of the graphic.
Texttop	Aligns the top of the tallest text with the top of the graphic.
Baseline	Aligns the baseline of the text with the bottom of the graphic. Same as Bottom.
Left	Places the graphic at the left side of the screen, and makes the text flow continuously around the graphic.
Right	Places the graphic at the right side of the screen, and makes the text flow continuously around the graphic. The Left and Right alignments are the only two alignment options that wrap text continuously around a graphic.

Table 26-2.   *Alignment Options for Placing Text Around Graphics*

To add a graphic to your page and align text around the graphic, follow these steps in FrontPage Express:

1. Click the Insert Image button on the toolbar. (You can also choose Insert |
   Image.) If you know the graphic's filename or URL, type it in the Image dialog
   box. If you don't know the filename, click the Browse button to look for the file.
   When you locate the file, select the filename and click Open. The graphic
   appears on your page.

2. To change the alignment option, right-click the graphic and select Image
   Properties. In the Image Properties dialog box, click the Appearance tab. Click
   the Alignment down-arrow and make your selection, as shown in Figure 26-9.
   Click OK.

You may need to adjust other options, besides the alignment option, in the Image
Properties dialog box. The Horizontal Spacing and Vertical Spacing fields control the
amount of distance between the edge of the graphic and the text. You can also enter a
specific size for the graphic, or resize the graphic manually by right-clicking it and
dragging the handles.

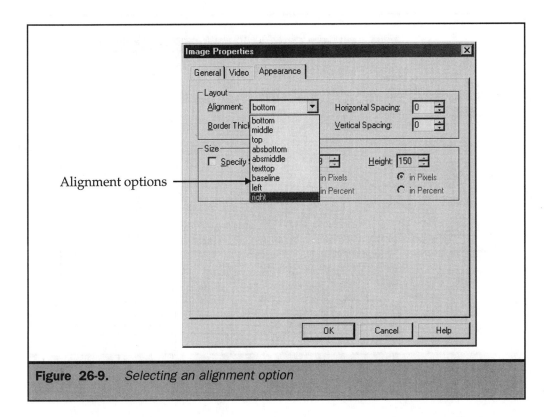

Figure 26-9.   *Selecting an alignment option*

Inserting Hyperlinks

Hyperlinks, or links, take you to other places (see "What Is the World Wide Web?" in Chapter 24). When you click a hyperlink, you move to another area of the page, jump to a completely different web page, or even access another resource on the Internet.

If you've used hyperlinks as the reader of a web page, you probably were grateful that the author included the links on the page. As the author of your own page, it's important to continue this tradition and provide your readers with links to other pages at your site, or to pages at other sites.

A hyperlink can be included in a line of text or added as a jump on a graphic. To insert a hyperlink in the text, click the Create Or Edit Hyperlink button on the toolbar, and enter the destination address, as shown in Figure 26-10. (You can also choose Insert | Hyperlink.)

HTTP is the protocol used to transmit web pages, and it appears at the default hyperlink type. To select a different type, click in the Hyperlink Type box and select the type you want from the drop-down list.

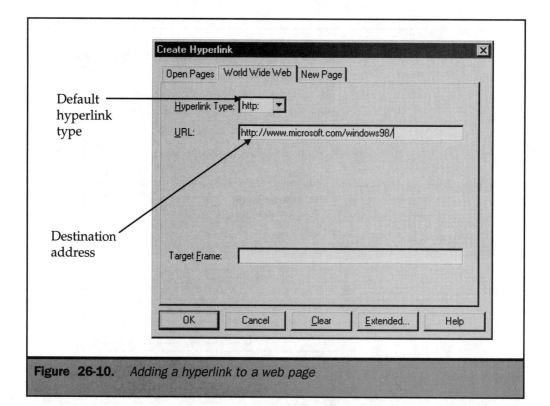

Figure 26-10.   *Adding a hyperlink to a web page*

To insert a hyperlink on a graphic, right-click the graphic and select Image Properties. In the Image Properties dialog box, type the complete destination address in the Location box.

Using WebBot Components

WebBot is the name that FrontPage Express gives to dynamic objects that you can add to your page.

Before adding a WebBot to your page, check with your web server administrator to be sure that your server supports the options you want to use. Your web server must run Microsoft's FrontPage software, which is not the most commonly run web server.

 If you're not sure which server your web pages will be stored on, or if there is a chance that the pages may move to another server in the future, avoid using WebBot components.

The available WebBots are the following:

- **Include**   Allows you to include another file in your page, by referencing the filename. When you add this WebBot to your page, you are asked to enter the URL of the web page you want to include.
- **Search**   Places a Search form on your web page.
- **Time Stamp**   Displays the date and/or time on your page.

To add a WebBot at the cursor location, follow these steps:

1. Click the Insert WebBot Component button on the toolbar. (You can also choose Insert | Insert WebBot Component.)

2. Select the component you want to add and click OK. If you select the Include component, FrontPage Express asks you to enter the URL of the page you want to include. If you select the Search component, you can accept the default search fields or fill in your own labels. If you select the Time Stamp component, you need to select the type of date you want to display and the format in which you want it to appear.

Testing Web Pages

Whenever you create or modify a web page, you should test the page in as many different browsers as possible, to make sure it looks the way you want it to look and to be sure all the links work. You can test your page without publishing it on the Web. When you click a link that requires Internet access, you either are prompted to connect to the Internet or receive an error message stating that the linked page cannot be found. (Of course, if you are testing the page at work and you have constant Internet access throughout the day, your links should work fine without any prompting or error messages.)

 If possible, test your page using both Netscape Navigator and Internet Explorer, including the latest version and other commonly used versions.

Before you test your page, check that the page has an appropriate title. The page title appears on the title bar whenever anyone accesses your page. To view or change the title in FrontPage Express, choose Format | Background and click the General tab. The Title box shows your page title. If necessary, modify the title to something that's more descriptive of the page. (You can also change the title in the Save As dialog box when you save the file.)

When the title is correct, choose File | Save As. Select the folder in which you want to store the file, enter a filename, and then click Save. You'll need to enter the full path name and filename in your browser to view the page.

To test your page in a browser, open your browser program and type the full path name and filename for your page on the Address or Location bar. Scroll down through the page to be sure it looks all right. Try each link to make sure the destinations are correct. You can't make changes in the browser; to modify your page, go back to FrontPage Express, enter the changes, and save the page again.

Publishing Web Pages

No one can see your page until you publish it on a *web server*, a computer running a web server program that sends web pages to web browsers over a network. In order to publish your page, you need information from your web server administrator or your Internet service provider regarding file locations, access, and publishing procedures.

Saving Your Web Pages onto a Web Server

Testing your pages in a browser before uploading them to a web server is always a good idea. However, you can publish your page directly from FrontPage Express without saving it as a local file. Choose File | Save As to run the Web Publishing Wizard. Type the file location you received from your administrator or ISP in the Page Location box. Continue working through the Wizard screens. When you are finished, your page is posted on the Web.

Note *The Web Publishing Wizard may not have been installed on your system. If not, install it from your Windows 98 CD-ROM or floppy disks: open Control Panel, open Add/Remove Programs, click the Windows Setup tab, choose the Internet Tools category from the Components list, click Details, and choose Web Publishing Wizard (see "Installing and Uninstalling Programs that Come with Windows 98" in Chapter 3).*

Uploading Web Pages Using Ftp

Most people transfer their finished web pages to their web server by using an FTP (file transfer protocol) program. Windows 98 comes with one, called Ftp (see "Transferring Files Using Ftp" in Chapter 28). It's not particularly good, though, so you might want to consider downloading a better one from the World Wide Web, like WS_FTP (see "Downloading, Installing, and Running Other Internet Programs" in Chapter 28).

Using the Personal Web Server

If you're part of a corporate intranet, you might want to consider setting up your computer as a web server, which allows you to share your HTML files with others in a small-scale arrangement. You can install the Personal Web Server, which comes with Windows 98. This application is not intended to turn your computer into a server on the World Wide Web; it's neither fast nor robust enough to act as a public web server.

To install and set up the Personal Web Server, follow these steps:

1. Choose Start | Programs | Internet Explorer | Personal Web Server.

2. Insert the Windows 98 CD-ROM in your CD drive. Choose Start | Run. Type **d:\add-ons\pws\setup.exe** in the Open box (using your own CD-ROM drive letter instead of D, if different) and click OK. The Setup program starts.

3. Select the Typical configuration. Accept the default installation folder name. The files are installed.

4. Restart your computer. Right-click the Personal Web Server icon on the Taskbar and select Properties.

5. Click the Web Site button. The Home Page Wizard starts. Answer the questions on the screen to indicate what information you want to display on the home page.

When you're ready to publish a page to your Personal Web Server, you can either open the Publish icon on the desktop, or right-click the Personal Web Server icon on the Taskbar, select Properties, and then click the Publish button.

Tip   *You don't need to run the Personal Web Server in order for others on your intranet to view web pages stored on your computer. Just store the web page on a shared folder or drive to which others have access. Other intranet users can see your web pages by choosing File | Open or File | Open Page in their web browsers.*

Chapter 27

Conferencing Over the Internet
with Microsoft Chat and
NetMeeting

indows 98 comes with two programs for chatting and conferencing over the Internet. Microsoft Chat lets you participate in Internet Relay Chat, a real-time, Internet-wide set of chat rooms. Microsoft NetMeeting lets you use the Internet as a long distance phone service, including video conferencing, typed chat, and even sharing programs over the Internet.

This chapter describes how to use these two programs. You can download other Internet chat and conferencing programs from the Internet itself; Chapter 28 tells you how.

> **Note**   *Microsoft Chat and NetMeeting are not included in the standard Windows 98 installation. You can install them from your Windows 98 CD-ROM or floppy disks (see "Installing and Uninstalling Programs That Come with Windows 98" in Chapter 3). Open Control Panel, run the Add/Remove Programs program, click the Windows Setup tab, choose Communications from the list of components, click Details, and choose Microsoft Chat and NetMeeting.*

Chatting Online by Using Microsoft Chat

Microsoft Chat is a *chat client*, a program that lets you participate in real-time chat (also called *Internet Relay Chat* or *IRC*) with other people via the Internet. To chat, you connect to a *chat server*, which acts as a switchboard for all the messages of the participants. Since thousands of people may be participating at one time, the world of online chat is divided into *rooms* (also known as *channels*), so that each room can concentrate on a specific topic. (Unfortunately, the topic of the majority of rooms appears, from observation, to be flirting, talking dirty, and otherwise wasting time—but if a miracle occurs, this may change as the world of chat evolves.) After you enter a room, you type messages; seconds after you press ENTER to send your message, everyone else in the room sees your message. Likewise, you see the messages sent by everyone else in the room.

> **Tip**   *Internet Relay Chat has been around for years, and there's a lot to know about it. For general information about online chatting, how to find chat rooms of interest to you, how not to make a fool of yourself, and other important information, read the documentation at the web sites listed in the sidebar "How to Find IRC Servers."*

Microsoft Chat version 2.0 includes an innovative feature—rather than just seeing a list of the messages sent by the people in the room, you can use Comics View to see the conversation as a comic strip. You can choose what character you want to look like onscreen. The conversation looks more interesting as a comic strip, and the faces remind you that real human beings are behind the chat, not just a bunch of computers. However, you can see fewer messages on the screen with Comics View.

Note *Internet Relay Chat, in which Microsoft Chat lets you participate, does not connect with the chat systems run by online services. Specifically, you can't use Microsoft Chat to join America Online's or CompuServe's chat rooms. Similarly, only Microsoft Network (MSN) members can enter MSN's members-only chat rooms.*

Configuring the Program

To run Microsoft Chat, choose Start | Programs | Internet Explorer | Microsoft Chat. You see the Connect dialog box; click Cancel, and then OK, to take a moment to configure your program before connecting to a server. (If you've never used the program before, it asks for your *nickname*—the name by which you'll be known while chatting online.) Then follow these steps:

1. Choose View | Options (or press CTRL-Q) to display the Microsoft Chat Options dialog box, shown in Figure 27-1.

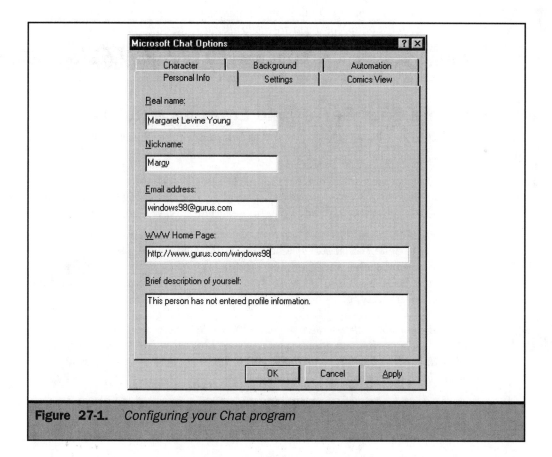

Figure 27-1. *Configuring your Chat program*

2. On the Personal Info tab, fill in as much information about yourself as you really want people in online chat rooms to know about you. You can leave boxes blank; only the Nickname box must contain an entry.

3. On the Settings tab, choose the options you want to use when you chat; you can prevent people from "whispering" to you (sending you private messages) or playing sounds on your computer's speakers.

4. On the Automation tab, you can create macros to record and play back comments you make frequently. (For example, if you type "Come here often?" to each person who enters the room, you can set ALT-1 to type that comment.)

5. If you are in Comics View, choose your options on the Comics View, Background, and Character tabs. If you are in Text View, choose your options on the Text View tab.

6. Click OK.

 The Content Advisor can screen out chats with offensive content. If you plan to allow children to chat online, or if you are easily offended, click the Settings tab on the Microsoft Chat Options dialog box. The Content Advisor can also screen out offensive web sites while browsing the World Wide Web (see "Avoiding What You Don't Want on the Web with Content Advisor" in Chapter 25).

Connecting to a Chat Server and Entering a Room

First, you connect to an IRC server, and then you enter a room (channel). Follow these steps:

1. When you start Microsoft Chat, the Connect dialog box (Figure 27-2) automatically appears. You can also display the Connect dialog box by clicking the Connect icon on the toolbar or by choosing File | New Connection.

2. Choose a server. If you have a Microsoft Network (MSN) account, you can connect to the default chat server (chat.msn.com). Otherwise, use a publicly accessible server by choosing a name from the Server list or by typing in a server name. See the sidebar "How to Find IRC Servers" to learn how to find the names of servers to type.

Tip *If you've already added chat servers to your Favorites list, you can choose a chat server from the Favorites box. If you want to connect to the same server that you used last time, and enter the same room, you'll find that those defaults already appear in the Connect dialog box.*

Figure 27-2. *Connecting to a chat server*

3. Choose a room. If you know the name of the chat room you want to join, you can type it in the Go To Chat Room box; otherwise, click Show All Available Chat Rooms. Then click OK. Microsoft Chat tries to connect to the IRC server. Servers are frequently full, having hit their maximum number of connections, so you may have to try several servers before you connect.

4. Once you are connected, if you specified the name of a room in step 3, you are ready to chat. Otherwise, you see the list of rooms (Figure 27-3). If the list is long, enter a number in the Min or Max boxes to specify the minimum or maximum number of people in the room. (Consider requiring a minimum of three to five people in a room, so that you enter a room with an active conversation.) To find a room whose title or description contains a particular word, type that word in the Display Chat Rooms That Contain box. When you see a likely looking room, double-click the room name to enter it.

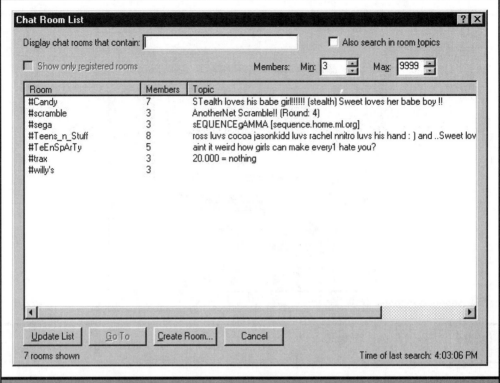

Figure 27-3.   *A list of chat rooms*

How to Find IRC Servers

Hundreds of IRC servers are active, and most are publicly accessible. IRC servers are organized into networks, and all the rooms (channels) on all the servers on a network are visible to anyone connected to any of the servers on that network. Servers come and go, but here are the web sites of some IRC server networks:

- EFNet (the original IRC server network): **http://www.irchelp.org**

- Undernet (one of the first alternative networks): **http://www.undernet.org**

- DALnet (the third of the Big Three networks): **http://www.dal.net**

- KidsWorld (just for kids): **http://www.kidsworld.org**

- AnotherNet (a smaller network): **http://www.another.org**

- StarLink (no sex-related or software-piracy rooms): **http://www.starlink.org**

Chatting

Once you are connected to an IRC server and in a room, you see the Microsoft Chat window. Figure 27-4 shows a conversation in Comics View, and Figure 27-5 shows a conversation in Text View. The conversation in the room begins to appear in the large box in the form of either comic strip panels (in Comics View) or lines of text (in Text View). The list of people in the room appears in the upper-right part of the window (scroll down to see the complete list, along with the character used by each person if you are in Comics View).You can tell who is talking by the character who appears in the comic strip panel (in Comics View) or by the name that precedes the message (in Text View).

In Comics View, you also see a picture of your own character, and a set of facial expressions from which to choose. (Click in the center of the circle for no particular expression.)

Sending Public or Private Messages

To send a message, type it in the small box at the bottom of the Microsoft Chat window, and then press ENTER (or click the Say button immediately to the right of the

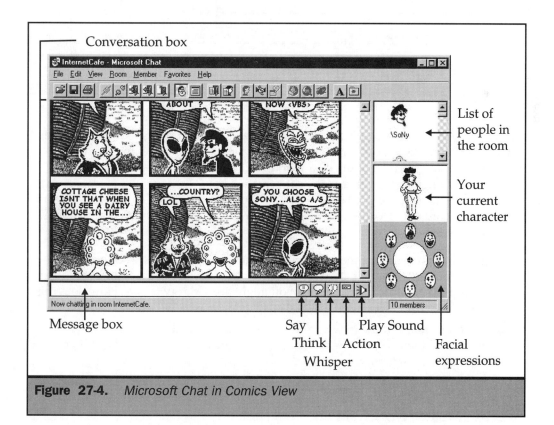

Figure 27-4.   *Microsoft Chat in Comics View*

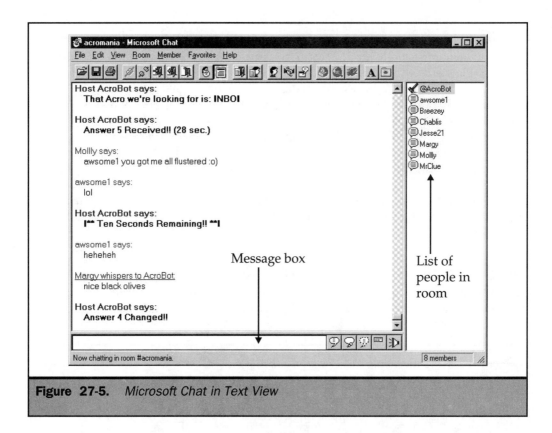

Figure 27-5.   *Microsoft Chat in Text View*

message box, or press CTRL-Y). Your message appears in the conversation box, preceded by your nickname. As the conversation proceeds, messages scroll off the top of the conversation area; if you want to go back and read what has scrolled off the top, use the scroll bar along the right side of the conversation box.

Normally, the messages you send are visible to everyone in the chat room. But you have other options. After you type a message in the message box, but before you press ENTER, you have the following options:

■ Type a message in the message box, without pressing ENTER, and then click the Think button (or press CTRL-T) to make the message appear as a thought rather than spoken words. For example, you might see, "Margy thinks: How does this program work?"

■ Type a message in the message box, click a name on the list of people in the room, and then click the Whisper button (or press CTRL-W) to whisper a private message to that person.

- Type an action in the message box, like "gets confused" or "scratches her head," and then click the Action button (or press CTRL-I). The action appears, preceded by your nickname, like this: "Margy gets confused."

- Click the Play Sound button and choose a sound from the list that appears. (To add sounds to that list, store other WAV files in the C:\Windows\Media folder.) The sound is played on the computers of the other people in the room, assuming that their computers have speakers, and that the same sound file is stored on their hard disks.

Leaving a Chat Room

To leave the room, click the Leave Room button or choose Room | Leave Room. You can click the Chat Room List button to see a list of rooms, and to choose another room to enter. Unlike most IRC chat client programs, Microsoft Chat lets you visit only one room at a time.

To disconnect from the IRC server, click the Disconnect button or choose Room | Disconnect.

Sending and Receiving Private Messages

You can send a single private message to someone else in your room by typing the message, selecting the person's name from the user list, and then clicking the Whisper button. For a private conversation, you can open a whisper box with another person in your room. Select the person's name from the user list, and then click the Whisper Box button on the toolbar (or choose Member | Whisper Box). A window appears in which your private conversation is shown; type in the message box at the bottom of the window to send a private message.

If someone sends you a private message, a whisper box appears with that person's message. Sometimes, private messages can be obtrusive or downright offensive. You can click the Ignore User button if one person keeps bothering you.

Anyone can send you a private message inviting you to join his or her chat room. You see a dialog box asking whether you want to join. Watch out for these invitations, which can be come-ons of one sort or another. If you don't want to be bothered by invitations, choose View | Options (or press CTRL-Q) to see the Microsoft Chat Options dialog box, click the Settings tab, and then deselect the Receive Chat Invitations option.

Creating Your Own Chat Room

You can create your own chat room on the IRC server to which you are connected. Follow these steps:

1. Click the Create Room button on the toolbar, or choose Room | Create Room. You see the Create Chat Room dialog box (shown in Figure 27-6).

2. Type a name (on most IRC servers, names must begin with a #) and topic for the chat room, and then choose the other options shown on the dialog box. Then click OK. The IRC server creates the room and displays it with only you in it. You are the *chanop* (channel operator) for the room, which means that you set the topic and can kick out other people.

3. Wait for people to enter your room. You can invite in other currently connected people if you know their nicknames; click the Invite button (or choose Member | Invite) and type the nickname(s) of people to invite in.

If people get unruly, you can ask them to leave. You can even kick them out of your room by selecting the person from the user list and choosing Member | Host | Kick. To ban someone permanently from the room, so the person can't come back (at least, not with the same nickname), choose Member | Host | Ban.

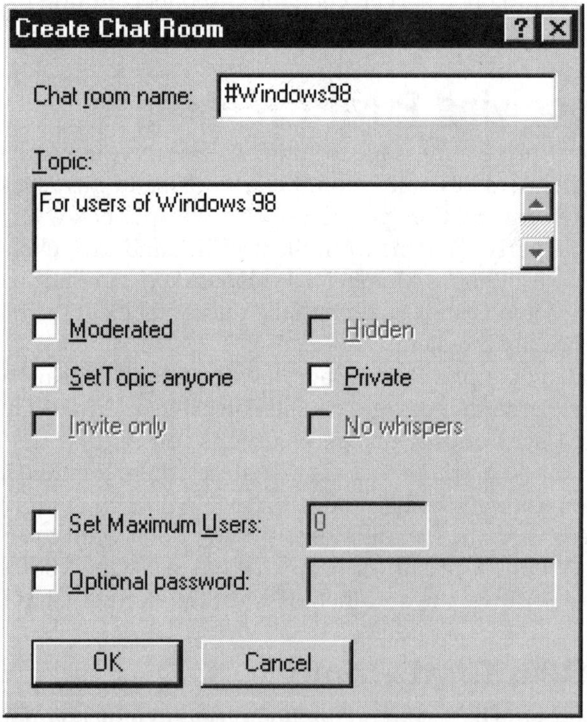

Figure 27-6.   *Creating your own chat room*

Other Things You Can Do

Here are other things you can do while chatting:

- Switch between Comics View and Text View anytime by clicking the Comics View and Text View buttons on the toolbar, or by choosing either View | Comics Strip or View | Plain Text.

- Save a transcript of the conversation in a file. In Text View, you can save a transcript in RTF (Rich Text Format), which is readable with formatting by most word processors, or in CCC format (Chat Conversation), which is readable by Microsoft Chat (open a CCC file by choosing File | Open).

- Look at information about the people in your chat room. Click the User List button or choose Member | User List. The User List dialog box shows all the people connected to the same server as you are; if the list is empty, click Update List. On the list of people, you can select one person and click the Whisper button to open a Whisper box that allows the two of you to have a private conversation. Or, you can select a person and click Invite to invite the person to join the room you are in.

- Get more information about a person in your chat room by selecting that person from the user list and clicking the Get Identity button (or choosing Member | Get Identity). You see the person's e-mail address, or at least the person's user name and the domain name of the computer to which he or she is connected. If the person's profile includes an e-mail address, you can click the Send E-mail button on the toolbar (or choose Member | Send E-mail) to send an e-mail message using your e-mail program (see Chapter 23). If the person's profile includes a URL in his or her profile, you can click the Visit HomePage button on the toolbar (or choose Member | Visit Home page) to run your web browser and see the specified web page (see Chapter 24). If the person's profile includes NetMeeting information, you can click the NetMeeting button on the toolbar (or choose Member | NetMeeting) to contact the person by using Microsoft NetMeeting (described in the next section).

- Send a file to someone (this may not work, depending on what IRC client program the person uses) by right-clicking the person on the user list and choosing Send File from the menu that appears. If someone tries to send you a file, Microsoft Chat asks whether you want to receive it. (Warning: Files sent over IRC can be incredibly rude, so watch out.) If you never want to receive files, choose View | Options, click the Settings tab, and then deselect the Receive File Transfer Requests option.

The more completely and truthfully you fill in the Personal Info section of the Microsoft Chat Options dialog box, the more potential there is that you will receive unwanted attention from other Internet users, in the form of unsolicited e-mail, invitations to chat, or "whispers."

Conferencing Using Microsoft NetMeeting

Microsoft NetMeeting is like a specialized chat program with lots of extra features. In addition to typing messages to other people in the chat room, all participants can draw on a shared virtual whiteboard, transfer files to each other, or edit a file together. If you have microphones, speakers, and video cameras, you can even use NetMeeting for voice or video conferences.

In order to connect to the other people with whom you want to meet, NetMeeting uses a *directory server* that stores the addresses of people who use NetMeeting. (The directory server is analogous to the IRC server that chat programs connect to.) When you are logged onto a directory server, your name appears on its lists, so that anyone else can "call" you. Once you have connected to a directory server, you can call another person, or several other people. You can start a new call, or join an existing call.

When you're connected to one or more people, you can do the following:

- Converse using audio, assuming that all callers' computers have microphones and speakers (audio is limited to two-person calls). You must have a reasonably fast Internet connection (at least a 28.8 bps modem) for acceptable audio quality.

- Chat by typing messages, very much like Text View in Microsoft Chat.

- Share a whiteboard, so that everyone can see what everyone else is drawing.

- See the person you are calling, if all callers' computers have video cameras (video is limited to two-person calls, too).

- Transfer files from one caller to another.

- Collectively edit a file—such as a word processing document, graphics file, or database—so that everyone in the call can see the changes everyone else has made.

NetMeeting lets you connect only with other people who use NetMeeting: it doesn't conform to any Internet conferencing standards. For example, you can't join a meeting with people who use Internet Relay Chat (IRC) or CU-SeeMe, PowWow, or Internet Phone (other online chat programs).

This section describes NetMeeting version 2.1.

Configuring NetMeeting

To run NetMeeting, choose Start | Programs | Internet Explorer | Microsoft NetMeeting. If you haven't already configured NetMeeting, you see a series of windows that tell you about the program and ask for the following information:

- **Which directory server to use**   The default is Microsoft's public server, at ils.microsoft.com. A number of other public directory servers are also available. If your organization uses NetMeeting, you may use a private directory server.

- **Your name, e-mail address, city, state, country, comments, and type of usage** You have to type your name and e-mail address, but you can leave the rest of the information blank. In fact, we recommend that you leave everything but your name blank and type a fake e-mail address, to avoid receiving unsolicited e-mail from unscrupulous Internet users. NetMeeting also asks you to categorize your use as either personal, business, or adults-only; this information is visible to others connected to the directory server.

- **Connection Speed**   Choose the speed of your modem, or specify that you are connected via a local area network. NetMeeting uses this information when sending audio or video data to you. It runs the Audio Tuning Wizard to make sure that your speakers are working.

When it's done, the configuration program displays the NetMeeting window. You may want to make some other changes to your configuration by choosing Call | Change My Information (or Tools | Options). On the Options dialog box that appears (shown in Figure 27-7), you can set these types of options:

- On the General tab, specify where to save files sent by other callers, whether to automatically accept incoming calls, whether to display icons for NetMeeting and the Intel Connection Advisor (a troubleshooting program that comes with NetMeeting) on the system tray, and other options.

- On the My Information tab, make changes to the information you typed when you first ran NetMeeting.

- On the Calling tab, specify which directory server to use and when to define SpeedDials (an address book that stores information about how to call people you plan to call often).

- On the Audio tab, configure NetMeeting to work with your microphone and speakers.

- On the Video tab, specify the size and quality of video images to display.

- On the Protocols tab, tell NetMeeting which network protocol to use to connect (choose TCP/IP for Internet connections).

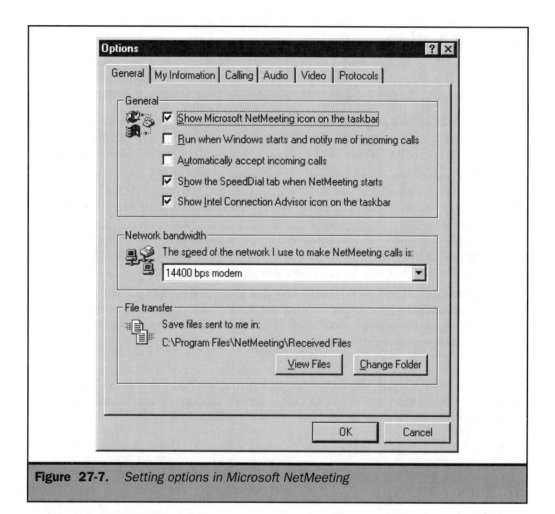

Figure 27-7. *Setting options in Microsoft NetMeeting*

Connecting to a Directory Server

When you start NetMeeting, it connects to a directory server. When you connect to a directory server, you see the Directory window within the NetMeeting window, showing a listing of the people connected to the same server (Figure 27-8). If you don't see a listing, click the Directory icon along the left side of the NetMeeting window. The little icon to the left of each person's e-mail address shows their status.

A PC icon with a blue screen and red twinkle means that the person is currently in a call, while a gray PC icon means that the person is not in a call. A little yellow speaker icon indicates that the person can communicate via audio. A little gray camera icon means that the person can communicate via video. By clicking in the Category

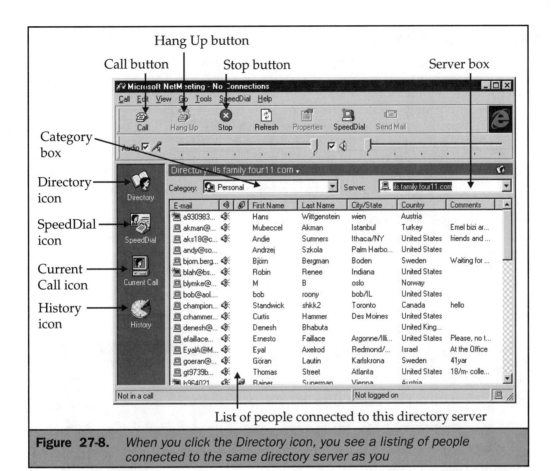

Figure 27-8. *When you click the Directory icon, you see a listing of people connected to the same directory server as you*

box, you can choose whether to see people who are running NetMeeting for personal use, business use, those in a call, those not in a call, those with video cameras, or all people.

On the listing of people, click the column headings to sort by that column; sorting by last name or e-mail address makes finding the person you want easier.

Tip   *If you want to choose a different server, click the Stop button on the toolbar (if NetMeeting is trying to connect to the wrong server), choose Call | Change My Information (or Tools | Options), click the Calling tab, choose the directory server from the Server name list, click OK, and then choose Call | Log On To (which includes the name of the selected directory server at the end of the command name). If you can't connect to a directory server, you can use the Web Directory instead. Choose Go | Web Directory.*

Making or Receiving a Call

To call someone, double-click the person's name on the directory list. NetMeeting contacts the directory server to make the connection, and then displays a dialog box on that person's computer screen, asking whether they want to connect with you. If the person accepts your call, you see the Current Call window within the NetMeeting window (Figure 27-9). (You can see this window any time by clicking the Current Call icon along the left side of the NetMeeting window.)

When someone calls you, you see a dialog box asking whether you want to take the call; click Accept if you do. You see the Current Call window.

Once you are connected to at least one other person, if both of you have microphones and speakers, you can just begin talking. Speak slowly, one at a time (as though you were using a walkie-talkie—over!). Unless you have a very fast connection, you may experience "breaking up"—the sound may be interrupted and "staticky." Keep your microphone away from the speakers to avoid feedback.

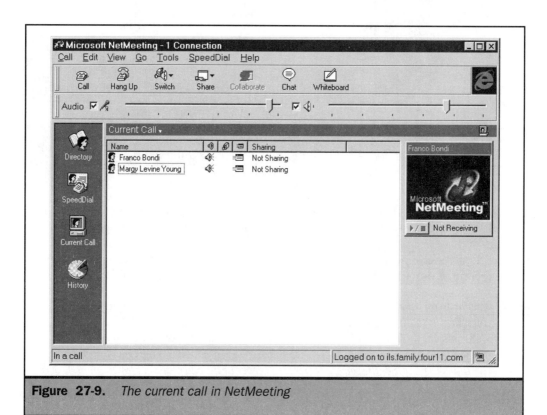

Figure 27-9.   *The current call in NetMeeting*

If one other person in the call has a video camera connected to the computer, video of the other person appears in the small Remote Video box on the right side of the NetMeeting window (see "Seeing Callers on Video").

Another way to make a call is to choose Call | New Call, or press CTRL-N. You see the New Call dialog box (Figure 27-10). In the Address box, type the name of the directory server to which the person is connected, followed by a slash (/) and the e-mail address of the person you want to call. If the person you are calling uses a computer with its own computer name or IP address, you can type that instead. Then click the Call button.

Hanging Up

When you are done with a call, click the Hang Up button on the toolbar. NetMeeting maintains its connection with the directory server, but disconnects from the call.

Creating and Using SpeedDials

A *SpeedDial* lets you store the connection information for people you plan to call more than once. To see a list of your SpeedDials, click the SpeedDial button on the left side of the NetMeeting window. NetMeeting usually creates a SpeedDial whenever you make

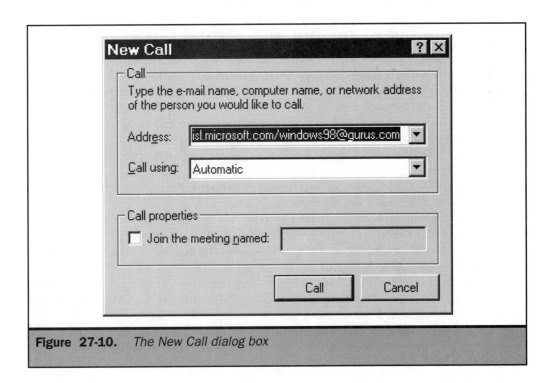

Figure 27-10.   *The New Call dialog box*

or receive a call; if you don't want SpeedDials created automatically, choose Tools | Options, click the Calling tab, and then choose the Automatically Add SpeedDials For People I Call And People Who Call Me setting that you want.

To add someone to your SpeedDials list, click either the Directory, Current Call, or History icon at the left of the NetMeeting window. Right-click the name of a person, and then choose Add SpeedDial from the menu that appears. Or, click the SpeedDial icon on the toolbar (or choose Call | Create SpeedDial) and fill out the dialog box:

- If you connect with the person by using a directory server, set the Call Using box to Directory Server. In the Address box, type the name of the directory server to which the person is connected, followed by a slash (/) and the e-mail address of the person you want to call. If the person is always connected to the same directory server that you are, you can omit the directory server name and the slash.

- If the person you are calling uses a computer with its own computer name or IP address, set the Call Using box to TCP/IP. In the Address box, type the host name or IP address.

After you create a SpeedDial, calling someone is easy—display your list of SpeedDials, and then double-click a name. Or, choose SpeedDials from the menu bar, and then choose the name from the menu that appears.

Hosting a Meeting or Joining an Existing Meeting

In addition to calls, you can communicate in *meetings*, calls that are scheduled in advance. To host a meeting, let everyone invited to the meeting know when the meeting will take place and how to call you using NetMeeting. At the time the meeting is scheduled to begin, choose Call | Host Meeting. NetMeeting displays the Current Call window, with only you listed as a caller. When the other callers connect, you see a dialog box asking whether they can join; click Accept or Ignore.

Because you are the host of the meeting, the meeting ends when you hang up. Other participants can come and go without ending the meeting. As the host, you can also throw people out of your meeting; right-click the person's name on the list of callers and choose Remove from the menu that appears.

To join an existing meeting, call someone who is in the meeting. You see a message that the person is currently in a meeting, asking whether you want to try to join the meeting; click Yes. When the person you called leaves the meeting, you leave too, so it's best to call the person who is hosting the meeting.

A *named meeting* is a meeting hosted by a teleconferencing company or some other meeting server. To join a named meeting, click the Call button on the toolbar to display the New Call dialog box. Then, in the Address box, type the network address of the host of the meeting, click the Join The Meeting Named box, and then type the name of the meeting (be sure to use the exact spelling and capitalization provided by the meeting host).

If you don't want anyone else to join the meeting (or any NetMeeting call), choose Call | Do Not Disturb. Remember to choose the same command again when you want to re-enable receiving calls.

Typing Messages in a Call

During a call, you can use written words, as well as a voice (especially useful if you don't have a microphone and speakers on your computer). Click the Chat button on the toolbar; NetMeeting displays a Chat window (Figure 27-11). To send a message to everyone in the call, type the message in the Message box, and then press ENTER. To send a message to one caller, click that person's name in the Send To box, type the message in the Message box, and then press ENTER.

The Chat window is a good place to take notes on the call. You can save a transcript of the meeting (the typed chat part, anyway) by choosing File | Save from the Chat

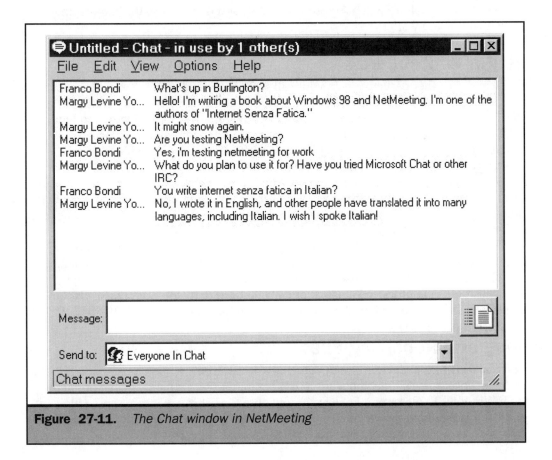

Figure 27-11. *The Chat window in NetMeeting*

window's menu bar. NetMeeting saves the messages in a text file with the filename you specify. Then you can e-mail your notes to the others in your call.

Seeing Callers on Video

If other people in your call have video cameras (even if you don't have one), you can see video from one of their cameras (one at a time) in your NetMeeting window. The video appears in the Remote Video window, a small box on the right side of the window when the Current Call icon is selected. If you don't see the video, click the button at the bottom of the Remote Video window.

To set your video options, choose Tools | Options, and then click the Video tab. You can tell NetMeeting to automatically enable your video camera when you make a call, set the size of the video image, choose between faster low-quality video and slower high-quality video, and specify the properties of your camera. If you have a camera, be sure to light your face (or whatever the camera points at) from the front.

You can't see more than one person at a time; to switch which person in the call you can see, choose Tools | Switch Audio And Video, and then choose the name of the person whom you want to see.

Sharing a Whiteboard

If you and the other participants in your call want to draw diagrams or pictures that are visible by everyone in the call, use the Whiteboard feature. When you click the Whiteboard button on the toolbar, you see the Whiteboard window (shown in Figure 27-12), which works similarly to Microsoft Paint (see "Drawing Pictures Using Microsoft Paint" in Chapter 5). When anyone in the call makes a change to the Whiteboard window, everyone in the call sees the change.

Unlike real whiteboards, the Whiteboard window can have as many pages as you want. (Maybe it's actually a flip chart.) To create a new page, click the Insert New Page button in the lower-right corner of the Whiteboard window. You can use the buttons to its left to switch from page to page.

If you want to take control of the whiteboard for a while, choose Tools | Lock Controls from the menu bar in the Whiteboard window. Only you can make changes to the whiteboard, until you choose the command again.

When you have produced a useful drawing or diagram, you can save or print the contents of the whiteboard by choosing File | Save (or Print).

Sending and Receiving Files

You can send files to anyone else in your call. Choose Tools | File Transfer | Send File, and then specify which file you want to send. Alternatively, drag the name of the file from Windows Explorer or a Folder window onto the list of callers. To send a file to one caller rather than to everyone in the call, right-click the person's name in the list of callers, and then choose Send File from the menu that appears.

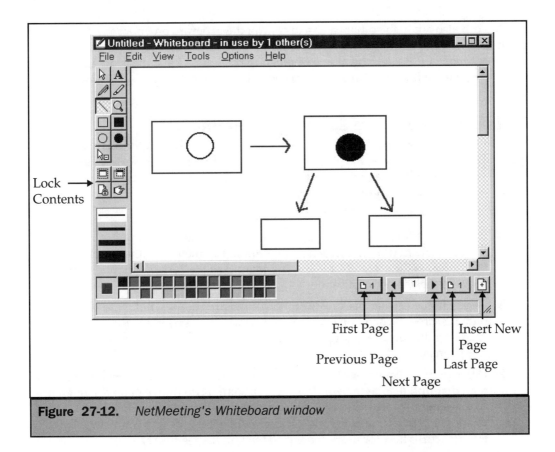

Figure 27-12. *NetMeeting's Whiteboard window*

If someone sends you a file, NetMeeting automatically receives the file, storing it in the C:\Program Files\NetMeeting\Received Files folder. You see a window telling you about the arrival of the file. To open the file with the default application for the type of file you received, click the Open button.

 Beware of viruses in executable files, and beware of generally offensive material when receiving files from people you don't know.

Sharing Programs

You and the other people in your meeting can share the windows of a running program that one member has on his or her screens. For example, you could show a group around your web site by running a browser on your machine, and then sharing the browser window so that the other callers can see the contents of the browser window on their screens, too.

You can also allow the other callers to control the program on your machine. For example, if you are working on a document in WordPerfect, all callers can edit the document together. Even if the other people in the call don't have the program you are using to create the file, you can give them control of your WordPerfect window to edit the file.

Letting Everyone Else See Your Program

To share a program with others in your call, run the program, click the Share button on the toolbar, and then choose the program from the list that appears. Now everyone in the call can see the program, even if they don't have the program on their computers. Only you can give commands to the program.

Here are a few pointers when sharing a program:

- Before you start to share an application, be sure to agree on a screen resolution for everyone to use. Using the same resolution as the rest of the people in the call prevents the screen from jumping around as the cursor and mouse pointer move in the shared application.

- Others in the call can see only as much of the program's window as you can see on your screen; when you click another window that overlaps the window that is editing the file, the obscured part of the window disappears on everyone else's screen, too.

- Unless you and everyone else in the call have fast Internet connections (faster than dial-up), displaying windows with a shared program can take a long time—a minute or two. Everyone in the call needs to wait for the shared window to appear, or everyone's screens will get hopelessly confusing. This feature works best for users connected by a high-speed LAN.

Letting Everyone Else Control a Shared Program

If you want the other callers to be able to control the shared program, you can let them. First, share the file by using the Share button, and then click the Collaborate button on the toolbar. Each person in the call who wants to participate clicks the Collaborate button on the toolbar, too. Now, anyone in the call can click in the application window to take control of the window, and then move the mouse or give commands. While another caller is controlling the shared program, the program's owner loses use of the cursor. The owner of the program can press ESC at any time to get control (and get the cursor back). Everyone else can still see the shared program's window. To let people take control again, click Collaborate again. To stop sharing the program, so that the other callers can no longer see the program's window, click the Share button on the toolbar again, and then choose the application to stop sharing.

Here are some tips about sharing control of a program:

- If you share Windows Explorer or a Folder window, all windows displayed by that application are shared with the other callers, including windows that you open after clicking the Share button.

- If you are going to edit a file collaboratively, make a backup copy of the file first, just in case. When you are done editing the file collaboratively, only the person who originally shared the file can save or print the file. If other callers want copies of the finished file, the owner of the file can send the file to the other callers.

- Each person in the call does not need to have the program that the call is sharing; mouse clicks and keystrokes are transmitted to the program's owner's computer.

Adding a NetMeeting Link to a Web Page

You can make it easy for other NetMeeting users to call you, by adding a NetMeeting-compatible *callto* link on your web page. On the web page, create a link (see "Inserting Hyperlinks" in Chapter 26) with the URL:

callto:servername/emailaddress

For example, a callto link might look like this:

<a href="callto:ils.family.four11.com/win98tcr@gurus.com>Call me!</a>

Other Things NetMeeting Can Do

Here are other things that you can do with NetMeeting:

- **See a history of calls**   Click the History icon on the left side of the NetMeeting window.

- **Send e-mail to someone**   Right-click a caller's name in the list of callers in the Current Call window or in the Directory listing, and then choose the Send Mail command from the menu that appears. NetMeeting runs Outlook Express to send the message; if you haven't configured Outlook Express, you see a dialog box asking you to do so.

- **Omit your name from the directory server listing**   Choose Tools | Options, click the Calling tab, and then select the Do Not List My Name In The Directory option. People can still call you by using the New Call dialog box, but they have to know your e-mail address and to which directory server you are connected.

Chapter 28

Other Internet Programs that Come with Windows 98

Working better with the Internet was one of Microsoft's main goals in creating Windows 98, so Windows 98 comes with lots of Internet-related programs. In addition to the automated sign-up software, the Internet Connection Wizard, and Dial-Up Networking, all described in Chapter 22, you get lots of Internet applications, which are described in the other chapters in this part of the book. Windows 98 also comes with these other useful Internet programs:

- HyperTerminal acts as a terminal emulator and lets you log into text-based systems, either over the Internet (like telnet) or by dialing directly.

- Telnet can also do terminal emulation over the Internet, faster but not as nicely as HyperTerminal.

- Ftp lets you transfer files to or from FTP servers.

- Virtual Private Networking lets your organization create a private local area network over the Internet.

This chapter describes how to use these programs. You can download other Internet programs from the Internet itself, and we recommend some programs that complement those that come with Windows 98 and suggest where to find the programs on the Web. In fact, you can use almost any Internet program that is Winsock-compatible (see "What Is Winsock?" in Chapter 22).

Logging in to Text-Based Systems Using HyperTerminal

HyperTerminal is Windows 98's built-in terminal-emulation program. It lets your powerful Windows computer, loaded with RAM, hard disk space, and other hardware, pretend to be a dumb terminal. HyperTerminal is useful for connecting to computers that are designed to talk to terminals, including UNIX shell accounts and bulletin board systems (see "UNIX Shell Accounts and Bulletin Board Systems" in Chapter 22). The computer you connect to by using HyperTerminal is called the *remote computer* (as opposed to your own *local computer*).

Note *HyperTerminal is not automatically installed when you install Windows 98; you may need to open the Control Panel, open the Add/Remove Programs icon, click the Windows Setup tab, choose Communications from the list of components, click Details, and then select HyperTerminal from among the Communications options. (See "Installing and Uninstalling Programs that Come with Windows 98" in Chapter 3.)*

You can use HyperTerminal in three ways:

- **Dial-up connections** You can use HyperTerminal to call another computer over a modem and phone line. No other communications program or account is involved. You use this method when connecting directly to a bulletin board system, UNIX shell account, or other text-based system that works with terminals. You tell HyperTerminal the modem to use to make the connection, along with the country, area code, and phone number to dial.

- **Direct cable connections**   You can use HyperTerminal to connect to a computer to which your computer is connected by a cable. You tell HyperTerminal the communications port (COM1 or COM2) to which the cable is connected. Alternatively, you can use the Direct Cable Connection program (see "Connecting Two Computers with Direct Cable Connection" in Chapter 19).

- **Telnet connections**   If you have an Internet account (or other TCP/IP-based connection), you can use HyperTerminal as a Winsock-compatible *telnet* program, a terminal program that works over the Internet. First, you connect to the Internet by using Dial-Up Networking. Then, you connect to a computer over the Internet by using a HyperTerminal telnet connection—you "telnet in." For example, you can look up books at the U.S. Library of Congress by making a telnet connection to the library's mainframe system and using its text-only interface. You tell HyperTerminal to connect using TCP/IP (Winsock), along with the port number and host address of the computer to which you want to connect. The standard *port number* (a number that tells an Internet host computer whether you are connecting for e-mail, the Web, telnet, or another Internet service) is 23 (see "What Is TCP/IP?" in Chapter 22). The *host address* is the Internet host name of the computer you want to telnet in to; for example, the host address of the U.S. Library of Congress is locis.loc.gov.

To dial up and connect to a computer, HyperTerminal creates a *HyperTerminal connection*, a configuration file with the specifications for the connection. HyperTerminal connection files have the extension .ht.

Running HyperTerminal

To run HyperTerminal, choose Start | Programs | Accessories | Communications | HyperTerminal. From the C:\Program Files\Accessories\HyperTerminal window that appears, run the Hypertrm.exe icon. (That is, click or double-click the icon, depending on whether your desktop uses Web style or Classic style—see "Choosing the Style of Your Desktop" in Chapter 1.) After you've created a HyperTerminal connection with all the information about the computer to which you want to connect, you can just click the icon for the connection rather than the Hypertrm icon.

Configuring HyperTerminal for Your Account

When you run HyperTerminal by using the Hypertrm icon (rather than running the icon for a HyperTerminal connection), it displays the Connection Description dialog box (Figure 28-1). Alternatively, if you are already running HyperTerminal, choose File | New Connection or click the New button on the toolbar.

When you see the Connection Description dialog box, follow these steps:

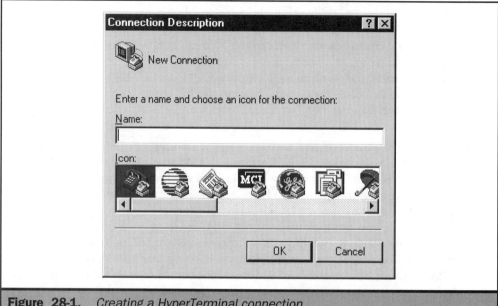

Figure 28-1. *Creating a HyperTerminal connection*

1. Type the name you want to use for the connection, choose an icon, and then click OK. You see the Connect To dialog box, asking for information about how to dial the phone to connect to the computer.

2. For a dial-up connection, set the Connect Using box to the modem to use for the connection, and then choose the country, type the area code, and type the phone number to dial. For a direct cable connection, set the Connect Using box to COM1 or COM2 (the communications port to which the cable is connected). For a telnet connection, set the Connect Using box to TCP/IP (Winsock), and then fill in the host address and port number.

3. Click OK. For dial-up connections, you see the Connect dialog box, shown in Figure 28-2. For telnet connections, skip to step 6.

4. If you want to change your dialing location (where you are dialing from) or use a calling card, click the Dialing Properties button (see "Configuring Windows for Dialing Locations" in Chapter 21).

5. To connect, click Dial. (If you don't want to connect right now, click Cancel. HyperTerminal saves your connection information.) For dial-up connections, HyperTerminal dials the phone. For telnet connections, if you're not already online, Dial-Up Networking displays its dialog box to get you connected to your Internet account; click Connect. When HyperTerminal has established a connection with the remote computer, you see the HyperTerminal window (Figure 28-3).

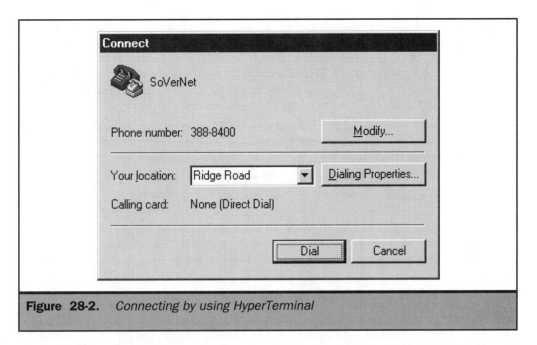

Figure 28-2. *Connecting by using HyperTerminal*

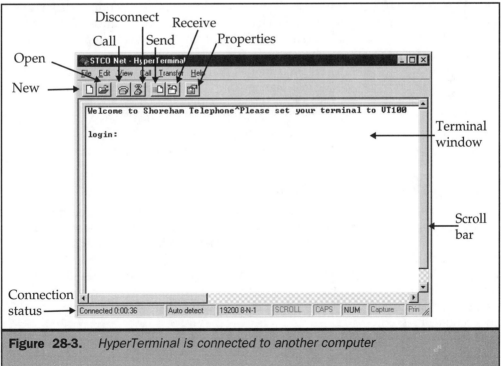

Figure 28-3. *HyperTerminal is connected to another computer*

6. Log in and use the remote computer, typing the commands that the remote computer requires. For example, if the remote computer displays a UNIX command line, you must type UNIX commands. You can use the scroll bar along the right side of the HyperTerminal window to see the *backscroll buffer*, which stores the last 500 lines of text that have scrolled up off the top of the terminal window (you can configure the buffer to be larger).

7. When you are done using the remote computer, log out by using the commands that it requires. HyperTerminal disconnects, too. If you have trouble getting disconnected, tell HyperTerminal to hang up by choosing Call | Disconnect from the menu bar (or by clicking the Disconnect icon on the toolbar).

8. When you exit from HyperTerminal, it asks whether you want to save the session (connection) you just created. Click Yes. (If you never plan to connect to this remote computer again, click No to throw away the connection information you typed above.) HyperTerminal creates an icon for the connection in the C:\Program Files\Accessories\HyperTerminal window.

Connecting with HyperTerminal

To connect to a computer for which you've already created a HyperTerminal connection, open the C:\Program Files\Accessories\HyperTerminal dialog box. Then open the icon for the connection. HyperTerminal runs and displays the Connect window; click Dial to make the connection. If you are using a telnet connection and you are not already connected to the Internet, Dial-Up Networking displays its window to prompt you to get online; click Connect.

If you are already running HyperTerminal, you can make a connection by choosing File | Open (or click the Open icon on the toolbar) and choosing the connection from the list. Then, click the Call icon on the toolbar, or choose Call | Call, to connect.

When you are done using the remote computer, log off by using whatever commands it requires; HyperTerminal should disconnect, too. If necessary, end the connection by choosing Call | Disconnect or by clicking the Disconnect icon on the toolbar.

Changing Information About a Connection

If the phone number for a remote computer changes, or you need to change the modem (or other information about the connection), run HyperTerminal by using the connection, but don't connect (click Cancel rather than Dial on the Connect dialog box). Click the Properties button on the toolbar or choose File | Properties to display the connection Properties dialog box (Figure 28-4). You can also display the Properties dialog box when you are using the connection. The settings on the Properties dialog box depend on the type of connection (dial-up, direct cable connection, or telnet).

In the Properties dialog box for the connection, you can set these types of options:

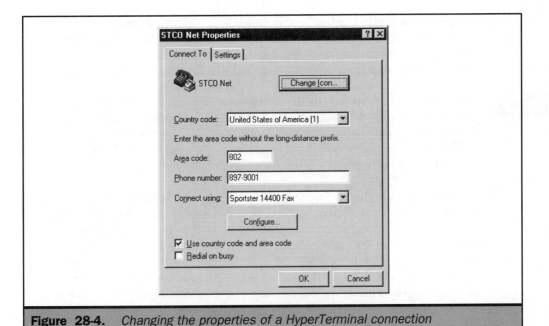

Figure 28-4.   *Changing the properties of a HyperTerminal connection*

- **Connection method**   On the Connect To tab, you specify the icon and how to connect: via modem, via cable (connected to your COM1 or COM2 port), or via TCP/IP (for a telnet connection). For dial-up connections, you also specify the phone number. For TCP/IP connections, you also specify the host address and port number (the default is 23, telnet's usual port). If you have Virtual Private Networking installed, VPN appears as an option (see "Connecting to Your Organization's Network Using Virtual Private Networking").

- **What keys do**   On the Settings tab, you specify whether the function keys, cursor motion keys, and control key combinations are transmitted to the other computer or are interpreted by Windows. For example, you can choose whether CTRL-C performs the task Windows usually assigns to CTRL-C—copying selected information to the Clipboard—or whether HyperTerminal passes the CTRL-C to the remote computer. You also control the actions of the BACKSPACE, DEL, and other keys.

- **Terminal emulation**   On the Settings tab, you tell HyperTerminal what type of terminal to emulate (act like). Most remote computers are configured to work with certain standard terminal types. HyperTerminal can emulate many of the most commonly used terminal types: ANSI, Minitel, TTY, Viewdata, VT100, and VT52. If you set the Emulation box to Auto Detect, HyperTerminal tries to figure out what type of terminal to emulate, based on information from the remote computer. If you click the Terminal Setup button, you can further configure HyperTerminal's actions, including how the cursor looks, what keys on the keypad do, and whether the terminal window displays 80 or 132 columns.

> **Note** *If you need HyperTerminal to emulate a Minitel (a widely used terminal in France), be sure to use the Arial Alternative font, which is the only font that contains all the special characters used by the French Minitel service. This font is on the Windows 98 CD-ROM in the \Add-ons\Minitel folder. For a list of what function keys to use with Minitel, see the HyperTerminal help.*

- **Character set** On the Settings tab, click the Terminal Setup button to control which character set it displays (ASCII, Special Graphics, or United Kingdom). Click the ASCII Setup button to control the characters that HyperTerminal sends and receives, including which character(s) HyperTerminal sends at the end of each line, whether HyperTerminal displays the characters you type or waits to display them until the remote computer echoes them back, and whether HyperTerminal waits a fraction of a second after each character or line it sends.

- **Other settings** You can specify how many lines of the text the backscroll buffer stores, and whether HyperTerminal beeps when connecting and disconnecting.

Transferring Files

HyperTerminal can send files from your computer to the remote computer, or receive files from the remote computer. A number of standard file transfer protocols exist; HyperTerminal can send and receive files by using the Xmodem (regular or 1K), Kermit, Ymodem, Ymodem-G, Zmodem, and Zmodem With Crash Recovery protocols. Choose a protocol that the remote computer can also handle. If you have a choice, use Zmodem With Crash Recovery.

Sending a File to the Remote Computer

To send a file to the remote computer:

1. Connect to the remote computer. If applicable, move to the directory on the remote computer in which you want to store the file.

2. If the file transfer protocol you plan to use requires you to give a command on the remote computer to tell it to expect a file, do so. For example, when transferring a file to a UNIX system by using Xmodem, you type the command **rx** *filename* on the remote computer. When transferring a file by using Zmodem (with or without Crash Recovery), no command is required; the UNIX system can detect when the file begins to arrive, and stores it automatically.

3. Click the Send button on the toolbar or choose Transfer | Send File. You see the Send File dialog box, shown here:

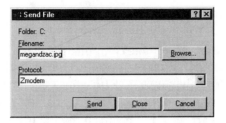

4. In the Filename box, type the name of the file you want to send, or click the Browse button to select the file.

5. Set the Protocol box to a file transfer protocol that the remote computer can use when receiving files.

6. Click the Send button. You see a window displaying the status of the file transfer (Figure 28-5). How much information the window displays depends on which file transfer protocol you use. You can click the Cancel button to stop the file transfer. Click the cps/bps button to control whether you see the transfer speed in characters per second (cps) or bits per second (bps). When the window disappears, file transfer is complete.

Figure 28-5. *HyperTerminal status while sending a file*

Receiving a File from the Remote Computer

To receive a file from the remote computer:

1. Connect to the remote computer. If applicable, move to the directory on the remote computer in which the file is stored.

2. Give the command on the remote computer to tell it to send the file. For example, to tell a UNIX system to transfer a file to your system by using Xmodem, you type the command **sx** *filename* on the remote computer.

3. If you are using Zmodem (with or without Crash Recovery), HyperTerminal detects that a file is arriving and begins receiving the file automatically (skip to step 8). Otherwise, click the Receive button on the toolbar or choose Transfer | Receive File. You see the Receive File dialog box, shown here:

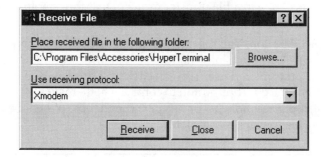

4. In the first box, type the path name of the folder in which you want to store the file, or click the Browse button to change the path name.

5. Set the Use Receiving Protocol setting to the file transfer protocol that the remote computer is using to send the file.

6. Click the Receive button.

7. For some protocols, HyperTerminal may need additional information. For example, when using Xmodem, the sending computer doesn't include the filename with the file, so HyperTerminal asks you what to name the file it receives. Type the additional information, and then click OK.

8. HyperTerminal displays a window similar to Figure 28-5, showing the progress of the file's transfer. You can click the Cancel button to stop the file transfer. Click the cps/bps button to control whether you see the transfer speed in characters per second (cps) or bits per second (bps). When the window disappears, the file transfer is complete.

Sending Text Files

You may want to send text to the other computer as though you were typing it. For example, if the remote computer asks a question to which you have an answer stored in a small text file, you can send the text file rather than retyping it; the remote computer doesn't realize that you are sending a file and accepts the text as though you typed it. You can also send text that is displayed by some other program; for example, you might want to send a number that is displayed in your spreadsheet program.

You can send small amounts of text by using either of two methods:

■ **Copy-and-paste it**   Display the text file in another program and copy it to the Windows Clipboard (see "What Is the Clipboard?" in Chapter 7). In HyperTerminal, choose Edit | Paste To Host.

■ **Transfer it**   Choose Transfer | Send Text File. When you see the Send Text File dialog box, choose the file to send. (Make sure that it's a small text file; large files, or files that contain non-text information, usually don't arrive intact.) HyperTerminal sends the contents of the file to the remote computer in the same way that it sends characters that you type.

CTRL-C and CTRL-V don't work for cut-and-paste in HyperTerminal. Choose Edit | Copy and Edit | Paste from the menu bar instead.

Capturing Text from the HyperTerminal Window

If the remote computer displays interesting information in the HyperTerminal window, you may want to save it. You can use these three methods to save text:

■ **Copy-and-paste it**   Select the text and choose Edit | Copy from the toolbar. You can use the scroll bar to see, and to select, text that has already scrolled up off the top of the HyperTerminal window. HyperTerminal copies the text to the Windows Clipboard. You can paste this text into the Windows Notepad, Wordpad, your word processing program, or any other program that accepts blocks of text.

■ **Capture it**   Choose Transfer | Capture Text. When you see the Capture Text dialog box, type the folder and name of the file into which you want to store the text. (Click Browse to select the folder.) Then click Start. All the text that appears in the terminal window from this point forward is also stored in the file. To stop capturing text, choose Transfer | Capture Text | Stop. To stop temporarily, choose Transfer | Capture Text | Pause; to later restart the text capture into the same file, choose Transfer | Capture Text | Resume. While HyperTerminal is capturing text to a file, the word Capture appears on the status bar along the bottom of the HyperTerminal window.

■ **Print it**   To tell HyperTerminal to print the information as it arrives in the terminal window, choose Transfer | Capture To Printer from the menu bar. As the remote computer sends text to your computer and HyperTerminal displays it, the text is printed, too. To stop printing, choose Transfer | Capture To

Printer again. While HyperTerminal is printing all incoming text, the words Print Echo appear on the status bar.

■ **Print the whole session**   To print the entire session with the remote computer, starting at the beginning of the backscroll buffer, choose File | Print.

Other HyperTerminal Commands

Here are a few other things you can do with HyperTerminal:

■ Tell HyperTerminal to answer incoming calls. If you are expecting a remote computer to dial into your computer, you can set your modem and HyperTerminal to answer the phone. Choose Call | Wait For A Call. The words Waiting For A Call appear on the status line. If an incoming call arrives on the phone line to which your modem is connected, your modem answers the phone, and HyperTerminal tries to connect to a computer on the other end of the phone line. To turn off auto-answer, choose Call | Stop Waiting.

■ Change the font that HyperTerminal displays in the terminal window. Choose View | Font.

■ Set the size of the HyperTerminal window to fit the terminal window exactly. Choose View | Snap.

Logging in to Other Computers Using Telnet

Windows 98 also comes with a Telnet program. Unlike HyperTerminal, it can connect only over the Internet; the Telnet program can't dial the phone (see "Logging in to Text-Based Systems Using HyperTerminal"). If you do much telnetting, HyperTerminal is a much nicer program, because it can remember the settings for multiple host computers, transfer files, and emulate a wider variety of terminals. The only advantage of the Windows 98 Telnet program is that it's faster over a LAN connection.

Running Telnet

To run Windows 98's built-in Telnet program:

1. Choose Start | Run, type **telnet**, and then click OK. You see the Telnet window, shown in Figure 28-6.

2. To connect to a remote computer over the Internet, choose Connect | Remote System. You see the Connect dialog box, shown here:

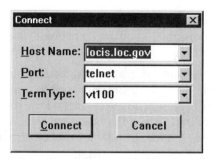

If you want to connect to a computer that you've connected to before, the host name may appear on the File menu; if so, choose the host name from the File menu and skip to step 7.

3. In the Host Name box, type the host name (host address) of the computer to which you want to connect. For example, the host name of the U.S. Library of Congress is locis.loc.gov. If you've connected to this host computer before, you can click the button at the right end of the Host Name box and choose the name from the drop-down list that appears.

4. Leave the Port box set to telnet. The other options connect to the host computer to use different Internet services, something that's useful only for network debugging.

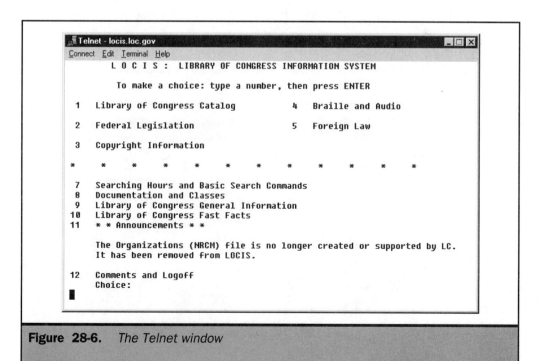

Figure 28-6.   *The Telnet window*

5. Set the TermType box to the string of characters to send to the remote computer, if it asks what type of terminal you are using. Note that this setting does not control the type of terminal that Telnet emulates (see the next section).

6. Click Connect. If your computer is not connected to the Internet, you see the Dial-Up Networking window, prompting you to connect; click the Connect button. Once you are online, Telnet connects to the remote computer. The Telnet window contains the terminal window, showing the text that you receive from the host computer, and your replies (Figure 28-6).

7. Log in and use the remote computer, typing the commands that the remote computer requires. You can use the scroll bar at the right side of the window to see lines of text that have scrolled up off the top edge of the window.

8. When you are done using the remote computer, log out by using the commands that it requires. Telnet disconnects, too. If you have trouble disconnecting, choose Connect | Disconnect to tell Telnet to hang up.

Configuring Telnet

You can configure the way the Telnet window looks by choosing Terminal | Preferences. You see the Terminal Preferences dialog box, shown in Figure 28-7. You can control the following settings:

- **Local Echo**   Whether the Telnet program displays what you type, or whether it waits and displays the text that the remote computer echoes back. This is turned off by default.

- **Appearance**   You can choose a blinking or block-style cursor, choose the font, and set the background color of the Telnet window.

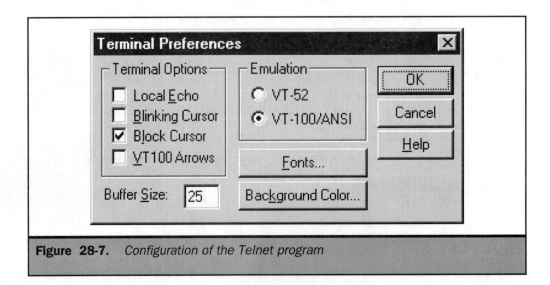

Figure 28-7.   *Configuration of the Telnet program*

- **Emulation**   You can control which terminal Telnet emulates (acts like). Telnet can emulate only two terminals: the DEC VT-100 and the DEC VT-52. (If the remote computer you want to use requires emulation of a different terminal, consider using the HyperTerminal program rather than Telnet.) If you choose to emulate a VT-100, you may also want to choose the VT100 Arrows options, so that the cursor motion keys send the same character sequences as would the same keys on a VT-100 terminal.

- **Buffer Size**   The Telnet program stores lines of text that have scrolled up off the top of the terminal window; you can choose how many lines are stored.

Other Telnet Commands

Here are other things that you can do with the Telnet program:

- The Telnet program doesn't handle file transfer (if you can telnet somewhere, you may be able to use FTP), but you can cut-and-paste by using the Windows Clipboard (see "What Is the Clipboard?" in Chapter 7). In addition to Edit | Copy (for copying selected text to the Clipboard) and Edit | Paste (for sending the Clipboard contents to the remote computer as if you had typed it), you can also use Edit | Select All to select the entire contents of the terminal window, and Edit | Copy All to copy the entire contents of the window to the Clipboard. See the next section for how to use FTP to transfer files.

- You can capture the text that appears in the Telnet window by choosing Terminal | Start Logging. Telnet asks you for the folder and name of the log file in which to store the text. If the log file already exists, Telnet deletes its previous contents and replaces it with the log of this terminal session. To stop storing the terminal text, choose Terminal | Stop Logging.

> **Note**   *CTRL-C and CTRL-V don't work for cut-and-paste in Telnet. Choose Edit | Copy and Edit | Paste from the menu bar instead.*

Transferring Files Using Ftp

FTP (File Transfer Protocol) is a system for transferring files over the Internet. An *FTP server* stores files, and *FTP clients* can log into FTP servers to either *upload* (transfer) files to the FTP server or (more commonly) download files from the FTP server. To use FTP, you must have an FTP client program.

Most web browsers, including Internet Explorer and Netscape Navigator, include an FTP client program that you can use to download files (see Chapter 24). Some web sites can also let you upload files to an FTP server. However, you can also use a separate FTP client program to upload files to, or download files from, an FTP server.

Windows 98 comes with a basic command-driven FTP client program called Ftp. If you plan to do much file transfer, especially uploading, you'll want a better FTP client program, such as WS_FTP (see "Downloading, Installing, and Running Other Internet Programs").

Basics of FTP

To connect to an FTP server, you specify the host name of the server (for example, rtfm.mit.edu), and then you log in. You have two choices:

- If you have an account on the FTP server, log in with your user name and password. You can access all the files that your user name gives you permission to use.

- If you don't have an account on the FTP server, the server may accept connections from guests. Connection without an account on the FTP server is called *anonymous FTP*. To use anonymous FTP, type **anonymous** for the user name and your own e-mail address as the password. Thousands of FTP servers on the Internet allow you to use anonymous FTP to download files, although some are so busy that it may be hard to get connected.

Once you are connected to an FTP server, it displays lots of messages to let you know what's going on. These messages all start with three-digit numbers, which you can ignore. For example, when you have transferred a file, you see the message 226 Transfer Complete.

When you transfer a file—by either uploading or downloading—you must choose between two modes:

- **ASCII Mode**   When transferring text files, use ASCII mode. Different computer systems use different characters to indicate the ends of lines. In ASCII mode, the Ftp program automatically adjusts line endings for the system to which the file is transferred.

- **Binary or Image Mode**   When transferring files that consist of anything but unformatted text, use Binary mode. In Binary mode, the Ftp program does not make any changes to the contents of the file during transfer. Use Binary mode when transferring graphics files, audio files, video files, programs, or any other kind of file other than plain text.

Running the Ftp Program

The Ftp program connects to an FTP server over the Internet, and then you type commands to move from directory to directory on the FTP server, upload or download files, and disconnect. Each command consists of a word that may be followed by additional information (called *arguments*); press ENTER after typing the command line.

For example, to download a file, you type the **get** command, followed by the name of the file you want to download, and then press ENTER.

To run Windows 98's built-in Ftp program:

1. Choose the Start | Run command, and then type **ftp**, followed by a space and the host name of the FTP server. Then click OK. If you are not connected to the Internet, you see the Dial-Up Networking window; click Connect. You see the Ftp window, shown in Figure 28-8.

2. You see a message confirming that you are connected. (Alternatively, you see a message saying that the host name is unknown or that the maximum number of connections to this host are already in use.) Then, the FTP server asks for a user name and password. If you have an account on the server, type your user name, press ENTER, type your password, and then press ENTER again. If you don't have an account on the server, type **anonymous**, press ENTER, type your e-mail address, and then press ENTER again.

3. If you connect successfully to the FTP server, you see a welcome message. Some FTP servers display a long welcome message dozens of lines long, detailing the contents of, and rules for, using the FTP server. Scroll up to read the welcome message if it scrolls up off the top of the Ftp window. The program displays the prompt ftp> to ask you to type a command.

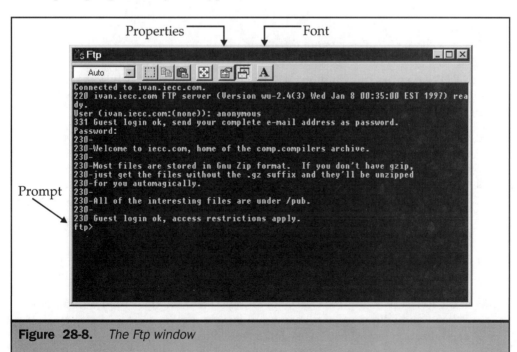

Figure 28-8.   *The Ftp window*

4. Once you are connected, type commands to move to the directory that contains the file you want to download or to which you want to upload a file. Then, give commands to upload or download files. These commands are described in the following sections.

5. When you are done transferring files, type **quit** or **bye** to disconnect from the FTP server. A message confirms that you have left the FTP server.

> **Tip** *If you want to disconnect from the FTP server and connect to a different server, you don't have to exit the Ftp program. Instead, type the **close** or **disconnect** command, and then press ENTER to disconnect from the FTP server. Next, type the **open** command, followed by a space, the host name of another FTP server, and then press ENTER to connect to the other server.*

Changing Directories on the FTP Server

Once you are connected to an FTP server, you must move to the directory (folder) to which you want to upload a file or from which you want to download a file. To change directories, type **cd**, followed by the name of the directory to which you want to move. To find out the name of the current directory, type the **pwd** command. For example, you might see the following (what you type appears in boldface; what the FTP server types appears in regular type):

ftp> **pwd**
257 "/usr/home/ivan" is current directory.

Each FTP server has its own directory structure. On many publicly accessible FTP servers, all the downloadable files are in a directory called pub. Here are a few tips for moving to the directory you want:

■ To move to the parent directory of the current directory, type **cd ..** (that is, the **cd** command followed by two dots).

■ To move to the top-level directory on the FTP server, also called the *root directory*, type **cd /** (that is, the **cd** command followed by a forward slash). Most FTP servers run the UNIX operating system, which uses slashes in place of the backslashes used in Windows.

■ You can move directly to a directory by typing its full path name, starting at the root; the full path name starts with a / to represent the root directory.

■ If the FTP server runs the UNIX operating system, capitalization is important. When typing directory or filenames, be sure to use the correct capitalization—most names use lowercase letters.

Seeing What's in the FTP Server's Current Directory

To see a list of files and subdirectories in the current directory on the FTP server, type the **dir** command. The exact format of the listing depends on the FTP server's operating system. Figure 28-9 shows a typical listing.

If the dir command produces a long listing, you can use wildcards to limit the files and directories that are included. The wildcard character * matches any number of characters. For example, type **dir c*** to list the file and directory names that begin with C. You can also tell the Ftp program to store the file listing in a file on your computer. Type this command:

dir . *filename*

The dot specifies that you want a listing of the current directory. Replace *filename* with the name of the file on your own computer in which you want to store the file listing (you can type a full path name to specify which folder in which to store the file). Ftp stores the file in your C:\Windows folder.

Tip   *If you want to see filenames only, with no other information, you can use the ls command.*

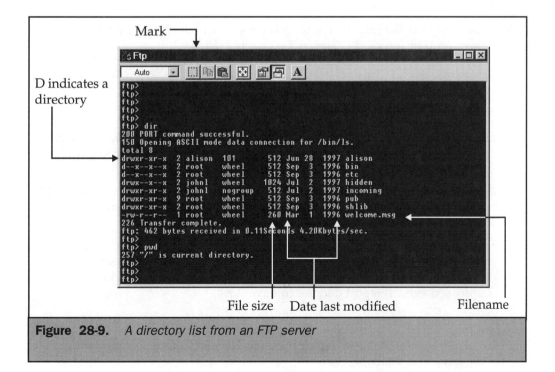

Figure 28-9.   *A directory list from an FTP server*

Selecting the Current Folder on Your Computer

Before you upload or download files, set the *current local directory*, the currently selected folder on your computer. This is the folder from which Ftp can upload files and to which it can download files.

To change the current local directory, type **lcd** (local directory), followed by the name of the folder on your computer. If the path name of the folder contains spaces, enclose the path name in quotes. To move to the parent folder of the current folder, type **lcd ..** (the **lcd** command followed by two dots).

For example, this command changes the current local directory to C:\My Documents:

> ftp> **lcd "C:\My Documents"**
> Local directory now C:\My Documents.

To see what's in the current local directory, use Windows Explorer or a Folder window.

Uploading Files

You use the put command to upload the files. To upload a group of files, you can use the mput command.

You can upload files only if you have write permission in the directory on the FTP server. Most anonymous FTP servers don't accept uploads, or they accept them into only one specific directory; read the welcome message to find out the rules for the FTP server you are using.

To upload a file, follow these steps:

1. Connect to the FTP server, move to the directory on the FTP server in which you want to store the file, and then set the current local directory to the folder on your computer that contains the files you want to upload.

2. If the file or files you want to upload contain anything but unformatted ASCII text, type **binary** to select Binary mode (see "Basics of FTP"). To switch back to ASCII mode to transfer text files, type **ascii**.

3. Type **put**, followed by a space, followed by the filename on your computer, followed by a space, followed by the filename to use on the FTP server. Then press ENTER. For example, to upload a file named draft13.doc and call the uploaded version report.doc, the command is

   put draft13.doc report.doc

4. You see a series of messages; the message Transfer Complete appears when the file transfer is done.

If a file with the name that you specify already exists on the FTP server, the put command may overwrite the existing file with the uploaded file.

5. If you want to check that the file is really on the FTP server, type **dir** to see a listing of files in the current directory.

You can copy a group of files to the FTP server by typing the mput (multiple put) command. Type **mput**, followed by a wildcard pattern that matches the names of the files you want to upload. The pattern * indicates that all files in the current directory on your computer should be copied.

For example, to upload all the files with the extension .html, you would type this command:

mput *.html

As it copies the files, the mput command asks you about each file. Type **y** to upload the files or **n** to skip it.

 If you don't want the mput command to ask you about each file before uploading it, include the prompt command first before giving the mput command. The prompt command turns off filename prompting.

Downloading Files

To download files from the FTP server to your computer, follow these steps:

1. Connect to the FTP server, move to the directory on the FTP server that contains the file that you want to download, and then set the current local directory to the folder on your computer in which you want to store the files you download (see "Changing Directories on the FTP Server").

2. If the file or files you want to download contain anything but unformatted ASCII text, type **binary** to select Binary mode (see "Basics of FTP"). To switch back to ASCII mode to transfer text files, type **ascii**.

3. Type **get**, followed by a space, followed by the filename on the FTP server, followed by a space, followed by the filename to use on your computer. The press ENTER. (You can't use filenames with spaces.) For example, to download a file named bud9812.doc and call the downloaded version budget.dec1998.doc, the command is

get bud9812.doc budget.dec1998.doc

4. You see a series of messages; the message Transfer Complete appears when the file transfer is done. To interrupt the file transfer, press CTRL-C. Sometimes that doesn't work, and the only way to interrupt the transfer is to close the FTP window.

5. If you want to check that the file really is downloaded, use Windows Explorer or a Folder window to see a listing of files on your computer.

You can copy a group of files to the FTP server by typing **mget**, followed by a wildcard pattern that matches the names of the files that you want to download. The pattern * means that all files in the current directory on your computer should be copied. For example, to download all the files whose names start with d, you would type this command:

      mget d*

As it copies the files, the mget command asks you about each file. Type **y** to download the files or **n** to skip it.

 If you download a non-text file and it is unusable, you probably forgot to issue the binary command before downloading the file.

Listing of Ftp Commands

Table 28-1 lists all the commands you can use with the Ftp program.

Command	Description
!	Runs a DOS command shell and displays a DOS prompt. You can type DOS commands, such as **dir**, which displays the contents of a folder (see Chapter 41). To exit from DOS and see the ftp> prompt again, type **exit**.
?	Displays a list of the commands that Ftp can perform (that is, the commands in this table).
append	Uploads a file and appends it to an existing file. Type **append**, followed by the name of the file on your computer that you want to upload, and then the name of the file on the FTP server to which you want to append the file.
ascii	Transfers files in ASCII mode (used for text files).
bell	Turns *bell mode* on or off; when bell mode is on, Ftp beeps whenever it completes a command.

Table 28-1. *Listing of Ftp Commands*

binary	Transfers files in Binary or Image mode (used for all files except text files).
bye	Disconnects from the FTP server and exits the Ftp program.
cd *dir*	Changes to the *dir* directory on the FTP server. If you omit the *dir*, Ftp says Remote Directory, and then waits for you to type the directory name and press ENTER.
close	Disconnects from the FTP server, without exiting the Ftp program.
debug	Turns on and off debugging mode (which displays more information about what Ftp is doing).
delete *name*	Deletes the file *name* on the FTP server. If you omit the *name*, Ftp says Remote File, and then waits for you to type the filename and press ENTER. Most publicly accessible FTP servers don't let you delete files.
dir *pat*	Lists the files in the current directory on the FTP server that match the wildcard pattern *pat*, with full information about the files. Omit *pat* to list all the files.
disconnect	Disconnects from the FTP server, without exiting the Ftp program.
get *old new*	Downloads the file *old* to your computer and names it *new*. Omit *new* to use the same name.
glob	Turns on and off metacharacter expansion of local filenames. When on, the Ftp program replaces wildcard patterns with the list of filenames they match. When off, Ftp passes wildcard patterns along to the FTP server.
hash	Turns on and off hash mode (in which Ftp displays a # for each block transferred).
help	Displays a list of the commands that Ftp can perform (that is, the commands in this table). Type the **help** command, followed by a space and a command name to get a short description of that command.
lcd *dir*	Changes to the folder *dir* on your computer.

Table 28-1. *Listing of Ftp Commands* (continued)

literal *command*	Sends a command to the FTP server that the Windows 98 Ftp program doesn't support. Type **literal**, followed by a space and the command you want to send.
ls *pat*	Lists only the filenames of the files in the current directory on the FTP server that match the wildcard pattern *pat*. Omit *pat* to list all the files.
mdelete *pat*	Deletes the files that match the wildcard pattern *pat* on the FTP server.
mget *pat*	Downloads the files to your computer that match the wildcard pattern *pat*.
mkdir *dir*	Creates a directory named *dir* on the FTP server (assuming that you have permission to do so).
mls *dir filename*	Stores a listing of the contents of the *dir* directory on the FTP server, and all of its subdirectories, in the file *filename* on your computer. Type * as *dir* to list all files.
mput *pat*	Uploads the files to the FTP server that match the wildcard pattern *pat*.
open *hostname*	Connects to the FTP server named *hostname*.
prompt	Turns on or off filename prompting for mput and mget commands. When prompting is on, Ftp asks before transferring each file.
put *old new*	Uploads the file *old* to the FTP server and names it *new*. Omit *new* to use the same name.
pwd	Displays the current directory on the FTP server.
quit	Disconnects from the FTP server and exits the Ftp program.
quote *command*	Sends a command to the FTP server that the Windows 98 Ftp program doesn't support. Type **quote**, followed by a space and the command you want to send.
recv *old new*	Downloads the file *old* to your computer and names it *new*. Omit *new* to use the same name.

Table 28-1.   *Listing of Ftp Commands* (continued)

remotehelp *command*	Displays the help information provided by the FTP server. Omit *command* to see a list of the commands the FTP server supports.
rename *old new*	Renames the file named *old* on the FTP server, using the filename *new* (assuming that you have permission to do so).
rmdir *dir*	Deletes the directory *dir* on the FTP server (assuming that you have permission to do so).
send *old new*	Uploads the file *old* to the FTP server and names it *new*. Omit *new* to use the same name.
status	Displays the status of the Ftp program, including the name of the FTP server to which you are connected, the file transfer mode (ASCII or Binary), and the bell mode.
trace	Turns packet tracing on and off.
type *transfertype*	Sets the transfer type (see "Basics of FTP"). *Transfertype* must be ascii, binary, or image.
user *name password*	Logs into the FTP server using a different user name. If you omit *name* and *password*, Ftp prompts you for them.
verbose	Turns verbose mode on and off. When verbose mode is off, Ftp displays fewer messages.

Table 28-1.   *Listing of Ftp Commands* (continued*)*

Other Ftp Tips

Here are other things you can do with the Ftp program:

- You can select a block of text and copy it to the Windows Clipboard (see "What Is the Clipboard?" in Chapter 7). Click the Mark button on the toolbar (the dotted box button), select the block of text to copy, and then click the Copy button (to the right of the Mark button). These commands are also available by clicking the System Menu button (the MS-DOS icon in the upper left corner of the Ftp window) and choosing Edit | Mark or Edit | Copy from the drop-down menu.

- You can paste text from the Clipboard into the Ftp window; if the text isn't an Ftp command or filename, Ftp will probably get confused. Click the Paste button on the toolbar (the button showing a clipboard). Or click the System Menu button and choose Edit | Paste from the system menu.

■ You can change the size of the Ftp window and the font it displays. To maximize the Ftp window, click the Full Screen button on the toolbar (the button with four red arrows). To return to running Ftp in a window, press ALT-ENTER. To choose a font size, click the Font box (the leftmost item on the toolbar) and choose the size you want; sizes are shown in pixels. Alternatively, you can click the Font button (the rightmost button on the toolbar) to choose the font size and style.

■ You can change other properties of the Ftp program by clicking the Properties button on the toolbar (the third button from the right). See Chapter 41 for a description of the properties of DOS programs.

Connecting to Your Organization's Network Using Virtual Private Networking

Many large organizations have private networks that are accessible to computers attached to local area networks within the organization (see Chapter 29). Although the private network is connected to the Internet, users on the Internet can't access information on computers on the private network; a computer called a *firewall* connects the private network to the Internet and controls what information can pass through.

But what if you work for such an organization and you are on a business trip? You can connect to the Internet by using an Internet provider, but how can you access your organization's private network? *Virtual Private Networking* (VPN) provides a way for an authorized computer on the Internet to "tunnel" through the firewall and connect to a private network.

To work, your organization's firewall must support *Point-to-Point Tunneling Protocol* (PPTP). PPTP lets VPN connect you through the firewall. Your organization's network administrator must have set up the firewall and a *virtual private networking server*, the program that provides PPTP. You'll need to contact your organization's system administrator to find out the host name of the virtual private networking server.

Note   *VPN is not automatically installed when you install Windows 98; you may need to open the Control Panel, open the Add/Remove Programs icon, click the Windows Setup tab, choose Communications from the list of components, click Details, and then select Virtual Private Networking from among the Communications options. (See "Installing and Uninstalling Programs that Come with Windows 98" in Chapter 3.)*

Follow these steps for using VPN to connect to a private network through a firewall:

1. Sign up with an Internet provider so that you can connect to the Internet from where you plan to be located. Configure Dial-Up Networking to connect to your Internet account (see Chapter 22). Test your Internet connection.

2. Create another Dial-Up Networking connection for your VPN connection. (Yes, you use two Dial-Up Networking connections at the same time, one for the physical modem connection, and one for the virtual link to the firewall.) Choose Start | Programs | Accessories | Communications | Dial-Up Networking to display the Dial-Up Networking window. Run the Make New Connection icon.

3. In the Make New Connection window, type a name for the connection (like VPN or the name of your organization) in the top box. Set the Select A Device box to Microsoft VPN Adapter. Click the Next button.

4. In the Host Name or IP Address box, type the host name of your organization's virtual private networking server. For example, you might type pptp.gurus.com. If your system administrator gives you the IP Address of the server, you can type that instead (see "Configuring a TCP/IP Connection" in Chapter 22). Click Next.

5. You see a window confirming that you have created a Dial-Up Networking connection; click Finish.

Now when you want to connect to your private network, connect to the Internet by using the Dial-Up Networking connection for your ISP, and then connect to the private network by using the connection you just created.

> **Tip** *Some Internet providers offer PPTP services that let you connect to your private network by using one Dial-Up Networking connection. If your Internet provider does offer these services, ask your ISP what to type in the User Name box in the Dial-Up Networking Connect To dialog box. You may need to type an entry in the format* name@companyname.com *rather than your usual user name. When you use this special user name, you connect both to the Internet and to your private network.*

Downloading, Installing, and Running Other Internet Programs

Once you have established a Dial-Up Networking connection with the Internet, you can run any Winsock-compatible program (see "What Is Winsock?" in Chapter 22). Although Windows 98 comes with some good Internet applications, you can supplement (or replace) them with other programs. For example, the Ftp program that comes with Windows 98 is not particularly powerful or easy to use; we vastly prefer the excellent shareware WS_FTP program, which shows you the contents of the local and remote directories, and lets you transfer files by clicking buttons rather than typing commands. (Read on to find out how to get it.)

Where to Get Internet Programs

Lots of Winsock-compatible Internet programs are available for downloading from the Internet itself. Some are *freeware* programs that are entirely free to use; some are *shareware* programs that require you to register the program if you decide that you like it; some are demo programs that let you try a partially disabled version of the program before you decide whether to buy the real program; and some are commercial programs that ask you to pay before downloading.

Many web-based libraries offer all types of programs. Here are our favorites:

- **The Ultimate Collection of Windows Software (TUCOWS)** at **http://www.tucows.com** classifies programs by operating system and type. It has lots of mirror sites (identical web sites) all over the globe, so it's rarely a problem to begin downloading even very popular programs. It's particularly easy to browse a long list of programs of a given type (browsers, or e-mail programs, for example) and compare reviews.

- **The CWApps List** at **http://cws.internet.com** is the original Winsock library, and is still excellent. Forrest Stroud set up this site when shareware and freeware Internet software were just starting to become available.

- **Shareware.com** at **http://www.shareware.com** also offers lots of non-Internet-related programs.

- **Download.com** at **http://www.download.com** has thousands of downloadable programs organized by category.

Installing and Running Internet Programs

Once you've downloaded a program from the Internet, it's a good idea to check it for *viruses*, self-replicating programs that may infect other programs on your computer. Windows 98 doesn't come with a virus checker, but you can download a good one from any of the software libraries in the preceding section. We like McAfee's antivirus programs, too (commercial software, downloadable from its web site at **http://www.mcafee.com**).

Most downloaded programs arrive as self-installing files; in Windows Explorer or a Folder window, run the file you downloaded. The program usually installs itself, asking you configuration questions along the way. Most programs either add themselves to the Start | Programs menu or add an icon to the desktop (or both). Other downloaded programs arrive in ZIP files, for which you need WinZip or another uncompressing program (see "Alternatives to Compressed Disks" in Chapter 35).

The first time you run a program, you may need to configure it further; check any documentation files that are installed along with the program. Look for a Tools | Options command or an Edit | Preferences command; these usually display configuration or preference dialog boxes.

Part V

Networking with Windows 98

Chapter 29

Understanding Local Area Networks

If you have more than one computer, you should consider connecting them with a local area network, or LAN. Windows 98 provides all the features needed to connect your computer to a LAN—no other software is needed.

This chapter introduces the basic concepts of LANs, including what a network is and why you might want one, the two major kinds of networks, and the equipment and configuration you need for setting up a LAN. You also see the Network dialog box and Network Neighborhood, two of Windows 98's networking tools. This chapter provides the background for the specifics covered in Chapters 30 and 31.

What Is a Network and Why Would You Need One?

A network provides a connection between computing resources, a way to share hardware and files, and a paperless way to communicate. A *local area network* (LAN) is a network that is limited to one building or group of buildings, in which the computers are usually connected by cables. A local area network can be as useful in a small office of two or three computers as it is in a large office. Each computer attached to a network is called a *node*.

Larger networks also exist. *Wide area networks* (WANs) connect computers that are geographically dispersed. And the *Internet*—the biggest network of them all—is a worldwide network of interconnected networks (see Chapter 22).

Sharing Hardware

Without a network, each *resource* (hard disk, CD-ROM drive, printer, or other device) is connected to only one computer (printers may be an exception if you have a switch box). Examples of resources in your office may include a hard drive on which the company's main database is stored, the color printer that everyone wants to use, and the 5¼ inch floppy drive that is needed only occasionally. Without a network, you can use a resource only from the computer to which the resource is attached. With a network, anyone using a computer attached to the network can print to the color printer, open the database, or access files on the diskette in the 5¼ inch drive down the hall. You may also want to share more specialized devices, such as CD-ROM recorders, ZIP drives, and tape drives.

The cheapest way to share resources is what some techie types call "sneakernet"—take a diskette, copy the file you need to print or share, and walk over (hence, "sneaker") to the computer with the printer, or the person who needs to use the file. But sneakernet is not very efficient—in the long run you'll save time and hassle (which of those 12 floppies has the current version of that file?) with a network. If you have a small office, using a network and just one printer to which everyone can print is more cost effective.

Sharing Files

If you want to share files without the danger of creating multiple versions, you need a network so that every person who accesses the file uses the same copy. Some software (notably database software) allows multiple users to use one file at the same time. Other software warns you when a file is being used by someone else on the network, and may even notify you when the file is available for your use.

When you work with large files that are too large to fit on a diskette, moving them to other computers is cumbersome without a network.

Communicating on the Network

A network allows you to communicate electronically. Applications like e-mail and WinPopup (described in Chapter 32) provide a way to disseminate information around the office without wasting paper. In addition, if you travel, you can use Dial-Up Networking to dial into your network and use the resources there even when you are out of town.

What Types of Networks Exist?

There are two basic types of networks—peer-to-peer and client-server. We describe them in the next two sections.

Understanding either kind of network requires having at least passing familiarity with two terms: client and server. A *client* is a computer that uses resources on the network. A printer client, for instance, is a computer that uses a network printer. A *server* is a computer (or a device that has a computer hidden inside) that has resources used by other devices on the network. For instance, a *file server* is a computer that stores files that are used by other computers; a *print server* is a computer with a printer attached to it—the print server lets other computers on the network send print jobs to the printer. The server makes a resource available to the network, and a client uses the resource.

Peer-to-Peer Networks

In a *peer-to-peer network*, as the term implies, all computers start out equal. All computers can function as both clients and servers. Security and permissions are administered from each computer in the network. Each computer in a peer-to-peer network can both request resources from other computers and share its own resources with other computers in the network. You can also configure the network so that some computers only share their resources and others only use resources. However, even in this situation, the network is still a peer-to-peer network, because each computer on the network is administered individually.

A peer-to-peer network is relatively easy to set up—any small office with more than one computer can create a small peer-to-peer network by using Windows to share printers and files and exchange e-mail. Only a small amount of hardware is required. Chapter 30 explains how to choose, install, and configure the hardware and software needed to create a peer-to-peer network using Windows.

Client-Server Networks

In a *client-server network*, server computers provide resources for the rest of the network, and client computers (also called *workstations*) only use these resources. No one uses the server computers as workstations; they are *dedicated servers*. For instance, a file server is used to store files that are shared on the network. Client computers use the files on this file server by running, opening, changing, saving, or deleting these files.

Client-server networks typically are more difficult and expensive to set up and administer than peer-to-peer networks, but they also have many advantages: they can handle more computers, they provide more-sophisticated administration and security options, and all resources are managed centrally on dedicated servers. Client-server networks require a *network operating system* (NOS)—Windows NT, Novell NetWare, and UNIX are common NOSs—as well as a greater initial outlay of time and money for setup and equipment, and a network administrator to create and maintain user IDs and permissions.

Table 29-1 lists differences between peer-to-peer and client-server networks. Chapter 31 describes how to set up your Windows 98 computer on an existing Novell or Windows NT network.

	Peer-to-Peer	**Client/Server**
Size	Good for small networks (under 12 computers, depending on the uses for the network). Keeping track of available resources and passwords for each resource becomes difficult on a large peer-to-peer network.	Good for medium to large networks. Since administration of network resources is central, the user can use all available resources with as few as one password (more passwords may be necessary if the network has more than one server).
Hardware	No dedicated file server is needed.	At least one computer must be a dedicated file server.

Table 29-1. *Differences Between Peer-to-Peer and Client-Server Networks*

	Peer-to-Peer	**Client/Server**
Operating System	Windows 98 will do.	Requires a network operating system (NOS).
Administrator Training	Little training for users to administer their own computers' resources for all users on the network.	System administrator must be trained.
Resource Control	Each computer's user has full control of that computer's resources.	The system administrator is in control of shared resources.
Resource Administration	Administered by the owner of each workstation.	Administered by network administrator.
Resource Security	Password is assigned to each resource.	Password is assigned to each user of a server. Each user is given permission to use certain resources by the network administrator.
Security Administration	Permissions are granted by the owner of each computer.	Only one password per user is required for the use of the resources associated with one server. Security is administered by a network administrator.

Table 29-1.   *Differences Between Peer-to-Peer and Client-Server Networks (continued)*

What Hardware Does a Network Require?

To connect a computer to either type of network, you need extra hardware:

- A *network interface card* (NIC) for each computer in the network.
- A connection among all the computers, most commonly copper wires, but can also be fiber-optic cable, infrared, radio waves, or a mixture.

This hardware is not expensive to install—it usually amounts to less than $50 per computer on the network.

A client-server network is more expensive, because it requires at least one computer to be a dedicated server.

How Do You Configure Windows 98 for a Network?

No matter what kind of network you're attaching your Windows 98 machine to, you must take some steps to configure it for the network. Specifically, you have to identify the client, the adapter, and the protocol the network uses. If you want to share your local resources (your hard drive or the printer attached to your computer, for instance), you also have to install a service. Further definitions are in order:

■ The *client* is determined by the type of network to which you are attaching: a Windows-compatible peer-to-peer network, a Microsoft NT Windows network, or a Novell NetWare network, for example.

■ The *adapter* identifies the specific network interface card that you have installed and the driver needed to make it work.

■ The *protocol* identifies the way information is passed between computers on the network. TCP/IP is the protocol used by the Internet, for example.

■ The *service* you define allows you to share resources on the computer (for example, file and printer sharing).

Displaying the Network Dialog Box

To configure the network, you use the Network dialog box, shown in Figure 29-1. There are two ways to display it:

■ Choose Start | Settings | Control Panel. Then click or double-click the Network icon (depending on whether you use Web style or Classic style on your desktop). (See "Choosing the Style of Your Desktop" in Chapter 1.)

■ Right-click the Network Neighborhood icon on the desktop and choose Properties from the shortcut menu.

You'll use the Network dialog box in the following chapters as you configure Windows 98 for your network. The tabs on the Network dialog box depend on what network software you have installed and configured.

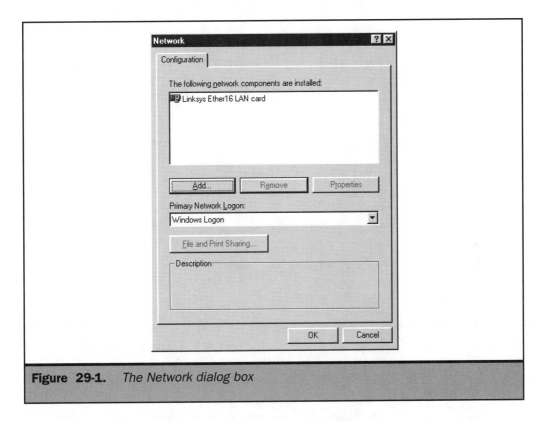

Figure 29-1. *The Network dialog box*

Displaying Your Network Neighborhood

Network Neighborhood is an icon that appears on your desktop after your network adapter is installed, which may happen when Windows 98 finds your network interface card. It looks like this:

When you open the Network Neighborhood icon, you see a Folder window with icons for each of the computers on your local area network. There is also an icon labeled Entire Network, which displays additional shared printers or disks, or computers on other LANs to which you have access.

Chapter 30

Creating a Windows
Peer-to-Peer Network

If you have a small number of computers (say, fifteen or less), and they all run some version of Windows (98, 95, 3.11, or NT), you can set up a peer-to-peer local area network (LAN) using Windows as your network operating system (see Chapter 29). First, you choose a networking technology (Token Ring or Ethernet), and then a cabling topology (star or bus). These choices dictate your choice of hardware, including network interface cards and cabling. Next you are ready to install your network hardware and configure Windows 98 to run over the network. Windows comes with some network troubleshooting tools.

This chapter covers setting up your network from scratch. However, if you are adding a Windows 98 computer to an existing Windows-based peer-to-peer network, or upgrading a computer on a network from an earlier version of Windows to Windows 98, the steps you need to follow are also found in this chapter—see the sidebars on "Adding to an Existing Network" and "Upgrading a Computer on an Existing Network."

What Do You Need to Do?

Setting up a network consists of four major tasks:

- Choosing the network technology.
- Choosing and buying the hardware.
- Installing the hardware.
- Configuring Windows to use the network.

While you don't need to be a network engineer to set up a small peer-to-peer network, you do need to have some knowledge about your computer. Ideally, you:

- Have some experience installing hardware. You need to install a network interface card in each computer that will be on the LAN (unless they have already been installed).

- Are comfortable using Folder windows or Windows Explorer to browse more than one disk. You'll need to find the other computers on the LAN using Folder windows or Windows Explorer (see "What Are Folder Windows and Windows Explorer Windows?" in Chapter 8).

- Are comfortable with dialog boxes with multiple tabs and options in dialog boxes. You'll be using the Network dialog box extensively, and it has a lot of different kinds of options.

If you feel that the preceding statements do not describe you, you may want to hire someone to install your hardware and configure your network. Just make sure you tell them what type of network you're expecting—a peer-to-peer network run by your Windows operating system.

Adding to an Existing Network

If you're adding a Windows 98 computer to an existing network, you can skip the beginning of this chapter regarding choosing a network technology and a topology—someone has already made those choices for you. Find out what technology is in use on your network, and then buy the appropriate network interface card for the computer that you want to add to the network. Also, if no leftover cable is on hand, buy the correct kind of cable for your network. Once you've done these things, you can dive into the steps in this chapter that start with the section "Installing Your Network Hardware."

Upgrading a Computer on an Existing Network

If you are upgrading the operating system of a computer on an existing network from an earlier version of Windows to Windows 98, you may find that your network works right away—open the Network Neighborhood icon on the desktop to see whether other computers on the network appear. If the network does not appear to be working, follow the steps in the section "Configuring Windows 98 for the LAN," later in this chapter.

Choosing a Technology for Your Network

Before you buy hardware for your network, you need to decide which standard you want to use to connect your network. The network interface cards and cabling that you choose must support the standard you choose.

Two network standards are commonly used: Token Ring and Ethernet.

Ethernet

Ethernet is a contention-based technology, which means that you have no control over which computers are allowed to send information over the network. This results in data collisions when two computers try to send information over the cables at the same time (data *contends* with other data when it collides). When two devices talk at exactly the same time, none of the data gets to where it's supposed to be going—both computers retransmit the data after a random interval, so the information gets through fine after this delay. Data contention can slow down a busy network, so Ethernet networks top out a little below their nominal fastest speed.

Using Ethernet technology is cheaper than Token Ring technology because Ethernet technology does not have a device controlling when a computer can begin to transmit. But when an Ethernet network has many users, lots of data collisions can lead to delays; overloaded Ethernet networks with many users can be slow. Ethernet is perfect for small or medium-sized offices and home offices. Ethernet network interface boards are relatively cheap, and are also available as PC Cards that fit most laptops.

There are two speeds of Ethernet. Original Ethernet has a speed of 10Mbps (megabits/second). "New" Ethernet, called *Fast Ethernet*, has a speed of 100Mbps. An even faster version, *Gigabit Ethernet*, is on the horizon and is intended to transmit data at a maximum speed of 1Gbps (gigabits/second), or ten times the Fast Ethernet standard.

Token Ring

With *Token Ring* technology, data transmission is controlled by means of a *token* (an electronic marker) that is passed around the ring of computers that make up the network. Only the machine with the token can transmit data. Once the data is transmitted and received, the token is passed to the next computer on the ring. There is no contention on a Token Ring network, because each computer has its turn to transmit, and no other computer is transmitting at that time.

Token Ring networks can operate at speeds of 4Mbps (oldest standard) to 16Mbps (current standard). A 100Mbps standard is in the works. Token Ring networks do not slow down much as more computers are added to the network—the token takes longer to get around the ring, but actual transmission always occurs at the standard rate.

Buying the hardware needed for a Token Ring network is much more expensive than the equivalent Ethernet hardware, even faster Ethernet hardware. Currently, Token Ring network interface cards can be five to eight times more expensive than Ethernet cards, and an additional piece of hardware called a MAU (multiple access unit) is also needed. On the other hand, Token Ring is a very reliable technology. It was developed by IBM and is found most often at companies that have (or had) IBM mainframe installations. Because switching from Token Ring to Ethernet usually requires new cabling, Token Ring hardware is still found in offices where it would be too expensive to rewire the building.

How to Choose

The standard you choose determines the hardware you buy. Each standard has advantages and disadvantages. However, if you are starting a network from scratch, you should choose the cheaper and more common Ethernet or Fast Ethernet. Most users choose Token Ring hardware only if they are adding to an existing Token Ring network.

From here on out, this chapter assumes that you are setting up an Ethernet network. Ethernet is the most common network standard, and the cheapest and easiest to set up in a small office. However, the steps outlined here do not differ much for setting up a Token Ring network; the major difference is that you would need to buy network interface cards and cabling that work with the Token Ring standard.

Choosing a Network Topology

The *topology* of a network determines the pattern of cabling you use to connect the computers. The topology usually also determines the type of cable you use. Because network interface cards must provide the correct connection for the chosen type of cable, you must choose the topology before buying network interface cards (although you can buy network interface cards that support both types of cable). So you must choose the network topology before shopping for hardware.

There are two typical ways for cabling an Ethernet network—bus and star topology:

■ **Bus topology**   The *bus* is the main cable to which all the other computers are attached. (Communication within a computer also happens along a bus.) See Figure 30-1 for a diagram of a network using bus topology.

■ **Star topology**   Each computer in the LAN is connected by a cable to a *hub*, the computer in the center of the star. See Figure 30-2 for a diagram of a network using star topology. In its simplest form, the hub provides a central connection point for the network.

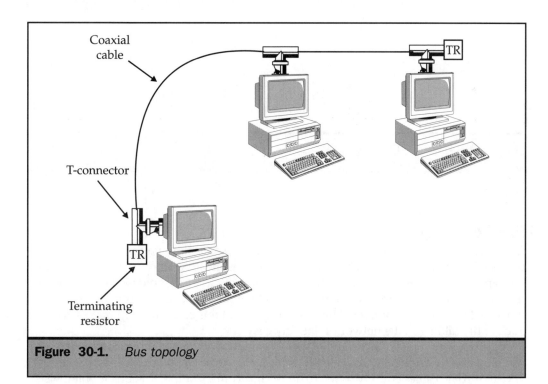

Figure 30-1.   *Bus topology*

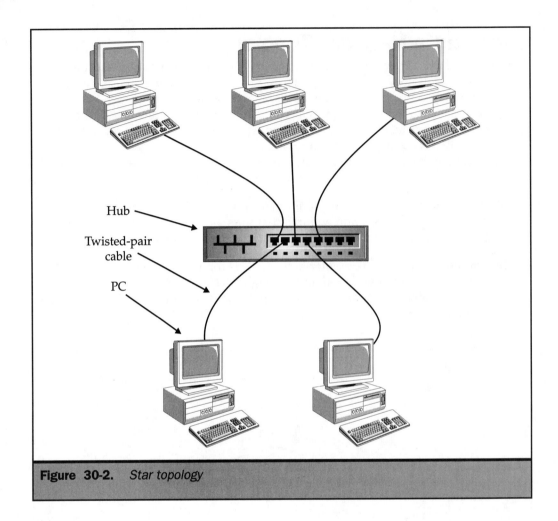

Figure 30-2.   *Star topology*

Bus Topology

Small networks commonly are connected with *coaxial cable* (known as coax or
10-Base-2) in a bus topology. This configuration uses the least amount of cable and the
least amount of hardware, because no hub is required. In bus topology, a coax cable is
connected from one computer to the next, in a long line, until all computers are
connected. Another advantage of bus topology is that this configuration makes keeping
track of the cabling in the network relatively easy.

Bus topology does have disadvantages. It can be awkward to move computers—
you may need new cables if the original cables are not long enough. You may even
have to reroute cables entirely to re-create the bus configuration. The bus topology is

vulnerable—if the LAN cable is unhooked in the middle, all the computers lose their network connection (the network works fine if computers are turned off). Similarly, if one piece of cable in the network is bad, many computers on the network can be affected (depending on the position in the bus of the bad cable). Troubleshooting a hardware problem with a network that uses bus topology can be more difficult than troubleshooting a network that uses star topology, because the problem can be harder to pinpoint. In general, bus topology is recommended only for networks of five or less computers. If you think your network may expand to include more than five computers, you may want to start out using star topology.

Star Topology

Medium and large networks often use a star topology. This configuration uses more cable and more hardware, but is easier to manage and less likely to fail. The cable used in Ethernet star topology is *unshielded twisted-pair* (also called 10Base-T).

In a star configuration, each computer is attached to a hub—one end of the cable plugs into a computer's network interface card, and the other end plugs into the hub, which provides a central connection point for the network cabling. Hubs come in different sizes (with different numbers of ports), and the more advanced hubs can correct signal errors and amplify signals.

Star topology is easy to set up, and the network is easier to troubleshoot than a bus network, since a damaged cable affects only one computer. On the down side, twisted-pair cable is usually more expensive than coax. Star topology requires much more cable, and a hub, all of which results in a bigger bill for the network. However, the difference in price is usually worth avoiding the inconvenience of trying to pinpoint a hardware problem in a large network.

You can also use hybrid networks, such as a set of hubs connected by a bus, which can minimize the amount of star cabling necessary.

Buying Network Hardware

You need the following hardware to set up your Ethernet network:

- A network interface card (or NIC) for each PC on the network.
- Enough cable to connect all the computers on your network. The amount and type of cable you need depends on the topology you choose for your network.
- A hub (if you choose star topology).

Note *If you are creating a small network, you may be able to buy a network kit that has all the hardware you need to set up a small network: network interface cards, cable, T-connectors, and terminators. Check at your local Staples or OfficeMax (or similar store).*

Buying Network Interface Cards

When you shop for your network interface cards, choose cards that:

- Match the type you've chosen for your network—Ethernet, Fast Ethernet, or Token Ring.
- Fit the cable you are using—coaxial cable or twisted-pair cable.
- Fit the computer you buy it for—computers with ISA, PCI, EISA, VESA, MCA, or PC Card slots.

All the network interface cards in each computer in the network must support the same standard—in an Ethernet network, for instance, all network interface cards must be Ethernet cards. Decide whether you want a speed of 10Mbps or 100Mbps (or a newer standard) and buy cards that are all the same speed (most people base their decision on price).

Check that each card you choose fits the cable that you are using. If you are using star topology and twisted-pair cable, choose a card that has a *RJ-45 connector*, which looks like a large phone jack. If you have chosen bus topology and coaxial cable, then choose a card that has a *BNC connector*, which looks like a sturdier version of a cable TV connector. Some cards have more than one type of connector.

Take inventory of every computer that will be on the LAN and make a note of the type of slot each has available; you have to buy a network interface card that fits a slot in each computer. The easiest way to determine slot types is to check the documentation for each computer. ISA, PCI, EISA, VESA, and MCA slots are all common. Laptops usually have PC Card slots, also called PCMCIA slots, that look like they fit a credit card. You may be able to tell which kind of slot your computer has by taking the cover off and looking, and then describing the slot to your local computer store expert—but it's safer to check your documentation for the type of architecture the motherboard has for each computer that will be on the LAN. You can and probably will mix cards of different slot types so long as the network type is consistent. For example, one of our networks has ISA, PCI, MCA, and PC Card interface cards all connected to a 10Mbps coax Ethernet.

Look for cards that are Windows 95 or 98 Plug-and-Play compatible, which includes cards made by most major manufacturers. Using a plug-and-play card makes configuring the card much easier, because Windows 98 can identify it automatically.

 Some newer computers come with a network interface card pre-installed. Check your system's documentation before you shop for your network interface cards.

Buying Cable

The type and amount of cable you choose depends on the topology you use in your network. We are assuming that the computers you are connecting are relatively near to each other. A general rule is not to run a cable more than 150 meters between computers (although the actual specifications for different types of cable in different types of networks may be greater). If you are connecting computers that are not close to each other, you need to do some research on how to create a network over medium distances.

 When you buy your cable, remember that you will be stringing it so that people don't trip over it. Measure carefully and allow extra—you can hide cable that is too long. If your cable is too short, you'll have to go shopping again.

Coaxial Cable

If you've chosen bus topology, you need to use coaxial cable. Coax cannot be plugged directly into a network interface card. Instead, a *T-connector* is attached to the BNC connector on the network interface card, and a cable is attached to either side of the T-connector. A diagram of the cable and T-connectors in a bus network is shown in Figure 30-1. The computer in the middle of the bus has a T-connector with cable attached to each side; computers at each end of the bus have cable on one side of the T-connector and a *terminating resistor* on the other side. You cannot have any cable between the T-connector and the computer.

When you shop for hardware for your Ethernet bus network using coax cable, you need to buy a T-connector for each computer, and a terminating resistor for each end of the bus (two terminating resistors for the whole network).

 You cannot just plug the coax cable directly into the computers on either end of your network. You must use a T-connector with the coax cable plugged in on one side, and a coax cable or a 50-ohm terminating resistor on the other side.

When determining how much cable you need, remember that computers are connected in an approximate line. Choose computers to be at the ends, and then measure the distance between each computer in the bus, allocating extra cable to go around furniture and out of the way of office traffic.

Twisted-Pair Cable

If you've chosen star topology, you need twisted-pair cable. The ends of these cables have RJ-45 connectors, which look like telephone cord connectors (the ones that plug into a telephone wall jack), but are about twice as big. When using twisted-pair cable, plug one end of each cable into a network interface card installed in a PC; plug the other end into the hub that is at the center of the star topology.

To determine how much cable you need, decide where you are going to place the hub, and then measure from each computer to the hub's location. Remember to allocate extra cable to go around furniture and out of the way of office traffic.

Although it's tempting, you cannot take a twisted-pair cable and connect two computers directly, unless you have a specially manufactured crossover cable. You need to connect the cable into a hub, because the hub manages which pairs of wires inside your cable are used for transmitting and receiving data. If you try to connect two computers directly with a standard cable, the transmit and receive wires will be incorrect on one end, and your connection will not work.

Buying a Hub

If you've chosen star topology with twisted-pair cable, you need a *hub*, a small box with lots of cable connectors. Buy a hub with enough connections for all the computers on your network. You may want a few extra connections so that you can add additional computers to the network later.

Installing Your Network Hardware

Now that you have all your parts—a network interface card for each computer, enough cabling, and a hub (for star topology) or T-connectors and terminators (for bus topology), you're ready to put it all together to create the physical network. Once you've completed the construction phase, you need to sit at each computer and configure Windows so that it knows about the network.

This whole procedure is best done when the computers are not in use and when you have a good chunk of time to devote to it—on a weekend.

Installing Network Interface Cards

The first step to installing your network hardware is to install your network interface cards in each computer that will be on the network. Turning off each computer, take the cover off, install the network card, and put the cover back on. For a laptop, this is usually as easy as sliding the card into the PC slot. For a desktop computer, this requires installing the card in a slot on the motherboard according to the manufacturer's installation instructions (see Chapter 15).

Once the card is installed, start the computer. Windows 98 should detect the new hardware and ask you to install the adapter drivers for it. (The driver tells the operating system how to talk to the hardware.) Later in the chapter, the section on installing your adapter walks you through the process of checking whether the network interface card (adapter) drivers have been automatically installed, and, if they haven't, installing them.

Stringing Cable

Once the card and its driver are installed, you can connect the cabling. The computers can be on when you connect the cables.

Cabling can be a simple job or an extravagant one, depending on your needs and how much time, effort, and money you're willing to put into it. A home office network that consists of two computers close together probably means cables running on the floor around the edge of the room and behind furniture. Cabling for an office probably means cables hidden by conduit, running inside walls, and running above dropped ceilings. You may want to hire someone if you have many computers to connect and want it done neatly. If you put cable inside ceilings or walls, be sure the installation conforms to fire and electrical codes.

When planning your wiring job, plan for the future. If you're wiring your office, add extra cables while the walls and ceiling are open. Put network jacks in the walls of any room that you think might have a computer in it some day. Plan your network cabling in the same manner you would plan phone extensions. Doing all the wiring now will make adding a computer to your network much easier in the future.

Coaxial Cable

If you're wiring coaxial cable, remember to use a T-connector on each network interface card. Each T-connector has cable attached to one side; the other side has either another cable or a terminating resistor.

Begin cabling at one end of the network—connect cable and a terminating resistor to the T-connector. Run the cable to the next computer, and then attach it to the T-connector. If this computer is in the middle of the bus, attach cable to the other side of the T-connector, and then run the cable to the next computer in the bus. When you reach the last computer, attach the cable to one side of the T-connector, and a terminating resistor to the other.

Twisted-Pair Cable

If you're using twisted-pair cable and star topology, run cable from each computer to the hub. The RJ-45 jacks are easy to use—just plug the cable into the network interface card as you would plug a phone wire into a phone jack.

 Don't run twisted-pair cable in a bundle with electrical power cable, because the electromagnetic interference can adversely affect the network, and a short-circuit between power and network cables could cause injury or fire.

Configuring Windows 98 for the LAN

After your hardware is installed, you still have to work the software side of the problem. You need to tell Windows 98 that the computer is now attached to a network, and you need to configure Windows to send and receive information using the network, no matter what type of network you are connecting to—a peer-to-peer network using Windows, or a Novell or Windows NT network.

As described at the end of Chapter 29, you now need to configure the network adapter, client, protocol, and, possibly, service. The steps from here to the end of the chapter must be completed on every computer in the network.

Before you start, it's a good idea to shut down all applications—when you're done using the Network dialog box, Windows reboots your computer, which is quicker if applications are already closed.

Displaying the Network Dialog Box

You use the Network dialog box (shown in Figure 30-3) repeatedly as you install your network. Open it by using one of the following methods:

■ Choose Start | Settings | Control Panel. Then open the Network icon—double-click or single-click depending on whether you use the Web style or Classic style desktop (see "Choosing the Style of Your Desktop" in Chapter 1).

■ Right-click the Network Neighborhood icon on the desktop, and choose Properties from the shortcut menu. (The Network Neighborhood icon appears only after your adapter is installed, which may happen when Windows 98 finds your network interface card. Read on for details.)

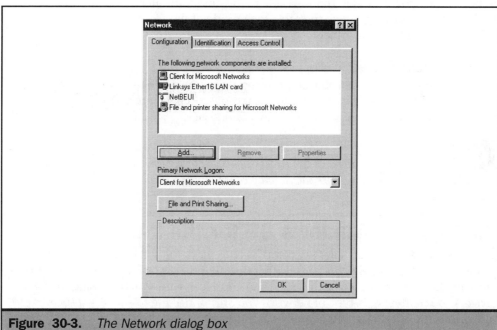

Figure 30-3. *The Network dialog box*

The Network dialog box displays all the installed components used for networking. Since using a PPP or SLIP connection to the Internet is also considered to be networking, you may see the TCP/IP protocol listed even though you do not (yet) have a LAN installed. The installed components can be one of four types—client, adapter, protocol, or service (see "How Do You Configure Windows 98 for a Network?" in Chapter 29). Different icons identify the different types of components:

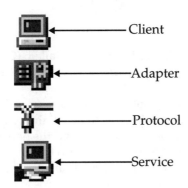

Client

Adapter

Protocol

Service

Installing Network Components

You start network component installation on the Configuration tab of the Network dialog box to install the four components: adapter, client, protocol, and service. In many cases, you won't have to install all four components manually—Windows 98 does some of the work for you. If you see that Windows 98 has already installed a component for you, skip to the next section.

Installing the Adapter

The *adapter* is the software driver that allows your PC to communicate with the network interface card in your PC. Every brand and model of network interface card has its own adapter that must be installed so that the client software knows how to package information and send it to the network interface card. If Windows 98 detects a Plug-and-Play network interface card, or if you upgraded to Windows 98 on a machine that was already connected to a network, you see the Network Neighborhood icon on your desktop, and the adapter appears in the Network dialog box.

If you're lucky (and smart enough to have bought and properly installed a good Plug-and-Play network interface card), you can skip installing the adapter, because Windows 98 notices when you install it and configures it automatically. To check whether an adapter is installed, or that the installed adapter is the correct one, look at the Network dialog box. Here's how to check whether an adapter is installed:

1. Display the Network dialog box, shown in Figure 30-3. Click the Configuration tab (if it's not already selected).

2. In the list at the top of the dialog box, look for a description of your network interface card with this icon next to it:

If you see the icon, then an adapter is already installed. (Check to see that the description shown matches your brand of network adapter—if not, install the correct adapter.)

If your network interface card is not Plug-and-Play, or if Windows 98 fails to recognize it, you use the Network dialog box to install the adapter for the card. You may want to give Windows 98 another chance to find the network interface card by using the Hardware Wizard, but if the Wizard doesn't find the card, you have to install the network interface card adapter yourself (see "Using the Add New Hardware Wizard" in Chapter 15). When the Hardware Wizard doesn't automatically find the card, it leaves you at step 4 of the following procedure. (A caveat: the dialog box you see is called Select Device, but it serves the same purpose and works the same way as the Select Network Adapters dialog box that you see if you install the network adapter by using the Network dialog box.)

If the adapter for your network interface card is not automatically installed, you need to know which driver you need to install. Windows comes with adapters for most network interface cards; however, your network interface card may have come with an adapter on a diskette or CD-ROM, and, additionally, an adapter for the card may be available at the manufacturer's web site or Microsoft's web site. Any of these drivers should work—look for the most recent one.

Here's how to install the adapter for your network interface card by using the Network dialog box:

1. Display the Network dialog box, shown in Figure 30-3. Click the Configuration tab (if it's not already selected).

2. Click the Add button. You see the Select Network Component Type dialog box, shown in Figure 30-4. You'll use this dialog box each time you need to add a new component to the Network dialog box.

3. Select Adapter, and then click the Add button. You see the Select Network Adapters dialog box, shown in Figure 30-5.

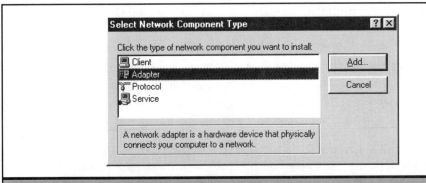

Figure 30-4. *Use the Select Network Component Type dialog box to select the type of network component to add*

4. If you want to use a driver on floppy disk or on your hard drive, click the Have Disk button, and then select the drive and folder containing the files to finish installing the driver.

5. Otherwise, select the manufacturer of your network interface card in the Manufacturers list box to see the adapters for cards made by that manufacturer.

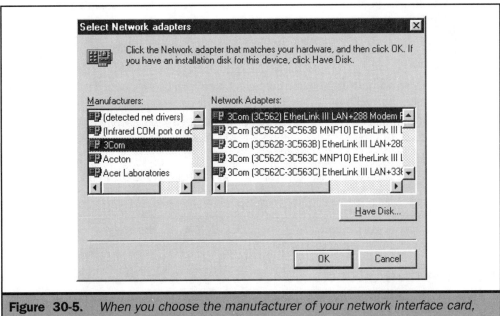

Figure 30-5. *When you choose the manufacturer of your network interface card, you see the available adapters*

6. Select the adapter from the Network Adapter list box, and then click the OK button. Wait while Windows finds and installs your adapter. Windows may ask you to insert your Windows 98 CD-ROM or floppy disk in the drive.

When the adapter is installed, you see the Network dialog box again. Not only has the adapter been installed, but Windows has also installed a client (Client for Microsoft Networks), and a protocol (TCP/IP). You will use the Client for Microsoft Networks, so if you see this client, you can skip the next section, "Installing the Client."

 In some cases, you may need to install more than one adapter; for instance, if you have two different network interface cards, because your computer is a node on two different networks, then you need to install two adapters. If you need more than one adapter installed, install them all now.

Installing the Client

The next step is to install the client component, which identifies the type of network your computer will be on. When you installed the adapter (or when Windows found your plug-and-play network interface card), Windows also installed a client, the Client for Microsoft Networks. If a client is installed, you can recognize it in the Network dialog box by its client icon (which looks like a little computer with a blue screen).

Since you are installing a peer-to-peer Windows network, the Client for Microsoft Networks is the one you need. If you've mistakenly deleted your Client for Microsoft Networks, follow these steps (these are also the steps you follow to install a client for a different kind of network):

1. Display the Network dialog box. Click the Configuration tab (if it's not already selected).

2. Click the Add button. You see the Select Network Component Type dialog box, shown in Figure 30-4.

3. Select Client as the type of network component you want to install, and then click the Add button. You see the Select Network Client dialog box, shown in Figure 30-6.

4. Choose the Manufacturer you want to use in order to see the available network clients. (Choose Microsoft if you're installing the Client for Microsoft Networks; that is, if you have a peer-to-peer network.)

5. Select the network client, and then click OK. You see the Network dialog box, with the client you just defined listed.

Installing the Protocol

Without a protocol, the computers on your network won't know how to talk to each other. The protocol is the language that your computer uses on the network. More than one protocol may be installed on a single computer, because computers can speak more

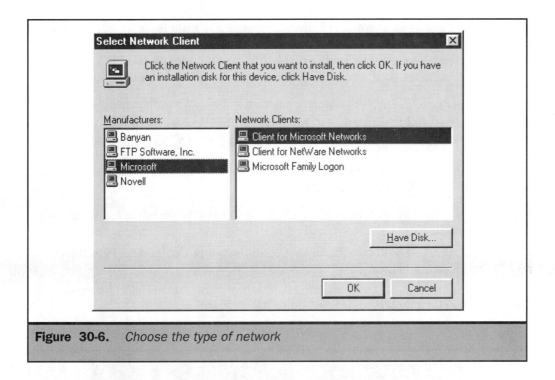

Figure 30-6. *Choose the type of network*

than one language. Networks that use Microsoft software (such as the peer-to-peer network you're creating now using Windows 98) support the three most common protocols—TCP/IP, IPX/SPX, and NetBEUI—as well as other less-common protocols:

- *TCP/IP* (Transmission Control Protocol/Internet Protocol) is the language spoken by computers on the Internet. Any computer using the Internet through a direct connection needs to have TCP/IP installed.

- *IPX/SPX* (Internetwork Packet eXchange/Sequenced Packet eXchange) is a protocol that was used primarily by Novell in their NetWare operating system. It is still widely used because of its ease of setup.

- *NetBEUI* (NetBIOS Extended User Interface) is used primarily by Microsoft in its networking products. It is fast and requires almost no configuration.

NetBEUI is by far the simplest protocol to use and configure. That simplicity has a drawback, however—NetBEUI is *non-routable*, which means that it can be used only on simple networks where routing devices are not used. *Routers* are devices used to connect multiple segments of networks; they can't transmit the NetBEUI protocol from one segment to another. Simple office and home-office networks usually don't require the use of routers, so NetBEUI is a good choice.

When you install an adapter, Windows automatically installs the TCP/IP protocol, in case you want to use TCP/IP for Internet communication. However, if you are setting up a simple peer-to-peer network, NetBEUI is an easier protocol to use—TCP/IP requires additional configuration that NetBEUI does not require.

You can delete the TCP/IP protocol, if you're sure you won't use it, but wait until you've installed the new protocol, NetBEUI, so that Windows doesn't also delete the client. If you're not sure whether the computer uses TCP/IP, don't delete it.

Installing a protocol is similar to installing other network components. Follow these steps to install NetBEUI or another protocol:

1. Display the Network dialog box. Click the Configuration tab (if it's not already selected).

2. Click the Add button to display the Select Network Component Type dialog box, shown in Figure 30-4.

3. Select Protocol, and then click the Add button. You see the Select Network Protocol dialog box, shown in Figure 30-7.

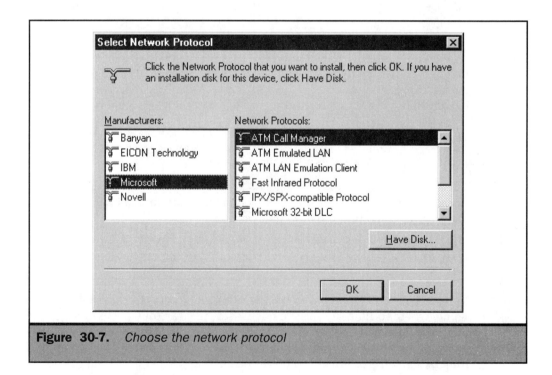

Figure 30-7. *Choose the network protocol*

4. If you are installing NetBEUI, select Microsoft as the manufacturer. Otherwise, select the manufacturer of the protocol you want to install.

5. Select NetBEUI (or the protocol you chose) as the Protocol, and then click OK. You see the Network dialog box, with the protocol you just added listed as an installed network component.

 When you install any protocol, Windows installs the Client for Microsoft Networks too, if it isn't already installed.

Installing the Service

A service is the last network component that you install—it also is the only optional component. Your network can work fine without a service, but no one on the network will be able to share resources, such as hard disks, CD-ROM drives, files, or printers. If you don't want to share resources, don't install a service.

 Even when a service has been defined, you can add some security measures to ensure that the resources on your computer are not abused (see "Limiting Access to a Shared Drive" in Chapter 32).

If you are creating a peer-to-peer network of Windows computers, you should install Microsoft's File And Printer Sharing For Microsoft Networks service. Install a service in the same way that you installed the other network components:

1. Display the Network dialog box. Click the Configuration tab (if it's not already selected).

2. Click the Add button to display the Select Network Component Type dialog box, shown in Figure 30-4.

3. Select Service, and then click the Add button. You see the Select Network Service dialog box, shown in Figure 30-8.

4. Select the File And Printer Sharing For Microsoft Networks service, and then click OK. You see the Network dialog box, with the service you just added listed.

The Configuration tab of the Network dialog box should now look like Figure 30-3 (additional components may also appear). If it doesn't look like this, install any additional components that are needed.

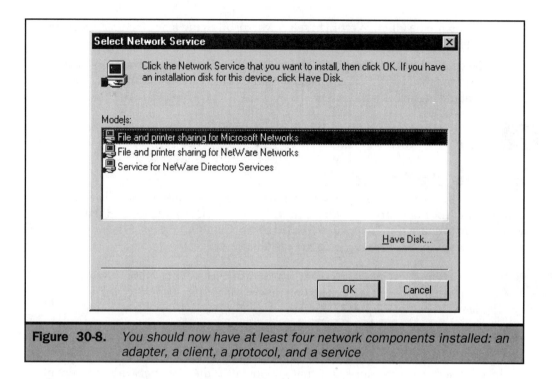

Figure 30-8.   *You should now have at least four network components installed: an adapter, a client, a protocol, and a service*

Setting the Properties of Your Network Components

Install all the network components before setting the properties of each component, because the components are interrelated. When components are installed before they are configured, Windows provides many of the correct configuration settings, thereby reducing the amount of work you have to do.

To configure an installed network component, display its properties by selecting the component on the Network dialog box and clicking the Properties button. In some cases, the default setting may be exactly what you need.

Configuring the Adapter

Follow these steps on each computer in the network to configure the properties of the adapter and protocol:

1. Display the Network dialog box. Click the Configuration tab (if it's not already selected).

2. Select the network adapter in the Network Components box of the Network dialog box.

3. Click the Properties button. You see the Properties dialog box for the adapter. Figure 30-9 shows the Properties dialog box for one network adapter, but the exact contents depend on the adapter driver.

4. Click the Driver Type tab. Check that the Enhanced Mode NDIS Driver radio button is selected.

5. Click the Bindings tab, which lists the protocols the card is bound to. If your network uses the NetBEUI protocol, only NetBEUI should be selected, so that the computer doesn't have to do extra work—click any other protocols to deselect them, if necessary.

6. Close the Properties dialog box.

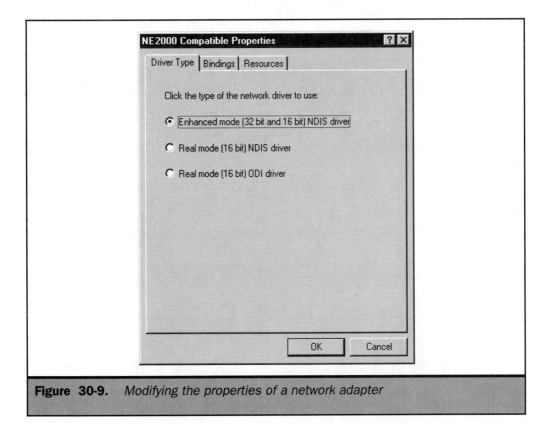

Figure 30-9. *Modifying the properties of a network adapter*

Configuring the Protocol

If you use the NetBEUI protocol, follow these steps (if you use another protocol, follow steps 1 and 2, and then determine what settings to change, if any):

1. Display the Network dialog box. Click the Configuration tab (if it's not already selected).

2. Select the NetBEUI protocol in the Network Components box of the Network dialog box.

3. Click the Properties button. You see the NetBEUI Properties dialog box, shown in Figure 30-10.

4. On the Bindings tab, check that the NetBEUI protocol is bound to Client for Microsoft Networks (there should be a check mark in the Client for Microsoft Networks box).

5. Close the NetBEUI Properties dialog box.

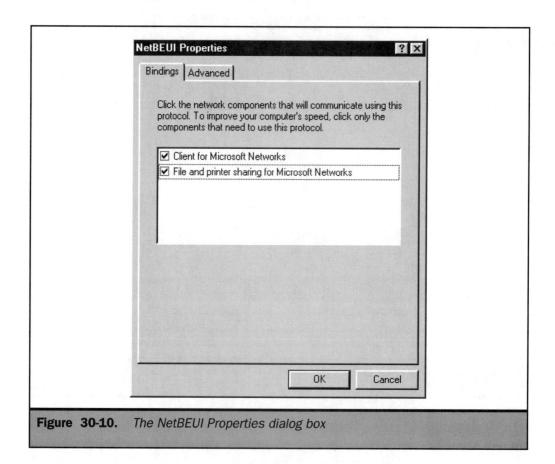

Figure 30-10.   *The NetBEUI Properties dialog box*

Configuring File and Print Sharing

If you plan to share resources on the computer, complete these additional steps:

1. Display the Network dialog box. Click the Configuration tab (if it's not already selected).

2. Click the File And Print Sharing button. You see the File And Print Sharing dialog box, shown here:

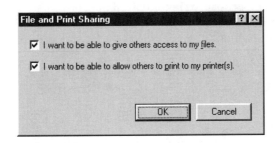

3. Select the check box(es) for the resources you want to share: files on any drives, and/or printers attached to the computer.

4. Click OK to return to the Network dialog box.

Enabling file and printer sharing only makes it possible for you to share resources—it does not automatically share resources, which might compromise security. In other words, your computer has the ability to allow others to print to your printer, or access files on your drives, but until you actually give others that permission, the resources remain unusable to others. The procedure for sharing resources is covered in Chapter 32.

Identifying the Computer

Once you have added and configured all the network components, you need to name the computer with a unique name, and identify the workgroup:

■ Naming your computer allows the users of other computers to refer to your computer by name. Some people pick a convention to use to name all their computers: cartoon characters, planets, friends, grade-school teachers, and so on. You may want to name your computers according to their primary function.

■ The *workgroup* is a group of computers on your network. The computers in a workgroup do not need to be physically close to each other, but they should be used by people who work together. The workgroup is a way to organize your peer-to-peer network's computers, similar to the way folders and subfolders organize the files on your PC.

For example, a small network of five computers may all belong to the same workgroup called Office. There's probably no reason to complicate things beyond that. Within the workgroup, the computers might be named Pluto, Neptune, Jupiter, Saturn, and Mars.

A larger organization with a larger network might need many workgroups to categorize their computers. Workgroups might be named Admin, Accounting, Shipping, and Maintenance. The computers within these workgroups each have their own names. However, a peer-to-peer network is not the best way to network many computers. Since you are probably creating a small peer-to-peer network, you should stick with one workgroup.

Here's how to give each PC a name and assign it to a workgroup:

1. Display the Network dialog box (if it isn't already displayed).

2. Click the Identification tab to see the identification settings, shown in Figure 30-11.

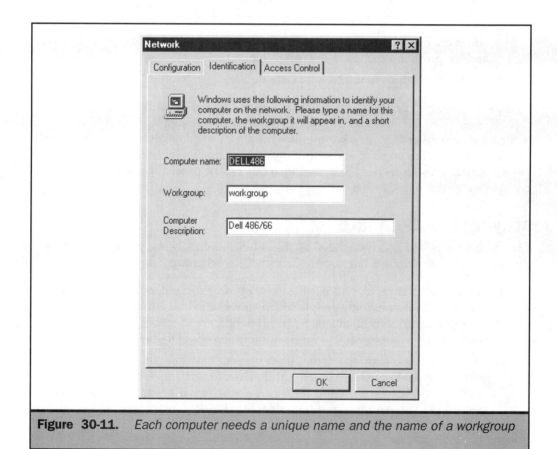

Figure 30-11. *Each computer needs a unique name and the name of a workgroup*

3. Type a name for the computer in the Computer Name box. Each computer in a workgroup needs a unique name.

4. Type a name for the workgroup in the Workgroup box.

Restarting the Computer

When you've installed and configured the adapter, client, protocol, and services for each computer, you're finished with the Network dialog box. Close the dialog box by clicking OK. Restart the computer when prompted to do so. You may be asked to insert your Windows 98 CD-ROM (the one you used to install the operating system) or floppy disk, so keep it on hand.

Checking Whether the Network Works

Once you've installed and configured the network components for a computer, you need to see whether your network works. Sit down at any of the computers on the network and follow these steps:

1. Open the Network Neighborhood icon on the desktop. You see the Network Neighborhood window (Figure 30-12), listing all the computers on the network.

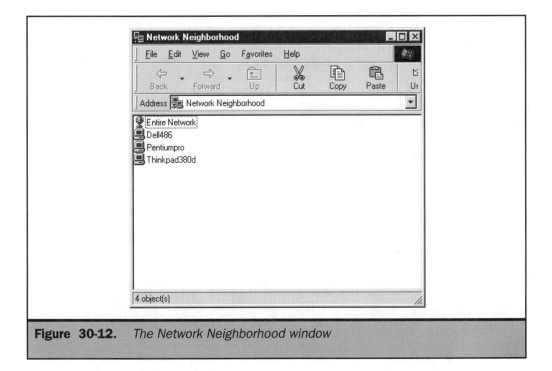

Figure 30-12.   *The Network Neighborhood window*

2. If you don't see the names of all the computers on the network, double-click the Entire Network icon, and then the Workgroup icon. Wait a minute or two. Your computer needs time to chat with the other computers on your network to find out who's out there and to build a list.

3. If you still don't see icons for the other computers on the network, read through the section "Troubleshooting Your Network" to find and fix the problem. If you see only your own computer in the list, there is some breakdown in the communication with the other computers. It could be physical, like a bad cable, or it could be software configuration, like the wrong protocol being used. Check the configuration of computers that are working (make sure that you've followed all the steps in this chapter). It's a good way to see whether you've missed something.

Once your network is working, the next step is to use it by sharing resources (see Chapter 32).

Logging In and Out

Each time you start Windows 98 after you have configured Windows to connect to a LAN, you see the Enter Network Password dialog box. Type your user name in the User Name box (the name you used the last time already appears in the box). Type your password in the Password box and click OK. If you use Windows 98 user profiles, and your network user name is different from your user profile name, you may have to log in again with your Windows user profile name and password. Then the desktop and Taskbar appear. You now have access to the shared resources on the LAN and can share your own computer's resources with others, as described in Chapter 32.

Note   *If you do not see the Enter Network Password dialog box, choose Start | Log Off to log in with your user name.*

When you are done working, you can log off the network to prevent anyone else from using your computer with your user name. Choose Start | Log Off. When Windows asks if you really want to log off, click Yes. Windows 98 closes all applications and displays the Enter Network Password dialog box.

Troubleshooting Your Network

Although Windows networking generally works well, you may have trouble with one computer, or all the computers on the network, especially when you first set up the network. This section recommends some steps to take to solve your problems.

The Windows 98 online help system has a useful Troubleshooter (see "Diagnosing Problems Using Troubleshooters" in Chapter 37). Find it by starting Help (choose Start | Help), and using the index to find "Network or LAN Troubleshooter."

The most common problems and solutions follow.

Some Computers Do Not Appear in Network Neighborhood

If you see some but not all computers in the network in Network Neighborhood, one of these problems may be the culprit:

- The computers that don't appear in Network Neighborhood may not be turned on or logged into the network.

- One of the other computers may have a loose cable connection, or a network interface card that is not working properly. Open Network Neighborhood on that computer to see whether the network can be seen from there.

Only Your Computer Appears in Network Neighborhood

If no other computers on the network appear in Network Neighborhood, you may have one of these problems:

- You need to log in. Sometimes Windows doesn't display the Enter Network Password dialog box. If you don't see the Enter Network Password dialog box, choose Start | Log Off. Windows shuts all open windows and displays the Enter Network Password dialog box.

- A cable may be loose or bad. Check all the connections of the cables. Occasionally, cables become damaged, so you may want to try replacing a suspect length of cable with one that you know is good.

- A protocol may be missing or incorrectly configured. Check to see that your computer is speaking the same language as all the others. If the other computers are using IPX/SPX and you are trying to use NetBEUI, then you can't communicate with them. The protocol must be an installed network component, and the network interface card must be bound to the protocol (display the Bindings tab of the network interface card's Properties dialog box to make sure that the card is bound to the NetBEUI protocol).

- You may have a hardware conflict. Your PC may have a problem using the network interface card. Open Control Panel, and then open the System icon. Click the Device Manager tab. If the network interface card appears with a yellow exclamation point, the card is not working properly. Check the installation instructions for your card.

No Network Neighborhood Icon Appears on the Desktop

Network Neighborhood does not appear unless a network interface card has been recognized. Install the network interface card, and install its driver (adapter) to see Network Neighborhood.

You Can't Use Resources on Another Computer

The resources may not have been set up yet to be shared. See Chapter 32 for more information on sharing resources.

Chapter 31

Connecting to Novell NetWare
and Windows NT Networks

peer-to-peer network, described in Chapter 30, can be very useful for connecting a small number of computers. However, if you work in a larger office, you may already have a client-server network installed. Currently, two of the most common operating systems for client-server networks are Novell NetWare and Windows NT. If you have either one of these types of networks, you can connect your Windows 98 computer to it by following the steps in this chapter: Install the network hardware, install the Windows 98 networking components, and configure the components for a Novell NetWare or Windows NT network. Then you can log in and out, share your computer's resources on the network, and find other computers on the network. To use the resources on other computers on the network, see Chapter 32.

> **Note**   *If your office uses a different type of network operating system, in all likelihood, you can still connect your computer to the network, but the specific steps are not included in this book. However, you may benefit from reading this chapter—the steps for putting a Windows 98 computer on any client-server network are much the same.*

A brief note about terminology: When you put your Windows 98 computer on a Novell NetWare network or Windows NT LAN (local area network), you are making it a client on the network. A client computer uses the resources on the network. Even though your computer may also share its resources with others, it is still referred to as a client of the network. (In client-server networks, the servers are computers that are dedicated to being servers—they usually are not also used as workstations.)

Although this chapter covers connecting a Windows 98 computer to a Novell or Windows NT network and sharing your computer's resources on the LAN, it does not cover how to create or administer either type of network—that topic is a large one, and beyond the scope of this book. Please refer to Chapter 29 for general LAN concepts and Chapter 30 for descriptions of Windows 98's built-in networking components.

How Do You Add a Client to a Client-Server Network?

This chapter covers the specific steps you need to take to connect your Windows 98 computer to an existing Novell NetWare or Windows NT network. Many of the steps you need to take are the same for both networks—the only real differences are the components you choose. Also, many steps are the same steps you would follow to connect your computer to a peer-to-peer network, described in the preceding chapter. Here's a road map of what you need to do:

1. Install the hardware: You need a network interface card and cable to attach your PC to the network (see "Buying Network Hardware" in Chapter 30). Buy a card and cable that match the existing LAN.

2. Install and configure network components: The specific components that you need to connect to either a Novell NetWare or Windows NT network are covered in this chapter.

Once you've completed these two steps, you need to log in to the network. In order to log in, you first need to restart your computer, which causes all the additions that you made to take effect. You also need a user name and password, assigned to you by the network administrator.

Of course, you'll probably want to use resources on the network, specifically files and printers (see Chapter 32). You may want to share resources that are attached to your computer with the rest of the network, or just with specific users of the network (see "Letting Others Use Your Computer's Resources"). For help with other tasks related to sharing hardware or software, talk to your network administrator.

Connecting to a Client-Server LAN

Once you have installed the necessary hardware, setting up a Windows 98 computer to be a client is very similar to setting it up to be connected to a Windows peer-to-peer network.

Displaying the Network Dialog Box

To begin, open the Network dialog box (shown later in this chapter, in Figure 31-2) by using one of the following methods:

- Open the Network icon on the Control Panel. Click or double-click the icon depending on whether you use Web style or Classic style for your desktop (see "Choosing the Style of Your Desktop" in Chapter 1).
- Right-click Network Neighborhood and choose Properties. (Network Neighborhood appears on the desktop when an adapter is installed. It also appears in Windows Explorer in the folder tree.)

Your Network dialog box may show some network components already installed.

Installing Network Components

You need to install three network software components—a client (which tells your computer what type of network operating system you use), an adapter (which communicates with the network interface card in your computer), and a protocol (which identifies the low-level language in which the network communicates). (See "How Do You Configure Windows 98 for a Network?" in Chapter 29.) Each is an independent component that works with the others to provide a connection to your LAN. If your computer has resources that you want to share with the rest of the network, you also need to install a fourth component—a service, the software that tells your computer to share its resources (such as printers or files) with other computers on the network.

If you are connecting your computer to a Novell NetWare network, read the following section to find out how to install the client, adapter, and protocol you need. If you are connecting your computer to a Windows NT network, skip to the section "Connecting Your Windows 98 Computer to a Windows NT LAN." If you plan to share your computer's resources with others on the LAN—whether you use a Novell NetWare or Windows NT network—also read the section "Letting Others Use Your Computer's Resources" to find out how to install the network services you need.

Configuring Your PC for a Novell NetWare LAN

To configure Windows 98 to recognize a Novell NetWare network, display the Network dialog box, as described earlier—you use it a lot as you set up your PC to be a Novell NetWare client. This section describes how to install the client, adapter, and protocol that you need, configure each component, and identify your computer to the network.

Installing Networking Components for Novell NetWare

For a Novell NetWare LAN, you install the adapter (unless it was installed automatically when Windows detected your network interface card), client, and protocol as described it the following sections. If you want to share your computer's resources over the network, you need to install a service, too.

Installing the Adapter

If your adapter wasn't installed automatically when Windows detected your network interface card, you must install the adapter manually. Check your card's documentation for information about which adapter to install. If you don't have an adapter installed, the Select Network Adapters dialog box appears automatically, once you have selected a client.

To install the adapter for your network interface card, follow these steps:

1. Display the Network dialog box (if it isn't already displayed).

2. Click the Add button on the Configuration tab to display the Select Network Component Type dialog box, shown here:

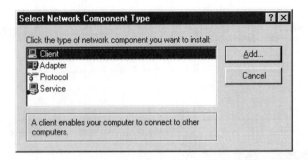

3. Select Adapter as the type of network component you want to add.

4. Click the Add button to see the Select Network Adapter dialog box, which shows a list of specific components available to you.

 If you have a disk with the adapter software you want to install, click the Have Disk button and then browse to the file you need.

5. Choose the manufacturer of the component in the left column of the Select Network Adapter dialog box. The specific adapters available from that manufacturer appear in the right column.

6. Choose the specific adapter in the right column of the Select Network Adapter dialog box.

7. Click OK to install the component and return to the Network dialog box. You may be prompted to insert your Windows 98 CD in the CD-ROM drive.

Installing the Client

Install Microsoft's Client For NetWare Networks. This may not seem to be the obvious choice. When looking at the Manufacturers list box, you may be tempted to select Novell, because you want to connect to a Novell network. However, Microsoft makes a good client for Novell networks. When you install the client, Microsoft's IPX/SPX-compatible Protocol is installed automatically.

To install the Client For NetWare Networks, follow these steps:

1. Display the Network dialog box.

2. Click the Add button on the Configuration tab to display the Select Network Component Type dialog box (shown in the previous section).

3. Select Client as the type of network component you want to add.

4. Click the Add button to see the Select Network Client dialog box, shown in Figure 31-1.

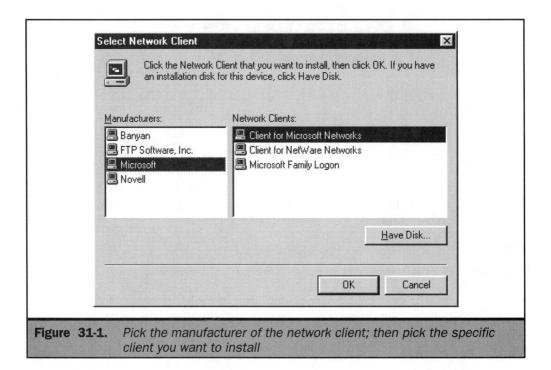

Figure 31-1.   *Pick the manufacturer of the network client; then pick the specific client you want to install*

Note   *If you have a disk with the client you want to install, click the Have Disk button and then browse to the file you need.*

5. Choose Microsoft as the manufacturer of the component in the left column of the Select Network Client dialog box. The specific clients available from Microsoft appear in the right column.

6. Choose Client For NetWare Networks in the right column of the Select Network Client dialog box.

7. Click OK to install the client and return to the Network dialog box. You may be prompted to insert your Windows 98 CD in the CD-ROM drive.

Installing the Protocol

The protocol you choose should be the one that is used by the network to which you are connecting. In most cases, you should install Microsoft's IPX/SPX-compatible Protocol (if it is installed when you install the client, you can skip this step). Some NetWare networks use TCP/IP, which requires more configuration (a unique address must be given to each computer on the LAN). If your Novell NetWare network uses TCP/IP, install Microsoft's TCP/IP protocol. This book does not provide the details on how to configure a client of a NetWare network using TCP/IP.

Follow these steps to install the network protocol:

1. Display the Network dialog box.

2. Click the Add button on the Configuration tab to display the Select Network Component Type dialog box.

3. Select Protocol as the type of network component you want to add.

4. Click the Add button to see the Select Network Protocol dialog box, which shows a list of specific components available to you.

5. In most cases, you should choose Microsoft as the manufacturer of the protocol in the left column. The specific protocols available from Microsoft appear in the right column. If you are using a protocol from a different manufacturer, choose that manufacturer.

6. Choose the specific protocol in the right column. Most NetWare networks use Microsoft's IPX/SPX-compatible Protocol, although some use Microsoft's TCP/IP protocol. Pick the one used by your network from the list of Microsoft's versions of these protocols in the right column.

7. Click OK to install the component and return to the Network dialog box. You may be prompted to insert your Windows 98 CD in the CD-ROM drive.

Do You Have the Components You Need?

Once you've completed these steps, your Network dialog box should look like Figure 31-2. Your adapter may be different, and you may have additional components listed, but you should see the following components:

- The adapter that works with your network interface card.

- The Microsoft Client for NetWare Networks.

- The IPX/SPX-compatible Protocol, or if your Novell NetWare network uses TCP/IP, the TCP/IP protocol.

Configuring Network Components for Novell NetWare

The next step is to check the properties of each of the network components. To check the properties of a component, select the component on the Network dialog box and click the Properties button.

Once the configuration is complete, close the Network dialog box and reboot the computer.

Setting Client Properties

To configure the client to work with the Novell NetWare network, follow these steps:

1. Select Client For NetWare Networks in the Network dialog box (on the Configuration tab).

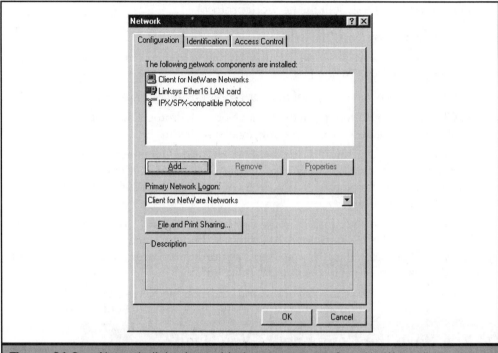

Figure 31-2.   *Network dialog box, with the components for a NetWare client*

2. Click the Properties button to display the Client For NetWare Networks Properties dialog box. If the General tab is not displayed, click the General tab. If you are connecting to either a NetWare 4.x network that is running "bindery mode" or to a NetWare 3.x network, you must enter the name of the Preferred server that authenticates your login. If you are connecting to a NetWare 4.x network that is using NDS (NetWare Directory Services), you must enter the name of the preferred directory tree and context for logging in. Ask your network administrator for these values.

3. In the First Network Drive box, select the letter of your first network drive—the default is the F drive. The first network drive is the first letter in the alphabet that is not assigned to a local resource, such as a floppy drive, hard drive, or CD-ROM drive.

4. Be sure the Enable Logon Script Processing check box is selected if you want to run NetWare login scripts. If your network administrator has created a logon script for you to map network drives or to do other tasks, you need to select this option for the script to run when you log on.

5. Click OK to return to the Network dialog box.

Setting Adapter Properties

Adapter properties are unique to your network interface card; however, we can tell you some properties that you can check for any adapter. To configure the adapter to work with the Novell NetWare network, follow these steps:

1. Select the installed adapter in the Network dialog box (on the Configuration tab).

2. Click the Properties button to display the Properties dialog box for the adapter that you installed. If the Driver Type tab is not displayed, click the Driver Type tab.

3. Select the Enhanced Mode (32 bit and 16 bit) NDIS Driver.

4. Click the Bindings tab. Check that the adapter is bound to the IPX/SPX-compatible Protocol (if your network uses TCP/IP, the adapter should be bound to TCP/IP). Be sure there is a check in the check box next to the protocol that the adapter uses. (Your adapter card may be bound to more than one protocol.)

5. Click the Resources tab. Resource settings are dependent upon the make and model of your network interface card. If your card needs to be configured by jumpers or switches on the card itself, make sure the settings in these list boxes match those you have set on the card. Note that an asterisk next to a value indicates a conflict with other hardware—you need to change the setting and make sure that the configuration of the card matches the new setting—network interface cards are configured using switches on the card itself or software utilities.

6. Click OK to close the Properties dialog box and return to the Network dialog box.

Setting Protocol Properties

To configure the protocol to work with the Novell NetWare network, follow these steps:

1. Select the protocol used by your NetWare network in the Network dialog box (on the Configuration tab).

2. Click the Properties button to display the Properties dialog box for the protocol.

3. Click the Bindings tab. The check box labeled Client For NetWare Networks must be checked. This tells the Client For NetWare Networks to use this protocol for its network communication.

4. Click OK to return to the Network dialog box.

Identifying the PC to Novell NetWare

Your PC must have a unique name, and the workgroup it is part of must be identified. Complete these steps to identify your computer:

1. Display the Identification tab of the Network dialog box (shown in Figure 31-3).

2. Type a name for your computer in the Computer Name box.

3. Type the name of the workgroup your computer belongs to in the Workgroup box.

Rebooting the PC

Once you have added and configured the necessary components and have identified the PC, you are ready to see whether the network works:

1. Click OK to close the Network dialog box.

2. Reboot the computer as prompted.

When the computer reboots, you should see the dialog box asking you to log in. You are done installing and configuring the software you need to connect to the network. Skip to the section "Logging In and Out" and continue with the following sections in this chapter.

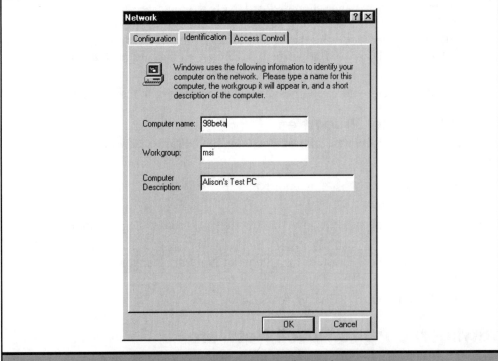

Figure 31-3. *Each PC needs a unique name and a workgroup name*

Connecting Your Windows 98 Computer to a Windows NT LAN

To configure Windows 98 to connect to a Windows NT network, display the Network dialog box, as described earlier—you'll use it a lot as you set up your PC to be a Windows NT client. This section describes how to install the client, adapter, and protocol that you need, configure each component, and identify your computer to the network.

Installing Components

In order to get your computer onto a Windows NT LAN, you need to install the adapter, client, and protocol as described it the following sections. If you want to share your computer's resources over the network, you need to install a service, too (see "Letting Others Use Your Computer's Resources").

Installing the Adapter

You must install the adapter for the network interface card you use to attach to the Windows NT network (your computer may have more than one network interface card). Check your card's documentation for information about which adapter to install. If you don't have an adapter installed, the Select Network Adapters dialog box appears automatically after you select a client.

To install the adapter for your network interface card, follow these steps:

1. Display the Network dialog box (if it isn't already displayed).

2. Click the Add button on the Configuration tab to display the Select Network Component Type dialog box.

3. Select Adapter as the type of network component you want to add.

4. Click the Add button to see the Select Network Adapter dialog box, which includes a list of specific components available to you.

Note   *If you have a disk with the adapter software you want to install, click the Have Disk button and then browse to the file you need.*

5. Choose the manufacturer of the component in the left column of the Select Network Adapter dialog box. The specific adapters available from that manufacturer appear in the right column.

6. Choose the specific adapter in the right column of the Select Network Adapter dialog box.

7. Click OK to install the component and return to the Network dialog box. You may be prompted to insert your Windows 98 CD in the CD-ROM drive.

Installing the Client

Install Microsoft's Client For Microsoft Networks. Although you may be looking for a Windows NT client, you won't find one—instead, you need the Client For Microsoft Networks. When you install the Client, the TCP/IP protocol is installed automatically, if no other protocol is already installed.

To install the Client For Microsoft Networks, follow these steps:

1. Display the Network dialog box.

2. Click the Add button on the Configuration tab to display the Select Network Component Type dialog box.

3. Select Client as the type of network component you want to add.

4. Click the Add button to see the Select Network Client dialog box (Figure 31-1).

5. Choose Microsoft as the manufacturer of the component in the left column of the Select Network Client dialog box. The specific clients available from Microsoft appear in the right column.

6. Choose the Client For Microsoft Networks in the right column of the Select Network Client dialog box.

7. Click OK to install the client and return to the Network dialog box. You may be prompted to insert your Windows 98 CD in the CD-ROM drive.

Installing the Protocol

The protocol you choose should be the one that is used by the network to which you are connecting. Windows NT networks may use IPX/SPX, NetBEUI, or TCP/IP as their protocol—you need to find out which protocol is used on the network to which you are connecting and then install that protocol. NetBEUI and IPX/SPX require almost no configuration; TCP/IP requires that each computer on the network have a unique network address. If the network you are using uses TCP/IP, check with the network administrator for details on how to configure the protocol.

Follow these steps to install the network protocol:

1. Display the Network dialog box.

2. Click the Add button on the Configuration tab to display the Select Network Component Type dialog box.

3. Select Protocol as the type of network component you want to add.

4. Click the Add button to see the Select Network Protocol dialog box, which includes a list of specific components available to you.

5. Choose Microsoft as the manufacturer of the protocol in the left column. The specific protocols available from Microsoft appear in the right column.

6. Choose the specific protocol in the right column. Windows NT networks may use Microsoft's IPX/SPX-compatible Protocol, TCP/IP, or NetBEUI. Pick the one used by your network.

7. Click OK to install the protocol and return to the Network dialog box. You may be prompted to insert your Windows 98 CD in the CD-ROM drive.

Repeat these steps to install an additional protocol if your network uses more than one protocol.

Do You Have the Components You Need?

Once you've completed these steps, your Network dialog box should look like Figure 31-4. Your adapter may be different, and you may have additional components listed, but you should see the following components:

■ The adapter that works with your network interface card.

■ The Client For Microsoft Networks.

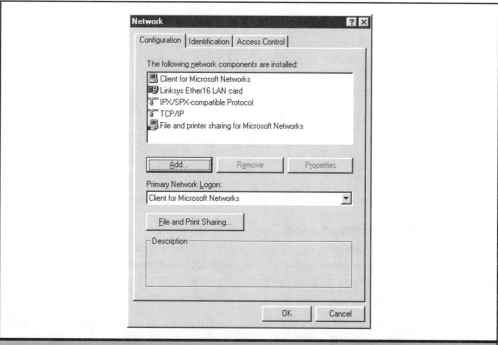

Figure 31-4. Network dialog box, with the components for a Windows NT client

■ The protocol that your network uses: IPX/SPX-compatible Protocol, TCP/IP, or the NetBEUI protocol (or a combination).

Configuring Network Components for a Windows NT Network

The next step is to check the properties of each of the network components. To check the properties of a component, select the component on the Network dialog box and then click the Properties button.

Once the configuration is complete, close the Network dialog box and reboot the computer.

Setting Client Properties

To configure the client to work with the Windows NT network, follow these steps:

1. Select the installed client in the Network dialog box (on the Configuration tab).

2. Click the Properties button to display the Client For Microsoft Networks Properties dialog box, shown in Figure 31-5.

3. Check that the Log On To Windows NT Domain option is selected.

4. Type the name of the domain that you are logging into in the Windows NT Domain box. This is not a specific server name. Instead, it is a name that may represent a whole group of computers in your company. The server that needs to authenticate your login will find you.

5. Choose whether you want Quick Logon or Logon And Restore Network Connections each time you log on. Quick Logon speeds up your initial login time, but means that using a network resource the first time in each session takes a little longer. Quick Logon is a better option if network resources are not always available.

6. Click OK to return to the Network dialog box.

Setting Adapter Properties

Adapter properties are unique to your network interface card, so you should check your card's documentation for instructions on how to configure the adapter properties. However, you should check some properties for any adapter. To configure the adapter to work with the Windows NT network, follow these steps:

1. Select the installed client in the Network dialog box (on the Configuration tab).

2. Click the Properties button to display the Properties dialog box for the adapter that you installed. If the Driver Type tab is not displayed, click the Driver Type tab.

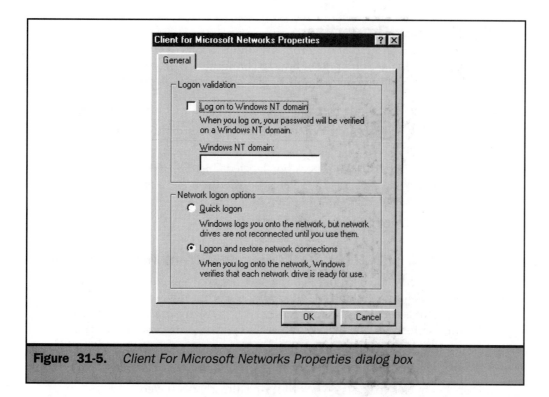

Figure 31-5.   *Client For Microsoft Networks Properties dialog box*

3. Select the Enhanced Mode (32 bit and 16 bit) NDIS Driver.

4. Click the Bindings tab. Check that the adapter is bound to the protocol that is in use in the network to which you are connecting (there should be a check mark next to the protocol in use). (Your adapter card may be bound to more than one protocol.)

5. Click the Resources tab. Check for an asterisk indicating that the network interface card is conflicting with other resources.

Note
Resource settings are dependent upon the make and model of your network interface card. If you have a resource conflict, you need to check your card's documentation to find out how to configure your card, so that it doesn't conflict with other resources (see "Troubleshooting Your Hardware Configuration" in Chapter 15). It may be configured by jumpers or switches on the card, or by software.

6. Click OK to close the Properties dialog box and return to the Network dialog box.

Setting Protocol Properties

You may need to change some of the properties of the protocol you are using. If you are using TCP/IP, you need to find out how to configure the protocol from your network administrator. If you are using IPX/SPX or NetBEUI, follow these steps:

1. Select the protocol in the Network dialog box (on the Configuration tab).
2. Click the Properties button to display the Properties dialog box for the protocol that you installed.
3. Click the Bindings tab. The check box labeled Client For Microsoft Networks must be checked. This tells the Client For Microsoft Networks to use this protocol for its network communication.
4. Click OK to return to the Network dialog box.

Identifying the Computer to Your Windows NT Network

Once you have added and configured all the network components, you need to name the computer with a unique name and identify the workgroup.

The workgroup is a group of computers on your network (see "Identifying the Computer" in Chapter 30). The workgroup is a way to organize your network's computers, similar to the way folders and subfolders organize the files on your PC.

Follow these steps to give the PC a name and assign it to a workgroup:

1. Display the Network dialog box (if it isn't already displayed).
2. Click the Identification tab to see the identification settings.
3. Type a name for the computer in the Computer Name box. Each computer in a workgroup needs a unique name.
4. Type a name for the workgroup in the Workgroup box.

Rebooting the PC

Once you have added and configured the necessary components and identified the PC, you are ready to see whether the network works:

1. Click OK to close the Network dialog box.
2. Reboot the computer, as prompted.

When the computer reboots, you should see the dialog box that asks you to log in. You are done configuring your computer to connect to a Windows NT network; continue with the following sections in this chapter to learn how to use it.

Logging In and Out

Microsoft uses the terms log on *and* log off, *while Novell uses* log in *and* log out. *Both sets of terms refer to the same actions—accessing and ending access to the network.*

When your computer is correctly connected and configured, the Enter Network Password dialog box appears when Windows 98 is restarted. Type your user name and password and then press ENTER or click OK. You now have access to NetWare or NT network resources.

If you do not see the Enter Network Password dialog box, choose Start | Log Off. Windows 98 closes all applications and displays a Log In dialog box.

When you log in, Windows processes your system's login scripts. *Login scripts* are batch files that contain mostly command-line commands, usually to map network drives and synchronize the PC time with the server time. Your system administrator creates login scripts, which can run for all users, groups of users, or specific individuals (you can create or edit a system login script only if you have administrator permissions on the network).

If you have trouble logging in, it may be because you do not have a name and password on the network. Ask your network administrator to set you up as a user. If you don't see the Enter Network Password window, try logging out by choosing Start | Log Off.

If you ever need to log off the network (perhaps so that unauthorized users can't access network resources when you're away from your computer), ask your network administrator how you should do it. In most cases you can use one of the following methods:

- Choose Start | Shut Down, select Close All Programs And Log On As A Different User, and then click OK. Windows 98 closes all programs and logs off the network.
- Choose Start | Log Off.
- Right-click any server displayed in Network Neighborhood or Windows Explorer and select Logout.

For information about changing your password, see Chapter 33.

Once you are connected to the LAN, you can use the shared resources on other people's computers, as described in the next chapter, as well as sharing your own computer's resources, described in the next section.

Letting Others Use Your Computer's Resources

Even though Novell NetWare and Windows NT are client-server network operating systems, your PC can share resources with the rest of the network, in addition to using the resources provided by the network (acting as a server for these specific resources). Resources that you might want to share include a local printer attached to the PCs parallel port, a CD-ROM drive, and files on the hard drive.

Unlike Windows peer-to-peer networking, NetWare and Windows NT provide both *user-level access control* (in which you can designate a list of people allowed to use the resource) and *share-level access control* (in which anyone who knows the resource's password can use the resource). If you have resources on your computer that you want to share with other users of the network, set up your computer to share your resources by using user-level access control rather than share-level access control. In a peer-to-peer network, your only choice is share-level control.

You should check with your network administrator before you share any resources over the LAN.

To share your computer's resources with other users on the LAN, you need to do three things:

- Install a service.
- Decide the type of access control you want to use.
- Change the resource's properties to make the resource visible over the network.

This section describes how to install the service you need for sharing resources and how to set the type of access control. To set a printer's properties to make it sharable, see "Sharing Printers" in the next chapter. To share a disk drive or folder, see "Sharing Disk Drives" in the next chapter.

Follow these steps to install and configure the service:

1. Open the Network dialog box. Display the Configuration tab of the dialog box (if it isn't already displayed).

2. Click the Add button to display the Select Network Component Type dialog box.

3. Select Service and click Add to display the Select Network Service dialog box.

4. Select Microsoft as the Manufacturer and File And Printer Sharing For Microsoft Networks as the service.

5. Click OK to close the dialog box and return to the Network dialog box. The additional component appears on the Network dialog box.

6. Click the File And Print Sharing button to display the File And Print Sharing dialog box.

7. Select the appropriate settings—if you want to share files on your local drives, make sure the first option is selected; if you want to share a local printer, select the second option.

8. Click OK to return to the Network dialog box.

9. Click the Access Control tab.

10. Check that the User-Level Access Control radio button is selected.

11. Type the name of a server or domain where user names are stored. (This is probably the same server or domain name you specified to log in.)

12. Click OK to close the Network dialog box. You need to reboot the computer to enable resource sharing.

Note
To share resources on a Novell NetWare client computer, you must be using the Microsoft Client For NetWare Networks. Other NetWare clients do not support resource sharing.

These steps enable you to take further steps to share files and printers—they don't actually make your files and printers available to other users on the network.

If you want users of Novell's NETX and VLM clients to be able to access the shared resources, you need to enable SAP Advertising, by doing the following:

1. Select the new component, File And Printer Sharing For NetWare Networks, and then click Properties.

2. Enable SAP Advertising by selecting it in the Property box and changing the Value setting to Enabled.

3. Click OK to close the Properties dialog box.

Note
Enabling SAP Advertising may add unwanted network traffic to the LAN.

To make sure that you are taking advantage of your network's access control, follow these steps:

1. Click the Access Control tab of the Network dialog box to see the options shown in Figure 31-6.

2. Click the User-Level Access Control radio button.

3. Type the name of a domain or server where the user information for the network can be accessed in the Obtain List Of Users And Groups box.

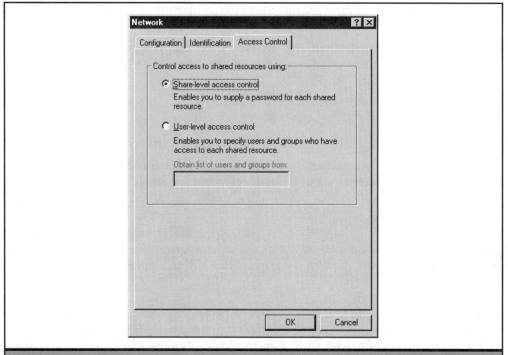

Figure 31-6. *Take advantage of user-level access to resources when you have a client-server network*

Finding Computers on the Network

Most peer-to-peer networks aren't large enough to lose computers on, but NetWare and Windows NT networks can be huge, connecting hundreds of computers. Windows 98 gives you a way to search for computers on your LAN if you know the name of the computer. Choose Start | Find | Computer to display the Find Computer dialog box. Type a computer name into the Named box (or choose a name from its pull-down menu) and click Find Now.

Chapter 32

Sharing Drives and Printers

If you have a LAN, you probably set it up because you have resources that you want to share. Perhaps you have three computers and only one printer. Perhaps several people use a database from different computers, and you want to make sure that they're always working with updated information. Whatever the reason, your LAN isn't much good if you don't know how to share your hardware.

This chapter tells you how to use shared resources on other computers, enable sharing the resources of your own computer, and share printers and disk drives so that everyone on your LAN can use them. It also tells you how you can limit use of shared resources through passwords and other means, as well as monitoring who is using the resources on your computer. The last section of this chapter explains how to use WinPopup to exchange messages with people over the LAN.

> **Note**   *This chapter assumes that you have connected your computer to a LAN and installed file-sharing and printer-sharing services (see Chapters 30 and 31).*

Using Shared LAN Resources

The main purpose of connecting to a network is to use the shared network resources, primarily files and printers (you may also want to receive e-mail). The steps you need to take to use a network drive or printer are similar whether you are connected to a peer-to-peer or client-server network. This section describes how to use the shared resources on other computers; to make printers and files on your own computer sharable, see "Enabling Hardware Sharing."

Using Network Drives

Network drives (disk drives that are shared on the network) are available from any computer on the LAN. There are two ways that you can access the drive:

- You may only use the drive only occasionally, in which case you can use Network Neighborhood to access the drive.

- You may use the drive frequently, in which case you will find it convenient to *map the drive*, which means that you assign the drive a letter so that it appears on the drop-down list of drives in Open and Save As dialog boxes.

Navigating Network Drives with Network Neighborhood

Once you have shared a drive, you can access it by using the Network Neighborhood icon on the desktop or the Network Neighborhood icon found in Windows Explorer.

The address of any shared resource appears using the UNC (Universal Naming Convention) form—that is, if the resource is on another computer, the path name is preceded by two backslashes followed by the name of the computer (see "What Are Addresses?" in Chapter 8).

Network Neighborhood displays shared drives on the network in Folder windows. Open the Network Neighborhood icon on the desktop or in Windows Explorer to see the name of all the computers on the LAN; click or double-click the icon, depending on whether your desktop uses Web style or Classic style (see "Choosing the Style of Your Desktop" in Chapter 1). If you don't see a list of computer names, you may need to troubleshoot your network (see Chapters 30 and 31). To access a shared drive, open the icon for the computer to which the drive is attached. Figure 32-1 shows the shared drives on a computer called Lamb. Three drives are available on Lamb: the first, Books, is a folder that has been shared, the second is the CD-ROM drive, and the third is the C drive, the main hard drive on Lamb.

You know you're looking at another computer on the network because of the computer icon in the Address box and the double slash used to address another computer. Once you see the drive, you can work with it as you do any drive on your own computer (see "Working with Folder Windows and Windows Explorer Windows" in Chapter 8).

You can also use the Network Neighborhood icon in Windows Explorer to find and open files on a shared drive. The Network Neighborhood icon in Windows Explorer gives you access to the same computers and drives as the Network Neighborhood icon on the desktop. The difference is whether you prefer the Windows Explorer presentation, with the hierarchy in the left pane, or if you prefer a Folder window. Figure 32-2 shows the same drives on Lamb as Figure 32-1—the only difference is the display.

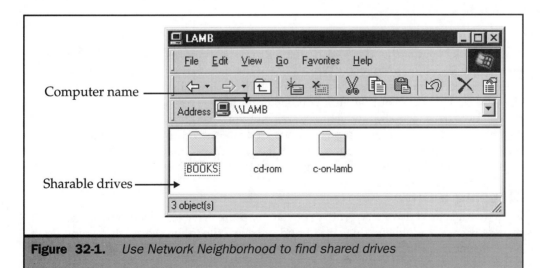

Figure 32-1. *Use Network Neighborhood to find shared drives*

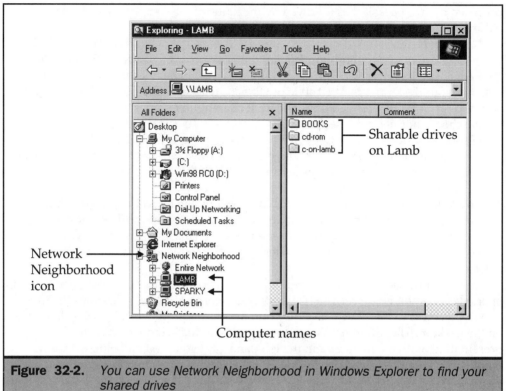

Figure 32-2. *You can use Network Neighborhood in Windows Explorer to find your shared drives*

Network Neighborhood is also available from dialog boxes of any applications you use. Figure 32-3 shows Microsoft Word's Open dialog box with a Network Neighborhood icon displayed. Use the Look In drop-down list to choose Desktop, or click the Up One Level button until you have reached the top of the folder tree to see the contents of the Desktop (which includes Network Neighborhood). Network Neighborhood is also an option on the Look In drop-down list. Once you have opened Network Neighborhood, you can see the drive you want—open the computer that owns the drive to see the drive, and then move to the folder you want.

Mapping a Drive

If you use a shared drive frequently, you can map the drive to a drive letter. The process is easy, and when you want to find or save a file to the shared drive, you don't have to spend so much time navigating through Network Neighborhood to find it.

Network Neighborhood icon

Look In box

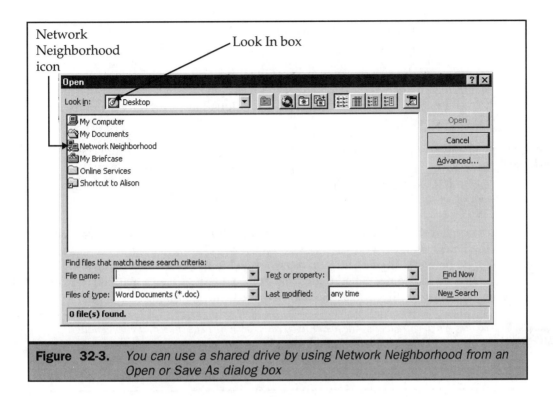

Figure 32-3.   *You can use a shared drive by using Network Neighborhood from an Open or Save As dialog box*

Here's the easiest way to map a drive to a drive letter:

1. Find the drive by using Network Neighborhood in a Folder window or Windows Explorer.

2. Right-click the drive and choose Map Network Drive to display the Map Network Drive dialog box, shown here:

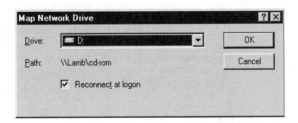

3. Choose a drive letter for the drive. Use the drop-down list to see the available letters.

4. Close the dialog box. If the shared drive requires a password, Windows prompts you to type it.

In Windows Explorer, you can also select the drive and choose Tools | Map Network Drive to display the Map Network Drive dialog box. However, using the Map choice on the shortcut menu is simpler—you don't have to specify the path of the drive you are mapping.

> **Note**   *You can also map a drive by using the Map Drive button on the Windows Explorer toolbar if it appears. (If it doesn't appear, choose View | Folder Options to display the Folder Options dialog box, click the View tab, look in the Advanced Settings box, and select the Show Map Network Drive Button In Toolbar setting.)*

Once you have mapped a drive, it appears in the folder tree with your local drives, and in the Folder window you see when you open My Computer. Figure 32-4 shows two mapped network drives: The E drive is mapped to the C drive on Lamb and the F drive is mapped to a folder called Books on Lamb. You can access a mapped network drive in the same way that you access a local drive from any dialog box.

> **Note**   *To map a drive to a folder, the folder itself must be defined as shared. It is not enough to share the drive on which the folder resides.*

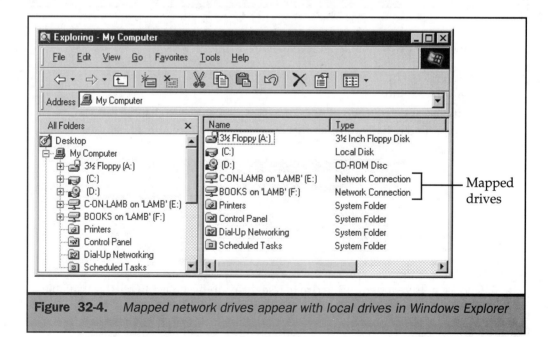

Figure 32-4.   *Mapped network drives appear with local drives in Windows Explorer*

Tips for Mapping

When you map a drive, you only map it for only one computer at a time. If you want the drive mapped for other computers in the LAN, you need to sit down at each of them and repeat the steps in the preceding section. That is, if you want all the computers in your office to be able to use the drive letter F to refer to the Books folder on the Lamb computer, you must map the Books folder to the F drive on each computer in the LAN.

If you use a shared network drive from more than one computer, you may want to spend a moment considering which drive letter to map the drive to. You will find it more convenient if the shared network drive has the same drive letter on each computer in the LAN—that way you won't have to refer to "the C drive on the computer in the corner near the door—the one called Bambi." Instead, you can just call it the F drive (the exception, of course, is the person who uses the computer called Bambi, for whom it's just the C drive). Before you assign the drive letter, you may want to make sure that letter is available on the other computers on the LAN.

You may have noticed the Reconnect At Logon check box on the Map Network Drive dialog box. When this option is selected, your computer checks that the shared resource is available each time you log on. Reconnecting at logon slows down the log on process slightly, but means that using the drive the first time is quicker, because the drive is already connected. If you are mapping a drive only temporarily (you need it only for the next twenty minutes, for example), turn off the Reconnect At Logon option.

Unmapping a Drive

If you want to "unmap" a drive, you can do so by disconnecting it: right-click the drive (in either a Folder window or Windows Explorer) and choose Disconnect from the shortcut menu. The drive remains accessible through Network Neighborhood, but a drive letter is no longer mapped to it. (To make a drive inaccessible even through Network Neighborhood, you must disable sharing from the computer that owns the resource.)

Using Network Printers

In order to use a network printer, you need to install the printer driver for that printer on your computer. Choose Settings | Printers, run Add Printers, and then follow the instructions on the screen. Select Network Printer to get the right Wizard. See "Printing to a Network Printer from Another Computer" later in this chapter.

Enabling Hardware Sharing

In order to share your hardware with others on the LAN, you need to make sure that sharing is enabled. For a Windows peer-to-peer network, see "Installing the Service" in Chapter 30 to install file and printer sharing, then see "Configuring File and Printer

Sharing" in Chapter 30 to configure sharing on your computer. For a NetWare or Windows NT network, see "Letting Others Use Your Computer's Resources" in Chapter 31 for how to configure your computer to share printers, disks, and folders.

To see if you have allowed your computer's resources to be shared (which is different than sharing particular resources), follow these steps on the computer with the resources that you want other computers on the LAN to have access to:

1. Right-click Network Neighborhood, and then choose Properties to display the Network dialog box. (Or display the Control Panel and open the Network icon.) Click the Configuration tab.

2. Check to see whether File And Printer Sharing For Microsoft Networks is listed in the box that shows all installed network components.

3. If it is not listed, click the File And Print Sharing button to display the File And Print Sharing dialog box.

4. Select both options: I Want To Be Able To Give Others Access To My Files, and I Want To Be Able To Allow Others To Print To My Printer(s).

5. Click OK on both open dialog boxes. Windows 98 may prompt you to insert your Windows 98 installation CD-ROM. You need to reboot for file and printer sharing to take effect.

Installing file and printer sharing does not automatically share your printer and hard drive—that could compromise security. Instead, this feature allows you to choose exactly which of the resources to share on your computer, by using the techniques covered in this chapter.

You can monitor the use of shared resources by using Net Watcher, as explained later in this chapter (see "Monitoring Shared Resources by Using Net Watcher").

Sharing Printers

Sharing a printer on a LAN has at least two steps: First you have to sit at the computer that is directly attached to the printer and configure the printer to be a network printer (so that other computers on the network can print to it). Then you need to configure the other computers on the LAN so that they know about the network printer.

Making a Printer Sharable

The first step in sharing a printer is to install the printer on one computer and make sure that you can print to it from that computer (see "Adding a New Local Printer" in Chapter 16). Once the printer is correctly installed, you can share it so that other computers on the network can print to it.

The computer that the printer is attached to is called a print server. The print server can also be someone's PC, the usual arrangement on a small network.

To share the printer so that other computers on the LAN can print to it, follow these steps:

1. Choose Start | Settings | Printers to see the Printers folder.

2. Right-click the printer you want to share, and then choose Sharing from the Shortcut menu. You see the Properties dialog box for the printer, with the Sharing tab displayed, as shown in Figure 32-5 properties. (Depending on what type of network you use, you may see different settings.)

3. Click the Shared As radio button.

4. Give your printer a Share Name. A straightforward name makes it easier for others on the network to figure out which printer they are using. You can enter a comment, too.

5. If you don't use NetWare or Windows NT networking, skip to step 8. If you use a NetWare or Windows NT network, click the Add button to choose users who may use your printer. You see the Add Users dialog box.

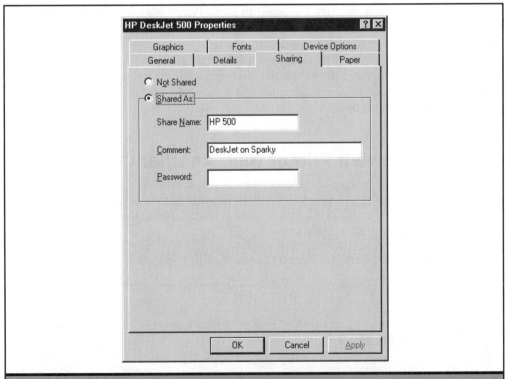

Figure 32-5. *Give the printer a name and description when you share it*

6. Select users who may use your printer by double-clicking their name or group, which adds them to the list on the right. Choose Everyone or The World to allow all users to use the printer.

7. Click OK to return to the printer's Properties dialog box.

8. Close the printer's Properties dialog box. You see the printer folder. The icon for the printer you just shared now has a hand under it, indicating the printer is shared, like this one:

If you want, you can limit the use of a shared printer by requiring that a password be supplied before anything can be printed to the network printer from another computer on the LAN. If you type a password into the Password box on the Sharing tab of the printer's Properties dialog box, anyone on the LAN wanting to print to your printer must supply that password in order to print. Windows asks you to confirm the password when you close the Properties dialog box. It is a good idea to make a note of the password, since you may not be using it yourself (when printing from the computer attached to the printer, no password is required).

To turn sharing off, open the Properties dialog box for the printer and select the Not Shared radio button on the Sharing tab. To remove the password, delete the contents of the Password box.

Printing to a Network Printer from Another Computer

Once you've set up the printer as a shared resource, you can use it from other computers on the LAN. You may even want to define it as the default printer on other computers. To use a network printer from another computer on the LAN, you need to install a driver for the printer. Here's how:

1. Choose Start | Settings | Printers to see the Printers folder.

2. Open the Add Printer icon. You see the Add Printer Wizard. The Wizard asks the following:

   ■ **Whether you're installing a local or network printer**   You're installing a network printer.

- **What the network path is for the printer**   Unless you can type the path for the printer from memory, use the Browse button to find it. To find the printer, first find the computer to which it is attached by expanding the Network Neighborhood hierarchy. Then, click the plus box next to the computer name and select the printer.

- **If you print from MS-DOS-based programs**   Usually the answer is No. Printing from DOS-based programs requires that Windows captures the output that the DOS program sends to a printer port (see "Adding a New Network Printer" in Chapter 16).

- **Which driver to install**   If you already have a driver installed for this type of printer, the Wizard asks whether you want to keep the existing driver or install a new one (one of these options will be recommended). If you don't have a driver installed, the Wizard prompts you to install one—you'll probably need your Windows CD-ROM, or a printer driver from another source (many can be found on the Internet).

- **What name you want to call the printer**   This should be a name that enables you to identify the printer. If you have six LaserJets on your network, you probably don't want to call it just "LaserJet"—instead, you might want to call it "Cindy's LaserJet" since it's attached to Cindy's machine. That way, when you print to this printer, you'll know where to go to pick up your printout.

- **If you want this printer to be your default printer**   If you want to print automatically to this printer every time you print, then the answer is Yes. If you usually want to print to another printer, choose No.

- **If you want to print a test page**   Choose Yes or No.

Once you've completed these steps, you can print to the network printer from this computer any time you want. If you defined the network printer as your default printer, then anything you print automatically goes to that printer. If you didn't define the network printer as the default printer, then you have to choose it from the list of defined printers before you print. This is usually done on the Print dialog box of the application you are using.

If a password is required for the shared printer, a dialog box appears asking you to provide the password after you give the print command. If the Save Password In Password List option is selected, you will not have to provide the password again when printing from the same computer and using the same user name.

If the network printer is unavailable, any print jobs will be held on your computer until the printer is again available.

For more information about printing, installing and configuring a printer, and changing the default printer, refer to Chapter 16.

Sharing Disk Drives

A disk drive that other computers can access over a network is called a *network drive.* There are a number of ways you might want to share a disk drive. You might want to permit all the computers on the LAN to access a CD-ROM drive, so that it can be used to install software, and so that you don't have to buy a CD-ROM drive for each computer. You may want to permit other users of the LAN to read a certain file on a particular hard drive—perhaps the file that contains the company personnel policy, so that you don't waste space on each computer saving the same file. You may want users to be able to read and write to one file, perhaps the one containing the database where orders are entered, so that the information each user sees is always the most up-to-date information available. Maybe there is one shared folder on your hard drive that you want other people to be able to use. Or maybe you just want to share everything— you want to allow everyone on the LAN to read and write to your hard drive.

Making a Drive Sharable

Sharing a drive is even simpler that sharing a printer—you only have to tell the computer that owns the drive that you want to share it in order for it to be visible to all the other computers on the LAN.

Follow these steps to share a drive:

1. Open a Folder window or Windows Explorer (see "What Are Folder Windows and Windows Explorer Windows?" in Chapter 8).

2. Right-click the drive you want to share, and then choose Sharing from the shortcut menu. (If you don't see Sharing, you need to install File And Printer Sharing from the Network dialog box.) You see the Sharing tab of the Properties dialog box for the drive (shown in Figure 32-6).

3. Click the Shared As radio button.

4. Give the drive the name that you want to appear in Folder windows and Windows Explorer as *name* on *'computer name'*. For instance, Figure 32-6 was created on a computer called Sparky. When we want to use the shared drive, we can look for the drive called C_DRIVE on 'Sparky'. If you want, you can provide a comment to further identify this drive. The comment is visible only when the properties are displayed, however.

5. Choose Full as the Access Type to allow users to read from and write to the drive. Read more about access types in the following section.

6. Close the Properties dialog box. You now see a hand as part of the drive icon, signifying that the drive is shared.

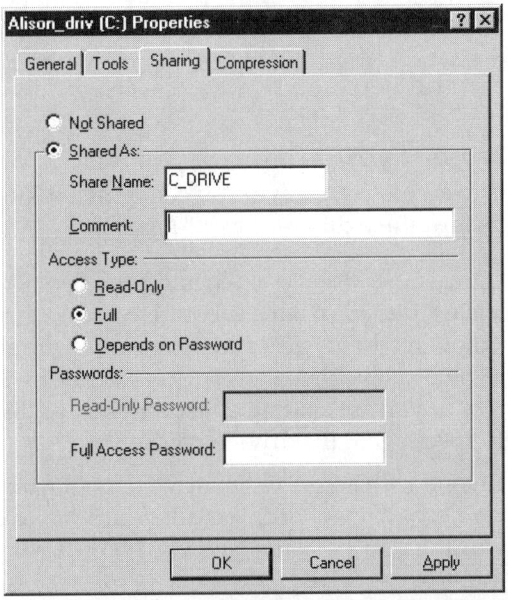

Figure 32-6.   *Sharing a disk drive*

Other users can use your files by navigating to them through Network Neighborhood. If they use the drive or folder often, they may want to map the drive (see "Mapping a Drive"). If you decide to turn off sharing of the drive, open the Properties dialog box for the drive and select the Not Shared radio button on the Sharing tab.

Limiting Access to a Shared Drive

There are some alternatives to sharing a whole drive with full read and write access:

- You can share just a folder.
- You can specify read-only rights.
- You can password-protect the drive.
- For NetWare and Windows NT networks, you can choose the users who can access the drive.

Making a Folder Sharable

To share just a folder, use a Folder window or Windows Explorer to view the folder. Then, right-click the folder and choose Sharing from the shortcut menu to display the

Properties dialog box for the folder. Follow the instructions in "Making a Drive Sharable" provided earlier in this chapter. From another computer on the LAN, the shared folder looks like a whole drive, but in fact, they can see and use only the shared folder.

Choosing an Access Type

When you allow others to access your drive, you choose what kind of access to give them. You have the choice of three different *access types*:

- **Read-Only**   Allows other users to open and copy files, but not alter a file, save a new file, or delete a file, all of which require write access. If you type a password, you allow read-only access only to those who know the password. If you leave the password box blank, anyone on the LAN will have read-only access to the drive. If you are sharing a read-only drive, like a CD-ROM drive, it is a good idea to specify that the drive is read-only.

- **Full**   Allows anyone with access to the drive to read from the drive and write to the drive. If you type a password, you allow full access only to those who know the password. If you leave the password box blank, anyone on the LAN will have full access to the drive.

- **Depends On Password**   Allows users access dependent on which password they provide. When this option is selected, the Passwords section of the dialog box becomes enabled. You can define two different passwords—one for read-only access and one for full access. If you use different passwords, you can determine who has read-only access and who has full access by limiting who knows which password. If you leave a Password box blank, you prohibit that type of access.

When you close the folder's Properties dialog box, Windows asks you to confirm the passwords. Since you probably won't use these passwords yourself, you'll probably forget them easily—make a note of them and keep them in a private place.

Controlling Who Can Access a Drive or Folder

If you use a NetWare or Windows NT network, you can specify which users can have access to your shared drive or folder. Follow the steps in "Making a Drive Sharable" earlier in this chapter. When you have displayed the Properties dialog box for the driver or folder to share, click the Add button to display the Add Users dialog box, from which you can choose users who may use your shared disk drive. Select users who may use your drive, then click OK to return to the drive's Properties dialog box. The Add button doesn't appear if you use a Windows peer-to-peer network.

Windows 98's Access Control Method

You may have noticed a complication with using passwords to access shared resources—each resource has its own password. This is called *share-level access control*, which means that each resource has one password, and each user who wants access to that resource must use that resource's password. This can result in having to remember many passwords. In a peer-to-peer Windows network, this is the only option for using passwords to protect resources.

An alternative to this type of security is to give each user one password, and then define the resources that each user has access to. This is called *user-level access control*. In most client-server networks, such as a Novell NetWare or Windows NT network, user-level access control is the norm, and a network administrator is needed to define the permissions for each user. See "Letting Others Use Your Computer's Resources" in Chapter 31 for how to set up user-level access control on a NetWare or Windows NT network.

Monitoring Shared Resources by Using Net Watcher

Net Watcher is a Windows 98 utility that shows you who is using the resources on your computer. Before you can run Net Watcher, you have to install the Client For Microsoft Networks, as described in "Installing a Service" and "Configuring File and Printer Sharing" in Chapter 30 for a Windows peer-to-peer network and "Letting Others Use Your Computer's Resources" in Chapter 31 for a NetWare or Windows NT network.

Note *Net Watcher may not be installed on your computer. To install Net Watcher from the Windows 98 CD-ROM or floppy disks, open Control Panel, open Add/Remove Programs, click the Windows Setup tab, choose System Tools from the Components list, click Details, and choose Net Watcher (see "Installing and Uninstalling Programs That Come with Windows 98" in Chapter 3).*

To run Net Watcher, choose Start | Programs | Accessories | System Tools | Net Watcher. You see the Net Watcher window shown in Figure 32-7. The main part of the window lists the connections that other computers on the LAN have made to your computer.

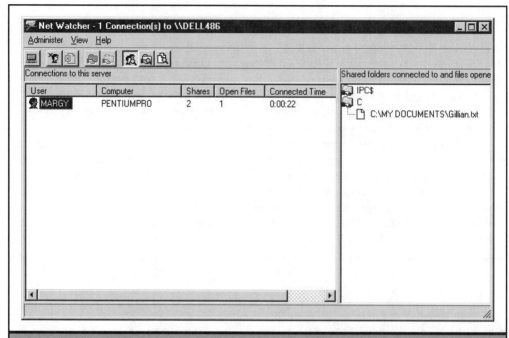

Figure 32-7.   *Net Watcher shows whether other people are using resources on your computer*

Seeing Who Is Using Resources

To see what resources other people are using on your computer, choose one of these commands:

- View | By Connections lists the people on your LAN who are connected to your computer. When you select a user from the list, the right pane of the Net Watcher window shows the files that person is using.

- View | By Shared Folders lists the folders on your computer that other people are connected to, including the folders for shared printers, shared drives, and shared folders. When you select a folder, the right pane shows the people who are connected to that folder.

- View | By Open Files lists the files on your computer that are open by other people. The Accessed By column shows who has opened the file.

Administering Your Shared Resources

Here are additional things you can do in Net Watcher:

- **Disconnect other users from the resources on your computer** Choose View | By Connections to see the list of users, and then choose Administer | Disconnect User.

- **Close a specific file that someone else has opened** Choose View | By Open Files to list the files that other people have opened, and then choose Administer | Close File.

- **Stop sharing a shared drive, folder, or printer** Choose View | By Shared Folder, select the item you want to stop sharing, and choose Administer | Stop Sharing Folder. Windows asks you confirm that you want to stop sharing the folder.

- **Look at the sharing properties of a shared folder** Choose View | By Shared Folder and select the shared item. Then choose Administer | Shared Folder Properties (or press ALT-ENTER). You see a dialog box that contains the same settings as the Sharing tab of the Properties dialog box for the shared item. Click OK when you are done working with the dialog box.

- **Share an additional drive or folder** Choose View | By Shared Folder and then choose Administer | Add Shared Folder. In the Enter Path dialog box that appears, type the path (address) of the item you want to share, or click the Browse button to find the drive or folder. Then click OK.

 Before disconnecting someone or closing a file, be sure to warn the user first, so that the person can save any open files.

Communicating over the LAN by Using WinPopup

WinPopup is a cute little program that allows you to receive messages from other people and devices on your LAN. WinPopup is not sophisticated—if you want reliable interoffice communication, you need to install and use e-mail. It can, however, be useful for sending short, urgent messages. For WinPopup to work, everyone who wants to send or receive messages has to be running the program. WinPopup is also available with Windows 95, and the two versions are completely compatible.

WinPopup may not be installed on your computer. To install WinPopup from the Windows 98 CD-ROM or floppy disks, open Control Panel, open Add/Remove Programs, click the Windows Setup tab, choose System Tools from the Components list, click Details, and choose WinPopup (see "Installing and Uninstalling Programs That Come with Windows 98" in Chapter 3).

For some reason WinPopup does not appear in the Start or Programs menu (you can put it there, of course—see Chapter 12 for details).

Running WinPopup

The WinPopup program file is stored in C:\Windows. The easiest way to run it is to look in C:\Windows using Windows Explorer or a Folder window. Once you see the WinPopup.exe file, you can open the icon to run WinPopup, create a shortcut on the desktop, or add a shortcut to the Start menu. The WinPopup window looks like this:

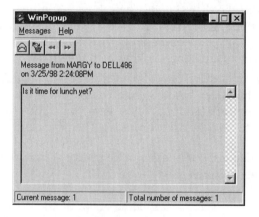

 If you plan to use WinPopup for office communication, add a shortcut to the C:\Windows\Start Menu\Programs StartUp folder on every computer in the office so that it runs each time Windows starts up (see "Running Programs When Windows 98 Starts" in Chapter 2).

Sending a Message

To send a message to another user, computer, or workgroup on your LAN, choose Messages | Send, press CTRL-S, or click the Send button on the WinPopup toolbar (the leftmost button). You see the Send Message dialog box, shown here:

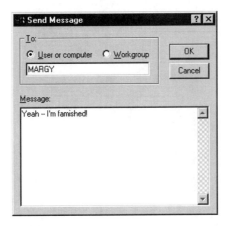

Use the To radio buttons to choose to send the message to a user or computer, or a whole workgroup. If you choose User Or Computer, you need to fill in the name of the user or computer where you want the message to show up. (Hint: the names of the computers are available in Network Neighborhood.) If you choose workgroup, WinPopup fills in the name of the workgroup you belong to; if you want to send the message to a different workgroup on the LAN, you need to know the name of the workgroup and fill it in. Type the message in the Message box and click the OK button to send it. A dialog box appears telling you that the message was successfully sent—this, however, does not mean that the message was actually received or read. WinPopup must be running for the message to be received, and the user must notice the beep that WinPopup makes when a message is received and display the WinPopup window to read the message.

Receiving a Message

When you receive a WinPopup message it appears in the WinPopup window. If that window is minimized, however, you may not even know that a message has been received. You can change WinPopup's options so that you are more likely to read a received message. Choose Messages | Options to display the three options. You can play a sound when a new message arrives, have the WinPopup window always on top, and display a dialog box when a message is received.

Messages are stored in WinPopup for as long as the program is running. You can see how many messages you have by looking at the status bar, and you can read different messages by using the Previous and Next buttons on the toolbar. Get rid of the displayed message by clicking the Delete button on the toolbar.

The
Complete
Reference

Chapter 33

Computer and Network Security

W indows 98 is designed for use by one person at a time, so it offers only limited security features compared to UNIX or Windows NT. This chapter examines Windows' security features, including password protection, user profiles, remote administration, and the security features in Internet Explorer and Netscape Navigator. Outlook Express and other e-mail programs also offer e-mail security features.

What Password Protection Does Windows Offer?

Windows has many different resources that can be password-protected. The major passwords are the following:

- **Windows password**   A largely cosmetic password that you enter when you enter a user name as you start up Windows 98 or switch from one user to another. Your Windows password controls whether your user profile is active. If you do not enter a password, Windows starts anyway. If you have a laptop or other computer with advanced power management that enters standby or hibernate modes to save power, you can set Windows to ask for your Windows password when it resumes from power saving mode. You can change your Windows password at any time (see "Setting the Windows Password").

- **Network password**   The password used to validate your user name to other host computers on the network. If your network password is missing or invalid, you can't gain access to remote disks or printers. The network password you use has to match the password required by the remote servers to which you connect. To change your network password, you have to ask the manager who controls the server(s) you use to change your password on the server. (The network password doesn't affect your use of Internet resources.)

- **Screen saver password**   A password used to leave screen saver mode. Without the password, the Windows screen savers won't resume what the computer was doing previously, although you can regain control by rebooting the computer. Screen saver passwords are useful on unattended print and file servers, to prevent casual or accidental misuse of the server, and can also be useful on your desktop computer if you're working on private or confidential materials, to prevent casual snooping when you're away from your desk (see "Setting the Screen Saver Password").

What Is a User Profile?

When two or more users share a computer, they don't have to argue about what color the background should be, or what programs should be on the Start menu, or whether

Web style is better than Classic style. Instead, each user can have a *user profile*, a folder in the directory C:\Windows\Profiles that contains files that describe each user's preferences. Each time a user logs in, Windows 98 finds the appropriate user profile and makes the appropriate changes. If you change any of your preferences—for example, by choosing a new wallpaper—that information is stored in your user profile, so that the change will still be there the next time you log in, but not the next time someone else logs in. Whenever your computer acquires a new user, you should establish a new user profile (see "Sharing a Computer").

Table 33-1 lists the settings that are stored separately for each user. These items are stored in the C:\Windows\Profiles*username* folder, where *username* is replaced by the name of the user profile (see "Understanding a User Profile").

Profile Item	Description
User.dat file (hidden)	Contains this user's configuration settings for the desktop, Folder windows, accessibility options, and other information.
Application Data folder	Contains this user's application program configuration settings.
Cookies folder	Contains cookies stored by this user's web browser (see "What Are Cookies?" in Chapter 25).
Desktop folder	Contains the items that appear on this user's desktop.
Favorites folder	Contains items this user has added to the Favorites folder.
History folder	Contains shortcuts to web sites this user has viewed recently.
My Documents folder	Contains the files and folders that appear in this user's My Documents folder.
NetHood folder (hidden)	Contains this user's network settings.
Recent folder (hidden)	Contains shortcuts to files this user has opened recently, for display on the Start	Documents menu.
Start Menu folder	Contains the shortcuts and folders that Windows uses to display the Start and Programs menus for this user.

Table 33-1. *Information Stored in User Profiles*

What Security Does Windows 98 Provide for Resources Shared with Other Computers?

When you share disks or printers with other computers on a NetWare or Windows NT-based LAN, you can use either share-level access control (where you assign a password to each shared resource) or user-level access control (where you create a list of people who are allowed access to each shared resource—see "Letting Others Use Your Computer's Resources" in Chapter 31). If your computer is on a peer-to-peer network, only share-level access control is available. (See Chapter 29 for definitions of these types of LANs.) Share-level passwords also apply when you use the Dial-Up Server to allow other computers to connect to your computer by using Dial-Up Networking (see "Connecting Two Computers by Using Dial-Up Networking" in Chapter 19).

What Is Remote Administration?

Remote administration permits someone on another computer to manage the resources on your computer. In corporate LANs, remote administration permits system managers to fix many networking and setup problems without physically visiting your computer. You specify the people who can administer your system (see "Managing Remote Administration").

 A remote administrator has almost complete access to all resources on your computer, so your security is only as good as your administrator's.

What Security Do Web Browsers Offer?

Internet Explorer and Netscape Navigator have complex security systems that control two completely separate aspects of Web use: communication security and downloaded object security.

Communication Security

Communication security ensures that the data you transmit and receive through the Internet or an intranet is sent to and received from the actual systems with which you intend to communicate, as opposed to another system impersonating the desired system. It also ensures that messages are sent and received without being intercepted or spied upon.

Browsers store *certificates*, cryptographic data that can identify your computer to remote computers, or vice versa. Certificates are issued by *certificate authorities*, each of which has its own certificate. Internet Explorer and Netscape Navigator are each delivered with about 30 *authority certificates* that they can use to check that the certificates presented to your computer by other sites are, in fact, issued by known certificate authorities. To provide secure communication with a remote web site, Internet Explorer and Navigator use *SSL* (Secure Sockets Layer) to provide a variation of the standard HTTP web protocol, called *HTTPS* (see "Keeping Your Web Communication Secure"). Web servers that use HTTPS are called *secure servers*.

You can also acquire a *personal certificate* to use to identify yourself when your Internet Explorer or Navigator contacts a web site. The most widely used authority for personal certificates is VeriSign, at **http://www.verisign.com**. See RSA Data Security's list of questions and answers at their web site, at **http://www.rsa.com/rsalabs/newfaq**, for more information about certificates.

Downloaded Object Security

Internet Explorer and Netscape Navigator use two different types of *downloaded object security*—security for information you download.

Internet Explorer's Downloaded Object Security

Internet Explorer can retrieve a wide variety of files and objects, ranging from innocuous plain text files and images to potentially destructive ActiveX controls and other executable programs. Internet Explorer's downloaded object security allows you to decide, based on both the web site where an object came from and the type of object, whether to retrieve an object, and once it's retrieved, what to do with it (see "Managing the Security of Files you Download from the Web with Internet Explorer"). Internet Explorer defines three levels of object access (low, medium, and high) to give varying amounts of access to your computer. You can also define custom access permissions, if the three standard settings don't meet your needs.

Internet Explorer divides the world into four *zones*:

- **Local Intranet**   Contains computers on your local network. They're usually considered fairly trustworthy, and objects are given a medium level of access to your computer.

- **Trusted Sites**   Includes the sites that you or Microsoft have listed as trustworthy. Objects from this zone generally are given the high level of access to your computer.

- **Restricted Sites**   Includes the sites that you have listed as untrustworthy. Objects from this zone are given the low level of access to your computer.

- **Internet**   Includes all sites that are not in one of the other three zones. Objects from this zone generally are given the medium level of access to your computer.

Downloaded ActiveX controls and other executable objects can and should be signed by their authors, using a certificate scheme similar to that used for validating remote servers.

Netscape Navigator's Downloaded Object Security

Since Netscape Navigator supports only Java and JavaScript, and doesn't support the intrinsically insecure ActiveX, it has a much simpler downloaded security system. It runs all Java and JavaScript programs in a "sandbox" that is designed to prevent deliberate or accidental damage to your system. The sandbox doesn't include the files and hardware on your system—only a limited amount of disk space, your keyboard, mouse, and screen. For example, a Java or JavaScript program can display a stock ticker on your screen, but it can't change or delete the files on your hard disk.

What Security Features Do Mail Programs Provide?

E-mail programs offer two kinds of security: signatures and encryption. Both depend on certificates that serve as electronic identity keys. The security system that Microsoft provides with Outlook Express, *S/MIME*, uses certificates issued by third parties, such as VeriSign. Another popular security system, *Pretty Good Privacy*, lets each user generate his or her own keys. Both are forms of *public-key cryptography*. Each certificate consists of a *public key* (also called a *digital ID*), a *private key*, and a *digital signature*. You keep your private key and digital signature secret, while you provide your public key (also called a *digital ID*) to anyone with whom you exchange secure mail, either directly or via a generally available key server.

Signatures allow you to add to your mail a *signature block*, generated with your private key, that verifies the author is indeed you, and that the message was not modified in transit. Anyone who wants to validate your signature can check it by using your public key. The signature is added as an extra block at the end of the message, without modifying the other contents, so that the recipient can read your message, regardless of whether he or she validates your signature.

Encryption scrambles a message so that only the recipient can decode it. A message encrypted with someone's public key can be decrypted only with that person's private key. You encrypt a message with the recipient's public key, and the recipient uses his or her private key to decode it. Anyone else looking at the message would see only unreadable gibberish. It's possible to both sign and encrypt the same message, so that only the designated recipient can decode the message, and so that the designated recipient can verify that the message is really from you.

Mail security depends on a *key-ring* of keys. On your key-ring, you need your own private key and digital signature, and the public key of everyone with whom you plan to exchange secure mail. Outlook Express security keeps your private key and digital signature as one of the properties of your Mail account, and keeps other people's public keys in the Address Book (see "Sending and Receiving Secure Mail").

For more information about encryption and signature, see RSA Data Security's web site at **http://www.rsa.com** and Network Associates' Pretty Good Privacy web site at **http://www.nai.com/products/security/security.asp**.

Sharing a Computer

When several users share a computer, user profiles allow each user to personalize the user interface, without inconveniencing the other users (see "What Is a User Profile?"). Profiles don't offer any security among users, since each user still has full access to every file on the computer, but profiles do offer a way for different users to share a computer more conveniently.

Setting Up for Multiple Users

By default, Windows 98 treats all users the same, even if they have different user names. The system has one set of preferences for everyone, and they are stored in subfolders of the C:\Windows folder. Anyone who changes a preference changes it for everyone else.

To give each user an independent profile, open the Passwords Properties dialog box by running the Passwords program from the Control Panel. Click or double-click the Passwords icon depending on whether you use the Web style or Classic style desktop (see "Choosing the Style of Your Desktop" in Chapter 1). Then click the User Profiles tab, shown in Figure 33-1.

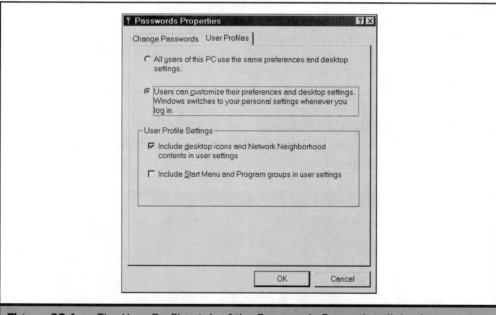

Figure   33-1.   *The User Profiles tab of the Passwords Properties dialog box*

At the top of the User Profiles tab are two choices:

- All Users Of This PC Use The Same Preferences And Desktop Settings.
- Users Can Customize Their Preferences And Desktop Settings. Windows Switches To Your Personal Settings Whenever You Log In.

The first choice is the default, and provides no independence among the users. The second choice allows different users to have different backgrounds, colors, fonts, and display resolutions. The differences even go down to the application level—one user can, for example, configure the toolbars in Word differently from another user.

The User Profile Settings check boxes at the bottom of the User Profile tab extend the independence of users even further. The first check box allows each user to have a different collection of shortcuts and other icons on the desktop, and to have different network settings—a different preferred server, for example, or access to a different collection of shared resources.

The second check box lets each user arrange his or her own Start menu and Programs menu. This option is handy if the different users use very different collections of software. An accountant might want to have a spreadsheet program at the top of the Start menu, while a graphic designer might want a drawing program there.

 If you choose maximum independence of users, be careful that the users don't inadvertently hide resources from each other. For example, when new software is installed, the installation program typically adds it to the Programs menu or makes a desktop shortcut for it automatically—for the user doing the installation. If the other users have their own Programs menu and desktop icons, they may not realize that the new software exists. We recommend that you install your application software and other resources before setting up user profiles.

Establishing a User Profile

Whenever your computer powers up, or one user logs off, the Welcome To Windows dialog box appears, as shown here:

Welcome to Windows	? X
Type a user name and password to log on to Windows.	OK
User name:	Cancel
Password:	

The User Name box may be blank, or Windows may suggest the name of the previous user. To establish a new user profile, follow these steps:

1. Type a new user name. If you want to have a password for this user profile, type a password. (If you leave the password line blank, then you have a blank password, so you won't need to enter one in the future.)

2. Windows requests that you type your password again (if you typed a password in Step 1) to insure that you typed it in correctly. Do so and click OK.

3. If Windows is configured to store separate settings for each user (see the previous section), Windows asks whether you want to store settings for this new user. Click Yes.

4. Windows sets up personalized settings for the desktop, Outlook Express, and other programs. Then you see the usual Windows 98 desktop.

Another way to create a user profile is to open the Control Panel and run the Users program. If you haven't set up user profiles before, Windows prompts to you create a user profile now by running the Add User Wizard. If you have already created users, you see the User Settings dialog box (shown in Figure 33-2). Click the New User button to create a user profile. The Add User Wizard asks you for the user's name and

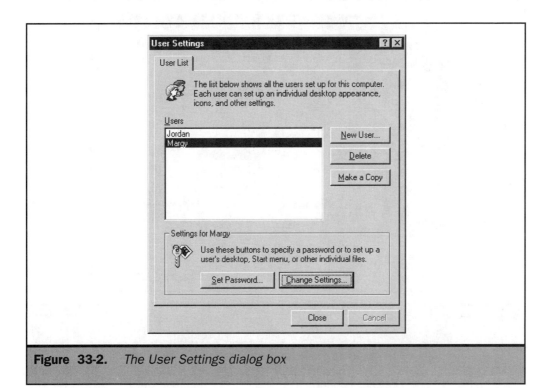

Figure 33-2.   *The User Settings dialog box*

password, and then displays the Personalized Items Setting dialog box shown in Figure 33-3. Choose the items that you want to store as part of the user profile.

Modifying a User Profile

To modify the information in your user profile, change your Windows 98 settings while you are logged in with your user name. The changes you make are stored as part of your user profile.

You can change the types of settings that are stored as part of your profile. Open the Control Panel and run the Users program to display the User Settings dialog box (shown in Figure 33-2). Select your name from the list of users and click the Change Settings button. You see the Personalized Items Settings dialog box (shown in Figure 33-3). Select the types of information you want in your user profile and click OK, then click Close to dismiss the User Settings dialog box.

You can also delete and copy user profiles from the User Settings dialog box. If you want to create a new user with the same settings as an existing user, you can copy the existing user's profile for the new person.

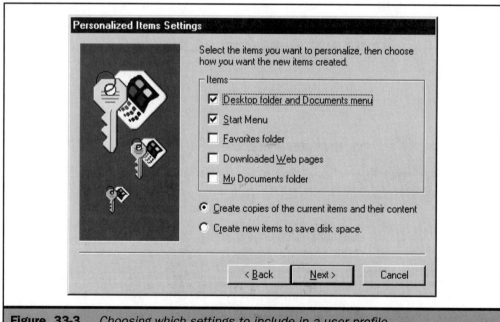

Figure 33-3.   *Choosing which settings to include in a user profile*

Understanding a User Profile

Information about the various users of your computer is contained in the folder C:\Windows\Profiles, with one subfolder for each user name (see Table 33-1 earlier in this chapter). Once you tell Windows to maintain user profiles for each user, whenever someone without a profile logs in, Windows asks whether to create one.

If you want to know what user names have been defined on your computer, look at the folders inside C:\Windows\Profiles.

You can get a good idea of what a user profile entails by looking at the subfolders that are created automatically inside each user name folder (see Figure 33-4). The folder Desktop, for example, contains the shortcuts, files, and folders that appear on that particular user's desktop. The folders Cookies, Favorites, History, and Temporary Internet Files contain the information necessary to customize the user's Internet browsing (see Chapter 24). Favorites chosen by one user, for example, remain in his or her Favorites folder, and are not noticed by other users (see "What Are Favorites and the Favorites Menu?" in Chapter 12). The Start Menu folder gives each user a separate Start menu, and the Recent folder makes sure that the Documents list on that Start menu is not affected when other users open documents. The NetHood folder allows

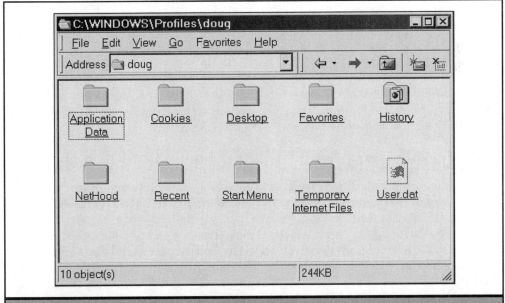

Figure 33-4.   *The subfolders of a user profile folder*

users to choose their own unique network settings, and the Application Data folder remembers the settings that they establish in Microsoft applications, such as the Quick Launch toolbar.

When a user profile is established, these folders are not empty. Instead, they are given the contents of the corresponding folders inside C:\Windows. So, for example, when Bob's user profile was established, the contents of C:\Windows\Favorites was copied into the new folder C:\Windows\Profiles\Bob\Favorites. As Bob adds or subtracts from his list of favorites, C:\Windows\Profiles\Bob\Favorites changes, but C:\Windows\Favorites does not. The other folders containing Bob's preferences behave similarly.

When user profiles are in effect, changing the contents of the C:\Windows\Desktop and C:\Windows\Start Menu folders don't affect your desktop or Start menu. These folders don't belong to any user, so they are never in effect. However, when you create a new user, the contents of these folders are copied to the new user's folders. If you create many new users, edit these folders to create a default Start menu and desktop for new users. Or create new users by copying the user profile of an existing user.

Switching Users

When Windows starts up, you choose which user to log in as by typing the user name in the Welcome To Windows dialog box. If Windows is already running, you can switch users by choosing Start | Log Off. (Actually, the command is named Log Off, followed by the name of the current user; for example, if Margy is currently logged in, the command appears as Log Off Margy.) All programs shut down, and you see the Welcome To Windows dialog box.

If you are logged in to a local area network, the Start | Log Off command logs you off of the network, too. When you log in, you may only see the Enter Network Password dialog box, rather than the Welcome to Windows dialog box.

Undoing User Profiles

You can make your computer treat all users equally again by returning to the User Profiles tab of the Passwords Properties box and selecting All Users Of This PC Use The Same Preferences And Desktop Settings.

After you do this, it may seem as if the system has "forgotten" your recent preferences. For example, anything you added to the Favorites menu during the period when your user profile was in use is no longer there. Any icons that you added to the desktop have disappeared. You can recover any or all of this information, since it is still in the C:\Windows\Profiles*YourUserName* folder. To recover the Favorites, for example, simply open the folder C:\Windows\Profiles*YourUserName*\Favorites and copy whatever shortcuts you want into the folder C:\Windows\Favorites.

Setting the Windows Password

You can change your Windows password at any time. Open the Passwords Properties dialog box from the Control Panel, click the Change Passwords tab if it's not already selected, and click the Change Windows Password button. In the window that opens, enter your existing password as the Old Password, and then enter the new password as the New Password and again as Confirm New Password for verification. Then click OK.

If you haven't assigned a password before, leave the Old Password blank. To remove a password, leave the two New Password fields blank.

Tip *If your Windows password and network password are the same, Windows prompts only for the network user name and password at startup time or when changing users. If the passwords are different, Windows prompts first for your network user name and password, and then your Windows user name and password. Microsoft recommends that you use the same password for both, which is more convenient although less secure than separate passwords.*

Setting the Screen Saver Password

To change the screen saver password, run the Display program from the Control Panel and click the Screen Saver tab. In the middle of the Display Properties dialog box is the Password Protected check box. Check it to enable the screen saver password. To change that password, click the Change button next to the check box and type a new password into both boxes on the Change Password dialog box that appears.

Managing Remote Administration

You can enable remote administration on your computer, so that someone else can manage its shared resources, or if you have remote administration privileges on another computer, you can administer that computer from your computer. (See "What Is Remote Administration?" earlier in this chapter.)

Controlling Remote Administration of Your Computer

To enable or disable remote administration on your computer, run the Passwords program from the Control Panel and click the Remote Administration tab, as shown in Figure 33-5. Click the Enable Remote Administration Of This Server check box to turn remote administration on or off. What information you have to supply depends on whether your LAN uses share-level access control or user-level access control (see "Windows 98's Access Control Method" in Chapter 32).

 Note *The Remote Administration tab appears only if File And Print Sharing For Microsoft Networks is installed (see "Enabling Hardware Sharing" in Chapter 32).*

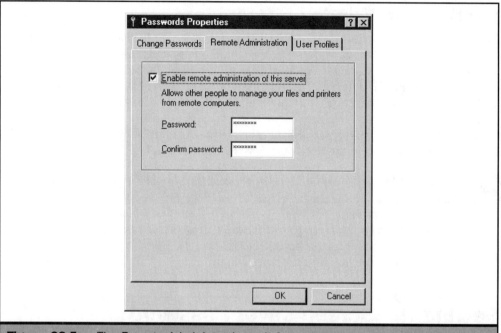

Figure 33-5.   *The Remote Administration tab for a computer using share-level access control*

■ If your LAN uses share-level access control, and if you're turning on remote administration for the first time, enter the password twice for validation (once in the Password box and once in the Confirm Password box).

■ If your LAN uses user-level access control, type the user or group names permitted to perform remote administration. Select the person's name from the list and click Add. To remove someone from the list, select the name and click Remove.

Managing Another Computer Remotely

If you have remote administration privileges on another computer, open the Network Neighborhood icon on your desktop, right-click the other computer, select Properties from the menu that appears, and then click the Tools tab in the Properties dialog box. The Properties dialog box shows three buttons:

- Net Watcher runs the Net Watcher program, which lets you see which files and printers are shared on this computer, and lets you add and remove shared drives (see "Monitoring Shared Resources by Using Net Watcher" in Chapter 32).

- System Monitor runs the System Monitor program, which lets you observe a variety of performance and tuning parameters (see "Using System Monitor" in Chapter 36).

- Administer lets you change file system settings. You see the remote computer's disk drives in a Folder window.

Any of these options may be grayed out if your access to the remote computer doesn't permit the access needed.

Keeping Your Web Communication Secure

Internet Explorer and Netscape Navigator handle communication security by using *SSL (Secure Sockets Layer)* to encrypt messages sent to and from remote servers, and *certificates* to verify who the party is at the other end of a connection (see "Communication Security"). For example, you use this type of security when you place a credit card order with a web-based retailer that uses a secure web server.

For the most part, SSL works invisibly, with all the security validation happening automatically. Internet Explorer and Netscape Navigator, by default, warn you when you switch between secure and normal pages. (We find these warnings annoying and turn them off.) You can tell whether the current page is secure in the following ways:

- Look at the URL for the page in the browser's Address or Location box to see whether the page's address starts with **https://** rather than **http://**.

- Look at the status bar at the bottom of the browser window to see whether a little lock icon appears. Netscape Navigator shows a padlock that is open (insecure) or closed (secure) in the lower left corner of its window. Internet Explorer shows a lock icon on the status bar when the connection is secure.

Whenever your browser opens an HTTPS connection to a server that supports SSL, the server presents a certificate to your computer. If the certificate is validated by one of the authority certificates known to your browser, and the name on the certificate matches the name of the web site, the browser uses the connection and displays web pages as usual. If either of those checks fail, the web browser warns you and gives you the option to continue. Figure 33-6 shows the warning window that Netscape Navigator displays when it can't validate a remote site's certificate, and Figure 33-7

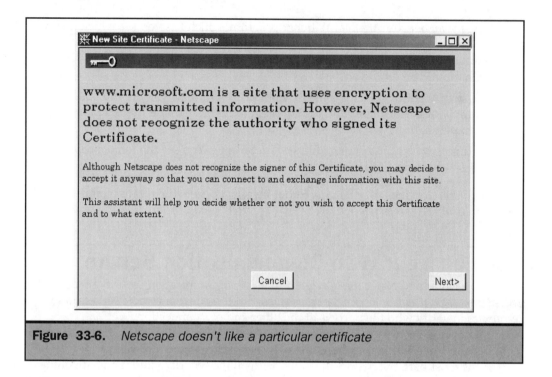

Figure 33-6. *Netscape doesn't like a particular certificate*

shows the corresponding Security Alert dialog box from Internet Explorer. Although it's possible to continue and use the connection despite the warning, this error usually means that there is a major software failure on the server, and you shouldn't believe anything else the server says, anyway.

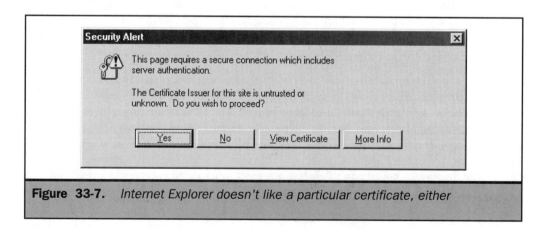

Figure 33-7. *Internet Explorer doesn't like a particular certificate, either*

Managing the Security of Files You Download from the Web with Internet Explorer

Internet Explorer has a complex security scheme for downloaded objects. For each of the four zones into which a web page can fall, you can set the security to high, medium, or low. For each zone, you can set exactly which remote operations you're willing to perform (see "Downloaded Object Security").

Download Security Settings

To check or view your download security settings, open the Internet Properties dialog box. You can open it either from the Control Panel or, in Internet Explorer, by selecting View | Internet Options. The dialog box is called Internet Properties in the first case and Internet Options in the second, but it's the same dialog box either way. Click the Security tab, as shown in Figure 33-8.

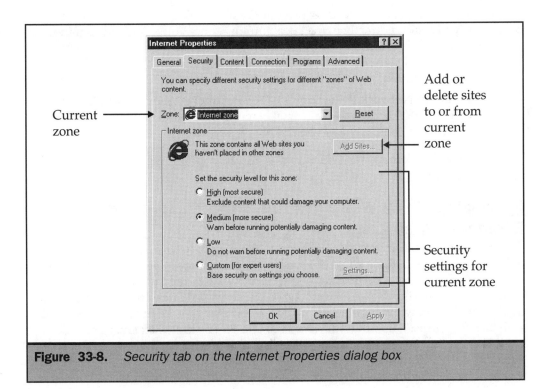

Figure 33-8.   *Security tab on the Internet Properties dialog box*

Displaying and Changing Settings for Zones

To see the current settings for a zone, select that zone in the Zone box. The rest of the information on the Security tab changes to show the settings for that zone.

To add or delete a web site from the Local Intranet, Trusted Sites, or Restricted Sites Zones, click the Add Sites button. (There's no button for the Internet Zone, since it contains all the web sites that are not contained in the other three zones.)

Controlling Which Web Sites Are in the Local Intranet Zone

The Local Intranet Zone normally contains sites on your own network, and is set up that way by your network administrator when he or she sets up the network. When you click Add Sites on the Security tab, Windows displays the Local Intranet Zone dialog box, with these three check boxes:

- **Include All Local (Intranet) Sites Not Listed In Other Zones**   Select this check box to include all other sites on the same local area network in the Local Intranet Zone. This check box is usually checked.

- **Include All Sites That Bypass The Proxy Server**   Many organizations have a *proxy server* that mediates access to sites outside the organization. Select this check box to include sites outside your organization to which your organization lets you connect directly in the Local Intranet zone. You can see a list of the sites that bypass the proxy server by displaying the Internet Properties or Internet Options dialog box, clicking the Connections tab, and clicking the Advanced button.

- **Include All Network Paths (UNCs)**   Select this check box to include all the sites with UNC addresses (Universal Naming Convention addresses), which apply only to computers on your LAN.

You can also click the Advanced button to add sites individually, as for Trusted and Restricted sites.

Controlling Which Web Sites Are in the Trusted and Restricted Sites Zones

The Trusted and Restricted Sites zones start with no web sites listed; you specify the web sites to include in these zones. To specify sites, select the zone to which you want to add sites, and then click Add Sites on the Security tab of the Internet Properties dialog box. You see the Trusted Sites Zone or the Restricted Sites Zone dialog box, the first of which is shown in Figure 33-9. To add a new site, type its full address, starting with **http://** or **https://**, into the Add This Web Site To The Zone box and then click Add. The web site appears in the Web Sites list. To remove a site, select it in the Web Sites list and click Remove. You can require a verified secure connection to all sites in this zone by clicking the Require Server Verification (https:) For All Sites In This Zone

Figure 33-9.   *Adding sites to the Trusted Sites zone*

check box at the bottom of the dialog box; when selected, this setting prevents you from adding any sites that don't support HTTPS (see "Communication Security").

Using Object Certificates When Downloading Files

Whenever Internet Explorer retrieves a web page that uses a hitherto unknown ActiveX or Java applet, Internet Explorer checks whether your settings permit you to download it. If your settings don't permit the download, Internet Explorer warns you and doesn't download the file. You see the dialog box shown here:

New applets usually are digitally signed by their authors; that is, each applet includes certificate information that identifies the applet's author and verifies that the applet wasn't tampered with since the author signed it. Unless a site is in the Trusted

Zone (in which case Internet Explorer accepts the applet without question), Internet Explorer displays information about the certificate, as in Figure 33-10 (see "Communication Security"). You see who the signer is, and who verified the signature. Assuming the signer is someone you're inclined to trust, such as a large reputable organization or someone you know personally, click Yes to accept the applet. If you expect always to accept applets from this signer, click the Always Trust Content From check box at the bottom of the dialog box to tell Internet Explorer not to ask about signatures from this signer in the future. (If you check the box and later change your mind, the list of signers you've checked is in the Internet Properties dialog box; click the Content tab and then click Publishers to examine and change the list.)

Managing Your Certificates

If you plan to download many programs (or display web pages that contain applets), you will end up with a collection of certificates with which Internet Explorer can verify the sources of the programs. You can also get your own certificate to identify yourself to secure remote web servers that demand user certificates for identification. (There are

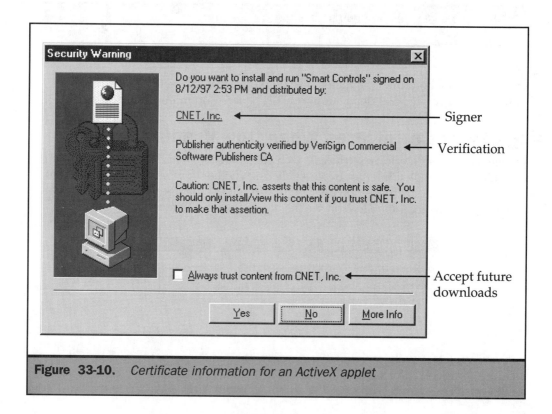

Figure 33-10. *Certificate information for an ActiveX applet*

almost no such servers now, but there probably will be in the future.) You can see lists of the certificates that you have received. Click the Content tab on the Internet Properties dialog box. Click the Personal, Authorities, or Publishers buttons in the Certificates section of the dialog box.

Managing Your Personal Certificates

Clicking the Personal button in the Certificates section of the Content tab displays the Client Authentication dialog box, shown in Figure 33-11. You see a list of the certificates you have installed on your computer that you can use to identify yourself. You can see the properties of a certificate by selecting it and clicking View Certificate.

If you receive a certificate and store it on your disk, click Import to read the certificate and include it on the list in this dialog box. Windows can read certificates stored in *personal certificate files* (with the extension .pfx). You can export a certificate and its associated information to a personal certificate file; select the certificate from the list on the Client Authentication dialog box and click Export. (See "Getting a Certificate" for how to get your own certificate.) If you get a certificate using Internet Explorer, you can export it to a file and then import the certificate from that file into Netscape Navigator, or vice-versa.

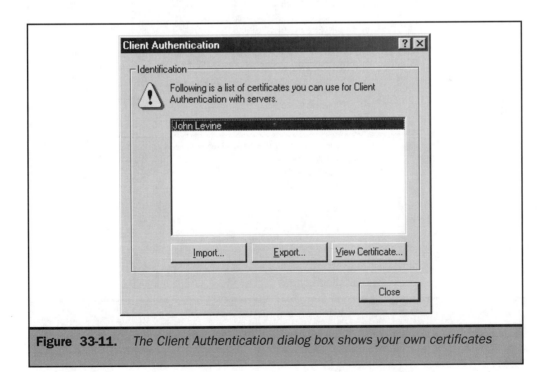

Figure 33-11. *The Client Authentication dialog box shows your own certificates*

Managing Certificates for Web Sites

Clicking the Authorities button on the Content tab displays the Certificate Authorities dialog box, shown in Figure 33-12. You see a list of the certificates that you have received from organizations that run web sites. Your browser may check these certificates before downloading information from the Internet.

Windows displays four kinds of certificates from four types of issuers:

- **Network server authentication**   Certificates that identify a remote network server for SSL sessions

- **Network client authentication**   Certificates that identify a local network client for SSL sessions

- **Secure e-mail**   Certificates used to sign and encrypt e-mail

- **Software publishing**   Certificates used to sign Java and ActiveX applets

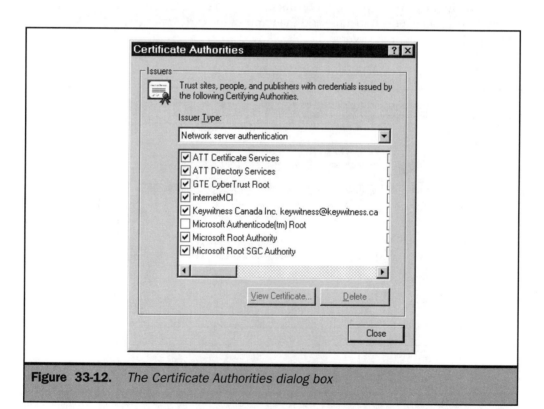

Figure 33-12.   *The Certificate Authorities dialog box*

Many certificates can be used for more than one type of issuer: Choose the issuer type by clicking in the Issuer Type box. You can click in the check box next to a certificate issuer's name to choose whether that certificate applies to that issuer type.

To see the properties of a certificate, select it from the list and click the View Certificate button. Figure 33-13 shows the Properties dialog box for a certificate: The left list shows the property names, and the right list shows the value of that property for this certificate.

You can delete a certificate by selecting it from the list and clicking Delete.

Managing Certificates from Certificate Publishers

Clicking the Publishers button on the Content tab displays the Authenticode Security Technology dialog box, shown in Figure 33-14. The dialog box lists certificates for software publishers which you have told your browsers to trust (by clicking the Always Trust Content From check box in the Security Warning dialog box, shown in Figure 33-10). New certificates are added when you download authenticated software

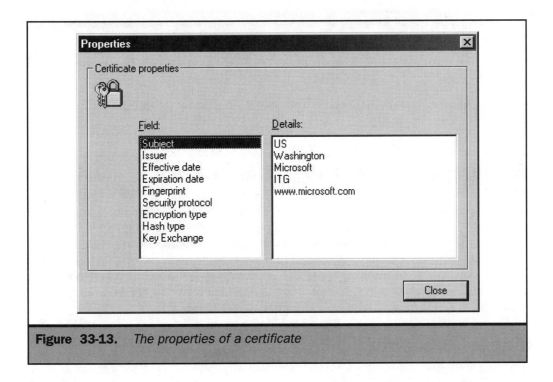

Figure 33-13. *The properties of a certificate*

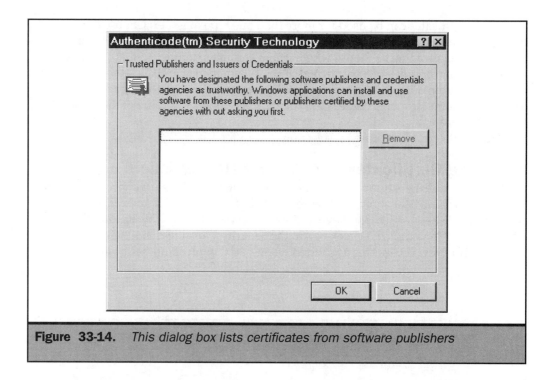

Figure 33-14. *This dialog box lists certificates from software publishers*

from the Internet. You can delete a certificate from this list by selecting it and clicking Remove.

Sending and Receiving Secure Mail

Outlook Express provides a certificate-based system (called S/MIME) for signing and encrypting mail (see "What Security Features Do Mail Programs Provide?" earlier in this chapter). *Signed* mail uses your own certificate to prove to the recipient that the author of the message is you, and that the message arrived without tampering (these are the same type of certificates described in the preceding sections for authenticating material you download from the Web). *Encrypted* mail uses the recipient's certificate to protect the message's contents, so that only the intended recipient can read the messages. A single message can be both signed and encrypted.

Getting a Certificate

The only source of certificates is a certificate authority, and for a certificate to be useful, the authority has to be one that is widely accepted. The best known certificate authority is VeriSign, at **http://www.verisign.com**. It provides a variety of certificates at various prices, usually including a free two-month trial of a personal certificate suitable for signing e-mail. The certificate authority's web site walks you through the process of getting a certificate. Details vary, but generally the steps include:

- You enter the basic information, including your e-mail address, into a form on the authority's web site.

- Your web browser automatically downloads your private key, part of the security information from the authority.

- The authority e-mails a confirmation code to the address you give. This ensures that the address you provide is really yours.

- You run Outlook Express and receive the message. It contains the URL of a page that will finish the registration, and a unique code to identify yourself when you get there. Use Windows' cut-and-paste tool to copy the code from your mail program to the browser window, rather than trying to retype it.

- The authority generates the public key that matches your private key and downloads it as well.

Note *This process of obtaining a certificate only verifies your e-mail address, not any other aspect of your identity. VeriSign offers more secure certificates with more careful identity checks, but the vast majority of certificates in use are this simplest kind.*

Sending Signed Mail

Once you have a certificate, sending signed mail is simple. While you're composing a message in Outlook Express, click the Digitally Sign Message button (the one with the little orange seal) to tell Outlook Express to sign the message as it's sent. Signed messages appear with the orange seal in the list of messages, as shown here:

Sending Encrypted Mail

Sending encrypted mail is only slightly harder than sending signed mail. The difference is that before you can send signed mail to someone, you have to have that recipient's digital ID (public key) in your Windows Address Book (see "Storing Addresses in Your Book" in Chapter 5). Once you have the digital ID, create the message as usual in Outlook Express, and click the Encrypt Message button (the envelope with the little blue lock) before sending the message. The encrypted mail icon looks like this:

There are three common ways to obtain someone's digital ID: from a signed message he or she sent, from an online directory, or from a file obtained elsewhere, such as a web-based lookup system.

Getting a Digital ID from Incoming Mail

Any time someone sends you a digitally signed message, you can get that person's digital ID from the message and add it to your Address Book. (Note that the digital ID is the equivalent of the sender's public key; the corresponding private key is not disclosed.) Open the message, select File | Properties, and then click the Security tab; you see the dialog box shown in Figure 33-15 (the title bar reflects the subject line of the message). Assuming that the signature is valid, click Add Digital ID To Address Book. The Address Book opens, creating a new entry for your correspondent (if one does not already exist). Click the Digital IDs tab and observe that a digital ID is listed; then click OK to update the Address Book.

Getting a Digital ID Through LDAP Search

If you know that your correspondent has a digital ID and you know which certificate authority issued it, you can look it up in that authority's directory.

In Outlook Express, open the Address Book and then click the Find button to open the search window, shown in Figure 33-16. In the Look In box, select the directory to search, which is most likely VeriSign for personal digital IDs. Enter the person's name or e-mail address and click Find Now.

The directory returns a list of entries that match your request. Double-click any entry in the list to see the details, which are arranged like an address book entry, and be sure it's the person you want. If it is, click Add To Address Book to turn it into an Address Book entry, edit as desired (adding more personal info, usually), and click OK to update the Address Book.

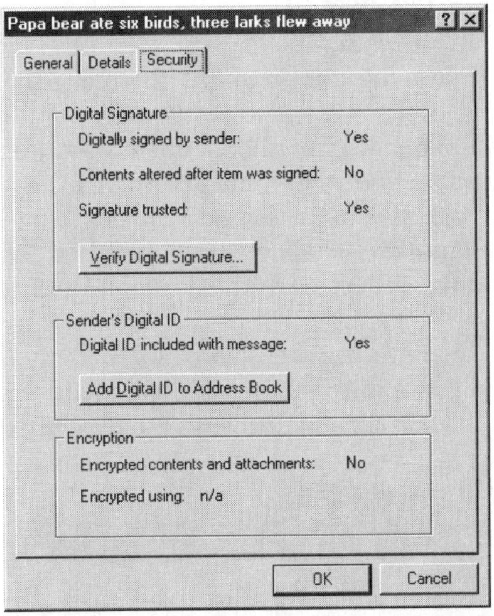

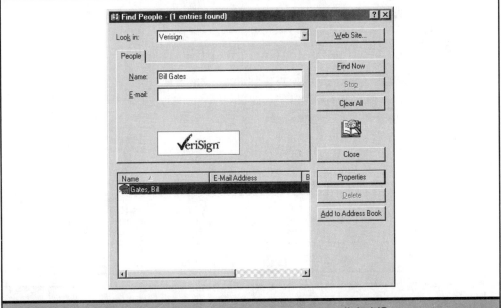

Figure 33-15.   *Getting a digital ID from a mail message*

Figure 33-16.   *Searching the VeriSign directory to get a digital ID*

Getting a Digital ID from a File

Digital IDs can be stored in *certificate files*, usually with the extension .cer. Someone can mail you a third party's ID as a file, or you might download the file from a web-based search system.

To add the digital ID to your Address Book, open the Address Book and create an entry for the person, including his or her e-mail address. (The e-mail address has to match the one to which the certificate is assigned.) Then click the Address Book's Digital IDs tab, shown in Figure 33-17. Click the Import button and select the file containing the ID. The Address Book reads the digital ID and adds it to the Address Book entry.

If you want to store someone's digital ID in a file, so that you can transfer it to another computer or send it to a third person, open the Address Book entry for that person, click the Digital IDs tab, click Export, and then specify the file to create.

Don't try to export your own digital ID this way; bugs in Windows keep it from working. Remember, you can send anyone your digital ID by sending a signed e-mail message.

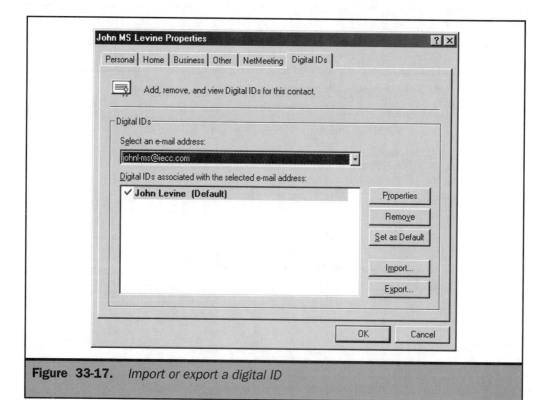

Figure 33-17. *Import or export a digital ID*

Receiving Encrypted or Signed Mail

Outlook Express automatically handles incoming encrypted or signed mail. Signed messages have a little orange seal at the right end of the Security line of the message headers; encrypted messages have a little blue lock (see Figure 33-18). When you open the message, Outlook Express automatically validates the signature or decrypts the message. The first time it does so, it displays a special window in place of the actual message, telling you what it did. Scroll down and click Continue to see the actual message. If you'd rather not see the special window in the future, a box above the Continue button lets you avoid the window in the future.

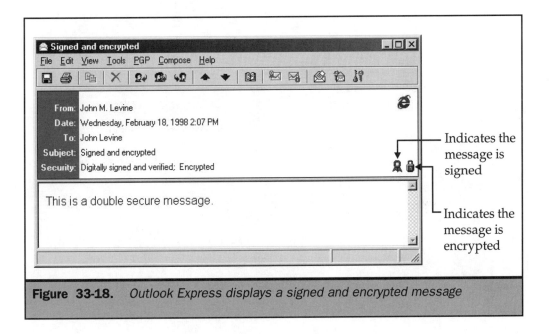

Figure 33-18. *Outlook Express displays a signed and encrypted message*

Part VI

Windows Housekeeping

Chapter 34

Keeping Your Disk Safe

Your disk contains an incredible amount of information; the hard disks on most Windows 98 machines hold at least 1GB (gigabyte, 1 billion bytes). Chapter 11 describes how information is stored on a hard disk and how to set up a hard disk for use with Windows 98. Some of the space on each disk is used to store the structure of the disk, including a table of the parts of the disk that are free (available for storing new information), a table of the files and folders on the disk, and which blocks of the disk store the information in which file.

If this structural information gets garbled, you can lose some of the information on the disk. It's wise to check the structure of the information on each hard disk regularly by using a Windows 98 program called ScanDisk, which not only checks the disk structure, but can also fix some of the errors that it finds.

Another disk problem arises when you create and delete many files over a long period of time. Files are stored in a series of sectors on your disk, and the sectors are not necessarily next to each other. The more you create and delete files, the more scattered, or *fragmented*, the available disk space becomes, and the more fragmented newly created files are. Scattered sectors are slower to find and read than sectors that are adjacent, so your disk access slows down.

To fix this problem, you can run the Disk Defragmenter utility that comes with Windows 98. Disk Defragmenter moves the information on your disk around to speed up access.

Many programs create temporary or backup files, which are not always deleted when they are no longer needed. The Disk Cleanup program can delete stale temporary files for you.

Windows 98 itself is stored in hundreds of files, and if any of these files go astray, Windows can crash or produce errors. You can run the System File Checker to see whether any of your Windows system files have unexpectedly changed or been deleted.

Does it sound like you have a lot to worry about to keep your Windows 98 system tidy? Luckily, you can schedule Windows 98 to run these housekeeping programs for you. In fact, you can tell the Scheduled Tasks program to run any program on a regular basis. Easier yet, run the Maintenance Wizard to ask the Wizard to schedule all the necessary housekeeping programs for your system.

Testing Your Disk Structure with ScanDisk

ScanDisk can both diagnose and repair errors on a wide variety of devices, including hard disks, diskettes, RAM drives, and laptop memory cards. ScanDisk can check the physical surface of disk drivers for bad sectors, and checks the file allocation table

(FAT), the directory structure, and the long filenames associated with many files. ScanDisk works both on uncompressed drives and on drives that have been compressed using Windows 98's DriveSpace program, or some older compression methods.

If Windows 98 crashes, or you turn off the computer without shutting down, when you restart Windows, it may suggest running ScanDisk to check your hard disk for errors resulting from Windows' unexpected termination. Take its suggestion.

Running ScanDisk

Follow these steps to run ScanDisk:

1. Choose Start | Programs | Accessories | System Tools | ScanDisk. You see the ScanDisk window, shown in Figure 34-1.

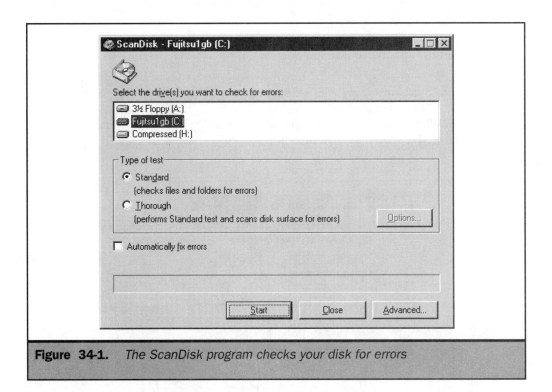

Figure 34-1.   *The ScanDisk program checks your disk for errors*

2. In the list of disk drives, click the disk you want to check. You can scan hard disks, floppy disks, and compressed disks (see "What Is Disk Compression?" in Chapter 35).

3. Click the type of test you want to run: Standard or Thorough. The Thorough test checks the physical surface of the disk for errors, while the Standard test does not.

4. If you chose to run a Thorough test, click the Options button to display the Surface Scan Options dialog box, shown in Figure 34-2. If you chose to run a Standard test, skip to step 6.

5. On the Surface Scan Options dialog box, choose which areas of the disk to scan, whether to perform write-testing (that is, writing information on the disk), and whether to repair bad sectors in which hidden or system files are stored. Then click OK.

6. If you do not want ScanDisk to ask your permission before it repairs each error it finds, make sure that an X appears in the Automatically Fix Errors box (click the box if no X appears).

7. Click the Advanced button to see your other options. Click OK when you have selected the options you prefer, or click Cancel to leave the options as they were.

8. Click the Start button in the ScanDisk window to begin scanning your disk for errors. As the program runs, it indicates what it is checking and how far it has gotten. When ScanDisk is done, you see the ScanDisk Results window, shown in Figure 34-3.

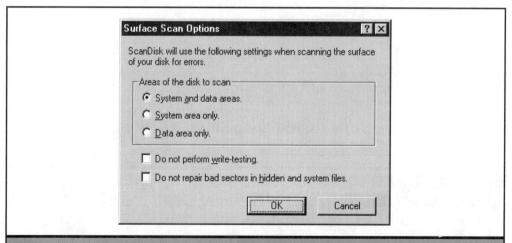

Figure 34-2.   *The Thorough ScanDisk test checks the physical surface of the disk*

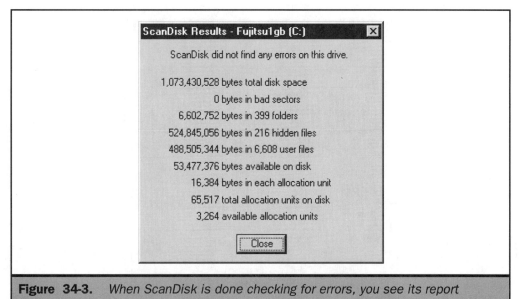

Figure 34-3.   *When ScanDisk is done checking for errors, you see its report*

9. Click the Close button to dismiss the Results window, and click Close again to close the ScanDisk program.

Running ScanDisk Each Time You Start Your Computer

If you restart your computer every day, or every few days, you can check your disks regularly by running the ScanDisk program automatically when Windows 98 starts. You can use the Maintenance Wizard to schedule when ScanDisk runs. If you'd like to choose ScanDisk's settings, follow these steps:

1. Using Windows Explorer or a Folder window, copy the ScanDisk shortcut to your C:\Windows\Start Menu\Programs\Startup folder. (If Windows is installed in a folder other than C:\Windows, adjust the folder name accordingly.) You can copy the shortcut from the C:\Windows\Start Menu\Programs\Accessories\System Tools folder (select it and press CTRL-C), and then paste it in the Startup folder (press CTRL-V).

2. Right-click the ScanDisk icon in your C:\Windows\Start Menu\Programs\ Startup folder, and then choose Properties from the menu that appears. You see the ScanDisk Properties window.

3. Click the Shortcut tab. The Target box shows the command that runs ScanDisk (as shown in Figure 34-4). The command is usually C:\WINDOWS\ SCANDSKW.EXE.

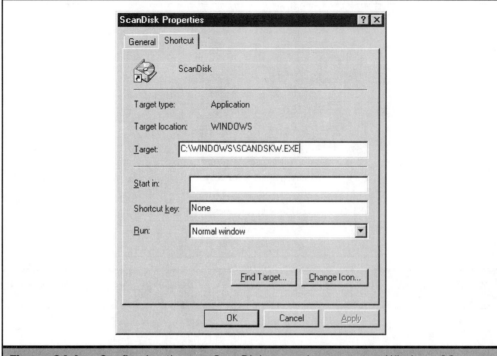

Figure 34-4. Configuring the way ScanDisk runs when you start Windows 98

4. Click in the Target box, and then press the END key to move your cursor to the end of the command that appears in the box. You are ready to type command-line options to control which drives ScanDisk will check each time you start Windows.

5. To tell ScanDisk to scan all the hard disks that are installed on your machine (skipping removable disks, such as diskettes and ZIP disks), type a space and type **/a** in the Target box, adding to the text already in the box. Or, to specify one or more drives to check, type a space, type the letter of the drive you want to check, and then type a colon (for example, to test drive D:, type **d:**). To specify another drive, repeat this step with another drive letter.

6. To tell ScanDisk to start, run, and close automatically, without asking you for input, type a space and type **/n** in the box.

7. Click OK to save your settings.

The next time you start Windows 98, ScanDisk will check the hard disk(s) you specified.

If you want ScanDisk to check your disk without correcting any errors, add the /p option to the end of the command in step 6.

Defragmenting Your Disk

As you create and delete files, Windows 98 may have to split up the information into many chunks when it stores a file on disk. The more chunks a file is split into, the slower Windows accesses the file, because the disk drive heads have to move all over the disk to find pieces of the file. To move the contents of files around on your hard disk so that each file is stored as one big chunk, run the Disk Defragmenter. It runs in the background—you can go on working while the program defragments your disk; your system may just be a little slow.

When Disk Defragmenter is done, nothing will appear to have changed. Your folders and files won't look any different in Windows Explorer and Folder windows. But your system will act a little perkier when you open large files. Defragmentation is especially important if you are using compressed disks and change the size of the compressed disk; when you make a compressed disk smaller, defragmentation is essential, so that Windows can find the empty space in the compressed disk.

If you use new hard disks, fragmentation doesn't affect speed as much as it does on older hard disks. One reason is that newer disks read an entire track (concentric circle of information) at a time from the disk into memory, so it doesn't matter if the sectors of the track contain information in the wrong order. Another reason is that newer disks have much faster access times, so that disk-reads don't cause long delays.

Running Disk Defragmenter

Follow these steps to run Disk Defragmenter.

1. Choose Start | Programs | Accessories | System Tools | Disk Defragmenter. You see the Select Drive dialog box, shown here:

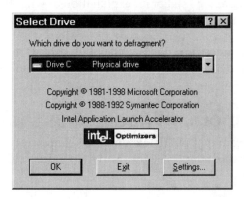

2. Choose the drive you want to defragment by clicking the box and choosing from the list that appears. The list of drives includes physical drives (actual disk drives) and compressed drives, which may actually be stored in files on other disk drives. The list does not include networked drives on other systems (see Chapter 32).

3. Click OK. Disk Defragmenter starts to work, and displays the Defragmenting Drive window shown here:

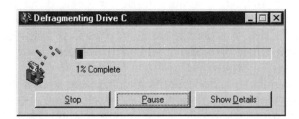

4. If any running program makes a change to a file on disk, Disk Defragmenter notices that the contents of the hard disk have changed and may opt to start over. You can stop or pause any time by clicking the Stop or Pause button. It's safe to stop and resume later. Pause lets you do some work and then continue where you left off.

5. When Disk Defragmenter is done, a message asks whether you want to exit the program; click Yes.

Tips for Defragmenting

When Disk Defragmenter is running, you can see a map of the sectors on your hard disk. Click the Show Details button on the Defragmenting Drive window. The screen fills with a grid of rectangles, each representing one sector of your hard disk. The amount of information stored in each sector is the same for your entire hard disk; the sector size of your disk depends on its format (see "What Are Partitions, File Systems, and Drive Letters?" in Chapter 11). For an explanation of what the colors of the rectangles mean, click the Legend button. When you are done looking at the map, click the Hide Details button.

On the Select Drive dialog box, you can click the Settings button to change settings that control how defragmentation is done, as shown in Figure 34-5.

Deleting Temporary Files Using Disk Cleanup

Disk Cleanup is a program that can delete unneeded temporary files from your hard disk. Some programs create temporary files and then forget to delete the files when

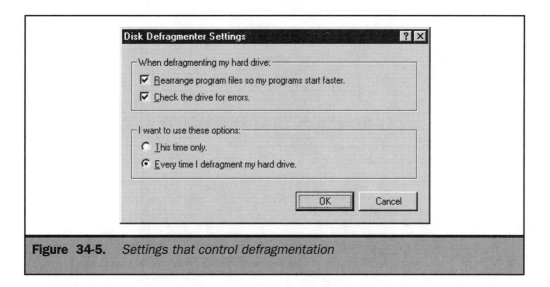

Figure 34-5.   *Settings that control defragmentation*

they are through with them. If a program, or Windows itself, exits unexpectedly (or "crashes"), temporary files may be left on your hard disk. It's a good idea to delete these files from time to time, not only because they take up space, but also because their presence may confuse the programs that created them.

Deleting Files Once

Here's how to run Disk Cleanup:

1. Choose Start | Programs | Accessories | System Tools | Disk Cleanup.

2. The Disk Cleanup program runs and asks which disk you want to clean up. Choose a disk drive and click OK. The Disk Cleanup window (shown in Figure 34-6) tells you how much disk space you can reclaim by deleting temporary files right now. Of course, this may include temporary files that your programs are currently using!

3. Click the box for each type of temporary file you want Disk Cleanup to delete. For more information on a type of temporary file, click the description; the program displays an explanation of what the files are, and what folders Disk Cleanup will delete them from.

4. For additional options, click the More Options tab. You see three buttons that provide some other ways to free up disk space, including deleting Windows components you don't use, uninstalling programs, or converting your disk to

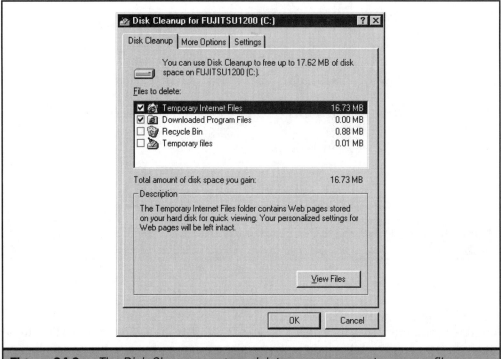

Figure 34-6. *The Disk Cleanup program deletes unnecessary temporary files*

FAT32 (see "What Are the FAT16 and FAT32 File Systems?" in Chapter 11). Click the corresponding button to try any of these methods.

5. If you'd like Windows to delete unneeded files whenever your disk gets full, click the Settings tab and click the check box labeled If This Drive Runs Low On Disk Space Automatically Run Disk Cleanup.

6. To begin deleting files, click OK. The program asks whether you are sure you want to delete files. Click Yes.

The methods of freeing up disk space that are shown on the windows displayed by the More Options tab are one-time operations. If you schedule the Disk Cleanup program to run on a regular basis (using the Task Scheduler or Maintenance Wizard), these additional options do not run.

Deleting Files Regularly

Run the Maintenance Wizard or Task Scheduler to tell Windows to run the Disk Cleanup program regularly (see "Running Programs on a Schedule Using Task

Scheduler" in Chapter 2). If you use Task Scheduler to schedule running the program, be sure to run Disk Cleanup once following the steps in the preceding section, so that you can choose the types of files to delete. If you use the Maintenance Wizard to schedule running the program, click the Settings button to choose the files to delete.

Checking Your Windows System Files

Windows requires many files in order to run. If any of the files is deleted, renamed, replaced, or corrupted, Windows can crash or behave unpredictably. System File Checker can warn you if any of the files that make up Windows 98 have changed or are missing. When you run the System File Checker program, it maintains a verification data file, named Default.sfc, and a log file, named Sfclog.txt, in your Windows program folder (usually C:\Windows). This verification data file contains information about the hundreds of files that make up Windows 98, including the filename, location, date last modified, version number, and a *CRC* (cyclical redundancy checking) code that is computed from the contents of the file.

When you run System File Checker, it compares your current system files with the information in the verification data file. If any of the files are missing, the program alerts you and asks what you want to do. Your options are covered in "Tips for Checking Windows System Files."

Running System File Checker

To run System File Checker, follow these steps:

1. Choose Start | Run, type **c:\windows\system\sfc.exe** and then press ENTER. You see the System File Checker window, shown in Figure 34-7.

2. Click the Start button in the System File Checker window to begin the scan of your files. The program compares your system files with the information in the verification data file.

3. If a file is missing or has changed, the program displays a message, like the one shown in Figure 34-8, and you must tell the program what to do about it. If you deleted or changed the file and want System File Checker to update the information in the verification data file to reflect this, click Update Verification Information. If you deleted or changed a number of files, and you don't want the program to flag each one, choose Update Verification Information For All Deleted/Changed Files. If this file should not have changed or vanished, choose Restore File, and the program prompts you to insert your Windows 98 installation diskettes or CD-ROM to reinstall the file. If you're not sure whether the file should have changed or vanished, you can choose Ignore to skip this file for now (without changing the information in the verification data file); the next time you run System File Checker, the program will check this file again.

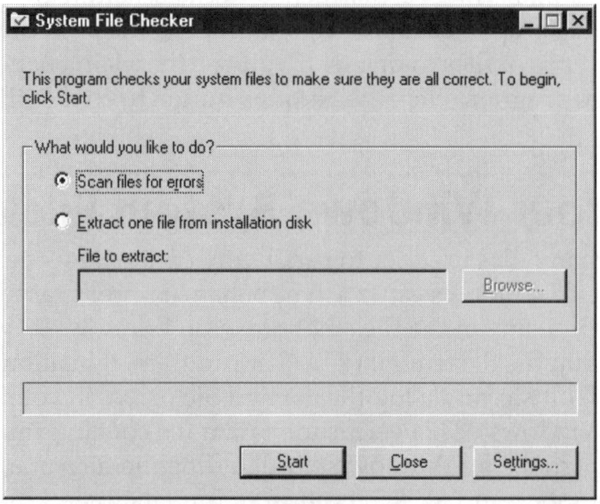

Figure 34-7.   *The System File Checker program*

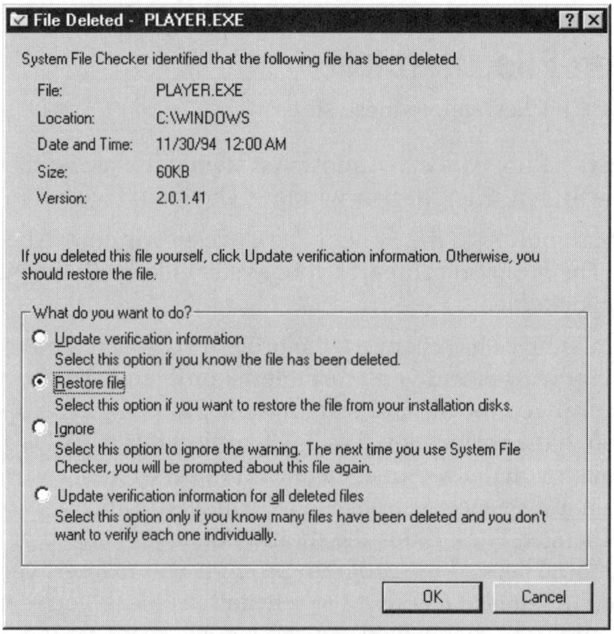

Figure 34-8.   *Choosing what to do when System File Checker detects that a file is missing*

4. When the program is done, you see the Finished window. Click the Details button in the window that appears to see a report like the one shown here:

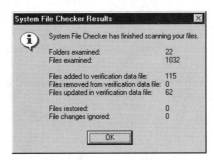

5. Click OK to clear the System File Checker Results window, and click OK again to clear the Finished window. Click Close to exit System File Checker.

Tips for Checking Windows System Files

You can tell System File Checker which folders to check for your system files. Click the Settings button on the System File Checker window, and change the list of folders that the program looks in. You can also change the types of files that the program looks for; the program usually looks for executable files, drivers, and other program-related files.

System File Checker normally checks only whether files have been deleted or whether new files have appeared. If you want the program to check that the contents of each file have not changed, click the Settings button on the System File Checker window, click the Settings tab, and then click the Check For Changed Files check box so that it contains a check mark. Checking the contents of files slows down the program.

If your verification data file (usually C:\Windows\Default.sfc) is corrupted, you can restore it to the original set of files that ship with Windows 98. If you restore the default list, the next time you run the System File Checker, it will ask you about each system file that has changed since you installed Windows 98.

The Maintenance Wizard doesn't schedule System File Checker to run automatically. Run it yourself every few months or if Windows is acting strangely. It can't run unattended, because you need to tell it what to do if it encounters a change in the system files.

Scheduling Your Disk Maintenance Programs

Windows 98 comes with the Maintenance Wizard, which can schedule Windows' disk housekeeping programs to run automatically.

To run the Maintenance Wizard, follow these steps:

1. Choose Start | Programs | Accessories | System Tools | Maintenance Wizard.

2. Follow the instructions in the Maintenance Wizard window to optimize your compressed drives (if you have any) by using Compression Agent, speed up your favorite programs by using Disk Defragmenter, scan your hard disk for errors by using ScanDisk, and delete unneeded temporary files by using Disk Cleanup. Select a Custom installation to choose settings for these progams. If you choose to delete your unnecessary temporary files, click the Settings button to tell the Wizard which files you'd like to delete. If you have Windows networking software installed, the Wizard asks how you use networking and offers to disable unneeded network software.

3. When you click Finish, the Wizard schedules your selected programs to run at the times you specified.

If you want to check, change, or stop any of the programs that the Maintenance Wizard scheduled, double-click the Task Scheduler icon in the system tray on the Taskbar (see "Running Programs on a Schedule Using Task Scheduler" in Chapter 2).

Chapter 35

Compressing Disks and
Partitions

W indows 98 and the application programs that you run with it take up space on your computer's hard disks—lots of space. If you are running out of space on your hard disks, you can use compression to store the same information in less space. Windows 98 comes with DriveSpace 3, a program that you can use to create compressed disks on your hard disks, delete or compress information, adjust the settings of your compressed disks, or upgrade compressed drives created with older compressing programs. Alternatively, you can use zip files to save disk space.

What Is Disk Compression?

Normally, when a program creates a disk file, Windows writes the file on the disk exactly as the program presents it. As an alternative, the system can examine the file's data for repeated or systematic content, and recode the file to remove some of the repeats as the file is stored on the disk. When a program calls to read the file from the disk, the system can reverse the process and re-create the original data. This process is somewhat inaccurately known as *compression*, because although the recoded data usually takes up less disk space than the original data, the saved disk space comes at the cost of the extra CPU time that the system uses to do the recoding.

Compressed disks involve a trade-off between disk space and speed—the system gets better compression by spending more time recoding, but reading and writing compressed files is slower than reading or writing uncompressed files. Earlier versions of DOS and Windows offered only a single degree of compression, but DriveSpace 3, the Windows 98 compression system, offers multiple degrees, so that you can, for example, tell the system to compress only the files that you haven't used for a long time, or compress only when the disk is nearly full. The new Compression Agent program lets you change your compression preferences, and lets you recompress files based on how long it's been since you last used them.

> **Note** *Windows 98 can compress space on FAT16 drives, but not on FAT32 drives (see "What Is a File System?" in Chapter 11). Windows 98 is compatible with some non-Microsoft compression programs, including Stacker (versions 2.x and greater) and Superstore (all versions).*

How Much Space Can Compression Save?

The rule of thumb is that a file can be compressed by 50 percent, but some files are considerably more compressible than others. We've seen compression save anywhere from 95 percent of the space occupied by a file, to no savings at all. You can roughly predict how well a file will compress by the type of file it is, based on its filename extension. In Table 35-1, high compressibility means 60 percent or more space saved, moderate means 40-50 percent saved, and low means 20 percent or less saved.

A few file types, such as GIF, JPG, CAB, and ZIP, already use the same kind of recoding that disk compression does, so those files do not become any smaller if you try to compress them.

Type	Compressibility	Description
EXE, DLL	Moderate (see text)	Runnable program
TXT, DOC	High	Text
XLS	High	Spreadsheet
BMP, DIB	Very high	Bitmap images
PCX	High	Bitmap images
WAV	Low	Sound file
GIF, JPG	Low to none	Bitmap images
CAB	None	"Cabinet" distribution files
ZIP	None	Archive file

Table 35-1. *File Types and Data Compression*

Executable files, with extensions EXE and DLL, are a special case. Compressing them usually saves about 50 percent of the space they occupy, but the speed penalty involved in using them is particularly severe due to the way that Windows creates a running program from EXE and DLL files.

In general, disk compression works well on many types of data files, and is acceptably fast on Pentium and faster processors. On a 486 computer, we recommend avoiding compression, except for very infrequently used files where the speed penalty isn't a big issue. (But there are other ways to save space with infrequently used files—see "Alternatives to Compressed Disks.")

How Does Windows Handle Compressed Disks?

A Windows compressed disk is actually a large file that resides on a regular disk or disk partition. All the files on the compressed disk are stored inside that large file. This design has two interesting results: uncompressed files can reside on the same real disk as the compressed files, and two or more compressed disks can reside on the same real disk.

Compressed disks have names like Drvspace.001 in the root folder of the real disk.

 Never try to delete, rename, or move a compressed disk's file. You can both lose the contents of the compressed disk and crash Windows.

What Is a Compressed Virtual Disk?

Windows provides two slightly different ways to create a compressed disk. You can compress an existing disk "in place," or you can create a new compressed disk that resides on an existing real disk. Either way, you create a *virtual disk*, something that acts like a disk but is actually part of another disk.

When you compress a disk in place, Windows actually creates a new compressed disk on the existing disk and moves all the existing disk's files to the new compressed disk. Then, it changes the drive letters so that the new compressed disk has the original disk's drive letter, and the original disk has a new drive letter. For example, if you have an existing disk D that you compress, the new compressed disk will be drive D, and the original disk will be moved to a previously unused letter, such as H.

If you compress C, the boot disk, Windows leaves copies of a few crucial system startup files on the original disk that it uses to get started. The startup process works the same as always, except slower.

You can also create a new compressed disk by telling DriveSpace which real disk to use and how much of its free space to assign to the new virtual disk. You can create as many compressed disks as you want in this way. For older programs that insist on having their own disk drive to use, or insist on using inconvenient file and folder names in the root folder of a drive, a small compressed disk dedicated to the program can sometimes be the best way to keep your system organized.

Can You Compress Floppy Disks?

You can compress a floppy disk (and most other removable disks) the same way that you can compress any other disk, but we don't recommend doing so. If you compress a disk with DriveSpace 3, the files on that disk will be readable *only* on Windows 98, not on Windows 95, Windows 3.1, DOS, or any of the other systems that can read DOS-formatted disks. DriveSpace offers the option of compressing floppy disks by using the older Doublespace compression scheme, but that still limits you to recent versions of DOS and Windows that support Doublespace.

Instead, we suggest using ZIP files, which are much more portable (see "Alternatives to Compressed Disks").

Compressing Existing Disks and Creating Compressed Virtual Disks

You compress disks by using the DriveSpace program, which you can run from a Folder window, Windows Explorer, or the Start menu.

Windows 98's compression programs may not be installed on your computer. If they don't appear on the menus described in the rest of this chapter, install them from the Windows 98 CD-ROM or floppy disks: Open Control Panel, open Add/Remove Programs, click the Windows Setup tab, choose System Tools from the list of categories, click Details, and choose Disk Compression Tools (see "Installing and Uninstalling Programs That Come with Windows 98" in Chapter 3).

Compressing Existing Disks

To compress an existing drive, follow these steps:

1. In a Folder window or Windows Explorer, right-click the drive you want to compress, and then choose Properties on the menu that appears. You see the disk's Properties dialog box, shown in Figure 35-1. Ensure that the File System is FAT16 (also called simply FAT), not FAT32 or anything else. Only FAT16 disks and partitions can be compressed (see "What Are the FAT16 and FAT32 File Systems?" in Chapter 11).

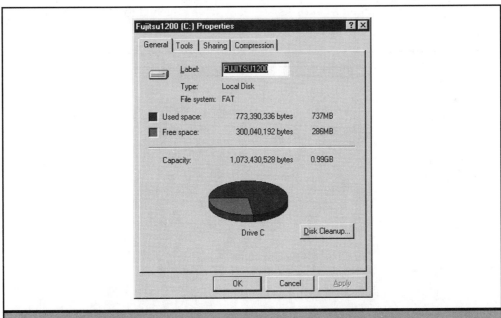

Figure 35-1.   *Properties of a hard disk, including space usage*

2. Click the Compression tab at the top of the dialog box to show the compression information (see Figure 35-2). If the disk isn't already compressed, you see your options: Compress the existing disk or create a new compressed volume.

3. To compress the existing disk, click Compress Drive. This starts the DriveSpace program and opens the Compress A Drive dialog box, showing how much free space the drive has now and how much free space it would have after compression.

Alternatively, choose Start | Programs | Accessories | System Tools | DriveSpace. You see a list of all the computer's disks. Select the one you want to compress and choose Drive | Compress to display the Compress A Drive dialog box.

4. To check or change your compressing options, click the Options button to display the Compressing Options dialog box. You can select the drive letter to use for the original uncompressed drive after compression, the amount of free space to leave on the original drive, and whether or not to hide the original drive so that it doesn't appear in Windows Explorer or Folder windows. Although the Windows default is to hide the original drive, we prefer not to hide it, to remind us what disks we really have attached to our computer.

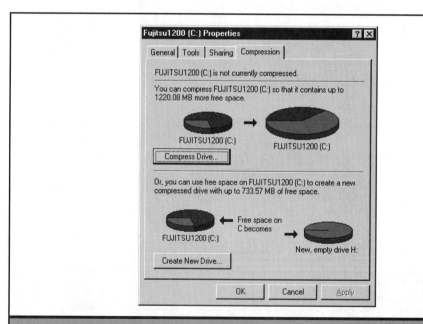

Figure 35-2.   *Options for compressing a hard disk*

5. Once you have the options set to your taste, click OK to return to the Compress A Drive dialog box, and then click the Start button in that dialog box. DriveSpace now compresses your disk in place. First, DriveSpace checks your disk for errors. Next, it reboots your computer into a special single-program mode, so that no other program can mess with the disk during the compression process. DriveSpace then compresses all the files and, finally, reboots your computer back into normal operation. Once your disk is compressed, you can use it the same way you always did.

Creating a compressed disk is very slow, and takes several hours during which your computer can't do anything else. You have to answer several "OK" questions, so you can't leave it overnight and expect it to be done in the morning. No other programs can run during disk compression.

Creating New Compressed Virtual Disks

You create a new compressed disk in much the same way that you compress an existing disk:

1. From a Folder window or Windows Explorer, open the Compression tab in the disk's Properties dialog box, as described in the preceding section, and then click Create New Drive. You see the Create New Compressed Drive dialog box, shown in Figure 35-3.

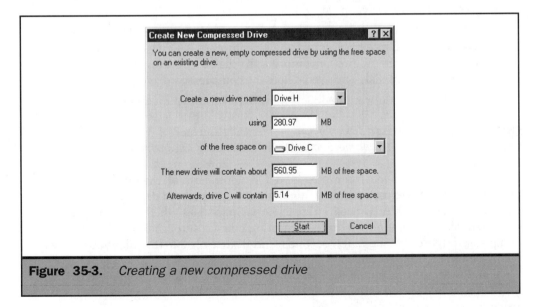

Figure 35-3.   *Creating a new compressed drive*

Alternatively, choose Start | Programs | Accessories | System Tools | DriveSpace. You see a list of all the computer's disks. Select the one on which you want to store the new compressed drive, and choose Advanced | Create Empty.

2. Change any parameters you want, which most likely includes the amount of real disk space to use for the new drive. By default, Windows allocates almost all the space on the real disk to the new compressed disk, which may or may not be what you intended.

3. Click the Start button in the Create New Compressed Drive dialog box. DriveSpace creates the new drive. (The program may recommend that you reboot so that all applications see the new drive.) Click Close if the dialog box still appears.

Caution   *Creating a new compressed disk isn't as slow as compressing an existing disk, but it can still take over an hour.*

Deleting and Uncompressing Disks

If you decide that you'd rather not use disk compression, you can uncompress and delete compressed disks. To uncompress a disk, follow these steps:

1. Run the DriveSpace program by choosing Start | Programs | Accessories | System Tools | DriveSpace.

2. Highlight the disk you want to uncompress, and then select Drive | Uncompress. DriveSpace shows the Uncompress A Drive dialog box that describes how it will first uncompress the disk by transferring the files to the underlying real disk, and then delete the compressed drive.

3. If that's want you want to do, click the Start button in the dialog box.

Caution   *You can uncompress a disk only if all the files will fit on the real drive. If they won't fit, you have to delete or move some files before you can uncompress.*

You can also just delete a compressed drive, wiping out all the files that drive contains. In the DriveSpace window, highlight the compressed drive you want to delete, and then select Advanced | Delete. DriveSpace asks whether you're sure you want to delete the compressed drive. Assuming you are sure, click Yes. Deleting a compressed disk only takes a few seconds, and it's irrevocable (the files you delete are *not* moved to the Recycle Bin).

If you want to wipe out all the files on a compressed disk, but not delete the disk, you can reformat the disk. In DriveSpace, select Drive | Format. Reformatting is usually faster than deleting the files by hand.

Adjusting and Tuning Compressed Disks Using DriveSpace and Compression Agent

Once you've created a compressed disk, DriveSpace and the new Compression Agent program allow you to adjust and tune your compressed disks. Changes you can make include:

- Adjust the size of a compressed disk
- Change the estimated compression on the disk
- Change the compression strategy for new files
- Recompress existing files to improve performance

Adjusting the Sizes of Compressed Disks

You can adjust the size of a compressed disk, either by taking free space from the underlying real disk and adding it to the compressed disk, or by releasing free space on the compressed disk back to the real disk. Follow these steps:

1. Run DriveSpace by choosing Start | Programs | Accessories | System Tools | DriveSpace.

2. Select the compressed disk and choose Drive | Adjust Free Space. DriveSpace opens the Adjust Free Space dialog box (Figure 35-4) showing the amounts of free space on the compressed disk and real disk, in megabytes, with a slider bar at the bottom. The closer to the left end of the slider bar the slider is, the more space is available on the compressed disk; the closer to the right end, the more space is available on the underlying disk.

3. Adjust the free space either by typing the amount of free space you want, in megabytes, into the free space field for either the compressed or real disk, or by sliding the slider back and forth.

4. Click OK. Adding space to the compressed disk is relatively fast, while releasing space back to the real disk can take an hour or two due to the need to reorganize the compressed disk.

Adjusting Free Space Estimates

The amount of free space reported on a compressed disk is an estimate, based on a guess of the *compression ratio*, the degree to which files can be compressed, and this estimate is usually wrong. You can adjust the estimate to be more accurate by following these steps:

1. In a Folder window or in Windows Explorer, right-click the compressed drive you want to adjust, select Properties from the menu that appears, and then click

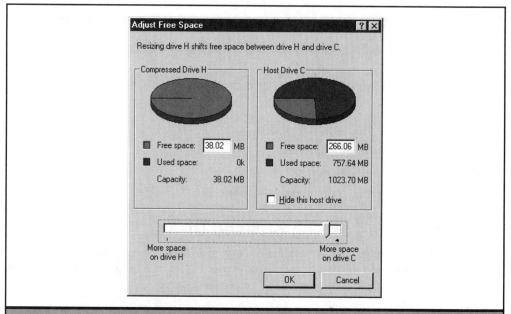

Figure 35-4. *Adjusting the amount of space in a compressed disk*

the Compression tab on the Properties dialog box. You see a table showing the actual and estimated compression on the disk. In the disk shown in Figure 35-5, the estimated compression of free space is 2.0 (that is 50 percent space savings), while the actual compression is 2.35. The estimated ratio appears in the Free Space row and Compression Ratio column of the table, while the actual ratio appears in the Total row in the same column.

2. To change the estimated compression ratio, run DriveSpace by clicking the Advanced button and the clicking the Run DriveSpace button. (Alternatively, you can choose Start | Programs | Accessories | System Tools | DriveSpace.)

3. Select the disk you want to change, and then select Advanced | Change Ratio to display the Compressing Ratio For Drive dialog box. You see the actual compression ratio (which you can't change) and the estimated ratio (which you can).

4. To change the estimated ratio, enter the actual value either by using the slider or by typing the value into the Estimated box.

5. Click OK. You can't change the ratio if any files are open on the drive or any programs are being run from the drive; if any files are open or any programs

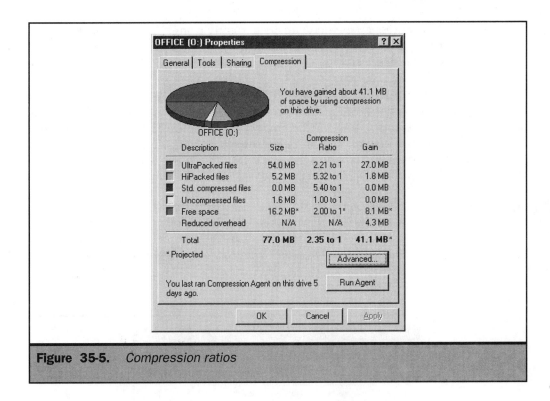

Figure 35-5.   *Compression ratios*

are running, DriveSpace offers to reboot the computer to close the offending files.

Changing the Compression Strategy and Recompressing Files

DriveSpace can use these compression techniques:

■ **UltraPack** is the most efficient and slowest compressing method. We suggest you use UltraPack only for files that haven't been used in a while and only if you have a fast computer (a Pentium Pro or better).

■ **HiPack** is almost as efficient and not quite as slow. HiPack makes sense if you have a very fast computer or compressed files that you use infrequently.

■ **Standard compression** usually provides a better trade-off between speed and space.

You can also tell DriveSpace to compress only when you're about to run out of space, or you can tell it to temporarily turn off compression altogether. DriveSpace can show you which compression method you are currently using. You can change the strategy that DriveSpace uses to compress files, and you can use Compression Agent to change the way that files are stored.

Changing DriveSpace's Compressing Strategy

To change the compression strategy, run DriveSpace and select Advanced | Settings to see the Disk Compression Settings dialog box, shown in Figure 35-6. The settings apply to all compressed disks on your system. Select the setting you want on the Disk Compression Settings dialog box, and then click OK. (If you want to use UltraPack, use the Compresion Agent as described in the next section.)

 The Automatically Mount New Compressed Drives check box applies to compressed removable disks, like floppy disks or Zip disks. If this box is not selected, then whenever you insert a compressed floppy disk or other removable disk, you must choose Advanced | Mount from the DriveSpace menu before you can use the disk.

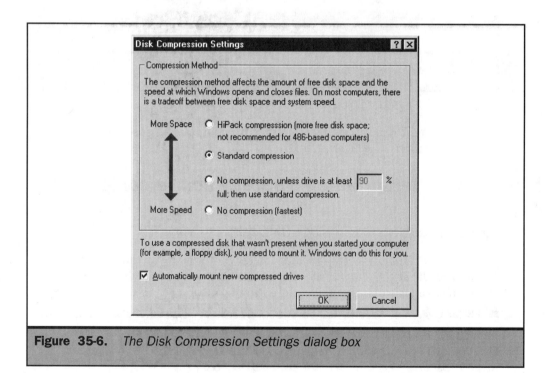

Figure 35-6. *The Disk Compression Settings dialog box*

Recompressing a Drive

Changing the settings doesn't change the way that existing files are stored. Compression Agent takes care of that. Follow these steps to fine-tune your compression strategies and to recompress your compressed drives:

1. Run Compression Agent by choosing Start | Programs | Accessories | System Tools | Compression Agent (see Figure 35-7). When Compression Agent starts, it shows how much space you could gain by changing compression methods.

After you run Compression Agent one time and set its parameters, it usually is more convenient to use the Task Scheduler to run it once or twice a week in the middle of the night (see "Running Programs on a Schedule Using Task Scheduler" in Chapter 2).

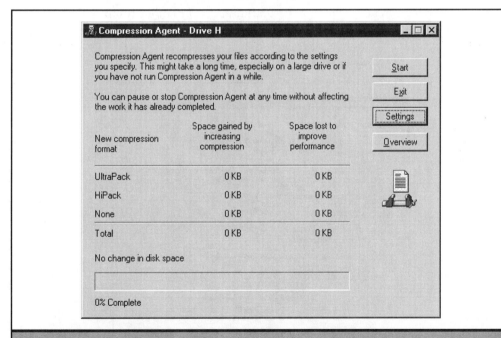

Figure 35-7. *The Compression Agent can recompress drives to improve efficiency*

2. To choose how to recompress your disks, click Settings to display the Compression Agent Settings dialog box, shown in Figure 35-8. Compression Agent can repack files into the highly compressed UltraPack form, which is even smaller than HiPack, but quite slow to read.

3. For further fine-tuning, click the Exceptions button to tell Compression Agent to use particular kinds of compression in specified folders or for particular types of files. Click Add to display the Add Exceptions dialog box, on which you specify the type of compressing to use for specific items. We tell it not to compress DLL or EXE files, due to the performance loss of running programs from compressed files. On a Pentium, it's OK to HiPack everything else, while on slower computers, it's faster not to compress anything else unless you're short on space (a setting you can make in DriveSpace). Click OK to return to the Compression Agent Settings dialog box.

4. Click OK to return to the Compression Agent dialog box, and then click the Start button in the dialog box to proceed with recompression.

Recompressing can take several hours, but unlike every other compression operation, you can pause or stop it at any time and resume later.

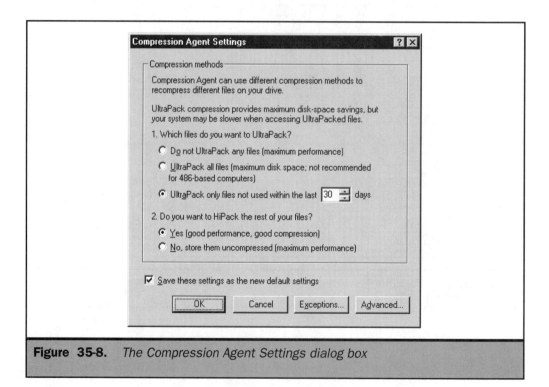

Figure 35-8. *The Compression Agent Settings dialog box*

Converting Older Compressed Disks

Windows 98 offers DriveSpace 3, a more advanced compression scheme than was offered on Windows 95, Windows 3.1, or DOS. Although Windows 98 handles the older compressed disks without trouble, if you upgrade a system with existing compressed disks, you'll get better performance if you upgrade your compressed drives to DriveSpace 3. To do so, run DriveSpace, highlight the compressed drive, and then select Drive | Upgrade. The upgrade process can take anywhere from a few minutes to several hours, depending on the number of files on the disk.

 Earlier versions of Windows and DOS cannot read a DriveSpace 3 disk. Do not upgrade your disks until you're sure you won't be going back to an earlier version of DOS or Windows.

DriveSpace can not upgrade a compressed floppy disk. Instead, it tells you to copy the files from the floppy disk to the hard disk, reformat the floppy disk, compress it with DriveSpace 3, and then copy the files back. We don't think it's worth the trouble to do so.

Alternatives to Compressed Disks

The popular WinZip (from Nico Mak Computing, **http://www.winzip.com**) and PKZIP (from PKWARE, **http://www.pkware.com**) programs create and manage *ZIP files*, highly compressed archives of files. Both programs work well, and the ZIP files they create are interchangeable, but we find WinZip easier to use. Or, consider buying ZipMagic which makes ZIP files as easy to use as folders. You can download an evaluation copy from **http://www.mijenix.com**. You can store information in ZIP files instead of using compressed disks.

A single ZIP file is analogous to a Windows folder, and can contain any number of files. Unlike a Windows folder, ZIP files can be copied around like any other files, and the ZIP format is well documented and standardized, so compatible ZIP programs are available for DOS, Macintosh, UNIX, and other systems.

To create a ZIP file using WinZip, run WinZip, open a Folder window or Windows Explorer that displays the files you want to add to the archive, and then drag the files into the WinZip window. WinZip asks for the name of the archive to create. To unpack a ZIP archive, open the archive in WinZip and select Extract, or drag the files from the WinZip window to a Folder window or Windows Explorer. WinZip has lots of other options, notably the ability to create floppy disk archives that span more than one disk, for large files and backups of large folders.

To create a ZIP file using ZipMagic, just rename a folder so that the new folder name has the extension .zip. The ZIP file looks and acts just like a folder in Windows Explorer and Folder windows.

Chapter 36

Tuning Windows 98 for
Maximum Performance

Windows 98 automatically sets itself up to give you adequate performance. Several tools allow you to tune your configuration to improve performance, primarily disk performance. The System Properties dialog box shows you hardware settings, including tuning settings. You may also want to track the system resources of your computer by using the Resource Meter program or monitor system usage by using the System Monitor program.

In our experience, few of the tuning techniques make a noticeable difference on a balanced system with adequate memory and disk, although they do make some difference on small systems with slow disks. The best ways to improve system performance remain to add more memory and a faster disk, in that order.

What Are System Resources and How Can You Monitor Them?

To keep Windows running smoothly, it helps to know when your system resources are running low.

What Are System Resources?

System resources are fixed-size areas of memory used by Windows applications. There are three resource pools:

- *System pool*, used for communication between applications and the system.
- *User pool*, used to manage windows, menus, and other parts of the Windows user interface.
- *GDI (graphic device interface) pool*, used to manage fonts, colors, and other tools that are used to create screen and printer images.

The primary reason you need to care about these resources is that if any of the pools runs out of space, applications—and sometimes Windows itself—fail in unpredictable ways. The Resource Meter program lets you trace how much space is left in each of these pools, so that you can see whether you're in danger of running out of space (see "Using Resource Meter"). A distressingly common error in Windows applications is *resource leakage*—applications allocate resource memory but fail to release it when done. If you suspect an application is leaking, you can use Resource Meter to compare available resources before and after you run the application. Assuming the system is otherwise quiet, after you run an application, the resources should return to the level they were before the application started.

If you do run out of system resources, the only reliable way to recover is to restart Windows.

How Can You Monitor System Usage?

Windows, like any computer system, can monitor many aspects of its own operation, including CPU usage, the software disk cache, disk operations, serial port operations, and network operations. Sometimes, when system performance is unacceptable, you can monitor key aspects and determine where the bottleneck is occurring. This helps determine whether the most effective improvements would be through software reconfiguration or a hardware upgrade, such as adding more memory. The System Monitor program displays and, optionally, logs performance data (see "Using System Monitor").

Tuning Your Computer's Performance with the System Properties Performance Tab

The System Properties dialog box includes all the hardware settings that you can change and offers several tuning features that can improve performance, or at least make the system crash less often. Open the System icon in the Control Panel to display the System Properties dialog box. Click or double-click the System icon depending on whether your desktop uses Web style or Classic style (see "Choosing the Style of Your Desktop" in Chapter 1). Alternatively, you can press WINDOWS-BREAK if your keyboard has a WINDOWS key (with the Windows logo on it) or right-click the My Computer icon on the desktop and select Properties.

The System Properties dialog box has the following tabs:

- General, showing the Windows version and registration information.
- Device Manager (see "Using the Device Manager" in Chapter 15).
- Hardware Profiles (see "Creating and Using Hardware Profiles" in Chapter 19).
- Performance, which lets you tune features related to disks, virtual memory, and the screen—see Figure 36-1, although the dialog box may look different depending on your installed file systems.

Tuning the File System

Click the File System button on the Performance tab of the System Properties dialog box to see the File System Properties dialog box. We cover each of its five tabs in turn.

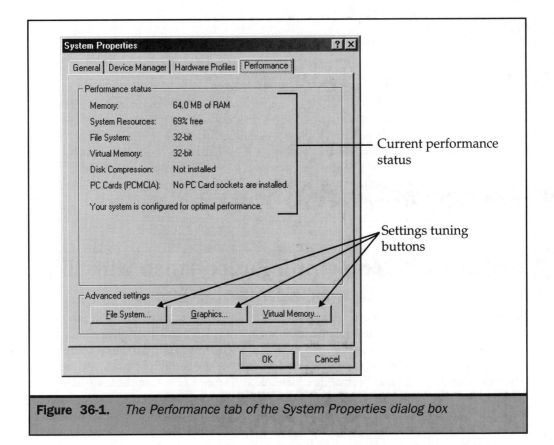

Figure 36-1.   *The Performance tab of the System Properties dialog box*

Hard Disk Tuning

The Hard Disk tab of the File System Properties dialog box, shown in Figure 36-2, lets you choose from three settings that describe the way you use your computer: Laptop, Desktop, or Server. Choose the one that most closely describes your computer. The Read-Ahead Optimization slider lets you adjust the amount of disk *read-ahead* the system uses—the amount of extra information Windows reads from the disk and stores in memory. Unless your system is extraordinarily short on memory (less than 8MB), use Full read-ahead.

Floppy Disk Tuning

The only setting on the Floppy Disk tab of the File System Properties dialog box, shown in Figure 36-3, tells Windows whether to search for new floppy disk drives as it boots. Unless you have an unusual setup in which Windows finds "phantom" drives that don't actually exist, leave it checked. (On the other hand, Microsoft points out that your system starts slightly faster if the box is not checked.)

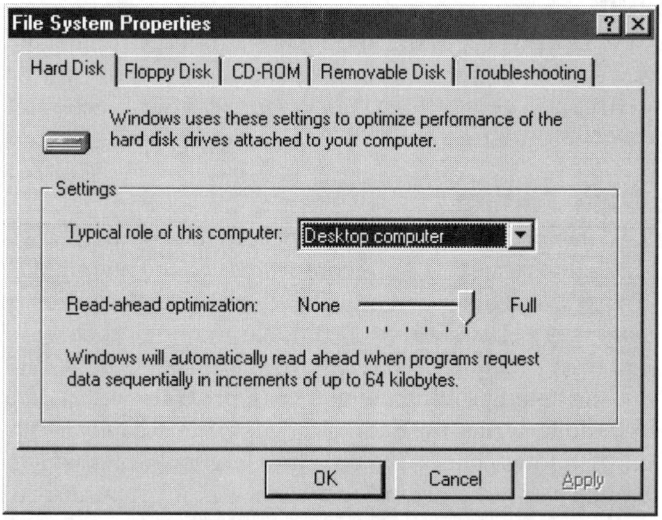

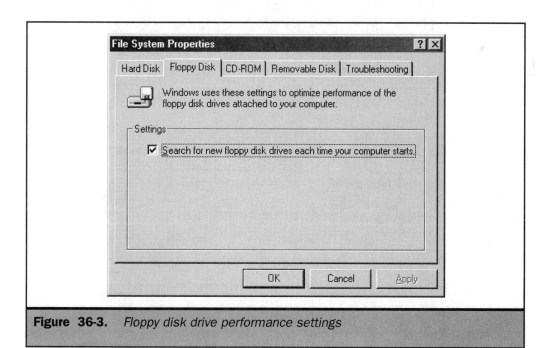

Figure 36-2. *Hard disk drive performance settings*

Figure 36-3. *Floppy disk drive performance settings*

CD-ROM Tuning

The settings on the CD-ROM tab of the File System Properties dialog box, shown in Figure 36-4, let you set the CD-ROM cache size and the speed of your drive. Unless you have a very slow drive and very little memory, use the largest cache and the Quad-Speed Or Higher setting.

Removable Disk Tuning

The Removable Disk tab of the File System Properties dialog box, shown in Figure 36-5, offers a single setting that turns on or off *write-behind caching* on removable disk drives (floppy disks, ZIP disks, and other drives from which the disk can be removed—see "What Are the Properties of Disk Drives, Partitions, and Logical Drives?" in Chapter 11). This setting entails a trade-off between performance and safety. With write-behind caching turned off (the default setting), whenever a program writes data to a file on a removable disk, Windows writes the data to the disk immediately. With write-behind caching turned on, Windows collects the data into larger chunks, which it can write faster. The disadvantage of write-behind caching is that if you remove a disk while a file is open for writing (or if the power should go out), the file may not be written to the disk and the file and file system may be damaged slightly, although the ScanDisk program can fix them.

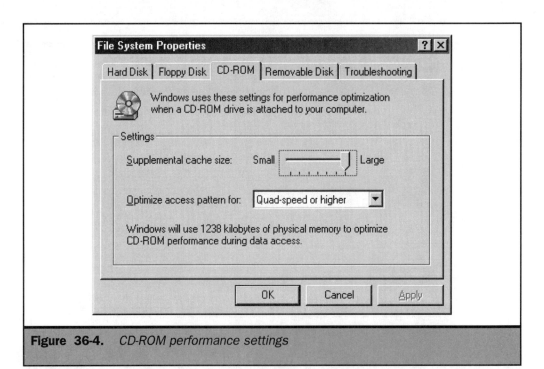

Figure 36-4. *CD-ROM performance settings*

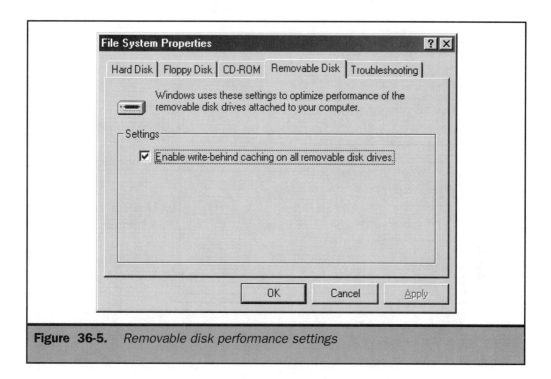

Figure 36-5.   *Removable disk performance settings*

Unless you have trouble telling when a program has finished writing a file to a removable disk, we recommend that you turn on write-behind caching.

Troubleshooting File System Problems

The Troubleshooting tab of the File System Properties dialog box, shown in Figure 36-6, lists settings that advanced users can use to diagnose and work around disk problems. Unless you have disk problems, don't use these settings.

Each of the first two settings turns off a specific performance feature that occasionally causes trouble with old and badly designed applications. The rest of the settings turn off features that occasionally cause trouble with old or badly designed disk controllers. If you have inexplicable disk errors, select all the troubleshooting setting check boxes and see whether the trouble goes away. If it goes away, clear the check boxes one at a time until the problem reappears, at which point you know that the setting you just turned off has triggered the problem. If it's one of the application settings (the first two settings), get an updated version of the application that causes the problem. If it's one of the disk controller settings, get a new disk controller.

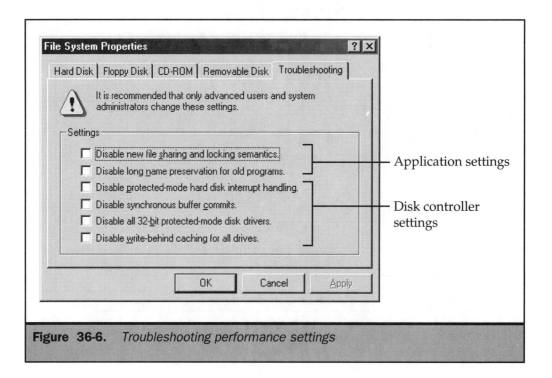

Figure 36-6.   *Troubleshooting performance settings*

Virtual Memory

Windows automatically manages program storage by using *virtual memory*, which moves chunks of program and data storage between disk and memory automatically, so that individual programs don't have to do all of their own memory management. Normally Windows manages virtual memory automatically, but in a few cases, you may want to change its parameters. Click the Virtual Memory button on the Performance tab of System Properties dialog box to see the Virtual Memory dialog box, shown in Figure 36-7. You can specify the disk drive on which Windows stores its *swap file* (the file to which virtual memory is copied), along with the minimum and maximum sizes of the swap file.

There are two likely cases in which you might want to set your own virtual memory settings:

■ If you have more than one disk, Windows normally puts the swap file on the boot drive (the disk drive from which Windows loads). If you have another drive that is larger or faster, you might want to tell Windows to swap to that other drive, instead (that is, store the swap file on that drive).

■ If you are extremely short of disk space, you can decrease the amount of virtual memory, and hence the disk space, that Windows allocates. If you decrease

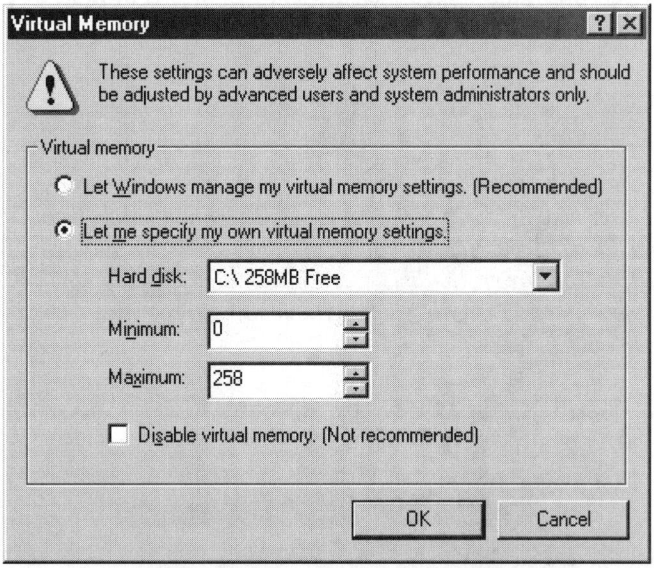

Figure 36-7. *Virtual Memory settings*

virtual memory too far, programs may fail as they run out of memory. There's generally no advantage to increasing the amount of virtual memory beyond the default, since extra virtual memory doesn't make the system run any faster.

You can also disable virtual memory altogether, which is usually a bad idea unless you have an enormous amount of RAM.

  The Graphics button on the System Properties dialog box displays the Advanced Graphics Settings dialog box, which is discussed in "Diagnosing Display Problems" in the next chapter.

Using Resource Meter to Track System Resources

Resource Meter is a small application that displays the amount of each of the three system resource pools currently in use (see "What Are System Resources?"). You can run Resource Meter by choosing Start | Programs | Accessories | System Tools | Resource Meter. The first time Resource Meter runs it displays a warning that it, too, uses some resources, and then appears as a small icon in the system tray, with bars that indicate how much resource space remains in each resource pool.

Resource Meter may not have been installed with Windows 98. To install it, open the Control Panel, open Add/Remove Programs, click the Windows Setup tab, choose System Tools from the list of categories, click Details, and click System Resource Meter (see "Installing and Uninstalling Programs That Come with Windows 98" in Chapter 3).

If you double-click that icon, you see the Resource Meter window, shown here, which displays each resource pool as a bar.

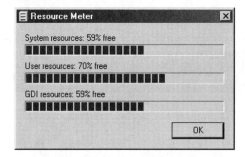

To get rid of the Resource Meter window, click OK or the Close button. To exit the program, right-click the icon in the system tray to see a menu, and then select Exit.

 ## Using System Monitor to Display Performance Data

System Monitor displays and logs information about the way your Windows 98 system is operating. System Monitor can display information in a variety of formats, can log the information to a file for later analysis, and can monitor remote systems.

System Monitor may not have been installed with Windows 98. To install it, open the Control Panel, open Add/Remove Programs, click the Windows Setup tab, choose System Tools from the list of categories, click Details, and click System Monitor (see "Installing and Uninstalling Programs That Come with Windows 98" in Chapter 3).

To start System Monitor, choose Start | Programs | Accessories | System Tools | System Monitor. The program starts by displaying one item (Kernel Processor Usage, a measure of CPU load) as a line chart, as shown in Figure 36-8.

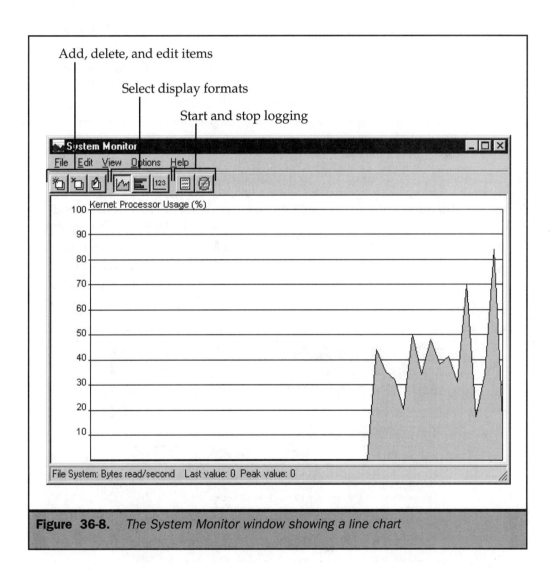

Figure 36-8.   *The System Monitor window showing a line chart*

Customizing the Display

System Monitor offers extensive customization of the displayed data.

Selecting Data to Display

You can add, edit, and delete displayed items. To add an item, follow these steps:

1. Click the Add button on the toolbar (the leftmost button). System Monitor displays the Add Item dialog box with a list of categories (see Figure 36-9).

2. Click a category of interest (in the left-hand box), and System Monitor displays a list of items in that category (in the right-hand box). (To see a description of an item, click a category and an item, then click the Explain button.)

3. Select the item(s) of interest and then click OK. The newly selected items appear in the System Monitor window. You may want to expand the window to make the display easier to read.

The categories and useful items in each category include:

- **Dial-Up Adapter**   Usually the COM1 serial port. Frames Received/Second and Frames Transmitted/Second provide an estimate of network throughput.

- **Dial-Up Adapter #2**   Usually the COM2 serial port (if your system has one).

- **Disk Cache**   Software component that manages disk data. Cache Hits and Cache Misses give an estimate of how effectively the cache is managing data.

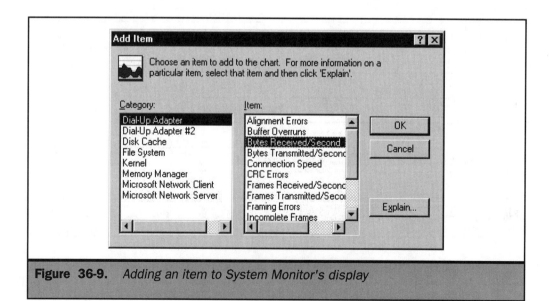

Figure 36-9.   *Adding an item to System Monitor's display*

- **File System**   Software component that transfers data between disk and memory. Reads/Second and Writes/Second provide an estimate of disk throughput. (Note that this interacts with the cache—in many cases, data read previously can be re-read from the cache, avoiding a second read from the disk.)

- **Kernel**   Fundamental Windows functions. Processor Usage (%) tells how CPU-bound your system is (that is, to what extent delays are due to your CPU speed).

- **Memory Manager**   Virtual memory functions. Page-Ins and Page-Outs (per second) provide an estimate of how much disk activity is related to virtual memory.

- **Microsoft Network Client**   Network client functions, such as use of disks on other computers on the LAN. Bytes Read/Second, Bytes Written/Second, and Transactions/Second estimate how much use is being made of remote disks.

- **Microsoft Network Server**   Network server functions, such as providing shared disks to other computers on a LAN. Bytes Read/Sec and Bytes Written/Second estimate the amount of disk activity requested by other systems on the LAN.

To remove an item from the display, click the Remove button on the System Monitor toolbar (the second button from the left), select the desired item from the menu, and then click OK.

Selecting the Display Format

The default scales and colors that System Monitor uses are usually acceptable, but you can customize them if you want. To change the displayed color or scale of an item, click the Edit button on the toolbar (the third button from the left), select the item that you want to change from the menu, and then click OK. You se the Chart Options dialog box, shown here:

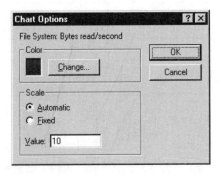

To change the color, click the Change button, select a color from the Color dialog box that appears, and click OK. Choose either automatic scaling (which asks Windows to set the scale based on the actual values of the item), or manually set a maximum displayed value. Then click OK.

System Monitor offers three formats:

- **Line charts**   Display how values of each item have changed over time (shown in Figure 36-8).

- **Bar charts**   Show the current value of each item graphically (shown in Figure 36-10). In each bar chart, the bar shows the current reading, and a narrow stripe shows the maximum reading since the program was started.

- **Numeric charts**   Show the current value of each items as numbers; numeric chart are useful when displaying a lot of items.

To switch among the three views, click the Line Charts, Bar Charts, and Numeric Charts buttons on the toolbar.

System Monitor rearranges the displayed items as you resize its window, and inserts or deletes captions, depending on the layout. Try changing the size and shape of the window until you get a layout that you like.

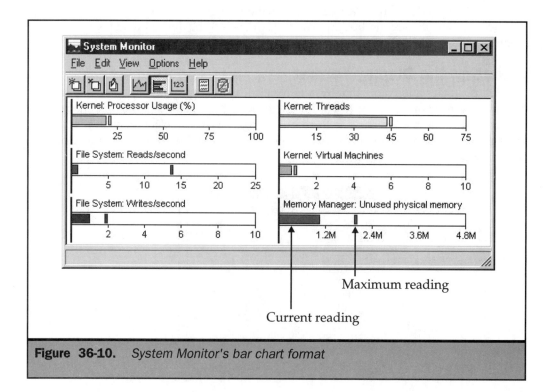

Figure 36-10.   *System Monitor's bar chart format*

Other Customizations

To display the maximum amount of data, select View | Hide Title Bar to remove all borders and titles around the System Monitor window. Press ESC to restore the display.

Normally System Monitor updates its display every three seconds. To change the interval at which it updates and logs data, select Options | Chart. You can select an interval as short as one second or as long as an hour.

Logging to a File

System Monitor can log data to a file for later analysis. System Monitor writes a comma-delimited text file that any spreadsheet or database package can read directly.

First, select the items you want to log and select the interval at which you want to log them. Then click the Start Logging button on the toolbar and choose the file to which the data should be logged (the default filename is Sysmon.log). System Monitor logs performance data until you either stop logging (by clicking the Stop Logging button on the toolbar) or exit the program.

Each time you start logging, System Monitor overwrites any existing log file with the same name. A good plan is to create a daily log file, putting the date into the name of the file, such as Sysmon-980704.log.

Remote Monitoring

For remote monitoring to work, both the computer to be monitored and the computer doing the monitoring must have the Remote Registry service installed from the Windows Resource Kit (an extra-cost package available from Microsoft). Furthermore, the computer to be monitored must be enabled for remote administration, and you must know its administrative password (see "What Is Remote Administration?" in Chapter 33).

To monitor a remote computer from your computer, click File | Connect from the menu bar in the System Monitor window and then enter the name of the computer whose information you want to monitor.

Tuning Your Hard Disk's Performance

The most effective way to speed up most Windows systems, short of adding extra memory or a new disk, is to optimize your hard disk. After you use the settings on the Performance tab of the System Properties dialog box to tune performance (see "Tuning the File System"), here are other programs you can try.

Disk Defragmenter

The most important Windows 98 tuning program is the Disk Defragmenter (see "Defragmenting Your Disk" in Chapter 34). As it defragments your disk, this program can also rearrange your executable programs so that they can start and run faster.

Compression Agent

If you use compressed drives, the Compression Agent serves a similar function (see "Recompressing a Drive" in Chapter 35). It can arrange for frequently used files to be stored in less compressed but faster-to-access form than less-frequently used files. Unless you have a very slow disk drive, compressed drives are slower to read and write than uncompressed drives.

Chapter 37

Troubleshooting Windows 98

Usually, Windows 98 works quite well, but sometimes it hangs and crashes. Luckily, Windows 98 comes with a number of diagnostic tools that can help out. This chapter describes techniques for dealing with programs that hang or crash, stopping programs from running automatically, diagnosing other problems, using the built-in Troubleshooters, and if all else fails, reporting problems to Microsoft for resolution.

What Diagnostic Tools Does Windows 98 Provide?

Windows 98 provides a wide range of diagnostic tools that you can use for different kinds of problems. In addition to the tools listed here, see "Configuring Windows Using the System Configuration Utility" in Chapter 39.

Startup Modes

The worst problems prevent Windows from starting up at all. If the data on your hard disk are intact, you can start Windows in one of several special *startup modes* that provide limited function and help diagnose problems. The startup modes are the following:

- **Normal**   Windows starts normally.
- **Logged**   Windows starts normally, but logs all the drivers it loads in the file Bootlog.txt.
- **Step-By-Step Confirmation**   Windows processes its initialization files one line at a time, stopping and telling you each driver it's about to load.
- **Safe Mode**   Windows starts by using the simplest possible set of drivers and hardware devices.
- **Command Prompt Only**   Windows loads all drivers, but starts an MS-DOS command prompt, not the full Windows system.
- **Safe Mode Command Prompt Only**   Windows loads minimum drivers and displays an MS-DOS command prompt.

See "Starting in a Special Mode" for how to tell Windows to start in a special startup mode.

Startup Floppy Disk

If you installed Windows from a CD-ROM, one of the steps in the installation process created a startup floppy disk, or emergency boot disk. If the file system on your hard disk is damaged, you can often start your computer from the startup floppy disk and repair the damage enough to make the hard disk bootable (that is, make the startup files usable) again.

If you don't have a startup floppy disk, you can easily make one while Windows is running. You need a single 1.44MB floppy disk. Follow these steps:

1. Write-enable the disk and put it in the disk drive.

2. Open the Control Panel by choosing Start | Settings | Control Panel.

3. Select Add/Remove Programs. Single- or double-click the icon, depending on whether your system is configured for Web style or Classic style desktop (see "Choosing the Style of Your Desktop" in Chapter 1).

4. Click the Startup Disk tab.

5. Click the Create Disk button and follow the instructions that Windows displays. Windows creates a bootable startup disk.

6. Remove the disk from the drive, write-protect it, label it, and put it in a safe place.

 Be sure you have a startup floppy disk available at all times, and be sure to create one if you don't have one. If your computer breaks, you won't be able to create one when you need it.

Safe Mode

Safe mode is a limited operating mode used to diagnose problems. All of Windows' basic functions are available, but the screen runs in basic VGA mode (640x480, 16 colors) and no devices are available beyond the screen, keyboard, and disks (see Chapter 13 for more information).

System Configuration Information

The System Properties dialog box, started by opening the System icon in the Control Panel, includes information about all the devices and hardware drivers configured into your copy of Windows. This dialog box is the place to resolve hardware and driver problems, and includes the Device Manager (see "Using the Device Manager" in Chapter 15).

Another way to see information about your system configuration is to run the System Information program. Choose Start | Programs | Accessories | System Tools | System Information to display the System Information window shown in Figure 37-1. Click the plus boxes in the left pane to see all the categories of information the program can display. When you choose an item in the left pane, System Information displays information about that item in the right pane.

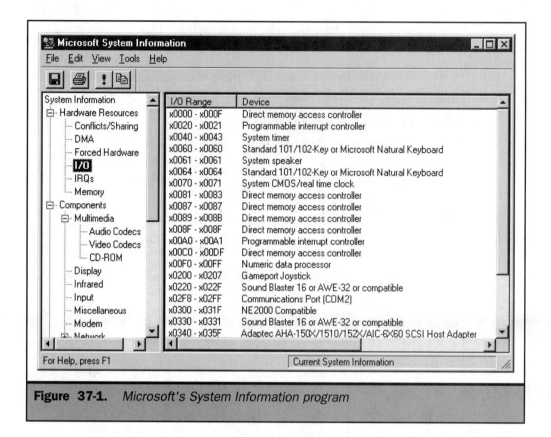

Figure 37-1. *Microsoft's System Information program*

You can print the displayed information by choosing File | Print or save the information in a text file by choosing File | Export. The Tools menu lists a number of other useful diagnostic programs you can run.

Windows Troubleshooters

For many problems, Microsoft provides a Troubleshooter that steps through some of the most common problems and offers suggestions on how to fix them (see "Diagnosing Problems Using Troubleshooters").

Debugging Tools

For hard-to-reproduce software problems, Microsoft includes Dr. Watson, a testing tool primarily used by software developers, which can be useful to report software errors (see "Reporting Problems Using Dr. Watson").

Dealing with Hung or Crashed Programs

Despite all the testing that software vendors do, Windows 98 and the applications you run under it have bugs, and sometimes *hang* (stop responding) or *crash* (fail altogether). When an application crashes, Windows displays a box telling you about it. There's not much you can do at that point, other than click OK. You may want to restart Windows if you're concerned that the program may have damaged files or Windows' internal operations.

When Internet Explorer crashes and you use the Active Desktop, Windows goes into a special recovery mode, with a white screen and explanatory messages. Click the link to restore the Active Desktop and get back to where you were.

If a program hangs, you generally can force Windows to stop the hung program. Press CTRL-ALT-DEL to open the Close Program dialog box, shown here:

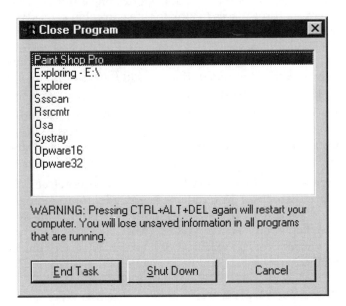

In the Close Program dialog box, a hung program usually has the notation "Not responding" after its name. Select the name of the program, and then click End Task. Normally the program then exits. If the program is hung badly, then after a few seconds, Windows reports that the program is not responding, and asks whether you really want to terminate it. You do.

If all else fails, press CTRL-ALT-DEL twice and Windows should restart. Windows runs ScanDisk if you didn't exit Windows properly, so that disk errors can be repaired (see "Testing Your Disk Structure with ScanDisk" in Chapter 34).

We recommend leaving your computer on all the time, so that Windows can run housekeeping and backup programs in the middle of the night. However, we find that we need to restart Windows every day or two to prevent Windows from eventually crashing. If programs you run leak resources (lose track of the memory they use), Windows finally runs out of memory. Run the Resource Meter so you can see when Windows is running low on memory (see "Using Resource Meter to Track System Resources" and "What Are System Resources?" in Chapter 36).

Stopping Programs from Running at Startup

When you start Windows, other programs may start up automatically, which can be very convenient (see "Running Programs When Windows 98 Starts" in Chapter 2). It's not always easy, however, to *stop* a program from running automatically when you start Windows. Here are three places to look for the entry that causes Windows to run the program:

- Make sure that a shortcut for the program isn't in the C:\Windows\Start Menu\Programs\Startup folder. If a shortcut for the program is there, delete it.

- Look for a line in your Win.ini file that runs the program (see "The Win.ini File" in Chapter 39). You can use the System Configuration Utility to display and edit the Win.ini file (but make a backup first). (See "Configuring Windows Using the System Configuration Utility" in Chapter 39.) The line would start with "run=" or "load=" line in the windows section.

- Examine the Registry for an entry that runs the program (see "What Is the Registry?" in Chapter 40). You can use Registry Editor to remove the offending entry, after making a backup of the Registry (see "Editing the Registry" in Chapter 40). Look in the HKEY_LOCAL_MACHINE\SOFTWARE\Microsoft\ Windows\CurrentVersion\RUN section, which lists programs that are run automatically.

Diagnosing Problems

If Windows doesn't start, or a piece of hardware is operating strangely, you may have either a hardware configuration problem or broken hardware.

Starting in a Special Mode

Starting Windows in one of the special startup modes is easy in principle, but can be tricky in practice. You have to press F8 the moment that your computer's hardware boot process transfers control to the Windows startup program. This usually is about one second after the last screen display from BIOS startup (such as screen and disk configuration messages). Usually, Windows displays a message like "Starting Windows 98..." at the moment you need to press F8, but often it flashes by too quickly to see. You can try holding down the F8 key during startup, until the keyboard beeps, and then letting up.

If you press F8 at the right time, Windows shows the Microsoft Windows 98 Startup Menu, with about six numbered choices. Type the number of the choice you need, and then press ENTER.

Diagnosing Hardware Problems

If Windows doesn't start up properly, start the system in Step-By-Step Confirmation mode. Windows prompts you to press Y or N at each stage of system startup. Press Y to each question until the system fails—whatever it just did caused the problem.

Restart Windows in Step-By-Step Confirmation mode again, but press N when it asks for the step that failed last time. With luck, you can get Windows running and then remove or reinstall the component that is causing trouble.

Another possibility, once you know which driver or component is causing trouble, is to restart Windows in Safe mode, and then remove or reinstall the troublesome component. After you start Windows in Safe mode, reconfigure or disable the offending driver by using the Device Manager (see "Using the Device Manager" in Chapter 15).

Diagnosing Display Problems

If your display is acting strangely, Windows offers several possible ways to fix the problem. This section describes the most common ways; also see "Diagnosing Problems Using Troubleshooters."

If the screen is utterly unreadable, restart Windows in Safe mode. After Windows is running in Safe or normal mode, open the Display Properties dialog box from the Control Panel and click the Settings tab (see "Changing Display Settings" in Chapter 13).

Your screen may not be able to handle whatever display resolution your adapter is using. Try setting the Screen Area to a smaller value to see whether the screen clears. (The number of colors doesn't matter—all modern screens can display an unlimited number of colors.)

Your screen may be able to handle the display resolution, but may not be able to handle the adapter's *refresh rate*, the number of times per second the adapter sends the image to the monitor. Click the Advanced button to display the Properties dialog box for your display adapter, and then click the Adapter tab. There may be a Refresh Rate box; if there is, try setting it to the slowest available refresh rate, usually 60 Hz. If that works, try faster rates until you find the fastest one that works reliably.

One final possibility is that the accelerator features in your display adapter aren't compatible with your computer. Symptoms typically are that the display is clear, but wrong, with lines or areas of the wrong color or wrong pattern on the screen. Click the Advanced button on the Settings tab in the Display Properties dialog box (as previously described) to display the Properties dialog box for your display adapter.

Click the Performance tab; depending on your display adapter, there may be a hardware acceleration slider ranging from None to Full. Try setting it to None; if this improves the display, try increasing the acceleration setting one notch at a time. (Another way to display this dialog box is to open the System icon on the Control Panel, click the Performance tab, and click the Graphics button.)

Diagnosing Problems Using Troubleshooters

Windows 98 includes fifteen *Troubleshooters*, step-by-step diagnostics that look for some of the most common problems and suggest solutions. The Troubleshooters vary in depth and usefulness; some are superficial, while others walk you through the details of significant system configuration changes.

All of the Troubleshooters are part of the Help system (see Chapter 6). Follow these steps to run a Troubleshooter:

1. Choose Start | Help to display the Windows Help window.

2. Click the Contents tab to display a list of topics, and then the Troubleshooting topic, and then Windows 98 Troubleshooters, shown in Figure 37-2.

3. Windows Troubleshooters are intended to be used in conjunction with whatever application is causing trouble, so arrange your screen so that both the Help window and your application window (if any) are visible.

4. Click the Troubleshooter you want to use. Windows displays a list of possible problems.

5. Click the one that most closely matches your problem, and then click Next. Windows suggests a possible solution.

6. Follow its advice. Windows asks whether its suggestion solved the problem.

7. Click Yes or No, and then click Next to try the rest of the Troubleshooter's suggestions.

The Troubleshooters that come with Windows 98 include:

- **Networking**   Problems related to networks, such as that you cannot connect to other computers, shared drives or printers don't work, or network adapters don't work. For more detailed instructions for troubleshooting LANs, see "Troubleshooting Your Network" in Chapter 30.

- **Modem**   Problems such as modem not detected, dialing problems, communication problems, or Internet access problems. For other ideas to try, see "Troubleshooting Your Modem" in Chapter 21.

- **Startup and Shutdown**   You get no response when starting or stopping, or mysterious messages at startup time. (You need another Windows machine in order to see this Troubleshooter, of course.)

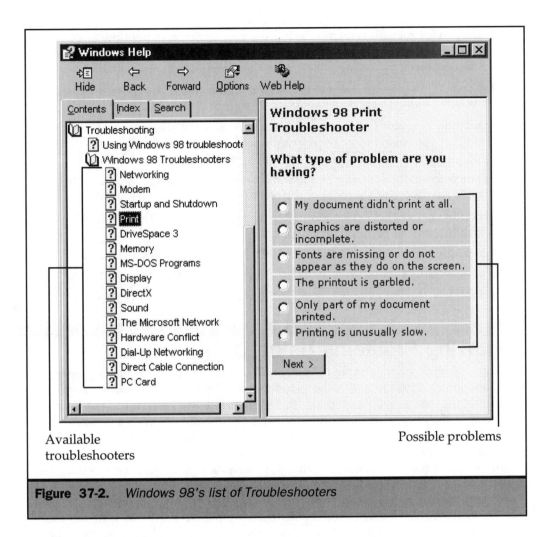

Available
troubleshooters

Possible problems

Figure 37-2.   *Windows 98's list of Troubleshooters*

- **Print**   Printing troubles such as no printing, incomplete or distorted printing, slow printing. (See Chapter 16 for how to install printers.)

- **DriveSpace 3**   Problems with the DriveSpace program and with compressed drives (see "What Is Disk Compression?" in Chapter 35).

- **Memory**   Out of memory errors, parity errors, Windows doesn't find all installed memory.

- **MS-DOS Programs**   DOS programs won't run under Windows, run incorrectly, or won't install (see Chapter 41).

- **Display**   Problems with display, videos and animations, multiple displays, and with a lot of DLL files that are not obviously related to display problems. (Best problem: My dialog boxes are not centered; solution: Tough luck.)

- **DirectX**   Problems related to the DirectX video system and related DLLs (see "What Is Video Data?" in Chapter 18).

- **Sound**   No sound, choppy or distorted sound, computer crashes when sounds play, or various error messages from sound components (see "Configuring Windows to Work with Sound" in Chapter 17).

- **The Microsoft Network**   Helps with various problems getting connected to MSN (see "Signing Up for Microsoft Network (MSN)" in Chapter 22).

- **Hardware Conflict**   Resolving a hardware conflict (see "Troubleshooting Your Hardware Configuration" in Chapter 15).

- **Dial-Up Networking**   A shortcut to the Modem Troubleshooter.

- **Direct Cable Connection**   A shortcut to the Networking Troubleshooter.

- **PC Card**   Problems with plug-in PC cards (see "PC Cards" in Chapter 15).

Reporting Problems Using Dr. Watson

Dr. Watson is a program that takes a "snapshot" of the system's state after a program fails. Software vendors can use the snapshot to try to figure out what went wrong. If you are having trouble with a program (including Windows itself), start Dr. Watson, and then run the troublesome program. When the program fails, you can immediately take a snapshot to document the current state of Windows and your programs, to aid in diagnosing the problem.

To use Dr. Watson, choose Start | Run, type **drwatson**, and then press ENTER. The program doesn't open a window, but adds a small icon to the system tray.

If your program fails, immediately double-click the Dr. Watson icon in the system tray. Dr. Watson creates a snapshot, reporting its progress as it does so. It then opens a report window in which it lists any possible trouble spots it noted, and lets you enter a sentence or two describing what you were doing when the program crashed, as shown in Figure 37-3. Next, select File | Save and save the report to a file. When you contact your software vendor, they may ask you to either open the saved report and read them some of the saved information or, more likely, e-mail or upload the entire log file to them.

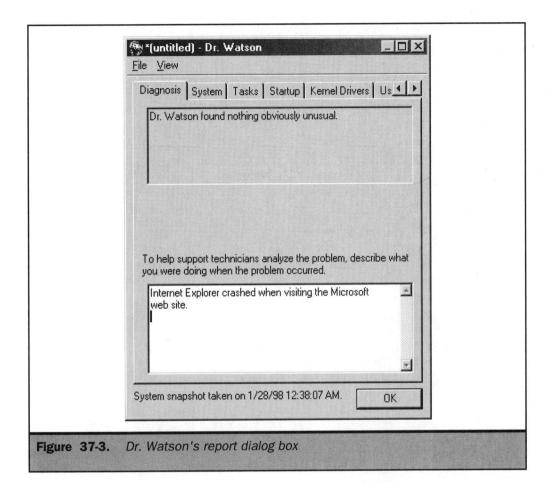

Figure 37-3. *Dr. Watson's report dialog box*

Chapter 38

Other Windows 98 Resources

Microsoft updates Windows 98 constantly to accommodate new hardware and software and to enhance features already found in the system. To stay up to date with these changes, you can run the Windows Update program to scan your system and look for outdated drivers and programs. You can also check the information that Microsoft provides on the Internet and do your own sleuthing by using resources and information available on the Internet.

This chapter explains how to update your computer by using the Windows Update program, and how to locate information about Windows 98 from Microsoft and other sources.

Tip *Before searching the Internet for information about Windows 98, take a look at the documentation that comes with the program. The Windows 98 CD-ROM contains a number of helpful text files in the \Readme folder. You can use WordPad to read these files (see "Taking Advantage of Free Word Processing with WordPad" in Chapter 4).*

Updating Your Computer with Windows Update

Windows Update is a program that is available from Microsoft's web site at **http://www.microsoft.com/windowsupdate**. Windows Update examines your computer and gives you a list of drivers and other files that can be updated. When the scan is complete, a list of available updates is presented, and you can choose which update(s) you want to install. In case you install an update that is not what you expected or does not work properly, Windows Update includes a Restore option that returns your computer to its condition prior to the update.

You can run Windows Update at any time to see whether new updates are available. It is especially important to run Windows Update before you install a new piece of hardware or a new software program, to be sure you have the drivers and files that you need on your system.

Windows Update uses a Wizard that guides you through the screens to complete the setup information. The first time you run Windows Update, you may be asked to register as a Windows user and supply some personal information, such as your name, location, and e-mail address. Windows Update uses Internet Explorer and your Internet settings to connect you to the Microsoft site on the Web. Before you start Windows Update, be sure your computer is connected or is ready to connect to the Internet (see Chapter 22).

To run Windows Update, follow these steps:

1. Choose Start | Windows Update. (If Windows Update is not listed at the top of your Start menu, choose Start | Settings | Windows Update.) The Internet Explorer window opens.

2. If you see the Dial-Up Connection dialog box, enter your user name and password and then click Connect. When you are connected to the Internet, the Windows Update page appears, as shown in Figure 38-1. The Windows Update page shows options that you can use to access the Update Wizard, get answers to technical support questions, or send your feedback about the Update page to Microsoft. (Since this page is on the Web, Microsoft may change its design at any time, but similar options will probably be available.)

3. Click Product Updates to open the Update page.

4. On the Product Updates page, click Device Drivers and System Files to start the Update Wizard. The Wizard takes you through the steps required to examine your system and determine whether updates are available. Follow the prompts on the screen until your system scan is complete and you see a list of available updates, as shown in Figure 38-2.

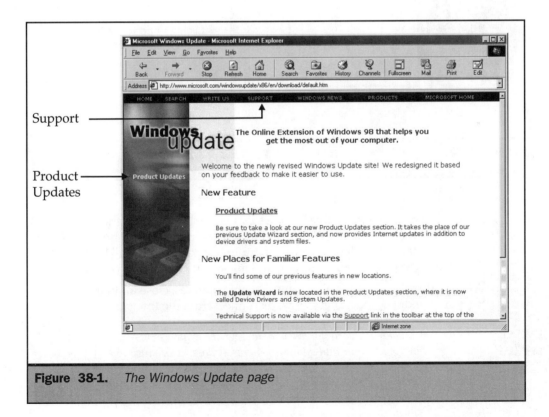

Figure 38-1.   *The Windows Update page*

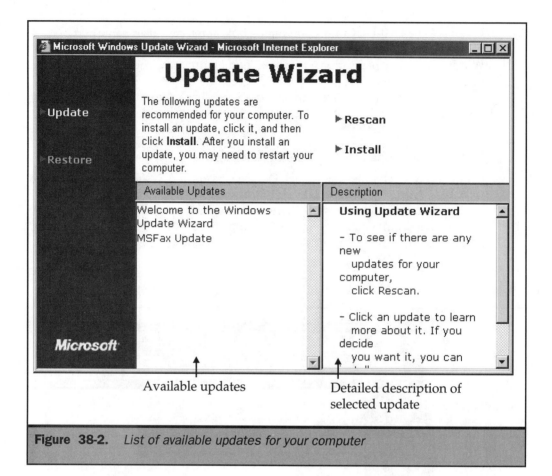

Available updates   Detailed description of
                           selected update

Figure 38-2.   *List of available updates for your computer*

5. Select an item on the Available Updates list. More details about the update, including the file size and download time, appear in the Description box. Click Install to install the update on your computer. Clicking the Install button downloads the file to your computer and installs the update on your system.

6. When you are finished installing the available updates, close all Internet Explorer windows and, if necessary, disconnect from the Internet.

Note   *Running the Update Wizard forces you to register your copy of Microsoft, including giving your name and address. Microsoft doesn't promise to keep this information confidential—in fact, they may sell this information to other companies for marketing or market research purposes. There have been several rumors about Microsoft gathering information about its customers surreptitiously during online registration, but these rumors have never been substantiated.*

What Materials Are Available from Microsoft?

In addition to using Windows Update to install updates on your computer, you can also use it to gather information and learn more about Windows 98. The Technical Support link on the Windows Update page gives you access to reference materials that are available from Microsoft, including articles dealing with program changes, work solutions, and better ways to use Microsoft products.

To access materials about Windows 98 from Windows Update, choose Start | Windows Update (or Start | Settings | Windows Update) and then click Support. You see the Support web page, shown in Figure 38-3. Make sure Windows 98 or All Products is selected in box 1, type the word or phrase you're looking for in box 2, and then click Find. (Since this pages is on the Web, Microsoft may change its content or design anytime, but we expect similar features to appear.)

When you click Find, a list of articles related to your topic appears. Click any article that looks interesting to see the full text of the article.

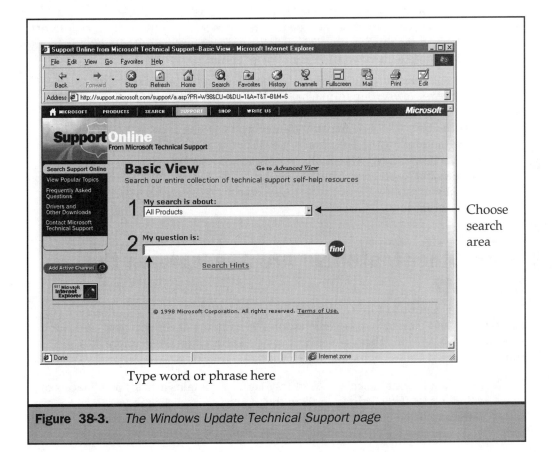

Figure 38-3.   *The Windows Update Technical Support page*

If you're confused by terminology and need to look up the definition of a word, click Glossary on the Technical Support page. In the Glossary, click the letter the word begins with, and then select Edit | Find (On This Page). Type the word you want to find and then click Find Next.

Other materials about Windows 98, besides those listed on the Technical Support page, are available from Microsoft:

■ The main Windows 98 page at **http://www.microsoft.com/windows98** is a good resource for general announcements and information about Windows 98. If you are upgrading from Windows 95 or Windows 3.1, click the All About link and select Features to see a list of the new features included in Windows 98. Keep scrolling down the page and you'll find a list of changes that have been made to the features you're familiar with from your version of Windows.

■ Each component included with Windows 98 has its own page at the Microsoft web site. For announcements and information about Internet Explorer, go to **http://www.microsoft.com/ie/ie40**. In the Contents area of the screen, click Features to see an overview of the new features incorporated as part of Internet Explorer. From the Features list, click the program, such as Outlook Express or NetMeeting, that you want to know more about.

■ Microsoft maintains hundreds of Usenet newsgroups on its news servers (see "What Are Newsgroups?" in Chapter 23). To add a Microsoft news server to your list of servers in Outlook Express, click Launch Outlook Express on the Taskbar. Select Tools | Accounts, and click the News tab. Click Add, choose News, and follow the prompts as the Wizard walks you through the steps to add the news server. The public Microsoft news server is named msnews.microsoft.com. After you add the server, download all the newsgroups so that you can see a list of what's available on the server. Several groups discuss Windows.

What Other Materials Are Available on the Internet?

Windows 98 is a popular topic on the Internet. A number of web sites, news services, newsgroups, and mailing lists cover Windows 98 and are not connected to or sponsored by Microsoft. These web sites provide information on a variety of computer-related issues, including Windows 98:

■ **http://www.winmag.com** *Windows Magazine* contains articles on all facets of Windows 98. Type **Windows 98** in the search box and click Search. Articles are rated and listed in order according to the best match. When you see an article you want to read, click the link to see the full article.

- **http://www.zdnet.com/pcmag** *PC Magazine* prints articles on a variety of computer topics, including Windows 98. To search for an article from the magazine, click Search and then type **Windows 98** in the Search box. The most recent articles are listed first.

- **http://www.cnet.com** The Computer Network (CNET) has the current news on all things related to computers. If you don't see an article on Windows 98 on the home page, click Search.Com and search for Windows 98. CNET searches resources around the Web to locate pages. Click a link to visit the site and view the information.

- **http://net.gurus.com/win98tcr** Our own web site for readers of the book. As we find useful information about Windows 98, we'll post it on this web site.

Channels are web sites that send information to you. Several channels are supplied with Windows 98, including many in the Technology field. From the Active Channel bar, click the News & Technology heading, type **Windows 98** in the search box, and then click Find (see "Subscribing to Channels" in Chapter 25).

Information on the Internet changes quickly. To search the Web for other Windows 98-related information, see "Finding What You Want on the Web" in Chapter 25.

Usenet Newsgroups

Newsgroups are discussion arenas on the Internet (see "What Are Newsgroups?" in Chapter 23). In addition to the newsgroups hosted by Microsoft, many other newsgroups, unaffiliated with Microsoft, discuss Windows 98 topics.

To find newsgroups about Windows 98, run Outlook Express or your favorite newsreader, and then search for newsgroups with **win** in the newsgroup name.

When you are searching for newsgroups, you can enter as few or as many characters as you like. The more characters you enter, the narrower the search. For example, a search for "Windows" will not show newsgroups with Win98 in the title.

If you can't find the type of discussion you want in the newsgroups listed on your ISP's news server, use the web site **http://www.dejanews.com** as a resource for newsgroup information. The Dejanews service is a web page that lets you search past newsgroup articles. You can search for newsgroup messages containing a word or phrase, or read messages from newsgroups that do not appear on your news server.

E-Mail Mailing Lists

Joining a mailing list is another way to obtain information via the Internet. A mailing list is like an e-mail based newsgroup—people sign up for the mailing list and receive all messages posted to the list. Whenever a member posts a message to the list, everyone on the list receives it as an e-mail message. Everyone who receives a message can respond to the list, and that's how discussions take place.

Each list has a list administrator who handles requests from people wanting to join the list. You can obtain information from the list administrator on how to subscribe and unsubscribe from the list. Many lists also offer the option of subscribing to a digest of postings, so that you receive a summary of messages instead of each individual e-mail message.

Mailing lists focus on specific topics. Whether you're interested in discussing Java programming or raising show dogs, there is probably a mailing list devoted to your subject.

The best way to find a mailing list is to seek recommendations from friends or colleagues. Traffic on a mailing list can become overwhelming (few people want hundreds of messages sent to their e-mail box each day), so it's important to find a list that not only fits the subjects you want to discuss, but also has the number of members that suits your needs.

If you can't locate a mailing list through recommendations, you can search the Web. Many web sites are available that show lists of mailing lists: our favorite is Liszt, at **http://www.liszt.com**.

You will get different results with each search engine. Use a few different search engines, and compile a short list of mailing lists you want to join. Try out each list until you locate the one(s) that discuss and distribute the information you need. Be sure to follow netiquette (see "What Is Netiquette?" in Chapter 23) and to read the FAQ (list of frequently asked questions) before asking questions of your own.

Part VII

Behind the Scenes: Windows 98 Internals

Chapter 39

Windows 98 Configuration and Control Files

W indows 98 stores its control and configuration information in a wide variety of files of different formats, including files for configuring both DOS and Windows. Windows comes with a program called System Configuration Utility (or Msconfig for short) to help make controlled changes to some of its configuration files. This chapter explains the configuration files used by Windows 98, as well as how to run the System Configuration Utility program. The last section, "Disk Formats and Coexisting with Other Operating Systems," contains some pointers for running both Windows 98 and another operating system (like UNIX) on the same computer.

What Kinds of Control Files Does Windows 98 Use?

Other than the Registry (described in Chapter 40), most of Windows' control information is stored in text files that you can open with Notepad or any other text editor. Although changing these files is usually a bad idea unless you're quite sure you know what you're doing, opening them and looking at their contents is entirely safe.

Hidden and Read-Only Files

Most of the control information is stored in hidden, system, and read-only files (see "What Are Attributes?" in Chapter 9). Hidden and system files are like any other files, except that they don't normally appear in file listings when you use Windows Explorer or a Folder window to display a folder that contains them. (Any file can be hidden, but only a couple of required files in the root folder of the boot drive are system files.) Read-only files can't be changed or deleted.

You can easily tell Windows to show you all the hidden files on your computer. In a Windows Explorer window that's displaying a folder, select View | Folder Options and then click the View tab. In the list of Advanced Settings are options for hidden and system files. Click Show All Files. If you just want to see the hidden files in this folder, click OK. To see hidden files whenever you open a folder, click Like Current Folder and then click OK. Hidden files appear listed with regular files, but their icons are paler than regular files.

You can change a file's hidden or system status by right-clicking the file and selecting Properties. Click the Hidden and Read-Only check boxes at the bottom of the Properties dialog box to select or deselect these attributes.

DOS Initialization Files

When you start Windows 98, it actually starts MS-DOS first, and then starts Windows from DOS. Several DOS configuration files control the DOS *boot* (startup) process. All of them reside in the root folder of the *boot disk*, usually C:\.

The Msdos.sys File

In versions of MS-DOS through 6.2, Msdos.sys was an executable program file that was run as part of the initial boot process. In Windows 95, it became a text file with commands to control the startup process. A typical Msdos.sys starts like this:

```
WinDir=C:\WINDOWS
WinBootDir=C:\WINDOWS
HostWinBootDrv=C
UninstallDir=C:\

[Options]
BootMulti=1
BootGUI=1
DoubleBuffer=1
AutoScan=1
```

Particularly if you're having trouble getting Windows to run reliably, you may want to make some changes to Msdos.sys to report in more detail the progress of the boot process. Rather than editing Msdos.sys directly, use the System Configuration Utility to make changes in a controlled fashion (see "Changing Your Startup Settings").

Special Setup for MS-DOS Programs

Although Windows 98 provides backward-compatible support for MS-DOS drivers, it's a good idea to avoid DOS drivers, if at all possible, since they run with full system privileges (meaning that any bugs can corrupt or crash the system) and can slow down the system.

If you have a DOS program that requires special setup or drivers, you can configure that program so that it runs in stand-alone DOS mode using its own Config.sys and Autoexec.bat files. If you have a DOS program that you run in a DOS window, you can put startup commands into a batch file and configure the DOS program so that the batch file runs just before the program starts (see "Controlling Startup and Basic Operation" in Chapter 41). In most cases, these techniques let you avoid loading DOS drivers into Windows 98.

The Config.sys File

MS-DOS gives you considerable control over its configuration. Config.sys contains commands that control the way DOS sets itself up, and also contains commands to load real-mode device drivers. On most Windows 98 systems, this file is empty, but it's available in case you have a device that has a DOS driver but no Windows driver, or an old MS-DOS application that requires special DOS drivers to work.

Microsoft includes two files that describe the contents of Config.sys, both of which you can open in Notepad:

- C:\Windows\Config.txt describes the commands that can appear in Config.sys.
- C:\Windows\Msdosdrv.txt describes the MS-DOS drivers provided with Windows 98. All the drivers either provide backward compatibility for old applications or support ancient hardware, such as EGA screen controllers.

To make changes to Config.sys, you can use Notepad or any text editor, but it's safer to use the System Configuration Utility (see "Configuring Windows Using the System Configuration Utility").

The Autoexec.bat File

Autoexec.bat complements Config.sys. While Config.sys is read during the DOS startup process, Autoexec.bat contains regular DOS commands to be run as soon as DOS has finished starting up. Although any DOS command is valid, the only command commonly used is SET, which defines environment variables used by some programs and drivers.

You can use Notepad or any text editor to make changes to Autoexec.bat, but it's safer to use the System Configuration Utility.

Windows Initialization Files

Windows 98 uses a combination of initialization files and the Registry to control its operations. The initialization files are, for the most part, a holdover from Windows 3.1, with newer control information placed in the Registry. Some Windows 3.1 applications stored their setup information in individual *INI files* (Windows initialization files), such as Progman.ini for the Windows 3.1 Program Manager, while others used sections in the general-purpose Win.ini file.

All INI files have the file extension .ini and nearly all reside in the C:\Windows folder. All INI files have a common format, of which the following is a typical example:

```
[Desktop]
Wallpaper=C:\WINDOWS\BLACKT~1.BMP
TileWallpaper=1
WallpaperStyle=0
Pattern=(None)

;; International settings
[intl]
iCountry=1
ICurrDigits=2
iCurrency=0
```

An INI file is divided into sections, with each section starting with a section name in square brackets. Within a section, each line is of the form *parameter=value*, where the value may be a filename, number, or other string. Blank lines and lines that start with a semicolon are ignored.

 In general, editing the Win.ini or System.ini file is a bad idea, but if you need to do so, use the System Configuration Utility.

The Win.ini File

In Windows 3.1, nearly every scrap of setup information in the entire system ended up in the Win.ini file in C:\Windows, meaning that if any program messed up Win.ini, the system could be nearly unusable. Windows 95 and 98 alleviated this situation by moving much of the information into the Registry, but Win.ini still contains a great deal of setup information, primarily from components that haven't changed much since the days of Windows 3.1. You'll typically find sections for many of your application programs in Win.ini, plus a little setup information for Windows itself.

Use the System Configuration Utility to edit the Win.ini file.

The System.ini File

In Windows 3.1, the System.ini file in C:\Windows listed all the Windows device and subsystem drivers to be loaded at startup. In Windows 98, some but not all of the driver information has moved into the Registry, but System.ini still contains a lot of driver configuration information. Use the System Configuration Utility to edit the System.ini file.

The Registry

The Windows Registry contains all of the configuration information not in an INI file, including the vast majority of the actual information used to control Windows 98 and its applications. Use Registry Editor to examine and manage the Registry (see Chapter 40).

Configuring Windows Using the System Configuration Utility

Microsoft provides the System Configuration Utility to help you make controlled changes to the various configuration files described earlier in this chapter. To run the System Configuration Utility, choose Start | Run, type **msconfig** in the Open box, and click OK. (Alternatively, click or double-click the Msconfig.exe filename in your C:\Windows\System folder using Windows Explorer or a Folder window). You see the System Configuration Utility window, shown in Figure 39-1.

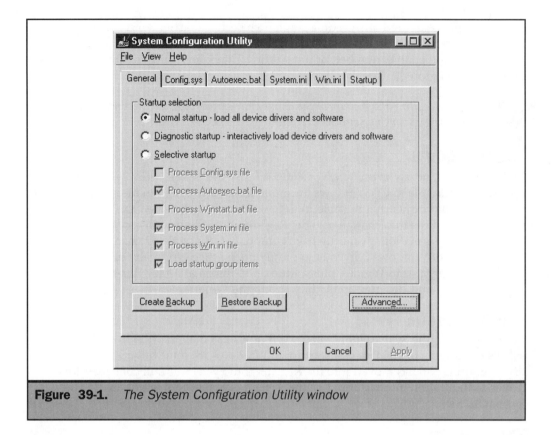

Figure 39-1.   *The System Configuration Utility window*

Some of the tabs in this window display information that disappears off the right side of the System Configuration Utility window. Drag the right edge of the window to make it wide enough to display some of the longer settings.

The System Configuration Utility includes a tab for each configuration file, along with the Startup tab, which lists information from the Registry about programs to be run at startup time. Changes you make don't take effect until the next time Windows restarts, so when you close the System Configuration Utility, it asks whether you want to save the changes you've made; if you click Yes, it offers to reboot Windows for you.

Choosing View from the System Configuration Utility menu bar displays a list of dialog boxes and windows that you might want to refer to when editing your system configuration (a nice convenience!).

Backing Up Your Configuration Files

Before you make any changes, click the Create Backup button on the General tab to make a backup copy of all the configuration files. The System Configuration Utility creates backups that have the same filenames as the original files, but the extension .pss. If you foul up any configuration files and have made a backup, you can click the Restore Backup button to copy the .pss backup files to their original names, overwriting the fouled-up versions of the files.

Restarting Windows with Various Startup Options

The General tab of the System Configuration Utility window can help you restart Windows in one of its startup modes that help diagnose problems (see "Startup Modes" in Chapter 37). To restart Windows in Step-By-Step Confirmation Mode, follow these steps:

1. Click the General tab, click the Diagnostic Startup setting, and then click OK. Windows asks whether you want to reboot your computer.

2. Click Yes. Windows shuts down, and then restarts. You see the Windows 98 Startup Menu.

3. Choose Step-By-Step Confirmation from the menu. Windows prompts you to press Y or N at each stage of system startup.

If you want to restart Windows and tell it to process only specific configuration files, click the Selective Startup setting on the General tab of the System Configuration Utility window, and then choose the files to process. When you click OK, Windows asks whether you want to reboot your computer. Click Yes. Windows restarts and processes only the files you specified. To save your changes without restarting Windows, click Apply (the changes to the files are saved, but still don't go into effect until you reboot).

Changing Advanced Settings

A number of settings can be changed using the System Configuration Utility, but Microsoft doesn't recommend changing them unless you know exactly what you are doing. To see and change these settings, click the Advanced button on the General tab of the System Configuration Utility window. You see the Advanced Troubleshooting Settings dialog box, shown in Figure 39-2. Table 39-1 describes each setting on the list. Be sure to click Cancel when exiting this dialog box unless you are absolutely sure you want to make changes.

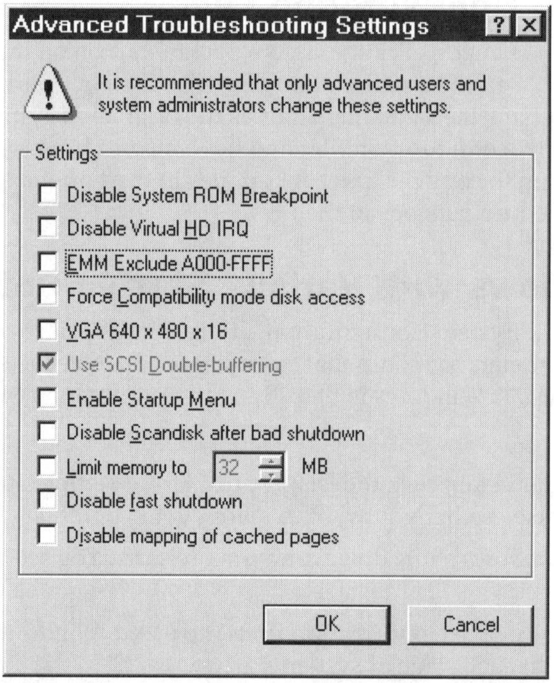

Figure 39-2.   *Changing advanced Windows configuration settings (use with care)*

Setting	Description
Disable System ROM Breakpoint	Specifies that Windows cannot use addresses in the ROM (read-only memory) address space for a breakpoint.
Disable Virtual HD IRQ	Specifies that program routines in your computer's ROM handle interrupts from the hard disk controller, rather than Windows handling them.
EMM Exclude A000-FFFF	Specifies that the upper memory area (address A000-FFFF), often used by the system's BIOS and by screen controllers, be excluded from Windows 98's memory space. This setting is usually selected.

Table 39-1.   *Advanced Windows Configuration Settings*

Setting	Description
Force Compatibility Mode Disk Access	Specifies that disk input and output (I/O) occur using your computer CPU's real mode.
VGA 640x480x16	Specifies that Windows use the low-resolution VGA display driver.
Use SCSI Double-Buffering	Specifies that Windows double-buffer information to and from SCSI devices (devices connected to your computer via a SCSI controller).
Enable Startup Menu	Specifies that every time your computer starts up, you see the Windows 98 Startup Menu rather than Windows starting.
Disable Scandisk After Bad Shutdown	Specifies that when you restart your computer after shutting down abnormally (for example, turning off the computer without shutting down Windows), Windows does not automatically run ScanDisk.
Limit Memory To xx MB	Specifies the maximum amount of memory that Windows uses. Use this setting when you suspect that bad memory locations are causing errors. Windows requires at least 16MB to load, so don't enter a number less than 16.
Disable Fast Shutdown	Specifies that Windows not use features that allow it to shut down faster.
Disable Mapping Of Cached Pages	Specifies that Windows not map cached pages, a feature that makes the virtual memory system run faster.

Table 39-1.   *Advanced Windows Configuration Settings* (continued)

Changing Your Config.sys and Autoexec.bat Files

The Config.sys and Autoexec.bat tabs in the System Configuration Utility window (Figure 39-3) show all the lines in your Config.sys and Autoexec.bat files. A check box appears to the left of each line (except for lines beginning with *REM*, which indicates a remark that Windows ignores).

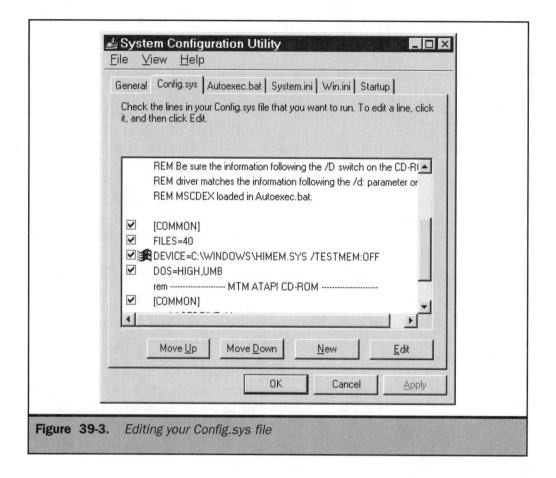

Figure 39-3. *Editing your Config.sys file*

To disable a line, click its check box to remove the check mark. The order in which drivers are loaded can make a difference as to how well they work; to change the order in which the lines of the file appear, click a line and click the Move Up or Move Down buttons. To edit a line, click the line, and then click the Edit button. To add a new line, click the line after which you want to insert the line, and then click the New button.

Changing Your System.ini and Win.ini Files

The System.ini and Win.ini tabs in the System Configuration Utility window (Figure 39-4) show a list of the sections in the System.ini and Win.ini files. To see the individual lines within a section, click the plus box to the left of the section name. To disable an entire section, click the check box to the left of the section name. To disable an individual line, click the check box to its left. You can also edit or change the order of the lines or insert new lines as described in the preceding section.

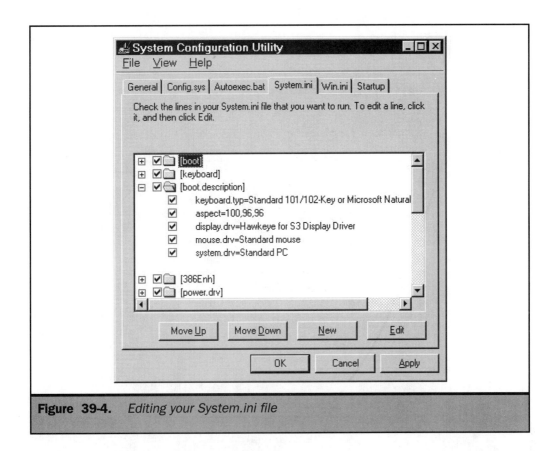

Figure 39-4.   *Editing your System.ini file*

Changing Your Startup Settings

The Startup tab in the System Configuration Utility window (Figure 39-5) shows the programs that run when Windows starts up, including the startup programs listed in the Registry, the programs in your Startup folder (usually stored in the C:\Windows\ Start Menu\Programs\Startup folder), and files mentioned in your Msdos.sys file. You can disable loading a program at startup by clicking its check box to remove the check mark. Unlike editing your Config.sys and Autoexec.bat files, you can't change the order in which the programs load.

Disk Formats and Coexisting with Other Operating Systems

Windows can share a hard disk with some other operating systems.

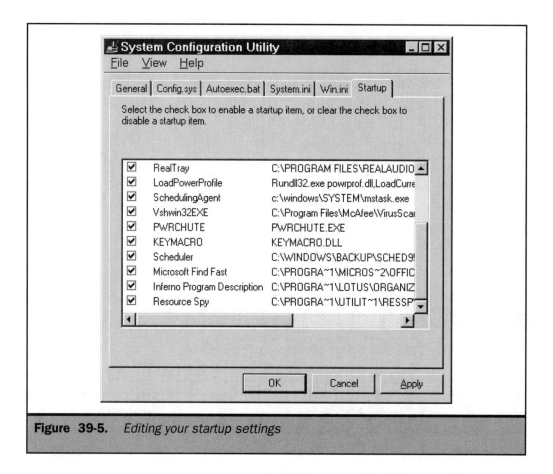

Figure 39-5. *Editing your startup settings*

FDISK and the Disk Partition Table

One way for multiple operating systems to be installed on a single hard disk is for each system to be assigned one or two partitions on the disk, and use its partition(s) when running. Windows 98 can share a system with OS/2 or UNIX this way. Windows uses a Primary DOS partition and, optionally, a Secondary DOS partition. Most other operating systems use a single partition. The Windows 98 FDISK utility creates Windows 98 partitions and respects partitions created by other systems, but cannot create a partition for any other system (see "Partitioning a Disk with the FDISK Program" in Chapter 11).

There are two ways to partition a disk between Windows 98 and another system:

■ **Install Windows 98 first** When running FDISK, tell it to use only as much of the disk as you want to assign to Windows, and leave the rest of the disk unassigned. Once Windows is installed, shut Windows down and install the other system, which generally creates its own partition using the rest of the disk.

■ **Install the other system first**   The equivalent of FDISK provided with most other operating systems can create a Primary DOS partition at the same time it creates its own partition. Once the other system is installed, shut the system down and install Windows 98, which automatically uses the existing Primary DOS partition.

A few systems offer other ways to coexist with Windows or DOS. For example, some versions of Linux (a popular, free UNIX-like system) can create a large file in a DOS partition and use that file as the Linux partition. This makes it possible to install Linux, even on a system that has Windows 98 preinstalled and assigns the entire disk to the DOS partition.

Other Operating Systems and Windows Files

Windows is completely unable to read or write files in anything other than a FAT16 or FAT32 DOS partition. It can't even read files in a Windows NT 4.x partition. (This says more about internal politics at Microsoft than about the technical difficulties involved.)

Fortunately, nearly every other operating system that runs on a PC can deal with DOS and Windows files. Most UNIX-like systems, for example, can logically mount a FAT16 DOS partition so that it appears to be part of the UNIX file system. Consult the documentation for your other operating system to find out how to give it access to your Windows files.

You cannot create a system that can run both Windows 98 and Windows 95. For information about running both Windows 98 and Windows 3.1 on the same system, see Appendix A.

Chapter 40

Registering Programs and File
Types

The Windows Registry stores configuration information about the programs you run, including which program is used to open, create, and edit each type of data file. You can use the Registry Editor program to edit the Registry, but do so with caution!

What Is the Registry?

Early versions of Windows scattered configuration settings among dozens of different files. Many settings were stored in C:\Windows\Win.ini and C:\Windows\System.ini, but programs were as likely to use their own INI files as the standard ones, and there was no consistency in the way that INI files were created and maintained (see "Windows Initialization Files" in Chapter 39). In Windows 95, Microsoft created the *Registry*, a single centralized database in which programs keep their setup information. It contains all of the information that the INI files contained, as well as other settings from around the system.

Most of the time, the Registry works automatically in the background, but in a few circumstances, you may want to change it yourself.

The Registry is stored in two hidden files, System.dat and User.dat, which are stored in your C:\Windows folder. Windows automatically makes backups of these files each time you start Windows, in cabinet files with names like C:\Windows\Sysbckup\rb002.cab. (It can keep several backups in several cabinet files.) The System.dat file stores information about the software on your computer system, and User.dat stores information about your usage of the software; if your computer is set up for several users, user-specific information about all users is stored in User.dat.

Associating File Types with Programs

In Windows, every file has a *file type*, determined by the three-letter file extension after the dot (see "What Are Extensions and File Types?" in Chapter 8). For example, My Proposal.doc has type DOC, so one usually calls it a DOC file. Every file type can be *associated* with a program or group of programs, so when you open a file of that type in Windows Explorer or a Folder window (by clicking or double-clicking the file), the associated program runs automatically to process the file. Most programs associate themselves with the appropriate file types when you install the program, but in a few circumstances, as described next, you may want to set your own associations:

- Sometimes there are *dueling programs*, where two or more programs can handle the same type of file, and whichever one you installed most recently wins, unless you intervene. This is particularly common with graphics formats such as GIF and JPG, because any graphics editing program and most web browsers can display them. You can change the association to whichever program you prefer. Another common pair of dueling programs are Microsoft Word and the

Word Viewer. Depending on how you prefer to work, when you click a DOC file, you may want Word to run as the default action, so that you can edit the file, or you may want Word Viewer to run, so that you can quickly look at the file.

■ Many files with unknown types are, in fact, known types in disguise, or close enough to known types that a program you have installed can handle them. For example, most LOG files are actually text files that WordPad or any other text editor can read. Word processors can almost all read each other's files; for example, if you run WordPerfect rather than Word, you can associate DOC files with WordPerfect.

The Windows file association facility is extremely complex and flexible. A file type can have several programs associated with it to do different actions, such as viewing and editing a file. The usual way to process a file is to open an application, but file associations can also use DDE (Dynamic Data Exchange), a Windows facility that enables one running program to send a message to another program (see "What Is DDE?" in Chapter 7).

For each registered file extension, there's a MIME type and an application to handle that type of file. The MIME type is a description used in e-mail and web pages; it's useful if you send and receive mail with attached files, but it's not essential (see "Attaching a File to a Message" in Chapter 23).

To see or change the details of a file association or to create a new association, open any disk drive or folder in Windows Explorer, and then choose View | Folder Options. In the Folder Options window, click File Types. Highlight a file type in the list of types, and then click Edit to see the Edit File Type dialog box, which contains a description of the type, the MIME type (if any), the usual extension for the type, and a list of actions (see "Creating or Editing an Association" in Chapter 3, which explains how to create or change a file association).

Tip *When you select a file whose extension isn't associated with any program, Windows opens an Open With window. You can create a file association by entering a short description of the file type and selecting the appropriate application from the list. Unless you uncheck the Always Use This Program To Open This File box, Windows saves the association permanently.*

Editing the Registry

The Windows Registry contains a great deal of information beyond the file associations discussed in the previous section. For the most part, you won't need to do any editing yourself, but occasionally, a bug fix or parameter change requires a change to the Registry, so you need to be prepared to do a little editing now and then. If you're interested in how Windows works, you can also spend as much time as you want nosing around the Registry to see what's stored in it. You use Windows Registry

Checker to make sure that the Registry is not corrupted and Registry Editor to look at or edit the Registry.

Checking the Registry for Consistency

Windows Registry Checker (also called Scanreg) checks the Registry for internal consistency. Use it before and after you do any Registry editing. To run Windows Registry Checker, follow these steps.

1. Choose Start | Run.
2. In the Run window, type **scanreg**, and press ENTER.
3. Windows Registry Checker checks the Registry. Then it offers to back up the registry.
4. Click Yes to make a backup copy of the Registry.

Making a Backup of the Registry Before Editing and Restoring from a Backup

Before you make any changes to the Registry, it's a good idea to make a backup of the two files in which the Registry is stored: C:\Windows\System.dat and C:\Windows\User.dat. To make backup copies, run Windows Registry Checker as just described. To skip the consistency check, type **scanreg /backup** in the Run window to force a backup.

If you corrupt the Registry while editing it, you can restore it to its state before the backup (see "In Case of Registry Disaster").

Running Registry Editor

Registry Editor (Regedit, for short) lets you edit anything in the registry. To run Registry Editor, select Start | Run, type **regedit**, and press ENTER.

Registry Editor has almost no built-in checks or validation, so be very sure that you make any changes correctly. Incorrect registry entries can lead to anything from occasional flaky behavior to complete system failure.

The Registry is organized much like the Windows file system. The Registry contains a large set of *keys* which are like folders, with keys stored within keys. Key name components are written with reverse slashes between them, much like filenames, so a typical key name is

HKEY_LOCAL_MACHINE\System\CurrentControlSet\
Services\VxD\VNETSUP

Each key is shown as a folder in the left pane of the Registry Editor window. Each key can have one or more *values*, each of which consists of a name and some data. The data can be a *string* (text), a *DWORD* (a numeric value), or a *binary string* (a sequence of binary or hexadecimal digits). Unlike the file system, a key at any level can contain any number of values, so in the example above, there could be values associated with HKEY_LOCAL_MACHINE\System\CurrentControlSet\Services or HKEY_LOCAL_MACHINE\System. (In practice, most of the values are stored at the lowest level or next-to-lowest level.) When you select a key in the left pane, the name and data of each of its values appear in the right pane.

Finding Registry Entries

If you know the name of the key you want, navigating through the key names is very similar to navigating through files in Windows Explorer. Registry Editor has a two-part window, shown in Figure 40-1, much like Windows Explorer. You can expand and contract parts of the name tree by clicking the + and - icons in the key area. Select any key to see the names and data of the values, if any, associated with that key.

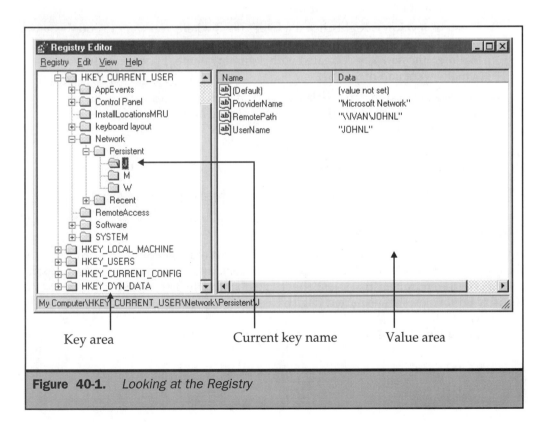

Figure 40-1. *Looking at the Registry*

If you don't know the name of the key, you can search for it by choosing Edit | Find. You can search for any combination of keys, value names, and value data. For example, if you mistyped your name at the time you set up Windows 98 and want to correct it, search for the mistyped name as value data. Use F3 to step from one match to the next.

Adding and Changing Registry Entries

You can add, edit, and delete registry entries (but be sure you backed up the registry first):

- **Change the data of a value** Double-click the name of the value (in the Name column of the right pane of the Registry Editor window). Registry Editor displays a dialog box in which you can enter the new data for the value. You can't change the type of a value, so you have to enter a text string, a numeric value, or a string of hexadecimal digits, depending on the type of the data.

- **Rename a key or a value** Right-click its name and choose Rename from the menu that appears.

- **Create a new key** Right-click the folder (key) where you want to add the new key and choose New | Key from the menu that appears. As in Windows Explorer, the new key is created with a dummy name. Type the name you actually want and press ENTER.

- **Create a new value** Right-click the key in which you want store the new value, choose New from the menu that appears, and choose the type of value (String Value, Binary Value, or DWORD). Once you've created a value, double-click the value's name to enter its data.

- **Delete a value or key** Select the value or key and press the DELETE key.

You can also rename and delete keys and values by using the Edit menu.

Editing the Registry as a Text File

Another way to edit the Registry is to export all or part of the Registry to a text file, edit the text file, and then import the changed values back into the Registry. You can export and import the entire registry or just one "branch" of the Registry's tree of keys. Registry Editor stores the exported Registry entries in a *registration file* with the extension .reg.

A registration file consists of a series of lines that look like this:

```
[HKEY_CLASSES_ROOT\.bfc\ShellNew\Config]
"NoExtension"="Temp"
```

The first line is the name of the key (enclosed in square brackets) and the lines that follow are the values in the key, in the format *"name"="value"*.

Follow these steps to edit the Registry by using a text editor:

1. Select a key in the left pane, choosing one that contains all the keys that you want to edit. To export the entire Registry, select the My Computer key, which is the key at the root of the Registry tree.

2. Choose Registry | Export to write the text file. Registry Editor asks you for the folder and filename to use for the registration file.

3. Edit the registration file in any text editor. Notepad works if you export only a section of the Registry. Make as few changes as possible to the file, then save the file.

4. In Registry Editor, choose Registry | Import to read the edited file back into the Registry. The keys and values in the imported file replace the corresponding keys and values in the Registry.

The Registry is quite large—an exported version of the whole thing can be three megabytes or more. If you do plan to edit it, just export the branch you plan to work on.

In Case of Registry Disaster

Each time you start Windows, it makes a backup of the entire Registry, and you can make additional backups whenever you want. If the Registry becomes seriously damaged, either due to an editing mistake or program failure, you can restore the Registry to its state as of the last time it was automatically backed up.

Restart Windows in Command Prompt Only mode (see "Starting in a Special Mode" in Chapter 37). At the DOS prompt, type **scanreg /restore** and press ENTER. Then restart Windows normally.

The Complete Reference

Chapter 41

Running DOS Programs and
Commands

Y ou may need to install and run older DOS programs on your Windows 98 system. Windows provides ways to run DOS programs and commands, cut-and-paste between DOS and Windows programs, and configure how DOS programs work with the screen, mouse, and keyboard. If you're an old hand at DOS, you may also wonder what's happened to two files that were crucial to DOS: Autoexec.bat and Config.sys. This chapter covers all of these topics.

What Is DOS?

MS-DOS (or *DOS* for short) is a simple operating system that was the predecessor to Windows. DOS version 1.0 was created in about 1981, at the same time as (but not originally for) the original IBM PC, and later versions—through DOS 6.22—added features and supported more recent hardware. Early versions of Windows (through 3.11) were add-ons for DOS—first you installed DOS on your computer, and then Windows, and then you started Windows from the DOS command prompt. Windows 95 and 98 still have a version of DOS buried inside them, although they integrate many of the DOS functions into Windows.

DOS provides only disk file management and the most rudimentary support for the screen, keyboard, mouse, timer, and other peripherals. As a result, interactive *DOS programs* (programs written to work with DOS rather than Windows) have to create their own user interfaces, usually by directly operating the hardware controllers for the screen and sometimes other devices. DOS supports only 640K of memory, so a variety of add-on drivers were developed by Microsoft and others to handle more memory than that.

DOS doesn't have a graphical user interface (GUI), doesn't usually display windows, and doesn't usually work with a mouse. Instead, you type commands at the *DOS prompt*, a symbol that indicates that DOS is waiting for you to type a *command line* (command, optionally followed by additional information). The default DOS prompt is C:\>.

Windows, on the other hand, provides extensive facilities to handle the screen and keyboard, and sophisticated memory management, which all Windows applications use. These facilities can make it difficult to run some DOS programs under Windows, because the DOS programs and Windows can't both control the same hardware at the same time.

How Does Windows Handle DOS Programs?

Windows can run DOS programs in two different ways: As an application running under Windows, or as a stand-alone program in a bare DOS environment. Alternatively, you can dispense with Windows altogether and restart your machine in MS-DOS mode.

The DOS Window

The most convenient way to run most DOS programs is in a DOS window while Windows is running. Windows creates a *virtual machine* for the DOS program, a special hardware and software environment that emulates enough of the features of a stand-alone environment to allow most DOS programs to run correctly. DOS programs that don't do extensive graphics can usually run within a DOS window, sharing the screen with Windows applications. Programs that require full access to the screen hardware can also take over the screen while Windows continues to run in the background.

Since Windows doesn't give the DOS program full control of the system, DOS programs running in a DOS window can run side-by-side with Windows applications and even with other DOS applications. You can cut-and-paste material between DOS programs and other programs.

Some DOS programs are *Windows aware* so that even though they don't run as Windows applications, they can check that they're being run under Windows and handle their screen and keyboard in a way that lets them run efficiently under Windows.

Stand-Alone DOS Mode

Some DOS programs, particularly some highly interactive games, require complete control of the computer. For those programs, Windows can run in stand-alone DOS mode, in which Windows shuts itself down, leaving only a small DOS system, starts the DOS application, and then restarts when the DOS application finishes.

Although this lets you run practically any DOS program, this procedure is extremely slow, since in effect it restarts Windows twice, once before the program starts and once after it runs. While the stand-alone DOS program is running, Windows isn't active, so no other programs can run.

MS-DOS Mode

If you want to use DOS and don't want to use Windows for a while, you can restart your computer without Windows. Choose Start | Shut Down, choose Restart In MS-DOS Mode, and click OK. Windows exits, DOS loads, and you see the DOS prompt. To restart Windows, type **win** and press ENTER.

 This MS-DOS mode is called Command Prompt Only mode on the Windows Startup menu (see "Startup Modes" in Chapter 37).

What Are the Config.sys and Autoexec.bat Files?

When DOS starts up, it reads configuration instructions from these two files in the root folder of the boot disk drive (usually C:\). Under Windows 98 these files are obsolete, since Windows has its own configuration management system, but they remain in place for backward compatibility with older programs. The Config.sys file contains configuration commands that DOS reads during the boot process, most notably DEVICE commands that load device drivers. The Autoexec.bat file contains DOS commands to be run as soon as DOS starts (see "DOS Initialization Files" in Chapter 39).

When you run DOS programs under Windows 98, Windows can provide Autoexec.bat and Config.sys files for programs that need them. For each program that runs in stand-alone DOS mode, Windows can create customized Config.sys and Autoexec.bat files with commands to be run before that program starts (see "Controlling Startup and Basic Operation").

Running DOS Programs

Once you run a DOS program, you can adjust the way it looks on the screen, copy-and-paste material to and from the Windows Clipboard, and finally exit.

If you have trouble running a DOS program, use the MS-DOS Troubleshooter (see "Diagnosing Problems Using Troubleshooters" in Chapter 37).

Starting DOS Programs

You run a DOS program the same way you run a Windows program, by clicking or double-clicking its icon or filename in the Windows Explorer window, a Folder window, or the Start menu, or by choosing Start | Run and typing its name into the Run window. Whether you single- or double-click icons to run programs depends on whether your system is configured with the Web style or Classic style desktop (see "Choosing the Style of Your Desktop" in Chapter 1).

You can also type DOS commands at a DOS prompt by selecting Start | Programs | MS-DOS Prompt (or by choosing Start | Run and typing **command**). You see the MS-DOS Prompt window in which you can type DOS commands, such as DIR, CHDIR, MKDIR, and DELETE, as well as run programs.

When you start either a DOS program or an MS-DOS Prompt window, you see a *DOS window*, shown in Figure 41-1. If you run a specific program to open the window, the program name appears in the title bar; if you choose the Start | Programs | MS-DOS Prompt command, the window is named MS-DOS Prompt.

To get help with DOS commands, type the command followed by /? (for example, type **copy /?** to get help with the DOS COPY command). To stop the help text from scrolling off the top of the DOS window, add | **more** to the end of the command line, like this:

```
copy /? | more
```

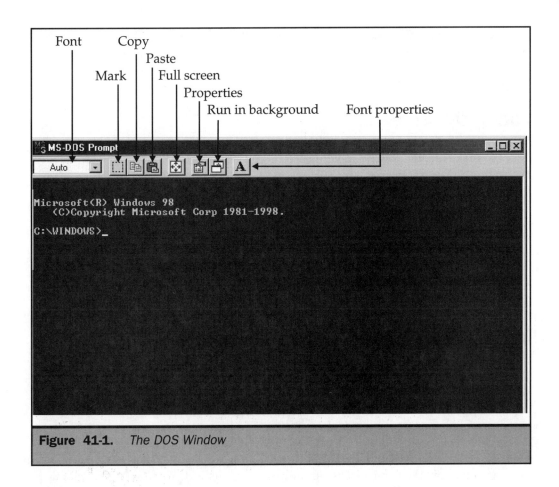

Figure 41-1. *The DOS Window*

Tip *If you can open a file by clicking or double-clicking it in Windows Explorer or a Folder window, you can open the file from the DOS prompt. Type **start** followed by a space and the path name (address) of the file. If the path name contains spaces, enclose it in double-quotes.The Start program opens the file (or folder) using the Windows file association.*

Exiting DOS Programs

Every DOS program has its own idiosyncratic command to exit. Some use a function key, some use a text command, and some use a menu command started with a slash or other character. Once the program exits, Windows changes the DOS window's title bar to Finished, but doesn't close the window to give you a chance to read any final output from the program. When you're done, click the Close button or press ALT-F4 to close the DOS window.

You can also force Windows to close a DOS window by clicking the Close button while the program is running. Windows warns you that closing the program will lose unsaved information, but if you click Yes, Windows stops the program and closes the window anyway.

Adjusting the Screen

Windows normally starts each DOS window as a 25x80 character window, choosing a font to make the window fit on your screen. You can select a different font from the Font box (the leftmost item on the toolbar), or by clicking the Font button (the rightmost button on the toolbar) to see the Font tab of the MS-DOS Prompt Properties window.

To switch between running in a window and using the full screen, click the Full screen button on the toolbar or press ALT-ENTER. (Once in a full screen, ALT-ENTER is the only way short of exiting the program to return the program to running in a window.)

To turn on and off the toolbar at the top of the DOS window, click the MS-DOS icon on the window's title bar (the System menu button) and select Toolbar from the System menu.

Using the Mouse and Clipboard

Early versions of DOS provided no mouse support at all, and even in later versions, DOS provided only the low-level support, leaving it entirely up to each application which (if any) mouse features to provide. As a result, most DOS programs provide no mouse support, so the primary use of the mouse is to cut-and-paste material to the Windows Clipboard (see "What Is the Clipboard?" in Chapter 7).

Using the Windows Clipboard

You can copy material from a DOS window to the Clipboard. To do so, first click the Mark button on the toolbar, or click the MS-DOS icon in the upper-left corner of the window and select Edit | Mark from the System menu that appears. Then use the mouse to highlight the area to copy, and click the Copy button on the toolbar or press ENTER to copy the selected area to the Clipboard.

Note   *DOS programs can place the screen (or the virtual screen emulated in a DOS window) into either text mode (which can display only text) or graphics mode (which can display any pattern of dots, including text). Windows copies the marked area as text if the screen is in text mode and as a bitmap if the screen is in graphics mode. Some programs, such as word processors, often use graphics mode to display text so that they can show font changes. Tell the DOS program to switch back to text mode before copying, to get text on the Clipboard.*

Windows lets you paste text from the Clipboard into DOS applications, too. The text is entered as though you had typed it on the keyboard, so it is up to the DOS application what to do with it. To paste, click the Paste button on the toolbar or select Edit | Paste from the System menu.

Using the Mouse in DOS Programs

In those DOS programs that do provide mouse support, using the mouse in a DOS window can be difficult. Since DOS provides no high-level mouse support, each application displays its own mouse pointer. In some Windows aware applications, the DOS mouse pointer is synchronized with the Windows mouse pointer, but more often than not, it isn't. In the latter case the best solution is usually to press ALT-ENTER to switch to full screen mode, so there's no Windows mouse pointer at all.

Printing from DOS Programs

Windows provides very limited support for printing from DOS programs. It offers a pass-through scheme that receives output from DOS programs and sends it directly to the printer. DOS programs have no access to the Windows printing subsystem, so each DOS application must have its own driver for any printer that it prints to.

DOS programs can print directly to a printer that is directly connected to your computer. Normally, Windows provides direct access to the printer, so DOS applications print directly to the printer port. In most cases it's preferable to configure your printer so that Windows intercepts the DOS output and *spools* the output as it does printer output from Windows applications (that is, Windows stores up the output and sends it to the printer). This provides more flexibility in printer management and avoids the possibility that a DOS program will interfere with an active print job from another program.

To spool DOS printer output to a local printer:

1. Select Start | Settings | Printers to open the Printers window, and then right-click the desired printer and select Properties to open the printer's Properties dialog box (see "Managing Printer Activity" in Chapter 16).

2. Click the Details tab and then the Port Settings button to get the Configure LPT Port dialog box (see "Configuring Printers" in Chapter 16).

3. Check the Spool MS-DOS Print Jobs check box.

4. Click OK in the Configure LPT Port dialog box, and then click OK in the printer Properties dialog box.

DOS programs can also print to network printers. Windows captures the output from a simulated printer port and then spools the printer output through the network in the same way that printer output is spooled from Windows programs.

To spool DOS printer output to a network printer:

1. Open the Properties dialog box for the printer you want to use, as previously described.

2. Click the Details tab, and then click Capture Printer Port to open the Capture Printer Port dialog box.

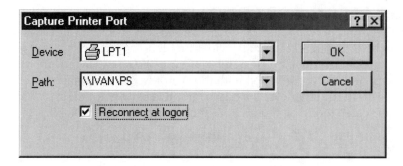

3. Select a device that does *not* correspond to a locally attached printer. (If you capture a port with a locally attached printer, you lose all access to that local printer.)

4. Enter the network path to the printer.

5. If you want this captured port to be available whenever you use Windows (most people do), check the Reconnect At Logon check box.

6. Click OK in the Capture Printer Port dialog box, and then click OK in the printer Properties dialog box.

To remove the connection between a captured printer port and a network printer, use the End Capture button on the Details tab of the printer Properties dialog box.

When you print from a DOS program to a spooled printer, either local or networked, Windows has no reliable way to tell when the DOS program is done printing. If your program doesn't print anything for several seconds, Windows assumes that it's done. This occasionally causes problems when an application prints part of a report, computes for a while, and then resumes printing, because Windows can interpret the pause in printing as the end of the print job. If this is a problem, use a locally connected printer and do *not* configure the printer to spool DOS print jobs.

Running Batch Files

DOS provides *batch files*, text files that contain a sequence of commands to be run as though typed at the DOS prompt. DOS batch files have the filename extension .bat. Windows treats a batch file as a DOS program, and opens a DOS window to run the batch file and any programs that the batch file runs. Since the Windows version of DOS lets you run any program, DOS or Windows, from the DOS prompt, you can use batch files as a poor man's script, listing a sequence of programs you want to run.

Coexisting with Other Programs

Windows normally assumes that a DOS program is interactive and can do no useful work when the DOS window is not active. Therefore, Windows suspends the program when you activate any other window. In a few cases, you do want the DOS program to continue running when its window is not active; for example, a long-running spreadsheet recalculation, or an application printing a long report. Click the Background button on the DOS window's toolbar to tell Windows to let the program continue to run in the *background* (in an inactive window).

Configuring the DOS Environment

Windows 98 provides a long list of settings for customizing the DOS environment. Nearly all the settings are parameters you can tweak to help a recalcitrant DOS program run in the Windows environment. More often than not, you can leave the settings alone and your program runs adequately, but if you need to tweak something, there are plenty of settings to tweak.

Earlier versions of Windows put the settings for DOS programs into separate *PIF files* (program information files). Windows 98 associates the settings directly with the executable file or a shortcut. (Nearly all settings can be associated with the executable file, except that if you change the icon that Windows displays for a program, Windows makes a shortcut, if you don't already have one.)

To see the properties for a DOS program, either click the Properties button on the toolbar while the program is running or right-click the program's icon in the Windows Explorer or Folder window and select Properties. If you open a DOS window by using the Start | Programs | MS-DOS Prompt command, changing the properties for that window affects all DOS windows, not whatever program happens to be running when you click the Properties button.

Tip *You can tell whether you are setting properties for all DOS windows or for a specific DOS program by looking at the title of the Properties dialog box. If the dialog box is entitled MS-DOS Prompt Properties, you are setting properties for the default DOS window. If the title bar includes the name of a program file, you are setting properties for a specific DOS program. Some DOS programs have Properties dialog boxes that display different settings from those described here.*

Although you can edit a program's properties while the program is running, most changes do not take effect until you close the program and run it again. (The main exception is changing fonts.) The following sections describe the settings on all the tabs of the MS-DOS Prompt Properties dialog box or the Properties dialog box for a DOS program.

Controlling Startup and Basic Operation

The settings on the Program tab of the MS-DOS Prompt Properties dialog box, Figure 41-2, control the startup and basic operation of a DOS program. At the top of the dialog box are the icon and name that appear on shortcuts or Start menu item for the program. The other settings include:

- **Cmd Line**   The command line to pass to the DOS program. The first thing on the command line must be the filename of the program. Many programs let you put parameters, switches, and file names in the command line as well. If you type a space followed by a question mark in the command line, Windows prompts you for command line data when you start the program and replaces the question mark with the data you enter.

- **Working**   The name of the folder to use as the program's working folder. The program reads and writes its files from this folder unless the program specifically names a different folder.

- **Batch File**   The name of a DOS batch file to run before the program starts: Rarely used.

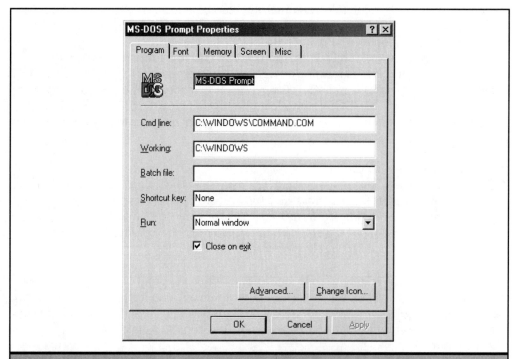

Figure 41-2.   *Choosing basic program properties for DOS programs*

- **Shortcut Key**   A key combination to use to start or activate the program (see "Running Programs Using Shortcut Keys" in Chapter 2). You can specify a CTRL- or ALT- key in combination with another key, or a plain function key.

 Any combination you specify as a shortcut can no longer be used as input by any other program running on your computer.

- **Run**   Whether to start the program in a normal, minimized, or maximized window (see "What Sizes Can Windows Be?" in Chapter 2). Most DOS programs can't handle a maximized window.

Two buttons appear at the bottom of the dialog box. The Change Icon button lets you select an icon to use for the program; the selection provided is rather nice. If you want to use an icon from another program, DLL file, or icon file (with extension .ico), click the Browse button on the Change Icon dialog box.

The Advanced button opens the Advanced Program Settings dialog box, shown in Figure 41-3. Normally, some settings on this dialog box are gray and unavailable; the figure has been modified to make all the settings readable.

The first two settings apply to programs that can run in a Window:

- **Prevent MS-DOS-based programs from detecting Windows**   Windows provides a standard technique that DOS programs can use to probe to determine whether Windows is running. Some older DOS programs behave badly when they detect Windows, generally because they are trying to work around bugs in early versions of Windows that are long-since fixed in Windows 98. This option tells Windows not to respond to the probe.

- **Suggest MS-DOS mode as necessary**   Windows normally monitors DOS programs running in a window for some operations that are unlikely to work in a Windows environment. Normally, if Windows detects one of those operations, it suggests that you switch to stand-alone DOS mode (see "Special Setup for MS-DOS Programs" in Chapter 39). If you uncheck this setting, Windows will let the program continue. Leave this setting checked unless you are absolutely sure that Windows has misdiagnosed one of those operations.

- **MS-DOS mode**   Run this program in stand-alone DOS mode.

If you select the MS-DOS mode setting, several other settings become active (see Figure 41-3).

- **Warn before entering MS-DOS mode**   Windows normally pops up a warning window when it's about to switch to stand-alone DOS mode. Uncheck this box if you like to live dangerously and let Windows shut down without warning when you run this program.

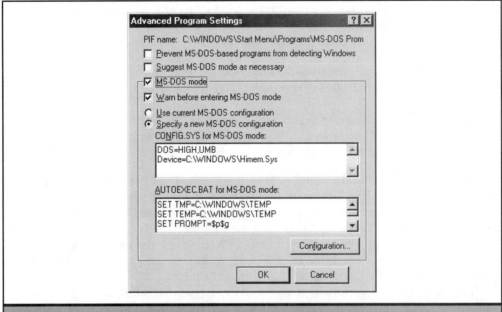

Figure 41-3.   *The Advanced Program Settings dialog box, with all settings visible*

■ **Use current MS-DOS configuration**   Use the Config.sys and Autoexec.bat files that Windows itself uses.

■ **Specify a new MS-DOS configuration**   This lets you enter Config.sys and Autoexec.bat entries to be run before this program starts.

■ **Configuration**   This button displays the Select MS-DOS Configuration Options dialog box (shown in Figure 41-4), which lets you specify some common DOS configuration options. When you click OK in this dialog box, Windows inserts appropriate lines in Config.sys and Autoexec.bat.

Controlling Fonts

The Font tab of the MS-DOS Prompt Properties dialog box, shown in Figure 41-5, lets you select the font to use in a DOS window. The Font tab doesn't let you do anything you can't do on the DOS window toolbar, but it is marginally more convenient.

You can choose among just bitmap fonts, just TrueType fonts, or both font types. Normally, you choose to display both.

The Window Preview box shows you how big your window will be relative to the Windows screen, and the Font Preview box shows what the text in the window will

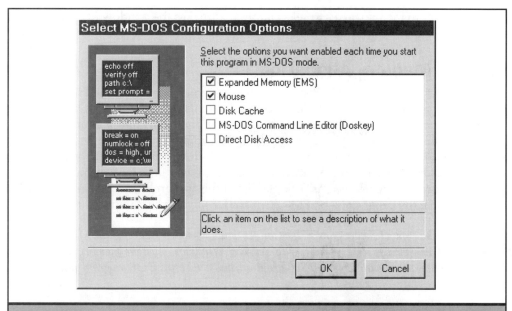

Figure 41-4.   *Selecting configuration options for starting a DOS window*

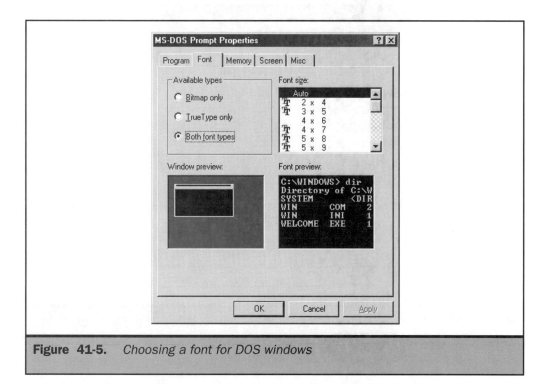

Figure 41-5.   *Choosing a font for DOS windows*

look like. Refer to the two boxes to select a font that makes the window fit on the screen and still be legible.

Controlling Memory Allocation

The Memory tab of the MS-DOS Prompt Properties dialog box, shown in Figure 41-6, controls how much memory is available to a program using each of the DOS addressing schemes. In nearly all cases, Windows automatically allocates an appropriate amount of each kind of memory to the program when it runs the program. A few programs fail if given as much memory as Windows makes available (at the time many DOS programs were written, most people never imagined that anyone would ever put as much as 4MB in a single PC). If this is a problem, determine the kind of memory that the program uses, EMS, XMS, or DPMI, and try limiting it to 8192K.

Select the Protected check box in the Conventional Memory section of the Memory tab. This setting tells Windows to protect Windows' system memory from accidental modification by the DOS program, and can keep a DOS program failure from crashing Windows.

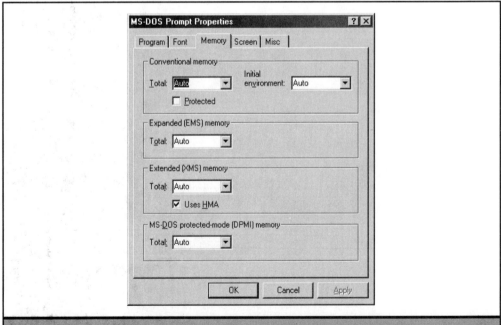

Figure 41-6.   *Setting how much memory to allocate to DOS programs*

Controlling Screen Properties

The Screen tab of the MS-DOS Prompt Properties dialog box, Figure 41-7, sets the initial size and resolution of the DOS application's window:

- **Usage**   You can choose between starting full-screen or in a window, and can select 25, 43, or 50 text lines on the screen by clicking the Initial Size box and choosing a number from the drop-down menu. (If you select more than 25, be sure that the program can handle the size you select.)

- **Window**   You can control whether to display the DOS window toolbar when the program starts, and whether to remember changes that the program makes to the screen setup from one run of the program to another. Check Restore Settings On Startup to tell Windows always to start the program with the initial settings.

- **Performance**   The two Performance settings make DOS emulation a little faster. Leave them checked, unless you observe errors in the screen display.

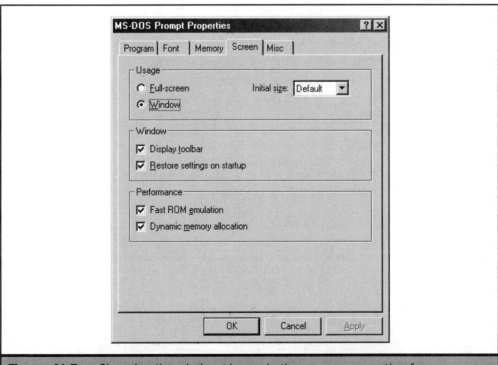

Figure 41-7.   *Choosing the window size and other screen properties for DOS windows*

Controlling Other Properties

The Misc tab of the MS-DOS Prompt Properties dialog box, Figure 41-8, controls a grab-bag of other DOS settings:

- **Allow Screen Saver** If checked, Windows can use its screen saver even when this program is in the foreground.

- **QuickEdit** If checked, any use of the mouse marks text as though you'd pressed the Mark button first. Check this box if your program makes no use of the mouse.

- **Exclusive Mode** Dedicate the mouse to this program. Not recommended, since it makes the mouse unusable as the Windows pointer until the program exits. Switch the DOS window to full-screen mode instead (by pressing ALT-ENTER), which makes the Windows mouse pointer vanish.

- **Always Suspend** Suspend this program whenever it's not the active window. Leave this box checked, unless the program does useful background activity.

- **Warn If Still Active** If checked, Windows pops up a warning box if you try to close this program before it exits.

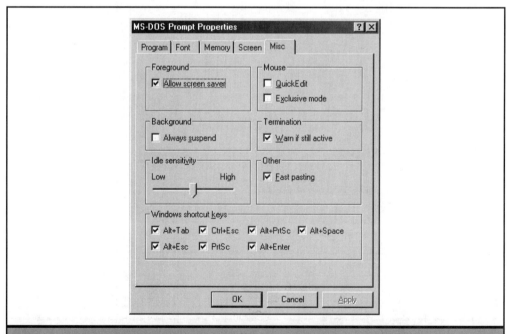

Figure 41-8.   *Choosing miscellaneous properties for DOS programs*

- **Idle Sensitivity** Windows attempts to detect when an active DOS program is idle and waiting for keyboard input, so that Windows can give more processor time to other applications. High sensitivity makes Windows give more time to other applications. Leave this alone, unless keyboard response to the program is sluggish, in which case make the sensitivity lower.

- **Fast Pasting** Windows uses an optimized technique for pasting text into a DOS window that fails with a few programs. If pasting doesn't work, turn this off.

- **Windows Shortcut Keys** The key combinations listed in this box normally perform Windows functions even when Windows is running a DOS program. If your DOS application needs to use any of these combinations itself, uncheck the ones it needs.

Installing DOS Programs

DOS provides no standard way to install programs. Most DOS programs include a simple installation batch file that copies the program's files from the installation disks to your hard disk. Once a program's files are installed, you can create shortcuts to the executable file and put those shortcuts in the Start menu or on the desktop, or both, just like native Windows applications.

Some DOS programs require that you install DOS drivers, which are loaded when Windows starts via lines in the Config.sys or Autoexec.bat files. Although Windows 98 provides surprisingly good backward-compatible support for DOS drivers, if you have an application that requires its own drivers, we recommend that you run it in a DOS window and use the Program settings on the Properties dialog box for the program to create customized Config.sys and Autoexec.bat files for that application. These files let you run your application with its drivers when you need to do so, but won't leave the drivers installed when running other Windows applications.

Chapter 42

Automating Tasks with the
Windows Scripting Host

If you've used computers long, you may remember *DOS batch files*, files containing lists of commands. Using batch files, you could store up a series of commands and run the whole series by giving just one command. When Windows supplanted DOS, many advanced users complained about the lack of a similar *scripting* capability in Windows. The Windows Scripting Host fills this lack by letting you create and run scripts. You can run scripts from Windows by using the Wscript program or from the DOS prompt by using the Cscript program. This chapter describes how to create script files, run them, configure the Wscript program, and store script settings.

What Is the Windows Scripting Host?

Windows 98 comes with the Windows Scripting Host (WSH), a program that can run scripts from either DOS or Windows. A *script* is a series of commands, like a batch file, and you can use scripts to automate repetitive tasks that you do often. Administrators of large Windows installations will find scripts an invaluable tool for creating and maintaining standard Windows configurations. For example, if you administer a large Windows installation, you can write a script that logs onto your organization's LAN, connects to various servers, and runs other housekeeping programs. You can use Windows 98's Task Scheduler and WSH to run the script on a schedule, or you can configure Windows to run WSH and the script automatically when Windows starts up (see "Running Programs When Windows 98 Starts" and "Running Programs on a Schedule Using Task Scheduler" in Chapter 2).

The Windows Scripting Host can run scripts written in a variety of languages, including VBScript (the scripting language used by Internet Explorer), and JavaScript (what Microsoft calls JScript). The makers of other scripting languages may also provide programs that will allow WSH to run scripts in their languages (Microsoft hopes that they do).

This chapter doesn't describe the VBScript or JavaScript languages; we suggest that you buy a book about the programming language you choose. Instead, this chapter describes how to use the Windows Scripting Host to run scripts after you've written them.

Note   *The Windows Scripting Host isn't automatically installed when you install Windows 98. To install it, open Control Panel, open Add/Remove Programs, click the Windows Setup tab, choose Accessories from the list of Windows 98 components, click Details, and choose Windows Scripting Host. WSH consists of the Wscript.exe and Cscript.exe programs, as well as a group of sample VBscript and JavaScript scripts stored in your C:\Windows\Samples\WSH folder.*

For more information about the Windows Scripting Host, visit its web sites at **http://www.microsoft.com/management** and **http://www.microsoft.com/scripting**.

What Is a WSH File?

If you plan to run a script frequently, you can store the configuration settings for the script in a text file with the extension .wsh (see "Creating WSH Files to Store Script Settings"). You can make more than one WSH file for a script; each WSH file runs the script using different settings.

Running Scripts from Windows

To run a script, just open the script's icon or filename in Windows Explorer, a Folder window, or the desktop. Click or double-click depending on whether your desktop uses Web style or Classic style (see "Choosing the Style of Your Desktop" in Chapter 1). The Wscript program, which is part of WSH and is stored in the C:\Windows folder, runs the script. Alternatively, you can choose Start | Run, type the full path name of the script you want to run into the Run dialog box, and then click OK.

Wscript is registered to run VBScript (with extension .vbs) and JavaScript (with extension .js) scripts, as well as WSH files (with extension .wsh). If you want to use Wscript to run scripts with other extensions, run the script's icon or filename, or type its filename into the Run dialog box as previously described; if Windows displays an Open With dialog box, you can tell Windows to run all scripts of this type using Wscript. Choose C:\Windows\Wscript.exe in the Open With dialog box and select the Always Use This Program To Open This File check box. In addition to running the script you specified, Windows registers Wscript to be the program used to open all files with this extension.

Tip   *To try out WSH, you can run one of the sample scripts that come with WSH. In Windows Explorer or a Folder window, look in your C:\Windows\Samples\ WSH folder and run one of the scripts listed. If you want to take a look at the text of a script, use Notepad to open the script (see "Reading Text Files with Notepad" in Chapter 4).*

Configuring the Wscript Program

Wscript has two properties that you can set (see Table 42-1). To see or set properties for Wscript, run Wscript with no script by running its filename (Wscript.exe) in the C:\Windows folder. Or choose Start | Run, type **wscript** in the Run dialog box, and then click OK. Either way, you see the Windows Scripting Host window, shown in Figure 42-1.

Option	Description
Stop scripts after specified number of seconds	Specifies a maximum number of seconds that a script can run, to prevent scripts that never terminate. (This setting is the equivalent of Cscript's //T:*nn* option or the WSH file Timeout setting.)
Display logo when scripts executed in MS-DOS prompt	Displays the version number for WSH each time Wscript runs a script. (This setting is the equivalent of Cscript's //logo or //nologo option or the WSH file DisplayLogo setting.)

Table 42-1.   *Properties of the Wscript Program*

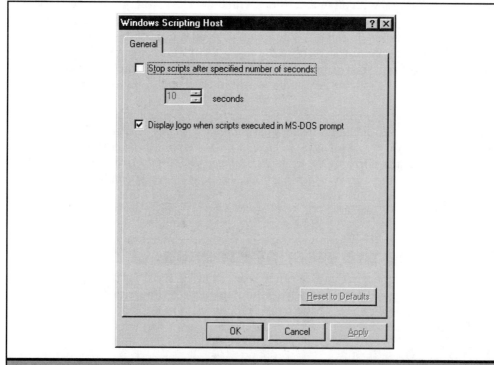

Figure 42-1.   *The Wscript program's Properties dialog box*

Running Scripts from the DOS Command Line

You can run scripts from the DOS command line by using the Cscript program (see "What Is DOS?" in Chapter 41). The Cscript.exe file is part of WSH and is installed in the C:\Windows\Command folder.

To run a script using Cscript, follow these steps:

1. Open a DOS window by choosing Start | Programs | MS-DOS Prompt. You see the DOS prompt, which is usually C:\Windows>.

2. Type **cscript** followed by a space and the full path name (file address) of the script you want to run. You can also type the command-line options listed in Table 42-2. Then press ENTER.

3. The script runs.

You can run one of the sample scripts that come with WSH. For the script name, type the name of one of the files in the C:\Windows\Samples\WSH folder.

You can use two kinds of command-line options with Cscript:

- **Host options**   Options that control WSH features. These options always start with two slashes (//).

- **Script options**   Information that is passed to the script itself. These options always start with one slash (/).

Table 42-2 lists the command-line options you can use with the Cscript command.

Creating WSH Files to Store Script Settings

To create a WSH file to store the settings for a script, follow these steps:

1. Right-click the filename of the script in Windows Explorer and choose Properties from the menu that appears. You see a Properties dialog box for the script. The General tab shows the name, size, and dates for the file. The Script tab shows the same settings that are shown in Figure 42-1.

2. Click the Script tab and choose the settings you want to use when you run the script with the WSH file.

3. Click OK. Windows creates a text file with the extension .wsh. The WSH file has the same name (except for the extension) as the script file and is stored in the same folder.

4. Run the WSH file the same way you run VBScript, JavaScript, and other script files, using Wscript or Cscript.

Option	Description
//?	Displays information about the Cscript command.
//B	Specifies running the script in batch mode, so that all user prompts and script errors are suppressed. This is the opposite of the //I option, and is the equivalent of the BatchMode=1 setting in a WSH file.
//H:*name*	Registers the program *name* (which must be either Cscript or Wscript) as the application for running this type of script. The default program for running scripts is Wscript.
//I	Specifies running the script in interactive mode, displaying all user prompts and script errors. (This is the default setting.) This is the opposite of the //B option, and is the equivalent of the BatchMode=0 setting in a WSH file.
//logo	Displays a banner when the script starts. (This is the default setting.) This is the opposite of the //nologo option, and is the equivalent of the DisplayLogo=1 setting in a WSH file.
//nologo	Specifies no display of the WSH banner. This is the opposite of the //logo setting, and is the equivalent of the DisplayLogo=0 setting in a WSH file.
//S	Saves the command-line options you use this time, so that they become the default.
//T:*nn*	Specifies the maximum number of seconds that the script can run before Cscript cancels the script. This is the equivalent of the Timeout=*nn* setting in a WSH file.

Table 42-2.   *Command-line Options for the Cscript Program*

A WSH file is a text file that looks like Figure 42-2. To look at the contents of a WSH file, open it in Notepad (see "Reading Text Files with Notepad" in Chapter 4). The file has two sections, ScriptFile and Options. Each section starts with the section name on a line by itself enclosed in square brackets. In each section, each setting appears on a line by itself in the format:

settingname=value

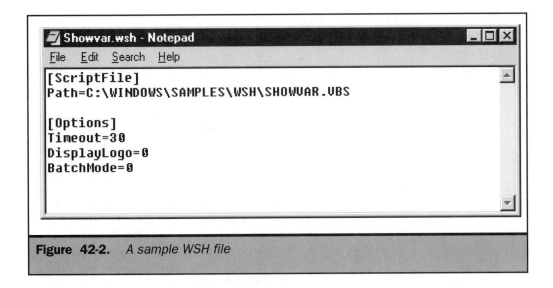

Figure 42-2.   *A sample WSH file*

The single line in the ScriptFile section of a WSH file contains a line like the following, specifying the name of the script to run:

Path=C:\WINDOWS\SAMPLES\WSH\SHOWVAR.VBS

Table 42-3 lists the settings in a WSH file.

Scripts can access any object present on a Windows system, including applications, networks, and the Windows Registry. See the sample scripts provided with Windows to see some examples of how this works.

Section	Setting Name	Description
ScriptFile	Path	Specifies the full path name of the script file to run.
Options	Timeout	Specifies the maximum number of seconds the script can run. If this value is 0, there is no maximum. This is the equivalent of the Stop Scripts After Specified Number Of Seconds setting on the script properties dialog box, or the //T:*nn* Cscript command-line option.

Table 42-3.   *Settings in a WSH File*

Section	Setting Name	Description
Options	DisplayLogo	Specifies whether to display (if the value is 1) or not display (if the value is 0) the WSH banner when the script runs. This is the equivalent of the Display Logo When Scripts Executed In MS-DOS Prompt setting on the script properties dialog box, or the //logo and //nologo Cscript command-line options.
Options	BatchMode	Specifies whether to run the script in batch mode (if the value is 1), suppressing user input and error messages, or in interactive mode (if the value is 0). This setting doesn't appear on the script properties dialog box; the only way to set it to 1 is to edit the WSH file. This setting is equivalent to the //B and //I Cscript command-line options.

Table 42-3. *Settings in a WSH File* (continued)

The Complete Reference

Installing or Upgrading to
Windows 98

Unless you buy a computer with Windows 98 already installed, you face the task of installing Windows 98—either installing it on a blank hard disk or upgrading your existing operating system. This chapter explains your installation options and details how to install, upgrade to, and uninstall Windows 98. You'll also find out how to check your installation, how to create a dual-boot installation, and other installation tips.

To install Windows 98, you need the following:

- A Windows 98 CD-ROM or a set of Windows 98 installation floppy disks

- A 486, Pentium, Pentium Pro, or compatible computer

- At least 16MB of RAM (32MB is better)

- At least 130MB of hard disk space, perhaps more (see "How Much Disk Space Does Windows 98 Require?")

- A blank floppy disk to use when creating an emergency boot disk

The Windows 98 CD-ROM (or the first of the series of floppy disks) contains an installation program called Setup. Windows 98 itself is stored in compressed format on the CD-ROM or floppies in a group of *cabinet files* with the extension .cab—Setup copies and decompresses the Windows 98 programs from the cabinet files during installation.

What Are Your Installation Options?

You can install Windows 98 in one of the following ways:

- Install Windows 98 on a blank formatted hard disk.

- Install it over Windows 3.1, Windows 3.11, Windows for Workgroups, Windows 95, Windows NT, OS/2, or DOS, replacing your previously installed operating system.

- Create a dual-boot installation with Windows 3.1 or Windows NT, or use OS/2's Boot Manager, so that you can choose to start your computer in either Windows 98 or your previously installed operating system.

Note *You cannot create a dual boot system with Windows 95 and Windows 98.*

Once you beginning the installation, Windows 98's Setup program gives you the following options:

- The Windows 98 Setup program installs Windows 98 in your *Windows program folder*. The default location for this folder is C:\Windows. During installation, Setup asks what folder to install Windows 98 in; you can specify a different folder to be your Windows program folder. Throughout this book, we assume that your Windows program folder is C:\Windows, as it is on the vast majority of Windows computers.

- Setup asks whether you want to be able to uninstall Windows 98 later and return to the operating system you used before. If you choose this option, Setup stores your existing operating system in a backup file which you can restore later (see "Uninstalling Windows 98"). Setup doesn't offer you this option if you are installing Windows 98 to a new Windows program folder (to create a dual-boot system) or if you are upgrading from a version of DOS earlier than 5.0.

Handling Version Conflicts

When installing Windows 98's new program files, if Setup sees that you have a more recent file of the same name in the same folder already on your hard disk, it copies its new file to your hard disk and makes a backup copy of the existing file. Setup stores the backup copies in the C:\Windows\VCM folder (VCM stands for Version Conflict Manager) and stores a list of the filenames in the C:\Windows\Verback.log text file.

To see which files were backed up, you can run the Version Conflict Manager program. Choose Start | Run and type **vcmui** to run Version Conflict Manager, which also lets you restore the previous backed-up versions.

How Much Disk Space Does Windows 98 Require?

During the installation process, the Setup program tells you how much disk space it will need. The amount of space required depends on:

- What operating system is already installed, if any.

- Whether you specify that Setup save the previous operating system (if any) to enable you to uninstall Windows 98 later. This optional uninstall file (a hidden file called C:\Winundo.dat) can be up to 65MB. You can tell Windows 98 to store this file on another partition or disk drive.

- The cluster size of the disk on which you are installing Windows 98 (see "What Are the FAT16 and FAT32 File Systems?" in Chapter 11). If you have a large disk that uses FAT16, even small files take up 32K each, bloating the space that Windows 98 occupies.

- How many optional programs you install along with Windows 98. Windows 98 comes with dozens of utilities and applications that aren't needed to run Windows 98, but that may come in handy.

Depending on these factors, Windows 98 can require anywhere from 130MB to almost 300MB during installation. About 45MB of this space is used by temporary files that are deleted when installation ends.

If you don't have enough space to install Windows 98, try emptying your Recycle Bin (if you are upgrading from Windows 95), deleting your web browser's cache (or the temporary file caches of other application programs), and deleting all temporary and backup files (with .tmp and .bak extensions, among others). If you still don't have enough space, you can uninstall programs and reinstall them later when Windows 98 is running. But Windows 98 requires lots of elbow room; if your disk space is tight, consider buying a larger hard disk.

If your system has more than one hard disk, the free space Windows 98 requires must be on the drive that contains your Windows program folder (usually C:\Windows). If you don't have quite enough space on that drive, and free space exists on another drive, you can use about 10MB of space on a second drive by starting the Setup program from the DOS command line with this command-line option:

setup /T:*path*

Replace *path* with the drive letter and path name (file address) of a temporary folder that Setup can use. (Setup creates this folder if it doesn't exist; if it does exist, Setup deletes the contents of this folder during installation.) For example, to use some space on drive E, using the Temp folder (which doesn't contain anything you want to keep), you type

setup /T:E:\Temp

What Is a Dual-Boot Installation?

A *dual-boot installation* is an installation of Windows 98 that leaves the installation of another operating system intact. When you start your computer, you can decide which operating system to run.

If Windows 3.1 or NT is installed on your computer, you can create a dual-boot installation with Windows 98 (as described later in this chapter). You can't dual-boot with Windows 95, because the two operating systems are too similar and share so many files. On a dual-boot system, you can't use FAT32, because Windows NT and Windows 3.1 don't support FAT32 (see "What Are the FAT16 and FAT32 File Systems?" in Chapter 11). OS/2's Boot Manager program allows OS/2 to dual-boot with Windows 98.

What Is an Emergency Boot Disk?

The *Emergency Boot Disk* (EBD) is a floppy disk that you create during the Windows 98 installation or upgrade process. Be sure to make an emergency boot disk when the

Windows 98 Setup program suggests it. You can use this floppy disk to restart your computer if you have a problem starting from your usual hard disk; put the floppy disk into the disk drive before you turn on your computer (see "Startup Floppy Disk" in Chapter 37). You can also use the Emergency Boot Disk to run Windows 98 if you reformat your hard disk.

The EBD contains generic CD-ROM drivers, so that if you need to start your computer from the floppy disk, your CD-ROM drive should work. The drivers provided don't work with all CD-ROM drives, though; if your CD-ROM drive came with a floppy disk containing drivers, make sure that you know where that disk is.

Caution   *If you use a computer that has one shared bay for both a CD-ROM and floppy disk drive, and you are installing from a CD-ROM, you cannot make an Emergency Boot Disk, because most computers require rebooting to switch from using the CD-ROM drive to the floppy disk drive. Click the Cancel button when Setup asks you to insert a floppy disk into the drive.*

You can create an EBD any time you are running Windows 98. Choose Start | Settings | Control Panel, open the Add/Remove Programs icon, and then click the Startup Disk tab. (Click or double-click the Add/Remove Programs icon depending on whether your Windows 98 desktop uses Web style or Classic style; see "Choosing the Style of Your Desktop" in Chapter 1.)

Preparing to Install Windows 98

Here are some tips, including suggestions from Microsoft, for a smoother installation:

- Run a virus-checker on your system before installing Windows 98, so that no viruses interfere with the installation. You can download several good virus-checkers from the Internet, including those from McAfee (at **http://www.mcafee.com**) and Symantec (at **http://www.symantec.com**).

- After running your virus-checker, disable it while installing Windows 98. Some computers have antivirus programs stored in the computer's BIOS; if your computer does, Setup won't run. If you see an error message reporting an antivirus program, check your system's documentation for instructions on how to disable virus-checking.

- Run ScanDisk (if you use Windows 95) or Chkdsk (if you use DOS or Windows 3.1) to clean up any formatting errors on your hard disk. Windows 98 runs ScanDisk again during installation, and it can't continue if it finds any errors.

- Make a backup copy of your Autoexec.bat and Config.sys files on a floppy disk. Then make a complete backup of your system. If that's not possible, make a backup of all of your data files.

- Make sure that you have enough free space on the hard disk on which your Windows program folder is (or will be) stored (see "How Much Disk Space Does Windows 98 Require?").

- If you have problems with hardware or software on your system, fix the problems first or uninstall the hardware or software.

- Remove unnecessary programs from your Autoexec.bat and Config.sys files, such as anti-virus programs or undelete utilities.

- Remove all LOAD= and RUN= files from your Win.ini file (which is in your Windows program folder, usually C:\Windows). (See "The Win.ini File" in Chapter 39). These lines run programs automatically when Windows starts. Edit the Win.ini file by using Notepad and insert a semicolon at the beginning of each LOAD= or RUN= line.

- If you run Windows 95, remove all programs from your C:\Windows\Start Menu\Programs\StartUp folder (see "Running Programs When Windows 98 Starts" in Chapter 2).

- Turn off your screen saver.

- Turn off any memory management programs, such as QEMM or 386MAX.

- Disable any non-Microsoft disk-caching programs, such as the caching programs that come with the Norton Utilities and PC Tools.

- Turn off other utilities that might interfere with installation, such as programs like CleanSweep that monitor software installations.

- Exit from all programs.

> **Note**
> *If you have Windows 98 on floppy disks, you cannot make copies of the disks. Microsoft uses a proprietary DMF format that allows the Windows 98 floppy disks to store more than the usual 1.4MB of data per disk.*

Installing Windows 98 on a Blank Hard Disk

If your hard disk has gotten full of junk, or your Windows 3.1 or 95 installation is unreliable, you may want to start from scratch rather than installing Windows 98 on top of what you already have on the hard disk. You can save the data files you want to keep, format the hard disk, install Windows 98, install the programs you want to use, and restore your data files.

To install Windows 98 from scratch, you must be able to create a floppy disk with enough of your existing operating system on it to let you start your computer in DOS and run the Windows 98 Setup program. If you are installing Windows 98 from a CD-ROM, this floppy disk must also include whatever drivers your CD-ROM drive needs (see "What Are Drivers?" in Chapter 15).

Formatting your hard disk deletes everything on it. You can't use the Recycle Bin or other unerase programs to get files back. Be sure to make and verify a backup copy of all the files you want to save.

Follow these steps to completely erase your hard disk and install Windows 98:

1. Back up all the data files that you want to save, so that you can restore them on your hard disk after you install Windows 98.

2. Make sure that you have the program disks for all the programs you want to install with Windows 98, including the program that can restore the files you backed up in step 1.

3. Using your old operating system, create a boot disk—a floppy disk from which you can start your computer, including drivers your CD-ROM drive requires (assuming you are installing Windows 98 from CD-ROM). You will need at least one blank floppy disk. If you run Windows 95, create a boot disk: choose Start | Settings | Control Panel, open the Add/Remove Programs icon, click the Startup Disk tab, and then click the Create Disk button (you may have to insert your Windows 95 CD-ROM or installation floppy disks, so have them handy). If you run Windows 3.1, use your DOS boot disk (or you can make one by using the DOS **FORMAT A: /S** command).

4. Look at the contents of the boot disk. If it doesn't contain the Format.com and Fdisk.exe files (which you will need to partition and format your hard disk), copy them from your hard disk. If you run Windows 95, these files are usually in the C:\Windows\Command folder. If you run Windows 3.1, these files are usually in your DOS directory.

5. Test the floppy disk to make sure that it works. If you plan to install Windows 98 from CD-ROM, make sure that the CD-ROM drive works. You may need to install CD-ROM drivers from a floppy disk that came with your CD-ROM drive. Insert the boot disk in the floppy disk drive, exit from Windows, and then restart the computer from the floppy. The computer should restart and display a DOS prompt.

6. Run the FDISK program to create a new DOS partition on your hard disk (see "Partitioning a Disk with the FDISK Program" in Chapter 11). Type **fdisk** and press ENTER. When you see the FDISK menu, delete all the partitions from your hard disk. Then create a new Primary DOS partition (Windows uses DOS partitions). Choose to make this partition active (that is, this partition is the one that the computer uses when starting up).

7. Restart the computer as directed by the FDISK program. Again, you see the DOS prompt. You can't use the DOS DIR command to list the contents of the hard disk, because you have not yet formatted it.

8. Run the Format program to reformat your hard disk. Use the /s command-line option to make the hard disk bootable. Assuming that your hard disk is drive C, type this command:

   format c:\ /s

9. Formatting takes a few minutes, depending on the size of your hard disk. When formatting is complete, type a volume label for the hard disk (any name for the disk or the computer, up to 11 characters, with no punctuation). Press ENTER.

10. When you see the DOS prompt again, run the Setup program from the Windows 98 CD-ROM to install Windows 98. If you are installing Windows 98 from CD-ROM, assuming that your CD-ROM drive is drive D, type **d:\setup** and press ENTER. If you are installing Windows 98 from floppy disks, put the first disk in the drive, type **a:\setup** and press ENTER.

11. Setup installs Windows 98. See "Upgrading from DOS" for what happens next.

Upgrading to Windows 98

You can upgrade to Windows 98 if your computer has Windows 95, Windows 3.1, Windows for Workgroups, MS-DOS, or OS/2. You can also install Windows 98 over Windows NT, replacing NT.

Upgrading from Windows 95

Windows 98 can use many of Windows 95's same configuration settings, so the process of upgrading from Windows 95 is quicker than upgrading from other operating systems. To upgrade from Windows 95 to Windows 98, follow these steps:

1. Start Windows 95.

2. If you are installing from a Windows 98 CD-ROM, put it in the CD-ROM drive. You may see a message asking whether you want to upgrade to Windows 98. If you don't see this message, you should see the Windows 98 CD-ROM window; click the Add/Remove Software icon and skip to step 4. If no window appears, run the Setup.exe program in the root folder of the CD-ROM drive (choose Start | Run, type **d:\setup**, and then press ENTER, assuming that your CD-ROM drive is drive D). Then skip to step 4.

3. If you are installing from floppy disks, insert the first disk in the drive, choose Start | Run, type **a:\setup**, and then press ENTER.

4. Follow the instructions that Setup displays, clicking the Next button to move to the next step. The process takes almost an hour.

Dealing with Disk Errors

Before installing Windows 98, the Setup program runs a version of ScanDisk to check your hard disk for errors. If it finds any errors, it can't proceed. If you see a message that ScanDisk has found an error, follow the steps appropriate to your situation, provided next, to fix the problem.

If you are upgrading from Windows 3.1, Windows 95, or MS-DOS:

1. Exit Windows so that you see the DOS prompt.

2. If you are installing from a Windows 98 CD-ROM, type this command (replace the d with the drive letter of your CD-ROM drive):

    d:\win98\scandisk.exe /all

3. If you are installing from floppy disks, insert disk 1 in the disk drive and type this command:

    a:scandisk.exe /all

4. ScanDisk runs and checks your hard disk. Follow the instructions on the screen to fix the problems that it finds.

5. Run the Windows 98 Setup program again.

If you are reinstalling Windows 98, follow these steps:

1. Exit the Setup program.

2. Choose Start | Programs | Accessories | System Tools | ScanDisk. The ScanDisk program runs.

3. Follow the instructions on the screen to fix the problems that it finds.

4. Run the Windows 98 Setup program again.

You can install from a CD-ROM that is connected over a local area network. Connect to the CD-ROM from your computer in the usual way (for example, in Windows Explorer, choose Tools | Map Network Drive). Display the contents of the root folder of the Windows 98 CD-ROM and run the Setup.exe program.

Note   *The Setup program asks in which folder to install Windows 98 (usually C:\Windows). If you choose a different folder than the one in which Windows 95 was installed, you must reinstall all of your application programs, and possibly all of your hardware drivers.*

Upgrading from Windows 3.1 or Windows for Workgroups 3.11

To upgrade from Windows 3.1 to Windows 98, follow these steps:

1. Start Windows 3.1.

2. If you are installing from a Windows 98 CD-ROM, put it in the CD-ROM drive. If you are installing from floppy disks, put the first one in the drive.

3. In File Manager or Program Manager, choose File | Run from the menu bar.

4. If you are installing from a Windows 98 CD-ROM, type **d:\setup** (if your CD-ROM isn't drive D, substitute the correct letter for d), and then press ENTER. If you are installing from floppy disks, type **a:\setup**, and then press ENTER.

5. Setup starts. Follow the instructions that Setup displays, clicking the Next button to move to the next step. The process takes almost an hour.

You can install Windows 98 from a CD-ROM connected over a local area network. Connect to the CD-ROM drive in the usual way (for example, by using File Manager, or by typing a NET USE command at the DOS prompt). In File Manager, display the contents of the root directory of the Windows 98 CD-ROM and run the Setup.exe program.

 If you want to be able to run either Windows 3.1 or Windows 98 when you start the computer, you can set up a dual-boot configuration (see "Creating a Dual-Boot Installation with Windows 3.1 or Windows for Workgroups").

Running Program Manager and File Manager

If you like to use the Windows 3.1 or 3.11 Program Manager and File Manager programs, you don't have to give them up when you upgrade to Windows 98. To run Program Manager, run Progman.exe in the C:\Windows folder. To run File Manager, run Winfile.exe in the C:\Windows folder.

Upgrading from DOS

You can upgrade to Windows 98 from a computer running DOS. (If any version of Windows is installed, though, Microsoft recommends running the Windows 98 Setup program from within Windows rather than from DOS.) Follow these steps:

1. If you are installing from a CD-ROM, put the Windows 98 CD-ROM in the CD-ROM drive, type **d:\setup** at the DOS prompt, and then press ENTER. (If your CD-ROM drive isn't drive D, substitute the correct letter.) If you are installing from floppy disks, put the first disk in the drive, type **a:\setup** at the DOS prompt, and then press ENTER.

2. Setup runs ScanDisk to check your hard disk for errors. When it's done, press x to exit from ScanDisk and continue with the installation.

3. You see the first Windows 98 Setup screen; follow the instructions to complete the installation, which can take up to an hour.

Upgrading from OS/2

To upgrade from OS/2, start the computer in MS-DOS mode and run the Setup.exe program in the root folder of the Windows 98 CD-ROM. After Windows is installed, you can no longer run OS/2.

You can't run Windows 98 under OS/2 or create a dual-boot configuration, but you may be able to use OS/2's Boot Manager to choose between the two operating systems when you start the computer (see "Creating a Dual-Boot Installation with OS/2").

Installing over Windows NT

Installing Windows 98 over Windows NT isn't exactly an upgrade—but it can be done. Start your computer from a floppy disk and then run the Setup.exe program in the root folder of the Windows 98 CD-ROM. If you want to continue to be able to run Windows NT, though, consider creating a dual-boot installation (see "Creating a Dual-Boot Installation with Windows NT").

Creating Dual-Boot Installations

You can create a dual-boot installation with Windows 3.1 or Windows NT. If you run OS/2, its Boot Manager can switch between OS/2 and Windows 98.

Creating a Dual-Boot Installation with Windows 3.1 or Windows for Workgroups

A dual-boot system is useful if you need to be able to run both operating systems, but it does require that you reinstall all of your programs for Windows 98. Your computer must run MS-DOS version 5.0 or later.

Installing Windows 98 in a New Folder

To create a dual-boot system, follow these steps:

1. Run Windows 3.1 and follow the instructions in "Upgrading from Windows 3.1 or Windows for Workgroups 3.11."

2. In step 5 of those instructions, when Setup asks for the directory in which to install Windows 98, choose Other Directory and click Next. This tells Setup to install Windows 98 in a different directory from the one in which Windows 3.1

is stored (usually a folder named C:\Windows). You see the Change Directory window.

3. Type the name of a new directory, like **c:\win98**, and then click Next. You see a message that warns you that if you install Windows 98 in a new directory, you'll have to reinstall all of your applications.

4. Click Yes to continue, and then click Next again.

5. Continue with the Windows 98 installation. You may need to answer questions about hardware if Windows 98 doesn't recognize all of your computer's components. When the Windows 98 installation is complete, Setup restarts the computer, running Windows 98.

6. Check that all of your hardware works, including CD-ROMs, tape drives, network cards, modems, and printers. You may need to reinstall these (see Chapter 15).

7. Reinstall the programs that you want to use with Windows 98, installing them in different folders from the Windows 3.1 installations. For example, install all the Windows 98 versions in subfolders of the C:\Program Files folder. When you are running Windows 98, you won't be able to run the programs you have installed in Windows 3.1.

Note *If you create a FAT32 partition using Windows 98, Windows 3.1 can't read any files stored in that partition.*

Once you have set up a dual-boot system, you control which operating system takes control when you start up the computer.

Starting the Computer in Windows 98

To turn on the computer and run Windows 98, let the startup process happen normally; Windows 98 takes control. If you are running Windows 3.1 and want to switch to Windows 98, follow these steps:

1. Choose File | Exit from Program Manager, and click OK to confirm.

2. When you see the DOS prompt, press CTRL-ALT-DEL to restart the computer in Windows 98.

Starting the Computer in Windows 3.1

Follow these steps to start your computer in Windows 3.1:

1. If the computer is off, turn on the computer and skip to step 4.

2. If you are running Windows 98, choose Start | Shut Down, click Restart, and then click OK.

3. If you see the DOS prompt, press CTRL-ALT-DEL to restart the computer.

4. When startup and copyright messages appear on your screen, *before* the Windows 98 "clouds" screen appears, press F4 as many times as you like. You see the message Now Loading Your Previous Version Of MS-DOS, Please Wait. Eventually, you see the MS-DOS prompt. If the command to start Windows 3.1 is in your Autoexec.bat file, Windows 3.1 starts automatically.

5. Start Windows 3.1 as you did before you installed Windows 98.

In step 4, when you see the startup and copyright messages, you can press F8 instead of F4. You see the Microsoft Windows 98 Startup Menu, with numbered options (see "Starting in a Special Mode" in Chapter 37). Press 7 and ENTER to select Previous Version Of MS-DOS. When you see the DOS prompt, start Windows 3.1 as usual.

 If you use the Restart In MS-DOS Mode option on the Shut Down menu to exit to DOS, and then try to run Windows 3.1, the DOS PATH command is set incorrectly for running Windows 3.1. Also, DOS 7 is running, the version that comes with Windows 98. Windows 3.1 will not run correctly.

Creating a Dual-Boot Installation with Windows NT

To create a dual-boot installation with Windows NT, first configure NT to multi-boot between NT and MS-DOS. Then start the computer in MS-DOS Mode and run the Setup.exe program on the Windows 98 CD-ROM. Be sure to install Windows 98 in a new folder in a FAT16 partition. Do not install Windows 98 in the Windows NT program folder, in a shared Windows NT/Windows 3.1 folder, or in a FAT32 partition.

 If you use NTFS partitions with Windows NT, Windows 98 can't read them. If you use FAT32 partitions with Windows 98, Windows NT can't read them.

Creating a Dual-Boot Installation with OS/2

The OS/2 Boot Manager program lets you choose operating systems when you start the computer. If you haven't installed Boot Manager, install it now. Then start OS/2 in MS-DOS mode and install Windows 98.

The Windows 98 Setup program disables Boot Manager so that Setup can restart the computer and finish its installation. When Setup is done and Windows 98 is running, re-enable Boot Manager by using the Windows 98 FDISK program (see "Partitioning a Disk with the FDISK Program" in Chapter 11). Choose Start | Run in Windows 98 and type **fdisk** in the Run dialog box. On the FDISK menu, choose 2 (Set Active Partition) and choose the number of the Boot Manager partition; the partition you want is a non-MS-DOS partition that is 1MB in size. When you quit FDISK and restart the computer, you can choose whether to run OS/2 or Windows 98.

Checking Your System After Installing Windows 98

If you didn't reformat your hard disk to install Windows 98 from scratch, and if you installed Windows 98 in the same directory as your previous version of Windows (that is, you didn't create a dual-boot installation), you shouldn't have to reinstall any of the application programs that were installed on your hard disk. The Setup program looks for installed programs and installs them in Windows 98, too.

Check that all of your hardware was correctly detected by Windows 98, including your modem, network cards, and printer. If they don't work right, refer to Chapter 15 to reinstall them.

If your computer is connected to a local area network, check that network communication is happening normally. If it's not, see "Troubleshooting Your Network" in Chapter 30, or talk to your LAN system administrator.

Uninstalling Windows 98

When you installed Windows 98, you may have chosen to back up your current operating system. You don't have this option if you installed over an earlier version of Windows 98, if you installed Windows 98 to a new directory (to create a dual-boot system, for example), or if you were running a version of MS-DOS older than version 5.0.

If you backed up your previous operating system, you can probably uninstall Windows 98 and return to that operating system. The uninstall program is called Uninstal.exe in the C:\Windows\Command folder.

If you have compressed the hard disk that contains your Windows program folder, you can't uninstall Windows 98 (see Chapter 35).

Running the Uninstall Program

Follow these steps to determine whether you can uninstall Windows 98:

1. Choose Start | Settings | Control Panel.

2. Run the Add/Remove Programs program. When you see the Add/Remove Programs Properties window, click the Install/Uninstall tab.

3. Look at the contents of the large box in the lower half of the window. If Uninstall Windows 98 is listed, you can uninstall it; select it and click the Add/Remove button.

If you can't uninstall Windows 98 because you can't get Windows to run, use your Emergency Boot Disk to start your computer in MS-DOS mode, then type **a:uninstal** and press ENTER at the DOS prompt to run the uninstallation program. (The uninstallation program is also stored in C:\Windows\Command\Uninstal.exe.)

Deleting the Uninstall Files

If you decide that you will never want to uninstall Windows and restore the previous operating system that you backed up, you can delete the backup files to gain about 8MB of free space on your hard disk. To delete the backed-up previous version of your operating system, follow these steps:

1. Choose Start | Settings | Control Panel.
2. Run the Add/Remove Programs program. When you see the Add/Remove Programs Properties window, click the Install/Uninstall tab.
3. Click Old Windows 3.x/MS-DOS System Files or Delete Windows 98 Uninstall Information on the list of installed programs, and then click the Remove button.

 This action prevents you from uninstalling Windows and returning to your previous operating system, without installing everything from scratch.

Glossary

10Base-T   *See* **unshielded twisted pair cable**.

16-bit application   Program designed to run with DOS and Windows 3.1. Windows 98 can run 16-bit applications.

32-bit application   Program designed to run with Windows 95, Windows 98, or Windows NT.

access control   Security feature that controls who has access to shared resources (hardware or files).

access type   Security feature that controls what people can do with a shared resource.

Accessibility   Features that allow people with disabilities to use Windows or other programs.

account   *See* **Internet account**.

ACPI   Advanced Configuration and Power Interface, a standard for saving power by automatically turning off computer hardware when it is not in use.

action   Part of the definition of a file type, specifying what Windows does with files of that type.

Active Channel bar   Internet Explorer window that displays information about Microsoft's recommended channels. *See also* **Channel bar**.

Active Desktop   Desktop configuration in which your desktop can display web pages.

active partition   The disk partition from which your computer starts, usually the Primary DOS partition.

Active Streaming Format   Streaming audio or video file format used by NetShow.

active window   The window that appears "on top" of other windows, obscuring parts of other windows that overlap. The active window is the window that is currently accepting input from the keyboard and mouse.

ActiveX controls   Small programs embedded in web pages that can automatically be downloaded and run on your computer to add features to web browsers.

adapter   Setting that identifies both the network interface card in a computer and the driver needed to make that card work.

adapter card   Printed circuit board that you can plug into an expansion slot inside your computer.

address   Information that tells you and Windows 98 where to find a piece of information. *See* **e-mail address; file address; I/O address; memory address; UNC address; URL.**

Address Bar toolbar   Toolbar that can appear in Folder windows and Windows Explorer windows, and includes only the Address box.

Address Book   Windows 98 utility that stores names and addresses.

Address box   Box appearing on the Address Bar toolbar in a Folder window or Windows Explorer window, in which the name of the open folder appears.

Address toolbar   Toolbar that can appear on the Taskbar, containing a box in which you can type a URL to view a web page.

America Online (AOL)   Popular online service geared toward individual rather than business users.

anonymous FTP   Connecting to a publicly available FTP server by using *anonymous* as the user name and your e-mail address as the password. *See* **FTP.**

AOL   *See* **America Online**.

APM   Advanced Power Management, a standard for saving power by automatically turning off computer hardware when it is not in use.

applet   Small application program, frequently received as part of a web page.

application or **application program**   Program for getting real-world work done, such as word processing programs, database programs, and spreadsheet programs.

Archive attribute   Setting regarding a file or folder that is used by backup programs. Many backup programs use the Archive attribute to indicate whether the file has been changed since the last time it was backed up.

area code rules Rules that describe when to dial 1 and/or the area code when dialing the phone.

argument Additional information you provide to a program, usually by typing the information on a command line following the program's name.

article Message posted to a newsgroup.

ASCII file *See* **text file**.

ASCII mode In FTP, a setting used to transfer files that contain only plain unformatted text. *See* **binary mode**.

ASF or **ASX** File extension for Active Streaming Format files, a streaming audio or video file format used by NetShow.

attached file or
attachment File that is sent as part of an e-mail message or newsgroup article.

attribute Setting regarding a file or folder. The four attributes are **Archive**, **Hidden**, **Read-Only**, and **System**.

audio CD Compact disk containing audio information (rather than containing a Windows 98-compatible file system).

authenticode Microsoft's technique for digitally signing ActiveX and Java applets, to identify the applet's author and verify that the applet was received without tampering or modification.

Auto Hide Feature that hides the Taskbar when you are not using it.

Autoexec.bat DOS batch file that runs automatically when the computer is started; Autoexec.bat must be stored in the root folder of the active partition.

Autorun Program on a CD-ROM that tells Windows 98 to run a program on the CD-ROM whenever the CD-ROM is inserted into the drive.

AVI file Video file, with extension .avi.

background Program running while its window is not active.

backscroll buffer Temporary storage for the last 500 lines of text that have scrolled up off the top of the HyperTerminal window.

backup Duplicate copy of information, stored separately, in case something happens to the original copy.

Backup job Specification of the information to be backed up by the Microsoft Backup program and the location to store the duplicate copy.

backup set Set of backed-up files, the result of running a Backup job.

baseline backup *See* **full backup**.

batch file List of DOS commands to execute, stored in a text file with the extension .bat.

BBS *See* **bulletin board system**.

Bcc Blind Carbon Copy; e-mail addresses to which to send a copy of an e-mail message, without the other recipients seeing the addresses.

bell mode In the Ftp program, whether the program beeps whenever it completes a command.

binary mode In FTP, a setting used to transfer files that contain information in a format other than plain unformatted text. *See* **ASCII mode**.

binary string Sequence of binary or hexadecimal digits used as the data portion of a value in the Registry.

binding Specification of which network protocols work with your network interface card.

BIOS setup Computer's low-level configuration information, including how much memory and what types of disks are installed.

bit Binary digit, which can be either 0 or 1.

bitmap Graphics format in which a picture or character is stored as a grid of dots. Standard Windows bitmap files have the extension .bmp. Older fonts are stored as bitmaps.

BMP file Graphics file in bitmap format (a Windows standard format for graphics files) with the extension .bmp.

BNC connector Connector used to connect network interface cards to coaxial cable in a bus topology network.

body   Text of an e-mail message (not including the header lines at the top of the message).

bookmark   Information about a web page that you might want to come back to, as stored by Netscape Navigator in its Bookmark.htm file.

boot   Start up or turn on your computer.

boot disk or
boot drive   Disk drive from which Windows loads on startup. *See also* **emergency boot disk**.

boot manager   Program that lets you select which partition to start from each time you restart your computer.

bps   Bits per second, a measure of data transmission speed. Sometimes confused with "baud."

briefcase   Folder containing files and subfolders to move between two computers.

browser   Program that your computer runs to communicate with web servers on the Internet and display web pages.

buffer   Temporary storage area.

**bulletin board
system (BBS)**   Text-based account that runs on a small computer (such as a PC). Many bulletin board systems are also connected to the Internet.

bus topology   Network topology in which each computer connects to a main cable (the *bus*).

byte   Eight bits, enough to hold one alphanumeric character.

cabinet file   File containing a group of files for installation, with the file extension .cab. The Windows 98 CD-ROM and floppy disks contain many cabinet files.

cache   Area on disk (usually a folder) for the temporary storage of information. Browsers store recently viewed web pages in a cache, in case you want to see them again. Windows also maintains caches for CD-ROMs and removable disks.

call log   List of calls you made by using Phone Dialer.

call waiting Telephone line feature that beeps when another call is coming in on the line.

calling card Telephone credit card, which you can configure Windows to use when dialing long-distance calls.

callto link Link on a web page that provides the information required to contact you by using an Internet-based conferencing system, such as NetMeeting.

Cc Carbon Copy; e-mail addresses to which to send a copy of an e-mail message.

CCC file Chat conversation file saved by Microsoft Chat.

CDF file Channel Definition Format file that allows web browsers to download information from the channel automatically.

CD-ROM Compact Disk/Read-Only Memory; compact disk containing digital (rather than audio) information.

central processing unit *See* **CPU**.

certificate Cryptographic data that can identify one computer or user to another. *See also* **digital ID**.

certificate authority Organization that issues certificates.

certificate file File containing a certificate (digital ID).

channel Method of organizing a web site according to a subscription model, so that your web browser can automatically download updates to the site. In Internet Relay Chat, a channel is a group of people who are chatting, also called a **chat room**.

Channel bar Window displayed on the Active Desktop that lists channels on the Web. *See also* **Active Channel bar**.

chanop Channel operator in an Internet Relay Chat channel.

Character Map Windows 98's utility for inserting special characters in your work.

chat Online communication in real-time (minimal delay between when you send a message and when the recipient receives it). The oldest chat system is Internet Relay Chat.

chat client Program that lets you participate in Internet Relay Chat.

chat room Group of people communicating together using Internet Relay Chat or another online chat system.

chat server Computer that serves the switchboard for online chat. Thousands of Internet Relay Chat servers are connected to the Internet.

check box Box onscreen that can either be blank or contain a check mark (or X), usually appearing in a dialog box. FrontPage Express comes with form templates to put check boxes on web page forms.

Classic style Desktop style in which icons (and filenames in Folder windows and Windows Explorer) run or open when double-clicked.

cleanup *See* **Disk Cleanup**.

client Program or computer that uses resources on a network. In Windows 98, a setting that identifies the type of network to which you are attaching the computer.

Client for Microsoft Networks Part of Windows 98 that handles using the resources of remote computers on a peer-to-peer network.

client-server network Network on which server computers provide resources for the rest of the network and client computers use only these resources.

Clipboard Temporary storage space in memory for storing cut-and-paste information.

clipboard file File saved by Clipboard Viewer, with the extension .clp.

clock *See* **system clock**.

Close button Button in the upper-right corner of a window; click this button to close the window and possibly exit the program.

CLP file Clipboard file, with extension .clp.

coaxial cable Type of cable used to connect computers in a bus topology.

codec System for audio or video compression and decompression.

collaboration NetMeeting feature that allows callers in a meeting to control a program running one person's computer and see the program's screen display.

color profile System for precisely representing colors on your monitor and printer.

COM1, COM2, COM3, COM4, or comm port *See* **serial port**.

command button Button that you can click to perform a command.

command line Command that you type at the DOS prompt, optionally followed by additional information.

Command Prompt Only mode Windows startup mode in which Windows loads all drivers, but starts an MS-DOS command prompt, not the full Windows system. Also called **MS-DOS mode**.

communication security Security that protects the data you transmit over the Internet or LAN.

compiled help module File displayed by Windows Help, stored with the extension .chm.

compressed disk Large file that resides on a regular disk or disk partition, and that Windows treats as a separate disk drive.

compressed virtual disk Large file that Windows treats like a disk, and that contains files in a compressed format.

compression System that examines data for repeated or systematic contents, and recodes the data to remove some of the redundancy. *Disk compression* stores files in a compressed format.

Compression Agent Windows 98 utility that recompresses compressed drives.

compression ratio Ratio of the compressed size to the original size of files on a compressed disk.

CompuServe Business-oriented online service owned by America Online.

Config.sys file DOS configuration file that controls the way DOS sets itself up.

connection *See* **Dial-Up Networking connection**.

contact list List of names and addresses in Address Book.

container file In OLE, file that contains a link to an object in another file, or that contains an embedded object from another file.

Content Advisor Microsoft's program for controlling the content that Internet Explorer displays. Content Advisor comes with Windows 98.

control character Character you type by holding down the CTRL key while pressing another key.

control files Files that Windows 98 uses to store parts of its own programs and configuration information.

Control Panel Window that displays icons for a number of programs that let you control your computer, Windows 98, and the software you have installed.

cookie Small (at most 4KB) file that a web server can cause your browser to store on your machine and return to the server.

copying As part of cut-and-paste, copying selected information from its current location and storing it (temporarily) on the Clipboard.

CPU Central processing unit, a computer chip that executes the instructions in programs. CPUs that can run Windows 98 and compatible programs include Intel 80486, Pentium, Pentium Pro, and Pentium II, as well as AMD and Cyrix chips.

CRC Cyclic Redundancy Checking, a code that System File Checker (and many other programs) use to check whether a file has changed.

CSLIP Compressed Serial Line Internet Protocol, a communications protocol for computers connected to the Internet. CSLIP has been superceded by PPP.

cursor Screen element (usually a blinking vertical bar) that indicates where the text you type will be inserted. Not to be confused with the *mouse pointer*.

Custom style Desktop style in which icons (and filenames in Folder windows and Windows Explorer) run or open as defined by the user.

cut-and-paste Feature of Windows that lets you select information from one file and move or copy it to another file (or another location in the same file).

cutting Removing selected information from its current location and storing it (temporarily) on the Clipboard.

data bits How many bits of information are included in each byte sent (usually eight).

DB-15 Standard display connector.

DB-25 Standard parallel or serial connector. *See* **parallel port** or **serial port**.

DB-9 Standard serial connector. *See* **serial port**.

DCC *See* **direct cable connection**.

DDE Dynamic Data Exchange, a way for programs to exchange information.

DDE action DDE command that defines how data moves to or from files of a specified type.

dedicated server Computer used only as a server on a client-server network; not used to run user applications.

default The information or mode that a program uses, unless you specify otherwise.

default printer The printer to which print jobs are sent, unless you specify otherwise.

default web browser The browser that Windows runs when you open a web page and no browser is running.

deferred printing Queuing print jobs on a computer without a printer, to be printed when you connect a printer to your computer later.

defragmenting Moving the contents of files around on your hard disk so that each file is stored as one big chunk, to speed up accessing the file.

DejaNews Web site where you can read Usenet newsgroups (**http://www.dejanews.com**).

deselecting Indicating that you do not want to include an item among the objects you are working with.

desktop The work area on your screen on which you see your programs. The desktop can contain windows, icons, and the Taskbar.

desktop scheme Group of desktop settings, including colors and fonts, saved with a name. Not the same as a **desktop theme**.

desktop style How the desktop, Folder windows, and Windows Explorer are configured to respond to mouse actions.

desktop theme Set of desktop background, cursor, font, and color settings to dress up your desktop. Like a **desktop scheme** but with a wider range of elements, including a screen saver, desktop background, mouse pointer, sounds, and icons.

Desktop toolbar Toolbar that can appear on the Taskbar, containing a button for each icon on the desktop.

Details view Way of representing the contents of a folder, in which items are listed with a tiny icon, the filename, the file's size, the file's type, when it was last modified, and its attributes.

device driver *See* **driver**.

Device Manager Windows program that lists all the devices that make up your computer and that lets you see and modify their configuration.

dialing location Location from which you place phone calls. You can tell Windows the area code and other information about the phone line at that location.

dialog box Special kind of window that allows you to change settings or give commands in a program. Most dialog boxes include OK and Cancel command buttons.

Dial-Up Adapter The Windows 98 network driver that enables Dial-Up Networking to connect to PPP, CSLIP, and SLIP accounts.

dial-up client The computer calling another computer via Dial-Up Networking.

Dial-Up Networking Windows 98 facility that lets your computer connect to the Internet and some other accounts.

Dial-Up Networking connection Icon with all the settings required to connect to an Internet account or other computer.

dial-up server   The computer running the Dial-Up Server or other remote server program, which allows that computer to receive calls via Dial-Up Networking.

Dial-Up Server   Program used to allow other computers to connect to a local area network using Dial-Up Networking.

digital camera   Device that digitizes video input (through the lens of the camera) for use by your computer.

digital ID   File containing encryption and digital identification information that you can use to digitally sign or encrypt e-mail and newsgroup messages in Outlook Express. *See also* **certificate**.

digital signature   Information added to the end of an e-mail message to prove who sent it.

digitize   Convert information into a digital format so that it can be processed by your computer.

DIN connector   Standard, round keyboard or mouse connector.

direct cable connection (DCC)   Connecting two computers with a serial cable to allow file or printing sharing. Also the name of the Windows 98 program that allows two computers to communicate over a direct cable connection.

Direct Memory Access   *See* **DMA**.

directory   *See* **folder**.

directory server   Computer that stores the addresses of people who use NetMeeting.

directory service   Searchable listing of names, e-mail addresses, and other information about people.

DirectX   Enhanced video system built into Windows 98.

Disk Cleanup   Windows 98 utility that deletes unneeded temporary files to free up space on your disk.

disk compression   *See* **compression**.

distribution file   *See* **installation file**.

DLL file Dynamic Link Library file, an executable file invoked from a running program, with the file extension .dll.

DMA Direct Memory Access, a system board facility used by a few medium-speed devices to communicate with the **CPU**.

DNS *See* **domain name server**.

DOC file Document file, with the file extension .doc. DOC files are usually (but not always) created by Microsoft Word or a compatible program.

docking station Hardware device into which you plug a laptop to provide connections to a monitor, keyboard, mouse, local area network, and/or additional PC Card slots.

Documents menu Menu of recently used files. Choose Start | Documents.

domain name The alphanumeric name of a computer or group of computers on the Internet; for example, microsoft.com.

domain name server (DNS) Computer on the Internet that translates between domain names and numeric IP addresses. You can specify two DNSs in Dial-Up Networking: a primary server and a secondary server.

DOS Disk Operating System, the operating system on which Windows runs. Sometimes called **MS-DOS**, but only by Microsoft.

DOS initialization file One of the files that DOS reads when starting up: Autoexec.bat, Config.sys, and Msdos.sys.

DOS program Program written to work with the DOS operating system.

DOS prompt Prompt that DOS displays when it is waiting for you to type a command.

DOS window Window in which a DOS program is running.

download Transfer a file from the Internet, other network, or mainframe to a PC.

downloaded object security Security for information you download from the Internet.

Dr. Watson Windows 98 utility that takes a snapshot of the system's state when a program fails.

drag-and-drop Method of moving or copying information from one file to another, or to another location in the same file.

drive letter Letter that identifies a disk drive or other storage device, or a partition of a drive.

driver Software that allows Windows to communicate with a device, such as a display or printer.

DriveSpace Windows 98's disk space compression system.

drop-down menu Menu that appears when you click a command on a menu bar. FrontPage Express comes with form templates to put drop-down menus on web page forms.

dual-boot installation Computer that can be started in either of two operating systems; for example, Windows 98 and Windows 3.1.

DVD Digital Versatile Disk or Digital Video Disk, a digital disk that can contain video material.

DWORD Type of Registry entry that contains a numeric value.

Dynamic HTML Microsoft's scheme to provide self-modifying web pages using JavaScript or VBScript.

EBD *See* **emergency boot disk**.

echo Whether a communications program displays what you type or waits and displays the text that the remote computer sends back.

ECMAScript *See* **JavaScript**.

EIDE *See* **IDE**.

EISA Enhanced Industry Standard Architecture, an improved version of ISA, now superceded by PCI.

electronic mail *See* **e-mail**.

e-mail Messages sent over a local area network, the Internet, or other network.

e-mail address   Address that identifies the recipient of an e-mail message. The e-mail address for comments or suggestions about this book is **win98tcr@gurus.com**.

embedding   In OLE, storing an object of one type file a file of another type, optionally maintaining linkage from the second file to the file that originally contained the object, for example, an Excel spreadsheet embedded in a Word Perfect document.

emergency boot disk   Floppy disk from which you can restart Windows in the event of trouble. Also called a *startup floppy disk*.

EML   File extension, used for e-mail messages, that is used by Outlook Express's Inbox Assistant to reply to messages automatically.

encrypted mail   E-mail that has been encoded so that only the intended recipient can read it.

encryption   Scrambling a message so that it can be read only by someone with a secret decryption key.

Enhanced ISA   *See* **EISA**.

error control   Feature of some modems that checks transmitted data for errors.

Ethernet   Type of local area network hardware.

event   Windows operation that can trigger a sound. For example, exiting a program is an event.

EXE or executable file   Program file with the file extension .exe.

expansion slot   Slot inside a computer into which you can insert an adapter card.

Explorer   *See* **Internet Explorer; Windows Explorer**.

Explorer bar   Left pane of a Windows Explorer window, usually displaying a folder tree.

Exploring window   Window displayed by the Windows Explorer program.

Extended DOS partition Section of a hard disk that stores an additional DOS or Windows file system.

extension The last part of a filename, attached to the rest of the filename by a period (.). Extensions are usually three letters long, and indicate the **file type**. For example, a file named Example.txt has the extension .txt.

external modem Modem that connects to your computer's serial port by using a serial cable.

FAQ Frequently Asked Questions (and their answers).

FAT *See* **file allocation table**.

FAT16 The file system used in all versions of DOS since DOS 2.0, as well as Windows 3.1 and Windows 95. FAT 16 is also supported in Windows 98 for disks up to 2GB.

FAT32 The new file system supported by Windows 98, in which data is stored more efficiently on disks larger than 500MB.

Favorites Files, folders, web pages, and programs to which you want easy access. Windows 98 stores shortcuts to Favorites in your Favorites folder and displays them on the Favorites menu.

Favorites menu Menu displayed by choosing Start | Favorites, listing files, shortcuts, and web sites that you have added.

FDISK DOS program that comes with Windows, used to create or delete partitions on disks.

file Collection of related information that is given a name and stored on a disk.

file address Address of a file on your computer or on a network to which your computer is attached. Also called a *path name*.

file allocation table The table that stores information about each sector on a disk.

file association Which program you use to open, edit, or print a specified type of file.

file attachment *See* **attached file**.

file icon Icon that represents a file; it looks like a piece of paper with the design of the program that created the file or that can open the file.

file server   Computer that stores files that are used by other computers on a network.

file system   The information that keeps track of which files are stored where on the disk. Its properties are displayed on the File System Properties dialog box.

File Transfer Protocol   *See* **FTP**.

file type   The type of information contained in a file, indicated by the extension portion of the filename.

filename   Name given to a file. The last part of a filename, after the last period, is the **extension**.

filter   Feature of Outlook Express and other mail clients that can automatically sort (or take other actions in response to) your incoming e-mail messages. Outlook Express and other newsreaders can also filter newsgroup articles for newsgroups to which you have subscribed.

FilterKeys   Accessibility feature that "filters out" repeated keystrokes.

firewall   Computer that connects a private network to the Internet and controls what information can pass through.

fixed spacing   Typeface design in which all letters in the typeface are the same width.

floppy disk   Also called a *diskette*, a removable disk that stores up to 2.8MB, depending on the capacity of the disk drive.

flow control   System that controls the flow of data between your modem and your computer.

folder   Special kind of file that contains a list of other files. Folders can contain other folders.

folder hierarchy   *See* **folder tree**.

folder icon   Icon that represents a folder; it looks like a manila folder.

folder list   *See* **folder tree**.

Folder Options   Command on the Start | Settings menu that helps you configure your desktop, Folder windows, and Windows Explorer windows.

folder tree   Diagram showing which folders are contained in which other folders. Also called a *folder hierarchy* or *folder list*.

Folder window Window displaying the contents of a folder. The My Computer icon on the desktop displays a Folder window when opened.

font All the characters in a typeface of a given size and style. Commonly but incorrectly used to mean **typeface**.

font substitution To speed up printing, using built-in printer fonts where possible for similar TrueType fonts.

Fonts folder Folder containing Windows font files.

Fonts window Windows displaying the installed fonts.

form Web page containing boxes that the reader can fill out, and buttons the reader can click to submit the information back to the web site.

form field Box on a form web page into which the reader can type, or from which the reader can choose options.

formatting Writing the file system on a disk.

Four11 Internet-based directory of people and companies.

fragmentation Inefficient storage of files in discontinuous groups of sectors on your disk.

freeware Programs that are entirely free to use and frequently downloadable from the Internet.

FTP File Transfer Protocol, a method for transferring files over the Internet. The built-in Windows program that transfers files by using FTP is called Ftp.

FTP client Program that lets you upload files to, or download files from, an FTP server. Windows 98 comes with the Ftp program. Internet Explorer and Netscape can also act as FTP clients.

FTP server Internet host computer that acts as a file archive, allowing other computers to upload or download files by using FTP.

full access Access type that allows other people to read from or write to a shared resource.

full backup Complete backup of all files and folders; also called a *baseline backup*.

game controller   Device that allows you to play arcade-style games on your computer.

GDI   Graphic Device Interface, the part of Windows 98 that formats program output for screens and printers.

GDI pool   Fixed-size area of memory used to manage fonts, colors, and other tools that are used to create screen and printer images.

GIF file   File in Graphics Information Format, a popular format for graphics files that is widely used in web pages. GIF files have the extension .gif.

Graphical User Interface (GUI)   Software design that allows you to control your computer by using a mouse, windows, and icons.

graphics mode   In a DOS window, the mode that displays any pattern of dots on the screen, including text.

guest computer   Computer that uses shared resources from other computers over a network or direct cable connection.

GUI   *See* **Graphical User Interface**.

hang   When a program or the Windows 98 system stops responding to input from the keyboard or mouse.

hard disk   Disk that is sealed into its disk drive.

hard disk controller   Adapter card that connects a hard disk to your computer.

hardware profile   Description of your computer's hardware resources.

header   Lines at the top of an e-mail message that contain the address, return address, date, and other information about the message, not including the **body** (text) of the message.

hidden file   File whose Hidden attribute is selected, so that the file doesn't appear in Folder windows or Windows Explorer.

hierarchical file system   System of storing files on disks, in which files are stored in folders and folders can contain other folders.

High Contrast   Accessibility option that uses a high contrast color scheme, and increases legibility wherever possible.

HiPack   Very effective but slow compressing method.

History List of recently displayed web pages, maintained by a browser.

home page The main (or starting) page of a web site. Also used to refer to a browser's **start page**.

host address On the Internet, address of a host computer.

host computer Computer that has the resources to be shared over a network or direct cable connection.

hot docking Docking or undocking a laptop without turning it off.

hover color The color a web page link turns when the mouse pointer is above it.

HSV Numerical way of describing a color by its hue, saturation, and luminescence value.

HTML Hypertext Markup Language, the language in which web pages are written. You can create files in HTML by using FrontPage Express or another web page editor.

HTML mail or
HTML messages E-mail messages formatted using HTML.

HTTP Hypertext Transfer Protocol, the language that web browsers and web servers use to communicate with each other.

HTTPS Secure version of HTTP, the protocol with which web browsers communicate with web servers.

hub Computer to which all other computers connect in a star topology.

hyperlink *See* link.

**HyperTerminal
connection** Configuration file (with extension .ht) containing the specifications HyperTerminal needs for connecting to another computer.

hypertext Interlinked text.

**Hypertext Markup
Language** *See* HTML.

hypertext template file File created by the Customize This Folder Wizard to store the appearance of a folder in Web view.

Hypertext Transfer Protocol *See* **HTTP**.

I/O Input and output.

I/O address Hexadecimal number that the CPU uses to identify a device.

icon Little picture on your screen that responds with an action when you point to it with the mouse, single-click it, or double-click it.

IDE Integrated Drive Electronics, a standard type of disk connection, used for hard disks and CD-ROM drives.

IE *See* **Internet Explorer**.

Image mode *See* **binary mode**.

Imaging *See* **Kodak Imaging**.

IMAP Internet Message Access Protocol, used for storing and delivering Internet e-mail.

incremental backup Backup of only those files that are new or have changed since the last backup.

Industry Standard Architecture *See* **ISA**.

INI file Initialization file, with the extension .ini.

initialization file File that contains configuration information used when a program loads. *See* **DOS initialization file**; **Windows initialization file**.

input device Hardware device used to digitize information so that it can be stored in your computer. Microphones, scanners, keyboards, and mice are input devices.

installation file File that contains all the files required for a program to run, along with an installation program.

InterLink cable See **null-modem cable**.

internal modem Modem on an adapter board inside your computer.

Internet Worldwide network of networks.

Internet account Account with an Internet service provider (**ISP**) that allows you to connect your computer to the Internet.

Internet address *See* **URL**.

Internet Explorer (IE) Microsoft's browser, which comes with Windows 98.

Internet Relay Chat (IRC) Internet-wide system of chat.

Internet service provider *See* **ISP**.

Internet shortcut File that acts as a placeholder for a web page, stored with the extension .url.

Internet zone Security zone that includes the computers that don't fall into any other zone.

interrupt Channels that a device can use to alert the CPU that the device needs attention.

intranet Network installed within an organization, with a web server that allows only people within the organization to view web pages from that server.

IP address Internet protocol address, the numerical address of a computer connected to the Internet.

IPX/SPX Internetwork Packet eXchange/Sequenced Packet eXchange, a protocol used primarily in Novell's NetWare operating system.

IRC *See* **Internet Relay Chat**.

IRC server *See* **chat server**.

ISA Industry Standard Architecture, a standard type of expansion slot or card.

ISDN Integrated Services Digital Network, a phone line that enables your computer to connect to another computer digitally.

ISDN terminal adapter   Device that connects your computer to an ISDN line (instead of a modem).

ISP   Internet Service Provider, an organization that provides dial-in Internet accounts, usually PPP, CSLIP, or SLIP accounts, but sometimes UNIX shell accounts.

Java   Language for writing applets that can be sent over the Web so that they can be executed by your computer.

JavaScript   Language often used for extending HTML by embedding scripts in web pages. Also called *JScript* (but only by Microsoft) and *ECMAscript*. JavaScript scripts are also stored in files with the extension .js.

joystick   Device that enables you to play arcade-style games on your computer.

JPEG or JPG file   File in the Joint Photographic Experts Group graphics format, a format well-suited for storing scanned photographs, and widely used in web pages. JPEG files have the extension .jpg.

JS file   File containing a JavaScript script.

JScript   *See* **JavaScript**.

kernel   Fundamental part of Windows (or of any operating system).

key   Component in the Registry. For information about encryption. *See* **private key; public key**.

key ring   Collection of cryptography data that you need for sending secure e-mail.

Kodak Imaging   Windows 98's built-in graphics editor for photos.

Kodak Review   Windows 98's built-in graphics viewer.

LAN   *See* **local area network**.

landscape   Print orientation in which lines of print are parallel to the long side of the paper.

LapLink cable   *See* **null-modem cable**.

Large Icons view Way of representing the contents of a folder, in which each item in the folder appears as a large icon with the file or folder name below it.

LDAP Lightweight Directory Access Protocol, a standard way for programs to search a directory service. Windows 98's Address Book uses LDAP.

link Word, phrase, or picture that you can click to display another related web page (or another page of the same web page). FrontPage Express lets you add links to your web pages. Also called *hyperlink*.

linking In OLE, storing a link in one file that links to an object in another file.

Links toolbar Toolbar that can appear on the Taskbar, containing the same buttons that appear on the Links toolbar in Internet Explorer. This toolbar can also appear in Folder windows and Windows Explorer windows.

list box Box that contains a list of options, one of which is selected, usually appearing on a dialog box.

List view Way of representing the contents of a folder, in which items are listed with a tiny icon and the filename.

Liszt Web site where you can search for mailing lists by topic (at **http://www.liszt.com**).

local File or device that is stored on or attached to the computer you are using (the **local computer**), rather than being stored on or attached to a computer connected to your computer by a network.

local area network (LAN) Network that connects computers that are in the same building or campus, usually with cables.

local computer Your own computer, rather than a computer connected to your computer over a network.

local disk Disk drive connected to your own computer (as opposed to a **network disk**).

Local Intranet zone Security zone that includes the computers on your own LAN.

local printer Printer attached to your own computer.

Logged mode Startup option similar to Windows 98's usual way of running, except that Windows logs all the drivers it loads in the file Bootlog.txt.

logon script File that specifies what prompts to wait for and what to type in response when logging in to an Internet account or local area network.

lurking Reading the messages in a newsgroup or mailing list without posting messages of your own. Entirely respectable.

magnification Size at which Windows displays text onscreen.

Magnifier Accessibility option that displays a window magnifying part of the screen.

mail *See* **e-mail**.

mail client Program for sending and receiving e-mail messages. Windows 98 comes with Outlook Express. Informally called an *e-mail program*.

mail gateway Computer that handles outgoing e-mail messages, sending them out to the Internet.

mail server Computer that handles incoming e-mail, storing it in mailboxes.

mailbox Location on your mail server where your e-mail is stored until you retrieve it using your mail client (such as Outlook Express).

mailing list E-mail-based discussion group.

Maintenance Wizard Windows 98 utility that schedules Windows' disk housekeeping programs to run automatically.

mapping Assigning a drive letter to a network drive on another computer.

Maximize button Button in the upper-right corner of a window that is clicked to maximize the window.

maximized window Window that takes up the entire screen, with no window borders.

MCA *See* **Microchannel**.

meeting NetMeeting call that is scheduled in advance.

memory The temporary storage your computer uses for the programs you are running and the files you currently have open. Also called *RAM*.

memory address Number that uniquely identifies one piece of memory storage.

Memory Manager Part of Windows 98 that handles virtual memory.

menu List of commands from which you can choose. *See* **drop-down menu; menu bar; pull-down menu; shortcut menu**.

menu bar Row of one-word commands that appears along the top of a window, just below the title bar.

Microchannel Type of expansion slots introduced by IBM for its PS/2 series.

Microsoft Exchange Personal Address Book Format Format for storing name and address information. Address Book can export files in this format.

Microsoft Network Microsoft's online service.

Microsoft Paint Windows 98's built-in graphics editor.

MID File extension used for MIDI-format music files (.mid).

MIDI Musical Instrument Digital Interface, a standard for digital musical instruments and the computer hardware and software that works with them.

MIDI channel Input from a MIDI device, containing one musical line. One MIDI input device can produce up to 16 channels; for example, one channel for each musical part or one channel for each instrument being simulated.

MIDI scheme Definition that indicates which MIDI instrument plays each MIDI channel.

MIME Multipurpose Internet Mail Extensions, the most widely used method of including non-text information, such as attached files, in e-mail messages. *See also* **S/MIME**.

Minimize button Button in the upper-right corner of a window that is clicked to minimize the window.

minimized window Window that is not displayed, so that only the window's button on the Taskbar appears on the screen.

modem driver Modem control program.

modulation Conversion of digital information from your computer into analog "sound" information for transmission over the phone.

motherboard *See* **system board**.

mouse Device for moving the mouse pointer on the screen and selecting the item the pointer points to.

mouse pointer Indicator on the screen that shows where the mouse is pointing. Also called the *pointer* or (incorrectly) the **cursor**.

MouseKeys Accessibility option that enables you to use the numeric keypad to control the pointer.

MPEG or MPG Video file format based on the **JPEG** graphics file format.

MS-DOS Microsoft Disk Operating System, also called **DOS**.

MS-DOS mode Mode in which Windows exits and you see only the DOS prompt. Also called **Command Prompt Only mode**.

MS-DOS name The eight-or-fewer-character name that resembles a file's real name, but that is legal under the pre-Windows 95 file-naming rules.

MSN *See* **Microsoft Network**.

multilink System that allows a single Dial-Up Networking to use multiple modems and phone lines for greater speed.

multimedia Information in a format other than plain text. Multimedia information can include pictures, movies, and sound.

multitasking Running multiple tasks at the same time. Windows 98 is a multitasking operating system, because it can run many tasks (programs) simultaneously.

My Computer Folder that contains items for each disk drive on your computer, along with a few other special subfolders.

named meeting NetMeeting meeting hosted by a teleconferencing company or some other meeting server.

navigating Changing your view from one folder to another, usually when looking for a folder or file.

Navigator *See* **Netscape Navigator**.

net *See* **Internet; local area network; network.**

Net Watcher Windows 98 utility that monitors and shows which resources on your computer other people are using.

NetBEUI NetBIOS Extended User Interface, the network protocol used primarily by Microsoft in its LAN networking products.

Netcaster Netscape's program for subscribing to web sites.

netiquette Net etiquette; etiquette on the Internet; conventions for what is appropriate in newsgroup and e-mail messages.

NetMeeting Microsoft's Internet-based conferencing program, which comes with Windows 98.

netnews *See* **Usenet.**

Netscape Navigator The world's most popular browsing program (as of early 1998).

Netstat Network diagnostic program that comes with Windows 98.

network Group of computers that are connected together. *See also* **Internet; local area network.** You can connect Windows 98 computers in a peer-to-peer network.

network client authentication certificate Certificate that identifies a remote network client for secure SSL sessions.

network disk or network drive Disk drive connected to a computer that your computer can access over a network (as opposed to a **local disk**).

network interface card Adapter that connects a computer to a local area network. Choose the card that is appropriate for a peer-to-peer network or other type of LAN.

Network Neighborhood Folder that contains entries for all the computers to which your computer is connected on a local area network or direct cable connection.

**network operating
system (NOS)**   Operating system that includes support for a client-server local area network.

network password   Password you use when logging into a LAN.

network printer   Printer that is attached to a computer on a local area network, and that can be used by other computers on the network.

**network server
authentication
certificate**   Certificate that identifies a remote network server for secure SSL sessions.

news account   Name of the news server to use when reading and posting to Usenet newsgroups.

newsgroup   Discussion group that is part of Usenet. Windows 98 comes with Outlook Express, which lets you read and post to newsgroups.

newsreader or
**newsreading
program**   Program for reading and posting to newsgroups. Windows 98 comes with Outlook Express, which is both a mail client and a newsreader.

nickname   Name by which you are known while chatting online.

NNTP   Net News Transfer Protocol, the protocol used by Usenet for distributing newsgroup articles.

node   Computer attached to a network.

**non-routable
protocol**   Network protocol that can be used only on a simple network where routing devices are not used.

Normal mode   Windows 98's usual way of running.

NOS   *See* **network operating system**.

Notepad   Windows 98's built-in text editor.

null-modem cable   Serial cable used to connect two computers in a direct cable connection (not to connect a computer to a modem).

object In OLE, a piece of information from a file; you can link or embed an object in a different file.

offline Not connected to any network or computer.

offline mode When your printer is not available (turned off or not connected to your computer).

OLE Object Linking and Embedding, a method of linking and combining information from files created by different applications.

online Connected to a computer or a network (a **local area network**, the **Internet**, or another network).

online help Helpful information stored on your computer that you can look at by using the Windows Help system.

online service Commercial service that allows you to connect to and access their proprietary information system.

OnNow Feature that allows Windows to power down the computer when nothing is happening, and to power back up when the computer is needed again, if the computer's hardware permits.

opening Displaying the contents of a file or folder, or running a program.

operating system (OS) Program that manages your entire computer system, including its screen, keyboard, disk drives, memory, and central processor. Windows 98 is an operating system.

Outlook Express Microsoft's e-mail program that is included with Windows 98 and with Internet Explorer 4.0.

output device Hardware device that can display, play, print, or otherwise use information from your computer. Printers, displays, and speakers are output devices.

packaged object In OLE, a piece of information from a file that you have linked or embedded in a different file.

packet Chunk of information transmitted on a network or other communications line.

Paint *See* **Microsoft Paint**.

pane   Section of a window.

parallel port   Connector on your computer used for parallel communications. You connect most printers to the parallel port.

parameter   Information provided to a program (usually on the command line or in an initialization file) to tell it how to run.

parity   Simple method of error-detection, in which the value of one bit is calculated from the values of a group of bits.

partition   Logical section of a hard disk.

pasting   Copying the information on the Clipboard to the location of the cursor in the active application.

path or **path name**   *See* **file address**.

PC Card   Credit-card-sized adapter cards used mainly in laptops. They fit in PC Card slots. Formerly called PCMCIA.

PC file transfer cable   *See* **null-modem cable**.

PCI   Personal Computer Interface, a standard type of expansion slot or card that fits into a PCI slot.

PCMCIA   *See* **PC Card**.

PCX file   Graphics file with extension .pcx.

peer-to-peer network   Network on which all computers can function as both clients and servers.

peripheral   Hardware device that is attached to your computer, such as a printer or modem.

personal certificate   Cryptographic information that identifies you when viewing web sites or sending e-mail.

Personal Computer Interface   *See* **PCI**.

Personal Web Server   Low-performance web server program that comes with Windows 98.

PGP   Pretty Good Privacy, a method of sending secure e-mail.

Phone Dialer Windows 98's built-in telephone dialer.

PICS Platform for Internet Content Selection, a method of labeling web site content, developed by the World Wide Web Consortium.

PIF file Program Information File with the extension .pif, containing configuration information for a DOS program.

ping Test message sent to find out whether another system will respond. Ping is also the name of a program that sends pings on the Internet; Windows 98 comes with a Ping program.

pixel Single dot that can take on any color on the screen.

PKZIP Program that creates and reads ZIP files by compressing and uncompressing files.

play list List of the tracks on an audio CD in the order in which you want to play them.

Plug and Play Type of device that can communicate with Windows to provide its own configuration information.

plug-in Program that "plugs in" to your browser program, adding new features to the browser.

plus box Small plus sign in a box that appears to the left of an item in a list, to show that the item contains sub-items. For example, a plus box to the left of a folder in a folder tree indicates that the folder contains sub-folders. Click the plus box to see the sub-items.

point In printing measurement, $\frac{1}{72}$ of an inch.

pointer See **mouse pointer**.

pointer scheme Set of shapes that the mouse pointer assumes.

pointer trail Shadowy trail left behind the moving mouse pointer.

Point-to-Point Protocol (PPP) Communications protocol for computers connected to the Internet by telephone (or telephone-like) lines.

Point-to-Point Tunneling Protocol (PPTP) Communications protocol used by Virtual Private Networking.

POP or **POP 3** Post Office Protocol 3, a program run by a mail server that stores your incoming e-mail until you retrieve it by using Outlook Express or another mail client.

port Connector on your computer to which you can connect a cable. *See* **parallel port; serial port**.

port number On the Internet, a number that tells an Internet host computer whether you are connecting for e-mail, the Web, telnet, or another Internet service.

port replicator Docking station that contains only additional ports.

portrait Print orientation in which lines of print are parallel to the short side of the paper.

power management Settings that automatically turn off computer components to save electricity. The Power Management icon on the Control Panel lets you configure these settings.

Power Meter Icon in the system tray that shows whether the computer is connected to AC power or running on batteries.

power scheme Group of settings that define when and if Windows should turn off the power to parts of your computer.

PPP *See* **Point-to-Point Protocol**.

PPP account Internet account that uses the PPP communications protocol; the most popular kind of Internet account.

PPTP *See* **Point-to-Point Tunneling Protocol**.

PPView program Windows 98 utility that displays Microsoft PowerPoint presentation files.

preference Setting or option that controls the way you want a program to work.

Pretty Good Privacy *See* **PGP**.

preview When viewing a folder as a web page, the small copy of the first page of the selected file that appears at the bottom of the left pane of the window.

primary DNS *See* **domain name server**.

Primary DOS partition Section of a hard disk that stores the main DOS or Windows file system.

print job Document sent to a printer.

print server Computer to which a printer is attached that is used by other computers on a network.

printer driver Printer control program.

printer port *See* **parallel port**.

printer window Window that displays the status of print jobs for one printer.

Printers folder Folder in which Windows stores printer drivers for the printers you have installed.

private key One of a pair of cryptographic keys. You use your private key to decode messages you receive that were encoded with your **public key** and to encode messages you want to sign.

process *See* **task**.

profile Group of settings stored with a name (also called a **scheme**). *See* **color profile**; **hardware profile**; **user profile**.

Profiles folder *See* **user profile**.

program Sequences of computer instructions that perform tasks.

program file File containing a program, usually with the extension .exe or .com.

Programs menu Menu displayed when you choose Start | Programs, showing a list of programs you can run.

property Setting that affects how an object works. You can set the properties of many objects by right-clicking the object and choosing Properties from the menu that appears, and then changing the settings on the resulting Properties dialog box.

proportional spacing Typeface design in which letters in the typeface are different widths.

protocol Setting that identifies the way information is passed between computers on the network.

proxy server Computer that acts as a gatekeeper between a LAN and the rest of the Internet.

PS/2 port Standard keyboard or mouse connector.

PSS file Backup of an initialization file (created by the System Configuration Utility), with the extension .pss.

public key One of a pair of cryptographic keys. You use a person's public key to encode a message so that it can be decoded only with the person's **private key** and to verify signed messages.

public-key cryptography Cryptography system that uses pairs of keys, one public and one private to the key's owner. Two forms are commonly used: PGP and S/MIME.

publishing Storing the files that make up one or more web pages on a web server so that others can view the pages.

pull-down menu Box onscreen with a downward-pointing triangle button at its right end, usually appearing in a dialog box.

push button In FrontPage Express, a button on a web page form that performs a command, usually sending the entries on the form back to the web server.

push technology Web-based Internet facility in which your web browser automatically downloads web pages to your computer.

QT file QuickTime video file, with the extension .qt.

query Information you want to search for. For example, when using a search engine, you type words or phrases to search for.

queue List of tasks waiting to be done. For example, a print queue is a list of print jobs waiting to be printed.

Quick Launch toolbar Toolbar on the Taskbar (usually at the left end, next to the Start button) with small icons for programs you run frequently.

Quick View Windows 98 utility that can display files in a variety of formats.

QuickTime Video file format with file extension .qt.

RA or RAM File extension (either .ra or .ram) used for RealAudio, a streaming audio file format.

radio button One of a group of round buttons that can either be blank or contain a dot, usually appearing in a dialog box. FrontPage Express comes with form templates to put radio buttons on web page forms.

RAM Random Access Memory; *see* **memory**. Also a file extension used for RealAudio files; *see* **RA**.

RAM drive Memory that simulates a disk drive.

read-ahead Extra information Windows reads from the disk and stores in memory, so that the information will be instantly available if Windows needs it.

read-only file File whose Read-Only attribute is selected, so that the file cannot be accidentally deleted or modified. Shared disks and folders can be designated read-only.

real-time chat *See* **chat**.

Recycle Bin Special folder in which Windows 98 stores files and folders you have recently deleted.

Recycled folder Folder that contains part or all of the Recycle Bin.

refresh Redisplay a window using updated information.

REG file *See* **registration file**.

Regedit Windows 98's Registry Editor utility for displaying and editing the Registry.

regional settings Windows settings that control how numbers, dates, times, and currency amounts appear.

registered file types *See* **file association**.

registration file File with the extension .reg, created by exporting part or all of the Registry.

Registry File in which Windows 98 stores a database of program and system setup information.

remote administration Facility that allows someone (usually a network administrator) at one computer to change the Windows settings on another computer.

remote computer Computer attached to the computer you are using over a local area network, Internet, or other network.

remote control Program that allows one computer to take control of another computer over a local area network, dial-up connection, the Internet, or other network.

remote node Computer that is attached to a local area network via Dial-Up Networking.

removable disk Disk that can be removed from its disk drive (unlike a hard disk). Floppy disks and ZIP disks are removable.

repartitioning Change the layout of partitions on a hard disk.

repeat delay Delay between starting to hold down a key and when the key begins repeating.

repeat rate How fast a key repeats once it starts repeating.

resolution Number of pixels (dots) your screen can display, expressed by a vertical and horizontal count. Standard screen resolutions include 640x480 (640 dots across and 480 dots high), 800x600, and 1024x768.

resource Hardware, software, or data that can be shared by users of a network. *See also* **system resources**.

resource leakage Loss of system resources when applications allocate memory but fail to release it when done.

Resource Meter Windows 98 utility that monitors system resources.

Restore button Button in the upper-right corner of a window that is clicked to restore the window (display the window within window borders).

restored window Window that appears within window borders—not maximized or minimized.

Restricted Sites zone Security zone that includes the computers you have told Windows not to trust.

RGB Numerical way of describing a color by its red, green, and blue components.

Rich Text Format *See* **RTF file**.

right-clicking Clicking with the right mouse button (unless you have configured your mouse to swap the functions of the buttons).

RJ-11 jack U.S. standard telephone connector.

RJ-45 connector Connector used to connect network interface cards to twisted pair cable in a star topology network.

RMI File extension used for MIDI-format music files.

room *See* **chat room**.

root Main or top-level folder (or directory) in a hierarchical file system.

router Specialized computer used to connect multiple segments of networks; for example, to connect a local area network to the Internet.

RSACi Recreational Software Advisory Council for the Internet, an organization that rates Web sites regarding topics that people might find offensive, so that your browser can screen out possibly offensive sites.

RTF file Rich Text Format, a portable format for storing documents, defined by Microsoft. WordPad can read and write RTF files, which have the extension .rtf.

RTS/CTS Request To Send/Clear To Send, a method of flow control used by some modems.

RV File extension (.rv) for RealVideo, a streaming video file format.

S/MIME Standard security system used by Outlook Express and other mail programs to send e-mail securely. *See also* **MIME**.

Safe mode Windows startup mode that provides minimal Windows functions by disabling all devices except the keyboard, screen, and disk.

Safe Mode Command Prompt Only The same as Safe mode, except that Windows displays only an MS-DOS command prompt.

sandbox Limited set of computer resources with which Netscape Navigator or Internet Explorer runs downloaded Java programs.

saved search Search criteria saved in a file with extension .fnd. You use the Start | Find | Files Or Folders command to rerun the search.

ScanDisk Windows utility that diagnoses and repairs disk errors.

scanner Device that digitizes pictures (or anything on paper) for use by your computer.

scheme Group of settings, stored with a name so that you can easily switch from one group of settings to another (similar to a **profile**). *See* **desktop scheme; MIDI scheme; pointer scheme; power scheme**.

scrap OLE object that has been left on the desktop or in a folder.

screen saver Program that displays an image, frequently one that moves, on your desktop when you are not using the computer.

screen saver password Password that lets you use your computer again after the screen saver appears.

screen shot Picture of what is on the screen.

script Program written using a scripting language such as JavaScript or VBScript. *See also* **batch file; logon script; Windows Scripting Host; WSH file**.

scroll bar Vertical or horizontal bar running along the right side or bottom of a window, allowing you to scroll the information displayed in the window.

SCSI Small Computer Systems Interface, a standard for connecting peripherals to computers. SCSI devices include hard disks, CD-ROMs, tapes, and scanners.

SCSI controller Adapter board for connecting SCSI devices to a computer.

SCSI device number Unique number of the SCSI device connected to one SCSI controller.

search engine Web site that helps you find information on the Web by searching the full text of the World Wide Web for the words or phrases you type.

secondary DNS *See* **domain name server.**

sector Physical block of storage on a disk.

secure e-mail E-mail that has been encoded so that only the intended recipient can read it.

secure e-mail certificates Certificates used to sign and encrypt e-mail.

secure server Web server that supports SSL (Secure Sockets Layer) to encrypt data sent between the server and your computer. Pages loaded from a secure server have URLs beginning with https://.

security Control over your computer system, who uses it, what programs run on it, and who reads or changes the information stored on your disks.

selecting Indicating the items you plan to work with. How you select files and folders on the desktop, in Folder windows, or in Windows Explorer depends on your desktop style.

selective startup Windows startup in which you choose which initialization files to process.

Send To menu Menu found on the File menu of Folder windows and Windows Explorer windows that allows you to copy files to preselected locations.

separator page Blank page between print jobs on a network printer.

serial port Connector on your computer that is used for serial communication. You connect serial mice, external modems, and serial printers to a serial port.

SerialKey Accessibility option that turns on support for alternate input devices attached to the serial port.

server Program or computer that provides resources that others can use on a network.

service Setting that allows you to share a computer's resources on a network.

Setup program Installation program, such as the Setup program that comes with Windows 98.

SGML   Standard Generalized Markup Language, the language on which HTML is based.

share name   Name by which a printer can be referred to by other users on a LAN.

shared resources   Hardware or files that are shared with other users on a LAN.

share-level access control   Method of controlling who can use shared network resources, in which anyone who knows the resource's password can use the resource.

shareware   Programs that require you to register and pay for the program if you decide that you like it. They are frequently downloadable from the Internet.

shell account   *See* **UNIX shell account**.

shortcut   File with a .lnk extension, used as a placeholder in your file system. *See also* **shortcut key; shortcut menu**.

shortcut icon   Icon that represents a shortcut, usually on the desktop or in a Folder window or Windows Explorer. Shortcut icons always include a little white curving arrow in the lower-left corner.

shortcut key   Combination of the CTRL key, the ALT key, and one other key; pressing these keys at the same time runs a specified shortcut.

shortcut menu   Menu that appears when you right-click an object. A shortcut menu contains commands that pertain to the object you right-clicked.

ShowSounds   Accessibility feature that displays a caption when the computer makes a sound.

signature   Lines that an e-mail program adds to the end of each message you send, usually containing your e-mail address, name, and a witty tag line. For encrypted e-mail, *see* **digital signature; signature block**.

signature block   Encryption-related text that is automatically added to the end of your outgoing e-mail messages.

signed mail   E-mail that has been encoded using your **private key**, to prove that you sent it.

SLIP Serial Line Internet Protocol, a communications protocol for computers connected to the Internet. SLIP has been superceded by PPP.

slot *See* **expansion slot; PC Card**.

Small Icons view Way of representing the contents of a folder, in which each item in the folder appears as a small icon with a file or folder name below it.

SMTP Simple Mail Transfer Protocol, the method used by mail gateways on the Internet to send outgoing messages.

software publishing certificates Certificates used to sign Java and ActiveX applets.

sound board Adapter board that lets you connect speakers or headphones (and possibly a microphone) to your computer.

SoundSentry Accessibility feature that displays a visual warning when the computer makes a sound.

special characters Characters that do not appear on the standard U.S. 101-key keyboard, such as fractions and accented letters.

SpeedDial Connection information for people you plan to call more than once, stored in NetMeeting. Phone Dialer also has a Speed Dial feature.

spooling Multitasking system that allows a program to send information to a printer while performing other tasks.

SSL Secure Sockets Layer, the method that web browsers use to provide secure encrypted communication.

Stand-alone DOS mode Windows mode in which DOS programs can run using their own Config.sys and Autoexec.bat files.

Standard Buttons toolbar Toolbar that can appear in Folder windows and Windows Explorer windows, and that displays standard buttons for switching folders, cut-and-paste, displaying properties, and controlling which view appears in the window.

star topology Network topology in which each computer connects to a central hub.

Start button Button labeled Start that usually appears at the left end of the **Taskbar**. When clicked, the Start button displays the Start menu.

Start command DOS program that switches to Windows to open a program or a file.

Start menu Menu displayed by clicking the Start button on the Taskbar. It contains commands and additional menus listing most of the programs that you can run on your computer.

Start Menu folder Usually C:\Windows\Start Menu, the folder that controls what appears on the Start menu, Programs menu, and their submenus.

start page The web page that the browser loads when you open the browser without asking for a specific page. Also referred to as **home page**.

startup floppy disk *See* **emergency boot disk**.

Startup folder Folder that contains programs that Windows runs automatically when you start Windows. Usually C:\Windows\Start Menu\Programs\Startup.

startup menu Menu that appears if you press F8 while Windows is loading.

startup modes Modes in which you can run Windows if you are having trouble starting Windows in the normal manner.

stationery HTML-based e-mail formats that you can use when composing e-mail to send to recipients whose e-mail programs can handle HTML messages.

status bar Section of a window that displays information about the program. The status bar is usually a gray bar running along the bottom of the window.

Step-By-Step Confirmation mode Way of starting Windows 98 in which Windows processes its initialization files one line at a time, stopping and telling you each driver it's about to load.

StickyKeys Accessibility option that lets you avoid pressing multiple keys by making keys such as CTRL, SHIFT, and ALT stay in effect after they have been released.

stop bits　How many extra bits of information are included after each byte sent through a serial port (usually one).

streaming audio　Audio (sound) data stored in a format that allows the beginning of the file to be played even before later parts of the file are read.

streaming video　Video (movie) data stored in a format that allows the beginning of the file to be played even before later parts of the file are read.

string　Series of text characters, including letters, numbers, spaces, and punctuation.

style　How desktop icons (and filenames in Folder windows and Windows Explorer) appear and react to clicks. The three styles are **Classic style; Custom style; Web style.**

subfolder　Folder contained in another folder.

submenu　Menu displayed by a command from another menu.

subscription　Automatic process for checking a web site for new content and optionally downloading it to your hard drive.

SUBST　DOS command that comes with Windows 98, used to assign a drive letter to a folder. Not recommended.

supervisor password　Password needed to make changes to Content Advisor settings.

surface scan　Scan of the physical surface of a disk to detect bad sectors.

suspend mode　When power is off to most of the components of your computer (usually a laptop), but the state of the computer, including running programs, is preserved.

Super-VGA (SVGA)　Type of display with higher resolution than a VGA monitor.

swap file　File to which Windows copies data in virtual memory.

switching　Choosing another window as the active window. Pressing ALT-TAB switches windows.

system board　The printed circuit board that carries the CPU and memory.

system clock　Digital clock that can appear on the system tray part of the Taskbar.

System Configuration Utility Windows 98 utility for editing Windows and DOS initialization files.

system file File or folder whose System attribute is selected, indicating that the file or folder stores part of the actual Windows 98 operating system.

System File Checker Windows 98 utility that checks that your Windows 98 system files have not been deleted, renamed, replaced, or corrupted.

System menu Menu displayed by clicking the System Menu button, pressing ALT-SPACEBAR, or right-clicking the title bar of the window. This menu was called the Control menu in Windows 3.1 and Windows 95.

System Menu button Tiny icon in the upper-left corner of each window, at the left end of the window's title bar. Click this button to display the System menu. This button was called the Control menu button in Windows 3.1 and Windows 95.

System Monitor Windows 98 utility that displays and logs information about the way your system is operating.

system pool Fixed-size area of memory used for communication between applications and Windows.

System Properties dialog box Window that displays all the configurable hardware settings for your computer system.

system resources Fixed-size areas of memory used by Windows applications.

system tray or **systray** Section of the Taskbar (usually the right end) that displays a group of tiny icons, along with the system clock.

systems program Program that performs a computer-oriented task, such as a printer driver or hard disk housekeeping program.

table Web page feature that allows you to present information in rows and columns.

tag HTML code, enclosed in angle brackets (< >).

task Series of instructions that your computer is executing. A program can create one or more tasks. For example, a word processing program might run one task that displays the program window and accepts your input to edit a file, and a second task that prints a file at the same time.

Task Manager The part of the Taskbar that shows a button for each program that is running.

Task Scheduler The Windows 98 program that can run programs automatically on a schedule you establish.

Taskbar Row of buttons and icons that usually appears along the bottom of the screen.

T-connector Connector used with network interface cards and coaxial cable in a bus topology Ethernet network.

TCP/IP Transmission Control Protocol/Internet Protocol, the system that computers use to communicate with each other on the Internet.

TCP/IP stack Communications program that Windows programs use for communicating via TCP/IP.

telephony driver Configuration file containing information that will eventually be used for making phone calls over the Internet.

telnet Program that emulates a terminal over the Internet. Windows 98 comes with two: Telnet and HyperTerminal.

template File that you can use when creating a document, containing formatting and other generic information. FrontPage Express comes with templates for creating web pages.

terminal window Window that allows you to see a communications session and type commands to the remote computer.

terminal-emulation program Program that makes your computer act like a terminal, for communicating with computers that are designed to attach to terminals. You use a terminal-emulation program, such as HyperTerminal, to connect to a UNIX shell account.

terminating resistor Terminator used with network interface cards and T-connectors in a bus topology network.

text box   Box onscreen in which you can type information, usually appearing on a dialog box. FrontPage Express comes with form templates to put text boxes on web page forms.

text file   File that contains only letters, numbers, and special characters that appear on the keyboard. Text files frequently have the extension .txt.

text mode   In a DOS window, mode that displays only text.

thumbnail   Tiny version of a picture.

Thumbnail view   Way of representing the contents of a folder, in which items are listed with a small icon followed by the filename. The icon is a miniature version of the first page of the file.

TIF or **TIFF file**   File in Tagged-Image Format, a graphics file format. TIF files have the extension .tif.

tiling   Repeating a graphic to fill up a space (such as the desktop).

title bar   The colored bar that runs along the top of a window.

ToggleKeys   Accessibility feature that sounds a tone when the CAPS LOCK, SCROLL LOCK, and NUM LOCK keys are activated.

token   Electronic marker passed from computer to computer on a Token Ring network.

Token Ring   Type of local area network hardware.

tool tips   Little informational boxes that appear when you leave the mouse pointer on something for a few seconds, usually used for buttons on toolbars.

toolbar   Row of small buttons with icons on them. Toolbars appear just below the menu bar in many windows, as well as on the Taskbar.

toolbar handle   Raised vertical bar on the left end of a toolbar on the Taskbar, used for dragging the toolbar to a different location.

topology   Pattern of cabling that is used to connect computers together into a network.

Tracert   Trace route; program that traces the route that packets take on the Internet.

track   Concentric circle on which information is stored on a disk. Tracks are divided into **sectors**.

transfer protocol Method that a computer needs to use to access a file over the Internet: the first part of a URL.

Troubleshooter Part of the Windows Help system that asks a series of questions to help you track down and solve hardware or software problems.

TrueType Method of storing typefaces as a set of formulas for drawing the characters at almost any size.

Trusted Sites zone Security zone that includes the computers you or Microsoft have told Windows to trust.

TTL Time To Live; how many times a packet can be passed from one computer to another while in transit on the Internet.

TV tuner card Adapter board you can install in your computer that allows you to connect your computer to a television antenna or cable and watch television programs on your computer screen.

TWAIN Standard for communications between scanners and computer software.

twisted pair *See* **unshielded twisted pair cable.**

TXT file Text file, with the file extension .txt.

typeface Set of shapes for letters, numbers, and punctuation (for example, Times Roman). A **font** is a typeface at a specific size and weight (for example, 12-point Times Roman Bold).

UART Universal Asynchronous Receiver/Transmitter, a chip used in serial communication ports.

UNC address Universal Naming Convention addresses, used when referring to files on some local area networks.

undeleting Reversing the action of deleting something.

Unicode Character codes that allow you to use characters from practically every language on Earth.

Universal Serial Bus (USB) New standard type of connector introduced on Windows 98 computers.

UNIX Operating system widely used on Internet host computers.

UNIX shell account   Type of Internet account that gives you access to a computer running the UNIX operating system, which you control by typing UNIX commands.

unshielded twisted pair cable   Type of cable used to connect computers in a star topology.

upload   Transfer a file from a PC to the Internet, other network, or mainframe.

URL   Uniform Resource Locator, the address of a piece of information on the Internet, usually a web page.

USB   *See* **Universal Serial Bus**.

Usenet   Internet-based system of tens of thousands of newsgroups (discussion groups). Windows 98 comes with Outlook Express, which lets you read and post to Usenet newsgroups.

user pool   Fixed-size area of memory that is used to manage windows, menus, and other parts of the Windows user interface.

user profile   Windows settings that are stored for use when you log into the computer. Each user's user profile can contain different settings.

User.dat   File that contains user profile settings for the desktop, Folder windows, and accessibility options from the Registry.

user-level access control   Method of controlling who can use shared network resources, in which each resource has a list of users who can use the resource.

value   Element stored in a key in the Registry. Each value consists of a name and some data.

VBS file   File containing a VBScript script, with extension .vbs.

VBScript   Language resembling Microsoft's Visual Basic that can be used to add scripts to web pages or other applications.

vCard   Virtual business card format, exportable from Address Book.

VCF file   Virtual business card file, with extension .vcf.

VCMUI Version Conflict Manager User Interface. *See* **Version Conflict Manager**.

VeriSign Widely used certificate authority for personal certificates.

Version Conflict Manager Windows 98 installation utility that displays a list of the files that Windows 98 Setup backed up before replacing the files with new versions.

VGA Type of display. *See also* **Super-VGA**.

video capture device Hardware device that digitizes video information for use by your computer; for example, a digital video camera.

view settings Settings that control how folders appear in Folder and Windows Explorer windows.

Viewer program Windows 98 utility that displays Microsoft Excel spreadsheet files.

virtual business card file File with extension .vcf that contains information about a person.

virtual disk Large file that Windows treats like a disk. Virtual disks are usually compressed. *See* **compressed virtual disk**.

virtual machine Hardware and software environment that emulates enough of the features of a stand-alone DOS environment to allow most DOS programs to run correctly.

virtual memory System that moves chunks of program and data storage between disk and memory automatically, so that individual programs don't have to do all of their own memory management.

Virtual Private Networking Program that allows an authorized computer on the Internet to "tunnel" through the firewall and connect to a private network.

virus Self-replicating program, frequently with destructive side-effects.

wait time Length of time that your system is inactive before the screen saver starts up.

wallpaper The background pattern behind all the windows, icons, and menus on your desktop.

WAN *See* **wide area network**.

WAV file Audio file with extension .wav.

Web *See* **World Wide Web**.

web address *See* URL.

web browser *See* **browser**.

web directory Web site that helps you find information on the Web by categorizing web pages by subject.

web editor *See* **web page editor**.

web guide *See* **web directory**.

web page HTML file stored on a web server.

web page editor Program for creating and editing files in HTML format for use as web pages. Windows 98 comes with FrontPage Express.

Web Publishing Wizard Wizard that uploads web pages from FrontPage Express to a web server.

web server Computer that stores web pages and responds to requests from web browsers.

web site Collection of web pages belonging to a particular person or organization.

Web style Desktop style in which icons (and filenames in Folder windows and Windows Explorer) run or open when single-clicked.

Web view View of a folder as if it were a web page.

WebBot In FrontPage Express, dynamic objects you can add to web pages.

WebTV for Windows Programs bundled with Windows 98 that allow your computer, when equipped with a television-tuner adapter card, to display broadcast television. Not to be confused with WebTV, the box that you can connect to a television and phone line in order to browse the Web and send and receive e-mail, without a separate computer.

whiteboard Feature of NetMeeting that allows callers to draw a shared picture that all callers can edit and see.

wide area network (WAN) Network that connects computers that are not all in the same building or campus.

wildcard Special character (* or ?) used when specifying filenames or folder names.

Win.ini file Windows 3.1 initialization file, which is still used by Windows 98.

win98tcr@ gurus.com E-mail address for comments or corrections about this book.

window Rectangular area on the screen that displays information from a running program.

window borders Gray border running around the sides of a restored window.

Windows Clipboard *See* **Clipboard**.

Windows Explorer File-and-folder-manipulating program that comes with Windows 98.

Windows initialization file One of the configuration files that Windows reads during startup. These files have the extension .ini. *See also* **Registry**.

Windows key On some keyboards, the key with the Microsoft Windows logo. Pressing the Windows key displays the Taskbar and Start menu. Equivalent to pressing CTRL-ESC.

Windows password Password you use when starting Windows 98 or switching from one user to another.

Windows program folder Folder that contains the Windows program files (along with many subfolders with Windows-related files), usually C:\Windows.

Windows Registry Checker Windows 98 utility that checks and backs up the Registry.

Windows Resource Kit Extra-cost package available from Microsoft, containing programming and system administration tools.

Windows Scripting Host (WSH) Windows 98 utility that can run JavaScript or VBScript scripts from either Windows or DOS.

Windows Update Program that can update Windows over the Internet by using updates from the Microsoft web site.

Windows-aware DOS program Type of DOS program that handles its screen and keyboard in a way that lets it run efficiently under Windows.

WinPopup Program that allows you to send and receive messages over a LAN.

WINS Microsoft's Windows Internet Naming Service, which automatically manages network parameters.

Winsock The standard way for Windows programs to work with Internet connection software. Most popular Internet programs are Winsock-compatible, including Internet Explorer, Netscape Navigator, and Outlook Express.

WinZip Program that creates and reads ZIP files by compressing and uncompressing files.

Wizard Program that steps you through the process of creating or configuring something. Wizards come with Windows 98 and other Microsoft products.

Word Viewer Program that can display document files in Microsoft Word format.

word wrap Feature of text editors and word processors that allows the program to insert line endings automatically.

WordPad Windows 98's built-in word processor.

workgroup Group of computers on a local area network.

working folder Folder in which a program reads and writes files, unless another folder is specified.

workstation Computer used by a person, rather than one used only as a server for people at other computers.

World Wide Web Collection of millions of files stored on thousands of web server computers all over the world.

write-behind caching Storing information in memory to be written to a removable disk, and then saving the information to the removable disk in large chunks.

Wscript program The part of Windows Scripting Host that runs scripts from Windows.

WSH *See* **Windows Scripting Host**.

WSH file Text file with the extension .wsh that contains configuration settings for a script to be run by Windows Scripting Host.

XON/XOFF Method of flow control used by some modems.

Zip disk Removable disk that stores about 100MB.

ZIP file File that contains compressed versions of one or more files, compressed by WinZip, PKZIP, ZipMagic, or a compatible compression program. ZIP files have the extension .zip.

zone Categorization of the sources of downloaded information, for security purposes.

Index

About the *Windows 98: The Complete Reference* CD-ROM

Inside the back cover of this book is a CD-ROM containing a web version of the entire text of this book. Using Internet Explorer, Netscape Navigator, or any other web browser, you can read the text of this book online. What's the advantage of reading about Windows 98 on your screen? The web version contains thousands of links throughout the book: If you see a reference to a topic you need more information about, click the link to see the chapter about that topic.

Using the CD

The *Windows 98: The Complete Reference* CD-ROM doesn't contain software—it doesn't have to, because Windows 98 comes with a web browser. Follow these steps to read the web version of the book:

1. Put the CD-ROM into your CD-ROM drive. If your drive's autorun feature works, your web browser runs and you see the title web page for the book. Skip to step 3.

2. If the web page for the book doesn't appear, run Windows Explorer or open a Folder window and display the contents of the root folder of the CD-ROM. Click or double-click the filename Win98tcr.htm depending on whether you use the Web style or Classic style desktop (see "Choosing the Style of Your Desktop" in Chapter 1). Your browser runs and displays the title web page for the book.

3. Click links as usual to browse the contents of the book.

If you want to read the CD-ROM web pages in the same order in which they appear in the book, click the Next link at the top of each web page to move to the next web page in the chapter. The Previous link takes you to the previous web page in the chapter.

Searching for Information in the Book

The web version of the book includes a complete Glossary with links to the places that the terms appear. From the title web page, click the Glossary link, click the first letter of the term you are looking for, and find and click the term. The topic you are looking for may not appear on the screen immediately: you may have to search the web page for it.

To search for information on the web page you are looking at:

- In Internet Explorer, choose Edit | Find (on this page) from the menu bar, type the word or phrase to search for, and click the Find Next button.

- In Netscape Navigator, choose Edit | Find In Page from the menu bar, type the word or phrase to search for, and click the Find Next button.

What if the word or phrase you are looking for doesn't appear in the Glossary?

1. Choose Start | Find | Files Or Folders to display the Find All Files dialog box.

2. Type a word or phrase in the Containing Text box.

3. Set the Look In box to your CD-ROM drive (which is D: on most computers). Then click Find Now.

Windows displays a list of the CD-ROM web pages that contain the word or phrase you typed. Double-click the name of a web page to display that page.

If You Run into Trouble

If you run into trouble, write to the authors of this book at **win98tcr@gurus.com**. We'd also be interested in your comments about the book. Don't write to us with Windows 98 questions, though—we're not equipped to replace Microsoft's Technical Support department!